U.S. DEPARTMENT OF TRANS
FEDERAL AVIATION ADMINISTRATION
Air Traffic Organization Policy

JO 7110.65AA

Effective Date:
April 20, 2023

SUBJ: Air Traffic Control

This order prescribes air traffic control procedures and phraseology for use by personnel providing air traffic control services. Controllers are required to be familiar with the provisions of this order that pertain to their operational responsibilities and to exercise their best judgment if they encounter situations not covered by it.

NATASHA A. DURKINS — Digitally signed by NATASHA A. DURKINS Date: 2023.03.03 12:50:09 -05'00'

Natasha A. Durkins
Vice President, Mission Support Services
Air Traffic Organization

Distribution: ZAT-710, ZAT-464

Initiated By: AJV-0
Vice President, Mission Support Services

RECORD OF CHANGES

DIRECTIVE NO. JO 7110.65AA

CHANGE TO BASIC	SUPPLEMENTS			OPTIONAL	CHANGE TO BASIC	SUPPLEMENTS			OPTIONAL

FAA Form 1320-5 (6-80) USE PREVIOUS EDITION

Explanation of Changes
Basic

Direct questions through appropriate facility/service center office staff to the Office of Primary Interest (OPI)

a. 1–2–6. ABBREVIATIONS
5–1–2. ATC SURVEILLANCE SOURCE USE
5–5–4. MINIMA
5–5–7. PASSING OR DIVERGING
5–5–9. SEPARATION FROM OBSTRUCTIONS
5–13–8. CONTROLLER INITIATED COAST TRACKS

This change adds operational guidance associated with the use of the Standard Terminal Automation Replacement System (STARS) Multi–Sensor Mode when the sensor environment does not support the use of FUSION and the use of single sensor does not provide sufficient surveillance coverage. Enhanced Backup Surveillance (EBUS) has been decommissioned throughout the National Airspace System (NAS) and references have been removed.

b. 1–2–6. ABBREVIATIONS
5–3–4. TERMINAL AUTOMATION SYSTEMS IDENTIFICATION METHODS
5–4–6. RECEIVING CONTROLLER HANDOFF

This change reinstates "AM" to paragraphs 5–3–4 and 5–4–6 and updates 5–4–6 to include Micro–En Route Automated Radar Tracking System (MEARTS). This change also adds the definition of "AM" to 1–2–6, and updates the current definition of AMB to remove the 2–mile disparity value as it is locally adaptable and not uniform across all facilities.

c. 2–1–4. OPERATIONAL PRIORITY
2–4–20. AIRCRAFT IDENTIFICATION
9–2–17. SAMP FLIGHTS

This change modifies the statement in paragraph 2–4–20 that the "SAMP" call sign will be followed by a three–digit flight number instead of specifying the last three digits of the aircraft's tail number. Other general edits and reference changes are made to paragraphs 2–1–4, 2–4–20, and 9–2–17 for clarity.

d. 2–1–4. OPERATIONAL PRIORITY
9–2–22. OPEN SKIES TREATY AIRCRAFT

This change removes all documentation and references to Open Skies Treaty flights in paragraph 2–1–4. This change deletes paragraph 9–2–22, Open Skies Treaty Aircraft.

e. 2–1–27. PILOT DEVIATION NOTIFICATION

This change renames the paragraph title and also adds a note to the paragraph identifying "Brasher Notification or Brasher Warning" as terms sometimes used to reference the phraseology for notifying a pilot of a possible pilot deviation.

f. 2–6–4. ISSUING WEATHER AND CHAFF AREAS
5–4–10. EN ROUTE FOURTH LINE DATA BLOCK USAGE

This change harmonizes the language in FAA Order JO 7110.65 2–6–4k and 5–4–10f Note 2 and Note 3 in which it explains the use of /NAVAID, /waypoint, and /F entries in the 4th line of the Full Data Block (FDB) when an aircraft has been cleared to deviate for weather. Additionally, the designated characters used for coordinating deviations between two specified headings in FAA Order JO 7110.65 5–4–10f were changed to eliminate ambiguity.

g. 2–6–6. HAZARDOUS INFLIGHT WEATHER ADVISORY

This change acknowledges that controllers are no longer required to disseminate Airmen's Meteorological Information (AIRMET) over the contiguous United States (CONUS). It updates the language in FAA Order

JO 7110.65, Air Traffic Control, paragraph 2–6–6, to reflect the change. ATC facilities in the CONUS will no longer receive AIRMET advisories to broadcast; operators have other methods of receiving AIRMET information over the CONUS.

h. 5–2–7. VFR CODE ASSIGNMENTS

This change adds a Note advising that data blocks displaying beacon code 1203 represent the lead aircraft of a Visual Flight Rules (VFR) standard formation flight not receiving ATC services.

i. 5–4–10. EN ROUTE FOURTH LINE DATA BLOCK USAGE

This change modifies FAA Order JO 7110.65, 5–4–10g and 5–4–10h, to accommodate the current En Route Automation Modernization (ERAM) display methods of assigned speed data. The use of the designation characters "M", "S", "+", "–" and "." will be included as acceptable methods to display speed assignment utilizing the four character limit for speed entries in the fourth line of the Full Data Block (FDB).

j. 6–4–3. MINIMA ON OPPOSITE COURSES
6–5–4. MINIMA ALONG OTHER THAN ESTABLISHED AIRWAYS OR ROUTES
6–5–5. RNAV MINIMA- DIVERGING/CROSSING COURSES

This change replaces the term "expanded route" in paragraphs 6–4–3(c) and (d) and 6–5–5(b) with language that will explicitly define when to apply the 18 mile separation standard. Also Figure 6–5–4 will be corrected.

k. 8–7–4. LATERAL SEPARATION
8–8–4. LATERAL SEPARATION
8–9–4. LATERAL SEPARATION
8–10–4. LATERAL SEPARATION

This change reduces the lateral separation minima from 30 NM to 23 NM in the oceanic airspaces of Oakland ARTCC, New York ARTCC, and portions of Anchorage ARTCC. This change also clarifies where 50 NM separation is used by removing the references to airspace that has been designated as Offshore Airspace from 8–7–4 subparagraph b, and 8–8–4 subparagraph b, by defining where it is used in New York's and San Juan's airspace. This change cancels and incorporates N JO 7110.788, which was effective December 21, 2022.

l. 9–2–12. LAW ENFORCEMENT OPERATIONS

This change retitles paragraph 9–2–12, reformats the paragraph by reorganizing and modifying the existing subparagraphs a. and b., and adds procedures required to ensure the effective use of sensitive government mission beacon codes and call signs. This change also eliminates outdated terminology and aligns the language with updates to other orders. This change cancels and incorporates N JO 7110.787, which was effective December 01, 2022.

m. 13–1–1. DESCRIPTION

This change amends "flight plan data" to "current plan data" which is a more accurate depiction of how the En Route Decision Support Tool (EDST) calculates trajectories and predicts conflicts. It also adds a NOTE to define what is meant by "current plan."

n. Editorial Changes

Editorial changes include updating references to re–numbered paragraphs, changing "operational supervisor" to "operations supervisor" where applicable, making the acronym DoD consistent throughout the order, changing "runway extended" to "extended runway" in paragraph 7–4–4 to make consistent with the rest of the order, and deleting the obsolete ARTS to non–ARTS transition info in paragraph 2–3–4.

o. Entire publication

Additional editorial/format changes were made where necessary. Revision bars were not used because of the insignificant nature of these changes.

U.S. DEPARTMENT OF TRANSPORTATION
FEDERAL AVIATION ADMINISTRATION
Air Traffic Organization Policy

JO 7110.65AA
CHG 1

Effective Date:
October 5, 2023

SUBJ: Air Traffic Control

1. Purpose of This Change. This change transmits revised pages to Federal Aviation Administration Order JO 7110.65AA, Air Traffic Control, and the Briefing Guide.

2. Audience. This change applies to all Air Traffic Organization (ATO) personnel and anyone using ATO directives.

3. Where Can I Find This Change? This change is available on the FAA website at http://faa.gov/air_traffic/publications and https://employees.faa.gov/tools_resources/orders_notices/.

4. Explanation of Policy Change. See the Explanation of Changes attachment that has editorial corrections and changes submitted through normal procedures. The Briefing Guide lists only new or modified material, along with background.

5. Distribution. This change is distributed to select offices in Washington headquarters, service area offices, the William J. Hughes Technical Center, the Mike Monroney Aeronautical Center, air traffic field facilities, and international aviation offices. This change is distributed electronically to all who subscribe to receive email notification through the FAA's website. All organizations are responsible for viewing, downloading, and subscribing to receive email notifications when changes occur to this order. Subscriptions to air traffic directives can be made through the Air Traffic Plans and Publications website at https://www.faa.gov/air_traffic/publications/ or directly via the following link: https://public.govdelivery.com/accounts/USAFAA/subscriber/new?topic_id=USAFAA_39.

6. Disposition of Transmittal. Retain this transmittal until superseded by a new basic order.

7. Page Control Chart. See the page control chart attachment.

NATASHA A. DURKINS
Digitally signed by NATASHA A. DURKINS
Date: 2023.08.03 14:31:18 -04'00'

Natasha A. Durkins
Vice President, Mission Support Services
Air Traffic Organization

Distribution: ZAT-710, ZAT-464

Initiated By: AJV-0
Vice President, Mission Support Services

Explanation of Changes
Change 1

Direct questions through appropriate facility/service center office staff to the Office of Primary Interest (OPI)

a. 2–1–4. OPERATIONAL PRIORITY

This change updates procedures and information regarding National Airborne Operations Center (NAOC) and Special Air Missions (SCOOT) missions, including mission notification procedures; clarifying use of the terms NAOC and SCOOT in air/ground communications; and approving special handling requests.

b. 5–2–15. VALIDATION OF MODE C READOUT

This change modifies the reference of "coast/suspend tabular list" to a more generic "Coast/Suspend Status" to accommodate differences in operating systems used in the NAS. Additionally, formatting changes were made to subparagraphs to improve clarity.

c. 5–5–4. MINIMA
5–5–9. SEPARATION FROM OBSTRUCTIONS

This change replaces current references to terminal airport surveillance radar systems ASR–9 and ASR–11, and their associated secondary radar systems with new terminology associated with the Mode S Beacon Replacement System (MSBRS).

d. 5–9–7. SIMULTANEOUS INDEPENDENT APPROACHES– DUAL & TRIPLE

This change revises the currently published high update rate surveillance (HUR) runway centerline spacing (RCLS) distances to those articulated within the report with improved surveillance update rate conditions. Additionally, runway centerline distances articulated for monitoring approaches is revised to account for recently changed offset approach distances.

e. 7–4–6. RNAV VISUAL FLIGHT PROCEDURES (RVFP)

This change provides specific guidance in the conduct of RNAV Visual Flight Procedures which have historically been covered in Flight Standards orders while the air traffic order has been silent.

f. Editorial Changes

Editorial changes include reference updates in paragraphs 2–2–10 and 2–6–2; updating reference in 10–2–19; updating references in 19 paragraphs throughout to align with JO 7610.4 and JO 7610.14 content division; removal of the abbreviation FMSP for Flight Management System Procedure; replacing the term TARGET MARKERS with DATA BLOCKS in paragraphs 5–3–8 and 5–3–9; and updating the distribution, subscription, and purchase information in Chapter 1, Section 1 and in the Change cover pages.

g. Entire publication

Additional editorial/format changes were made where necessary. Revision bars were not used because of the insignificant nature of these changes.

U.S. DEPARTMENT OF TRANSPORTATION
FEDERAL AVIATION ADMINISTRATION
Air Traffic Organization Policy

JO 7110.65AA
CHG 2

Effective Date:
March 21, 2024

SUBJ: Air Traffic Control

---

1. Purpose of This Change. This change transmits revised pages to Federal Aviation Administration Order JO 7110.65AA, Air Traffic Control, and the Briefing Guide.

2. Audience. This change applies to all Air Traffic Organization (ATO) personnel and anyone using ATO directives.

3. Where Can I Find This Change? This change is available on the FAA website at http://faa.gov/air_traffic/publications and https://employees.faa.gov/tools_resources/orders_notices/.

4. Explanation of Policy Change. See the Explanation of Changes attachment that has editorial corrections and changes submitted through normal procedures. The Briefing Guide lists only new or modified material, along with background.

5. Distribution. This change is distributed to select offices in Washington headquarters, service area offices, the William J. Hughes Technical Center, the Mike Monroney Aeronautical Center, air traffic field facilities, and international aviation offices. This change is distributed electronically to all who subscribe to receive email notification through the FAA's website. All organizations are responsible for viewing, downloading, and subscribing to receive email notifications when changes occur to this order. Subscriptions to air traffic directives can be made through the Air Traffic Plans and Publications website at https://www.faa.gov/air_traffic/publications/ or directly via the following link: https://public.govdelivery.com/accounts/USAFAA/subscriber/new?topic_id=USAFAA_39.

6. Disposition of Transmittal. Retain this transmittal until superseded by a new basic order.

7. Page Control Chart. See the page control chart attachment.

Natasha A. Durkins
Digitally signed by Natasha A. Durkins
Date: 2024.01.29 15:28:28 -05'00'

Natasha A. Durkins
Vice President,
Mission Support Services

Distribution: ZAT-710, ZAT-464

Initiated By: AJV-0
Vice President, Mission Support Services

Explanation of Changes
Change 2

Direct questions through appropriate facility/service center office staff to the Office of Primary Interest (OPI)

a. 3–9–4. LINE UP AND WAIT (LUAW)
3–10–5. LANDING CLEARANCE
3–10–10. ALTITUDE RESTRICTED LOW APPROACH

This change removes use of the word "unrestricted" associated with low approach in FAA Order JO 7110.65, Air Traffic Control, paragraphs 3–9–4, Line Up and Wait (LUAW), and 3–10–5, Landing Clearance. An "unrestricted" low approach is itself a low approach; the term "unrestricted" is not deemed necessary. Additional edits were made to enhance the distinction between aircraft holding on a runway (for example, an aircraft authorized holding on the runway for an engine run-up) and an aircraft authorized LUAW.

b. 3–9–8. INTERSECTING RUNWAY/INTERSECTING FLIGHT PATH OPERATIONS
3–10–4. INTERSECTING RUNWAY/INTERSECTING FLIGHT PATH SEPARATION

This change adds the provisions of the Land and Hold Short Operations (LAHSO) order to FAA Order JO 7110.65 as it pertains to the authorized circumstances of how LAHSO is used.

c. 5–1–2. ATC SURVEILLANCE SOURCE USE

This change clarifies that the provisions of subparagraph 5–1–2a are not applicable when operating in FUSION, except when required by facility directive.

d. 5–2–11. CODE MONITOR

This change adds dedicated beacon code 1203 to other visual flight rules (VFR) codes that are specifically monitored by ATC.

e. 5–2–15. VALIDATION OF MODE C ALTITUDE READOUT

This change corrects the subject of the sentences in subparagraphs 5–2–15e and 5–2–15f to improve clarity by modifying the sentence structure to more accurately describe the conditions being addressed.

f. 5–7–2. METHODS

This change to paragraph 5–7–2 permits speed adjustments of a specified number of knots to be expressed in group form and single–digit form for adjustments to specified speed in knots.

g. 8–1–10. PROCEDURES FOR WEATHER DEVIATIONS AND OTHER CONTINGENCIES IN OCEANIC CONTROLLED AIRSPACE
8–7–5. PROCEDURES FOR WEATHER DEVIATIONS IN NORTH ATLANTIC (NAT) AIRSPACE
8–9–5. PROCEDURES FOR WEATHER DEVIATIONS AND OTHER CONTINGENCIES IN OCEANIC CONTROLLED AIRSPACE

This change removes the "Procedures for Weather Deviations and Other Contingencies in Oceanic Controlled" paragraphs from Sections 7 and 9 and places language into Section 1, General, which will make it clear that the necessary guidance is applicable to all ICAO regions containing oceanic-controlled airspace.

h. 9–2–5. FLYNET

These changes remove references to the term FLYNET in the remarks section of a flight plan and add information that the code word FLYNET will be used in conjunction with the aircraft call sign to request priority handling of a nuclear/radiological or potential nuclear/radiological event.

i. Editorial Changes

Editorial changes include updates to references to Automated Information Transfer procedures in JO 7210.3; a change removing the term "appropriate stratum" from subparagraph 10–4–4c2; a removal of the acronym

STR for Strategic Training Routes, to not conflict with Standard Taxi Routes; a subparagraph reference correction in subparagraph 3−9−6e; updates to references to the Chart Supplement throughout the order; a simple reference correction in paragraphs 5−2−14 and 5−2−22; adding references and links to relevant Interpretations throughout the order; an update to the abbreviation for West Atlantic Route System (WATRS) to its new name, West Atlantic (WAT); correcting the spelling of "Juliet" to "Juliett" throughout; and replacing Operations−Headquarters, AJT−2 with their current office name as Operational Policy and Implementation, AJT−2.

j. Entire publication

Additional editorial/format changes were made where necessary. Revision bars were not used because of the insignificant nature of these changes.

Table of Contents

Chapter 1. General

Section 1. Introduction

Section 2. Terms of Reference

Chapter 2. General Control

Section 1. General

Section 2. Flight Plans and Control Information

Section 3. Flight Progress Strips

Section 4. Radio and Interphone Communications

Paragraph **Page**

Section 5. Route and NAVAID Description

Section 6. Weather Information

Section 7. Altimeter Settings

Section 8. Runway Visibility Reporting– Terminal

Section 9. Automatic Terminal Information Service Procedures

Section 10. Team Position Responsibilities

Paragraph **Page**

Chapter 3. Airport Traffic Control– Terminal

Section 1. General

Section 2. Visual Signals

Section 3. Airport Conditions

Section 4. Airport Lighting

Paragraph **Page**

Section 5. Runway Selection

Section 6. Airport Surface Detection Procedures

Section 7. Taxi and Ground Movement Procedures

Section 8. Spacing and Sequencing

Section 9. Departure Procedures and Separation

Section 10. Arrival Procedures and Separation

Paragraph **Page**

Section 11. Helicopter Operations

Section 12. Sea Lane Operations

Chapter 4. IFR

Section 1. NAVAID Use Limitations

Section 2. Clearances

Section 3. Departure Procedures

Section 4. Route Assignment

Section 5. Altitude Assignment and Verification

Section 6. Holding Aircraft

Section 7. Arrival Procedures

Paragraph **Page**

Section 8. Approach Clearance Procedures

Chapter 5. Radar

Section 1. General

Section 2. Beacon/ADS–B Systems

Section 3. Radar Identification

Section 4. Transfer of Radar Identification

Section 5. Radar Separation

Paragraph Page

Section 6. Vectoring

Section 7. Speed Adjustment

Section 8. Radar Departures

Section 9. Radar Arrivals

Section 10. Radar Approaches– Terminal

Chapter 6. Nonradar

Section 1. General

Section 2. Initial Separation of Successive Departing Aircraft

Section 3. Initial Separation of Departing and Arriving Aircraft

Section 4. Longitudinal Separation

Section 5. Lateral Separation

Section 6. Vertical Separation

Section 7. Timed Approaches

Chapter 7. Visual

Section 1. General

Paragraph **Page**

Section 2. Visual Separation

Section 3. VFR-On-Top

Section 4. Approaches

Section 5. Special VFR (SVFR)

Section 6. Basic Radar Service to VFR Aircraft– Terminal

Section 7. Terminal Radar Service Area (TRSA)– Terminal

Section 4. Lateral Separation

Section 5. Offshore/Oceanic Transition Procedures

Section 6. Separation from Airspace Reservations

Section 7. North Atlantic ICAO Region

Section 8. Caribbean ICAO Region

Section 9. Pacific ICAO Region

Section 10. North American ICAO Region

Chapter 9. Special Flights

Section 1. General

Paragraph **Page**

Section 2. Special Operations

Section 3. Special Use, ATC–Assigned Airspace, and Stationary ALTRVs

Section 4. Fuel Dumping

Section 5. Jettisoning of External Stores

Section 6. Unmanned Free Balloons

Section 7. Parachute Operations

Section 4. Control Actions

Section 5. Miscellaneous Operations

Section 6. Oceanic Emergency Procedures

Section 7. Ground Missile Emergencies

Chapter 11. Traffic Management Procedures

Section 1. General

Chapter 12. Canadian Airspace Procedures

Section 1. General Control

Chapter 13. Decision Support Tools

Section 1. ERAM – En Route

Section 2. ATOP - Oceanic

Appendices

Chapter 1. General

Section 1. Introduction

1-1-1. PURPOSE OF THIS ORDER

This order prescribes air traffic control procedures and phraseology for use by persons providing air traffic control services. Controllers are required to be familiar with the provisions of this order that pertain to their operational responsibilities and to exercise their best judgment if they encounter situations that are not covered by it.

1-1-2. AUDIENCE

This order applies to all ATO personnel and anyone using ATO directives.

1-1-3. WHERE TO FIND THIS ORDER

This order is available on the FAA's Air Traffic Plans and Publications website at http://faa.gov/air_traffic/publications and Orders & Notices website at https://www.faa.gov/regulations_policies/orders_notices/.

1-1-4. WHAT THIS ORDER CANCELS

FAA Order JO 7110.65Z, Air Traffic Control, dated June 17, 2021, and all changes to it are canceled.

1-1-5. EXPLANATION OF CHANGES

The significant changes to this order are identified in the Explanation of Changes page(s). It is advisable to retain the page(s) throughout the duration of the basic order.

1-1-6. EFFECTIVE DATES AND SUBMISSIONS FOR CHANGES

a. This order and its changes are scheduled to be published to coincide with AIRAC dates. (See TBL 1-1-1.)

b. The "Cutoff Date for Completion" in the table below refers to the deadline for a proposed change to be fully coordinated and signed. Change initiators must submit their proposed changes well in advance of this cutoff date to meet the publication effective date. The process to review and coordinate changes often takes several months after the change is initially submitted.

TBL 1-1-1
Publication Schedule

Basic or Change	Cutoff Date for Completion	Effective Date of Publication
JO 7110.65AA	11/3/22	4/20/23
Change 1	4/20/23	10/5/23
Change 2	10/5/23	3/21/24
Change 3	3/21/24	9/5/24
JO 7110.65BB	9/5/24	2/20/25
Change 1	2/20/25	8/7/25
Change 2	8/7/25	1/22/26
Change 3	1/22/26	7/9/26

1-1-7. DELIVERY DATES

a. This order will be available on the FAA's website 30 days prior to its effective date.

b. If an FAA facility **has not** received the order/changes at least 30 days before the above effective dates, the facility must notify its service area office distribution officer.

c. If a military facility **has not** received the order/changes at least 30 days before the above effective dates, the facility must notify its appropriate military headquarters. (See TBL 1-1-2.)

TBL 1-1-2
Military Distribution Contacts

Military Headquarters	DSN	Commercial
U.S. Army USAASA	656-4868	(703) 806-4868
U.S. Air Force HQ AFFSA	884-5509	(405) 734-5509
U.S. Navy CNO (N980A)	224-2638	(703) 614-2638

1-1-8. RECOMMENDATIONS FOR PROCEDURAL CHANGES

The office of primary responsibility (OPR) for this order is:

FAA Headquarters, Mission Support Services
Policy (AJV-P)
600 Independence Avenue, SW
Washington, DC 20597

a. Personnel should submit recommended changes in procedures to facility management.

b. Recommendations from other sources should be submitted through appropriate FAA, military, or industry/user channels.

c. Proposed changes must be submitted electronically to 9-AJV-P-HQ-Correspondence@faa.gov. The submission should include a description of the recommended change, and the proposed language to be used in the order.

NOTE-
For details on the submission process as well as additional AJV-P processing responsibilities, please see FAA Order JO 7000.5, Procedures for Submitting Changes to Air Traffic Control Publications.

d. Procedural changes will not be made to this order until the operational system software has been adapted to accomplish the revised procedures.

1-1-9. REQUESTS FOR INTERPRETATIONS OR CLARIFICATIONS TO THIS ORDER

a. Interpretation requests from field air traffic personnel must be submitted as follows:

1. The request must be submitted, in writing, by an Air Traffic Facility/General manager to their Service Area Director.

2. The Service Area Director must review the request and determine if more than one interpretation on the intent of the language can be inferred.

3. If it is determined that an interpretation is required, the Service Area Director must submit the request, in writing, to the Policy Directorate, for a response.

b. If a request does not require an interpretation but further clarification is needed it must be forwarded to the Service Center Operations Support Group for a response.

1. The Service Center Operations Support Group may consult with the Policy Directorate when preparing their response.

2. The Service Center Operations Support Group must provide a written response to the requestor and forward the response to the Policy Directorate.

c. Interpretation requests from all other sources must be submitted to the Policy Directorate at 9–AJV–P–HQ–Correspondence@faa.gov.

NOTE–
Interpretations can be accessed through the Air Traffic Control Interpretation link at the following website: https://my.faa.gov/org/linebusiness/ato/mission_support/psgroup/atc_interpretations.html.

1–1–10. PROCEDURAL LETTERS OF AGREEMENT (LOA)

Procedures/minima which are applied jointly or otherwise require the cooperation or concurrence of more than one facility/organization must be documented in a letter of agreement. LOAs only supplement this order. Any minima they specify must not be less than that specified herein unless appropriate military authority has authorized application of reduced separation between military aircraft.

REFERENCE–
FAA Order JO 7110.65, Para 2–1–1, ATC Service.
FAA Order JO 7210.3, Para 4–3–1, Letters of Agreement.

1–1–11. CONSTRAINTS GOVERNING SUPPLEMENTS AND PROCEDURAL DEVIATIONS

a. Exceptional or unusual requirements may dictate procedural deviations or supplementary procedures to this order. Prior to implementing supplemental or any procedural deviation that alters the level, quality, or degree of service, obtain prior approval from the Vice President, Mission Support Services.

b. If military operations or facilities are involved, prior approval by the following appropriate headquarters is required for subsequent interface with FAA. (See TBL 1–1–3.)

TBL 1–1–3
Military Operations Interface Offices

Branch	Address
U.S. Navy	Department of the Navy Chief of Naval Operations N980A, NAATSEA 2000 Navy Pentagon (5D453) Washington, D.C. 20350–2000
U.S. Air Force	HQ AFFSA 5316 S. Douglas Blvd Bldg 8400, Room 232 Oklahoma City, OK 73150
U.S. Army	Director USAASA (MOAS–AS) 9325 Gunston Road, Suite N319 Ft. Belvoir, VA 22060–5582

NOTE–
Terminal: Headquarters Air Force Flight Standards Agency is the approval authority for any USAF procedures or minima that differ from those specified herein and that involve military aircraft only.

REFERENCE–
FAA Order JO 7110.65, Para 2–1–12, Military Procedures.
FAA Order JO 7110.65, Para 3–1–3, Use of Active Runways.

1-1-12. SAFETY MANAGEMENT SYSTEM (SMS)

Every employee is responsible to ensure the safety of equipment and procedures used in the provision of services within the National Airspace System (NAS). Risk assessment techniques and mitigations, as appropriate, are intended for implementation of any planned safety significant changes within the NAS, as directed by FAA Order 1100.161, Air Traffic Safety Oversight. Direction regarding the SMS and its application can be found in the FAA Safety Management System Manual and FAA Order 1100.161. The SMS will be implemented through a period of transitional activities. (Additional information pertaining to these requirements and processes can be obtained by contacting the service area offices.)

1-1-13. REFERENCES TO FAA NON-AIR TRAFFIC ORGANIZATIONS

When references are made to regional office organizations that are not part of the Air Traffic Organization (i.e., Communications Center, Flight Standards, Airport offices, etc.), the facility should contact the FAA region where the facility is physically located – not the region where the facility's service area office is located.

1-1-14. DISTRIBUTION

a. This order is distributed to selected offices in Washington headquarters, regional offices, service area offices, the William J. Hughes Technical Center, the Mike Monroney Aeronautical Center, and to all air traffic field facilities and international aviation field offices.

b. This order is distributed electronically to all who subscribe to receive email notifications through the FAA's website. All organizations are responsible for viewing, downloading, and subscribing to receive email notifications when changes occur to this order. Subscriptions to air traffic directives can be made through the Air Traffic Plans and Publications website at https://www.faa.gov/air_traffic/publications/ or directly via the following link: https://public.govdelivery.com/accounts/USAFAA/subscriber/new?topic_id=USAFAA_39.

Section 2. Terms of Reference

1–2–1. WORD MEANINGS

As used in this order:

a. "Shall" or "must" means a procedure is mandatory.

b. "Shall not" or "must not" means a procedure is prohibited.

c. "Should" means a procedure is recommended.

d. "May" or "need not" means a procedure is optional.

e. "Will" means futurity, not a requirement for the application of a procedure.

f. Singular words include the plural.

g. Plural words include the singular.

h. "Aircraft" means the airframe, crew members, or both.

i. "Approved separation" means separation in accordance with the applicable minima in this order.

j. "Altitude" means indicated altitude mean sea level (MSL), flight level (FL), or both.

k. "Miles" means nautical miles unless otherwise specified, and means statute miles in conjunction with visibility.

l. "Course," "bearing," "azimuth," "heading," and "wind direction" information must always be magnetic unless specifically stated otherwise.

m. "Time" when used for ATC operational activities, is the hour and the minute in Coordinated Universal Time (UTC). Change to the next minute is made at the minute plus 30 seconds, except time checks are given to the nearest quarter minute.

n. "Runway" means the runway used by aircraft and, unless otherwise specified, does not include helipads and/or their accompanying takeoff/landing courses. (See Pilot/Controller Glossary terms – Runway and Helipad.)

o. Flight operations in accordance with the options of "due regard" or "operational" have the following requirements:

1. Obligates the authorized state aircraft commander to:

(a) Separate his/her aircraft from all other air traffic; and

(b) Assure that an appropriate monitoring agency assumes responsibility for search and rescue actions; and

(c) Operate under at least one of the following conditions:

(1) In visual meteorological conditions (VMC); or

(2) Within an area that is covered by an ATC surveillance source and in communications with ATC, or within surveillance source service volume and radio communications range of a facility, Department of Homeland Security or DoD unit capable of providing the pilot assistance to operate with due regard to other aircraft; or

(3) Be equipped with airborne radar that is sufficient to provide separation between his/her aircraft and any other aircraft he/she may be controlling and other aircraft; or

(4) Operate within Class G airspace.

2. An understanding between the pilot and controller regarding the intent of the pilot and the status of the flight should be reached before the aircraft leaves ATC frequency.

NOTE–

1. *A pilot's use of the phrase "Going Tactical" does not indicate "Due Regard."*

2. *The above conditions provide for a level of safety equivalent to that normally given by International Civil Aviation Organization (ICAO) ATC agencies and fulfills U.S. Government obligations under Article 3, paragraph d, of the Chicago Convention of 1944, which stipulates there must be "due regard for the safety of navigation of civil aircraft" when flight is not being conducted under ICAO flight procedures.*

REFERENCE–
DoD Instruction (DoDI) 4540.1, Enclosure 3, Para 3c(1)(c).
DoD Flight Information Publication (FLIP), Section 8–6c(1).

p. "CFR" means Code of Federal Regulations.

FIG 1–2–1
Divergence

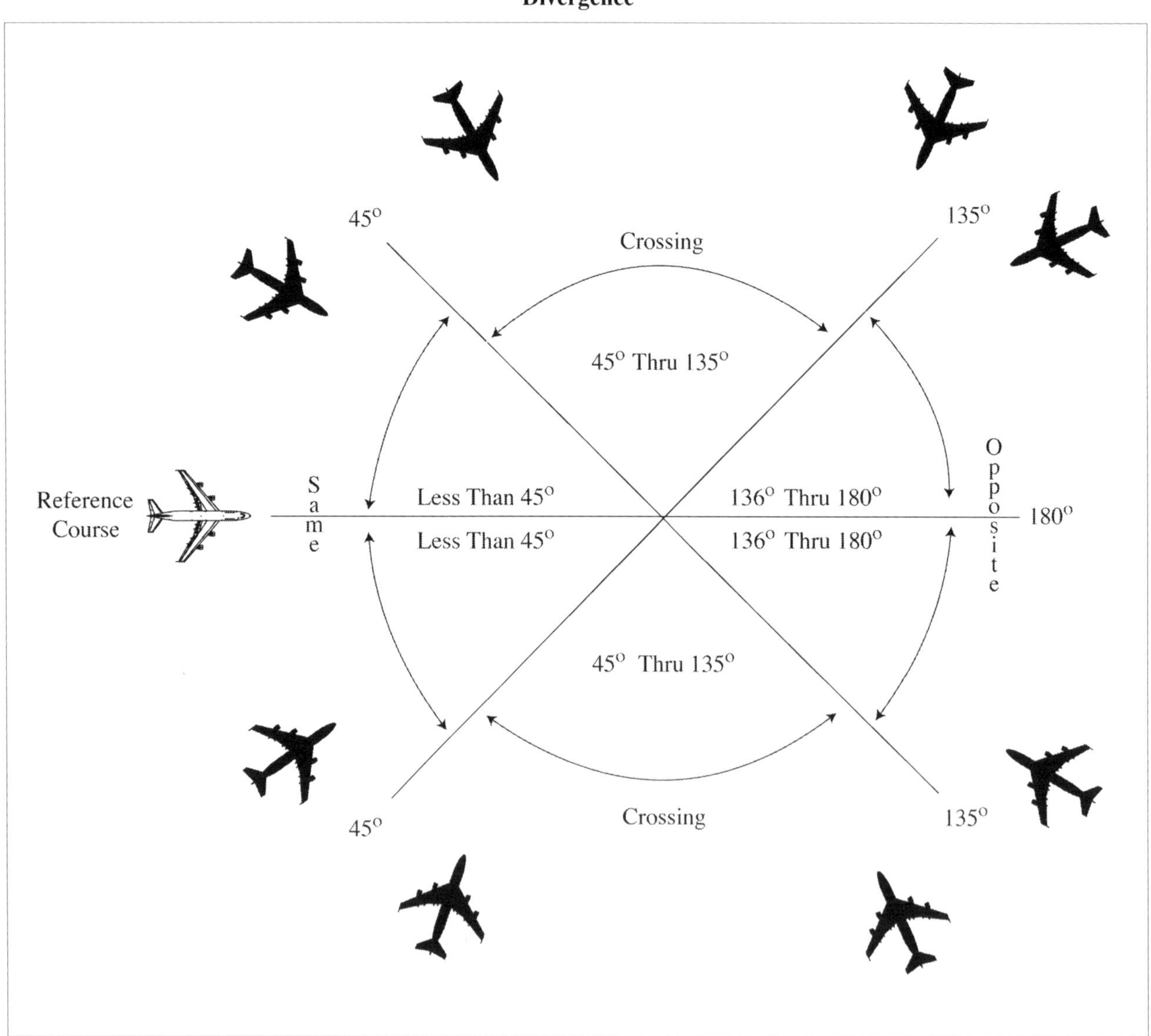

1–2–2. COURSE DEFINITIONS

The following definitions must be used in the application of the separation criteria in this order.

NOTE–
The term "protected airspace," as used in this paragraph, is the airspace equal to one half the required applicable lateral separation on either side of an aircraft along its projected flight path. If the protected airspace of two aircraft does not overlap, applicable lateral separation is ensured.

a. *SAME COURSES* are courses whose protected airspaces are coincident, overlap, or intersect and whose angular difference is less than 45 degrees. (See FIG 1–2–1.)

b. *CROSSING COURSES* are intersecting courses whose angular difference is 45 through 135 degrees inclusive. (See FIG 1–2–1.)

c. *OPPOSITE/RECIPROCAL COURSES* are courses whose protected airspaces are coincident, overlap, or intersect and whose angular difference is greater than 135 degrees through 180 degrees inclusive. (See FIG 1–2–1.)

1–2–3. NOTES

Statements of fact, or of a prefatory or explanatory nature relating to directive material, are set forth as notes.

1–2–4. REFERENCES

As used in this order, references direct attention to an additional or supporting source of information such as FAA, NWS, and other agencies' orders, directives, notices, CFRs, and Advisory Circulars (ACs).

1–2–5. ANNOTATIONS

Revised, reprinted, or new pages are marked as follows:

a. The change number and the effective date are printed on each revised or additional page.

b. A page that does not require a change is reprinted in its original form.

c. Bold vertical lines in the margin of changed pages indicate the location of substantive revisions to the order. Bold vertical lines adjacent to the title of a chapter, section, or paragraph means that extensive changes have been made to that chapter, section, or paragraph.

d. Paragraphs/sections annotated with *EN ROUTE, OCEANIC,* or *TERMINAL* are only to be applied by the designated type facility. When they are not so designated, the paragraphs/sections apply to all types of facilities (en route, oceanic, and terminal).

e. The annotation, *USAF* for the U.S. Air Force, *USN* for the U.S. Navy, and *USA* for the U.S. Army denotes that the procedure immediately following the annotation applies only to the designated service.

REFERENCE–
FAA Order JO 7110.65, Para 2–1–12, Military Procedures.

f. WAKE TURBULENCE APPLICATION inserted within a paragraph means that the remaining information in the paragraph requires the application of wake turbulence procedures.

g. The annotation ***PHRASEOLOGY*** denotes the prescribed words and/or phrases to be used in communications.

NOTE–
Controllers may, after first using the prescribed phraseology for a specific procedure, rephrase the message to ensure the content is understood. Good judgment must be exercised when using nonstandard phraseology.

h. The annotation ***EXAMPLE*** provides a sample of the way the prescribed phraseology associated with the preceding paragraph(s) will be used. If the preceding paragraph(s) does (do) not include specific prescribed phraseology, the ***EXAMPLE*** merely denotes suggested words and/or phrases that may be used in communications.

NOTE–
The use of the exact text contained in an example not preceded with specific prescribed phraseology is not mandatory. However, the words and/or phrases are expected, to the extent practical, to approximate those used in the example.

1-2-6. ABBREVIATIONS

As used in this order, the abbreviations listed below have the following meanings indicated. (See TBL 1-2-1.)

TBL 1-2-1
FAA Order JO 7110.65 Abbreviations

Abbreviation	Meaning
AAR	Adapted arrival route
AAR	Airport arrival rate
AC	Advisory Circular
ACC	Area Control Center
ACE-IDS ...	ASOS Controller Equipment- Information Display System
ACL	Aircraft list
ACLS	Automatic Carrier Landing System
ADAR	Adapted departure arrival route
ADC	Aerospace Defense Command
ADIZ	Air Defense Identification Zone (to be pronounced "AY DIZ")
ADR	Adapted departure route
ADS	Automatic Dependent Surveillance
ADS-B	Automatic Dependent Surveillance-Broadcast
ADS-C	Automatic Dependent Surveillance-Contract
AFP	Airspace Flow Program
AIDC	ATS Interfacility Data Communications
AIM	Aeronautical Information Manual
AIRMET ...	Airmen's meteorological information
ALDARS ...	Automated Lightning Detection and Reporting System
ALERFA ...	Alert phase code (Alerting Service)
ALNOT	Alert notice
ALS	Approach Light System
ALTRV	Altitude reservation
AM	Ambiguity-A disparity greater than a locally adapted distance exists between the position declared for a target by MEARTS and another facility's computer declared position during interfacility handoff
AMASS	Airport Movement Area Safety System
AMB	Ambiguity-A disparity greater than a locally adapted distance exists between the position declared for a target by STARS and another facility's computer declared position during interfacility handoff
AMVER	Automated Mutual Assistance Vessel Rescue System
ANG	Air National Guard
APR	ATC preferred route
APREQ	Approval Request
ARAC	Army Radar Approach Control facility (US Army)
ARINC	Aeronautical Radio Incorporated
ARIP	Air refueling initial point
ARSR	Air route surveillance radar
ARTCC	Air Route Traffic Control Center
ASD	Aircraft Situation Display
ASDE	Airport surface detection equipment
ASDE-X ...	Airport Surface Detection Equipment System - Model X
ASF	Airport Stream Filters
ASOS	Automated Surface Observing System
ASR	Airport surveillance radar
ASSC	Airport Surface Surveillance Capability
ATC	Air traffic control
ATCAA	ATC assigned airspace
ATCSCC	David J. Hurley Air Traffic Control System Command Center
ATD	Along-Track Distance
ATIS	Automatic Terminal Information Service
ATO	Air Traffic Organization
ATO COO ..	Air Traffic Organization Chief Operating Officer
ATOP	Advanced Technologies and Oceanic Procedures
ATS	Air Traffic Service
AWOS	Automated Weather Observing System
BASE	Cloud base
CA	Conflict Alert
CARCAH ...	Chief, Aerial Reconnaissance Coordination, All Hurricanes
CARF	Central Altitude Reservation Function
CAT	Clear air turbulence
CDT	Controlled departure time
CEP	Central East Pacific
CERAP	Combined Center/RAPCON
CFR	Code of Federal Regulations
CFR	Call for Release
CIC	Controller-in-Charge

Abbreviation	Meaning
CNS	Continuous
CPDLC	Controller Pilot Data Link Communications
CPME	Calibration Performance Monitor Equipment
CTA	Control Area
CTRD	Certified Tower Radar Display
CVFP	Charted Visual Flight Procedure
CWA	Center Weather Advisory
DETRESFA .	Distress Phase code (Alerting Service)
DH	Decision height
DL	Departure List
DME	Distance measuring equipment compatible with TACAN
DOE	Department of Energy
DP	Instrument Departure Procedure
DR	Dead reckoning
DRT	Diversion recovery tool
DSR	Display System Replacement
DTAS	Digital Terminal Automation Systems
DTM	Digital Terrain Map
DVFR	Defense Visual Flight Rules
DVRSN	Diversion
EA	Electronic Attack
EAS	En Route Automation System
EDCT	Expect Departure Clearance Time
EDST	En Route Decision Support Tool
EFC	Expect further clearance
EFVS	Enhanced Flight Vision System
ELDB	Enhanced Limited Data Block
ELP	Emergency Landing Pattern
ELT	Emergency locator transmitter
EoR	Established on RNP
EOVM	Emergency obstruction video map
EOS	End Service
ERAM	En Route Automation Modernization
ERIDS	En Route Information Display System
ERT	Embedded route text
ETA	Estimated time of arrival
FAA	Federal Aviation Administration
FANS	Future Air Navigation System
FDB	Full Data Block
FDIO	Flight Data Input/Output
FDP	Flight data processing
FICON	Field Condition
FIR	Flight Information Region
FL	Flight level
FLIP	Flight Information Publication
FLY	Fly or flying
FMS	Flight Management System
FSM	Flight Schedule Monitor
FSS	Flight Service Station
GCA	Ground controlled approach
GNSS	Global Navigation Satellite System
GPD	Graphics Plan Display
GPS	Global Positioning System
GS	Ground stop
HF/RO	High Frequency/Radio Operator
HIRL	High intensity runway lights
IAFDOF	Inappropriate Altitude for Direction of Flight
ICAO	International Civil Aviation Organization
IDENT	Aircraft identification
IDS	Information Display System
IFR	Instrument flight rules
IFSS	International Flight Service Station
ILS	Instrument Landing System
INCERFA ...	Uncertainty Phase code (Alerting Service)
INREQ	Information request
INS	Inertial Navigation System
IR	IFR military training route
IRU	Inertial Reference Unit
ISR	Increased Separation Required
ITWS	Integrated Terminal Weather System
JATO	Jet assisted takeoff
LAHSO	Land and Hold Short Operations
LOA	Letter of Agreement
LLWAS	Low Level Wind Shear Alert System
LLWAS NE .	Low Level Wind Shear Alert System Network Expansion
LLWAS–RS .	Low Level Wind Shear Alert System Relocation/Sustainment
L/MF	Low/medium frequency
LORAN	Long Range Navigation System
Mach	Mach number
MALS	Medium Intensity Approach Light System
MALSR	Medium Approach Light System with runway alignment indicator lights

Abbreviation	Meaning
MAP	Missed approach point
MARSA	Military authority assumes responsibility for separation of aircraft
MCA	Minimum crossing altitude
MCI	Mode C Intruder
MDA	Minimum descent altitude
MDM	Main display monitor
MEA	Minimum en route (IFR) altitude
MEARTS ...	Micro En Route Automated Radar Tracking System
METAR	Aviation Routine Weather Report
MIA	Minimum IFR altitude
MIAWS	Medium Intensity Airport Weather System
MIRL	Medium intensity runway lights
MNPS	Minimum Navigation Performance Specification
MNT	Mach Number Technique
MOA	Military operations area
MOCA	Minimum obstruction clearance altitude
MRA	Minimum reception altitude
MSAW	Minimum Safe Altitude Warning
MSL	Mean sea level
MTI	Moving target indicator
MTR	Military training route
MVA	Minimum vectoring altitude
NADIN	National Airspace Data Interchange Network
NAR	National Automation Request
NAS	National Airspace System
NAT	ICAO North Atlantic Region
NAT HLA ...	North Atlantic High Level Airspace
NBCAP	National Beacon Code Allocation Plan
NDB	Nondirectional radio beacon
NHOP	National Hurricane Operations Plan
NM	Nautical mile
NOAA	National Oceanic and Atmospheric Administration
NOPAC	North Pacific
NORAD	North American Aerospace Defense Command
NOS	National Ocean Service
NOTAM	Notice to Air Missions
NOWGT	No weight. The weight class or wake category has not been determined
NRP	North American Route Program

Abbreviation	Meaning
NRR	Nonrestrictive Route
NRS	Navigation Reference System
NTZ	No transgression zone
NWS	National Weather Service
NWSOP	National Winter Storm Operations Plan
ODALS	Omnidirectional Approach Lighting System
ODP	Obstacle Departure Procedure
OID	Operator Interface Device
OS	Operations Supervisor
OTR	Oceanic transition route
PAPI	Precision Approach Path Indicators
PAR	Precision approach radar
PBCT	Proposed boundary crossing time
P/CG	Pilot/Controller Glossary
PDC	Pre–Departure Clearance
PIREP	Pilot Weather Report
PPI	Plan position indicator
PTP	Point–to–point
PVD	Plan view display
RA	Radar Associate
RAIL	Runway alignment indicator lights
RAPCON ...	Radar Approach Control facility (USAF, USN and USMC)
RATCF	Radar Air Traffic Control Facility (USN and USMC)
RBS	Radar bomb scoring
RCC	Rescue Coordination Center
RCLS	Runway Centerline System
RCR	Runway condition reading
RE	Recent (used to qualify weather phenomena such as rain, e.g. recent rain = RERA)
REIL	Runway end identifier lights
RF	Radius–to–Fix
RNAV	Area navigation
RNP	Required Navigation Performance
RTQC	Real–Time Quality Control
RVR	Runway visual range
RVSM	Reduced Vertical Separation Minimum
RwyCC	Runway Condition Codes
RwyCR	Runway Condition Report
SAA	Special Activity Airspace

Abbreviation	Meaning
SAR	Search and rescue
SATCOM ...	Satellite Communication
SDP	Surveillance Data Processing
SELCAL	Selective Calling System
SFA	Single frequency approach
SFO	Simulated flameout
SID	Standard Instrument Departure
SIGMET	Significant meteorological information
SPA	Special Posting Area
SPECI	Nonroutine (Special) Aviation Weather Report
STAR	Standard terminal arrival
STARS	Standard Terminal Automation Replacement System
STMC	Supervisory Traffic Management Coordinator
STMCIC	Supervisory Traffic Management Coordinator–in–charge
STOL	Short takeoff and landing
SURPIC	Surface Picture
SVFR	Special Visual Flight Rules
TAA	Terminal arrival area
TAS	Terminal Automation Systems
TACAN	TACAN UHF navigational aid (omnidirectional course and distance information)
TAWS	Terrain Awareness Warning System
TCAS	Traffic Alert and Collision Avoidance System
TCDD	Tower cab digital display
TDLS	Terminal Data Link System
TDW	Tower display workstation
TDWR	Terminal Doppler Weather Radar
TDZL	Touchdown Zone Light System
TF	Track–to–Fix
TFMS	Traffic Flow Management System
TMC	Traffic Management Coordinator
TMU	Traffic Management Unit
TRACON ...	Terminal Radar Approach Control
TRSA	Terminal radar service area
UFO	Unidentified flying object
UHF	Ultra high frequency
USA	United States Army
USAF	United States Air Force
USN	United States Navy
UTC	Coordinated universal time
UTM	Unsuccessful transmission message
UUA	Urgent pilot weather report
VCI	Voice Communication Indicator
VFR	Visual flight rules
VHF	Very high frequency
VMC	Visual meteorological conditions
VNAV	Vertical Navigation
VOR	VHF navigational aid (omnidirectional course information)
VOR/DME ..	Collocated VOR and DME navigational aids (VHF course and UHF distance information)
VORTAC ...	Collocated VOR and TACAN navigation aids (VHF and UHF course and UHF distance information)
VR	VFR military training route
VSCS	Voice Switching and Control System
WAAS	Wide Area Augmentation System
WARP	Weather and Radar Processing
WAT	West Atlantic
WRA	Weather Reconnaissance Area
WSO	Weather Service Office
WSP	Weather System Processor
WST	Convective SIGMET

Chapter 2. General Control

Section 1. General

2-1-1. ATC SERVICE

a. The primary purpose of the ATC system is to prevent a collision involving aircraft operating in the system.

b. In addition to its primary purpose, the ATC system also:

1. Provides a safe, orderly, and expeditious flow of air traffic.

2. Supports National Security and Homeland Defense missions.

c. The ATC system must provide certain additional services to the extent permitted. The provision of additional services is not optional on the part of the controller, but rather required when the work situation permits. It is recognized that the provision of these services may be precluded by various factors, including, but not limited to:

1. Volume of traffic.

2. Frequency congestion.

3. Quality of surveillance.

4. Controller workload.

5. Higher priority duties.

6. The physical inability to scan and detect situations falling in this category.

d. Controllers must provide air traffic control service in accordance with the procedures and minima in this order, except when one or more of the following conditions exists:

1. A deviation is necessary to conform with ICAO Documents, National Rules of the Air, or special agreements where the U.S. provides air traffic control service in airspace outside the U.S. and its possessions or:

NOTE–
Pilots are required to abide by CFRs or other applicable regulations regardless of the application of any procedure or minima in this order.

2. Other procedures/minima are prescribed in a letter of agreement, FAA directive, or a military document, or:

NOTE–
These procedures may include altitude reservations, air refueling, fighter interceptor operations, law enforcement, etc.

REFERENCE–
FAA Order JO 7110.65, Para 1–1–10, Procedural Letters of Agreement (LOA).

3. A deviation is necessary to assist an aircraft when an emergency has been declared.

REFERENCE–
FAA Order JO 7110.65, Para 2–1–6, Safety Alert.
FAA Order JO 7110.65, Chapter 10, Emergencies.
FAA Order JO 7110.65, Para 5–1–4, Merging Target Procedures.

INTERPRETATION–
7110.65, 2–1–1 c, ATC Service; Emergencies and 10–1–1 d, Emergency Determinations (6–11–2015)

e. Air Traffic Control services are not provided for model aircraft operating in the NAS or to any UAS operating in the NAS at or below 400ft AGL.

NOTE–
1. *This does not prohibit ATC from providing services to civil and public UAS.*

2. *The provisions of this paragraph apply to model aircraft operating at any altitude. For all other UAS, this paragraph applies only to those UAS operating entirely at or below 400ft AGL.*

REFERENCE–
P/CG Term – Model Aircraft.

2–1–2. DUTY PRIORITY

a. Give first priority to separating aircraft and issuing safety alerts as required in this order. Good judgment must be used in prioritizing all other provisions of this order based on the requirements of the situation at hand.

REFERENCE–
FAA Order JO 7110.65, Para 2–1–6, Safety Alert.

NOTE–
Because there are many variables involved, it is virtually impossible to develop a standard list of duty priorities that would apply uniformly to every conceivable situation. Each set of circumstances must be evaluated on its own merit, and when more than one action is required, controllers must exercise their best judgment based on the facts and circumstances known to them. That action which is most critical from a safety standpoint is performed first.

b. Provide support to national security and homeland defense activities to include, but not be limited to, reporting of suspicious and/or unusual aircraft/pilot activities.

REFERENCE–
FAA Order JO 7610.4, Sensitive Procedures and Requirements for Special Operations.

c. Provide and/or solicit weather information in accordance with procedures and requirements outlined in this order.

NOTE–
Controllers are responsible to become familiar with and stay aware of current weather information needed to perform ATC duties.

d. Provide additional services to the extent possible, contingent only upon higher priority duties and other factors including limitations of radar, volume of traffic, frequency congestion, and workload.

2–1–3. PROCEDURAL PREFERENCE

a. Use automation procedures in preference to nonautomation procedures when workload, communications, and equipment capabilities permit.

b. Use automation procedures that provide closed loop clearances in preference to open loop clearances to promote operational advantage for time–based management (TBM) when workload permits. (e.g., a QU route pick that anticipates length of vector and includes the next fix that ties into the route of flight.)

c. Use radar separation in preference to nonradar separation when it will be to an operational advantage and workload, communications, and equipment permit.

d. Use nonradar separation in preference to radar separation when the situation dictates that an operational advantage will be gained.

NOTE–
One situation may be where vertical separation would preclude excessive vectoring.

2–1–4. OPERATIONAL PRIORITY

It is recognized that traffic flow may affect the controller's ability to provide priority handling. However, without compromising safety, good judgment must be used in each situation to facilitate the most expeditious movement of priority aircraft. Provide air traffic control service to aircraft on a "first come, first served" basis as circumstances permit, except the following:

NOTE−
It is solely the pilot's prerogative to cancel an IFR flight plan. However, a pilot's retention of an IFR flight plan does not afford priority over VFR aircraft. For example, this does not preclude the requirement for the pilot of an arriving IFR aircraft to adjust his/her flight path, as necessary, to enter a traffic pattern in sequence with arriving VFR aircraft.

a. An aircraft in distress has the right of way over all other air traffic.

REFERENCE−
14 CFR Section 91.113(c).

b. Treat air ambulance flights as follows:

1. Provide priority handling to civil air ambulance flights when the pilot, in radio transmissions, verbally identifies the flight by stating "MEDEVAC" followed by the FAA authorized call sign or the full civil registration letters/numbers. Good judgment must be used in each situation to facilitate the most expeditious movement of a MEDEVAC aircraft.

NOTE−
If a flight plan includes the letter "L" for "MEDEVAC" and/or includes "MEDEVAC" in Item 11 (Remarks) of the flight plan or Item 18 (Other Information) of an international flight plan, the entries are considered informational in nature only and not an identification for operational priority.

REFERENCE−
FAA Order JO 7110.65, Para 2−4−20, Aircraft Identification.

2. Provide priority handling to AIR EVAC and HOSP flights when verbally requested by the pilot.

NOTE−
If a flight plan includes "HOSP" or "AIR EVAC" in either Item 11 (Remarks) or Item 18 (Other Information) of an international flight plan, the entries are considered informational in nature only and not an identification for operational priority. For aircraft identification in radio transmissions, civilian pilots will use normal call signs when filing "HOSP" and military pilots will use the "EVAC" call sign.

3. Assist the pilots of MEDEVAC, AIR EVAC, and HOSP aircraft to avoid areas of significant weather and adverse conditions.

4. If requested by a pilot, provide additional assistance (i.e., landline notifications) to expedite ground handling of patients, vital organs, or urgently needed medical materials.

c. Provide priority handling and expedite the movement of presidential aircraft and entourage and any rescue support aircraft as well as related control messages when traffic conditions and communications facilities permit.

NOTE−
As used herein the terms presidential aircraft and entourage include aircraft and entourage of the President, Vice President, or other public figures when designated by the White House.

REFERENCE−
FAA Order JO 7110.65, Para 2−4−20, Aircraft Identification.
FAA Order JO 7110.65, Para 4−3−2, Departure Clearances.
FAA Order JO 7210.3, Para 5−1−1, Advance Coordination.

d. Provide priority handling and maximum assistance to SAR aircraft performing a SAR mission.

REFERENCE−
FAA Order JO 7110.65, Para 10−1−3, Providing Assistance.

e. Provide priority handling and maximum assistance to expedite the movement of interceptor aircraft on active air defense missions until the unknown aircraft is identified.

f. Provide priority handling to NIGHT WATCH "NAOC" (pronounced NAY−OCK) aircraft when notified via landline or when "NAOC" is used in air/ground communications. When the term "NAOC" is used, approve any request(s) as soon as practicable.

NOTE−
The term "NAOC" will not be a part of the Flight ID in the flight plan or used in conjunction with the call sign but may otherwise be used when the aircraft is airborne.

REFERENCE−
FAA Order JO 7610.4, Para 9−1−1, Applications.

g. Provide priority handling to any civil or military aircraft using the code name "FLYNET."

REFERENCE–
FAA Order JO 7110.65, Para 9–2–5, FLYNET.
FAA Order JO 7610.4, Para 9–4–1, "FLYNET" Flights, Nuclear Emergency Teams.

h. Provide priority handling to aircraft using the code name "Garden Plot" only when CARF notifies you that such priority is authorized. Refer any questions regarding flight procedures to CARF for resolution.

NOTE–
Garden Plot flights require priority movement and are coordinated by the military with CARF. State authority will contact the Regional Administrator to arrange for priority of National Guard troop movements within a particular state.

i. Provide priority handling to USAF or other government aircraft engaged in aerial sampling/surveying missions using the call sign "SAMP."

REFERENCE–
FAA Order JO 7110.65, Para 9–2–17, SAMP Flights.
FAA Order JO 7210.3, Para 5–3–2, Aerial Sampling/Surveying For Airborne Contamination.

j. Provide priority handling to Special Air Mission "SCOOT" aircraft when notified via landline or when "SCOOT" is used in air/ground communications. When the term "SCOOT" is used, approve any request(s) as soon as practicable.

NOTE–
The term "SCOOT" will not be a part of the Flight ID in the flight plan but may be used during radio communications in conjunction with the call sign.

REFERENCE–
FAA Order JO 7610.4, Para 9–6–1, Applications.

k. When requested, provide priority handling to TEAL and NOAA mission aircraft.

REFERENCE–
FAA Order JO 7110.65, Para 9–2–19, Weather Reconnaissance Flights.

l. Provide priority handling, as required to expedite Flight Check aircraft.

NOTE–
It is recognized that unexpected wind conditions, weather, or heavy traffic flows may affect controller's ability to provide priority or special handling at the specific time requested.

REFERENCE–
FAA Order JO 7110.65, Para 9–1–3, Flight Check Aircraft.

m. IFR aircraft must have priority over SVFR aircraft.

REFERENCE–
FAA Order JO 7110.65, Chapter 7, Section 5, Special VFR (SVFR).

n. Aircraft operating under the North American Route Program (NRP) are not subject to route limiting restrictions (e.g., published preferred IFR routes, letter of agreement requirements, standard operating procedures).

REFERENCE–
FAA Order JO 7110.65, Para 2–3–2, En Route Data Entries.
FAA Order JO 7110.65, Para 2–2–15, North American Route Program (NRP) Information.
FAA Order JO 7110.65, Para 4–2–5, Route or Altitude Amendments.
FAA Order JO 7210.3, Chapter 18, Section 17, North American Route Program.

o. If able, provide priority handling to diverted flights. Priority handling may be requested via use of "DVRSN" in the remarks section of the flight plan or by the flight being placed on the Diversion Recovery Tool (DRT).

REFERENCE–
FAA Order JO 7210.3, Para 18–4–5, Diversion Recovery.

p. If able, provide priority handling to FALLEN HERO flights when "FALLEN HERO" is indicated in the remarks section of the flight plan or requested in air/ground communications.

2–1–5. EXPEDITIOUS COMPLIANCE

a. Use the word "immediately" only when expeditious compliance is required to avoid an imminent situation.

b. Use the word "expedite" only when prompt compliance is required to avoid the development of an imminent situation. If an "expedite" climb or descent clearance is issued by ATC, and subsequently the altitude to maintain is changed or restated without an expedite instruction, the expedite instruction is canceled.

c. In either case, if time permits, include the reason for this action.

2-1-6. SAFETY ALERT

Issue a safety alert to an aircraft if you are aware the aircraft is in a position/altitude that, in your judgment, places it in unsafe proximity to terrain, obstructions, or other aircraft. Once the pilot informs you action is being taken to resolve the situation, you may discontinue the issuance of further alerts. Do not assume that because someone else has responsibility for the aircraft that the unsafe situation has been observed and the safety alert issued; inform the appropriate controller.

NOTE–
1. *The issuance of a safety alert is a first priority (see paragraph 2-1-2, Duty Priority) once the controller observes and recognizes a situation of unsafe aircraft proximity to terrain, obstacles, or other aircraft. Conditions, such as workload, traffic volume, the quality/limitations of the radar system, and the available lead time to react are factors in determining whether it is reasonable for the controller to observe and recognize such situations. While a controller cannot see immediately the development of every situation where a safety alert must be issued, the controller must remain vigilant for such situations and issue a safety alert when the situation is recognized.*

2. *Recognition of situations of unsafe proximity may result from MSAW/E-MSAW, automatic altitude readouts, Conflict/Mode C Intruder Alert, observations on a PAR scope, or pilot reports.*

3. *Once the alert is issued, it is solely the pilot's prerogative to determine what course of action, if any, will be taken.*

a. Terrain/Obstruction Alert. Immediately issue/initiate an alert to an aircraft if you are aware the aircraft is at an altitude that, in your judgment, places it in unsafe proximity to terrain and/or obstructions. Issue the alert as follows:

PHRASEOLOGY–
LOW ALTITUDE ALERT (call sign),

CHECK YOUR ALTITUDE IMMEDIATELY.

and, if the aircraft is not yet on final approach,

THE (as appropriate) MEA/MVA/MOCA/MIA IN YOUR AREA IS (altitude).

REFERENCE–
P/CG Term – Final Approach – IFR

b. Aircraft Conflict/Mode C Intruder Alert. Immediately issue/initiate an alert to an aircraft if you are aware of another aircraft at an altitude that you believe places them in unsafe proximity. If feasible, offer the pilot an alternate course of action. When an alternate course of action is given, end the transmission with the word "immediately."

PHRASEOLOGY–
TRAFFIC ALERT (call sign) (position of aircraft) ADVISE YOU TURN LEFT/RIGHT (heading),

and/or

CLIMB/DESCEND (specific altitude if appropriate) IMMEDIATELY.

EXAMPLE–
"Traffic Alert, Cessna Three Four Juliett, 12'o clock, 1 mile advise you turn left immediately."
or
"Traffic Alert, Cessna Three-Four Juliett, 12'o clock, 1 mile advise you turn left and climb immediately."

REFERENCE–
FAA Order JO 7110.65, Para 5–13–1, Conflict Alert (CA) and Mode C Intruder (MCI) Alert.
FAA Order JO 7110.65, Para 5–13–2, En Route Minimum Safe Altitude Warning (E–MSAW).
FAA Order JO 7110.65, Para 5–14–6, CA/MCI.
FAA Order JO 7110.65, Para 5–2–21, Altitude Filters.
FAA Order JO 7110.65, Para 2–1–21, Traffic Advisories.

2–1–7. INFLIGHT EQUIPMENT MALFUNCTIONS

a. When a pilot reports an inflight equipment malfunction, determine the nature and extent of any special handling desired.

NOTE–
Inflight equipment malfunctions include partial or complete failure of equipment, which may affect either safety, separation standards, and/or the ability of the flight to proceed under IFR, or in Reduced Vertical Separation Minimum (RVSM) airspace, in the ATC system. Controllers may expect reports from pilots regarding VOR, TACAN, ADF, GPS, RVSM capability, or low frequency navigation receivers, impairment of air–ground communications capability, or other equipment deemed appropriate by the pilot (e.g., airborne weather radar). Pilots should communicate the nature and extent of any assistance desired from ATC.

b. Provide the maximum assistance possible consistent with equipment, workload, and any special handling requested.

c. Relay to other controllers or facilities who will subsequently handle the aircraft, all pertinent details concerning the aircraft and any special handling required or being provided.

2–1–8. MINIMUM FUEL

If an aircraft declares a state of "minimum fuel," inform any facility to whom control jurisdiction is transferred of the minimum fuel problem and be alert for any occurrence which might delay the aircraft en route.

NOTE–
Use of the term "minimum fuel" indicates recognition by a pilot that his/her fuel supply has reached a state where, upon reaching destination, he/she cannot accept any undue delay. This is not an emergency situation but merely an advisory that indicates an emergency situation is possible should any undue delay occur. A minimum fuel advisory does not imply a need for traffic priority. Common sense and good judgment will determine the extent of assistance to be given in minimum fuel situations. If, at any time, the remaining usable fuel supply suggests the need for traffic priority to ensure a safe landing, the pilot should declare an emergency and report fuel remaining in minutes.

2–1–9. REPORTING ESSENTIAL FLIGHT INFORMATION

Report as soon as possible to the appropriate FSS, airport manager's office, ARTCC, approach control facility, operations office, or military operations office any information concerning components of the NAS or any flight conditions which may have an adverse effect on air safety.

NOTE–
FSSs are responsible for classifying and disseminating Notices to Air Missions.

REFERENCE–
FAA Order JO 7110.65, Para 3–3–3, Timely Information.
FAA Order JO 7210.3, Para 3–1–2, Periodic Maintenance.
USN, See OPNAVINST 3721.30.

2–1–10. NAVAID MALFUNCTIONS

a. When an aircraft reports a ground–based NAVAID malfunction, take the following actions:

1. Request a report from a second aircraft.

2. If the second aircraft reports normal operations, continue use and inform the first aircraft. Record the incident on FAA Form 7230–4 or appropriate military form.

3. If the second aircraft confirms the malfunction or in the absence of a second aircraft report, activate the standby equipment or request the monitor facility to activate.

4. If normal operation is reported after the standby equipment is activated, continue use, record the incident on FAA Form 7230−4 or appropriate military form, and notify technical operations personnel (the Systems Engineer of the ARTCC when an en route aid is involved).

5. If continued malfunction is reported after the standby equipment is activated or the standby equipment cannot be activated, inform technical operations personnel and request advice on whether or not the aid should be shut down. In the absence of a second aircraft report, advise the technical operations personnel of the time of the initial aircraft report and the estimated time a second aircraft report could be obtained.

b. When an aircraft reports a GPS or WAAS anomaly, request the following information and/or take the following actions:

1. Record the following minimum information:

(a) Aircraft make, model, and call sign.

(b) Location or position, and altitude at the time where GPS or WAAS anomaly was observed.

(c) Date/time of occurrence.

2. Request a report from a second aircraft.

3. Record the incident on FAA Form 7230−4 or appropriate military form.

4. Inform other aircraft of the anomaly as specified in subparagraph 4−8−1k, l, or m, as applicable.

PHRASEOLOGY−
ATTENTION ALL AIRCRAFT, GPS REPORTED UNRELIABLE (OR WAAS UNAVAILABLE) IN VICINITY/AREA (position).

EXAMPLE−
"Attention all aircraft, GPS reported unreliable (or WAAS unavailable) in the area 30 miles south of Waco VOR."

c. When a pilot reports a WAAS anomaly, determine from the pilot what indications he or she observes and record the information in accordance with subparagraph b above.

2−1−11. USE OF MARSA

a. MARSA may only be applied to military operations specified in a letter of agreement or other appropriate FAA or military document.

NOTE−
Application of MARSA is a military command prerogative. It will not be invoked indiscriminately by individual units or pilots. It will be used only for IFR operations requiring its use. Commands authorizing MARSA will ensure that its implementation and terms of use are documented and coordinated with the control agency having jurisdiction over the area in which the operations are conducted. Terms of use will assign responsibility and provide for separation among participating aircraft.

b. ATC facilities do not invoke or deny MARSA. Their sole responsibility concerning the use of MARSA is to provide separation between military aircraft engaged in MARSA operations and other nonparticipating IFR aircraft.

c. DoD must ensure that military pilots requesting special use airspace/ATCAAs have coordinated with the scheduling agency, have obtained approval for entry, and are familiar with the appropriate MARSA procedures. ATC is not responsible for determining which military aircraft are authorized to enter special use airspace/ATCAAs.

REFERENCE−
FAA Order JO 7110.65, Para 9−2−13, Military Aerial Refueling.

2-1-12. MILITARY PROCEDURES

Military procedures in the form of additions, modifications, and exceptions to the basic FAA procedure are prescribed herein when a common procedure has not been attained or to fulfill a specific requirement. They must be applied by:

a. ATC facilities operated by that military service.

EXAMPLE-
1. *An Air Force facility providing service for an Air Force base would apply USAF procedures to all traffic regardless of class.*

2. *A Navy facility providing service for a Naval Air Station would apply USN procedures to all traffic regardless of class.*

b. ATC facilities, regardless of their parent organization (FAA, USAF, USN, USA), supporting a designated military airport exclusively. This designation determines which military procedures are to be applied.

EXAMPLE-
1. *An FAA facility supports a USAF base exclusively; USAF procedures are applied to all traffic at that base.*

2. *An FAA facility provides approach control service for a Naval Air Station as well as supporting a civil airport; basic FAA procedures are applied at both locations by the FAA facility.*

3. *A USAF facility supports a USAF base and provides approach control service to a satellite civilian airport; USAF procedures are applied at both locations by the USAF facility.*

REFERENCE-
FAA Order JO 7110.65, Para 1-2-5, Annotations.

c. Other ATC facilities when specified in a letter of agreement.

EXAMPLE-
A USAF unit is using a civil airport supported by an FAA facility- USAF procedures will be applied as specified in a letter of agreement between the unit and the FAA facility to the aircraft of the USAF unit. Basic FAA procedures will be applied to all other aircraft.

2-1-13. FORMATION FLIGHTS

Control formation flights as a single aircraft. Separation responsibility between aircraft within the formation rests with the flight leader and the pilots of the other aircraft in the flight. This includes transition periods when aircraft within the formation are maneuvering to attain separation from each other to effect individual control during join-up and breakaway.

REFERENCE-
P/CG Term - Formation Flight.
FAA Order JO 7610.14, Chapter 7, Section 3, Military Formation Flight.
ICAO Annex 2, 3.1.8 Formation Flights.

a. Support formation flight join-up for two aircraft when all of the following occur:

1. Requested by any participating pilot.

2. All participating pilots concur.

3. Either of the participating pilots reports the other/s in sight.

EXAMPLE-
"ROOK01 has EAGLE03 in sight, request formation join-up with EAGLE03 at flight level two zero zero. EAGLE03 will be the lead."

"EAGLE03 verify requesting flight join-up with ROOK01."

If affirmative:

"ROOK01 climb and maintain flight level two zero zero. Report (advise) when formation join-up is complete."

b. If multiple single aircraft request to join–up, multiple formations are joining as one, or aircraft are joining an established formation, obtain confirmation of required items listed in subparagraph 2–1–13a, from the lead aircraft.

REFERENCE–
P/CG Term – Formation Flight

c. After join–up, aircraft beacon code assignment will be determined by formation type.

1. For a standard formation only the aircraft acting as the lead will squawk an ATC assigned beacon code. Ensure all other aircraft squawk standby.

2. For a nonstandard formation, each aircraft should squawk an ATC assigned beacon code. Controller discretion allows aircraft in a nonstandard formation to squawk standby if operationally advantageous.

REFERENCE–
FAA Order JO 7610.14, Para 7–3–6, Nonstandard Formation Tactics, Subpara b3.

EXAMPLE–
"N123JP squawk standby."

Or

"N123SP have N123JP squawk standby."

d. When formation break–up is requested, issue control instructions and/or clearances which will result in approved separation through the lead or directly to the requesting aircraft in the formation.

EXAMPLE–
"N5871S requesting flight break–up with N731K. N731K is changing destination to PHL."
"N731K squawk 5432, turn right, fly heading zero–seven–zero.

"Center, BAMA21. BAMA23 is requesting to RTB."
"BAMA21 have BAMA23 squawk 5544, descend and maintain flight level one–niner–zero and change to my frequency."

"Center, BAMA21. BAMA23 is requesting to RTB."
"BAMA23 squawk 5544. BAMA23 Radar contact (position if required). Cleared to SSC via direct. Descend and maintain flight level one–niner–zero."

REFERENCE–
FAA Order JO 7110.65, Para 5–5–8, Additional Separation for Formation Flights.
P/CG Term– Formation Flight.

e. Military and civil formation flights in RVSM airspace.

1. Utilize RVSM separation standards for a formation flight, which consists of all RVSM approved aircraft.

2. Utilize non–RVSM separation standards for a formation flight at or above FL 290, which does not consist of all RVSM approved aircraft.

3. If aircraft are requesting to form a formation flight to FL 290 or above, the controller who issues the clearance creating the formation flight is responsible for ensuring that the proper equipment suffix is entered for the lead aircraft.

4. If the flight departs as a formation, and is requesting FL 290 or above, the first center sector must ensure that the proper equipment suffix is entered.

5. If the formation flight is below FL 290 and later requests FL 290 or above, the controller receiving the RVSM altitude request must ensure the proper equipment suffix is entered.

6. Upon break–up of the formation flight, the controller initiating the break–up must ensure that all aircraft or flights are assigned their proper equipment suffix.

2–1–14. COORDINATE USE OF AIRSPACE

a. Ensure that the necessary coordination has been accomplished before you allow an aircraft under your control to enter another controller's area of jurisdiction.

b. Before you issue a control instruction directly to a pilot that will change the aircraft's heading, route, speed, or altitude, you must ensure that coordination has been completed with all controllers whose area of jurisdiction is affected by those instructions unless otherwise specified by a letter of agreement or facility directive. If your control instruction will be relayed to the pilot through a source other than another radar controller (FSS, New York Radio, San Francisco Radio, another pilot, etc.), you are still responsible to ensure that all required coordination is completed.

NOTE–
1. *It is good operating practice for controllers to confirm that required coordination has been/will be effected, especially in unusual circumstances, such as recently modified sector configurations, airspace changes, route changes, etc.*

2. *Ensuring that all required coordination has been completed does not necessarily imply that the controller issuing the control instruction directly to the pilot has to perform the coordination action.*

REFERENCE–
FAA Order JO 7110.65, Para 2–1–15, Control Transfer.
FAA Order JO 7110.65, Para 5–5–10, Adjacent Airspace.
FAA Order JO 7110.65, Para 5–4–5, Transferring Controller Handoff.
FAA Order JO 7110.65, Para 5–4–6, Receiving Controller Handoff.

2–1–15. CONTROL TRANSFER

a. Transfer control of an aircraft in accordance with the following conditions:

1. At a prescribed or coordinated location, time, fix, or altitude; or,

2. At the time a radar handoff and frequency change to the receiving controller have been completed and when authorized by a facility directive or letter of agreement which specifies the type and extent of control that is transferred.

REFERENCE–
FAA Order JO 7110.65, Para 2–1–14, Coordinate Use of Airspace.
FAA Order JO 7110.65, Para 5–4–5, Transferring Controller Handoff.
FAA Order JO 7110.65, Para 5–4–6, Receiving Controller Handoff.

b. Transfer control of an aircraft only after eliminating any potential conflict with other aircraft for which you have separation responsibility.

c. Assume control of an aircraft only after it is in your area of jurisdiction unless specifically coordinated or as specified by letter of agreement or a facility directive.

2–1–16. SURFACE AREAS

a. Coordinate with the appropriate nonapproach control tower on an individual aircraft basis before issuing a clearance which would require flight within a surface area for which the tower has responsibility unless otherwise specified in a letter of agreement.

REFERENCE–
FAA Order JO 7210.3, Para 4–3–1, Letters of Agreement.
14 CFR Section 91.127, Operating on or in the Vicinity of an Airport in Class E Airspace.
P/CG Term – Surface Area.

b. Coordinate with the appropriate control tower for transit authorization when you are providing radar traffic advisory service to an aircraft that will enter another facility's airspace.

NOTE–
The pilot is not expected to obtain his/her own authorization through each area when in contact with a radar facility.

c. Transfer communications to the appropriate facility, if required, prior to operation within a surface area for which the tower has responsibility.

REFERENCE–
FAA Order JO 7110.65, Para 2–1–17, Radio Communications.
FAA Order JO 7110.65, Para 3–1–11, Surface Area Restrictions.
FAA Order JO 7110.65, Para 7–6–1, Application.
14 CFR Section 91.129, Operations in Class D Airspace.

2-1-17. RADIO COMMUNICATIONS

a. Transfer radio communications before an aircraft enters the receiving controller's area of jurisdiction unless otherwise coordinated or specified by a letter of agreement or a facility directive.

b. Transfer radio communications by specifying the following:

NOTE-
Radio communications transfer procedures may be specified by a letter of agreement or contained in the route description of an MTR as published in the DoD Planning AP/1B (AP/3).

1. The facility name or location name and terminal function to be contacted. *TERMINAL*: Omit the location name when transferring communications to another controller within your facility, or, when the tower and TRACON share the same name (for example, Phoenix Tower and Phoenix TRACON).

EXCEPTION. Controllers must include the name of the facility when instructing an aircraft to change frequency for final approach guidance.

2. Frequency to use except the following may be omitted:

(a) FSS frequency.

(b) Departure frequency if previously given or published on a SID chart for the procedure issued.

(c) *TERMINAL:*

(1) Ground or local control frequency if in your opinion the pilot knows which frequency is in use.

(2) The numbers preceding the decimal point if the ground control frequency is in the 121 MHz bandwidth.

EXAMPLE-
"Contact Tower."
"Contact Ground."
"Contact Ground Point Seven."
"Contact Ground, One Two Zero Point Eight."
"Contact Huntington Radio."
"Contact Departure."
"Contact Los Angeles Center, One Two Three Point Four."

3. Time, fix, altitude, or specifically when to contact a facility. You may omit this when compliance is expected upon receipt.

NOTE-
AIM, paragraph 5-3-1, ARTCC Communications, informs pilots that they are expected to maintain a listening watch on the transferring controller's frequency until the time, fix, or altitude specified.

PHRASEOLOGY-
CONTACT (facility name or location name and terminal function), (frequency).

If required,

AT (time, fix, or altitude).

c. Controllers must, within a reasonable amount of time, take appropriate action to establish/restore communications with all aircraft for which a communications transfer or initial contact to his/her sector is expected/required.

NOTE-
For the purposes of this paragraph, a reasonable amount of time is considered to be 5 minutes from the time the aircraft enters the controller's area of jurisdiction or comes within range of radio/communications coverage. Communications include two-way VHF or UHF radio contact, data link, or high frequency (HF) radio through an approved third-party provider such as New York Radio or San Francisco Radio.

d. ERAM facilities, beginning with initial audio contact with an aircraft, must utilize the voice communication indicator to reflect the current status of voice communications.

e. In situations where an operational advantage will be gained, and following coordination with the receiving controller, you may instruct aircraft on the ground to monitor the receiving controller's frequency.

EXAMPLE–
"Monitor Tower."
"Monitor Ground."
"Monitor Ground Point Seven."
"Monitor Ground, One Two Zero Point Eight."

f. In situations where a sector has multiple frequencies or when sectors are combined using multiple frequencies and the aircraft will remain under your jurisdiction, transfer radio communication by specifying the following:

PHRASEOLOGY–
(Identification) CHANGE TO MY FREQUENCY (state frequency).

EXAMPLE–
"United two twenty-two change to my frequency one two three point four."

REFERENCE–
AIM, Para 4–2–3, Contact Procedures.

g. Avoid issuing a frequency change to helicopters known to be single-piloted during air-taxiing, hovering, or low-level flight. Whenever possible, relay necessary control instructions until the pilot is able to change frequency.

NOTE–
Most light helicopters are flown by one pilot and require the constant use of both hands and feet to maintain control. Although Flight Control Friction Devices assist the pilot, changing frequency near the ground could result in inadvertent ground contact and consequent loss of control. Pilots are expected to advise ATC of their single-pilot status if unable to comply with a frequency change.

REFERENCE–
AIM, Para 4–3–14, Communications.

h. In situations where the controller does not want the pilot to change frequency but the pilot is expecting or may want a frequency change, use the following phraseology.

PHRASEOLOGY–
REMAIN THIS FREQUENCY.

REFERENCE–
FAA Order JO 7110.65, Para 4–7–1, Clearance Information.
FAA Order JO 7110.65, Para 5–12–9, Communication Transfer.

2–1–18. OPERATIONAL REQUESTS

Respond to a request from another controller, a pilot or vehicle operator by one of the following verbal means:

a. Restate the request in complete or abbreviated terms followed by the word "APPROVED." The phraseology "APPROVED AS REQUESTED" may be substituted in lieu of a lengthy readback.

PHRASEOLOGY–
(Requested operation) APPROVED.

or

APPROVED AS REQUESTED.

b. State restrictions followed by the word "APPROVED."

PHRASEOLOGY–
(Restriction and/or additional instructions, requested operation) APPROVED.

c. State the word "UNABLE" and, time permitting, a reason.

PHRASEOLOGY–
UNABLE (requested operation).

and when necessary,

(reason and/or additional instructions.)

d. State the words "STAND BY."

NOTE–
"STAND BY" is not an approval or denial. The controller acknowledges the request and will respond at a later time.

REFERENCE–
FAA Order JO 7110.65, Para 2–1–21, Traffic Advisories.
FAA Order JO 7110.65, Para 4–2–5, Route or Altitude Amendments.
FAA Order JO 7110.65, Para 7–9–3, Methods.

2–1–19. WAKE TURBULENCE

a. Apply wake turbulence procedures to an aircraft operating behind another aircraft when wake turbulence separation is required.

NOTE–
Paragraph 5–5–4, Minima, subparagraphs f and g specify the required radar wake turbulence separations. Time-based separations are contained in paragraph 3–9–6, Same Runway Separation, paragraph 3–9–7, Wake Turbulence Separation for Intersection Departures, paragraph 3–9–8, Intersecting Runway Separation, paragraph 3–9–9, Nonintersecting Converging Runway Operations, paragraph 3–10–3, Same Runway Separation, paragraph 3–10–4, Intersecting Runway Separation, paragraph 6–1–4, Adjacent Airport Operation, paragraph 6–1–5, Arrival Minima, and paragraph 6–7–5, Interval Minima.

b. The separation minima must continue to touchdown for all IFR aircraft not making a visual approach or maintaining visual separation.

REFERENCE–
FAA Order JO 7110.65, Para 5–9–5, Approach Separation Responsibility.

2–1–20. WAKE TURBULENCE CAUTIONARY ADVISORIES

a. Issue wake turbulence cautionary advisories including the position, altitude if known, and direction of flight to aircraft operating behind an aircraft that requires wake turbulence separation when:

REFERENCE–
AC 90–23, Aircraft Wake Turbulence, Pilot Responsibility, Para 11.
FAA Order JO 7110.65, Para 5–5–4, Minima, subpara f.

1. *TERMINAL.* VFR aircraft not being radar vectored are behind the larger aircraft.

2. IFR aircraft accept a visual approach or visual separation.

REFERENCE–
FAA Order JO 7110.65, Para 7–4–1, Visual Approach.

3. *TERMINAL.* VFR arriving aircraft that have previously been radar vectored and the vectoring has been discontinued.

b. Issue cautionary information to any aircraft if in your opinion, wake turbulence may have an adverse effect on it. When traffic is known to be a Super aircraft, include the word *Super* in the description. When traffic is known to be a Heavy aircraft, include the word *Heavy* in the description.

NOTE–
Wake turbulence is generated when an aircraft produces lift. Because the location of wake turbulence is difficult to determine, the controller is not responsible for anticipating its existence or effect. Aircraft flying through a Super/Heavy aircraft's flight path may have an increased chance of a wake encounter.

REFERENCE–
AC 90–23, Aircraft Wake Turbulence.
P/CG Term– Aircraft Classes.
P/CG Term– Wake Turbulence.

PHRASEOLOGY−
CAUTION WAKE TURBULENCE (traffic information).

REFERENCE−
FAA Order JO 7110.65, Para 7−2−1, Visual Separation.

2−1−21. TRAFFIC ADVISORIES

Unless an aircraft is operating within Class A airspace or omission is requested by the pilot, issue traffic advisories to all aircraft (IFR or VFR) on your frequency when, in your judgment, their proximity may diminish to less than the applicable separation minima. Where no separation minima applies, such as for VFR aircraft outside of Class B/Class C airspace, or a TRSA, issue traffic advisories to those aircraft on your frequency when in your judgment their proximity warrants it. Provide this service as follows:

a. To radar identified aircraft:

1. Azimuth from aircraft in terms of the 12−hour clock, or

2. When rapidly maneuvering aircraft prevent accurate issuance of traffic as in 1 above, specify the direction from an aircraft's position in terms of the eight cardinal compass points (N, NE, E, SE, S, SW, W, and NW). This method must be terminated at the pilot's request.

3. Distance from aircraft in miles.

4. Direction in which traffic is proceeding and/or relative movement of traffic.

NOTE−
Relative movement includes closing, converging, parallel same direction, opposite direction, diverging, overtaking, crossing left to right, crossing right to left.

5. If known, type of aircraft and altitude.

REFERENCE−
FAA Order JO 7110.65, Para 2−4−21, Description of Aircraft Types.

PHRASEOLOGY−
TRAFFIC, (number) O'CLOCK,

or when appropriate,

(direction) (number) MILES, (direction)−BOUND and/or (relative movement),

and if known,

(type of aircraft and altitude).

or

When appropriate,

(type of aircraft and relative position), (number of feet) FEET ABOVE/BELOW YOU.

If altitude is unknown,

ALTITUDE UNKNOWN.

EXAMPLE−
"Traffic, eleven o'clock, one zero miles, southbound, converging, Boeing Seven Twenty Seven, one seven thousand."
"Traffic, twelve o'clock, one five miles, opposite direction, altitude unknown."
"Traffic, ten o'clock, one two miles, southeast bound, one thousand feet below you."

6. When requested by the pilot, issue radar vectors to assist in avoiding the traffic, provided the aircraft to be vectored is within your area of jurisdiction or coordination has been effected with the sector/facility in whose area the aircraft is operating. If unable to provide radar vectors, inform the pilot.

PHRASEOLOGY–
(Identification) UNABLE RADAR VECTORS (time permitting, a reason).

EXAMPLE–
"November 123, unable radar vectors, you are not under my jurisdiction."

REFERENCE–
FAA Order JO 7110.65, Para 2–1–18, Operational Requests.

7. Inform the pilot of the following when traffic you have issued is not reported in sight:

(a) The traffic is no factor.

(b) The traffic is no longer depicted on radar.

PHRASEOLOGY–
TRAFFIC NO FACTOR/NO LONGER OBSERVED,

or

(number) O'CLOCK TRAFFIC NO FACTOR/NO LONGER OBSERVED,

or

(direction) TRAFFIC NO FACTOR/NO LONGER OBSERVED.

b. To aircraft that are not radar identified:

1. Distance and direction from fix.

2. Direction in which traffic is proceeding.

3. If known, type of aircraft and altitude.

4. ETA over the fix the aircraft is approaching, if appropriate.

PHRASEOLOGY–
TRAFFIC, (number) MILES/MINUTES (direction) OF (airport or fix), (direction)–BOUND,

and if known,

(type of aircraft and altitude),

ESTIMATED (fix) (time),

or

TRAFFIC, NUMEROUS AIRCRAFT VICINITY (location).

If altitude is unknown,

ALTITUDE UNKNOWN.

EXAMPLE–
"Traffic, one zero miles east of Forsythe V–O–R, Southbound, M–D Eighty, descending to one six thousand."
"Traffic, reported one zero miles west of Downey V–O–R, northbound, Apache, altitude unknown, estimated Joliet V–O–R one three one five."
"Traffic, eight minutes west of Chicago Heights V–O–R, westbound, Mooney, eight thousand, estimated Joliet V–O–R two zero three five."
"Traffic, numerous aircraft, vicinity of Delia airport."

c. For aircraft displaying Mode C, not radar identified, issue indicated altitude.

EXAMPLE–
"Traffic, one o'clock, six miles, eastbound, altitude indicates six thousand five hundred."

REFERENCE–
FAA Order JO 7110.65, Para 3–1–6, Traffic Information.
FAA Order JO 7110.65, Para 7–2–1, Visual Separation.
FAA Order JO 7110.65, Para 7–6–10, VFR Departure Information.

2–1–22. UNMANNED AIRCRAFT SYSTEM (UAS) ACTIVITY INFORMATION.

a. Issue UAS advisory information for known UAS activity, when in your judgment their proximity warrants it. If known, include position, distance, course, type of unmanned aircraft (UA), and altitude.

EXAMPLE–
"U–A–S activity, 12 o'clock, 1 mile, southbound, quad copter, 400 feet and below."
"Unmanned aircraft system activity, 2 miles east of Brandywine Airport, 300 feet and below."

b. Issue UAS advisory information for pilot–reported or tower–observed activity, when in your judgment, their proximity warrants it. If known, include position, altitude, course, and type. Continue to issue advisories to potentially impacted aircraft for at least 15 minutes following the last report.

EXAMPLE–
"U–A–S activity reported, 12 o'clock, 1 mile, altitude reported one thousand two hundred."
"Unmanned aircraft system activity observed, 1 mile east of Trenton Airport, altitude unknown."

2–1–23. BIRD ACTIVITY INFORMATION

a. Issue advisory information on pilot-reported, tower-observed, or radar-observed and pilot-verified bird activity. Include position, species or size of birds, if known, course of flight, and altitude. Do this for at least 15 minutes after receipt of such information from pilots or from adjacent facilities unless visual observation or subsequent reports reveal the activity is no longer a factor.

EXAMPLE–
"Flock of geese, one o'clock, seven miles, northbound, last reported at four thousand."
"Flock of small birds, southbound along Mohawk River, last reported at three thousand."
"Numerous flocks of ducks, vicinity Lake Winnebago, altitude unknown."

b. Relay bird activity information to adjacent facilities and to FSSs whenever it appears it will become a factor in their areas.

2–1–24. TRANSFER OF POSITION RESPONSIBILITY

The transfer of position responsibility must be accomplished in accordance with the "Standard Operating Practice (SOP) for the Transfer of Position Responsibility," and appropriate facility directives each time operational responsibility for a position is transferred from one specialist to another.

2–1–25. WHEELS DOWN CHECK

USA/USN

Remind aircraft to check wheels down on each approach unless the pilot has previously reported wheels down for that approach.

NOTE–
The intent is solely to remind the pilot to lower the wheels, not to place responsibility on the controller.

a. Tower must issue the wheels down check at an appropriate place in the pattern.

PHRASEOLOGY–
CHECK WHEELS DOWN.

b. Approach/arrival control, GCA must issue the wheels down check as follows:

1. To aircraft conducting ASR, PAR, or radar monitored approaches, before the aircraft starts descent on final approach.

2. To aircraft conducting instrument approaches and remaining on the radar facility's frequency, before the aircraft passes the outer marker/final approach fix.

PHRASEOLOGY–
WHEELS SHOULD BE DOWN.

2–1–26. SUPERVISORY NOTIFICATION

Ensure supervisor/controller-in-charge (CIC) is aware of conditions which impact sector/position operations including, but not limited to, the following:

a. Weather.

b. Equipment status.

c. Potential sector overload.

d. Emergency situations.

e. Special flights/operations.

f. Aircraft/pilot activity, including unmanned aircraft system (UAS) operation that is considered suspicious, as prescribed in FAA Order JO 7610.4, paragraph 7–3–1, and for information more specific to UAS, FAA Order JO 7210.3, paragraph 2–1–34.

REFERENCE–
P/CG Term – Suspicious UAS.

2–1–27. POSSIBLE PILOT DEVIATION NOTIFICATION

When it appears that the actions of a pilot constitute a pilot deviation, notify the pilot, workload permitting.

PHRASEOLOGY–
(Identification) POSSIBLE PILOT DEVIATION ADVISE YOU CONTACT (facility) AT (telephone number).

NOTE–
The phraseology example identified in this paragraph is commonly referred to as the "Brasher Notification" or "Brasher Warning," which gives flight crews the opportunity to make note of the occurrence for future reference. The use of these terms during direct pilot communications is not appropriate.

REFERENCE–
FAA Order JO 8020.16, Air Traffic Organization Aircraft Accident and Aircraft Incident Notification, Investigation, and Reporting, Chapter 11, Para 3, Air Traffic Facility Responsibilities.

2–1–28. TCAS RESOLUTION ADVISORIES

a. When an aircraft under your control jurisdiction informs you that it is responding to a TCAS Resolution Advisory (RA), do not issue control instructions that are contrary to the RA procedure that a crew member has advised you that they are executing. Provide safety alerts regarding terrain or obstructions and traffic advisories for the aircraft responding to the RA and all other aircraft under your control jurisdiction, as appropriate.

b. Unless advised by other aircraft that they are also responding to a TCAS RA, do not assume that other aircraft in the proximity of the responding aircraft are involved in the RA maneuver or are aware of the responding aircraft's intended maneuvers. Continue to provide control instructions, safety alerts, and traffic advisories as appropriate to such aircraft.

NOTE–
When notified by the pilot of an RA, the controller is not prohibited from issuing traffic advisories and safety alerts.

REFERENCE–
FAA Order JO 7110.65, Para 2–1–6, Safety Alert.
FAA Order JO 7110.65, Para 2–1–21, Traffic Advisories.

c. Once the responding aircraft has begun a maneuver in response to an RA, the controller is not responsible for providing approved separation between the aircraft that is responding to an RA and any other aircraft, airspace, terrain or obstructions. Responsibility for approved separation resumes when one of the following conditions is met:

1. The responding aircraft has returned to its assigned altitude, or

2. A crew member informs you that the TCAS maneuver is completed and you observe that approved separation has been reestablished, or

3. The responding aircraft has executed an alternate clearance and you observe that approved separation has been reestablished.

NOTE–
1. *AC 120–55, Air Carrier Operational Approval and Use of TCAS II, suggests pilots use the following phraseology to notify controllers during TCAS events. When a TCAS RA may affect an ATC clearance, inform ATC when beginning the maneuver, or as soon as workload permits.*

EXAMPLE–
1. *"New York Center, United 321, TCAS RA."*

NOTE–
2. *When the RA has been resolved, the flight crew should advise ATC they are returning to their previously assigned clearance or subsequent amended clearance.*

EXAMPLE–
2. *"New York Center, United 321, clear of conflict, returning to assigned altitude."*

2–1–29. RVSM OPERATIONS

RVSM operations are conducted in RVSM airspace that is defined as any airspace between FL 290 and FL 410 inclusive, where eligible aircraft are separated vertically by 1,000 feet. Controller responsibilities must include but not be limited to the following:

a. Non–RVSM aircraft operating in RVSM airspace.

1. Ensure non-RVSM aircraft are not permitted in RVSM airspace unless they meet the criteria of excepted aircraft and are previously approved by the operations supervisor/CIC. The following aircraft are excepted: DoD, DoD-certified aircraft operated by NASA (T38, F15, F18, WB57, S3, and U2 aircraft only), MEDEVAC, manufacturer aircraft being flown for development/certification, and Foreign State aircraft. These exceptions are accommodated on a workload or traffic-permitting basis.

NOTE–
The operations supervisor/CIC is responsible for system acceptance of a non–RVSM aircraft beyond the initial sector–to–sector coordination following the pilot request to access the airspace. Operations supervisor/CIC responsibilities are defined in FAA Order JO 7210.3, Chapter 6, Section 9, Reduced Vertical Separation Minimum (RVSM).

2. Ensure sector–to–sector coordination for all non–RVSM aircraft operations within RVSM airspace.

3. Inform the operations supervisor/CIC when a non–RVSM exception flight is denied clearance into RVSM airspace or is removed from RVSM airspace.

b. Non–RVSM aircraft transitioning RVSM airspace.

Ensure that operations supervisors/CICs are made aware when non–RVSM aircraft are transitioning through RVSM airspace.

c. Apply appropriate separation standards and remove any aircraft from RVSM airspace that advises it is unable RVSM due to equipment while en route.

d. Use "negative RVSM" in all verbal ground–to–ground communications involving non–RVSM aircraft while cleared to operate within RVSM airspace.

EXAMPLE–
"Point out Baxter1 climbing to FL 360, negative RVSM."

e. For the following situations, use the associated phraseology:

1. To deny clearance into RVSM airspace.

PHRASEOLOGY–
"UNABLE CLEARANCE INTO RVSM AIRSPACE."

2. To request a pilot to report when able to resume RVSM.

PHRASEOLOGY–
"REPORT ABLE TO RESUME RVSM."

f. In the event of a change to an aircraft's RVSM eligibility, amend the RVSM qualifier ("W") in the ICAO equipment string in order to properly identify non–RVSM aircraft on the controller display.

NOTE–
Changing the equipment suffix instead of amending the equipment string may result in incorrect revisions to other ICAO qualifiers.

REFERENCE–
AIM, Para 5–1–9, International Flight Plan (FAA Form 7233–4) IFR Flights (For Domestic or International Flights).
AIM, TBL 5–1–4 Aircraft COM, NAV, and Approach Equipment Qualifiers.

g. ATC may allow aircraft to remain in RVSM airspace using reduced vertical separation minima after the loss of a transponder or Mode C altitude reporting.

NOTE–
In a transponder out situation, the aircraft's altitude–keeping capabilities required for flight in RVSM airspace should remain operational.

REFERENCE–
FAA Order JO 7110.65, Para 4–5–1, Vertical Separation Minima.
FAA Order JO 7110.65, Para 2–3–8, Aircraft Equipment Suffix.
14 CFR Section 91.215 ATC Transponder and Altitude Reporting Equipment and Use.
Advisory Circular AC 91–85B, Authorization of Aircraft and Operators for Flight in Reduced Vertical Separation Minimum (RVSM) Airspace.

2–1–30. TERRAIN AWARENESS WARNING SYSTEM (TAWS) ALERTS

a. When an aircraft under your control jurisdiction informs you that it is responding to a TAWS (or other on–board low altitude) alert, do not issue control instructions that are contrary to the TAWS procedure that a crew member has advised you that they are executing. Provide safety alerts regarding terrain or obstructions and traffic advisories for the aircraft responding to the TAWS alert and all other aircraft under your control jurisdiction, as appropriate.

b. Once the responding aircraft has begun a maneuver in response to TAWS alert, the controller is not responsible for providing approved separation between the aircraft that is responding to a TAWS alert and any other aircraft, airspace, terrain or obstructions. Responsibility for approved separation resumes when one of the following conditions is met:

1. The responding aircraft has returned to its assigned altitude, or

2. A crew member informs you that the TAWS maneuver is completed and you observe that approved separation has been reestablished, or

3. The responding aircraft has executed an alternate clearance and you observe that approved separation has been reestablished.

2–1–31. "BLUE LIGHTNING" EVENTS

Ensure that the supervisor/controller–in–charge (CIC) is notified of reports of possible human trafficking. These may be referred to as "Blue Lightning" events.

Section 2. Flight Plans and Control Information

2–2–1. RECORDING INFORMATION

a. Record flight plan information required by the type of flight plan and existing circumstances. Use authorized abbreviations when possible.

NOTE–
Generally, all military overseas flights are required to clear through a specified military base operations office (BASOPS). Pilots normally will not file flight plans directly with an FAA facility unless a BASOPS is not available. BASOPS will, in turn, forward the IFR flight notification message to the appropriate center.

b. *EN ROUTE.* When flight plans are filed directly with the center, record all items given by the pilot either on a flight progress strip/flight data entry or on a voice recorder. If the latter, enter in box 26 of the initial flight progress strip the sector or position number to identify where the information may be found in the event search and rescue (SAR) activities become necessary.

REFERENCE–
FAA Order JO 7110.65, Para 2–3–2, En Route Data Entries.

2–2–2. FORWARDING INFORMATION

a. Except during EAS FDP operation, forward the flight plan information to the appropriate ATC facility, FSS, or BASOPS and record the time of filing and delivery on the form.

b. *EN ROUTE.* During EAS FDP operation, the above manual actions are required in cases where the data is not forwarded automatically by the computer.

NOTE–
During EAS FDP operation, data is exchanged between interfaced automated facilities and both the data and time of transmission are recorded automatically.

c. *EN ROUTE.* Forward proposed tower en route flight plans and any related amendments to the appropriate departure terminal facility.

2–2–3. FORWARDING VFR DATA

TERMINAL

Forward aircraft departure times to FSSs or military operations offices when they have requested them. Forward other VFR flight plan data only if requested by the pilot.

2–2–4. MILITARY DVFR DEPARTURES

TERMINAL

Forward departure times on all DVFR departures from joint-use airports to the military operations office.

NOTE–
1. *Details for handling air carrier and nonscheduled civil DVFR flight data are contained in FAA Order JO 7610.4, Sensitive Procedures and Requirements for Special Operations.*

2. *Civil pilots departing DVFR from a joint-use airport will include the phrase "DVFR to (destination)" in their initial call-up to an FAA-operated tower.*

2–2–5. IFR TO VFR FLIGHT PLAN CHANGE

Request a pilot to contact the appropriate FSS if the pilot informs you of a desire to change from an IFR to a VFR flight plan.

2-2-6. IFR FLIGHT PROGRESS DATA

Forward control information from controller to controller within a facility, then to the receiving facility as the aircraft progresses along its route. Where appropriate, use computer equipment in lieu of manual coordination procedures. Do not use the remarks section of flight progress strips in lieu of voice coordination to pass control information. Ensure that flight plan and control information is correct and up-to-date. When covered by a letter of agreement/facility directive, the time requirements of subparagraph a may be reduced, and the time requirements of subparagraph b1 and paragraph 2-2-11, Forwarding Amended and UTM Data, subparagraph a may be increased up to 15 minutes when facilitated by automated systems or mandatory radar handoffs; or if operationally necessary because of manual data processing or nonradar operations, the time requirements of subparagraph a may be increased.

NOTE-

1. *The procedures for preparing flight plan and control information related to altitude reservations (ALTRVs) are contained in FAA Order JO 7210.3, paragraph 8-1-2, Facility Operation and Administration, ALTRV Flight Data Processing. Development of the methods for assuring the accuracy and completeness of ALTRV flight plan and control information is the responsibility of the military liaison and security officer.*

2. *The term facility in this paragraph refers to centers and terminal facilities when operating in an en route capacity.*

a. Forward the following information at least 15 minutes before the aircraft is estimated to enter the receiving facility's area:

1. Aircraft identification.

2. Number of aircraft if more than one, heavy aircraft indicator "H/" if appropriate, type of aircraft, and aircraft equipment suffix.

3. Assigned altitude and ETA over last reporting point/fix in transferring facility's area or assumed departure time when the departure point is the last point/fix in the transferring facility's area.

4. Altitude at which aircraft will enter the receiving facility's area if other than the assigned altitude.

5. True airspeed.

6. Point of departure.

7. Route of flight remaining.

8. Destination airport and clearance limit if other than destination airport.

9. ETA at destination airport (not required for military or scheduled air carrier aircraft).

10. Altitude requested by the aircraft if assigned altitude differs from requested altitude (within a facility only).

NOTE-

When an aircraft has crossed one facility's area and assignment at a different altitude is still desired, the pilot will reinitiate the request with the next facility.

REFERENCE-

FAA Order JO 7110.65, Para 4-5-8, Anticipated Altitude Changes.

11. When flight plan data must be forwarded manually and an aircraft has been assigned a beacon code by the computer, include the code as part of the flight plan.

NOTE-

When an airborne aircraft that has been assigned a beacon code by the ARTCC computer and whose flight plan will terminate in another facility's area cancels ATC service, appropriate action should be taken to remove flight plan information on that aircraft.

REFERENCE-

FAA Order JO 7110.65, Para 2-2-11, Forwarding Amended and UTM Data.

12. Longitudinal separation being used in nonradar operations between aircraft at the same altitude if it results in these aircraft having less than 10 minutes separation at the facilities' boundary, unless (otherwise) specified in a Letter of Agreement (LOA).

13. Any additional nonroutine operational information pertinent to flight safety.

NOTE–
EN ROUTE. This includes alerting the receiving controller that the flight is conducting celestial navigation training.

REFERENCE–
FAA Order JO 7110.65, Para 9–2–2, Celestial Navigation Training.

b. Forward position report over last reporting point in the transferring facility's area if any of the following conditions exist:

1. Time differs more than 3 minutes from estimate given.

2. Requested by receiving facility.

3. Agreed to between facilities.

2–2–7. MANUAL INPUT OF COMPUTER-ASSIGNED BEACON CODES

When a flight plan is manually entered into the computer and a computer-assigned beacon code has been forwarded with the flight plan data, insert the beacon code in the appropriate field as part of the input message.

2–2–8. ALTRV INFORMATION

EN ROUTE

When an aircraft is a part of an approved ALTRV, forward only those items necessary to properly identify the flight, update flight data contained in the ALTRV APVL, or revise previously given information.

2–2–9. COMPUTER MESSAGE VERIFICATION

EN ROUTE

Unless your facility is equipped to automatically obtain acknowledgment of receipt of transferred data, when you transfer control information by computer message, obtain, via Service F, acknowledgment that the receiving center has received the message and verification of the following:

a. Within the time limits specified by a letter of agreement or when not covered by a letter of agreement, at least 15 minutes before the aircraft is estimated to enter the receiving facility's area, or at the time of a radar handoff, or coordination for transfer of control:

1. Aircraft identification.

2. Assigned altitude.

3. Departure or coordination fix time.

b. Any cancellation of IFR or EAS generated VFR flight plan.

REFERENCE–
FAA Order JO 7110.65, Para 2–2–6, IFR Flight Progress Data.

2–2–10. TRANSMIT PROPOSED FLIGHT PLAN

EN ROUTE

a. Transmit proposed flight plans which fall within an ARTCC's Proposed Boundary Crossing Time (PBCT) parameter to adjacent ARTCC's via the Computer B network during hours of inter-center computer operation. In addition, when the route of flight of any proposed flight plan exceeds 20 elements external to the originating ARTCC's area, NADIN must be used to forward the data to all affected centers.

b. During nonautomated operation, the proposed flight plans must be sent via NADIN to the other centers involved when any of the following conditions are met:

1. The route of flight external to the originating center's area consists of 10 or more elements and the flight will enter 3 or more other center areas.

NOTE–
An element is defined as either a fix or route as specified in FAA Order JO 7110.10, Flight Services, paragraph 6–2–3, Control Messages.

2. The route of flight beyond the first point of exit from the originating center's area consists of 10 or more elements, which are primarily fixes described in fix-radial-distance or latitude/longitude format, regardless of the number of other center areas entered.

3. The flight plan remarks are too lengthy for interphone transmission.

2–2–11. FORWARDING AMENDED AND UTM DATA

a. Forward any amending data concerning previously forwarded flight plans except that revisions to ETA information in paragraph 2–2–6, IFR Flight Progress Data, need only be forwarded when the time differs by more than 3 minutes from the estimate given.

PHRASEOLOGY–
(Identification), REVISED (revised information).

EXAMPLE–
"American Two, revised flight level, three three zero."

"United Eight Ten, revised estimate, Front Royal two zero zero five."

"Douglas Five Zero One Romeo, revised altitude, eight thousand."

"U.S. Air Eleven Fifty–one, revised type, heavy Boeing Seven Sixty-seven."

REFERENCE–
FAA Order JO 7110.65, Para 2–2–6, IFR Flight Progress Data.

b. Computer acceptance of an appropriate input message fulfills the requirement for sending amended data. During EAS FDP operations, the amendment data are considered acknowledged on receipt of a computer update message or a computer–generated flight progress strip containing the amended data.

NOTE–
1. *The successful utilization of automation equipment requires timely and accurate insertion of changes and/or new data.*

2. *If a pilot is not issued a computer-generated ADR/ADAR/AAR and if amendment data is not entered into the computer, the next controller will have incorrect route information.*

c. Forward any amended control information and record the action on the appropriate flight progress strip. Additionally, when a route or altitude in a previously issued clearance is amended within 30 minutes of an aircraft's proposed departure time, the facility that amended the clearance must coordinate the amendment with the receiving facility via verbal AND automated means to ensure timely passage of the information. If the automated means of coordination are unavailable, then verbal coordination is sufficient.

NOTE–
The term "receiving" facility means the ATC facility that is expected to transmit the amended clearance to the intended aircraft/pilot.

d. *EN ROUTE.* Effect manual coordination on any interfacility flight plan data that is not passed through automated means.

e. EN ROUTE. When a controller receives a UTM notification to an FDIO only facility, they must effect manual coordination for the flight plan data. In addition, the controller must verify the flight plan data to the receiving facility within three minutes of the transfer of control point estimate.

NOTE–
FDIO only facilities are facilities with FDIO but without STARS.

2-2-12. AIRBORNE MILITARY FLIGHTS

Forward to FSSs the following information received from airborne military aircraft:

a. IFR flight plans and changes from VFR to IFR flight plans.

b. Changes to an IFR flight plan as follows:

1. Change in destination:

(a) Aircraft identification and type.

(b) Departure point.

(c) Original destination.

(d) Position and time.

(e) New destination.

(f) ETA.

(g) Remarks including change in fuel exhaustion time.

(h) Revised ETA.

2. Change in fuel exhaustion time.

NOTE–
This makes current information available to FSSs for relay to military bases concerned and for use by centers in the event of two–way radio communications failure.

2-2-13. FORWARDING FLIGHT PLAN DATA BETWEEN U.S. ARTCCs AND CANADIAN ACCs

EN ROUTE

a. *Domestic.* (Continental U.S./Canadian airspace except Alaska) Proposed departure flight plans and en route estimates will be handled on a 30 minute lead time (or as bilaterally agreed) between any ACC and ARTCC.

b. *International.* Any route changes (except SIDs) must be forwarded to the appropriate Oceanic/Pre-oceanic ACC or ARTCC with an optimum lead time of 30 minutes or as soon as this information becomes available.

c. Initially, if a flight goes from U.S. airspace into Canadian airspace and returns to U.S. airspace, the ACC will be responsible for forwarding the flight plan data to the appropriate ARTCC by voice transmission except for flights which traverse mutually agreed on airways/fixes. These airways/fixes will be determined on a case-by-case basis and will be based on time and distance considerations at the service area office.

2-2-14. TELETYPE FLIGHT DATA FORMAT- U.S. ARTCCs - CANADIAN ACCs

EN ROUTE

The exchange of flight plan data between Canadian ACCs and U.S. ARTCCs must be made as follows:

a. The U.S. ARTCCs will transmit flight data to the Canadian ACCs in one of the following formats:

1. NADIN II input format as described in the NAS Management Directives (MDs) for:

(a) Flight Plan Messages:

(1) Active.

(2) Proposed.

(b) Amendment messages.

(c) Cancellation messages.

(d) Response Messages to Canadian Input:

(1) Acknowledgment messages.

(2) Error messages.

(3) Rejection messages.

2. Transport Canada (TC) ACC Flight Strip Format: Where the data to be printed on the ACC strip form exceeds the strip form field size, the NADIN II input format in 1 above will be used. Input sequentially fields 1 through 8 in paragraph 2–2–6, IFR Flight Progress Data, subparagraph a.

b. TC's ACCs will transmit flight data to the FAA ARTCCs in the following format:

1. NADIN II input format as described in NAS MDs for:

(a) Flight Plan Messages:

(1) Active.

(2) Proposed.

(b) Amendment messages.

(c) Cancellation messages.

(d) Correction messages.

2–2–15. NORTH AMERICAN ROUTE PROGRAM (NRP) INFORMATION

a. "NRP" must be retained in the remarks section of the flight plan if the aircraft is moved due to weather, traffic, or other tactical reasons.

NOTE–
Every effort should be made to ensure the aircraft is returned to the original filed flight plan/altitude as soon as conditions warrant.

b. If the route of flight is altered due to a pilot request, "NRP" must be removed from the remarks section of the flight plan.

c. "NRP" must not be entered in the remarks section of a flight plan, unless prior coordination is accomplished with the ATCSCC or as prescribed by international NRP flight operations procedures.

d. The en route facility within which an international flight entering the conterminous U.S. requests to participate in the NRP must enter "NRP" in the remarks section of the flight plan.

REFERENCE–
FAA Order JO 7110.65, Para 2–1–4, Operational Priority.
FAA Order JO 7110.65, Para 2–3–2, En Route Data Entries.
FAA Order JO 7110.65, Para 4–2–5, Route or Altitude Amendments.
FAA Order JO 7210.3, Chapter 18, Section 17, North American Route Program.

Section 3. Flight Progress Strips

2–3–1. GENERAL

Unless otherwise authorized in a facility directive, use flight progress strips to post current data on air traffic and clearances required for control and other air traffic control services. To prevent misinterpretation when data is hand printed, use standard hand-printed characters.
En route: Flight progress strips must be posted.

REFERENCE–
FAA Order JO 7210.3, Para 6–1–6, Flight Progress Strip Usage.

a. Maintain only necessary current data and remove the strips from the flight progress boards when no longer required for control purposes. To correct, update, or preplan information:

1. Do not erase or overwrite any item. Use an "X" to delete a climb/descend and maintain arrow, an at or above/below symbol, a cruise symbol, and unwanted altitude information. Write the new altitude information immediately adjacent to it and within the same space.

2. Do not draw a horizontal line through an altitude being vacated until after the aircraft has reported or is observed (valid Mode C) leaving the altitude.

3. Preplanning may be accomplished in red pencil.

b. Manually prepared strips must conform to the format of machine-generated strips and manual strip preparation procedures will be modified simultaneously with the operational implementation of changes in the machine-generated format. (See FIG 2–3–1.)

c. Altitude information may be written in thousands of feet provided the procedure is authorized by the facility manager, and is defined in a facility directive, i.e., 5,000 feet as 5, and 2,800 as 2.8.

NOTE–
A slant line crossing through the number zero and underline of the letter "s" on handwritten portions of flight progress strips are required only when there is reason to believe the lack of these markings could lead to misunderstanding. A slant line crossing through the number zero is required on all weather data.

FIG 2-3-1

Standard Recording of Hand-printed Characters

Typed	Hand Printed	Typed	Hand Printed
A	A	T	T
B	B	U	U
C	C	V	V
D	D	W	W
E	E	X	X
F	F	Y	Y
G	G	Z	Ƶ
H	H		
I	I	1	1
J	J	2	2
K	K	3	3
L	L	4	4
M	M	5	5
N	N	6	6
O	O	7	7
P	P	8	8
Q	Q	9	9
R	R	0	Ø
S	S		

2-3-2. EN ROUTE DATA ENTRIES

FIG 2-3-2
Flight Progress Strip
(7230-19)

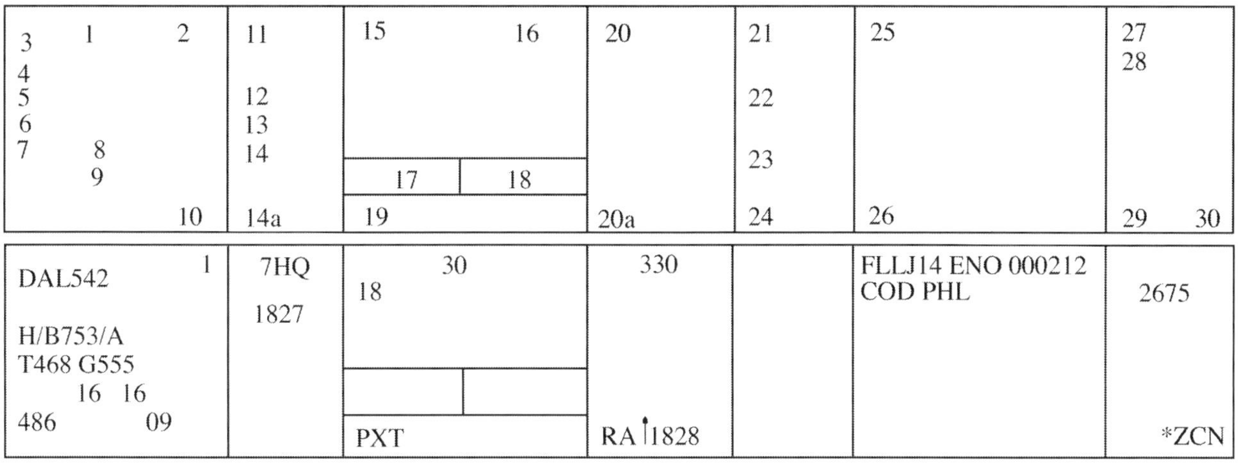

3 1 2 4 5 6 7 8 9 10	11 12 13 14 14a	15 16 17 18 19	20 20a	21 22 23 24	25 26	27 28 29 30
DAL542 1 H/B753/A T468 G555 16 16 486 09	7HQ 1827	30 18 PXT	330 RA↑1828		FLLJ14 ENO 000212 COD PHL	2675 *ZCN

a. Information recorded on the flight progress strips (FAA Forms 7230-19) must be entered in the correspondingly numbered spaces:

TBL 2-3-1

Block	Information Recorded
1.	Verification symbol if required.
2.	Revision number. DSR-Not used.
3.	Aircraft identification.
4.	Number of aircraft if more than one, heavy aircraft indicator "H/" if appropriate, type of aircraft, and aircraft equipment suffix.
5.	Filed true airspeed.
6.	Sector number.
7.	Computer identification number if required.
8.	Estimated ground speed.
9.	Revised ground speed or strip request (SR) originator.
10.	Strip number. DSR- Strip number/Revision number.
11.	Previous fix.
12.	Estimated time over previous fix.
13.	Revised estimated time over previous fix.
14.	Actual time over previous fix, or actual departure time entered on first fix posting after departure.
14a.	Plus time expressed in minutes from the previous fix to the posted fix.
15.	Center-estimated time over fix (in hours and minutes), or clearance information for departing aircraft.
16.	Arrows to indicate if aircraft is departing (↑) or arriving (↓).
17.	Pilot-estimated time over fix.
18.	Actual time over fix, time leaving holding fix, arrival time at nonapproach control airport, or symbol indicating cancellation of IFR flight plan for arriving aircraft, or departure time (actual or assumed).
19.	Fix. For departing aircraft, add proposed departure time.
20.	Altitude information (in hundreds of feet) or as noted below.
NOTE-	*Altitude information may be written in thousands of feet provided the procedure is authorized by the facility manager, and is defined in a facility directive, i.e. FL 330 as 33, 5,000 feet as 5, and 2,800 as 2.8.*

Block	Information Recorded
20a.	**OPTIONAL USE,** when voice recorders are operational; **REQUIRED USE,** when the voice recorders are not operating and strips are being use at the facility. This space is used to record reported RA events. The letters RA followed by a climb or descent arrow (if the climb or descent action is reported) and the time (hhmm) the event is reported.
21.	Next posted fix or coordination fix.
22.	Pilot's estimated time over next fix.
23.	Arrows to indicate north (↑), south (↓), east (→), or west (←) direction of flight if required.
24.	Requested altitude.
NOTE–	*Altitude information may be written in thousands of feet provided the procedure is authorized by the facility manager, and is defined in a facility directive, i.e., FL 330 as 33, 5,000 feet as 5, and 2,800 as 2.8.*
25.	Point of origin, route as required for control and data relay, and destination.
26.	Pertinent remarks, minimum fuel, point out/radar vector/speed adjustment information or sector/position number (when applicable in accordance with paragraph 2–2–1, Recording Information), or NRP.
27.	Mode 3/A beacon code if applicable.
28.	Miscellaneous control data (expected further clearance time, time cleared for approach, etc.).
29–30.	Transfer of control data and coordination indicators.

b. Latitude/longitude coordinates may be used to define waypoints and may be substituted for nonadapted NAVAIDs in space 25 of domestic en route flight progress strips provided it is necessary to accommodate a random RNAV or GNSS route request.

c. Facility air traffic managers may authorize the optional use of spaces 13, 14, 14a, 22, 23, 24, and 28 for point out information, radar vector information, speed adjustment information, or transfer of control data.

2–3–3. OCEANIC DATA ENTRIES

FIG 2–3–3

1 2 3 4 5 6	7 8 9	10 11	12 13	14 15	16 17	16 17	18 19 20	21 21 24	
22 23									

10000 B763 DAL210 M KZ M080 22 of 70 A	F370	BOS 0820	ACK 0820	TUK 0831	LACKS 0846	SLATN 0856	KBOS TXKF R	KZ C 70 87 1 of 2

a. The ATOP system displays information on electronic flight progress strips and, in the event of a catastrophic system failure, will print flight progress strips with data in the corresponding numbered spaces:

TBL 2-3-2

Block	Information Recorded
1.	Mode 3/A beacon code, if applicable.
2.	Number of aircraft, if more than one, and type of aircraft.
3.	Aircraft identification.
4.	Reduced separation flags. Indicators are available for: M – Mach Number Technique (MNT), R – Reduced MNT, D or 3 – Distance–based longitudinal separation using 50 NM (D) or 30 NM (3), and W– Reduced Vertical Separation Minimum (RVSM). These flags are selectable for aircraft whose flight plans contain the required equipment qualifiers for each separation criteria.
5.	Controlling sector number.
6.	Filed airspeed or assigned Mach number/True airspeed.
7.	Reported flight level. May contain an indicator for a flight that is climbing (↑) or descending (↓). Reports from Mode C, ADS or position reports are displayed in that order of preference.
8.	Cleared flight level. May contain an indicator for a future conditional altitude (*) that cannot be displayed.
9.	Requested flight level, if applicable.
10.	Previously reported position.
11.	Actual time over previously reported position.
12.	Last reported position.
13.	Actual time over last reported position.
14.	Next reporting position.
15.	In–conformance pilot's estimate or controller–accepted pilot's estimate for next reporting position.
16.	Future reporting position(s).
17.	System estimate for future reporting position(s).
18.	Departure airport or point of origin.
19.	Destination airport or filed point of flight termination.
20.	Indicators. Indicators and toggles for displaying or suppressing the display of the route of flight (F), second flight profile (2), radar contact (A), annotations (&), degraded Required Navigation Performance (RNP, indicator R) and clearance restrictions (X).
21.	Coordination indicator(s).
22.	Annotations.
23.	Clearance restrictions and conditions (may be multiple lines).
24.	Strip number and total number of strips (printed strips only).

b. Standard annotations and abbreviations for Field 22 may be specified by facility directives.

2-3-4. TERMINAL DATA ENTRIES

a. Arrivals:

Information recorded on the flight progress strips (FAA Forms 7230–7.1, 7230–7.2, and 7230–8) must be entered in the correspondingly numbered spaces. Facility managers can authorize omissions and/or optional use of spaces 2A, 8A, 8B, 9A, 9B, 9C, and 10–18, if no misunderstanding will result. These omissions and/or optional uses must be specified in a facility directive.

FIG 2-3-4

1		5	8	9	9B	10	11	12
2	2A	6	8A			13	14	15
3								
4		7	8B	9A	9C	16	17	18

TBL 2–3–3

Block	Information Recorded
1.	Aircraft identification.
2.	Revision number (FDIO locations only).
2A.	Strip request originator. (At FDIO locations this indicates the sector or position that requested a strip be printed.)
3.	Number of aircraft if more than one, heavy aircraft indicator "H/" if appropriate, type of aircraft, and aircraft equipment suffix.
4.	Computer identification number if required.
5.	Secondary radar (beacon) code assigned.
6.	(FDIO Locations.) The previous fix will be printed. (Non–FDIO Locations.) Use of the inbound airway. This function is restricted to facilities where flight data is received via interphone when agreed upon by the center and terminal facilities.
7.	Coordination fix.
8.	Estimated time of arrival at the coordination fix or destination airport.
8A.	**OPTIONAL USE.**
8B.	**OPTIONAL USE,** when voice recorders are operational; **REQUIRED USE,** when the voice recorders are not operating and strips are being used at the facility. This space is used to record reported RA events when the voice recorders are not operational and strips are being used at the facility. The letters RA followed by a climb or descent arrow (if the climb or descent action is reported) and the time (hhmm) the event is reported.
9.	Altitude (in hundreds of feet) and remarks.
NOTE–	*Altitude information may be written in thousands of feet provided the procedure is authorized by the facility manager, and is defined in a facility directive, i. e., FL 230 as 23, 5,000 feet as 5, and 2,800 as 2.8.*
9A.	Minimum fuel, destination airport/point out/radar vector/speed adjustment information. Air traffic managers may authorize in a facility directive the omission of any of these items, **except minimum fuel,** if no misunderstanding will result.
NOTE–	*Authorized omissions and optional use of spaces must be specified in the facility directive concerning strip marking procedures.*
9B.	**OPTIONAL USE.**
9C.	**OPTIONAL USE.**
10–18.	Enter data as specified by a facility directive. Radar facility personnel need not enter data in these spaces except when nonradar procedures are used or when radio recording equipment is inoperative.

b. Departures:

Information recorded on the flight progress strips (FAA Forms 7230–7.1, 7230–7.2, and 7230–8) shall be entered in the correspondingly numbered spaces. Facility managers can authorize omissions and/or optional use of spaces 2A, 8A, 8B, 9A, 9B, 9C, and 10–18, if no misunderstanding will result. These omissions and/or optional uses shall be specified in a facility directive.

FIG 2–3–5

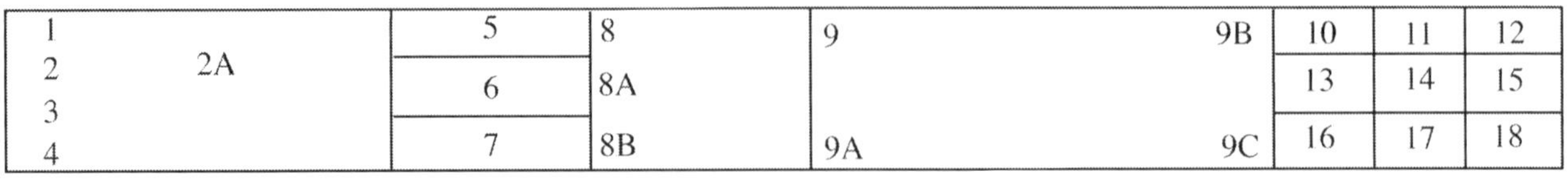

1		5	8	9	9B	10	11	12
2	2A	6	8A			13	14	15
3								
4		7	8B	9A	9C	16	17	18

TBL 2–3–4

Block	Information Recorded
1.	Aircraft identification.
2.	Revision number (FDIO locations only).
2A.	Strip request originator. (At FDIO locations this indicates the sector or position that requested a strip be printed.)
3.	Number of aircraft if more than one, heavy aircraft indicator "H/" if appropriate, type of aircraft, and aircraft equipment suffix.
4.	Computer identification number if required.
5.	Secondary radar (beacon) code assigned.
6.	Proposed departure time.
7.	Requested altitude.
NOTE–	*Altitude information may be written in thousands of feet provided the procedure is authorized by the facility manager, and is defined in a facility directive, i. e., FL 230 as 23, 5,000 feet as 5, and 2,800 as 2.8.*
8.	Departure airport.
8A.	**OPTIONAL USE.**
8B.	**OPTIONAL USE**, when voice recorders are operational; **REQUIRED USE,** when the voice recorders are not operating and strips are being used at the facility. This space is used to record reported RA events when the voice recorders are not operational and strips are being used at the facility. The letters RA followed by a climb or descent arrow (if the climb or descent action is reported) and the time (hhmm) the event is reported.

Block	Information Recorded
9.	**Computer–generated:** Route, destination, and remarks. Manually enter altitude/altitude restrictions in the order flown, if appropriate, and remarks.
9.	**Hand–prepared:** Clearance limit, route, altitude/altitude restrictions in the order flown, if appropriate, and remarks.
NOTE–	*Altitude information may be written in thousands of feet provided the procedure is authorized by the facility manager, and is defined in a facility directive, i.e., FL 230 as 23, 5,000 feet as 5, and 2,800 as 2.8.*
9A.	**OPTIONAL USE.**
9B.	**OPTIONAL USE.**
9C.	**OPTIONAL USE.**
10–18.	Enter data as specified by a facility directive. Items, such as departure time, runway used for takeoff, check marks to indicate information forwarded or relayed, may be entered in these spaces.

c. Overflights:

Information recorded on the flight progress strips (FAA Forms 7230–7.1, 7230–7.2, and 7230–8) shall be entered in the correspondingly numbered spaces. Facility managers can authorize omissions and/or optional use of spaces 2A, 8A, 8B, 9A, 9B, 9C, and 10–18, if no misunderstanding will result. These omissions and/or optional uses shall be specified in a facility directive.

FIG 2–3–6

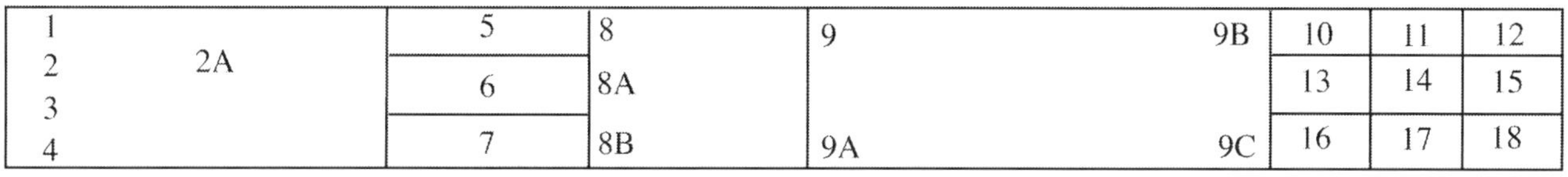

1 2 3 4	2A	5	8	9	9B	10	11	12
		6	8A			13	14	15
		7	8B	9A	9C	16	17	18

TBL 2-3-5

Block	Information Recorded
1.	Aircraft identification.
2.	Revision number (FDIO locations only).
2A.	Strip request originator. (At FDIO locations this indicates the sector or position that requested a strip be printed.)
3.	Number of aircraft if more than one, heavy aircraft indicator "H/" if appropriate, type of aircraft, and aircraft equipment suffix.
4.	Computer identification number if required.
5.	Secondary radar (beacon) code assigned.
6.	Coordination fix.
7.	Overflight coordination indicator (FDIO locations only).
NOTE-	*The overflight coordination indicator identifies the facility to which flight data has been forwarded.*
8.	Estimated time of arrival at the coordination fix.
8A.	**OPTIONAL USE.**
8B.	**OPTIONAL USE,** when voice recorders are operational; **REQUIRED USE**, when the voice recorders are not operating and strips are being used at the facility. This space is used to record reported RA events when the voice recorders are not operational and strips are being used at the facility. The letters RA followed by a climb or descent arrow (if the climb or descent action is reported) and the time (hhmm) the event is reported.
9.	Altitude and route of flight through the terminal area.
NOTE-	*Altitude information may be written in thousands of feet provided the procedure is authorized by the facility manager, and is defined in a facility directive, i.e., FL 230 as 23, 5,000 feet as 5, and 2,800 as 2.8.*
9A.	**OPTIONAL USE.**
9B.	**OPTIONAL USE.**
9C.	**OPTIONAL USE.**
10-18.	Enter data as specified by a facility directive.

NOTE-
National standardization of items (10 through 18) is not practical because of regional and local variations in operating methods; e.g., single fix, multiple fix, radar, tower en route control, etc.

d. Air traffic managers at automated terminal radar facilities may waive the requirement to use flight progress strips provided:

1. Backup systems such as multiple radar sites/systems are utilized.

2. Local procedures are documented in a facility directive. These procedures should include but not be limited to:

(a) Departure areas and/or procedures.

(b) Arrival procedures.

(c) Overflight handling procedures.

(d) Transition from radar to nonradar.

(e) Transition to or from ESL.

3. No misunderstanding will occur as a result of no strip usage.

4. Unused flight progress strips, facility developed forms and/or blank notepads shall be provided for controller use.

5. Facilities shall revert to flight progress strip usage if backup systems referred to in subparagraph d1 are not available.

e. Air traffic managers at FDIO locations may authorize reduced lateral spacing between fields so as to print all FDIO data to the left of the strip perforation. When using FAA Form 7230-7.2, all items will retain the same relationship to each other as they do when the full length strip (FAA Form 7230-7.1) is used.

2–3–5. AIRCRAFT IDENTITY

Indicate aircraft identity by one of the following using combinations not to exceed seven alphanumeric characters:

a. Civil aircraft, including the air-carrier letter-digit registration number which can include the letter "T" for air taxi, the letter "L" for MEDEVAC, or the 3-letter company designator specified in FAA Order JO 7340.2, Contractions, followed by the trip or flight number. Use the operating air carrier's company name in identifying equipment interchange flights.

EXAMPLE–
"N12345."
"TN5552Q."
"AAl192."
"LN751B."

NOTE–
The letter "L" is not to be used for air carrier/air taxi MEDEVAC *aircraft.*

b. Military Aircraft.

1. Prefixes indicating branch of service and/or type of mission followed by the last 5 digits of the serial number (the last 4 digits for CFC and CTG). (See TBL 2–3–6 and TBL 2–3–7.)

2. Pronounceable words of 3, 4, 5, and 6 letters followed by a 4–, 3–, 2–, or 1–digit number.

EXAMPLE–
"SAMP Three One Six."

3. Assigned double-letter 2–digit flight number.

4. Navy or Marine fleet and training command aircraft, one of the following:

(a) The service prefix and 2 letters (use phonetic alphabet equivalent) followed by 2 or 3 digits.

TBL 2–3–6
Branch of Service Prefix

Prefix	Branch
A	U.S. Air Force
C	U.S. Coast Guard
G	Air or Army National Guard
R	U.S. Army
VM	U.S. Marine Corps
VV	U.S. Navy
CFC	Canadian Forces
CTG	Canadian Coast Guard

TBL 2–3–7
Military Mission Prefix

Prefix	Mission
E	Medical Air Evacuation
F	Flight Check
L	LOGAIR (USAF Contract)
RCH	AMC (Air Mobility Command)
S	Special Air Mission

(b) The service prefix and a digit and a letter (use phonetic alphabet equivalent) followed by 2 or 3 digits.

5. Aircraft carrying the President, Vice President, and/or their family members will use the identifiers in the following tables. See TBL 2-3-8 and TBL 2-3-9.

TBL 2-3-8
President and Family

Service	President	Family
Air Force	AF1	EXEC1F
Marine	VM1	EXEC1F
Navy	VV1	EXEC1F
Army	RR1	EXEC1F
Coast Guard	C1	EXEC1F
Guard	G1	EXEC1F
Commercial	EXEC1	EXEC1F

TBL 2-3-9
Vice President and Family

Service	Vice President	Family
Air Force	AF2	EXEC2F
Marine	VM2	EXEC2F
Navy	VV2	EXEC2F
Army	RR2	EXEC2F
Coast Guard	C2	EXEC2F
Guard	G2	EXEC2F
Commercial	EXEC2	EXEC2F

c. Special use. Approved special use identifiers.

2-3-6. AIRCRAFT TYPE

Use the approved aircraft type designator, in accordance with FAA Order 7360.1, Aircraft Type Designators.

2-3-7. USAF/USN UNDERGRADUATE PILOTS

To identify aircraft piloted by solo USAF/USN undergraduate student pilots (who may occasionally request revised clearances because they normally are restricted to flight in VFR conditions), the aircraft identification in the flight plan shall include the letter "Z" as a suffix. Do not use this suffix, however, in ground-to-air communication.

NOTE-
USAF solo students who have passed an instrument certification check may penetrate cloud layers in climb or descent only. Requests for revised clearances to avoid clouds in level flight can still be expected. This does not change the requirement to use the letter "Z" as a suffix to the aircraft identification.

REFERENCE-
FAA Order JO 7110.65, Para 2-4-20, Aircraft Identification.
FAA Order JO 7610.14, Chapter 7, Section 2, USAF Undergraduate Flying Training (UFT)/Pilot Instructor Training (PIT)/Introduction To Fighter Fundamentals.

2-3-8. AIRCRAFT EQUIPMENT SUFFIX

a. The aircraft equipment suffix identifying communication, navigation and surveillance (CNS) capability is generated by automation using the equipment codes of the ICAO flight plan. To change a suffix, the CNS equipment codes must be modified, allowing automation to translate them into the proper suffix. If using unsupported automation platforms (OFDPS and FDP2000), verbally coordinate changes with adjacent supported facilities.

b. ERAM and ATOP are best suited for making changes to the equipment codes in an ICAO flight plan. For FDIO entries, if uncertain of the proper format to correctly amend an equipment code, verbally coordinate the change with the appropriate en route facility.

NOTE–
Directly changing the equipment suffix with a symbol preceded by a slant instead of amending the aircraft equipment codes may unintentionally alter or delete other equipment codes.

c. For VFR operations, indicate the aircraft's transponder and navigation capabilities by adding the appropriate symbol, preceded by a slant (See TBL 2–3–10).

d. GNSS-equipped aircraft:

1. Have an equipment suffix of /G, /L, /S, or /V.

2. May be determined by executing an ICAO flight plan readout and verifying a filed "G" in the ICAO equipment list.

3. May be determined by verifying with the pilot that the aircraft is GNSS-equipped.

e. When forwarding this information, state the aircraft type followed by the word "slant" and the appropriate phonetic letter equivalent of the suffix.

EXAMPLE–
"Cessna Three–ten slant Tango."
"A–Ten slant November."
"F–Sixteen slant Papa."
"Seven–sixty–seven slant Golf."

NOTE–
/H and /O are intended for ATC use only. These suffixes are not published in the Aeronautical Information Manual.

2–3–9. CLEARANCE STATUS

Use an appropriate clearance symbol followed by a dash (–) and other pertinent information to clearly show the clearance status of an aircraft. To indicate delay status use:

a. The symbol "H" at the clearance limit when holding instructions have been included in the aircraft's original clearance. Show detailed holding information following the dash when holding differs from the established pattern for the fix; i.e., turns, leg lengths, etc.

b. The symbols "F" or "O" to indicate the clearance limit when a delay is not anticipated.

TBL 2-3-10
Aircraft Equipment Suffixes

Separation Standard	Navigation Capability	Transponder Capability	Suffix
RVSM	Any	Failed transponder	/H
	Any	Failed Mode C	/O
	No RNAV, No GNSS	Transponder with Mode C	/W
	RNAV, No GNSS	Transponder with Mode C	/Z
	GNSS	Transponder with Mode C	/L
Non-RVSM	No DME	No transponder	/X
		Transponder, no Mode C	/T
		Transponder with Mode C	/U
	DME	No transponder	/D
		Transponder, no Mode C	/B
		Transponder with Mode C	/A
	TACAN	No transponder	/M
		Transponder, no Mode C	/N
		Transponder with Mode C	/P
	RNAV, No GNSS	No transponder	/Y
		Transponder, no Mode C	/C
		Transponder with Mode C	/I
	GNSS	No transponder	/V
		Transponder, no Mode C	/S
		Transponder with Mode C	/G

2-3-10. CONTROL SYMBOLOGY

Use authorized control and clearance symbols or abbreviations for recording clearances, reports, and instructions. Control status of aircraft must always be current. You may use:

a. Plain language markings when it will aid in understanding information.

b. Locally approved identifiers. Use these only within your facility and not on teletypewriter or interphone circuits.

c. Plain sheets of paper or locally prepared forms to record information when flight progress strips are not used. (See TBL 2-3-11 and TBL 2-3-12.)

d. Control Information Symbols.
(See FIG 2-3-7 and FIG 2-3-8.)

REFERENCE–
FAA Order JO 7110.65, Para 4-5-3, Exceptions.

TBL 2-3-11
Clearance Abbreviations

Abbreviation	Meaning
A	Cleared to airport (point of intended landing)
B	Center clearance delivered
C	ATC clears (when clearance relayed through non-ATC facility)
CAF	Cleared as filed
D	Cleared to depart from the fix
F	Cleared to the fix
H	Cleared to hold and instructions issued
L	Cleared to land
N	Clearance not delivered
O	Cleared to the outer marker
PD	Cleared to climb/descend at pilot's discretion
Q	Cleared to fly specified sectors of a NAVAID defined in terms of courses, bearings, radials or quadrants within a designated radius.
T	Cleared through (for landing and takeoff through intermediate point)
V	Cleared over the fix
X	Cleared to cross (airway, route, radial) at (point)
Z	Tower jurisdiction

TBL 2–3–12
Miscellaneous Abbreviations

Abbreviation	Meaning
BC	Back course approach
CT	Contact approach
FA	Final approach
FMS	Flight management system approach
GPS	GPS approach
I	Initial approach
ILS	ILS approach
MA	Missed approach
NDB	Nondirectional radio beacon approach
OTP	VFR conditions–on–top
PA	Precision approach
PT	Procedure turn
RA	Resolution advisory (Pilot reported TCAS event)
RH	Runway heading
RNAV	Area navigation approach
RP	Report immediately upon passing (fix/altitude)
RX	Report crossing
SA	Surveillance approach
SI	Straight–in approach
TA	TACAN approach
TL	Turn left
TR	Turn right
VA	Visual approach
VR	VOR approach

FIG 2–3–7

Control Information Symbols [Part 1]

Symbols	Meaning
T→ ( )	Depart (direction, if specified)
↑	Climb and maintain
↓	Descend and maintain
→	Cruise
@	At
X	Cross
~~M~~→	Maintain
⇉	Join or intercept airway/jet route/track or course
═	While in controlled airspace
△	While in control area
→△	Enter control area
△→	Out of control area
NW⊗ ⊘NE ⊖→E	Cleared to enter, depart or through surface area. Indicated direction of flight by arrow and appropriate compass letter. Maintain Special VFR conditions (altitude if appropriate) while in surface area.
250 K	Aircraft requested to adjust speed to 250 knots.
-20 K	Aircraft requested to reduce speed 20 knots.
+30 K	Aircraft requested to increase speed 30 knots.
Ⓦ	Local Special VFR operations in the vicinity of (name) airport are authorized until(time). Maintain special VFR conditions (altitude if appropriate).
>	Before
<	After or Past
170 (red)	Inappropriate altitude/flight level for direction of flight. (Underline assigned altitude/flight level in red).
/	Until
( )	Alternate instructions
Restriction	Restriction
⊤↓	At or Below
⊥↑	At or Above
-(Dash)	From-to (route, time, etc.)
(Alt)B(Alt)	Indicates a block altitude assignment. Altitudes are inclusive, and the first altitude shall be lower than the second. Example: 310B370
v <	Clearance void if aircraft not off ground by (time)

NOTE: The absence of an airway route number between two fixes in the route of flight indicates "direct"; no symbol or abbreviation is required.

FIG 2-3-8
Control Information Symbols [Part 2]

Symbols	Meaning
℄	Pilot canceled flight plan
√	EN ROUTE: Aircraft has reported at assigned altitude, Example: 80 √
√	TERMINAL/FSS: Information forwarded (indicated information forwarded as required)
◯ (red)	EN ROUTE: Information or revised information forwarded. (Circle, in red, inappropriate altitude/flight level for direction of flight or other control information when coordinated. Also circle, in red, the time (minutes and altitude) when a flight plan or estimate is forwarded. Use method in both inter-center and intra-center coordination.)
(50)	Other than assigned altitude reported (circle reported altitude)
H 10/6	DME holding (use with mileages)(Upper figure indicates distance from station to DME fix, lower figure indicates length of holding pattern.) In this example, the DME fix is 10 miles out with a 6 mile pattern indicated.
(mi.)(dir.)	DME arc of VORTAC, TACAN, or MLS.
C (freq.)	Contact (facility) or (freq.), (time, fix, or altitude if appropriate). Insert frequency only when it is other than standard.
R	Radar contact.
R	EN ROUTE: Requested altitude (preceding altitude information)
R (struck through)	Radar service terminated
R (crossed out)	Radar contact lost
RV	Radar vector
RV (V crossed out)	Pilot resumed own navigation
(R)	Radar handoff (circle symbol when handoff completed)
E (red)	EMERGENCY
W (red)	WARNING
P	Point out initiated. Indicate the appropriate facility, sector or position. Example: PZFW.
FUEL	Minimum fuel

NOTE: The absence of an airway route number between two fixes in the route of flight indicates "direct"; no symbol or abbreviation is required.

Section 4. Radio and Interphone Communications

2–4–1. RADIO COMMUNICATIONS

Use radio frequencies for the special purposes for which they are intended. A single frequency may be used for more than one function except as follows:

TERMINAL. When combining positions in the tower, do not use ground control frequency for airborne communications.

NOTE–
Due to the limited number of frequencies assigned to towers for the ground control function, it is very likely that airborne use of a ground control frequency could cause interference to other towers or interference to your aircraft from another tower. When combining these functions, it is recommended combining them on local control. The ATIS may be used to specify the desired frequency.

2–4–2. MONITORING

Monitor interphones and assigned radio frequencies continuously.

NOTE–
Although all FAA facilities, including RAPCONs and RATCFs, are required to monitor all assigned frequencies continuously, USAF facilities may not monitor all unpublished discrete frequencies.

2–4–3. PILOT ACKNOWLEDGMENT/READ BACK

Ensure pilots acknowledge all Air Traffic Clearances and ATC Instructions. When a pilot reads back an Air Traffic Clearance or ATC Instruction:

a. Ensure that items read back are correct.

b. Ensure the read back of hold short instructions, whether a part of taxi instructions or a LAHSO clearance.

c. Ensure pilots use call signs and/or registration numbers in any read back acknowledging an Air Traffic Clearance or ATC Instruction.

NOTE–
1. *ATC Clearance/Instruction Read Back guidance for pilots in the AIM states:*
a. *Although pilots should read back the "numbers," unless otherwise required by procedure or controller request, pilots may acknowledge clearances, control instructions, or other information by using "Wilco," "Roger," "Affirmative," or other words or remarks with their aircraft identification.*
b. *Altitudes contained in charted procedures, such as departure procedures, instrument approaches, etc., need not be read back unless they are specifically stated by the controller.*
c. *Initial read back of a taxi, departure or landing clearance should include the runway assignment, including left, right, center, etc. if applicable.*

2. *Until a pilot acknowledges a controller's clearance or instruction, a controller cannot know if a pilot will comply with the clearance or remain as previously cleared.*

EXAMPLE–
"Climbing to Flight Level three three zero, United Twelve" or "November Five Charlie Tango, roger, cleared to land runway four left."

REFERENCE–
P/CG Term – Air Traffic Clearance.
P/CG Term – ATC Instructions.
FAA Order JO 7110.65, 3–7–2. Taxi and Ground Movement Operations.
FAA Order JO 7110.65, 10–4–4. Communications Failure.
AIM Para 4-2-3, Contact Procedures.
AIM Para 4-4-7 Pilot Responsibility upon Clearance Issuance.
AIM Para 6-4-1, Two-way Radio Communications Failure.
Federal Register, April 1, 1999 14 CFR Part 91 Pilot Responsibility for Compliance with ATC Clearances and Instructions.

2–4–4. AUTHORIZED INTERRUPTIONS

As necessary, authorize a pilot to interrupt his/her communications guard.

NOTE–
Some users have adopted procedures to ensure uninterrupted receiving capability with ATC when a pilot with only one operative communications radio must interrupt his/her communications guard because of a safety related problem requiring airborne communications with his/her company. In this event, pilots will request approval to abandon guard on the assigned ATC frequency for a mutually agreeable time period. Additionally, they will inform controllers of the NAVAID voice facility and the company frequency they will monitor.

2–4–5. AUTHORIZED TRANSMISSIONS

Transmit only those messages necessary for air traffic control or otherwise contributing to air safety.

REFERENCE–
FAA Order JO 7210.3, Para 3–2–2, Authorized Messages Not Directly Associated with Air Traffic Services.

2–4–6. FALSE OR DECEPTIVE COMMUNICATIONS

Take action to detect, prevent, and report false, deceptive, or phantom controller communications to an aircraft or controller. The following must be accomplished when false or deceptive communications occur:

a. Correct false information.

b. Broadcast an alert to aircraft operating on all frequencies within the area where deceptive or phantom transmissions have been received.

EXAMPLE–
"Attention all aircraft. False ATC instructions have been received in the area of Long Beach Airport. Exercise extreme caution on all frequencies and verify instructions."

c. Collect pertinent information regarding the incident.

d. Notify the operations supervisor of the false, deceptive, or phantom transmission and report all relevant information pertaining to the incident.

2–4–7. AUTHORIZED RELAYS

a. Relay operational information to aircraft or aircraft operators as necessary. Do not agree to handle such messages on a regular basis. Give the source of any such message you relay.

b. Relay official FAA messages as required.

NOTE–
The FAA Administrator and Deputy Administrator will sometimes use code phrases to identify themselves in air-to-ground communications as follows:
Administrator: "SAFEAIR ONE."
Deputy Administrator: "SAFEAIR TWO."

EXAMPLE–
"Miami Center, Jetstar One, this is SAFEAIR ONE, (message)."

c. Relay operational information to military aircraft operating on, or planning to operate on IRs.

2–4–8. RADIO MESSAGE FORMAT

Use the following format for radio communications with an aircraft:

a. Sector/position on initial radio contact:

1. Identification of aircraft.

2. Identification of ATC unit.

3. Message (if any).

4. The word "over" if required.

b. Subsequent radio transmissions from the same sector/position must use the same format, except the identification of the ATC unit may be omitted.

TERMINAL. You may omit aircraft identification after initial contact when conducting the final portion of a radar approach.

REFERENCE–
FAA Order JO 7110.65, Para 2–4–20, Aircraft Identification.

2–4–9. ABBREVIATED TRANSMISSIONS

Transmissions may be abbreviated as follows:

a. Use the identification prefix and the last 3 digits or letters of the aircraft identification after communications have been established with a U.S. civil aircraft using the aircraft registration as identification.

b. Do not abbreviate:

1. Similar sounding aircraft identifications.

2. Aircraft call signs, including:

(a) Aircraft having an International Civil Aviation Organization three letter designator (ICAO 3LD) and other aircraft with an FAA authorized call sign (U.S. special or local).

(b) Aircraft with a military call sign.

3. Foreign aircraft using the foreign civil registration number as identification.

REFERENCE–
FAA Order JO 7110.65, Para 2–4–15, Emphasis for Clarity.
FAA Order JO 7110.65, Para 2–4–20, Aircraft Identification.
FAA Order JO 7610.12, Assignment and Authorization of Call Sign Designators and Associated Telephonies.

c. Omit the facility identification after communication has been established.

d. Transmit the message immediately after the callup (without waiting for the aircraft's reply) when the message is short and receipt is generally assured.

e. Omit the word "over" if the message obviously requires a reply.

2–4–10. INTERPHONE TRANSMISSION PRIORITIES

Give priority to interphone transmissions as follows:

a. First priority. Emergency messages including essential information on aircraft accidents or suspected accidents. After an actual emergency has passed, give a lower priority to messages relating to that accident.

b. Second priority. Clearances and control instructions.

c. Third priority. Movement and control messages using the following order of preference when possible:

1. Progress reports.

2. Departure or arrival reports.

3. Flight plans.

d. Fourth priority. Movement messages on VFR aircraft.

2–4–11. PRIORITY INTERRUPTION

Use the words "emergency" or "control" for interrupting lower priority messages when you have an emergency or control message to transmit.

2–4–12. INTERPHONE MESSAGE FORMAT

Use the following format for interphone intra/interfacility communications:

a. Both the caller and receiver identify their facility and/or position in a manner that ensures they will not be confused with another position.

NOTE–
Other means of identifying a position, such as substituting departure or arrival gate/fix names for position identification, may be used. However, it must be operationally beneficial, and the procedure fully covered in a letter of agreement or a facility directive, as appropriate.

EXAMPLE–
Caller: *"Albuquerque Center Sixty Three, Amarillo Departure."*

Receiver: *"Albuquerque Center."*

b. Between two facilities which utilize numeric position identification, the caller must identify both facility and position.

EXAMPLE–
Caller: *"Albuquerque Sixty Three, Fort Worth Eighty Two."*

c. Caller states the type of coordination to be accomplished when advantageous. For example, handoff or APREQ.

d. The caller states the message.

e. The receiver states the response to the caller's message followed by the receiver's operating initials.

f. The caller states his or her operating initials.

EXAMPLE–
1.
Caller: *"Denver High, R Twenty–five."*

Receiver: *"Denver High."*

Caller: *"Request direct Denver for Northwest Three Twenty–eight."*

Receiver: *"Northwest Three Twenty–eight direct Denver approved. H.F."*

Caller: *"G.M."*

2.
Receiver: *"Denver High, Go ahead override."*

Caller: *"R Twenty–five, Request direct Denver for Northwest Three Twenty–eight."*

Receiver: *"Northwest Three Twenty–eight direct Denver approved. H.F."*

Caller: *"G.M."*

3.
Caller: *("Bolos" is a departure gate in Houston ARTCC's Sabine sector)– "Bolos, Houston local."*

Receiver: *"Bolos."*

Caller: *"Request Flight Level three five zero for American Twenty–five."*

Receiver: *"American Twenty–five Flight Level three five zero approved, A.C."*

Caller: *"G.M."*

4.
Caller: *"Sector Twelve, Ontario Approach, APREQ."*

Receiver: *"Sector Twelve."*

Caller: *"Cactus Five forty-two heading one three zero and climbing to one four thousand."*

Receiver: *"Cactus Five forty-two heading one three zero and climbing to one four thousand approved. B.N."*

Caller: *"A.M."*

5.
Caller: *"Zanesville, Columbus, seventy-three line, handoff."*

Receiver: *"Zanesville."*

Caller: *"Five miles east of Appleton VOR, United Three Sixty-six."*

Receiver: *"United Three Sixty-six, radar contact, A.Z."*

Caller: *"M.E."*

g. Identify the interphone voice line on which the call is being made when two or more such lines are collocated at the receiving operating position.

EXAMPLE–
"Washington Center, Washington Approach on the Fifty Seven line."

"Chicago Center, O'Hare Tower handoff on the Departure West line."

h. *TERMINAL.* The provisions of subparagraphs a, b, c, e, f, g, and paragraph 2-4-13, Interphone Message Termination, may be omitted provided:

1. Abbreviated standard coordination procedures are contained in a facility directive describing the specific conditions and positions that may utilize an abbreviated interphone message format; and

2. There will be no possibility of misunderstanding which positions are using the abbreviated procedures.

2-4-13. INTERPHONE MESSAGE TERMINATION

Terminate interphone messages with your operating initials.

2-4-14. WORDS AND PHRASES

a. Use the words or phrases in radiotelephone and interphone communication as contained in the P/CG or, within areas where Controller Pilot Data Link Communications (CPDLC) is in use, the phraseology contained in the applicable CPDLC message set.

b. The word *super* must be used as part of the identification in all communications with or about super aircraft.

c. The word *heavy* must be used as part of the identification in all communications with or about heavy aircraft.

d. *EN ROUTE.* The use of the words *super* or *heavy* may be omitted except as follows:

1. In communications with a terminal facility about super or heavy aircraft operations.

2. In communications with or about super or heavy aircraft with regard to an airport where the en route center is providing approach control service.

3. In communications with or about super or heavy aircraft when the separation from a following aircraft may become less than 5 miles by approved procedure.

4. When issuing traffic advisories.

EXAMPLE–
"United Fifty–Eight Heavy."

NOTE–
Most airlines will use the word "super" or "heavy" following the company prefix and flight number when establishing communications or when changing frequencies within a terminal facility's area.

e. When in radio communications with "Air Force One" or "Air Force Two," do not add the heavy designator to the call sign. State only the call sign "Air Force One/Two" regardless of the type aircraft.

2–4–15. EMPHASIS FOR CLARITY

a. Treat aircraft with similar sounding aircraft identifications by emphasizing appropriate digits, letters, or similar sounding words to aid in distinguishing between similar sounding aircraft identifications. Do not abbreviate similar sounding aircraft identifications.

REFERENCE–
FAA Order JO 7110.65, Para 2–4–20, Aircraft Identification.
FAA Order JO 7110.65, Para 2–4–9, Abbreviated Transmissions.

b. Treat aircraft with similar sounding call signs by restating the call sign after the flight number.

EXAMPLE–
"United Thirty–one United."
"American Thirty–one American."

NOTE–
Similar sounding call signs procedures may apply to ICAO 3LD U.S. special, local, or military call sign.

c. Notify each pilot concerned when communicating with aircraft having similar sounding identifications.

EXAMPLE–
"United Thirty–one United, Miami Center, U.S. Air Thirty–one is also on this frequency, acknowledge."

"U.S. Air Thirty–one U.S. Air, Miami Center, United Thirty–one is also on this frequency, acknowledge."

d. Notify the operations supervisor–in–charge of any duplicate call signs or phonetically similar–sounding call signs when the aircraft are operating simultaneously within the same sector.

REFERENCE–
FAA Order JO 7210.3, Para 2–1–14, Aircraft Identification Problems.

2–4–16. ICAO PHONETICS

Use the ICAO pronunciation of numbers and individual letters. (See the ICAO radiotelephony alphabet and pronunciation in TBL 2–4–1.)

TBL 2–4–1
ICAO Phonetics

Character	Word	Pronunciation
0	Zero	ZE–RO
1	One	WUN
2	Two	TOO
3	Three	TREE
4	Four	FOW–ER
5	Five	FIFE
6	Six	SIX
7	Seven	SEV–EN
8	Eight	AIT
9	Nine	NIN–ER
A	Alfa	**AL**FAH
B	Bravo	**BRAH**VOH
C	Charlie	**CHAR**LEE
D	Delta	**DELL**TAH
E	Echo	**ECK**OH
F	Foxtrot	**FOKS**TROT
G	Golf	GOLF
H	Hotel	HOH**TELL**

Character	Word	Pronunciation
I	India	**IN**DEE AH
J	Juliett	**JEW**LEE ETT
K	Kilo	**KEY**LOH
L	Lima	**LEE**MAH
M	Mike	MIKE
N	November	NO**VEM**BER
O	Oscar	**OSS**CAH
P	Papa	PAH**PAH**
Q	Quebec	KEH**BECK**
R	Romeo	**ROW**ME OH
S	Sierra	SEE**AIR**AH
T	Tango	**TANG**GO
U	Uniform	**YOU**NEE FORM
V	Victor	**VIK**TAH
W	Whiskey	**WISS**KEY
X	X–ray	**ECKS**RAY
Y	Yankee	**YANG**KEY
Z	Zulu	**ZOO**LOO

NOTE–
Syllables to be emphasized in pronunciation are in bold face.

2–4–17. NUMBERS USAGE

State numbers as follows:

a. Serial numbers. The separate digits.

EXAMPLE–

Number	Statement
11,495	"One one four niner five."
20,069	"Two zero zero six niner."

b. Altitudes or flight levels:

1. Altitudes. Pronounce each digit in the number of hundreds or thousands followed by the word "hundred" or "thousand" as appropriate.

EXAMPLE–

Number	Statement
10,000	"One zero thousand."
11,000	"One one thousand."
17,900	"One seven thousand niner hundred."

NOTE–
Altitudes may be restated in group form for added clarity if the controller chooses.

EXAMPLE−

Number	Statement
10,000	"Ten thousand."
11,000	"Eleven thousand."
17,900	"Seventeen thousand niner hundred."

2. Flight levels. The words "flight level" followed by the separate digits of the flight level.

EXAMPLE−

Flight Level	Statement
180	"Flight level one eight zero."
275	"Flight level two seven five."

3. MDA/DH Altitudes. The separate digits of the MDA/DH altitude.

EXAMPLE−

MDA/DH Altitude	Statement
1,320	"Minimum descent altitude, one three two zero."
486	"Decision height, four eight six."

c. Time:

1. General time information. The four separate digits of the hour and minute/s in terms of UTC.

EXAMPLE−

UTC	Time (12 hour)	Statement
0715	1:15 a.m. CST	"Zero seven one five."
1915	1:15 p.m. CST	"One niner one five."

2. Upon request. The four separate digits of the hours and minute/s in terms of UTC followed by the local standard time equivalent; or the local time equivalent only. Local time may be based on the 24−hour clock system, and the word "local" or the time zone equivalent must be stated when other than UTC is referenced. The term "ZULU" may be used to denote UTC.

EXAMPLE−

UTC	Time (24 hour)	Time (12 hour)	Statement
2230	1430 PST	2:30 p.m.	"Two two three zero, one four three zero Pacific or Local." or "Two−thirty P−M."

3. Time check. The word "time" followed by the four separate digits of the hour and minutes, and nearest quarter minute. Fractions of a quarter minute less than eight seconds are stated as the preceding quarter minute; fractions of a quarter minute of eight seconds or more are stated as succeeding quarter minute.

EXAMPLE–

Time	Statement
1415:06	"Time, one four one five."
1415:10	"Time, one four one five and one–quarter."

4. Abbreviated time. The separate digits of the minutes only.

EXAMPLE–

Time	Statement
1415	"One five."
1420	"Two zero."

d. Field elevation. The words "field elevation" followed by the separate digits of the elevation.

EXAMPLE–

Elevation	Statement
17 feet	"Field elevation, one seven."
817 feet	"Field elevation, eight one seven."
2,817 feet	"Field elevation, two eight one seven."

e. The number "0" as "zero" except where it is used in approved "group form" for authorized aircraft call signs, and in stating altitudes.

EXAMPLE–

As Zero	As Group
"Field elevation one six zero." "Heading three zero zero." "One zero thousand five hundred."	"Western five thirty." "EMAIR One Ten." "Ten thousand five hundred."

f. Altimeter setting. The word "altimeter" followed by the separate digits of the altimeter setting.

EXAMPLE–

Setting	Statement
30.01	"Altimeter, three zero zero one."

g. Surface wind. The word "wind" followed by the separate digits of the indicated wind direction to the nearest 10–degree multiple, the word "at" and the separate digits of the indicated velocity in knots, to include any gusts.

EXAMPLE–
"Wind zero three zero at two five."
"Wind two seven zero at one five gusts three five."

h. Heading. The word "heading" followed by the three separate digits of the number of degrees, omitting the word "degrees." Use heading 360 degrees to indicate a north heading.

EXAMPLE–

Heading	Statement
5 degrees	"Heading zero zero five."
30 degrees	"Heading zero three zero."
360 degrees	"Heading three six zero."

i. Radar beacon codes. The separate digits of the 4–digit code.

EXAMPLE–

Code	Statement
1000	"One zero zero zero."
2100	"Two one zero zero."

j. Runways. The word "runway," followed by the separate digits of the runway designation. For a parallel runway, state the word "left," "right," or "center" if the letter "L," "R," or "C" is included in the designation.

EXAMPLE–

Designation	Statement
3	"Runway Three."
8L	"Runway Eight Left."
27R	"Runway Two Seven Right."

k. Frequencies.

1. The separate digits of the frequency, inserting the word "point" where the decimal point occurs.

(a) Omit digits after the second digit to the right of the decimal point.

(b) When the frequency is in the L/MF band, include the word "kiloHertz."

EXAMPLE–

Frequency	Statement
126.55 MHz	"One two six point five five."
369.0 MHz	"Three six niner point zero."
121.5 MHz	"One two one point five."
135.275 MHz	"One three five point two seven."
302 kHz	"Three zero two kiloHertz."

2. *USAF/USN.* Local channelization numbers may be used in lieu of frequencies for locally based aircraft when local procedures are established to ensure that local aircraft and ATC facilities use the same channelization.

EXAMPLE–

Frequency	Statement
275.8 MHz	"Local channel one six."

3. Issue TACAN frequencies by stating the assigned two or three–digit channel number.

l. Speeds.

1. The separate digits of the speed followed by "knots" except as required by paragraph 5–7–2, Methods.

EXAMPLE–

Speed	Statement
250	"Two five zero knots."
190	"One niner zero knots."

2. The separate digits of the Mach number preceded by "Mach."

EXAMPLE−

Mach Number	Statement
1.5	"Mach one point five."
0.64	"Mach point six four."
0.7	"Mach point seven."

m. Miles. The separate digits of the mileage followed by the word "mile."

EXAMPLE−
"Three zero mile arc east of Nottingham."
"Traffic, one o'clock, two five miles, northbound, D−C Eight, flight level two seven zero."

2−4−18. NUMBER CLARIFICATION

a. If deemed necessary for clarity, and after stating numbers as specified in paragraph 2−4−17, Numbers Usage, controllers may restate numbers using either group or single-digit form.

EXAMPLE−
"One Seven Thousand, Seventeen Thousand."
"Altimeter Two Niner Niner Two, Twenty Nine Ninety Two."
"One Two Six Point Five Five, One Twenty Six Point Fifty Five."

2−4−19. FACILITY IDENTIFICATION

Identify facilities as follows:

a. Airport traffic control towers. State the name of the facility followed by the word "tower." Where military and civil airports are located in the same general area and have similar names, state the name of the military service followed by the name of the military facility and the word "tower."

EXAMPLE−
"Columbus Tower."
"Barksdale Tower."
"Navy Jacksonville Tower."

b. Air route traffic control centers. State the name of the facility followed by the word "center."

c. Approach control facilities, including RAPCONs, RATCFs, and ARACs. State the name of the facility followed by the word "approach." Where military and civil facilities are located in the same general area and have similar names, state the name of the military service followed by the name of the military facility and the word "approach."

EXAMPLE−
"Denver Approach."
"Griffiss Approach."
"Navy Jacksonville Approach."

d. Functions within a terminal facility. State the name of the facility followed by the name of the function.

EXAMPLE−
"Boston Departure."
"LaGuardia Clearance Delivery."
"O'Hare Ground."

e. When calling or replying on an interphone line which connects only two non−VSCS equipped facilities, you may omit the facility name.

EXAMPLE−
"Bradford High, Handoff."

f. Flight service stations. State the name of the station followed by the word "radio."

EXAMPLE–
"Leesburg Radio."

g. Radar facilities having ASR or PAR but not providing approach control service. State the name of the facility, followed by the letters "G–C–A."

EXAMPLE–
"Corpus Christi G–C–A."
"Davison G–C–A."

2–4–20. AIRCRAFT IDENTIFICATION

Use the full identification in reply to aircraft with similar sounding identifications. For other aircraft, the same identification may be used in reply that the pilot used in his/her initial callup except use the correct identification after communications have been established. Identify aircraft as follows:

a. U.S. registry aircraft. State one of the following:

REFERENCE–
FAA Order JO 7110.65, Para 2–4–8, Radio Message Format.
FAA Order JO 7110.65, Para 2–4–9, Abbreviated Transmissions.
FAA Order JO 7110.65, Para 2–4–15, Emphasis for Clarity.
FAA Order JO 7110.65, Para 2–4–17, Numbers Usage.

1. Civil. State the prefix "November" when establishing initial communications with U.S. registered aircraft followed by the ICAO phonetic pronunciation of the numbers/letters of the aircraft registration. The controller may state the aircraft type, the model, the manufacturer's name, followed by the ICAO phonetic pronunciation of the numbers/letters of the aircraft registration if used by the pilot on the initial or subsequent call.

EXAMPLE–
Air traffic controller's initiated call:

"November One Two Three Four Golf."
"November One Two Three Four."

Responding to pilot's initial or subsequent call:

"Jet Commander One Two Three Four Papa."
"Bonanza One Two Three Four Tango."
"Sikorsky Six Three Eight Mike Foxtrot."

NOTE–
If aircraft identification becomes a problem when the procedures specified above are used, see paragraph 2–4–15, Emphasis for Clarity.

2. Aircraft having an ICAO 3LD and other FAA authorized call sign (U.S. special or local). State the call sign followed by the flight number in group form.

NOTE–
"Group form" is the pronunciation of a series of numbers as the whole number, or pairs of numbers they represent rather than pronouncing each separate digit. The use of group form may, however, be negated by four-digit identifiers or the placement of zeros in the identifier.

EXAMPLE–
"American Fifty–Two."
"Delta One Hundred."
"Eastern Metro One Ten."
"General Motors Thirty Fifteen."
"United One Zero One."
"Delta Zero One Zero."
"TWA Ten Zero Four."

NOTE–
For clarity, aircraft having an ICAO 3LD and other FAA authorized call sign may be pronounced using single digits if necessary.

EXAMPLE–
"United Five One Seven."
"United Five Seven Zero."

NOTE–
For procedures that address similar sounding call signs, see paragraph 2–4–15, Emphasis for Clarity.

REFERENCE–
FAA Order JO 7610.12, Assignment and Authorization of Call Sign Designators and Associated Telephonies.

3. Air taxi and commercial operators not having FAA authorized call signs. State the prefix "TANGO" on initial contact, if used by the pilot, followed by the registration number. The prefix may be dropped in subsequent communications.

EXAMPLE–
"Tango Mooney Five Five Five Two Quebec."
"Tango November One Two Three Four."

4. Air carrier/taxi ambulance. State the prefix "MEDEVAC" if used by the pilot, followed by the call sign and flight number in group form.

EXAMPLE–
"MEDEVAC Delta Fifty-One."

5. Civilian air ambulance. State the word *"MEDEVAC"* followed by the numbers/letters of the registration number.

EXAMPLE–
"MEDEVAC Two Six Four Six."

6. U.S. military. State one of the following:

(a) The service name, followed by the word "copter," when appropriate, and the last 5 digits of the serial number.

EXAMPLE–
"Navy Five Six Seven One Three."
"Coast Guard Six One Three Two Seven."
"Air Guard One Three Five Eight Six."
"Army Copter Three Two One Seven Six."

NOTE–
If aircraft identification becomes a problem, the procedures reflected in FAA Order JO 7210.3, Facility Operation and Administration, paragraph 2–1–14, Aircraft Identification Problems, will apply.

(b) Special military operations. State one of the following followed by the last 5 digits of the serial number:

(c) Air evacuation flights. "AIR EVAC," "MARINE AIR EVAC," or "NAVY AIR EVAC."

EXAMPLE–
"Air Evac One Seven Six Five Two."

(d) Rescue flights. (Service name) "RESCUE."

EXAMPLE–
"Air Force Rescue Six One Five Seven Niner."

(e) Air Mobility Command. "REACH."

EXAMPLE–
"Reach Seven Eight Five Six Two."

(f) Special Air Mission. "SAM."

EXAMPLE–
"Sam Niner One Five Six Two."

(g) USAF Contract Aircraft "LOGAIR."

EXAMPLE–
"Logair Seven Five Eight Two Six."

(h) Military tactical and training:

(1) U.S. Air Force, Air National Guard, Military District of Washington priority aircraft, and USAF civil disturbance aircraft. Pronounceable words of 3 to 6 letters followed by a 1 to 5 digit number.

EXAMPLE–
"Paul Two Zero."
"Pat One Five Seven."
"Gaydog Four."

NOTE–
When the "Z" suffix described in paragraph 2–3–7, USAF/USN Undergraduate Pilots, is added to identify aircraft piloted by USAF undergraduate pilots, the call sign will be limited to a combination of six characters.

(2) Navy or Marine fleet and training command aircraft. The service name and 2 letters, or a digit and a letter (use letter phonetic equivalents), followed by 2 or 3 digits.

EXAMPLE–
"Navy Golf Alfa Two One."
"Marine Four Charlie Two Three Six."

7. Presidential aircraft and Presidential family aircraft:

(a) When the President is aboard a military aircraft, state the name of the military service, followed by the word "One."

EXAMPLE–
"Air Force One."
"Army One."
"Marine One."

(b) When the President is aboard a civil aircraft, state the words "Executive One."

(c) When a member of the President's family is aboard any aircraft, if the U.S. Secret Service or the White House Staff determines it is necessary, state the words "Executive One Foxtrot."

REFERENCE–
FAA Order JO 7110.65, Para 2–1–4, Operational Priority.

8. Vice Presidential aircraft:

(a) When the Vice President is aboard a military aircraft, state the name of the military service, followed by the word "Two."

EXAMPLE–
"Air Force Two."
"Army Two."
"Marine Two."

(b) When the Vice President is aboard a civil aircraft, state the words "Executive Two."

(c) When a member of the Vice President's family is aboard any aircraft, if the U.S. Secret Service or the White House Staff determines it is necessary, state the words "Executive Two Foxtrot."

REFERENCE–
FAA Order JO 7110.65, Para 2–1–4, Operational Priority.

9. DOT and FAA flights. The following alphanumeric identifiers and radio/interphone call signs are established for use in air/ground communications when the Secretary of Transportation, Deputy Secretary of

Transportation, FAA Administrator or FAA Deputy Administrator have a requirement to identify themselves. (See TBL 2–4–2.)

TBL 2–4–2
DOT and FAA Alphanumeric Identifiers and Call Signs

Official	Identifier	Call Sign
Secretary of Transportation	DOT–1	Transport–1
Deputy Secretary of Transportation	DOT–2	Transport–2
Administrator, Federal Aviation Administration	FAA–1	Safeair–1
Deputy Administrator, Federal Aviation Administration	FAA–2	Safeair–2

10. Other Special Flights.

(a) Flight Inspection of navigational aids. State the call sign "FLIGHT CHECK" followed by the digits of the registration number.

EXAMPLE–
"Flight Check Three Niner Six Five Four."

(b) USAF or other government aircraft engaged in aerial sampling/surveying missions. State the call sign "SAMP" followed by a three–digit flight number.

EXAMPLE–
"SAMP Three One Six."

REFERENCE–
FAA Order JO 7110.65, Para 9–2–17, SAMP Flights.

11. Use a pilot's name in identification of an aircraft only in special or emergency situations.

b. Foreign registry. State one of the following:

1. Civil. State the aircraft type or the manufacturer's name followed by the letters/numbers of the full aircraft registration, or state the letters or digits of the full aircraft registration. Do not abbreviate.

EXAMPLE–
"Citation C–G–L–R–B."
"C–G–L–R–B."

NOTE–
1. *Letters may be spoken individually or phonetically.*

2. *Some foreign civil aircraft registrations begin with a number.*

REFERENCE–
FAA Order JO 7110.65, Para 2–4–9, Abbreviated Transmissions.

2. ICAO 3LD. State the associated telephony followed by the flight number in group form, or separate digits may be used if that is the format used by the pilot. Do not abbreviate.

EXAMPLE–
"Scandinavian Sixty–eight."
"Scandinavian Six Eight."

3. Foreign Military. Except for military services identified in FAA Order JO 7340.2, Contractions, state the name of the country and the military service followed by the separate digits or letters of the registration or call sign. For military services listed in FAA Order JO 7340.2, state the approved telephony followed by the separate digits of the flight number.

EXAMPLE–
"Canforce Five Six Two Seven."
"Brazilian Air Force Five Three Two Seven."

2-4-21. DESCRIPTION OF AIRCRAFT TYPES

Except for super and heavy aircraft, describe aircraft as follows when issuing traffic information.

a. Military:

1. Military designator, with numbers spoken in group form, or

2. Service and type, or

3. Type only if no confusion or misidentification is likely.

b. Air Carrier:

1. Manufacturer's model or type designator.

2. Add the manufacturer's name, company name or other identifying features when confusion or misidentification is likely.

EXAMPLE–
"L–Ten–Eleven."
"American MD–Eighty. Seven Thirty–Seven."
"Boeing Seven Fifty–Seven."

NOTE–
Pilots of "interchange" aircraft are expected to inform the tower on the first radio contact the name of the operating company and trip number followed by the company name, as displayed on the aircraft, and the aircraft type.

c. General Aviation and Air Taxi:

1. Manufacturer's model or type designator.

2. Manufacturer's name, or add color when considered advantageous.

EXAMPLE–
"Tri–Pacer."
"P A Twenty–Two."
"Cessna Four–Oh–One."
"Blue and white King Air."
"Airliner."
"Sikorsky S–Seventy–Six."

d. When issuing traffic information to aircraft following a super aircraft, specify the word s*uper* before the manufacturer's name and model.

e. When issuing traffic information to aircraft following a heavy aircraft, specify the word *heavy* before the manufacturer's name and model.

EXAMPLE–
"Super A-Three-Eighty" or "Super A-three-eighty-eight."
"Heavy C-Seventeen."
"Heavy Boeing Seven Forty-Seven."

REFERENCE–
FAA Order JO 7110.65, Para 2–1–21, Traffic Advisories.

2-4-22. AIRSPACE CLASSES

A, B, C, D, E, and G airspace are pronounced in the ICAO phonetics for clarification. The term "Class" may be dropped when referring to airspace in pilot/controller communications.

EXAMPLE–
"Cessna 123 Mike Romeo cleared to enter Bravo airspace."
"Sikorsky 123 Tango Sierra cleared to enter New York Bravo airspace."

Section 5. Route and NAVAID Description

2–5–1. AIR TRAFFIC SERVICE (ATS) ROUTES

Describe ATS routes as follows:

a. VOR/VORTAC/TACAN airways or jet routes. State the word "Victor" or the letter "J" followed by the number of the airway or route in group form.

EXAMPLE–
"Victor Twelve."
"J Five Thirty–Three."

b. VOR/VORTAC/TACAN alternate airways. State the word "Victor" followed by the number of the airway in group form and the alternate direction.

EXAMPLE–
"Victor Twelve South."

c. Colored/L/MF airways. State the color of the airway followed by the number in group form.

EXAMPLE–
"Blue Eighty–One."

d. Named Routes. State the words "North American Route" or "Bahama Route" followed by the number of the route in group form.

EXAMPLE–
"North American Route Sixty–Seven Bravo."
"Bahama Route Fifty–Five Victor."

e. Air Traffic Service (ATS) routes. State the letter(s) of the route phonetically, followed by the number of the route in group form.

EXAMPLE–
"Romeo Twenty."
"Alfa Fifty."
"Golf Sixty–one."
"Alfa Seven Hundred."

f. Military Training Routes (MTRs). State the letters "I–R" or "V–R" followed by the number of the route in group form.

EXAMPLE–
"I–R Five Thirty–one."
"V–R Fifty–two."

g. Published RNAV routes.

1. High Altitude – State the letter "Q" followed by the route number in group form.

EXAMPLE–
"Q One Forty–five."

2. Low Altitude – State the letter of the route phonetically, followed by the number of the route in group form.

EXAMPLE–
"Tango Two Ten."

2–5–2. NAVAID TERMS

a. Describe NAVAIDs as follows:

1. State the name or phonetic alphabet equivalent (location identifier) of a NAVAID when using it in a routing.

EXAMPLE−
"V6 Victor Whiskey Victor (Waterville) V45 Jackson"

2. When utilized as the clearance limit, state the name of the NAVAID followed by the type of NAVAID if the type is known.

PHRASEOLOGY−
CLEARED TO (NAVAID name and type)

EXAMPLE−
"Cleared to Grand Rapids VOR"

b. Describe radials, arcs, courses, bearings, and quadrants of NAVAIDs as follows:

1. VOR/VORTAC/TACAN/GPS Waypoint. State the name of the NAVAID or GPS Waypoint followed by the separate digits of the radial/azimuth/bearing (omitting the word "degrees") and the word "radial/azimuth/bearing."

EXAMPLE−
"Appleton Zero Five Zero Radial."

2. Arcs about VOR-DME/VORTAC/TACAN NAVAIDs. State the distance in miles from the NAVAID followed by the words "mile arc," the direction from the NAVAID in terms of the eight principal points of the compass, the word "of," and the name of the NAVAID.

EXAMPLE−
"Two Zero mile arc southwest of Kirksville VOR"

3. Quadrant within a radius of NAVAID. State direction from NAVAID in terms of the quadrant; i.e., NE, SE, SW, NW, followed by the distance in miles from the NAVAID.

EXAMPLE−
"Cleared to fly northeast quadrant of Phillipsburg VORTAC within Four Zero mile radius."

REFERENCE−
FAA Order JO 7110.65, Para 4−4−1, Route Use.
P/CG Term − Quadrant.

4. Nondirectional beacons. State the course to or the bearing from the radio beacon, omitting the word "degree," followed by the words "course to" or "bearing from," the name of the radio beacon, and the words "radio beacon."

EXAMPLE−
"Three Four Zero bearing from Randolph Radio Beacon."

5. MLS. State the azimuth to or azimuth from the MLS, omitting the word "degree" followed by the words "azimuth to" or "azimuth from," the name of the MLS, and the term MLS.

EXAMPLE−
"Two Six Zero azimuth to Linburgh Runway Two Seven MLS."

6. Navigation Reference System (NRS) Waypoint. State the single letter corresponding to the ICAO Flight Information Region (FIR) identifier, followed by the letter corresponding to the FIR subset (ARTCC area for the conterminous U.S.), the latitude increment in single digit or group form, and the longitude increment.

EXAMPLE−
"Kilo Delta Three Four Uniform."
"Kilo Delta Thirty Four Uniform."

2−5−3. NAVAID FIXES

Describe fixes determined by reference to a radial/localizer/azimuth and distance from a VOR-DME/VORTAC/TACAN/ILS-DME as follows:

a. When a fix is not named, state the name of the NAVAID followed by a specified radial/localizer/azimuth, and state the distance in miles followed by the phrase "mile fix."

EXAMPLE−
"Appleton Zero Five Zero radial Three Seven mile fix." "Reno localizer back course Four mile fix."

b. When a fix is charted on a SID, STAR, en route chart, or approach plate, state the name of the fix.

c. Use specific terms to describe a fix. Do not use expressions such as "passing Victor Twelve" or "passing J Eleven."

Section 6. Weather Information

2-6-1. FAMILIARIZATION

Controllers must become familiar with pertinent weather information when coming on duty, and stay aware of current and forecasted weather information needed to perform ATC duties.

NOTE–
Every phase of flight has the potential to be impacted by weather, and emphasis must be placed on gathering, reporting and disseminating weather information.

2-6-2. PIREP SOLICITATION AND DISSEMINATION

Emphasis must be placed on the solicitation and dissemination of Urgent (UUA) and Routine (UA) PIREPs. Timely dissemination of PIREPs alerts pilots to weather conditions and provides information useful to forecasters in the development of aviation forecasts. PIREPs also provide information required by ATC in the provision of safe and efficient use of airspace. This includes reports of strong frontal activity, squall lines, thunderstorms, light to severe icing, wind shear and turbulence (including clear air turbulence) of moderate or greater intensity, braking action, volcanic eruptions and volcanic ash clouds, detection of sulfur gases in the cabin, and other conditions pertinent to flight safety. Controllers must provide the information in sufficient detail to assist pilots in making decisions pertinent to flight safety.

NOTE–
Routine PIREPs indicating a lack of forecasted weather conditions, for example, a lack of icing or turbulence, are also valuable to aviation weather forecasters and pilots. This is especially true when adverse conditions are expected or forecasted but do not develop or no longer exist.

REFERENCE–
FAA Order JO 7110.65, Para 3-1-8, Low Level Wind Shear/Microburst Advisories.
FAA Order JO 7110.65, Para 3-3-4, Braking Action.
P/CG Term– Braking Action.
FAA Order JO 7210.3, Para 6-3-1, Handling of SIGMETs, CWAs, and PIREPs.
AIM, Para 7-5-9, Flight Operations in Volcanic Ash.
FAA Order JO 7210.3, Para 10-3-1, SIGMET and PIREP Handling.
FAA Order JO 7110.10, Chapter 8, Section 1, Pilot Weather Reports.

a. Solicit PIREPs when requested, deemed necessary or any of the following conditions exists or is forecast for your area of jurisdiction:

1. Ceilings at or below 5,000 feet. These PIREPs must include cloud bases, tops and cloud coverage when available. Additionally, when providing approach control services, ensure that at least one descent/climb–out PIREP and other related phenomena is obtained each hour.

2. Visibility (surface or aloft) at or less than 5 miles.

3. Thunderstorms and related phenomena.

4. Turbulence of moderate degree or greater.

5. Icing of light degree or greater.

6. Wind shear.

7. Braking action reports less than good.

8. Volcanic ash clouds.

9. Detection of sulfur gases (SO2 or H2S), associated with volcanic activity, in the cabin.

NOTE–
1. *The smell of sulfur gases in the cockpit may indicate volcanic activity that has not yet been detected or reported and/or*

possible entry into an ash–bearing cloud. SO2 is identifiable as the sharp, acrid odor of a freshly struck match. H2S has the odor of rotten eggs.

2. *Pilots may forward PIREPs regarding volcanic activity using the format described in the Volcanic Activity Reporting Form (VAR) as depicted in the AIM, Appendix 2.*

b. Record with the PIREPs:

1. Time.

2. Aircraft position.

3. Type aircraft.

4. Altitude.

5. When the PIREP involves icing include:

(a) Icing type and intensity.

(b) Air temperature in which icing is occurring.

c. Obtain PIREPs directly from the pilot, or if the PIREP has been requested by another facility, you may instruct the pilot to deliver it directly to that facility.

PHRASEOLOGY–
REQUEST/SAY FLIGHT CONDITIONS. Or if appropriate,
REQUEST/SAY (specific conditions; i.e., ride, cloud, visibility, etc.) CONDITIONS.
If necessary,
OVER (fix),

or

ALONG PRESENT ROUTE,

or

BETWEEN (fix) AND (fix).

d. Disseminate PIREPs as follows:

1. Relay pertinent PIREP information to concerned aircraft in a timely manner.

NOTE–
Use the word gain and/or loss when describing to pilots the effects of wind shear on airspeed.

EXAMPLE–
"Delta Seven Twenty–one, a Boeing Seven Thirty–seven, previously reported wind shear, loss of two five knots at four hundred feet."
"Alaska One, a Boeing Seven Thirty–seven, previously reported wind shear, gain of two–five knots between niner hundred and six hundred feet, followed by a loss of five zero knots between five hundred feet and the surface."

REFERENCE–
AIM, Para 7–1–22, Wind Shear PIREPs.

2. *EN ROUTE.* Relay all operationally significant PIREPs to the facility weather coordinator.

REFERENCE–
FAA Order JO 7210.3, Para 6–3–1, Handling of SIGMETs, CWAs, and PIREPs.

3. *TERMINAL.* Relay all operationally significant PIREPs to:

(a) The appropriate intrafacility positions.

(b) The OS/CIC for long line dissemination via an FAA approved electronic system (for example, AIS–R, or similar systems); or,

(c) Outside Alaska: The overlying ARTCC's Flight Data Unit for long–line dissemination.

(d) Alaska Only: The FSS serving the area in which the report was obtained.

NOTE–
The FSS in Alaska is responsible for long line dissemination.

REFERENCE–
FAA Order JO 7110.65, Para 2–1–2, Duty Priority.

(e) Other concerned terminal or en route ATC facilities, including non–FAA facilities.

2–6–3. REPORTING WEATHER CONDITIONS

a. When the prevailing visibility at the usual point of observation, or at the tower level, is less than 4 miles, tower personnel must take prevailing visibility_observations and apply the observations as follows:

1. Use the lower of the two observations (tower or surface) for aircraft operations.

2. Forward tower visibility observations to the weather observer.

3. Notify the weather observer when the tower observes the prevailing visibility decrease to less than 4 miles or increase to 4 miles or more.

b. Describe the wind as calm when the wind velocity is less than three knots.

REFERENCE–
FAA Order JO 7110.65, Para 3–5–3, Tailwind Components.
FAA Order JO 7110.65, Para 3–10–4, Intersecting Runway/Intersecting Flight Path Separation.

c. Forward current weather changes to the appropriate control facility as follows:

1. When the official weather changes to a condition:

(a) Less than a 1,000–foot ceiling or below the highest circling minimum, whichever is greater.

(b) Where the visibility is less than 3 miles.

(c) Where conditions improve to values greater than those listed in (a) and (b).

2. When changes which are classified as special weather observations during the time that weather conditions are below 1,000–foot ceiling or the highest circling minimum, whichever is greater, or less than 3 miles visibility.

d. Towers at airports where military turbo–jet en route descents are routinely conducted must also report the conditions to the ARTCC even if it is not the controlling facility.

e. If the receiving facility informs you that weather reports are not required for a specific time period, discontinue the reports.

f. *EN ROUTE.* When you determine that weather reports for an airport will not be required for a specific time period, inform the FSS or tower of this determination.

REFERENCE–
FAA Order JO 7110.65, Para 3–10–2, Forwarding Approach Information by Nonapproach Control Facilities.

2–6–4. ISSUING WEATHER AND CHAFF AREAS

a. Controllers must issue pertinent information on observed/reported weather and chaff areas to potentially affected aircraft. Define the area of coverage in terms of:

1. Azimuth (by referring to the 12–hour clock) and distance from the aircraft and/or

2. The general width of the area and the area of coverage in terms of fixes or distance and direction from fixes.

NOTE–
Weather significant to the safety of aircraft includes conditions such as funnel cloud activity, lines of thunderstorms,

embedded thunderstorms, large hail, wind shear, microbursts, moderate to extreme turbulence (including CAT), and light to severe icing.

REFERENCE–
AIM, Para 7–1–12, ATC Inflight Weather Avoidance Assistance.

PHRASEOLOGY–
WEATHER/CHAFF AREA BETWEEN (number) O'CLOCK AND (number) O'CLOCK (number) MILES, and/or (number) MILE BAND OF WEATHER/CHAFF FROM (fix or number of miles and direction from fix) TO (fix or number of miles and direction from fix).

b. Inform any tower for which you provide approach control services of observed precipitation on radar which is likely to affect their operations.

c. Use the term "precipitation" when describing radar–derived weather. Issue the precipitation intensity from the lowest descriptor (LIGHT) to the highest descriptor (EXTREME) when that information is available. Do not use the word "turbulence" in describing radar–derived weather.

1. LIGHT.

2. MODERATE.

3. HEAVY.

4. EXTREME.

NOTE–
Weather and Radar Processor (WARP) does not display light intensity.

PHRASEOLOGY–
AREA OF (Intensity) PRECIPITATION BETWEEN (number) O'CLOCK AND (number) O'CLOCK, (number) MILES, MOVING (direction) AT (number) KNOTS, TOPS (altitude). AREA IS (number) MILES IN DIAMETER.

EXAMPLE–
1. *"Area of heavy precipitation between ten o'clock and two o'clock, one five miles. Area is two five miles in diameter."*

2. *"Area of heavy to extreme precipitation between ten o'clock and two o'clock, one five miles. Area is two five miles in diameter."*

REFERENCE–
P/CG Term– Precipitation Radar Weather Descriptions.

d. *TERMINAL:* In STARS, correlate precipitation descriptors from subparagraph c as follows:

1. Level 1 = LIGHT

2. Level 2 = MODERATE

3. Levels 3 and 4 = HEAVY

4. Levels 5 and 6 = EXTREME

e. When precipitation intensity information is not available.

PHRASEOLOGY–
AREA OF PRECIPITATION BETWEEN (number) O'CLOCK AND (number) O'CLOCK, (number) MILES. MOVING (direction) AT (number) KNOTS, TOPS (altitude). AREA IS (number) MILES IN DIAMETER, INTENSITY UNKNOWN.

EXAMPLE–
"Area of precipitation between one o'clock and three o'clock, three five miles moving south at one five knots, tops flight level three three zero. Area is three zero miles in diameter, intensity unknown."

NOTE–
Phraseology using precipitation intensity descriptions is only applicable when the radar precipitation intensity information is determined by NWS radar equipment or NAS ground based digitized radar equipment with weather capabilities. This precipitation may not reach the surface.

f. *EN ROUTE.* When issuing Air Route Surveillance Radar (ARSR) precipitation intensity use the following:

1. Describe the lowest displayable precipitation intensity as MODERATE.

2. Describe the highest displayable precipitation intensity as HEAVY to EXTREME.

PHRASEOLOGY–
AREA OF (Intensity) PRECIPITATION BETWEEN (number) O'CLOCK and (number) O'CLOCK, (number) MILES, MOVING (direction) AT (number) KNOTS, TOPS (altitude). If applicable, AREA IS (number) MILES IN DIAMETER.

EXAMPLE–
1. *"Area of moderate precipitation between ten o'clock and one o'clock, three zero miles moving east at two zero knots, tops flight level three seven zero.*

2. *"Area of moderate precipitation between ten o'clock and three o'clock, two zero miles. Area is two five miles in diameter."*

g. Controllers must ensure that the highest available level of precipitation intensity within their area of jurisdiction is displayed unless operational/equipment limitations exist.

h. When requested by the pilot, provide radar navigational guidance and/or approve deviations around weather or chaff areas. In areas of significant weather, plan ahead and be prepared to suggest, upon pilot request, the use of alternative routes/altitudes.

1. An approval for lateral deviation authorizes the pilot to maneuver left or right within the lateral limits specified in the clearance.

REFERENCE–
AIM, Subpara 7–1–12b1(a), ATC Inflight Weather Avoidance Assistance.

2. When approving a weather deviation for an aircraft that had previously been issued a crossing altitude, including climb via or descend via clearances, issue an altitude to maintain and, if necessary, assign a speed along with the clearance to deviate. If you intend on clearing the aircraft to resume the procedure, advise the pilot.

PHRASEOLOGY–
DEVIATION (restrictions, if necessary) APPROVED, MAINTAIN (altitude), (if necessary) MAINTAIN (speed), (if applicable) EXPECT TO RESUME (SID/STAR, etc.) AT (NAVAID, fix/waypoint).

NOTE–
After a climb via or descend via clearance has been issued, a vector/deviation off of a SID/STAR cancels all published altitude and speed restrictions on the procedure. The aircraft's Flight Management System (FMS) may be unable to process crossing altitude restrictions once the aircraft leaves the SID/STAR lateral path. Without an assigned altitude, the aircraft's FMS may revert to leveling off at the altitude set by the pilot, which may be the SID/STAR published top or bottom altitude.

REFERENCE–
FAA Order JO 7110.65, Para 4–2–5, Route or Altitude Amendments.
FAA Order JO 7110.65, Para 5–6–1, Application.
FAA Order JO 7110.65, Para 5–6–2, Methods.

3. If a pilot enters your area of jurisdiction already deviating for weather, advise the pilot of any additional weather which may affect the route.

NOTE–
When aircraft are deviating around weather and transitioning from sector to sector, unless previously coordinated, the receiving controller should not assume that the transferring controller has issued weather affecting the aircraft's route of flight.

4. If traffic and airspace (i.e., special use airspace boundaries, LOA constraints) permit, combine the approval for weather deviation with a clearance on course.

PHRASEOLOGY–
DEVIATION (restrictions if necessary) APPROVED, WHEN ABLE, PROCEED DIRECT (name of NAVAID/WAYPOINT/FIX)

or

DEVIATION (restrictions if necessary) APPROVED, WHEN ABLE, FLY HEADING (degrees), VECTOR TO JOIN (airway) AND ADVISE.

EXAMPLE–
1. *"Deviation 20 degrees right approved, when able proceed direct O'Neill VORTAC and advise." En Route: The corresponding fourth line entry is "D20R/ONL" or "D20R/F."*

2. *"Deviation 30 degrees left approved, when able fly heading zero niner zero, vector to join J324 and advise." En Route: In this case the free text character limitation prevents use of fourth line coordination and verbal coordination is required.*

5. If traffic or airspace prevents you from clearing the aircraft on course at the time of the approval for a weather deviation, instruct the pilot to advise when clear of weather.

PHRASEOLOGY–
DEVIATION (restrictions if necessary) APPROVED, ADVISE CLEAR OF WEATHER.

EXAMPLE–
"Deviation North of course approved, advise clear of weather."
En Route: In this case the corresponding fourth line entry is "DN," and the receiving controller must provide a clearance to rejoin the route in accordance with paragraph 2–1–15c.

i. When a deviation cannot be approved as requested because of traffic, take an alternate course of action that provides positive control for traffic resolution and satisfies the pilot's need to avoid weather.

PHRASEOLOGY–
UNABLE REQUESTED DEVIATION, FLY HEADING (heading), ADVISE CLEAR OF WEATHER

or

UNABLE REQUESTED DEVIATION, TURN (number of degrees) DEGREES (left or right) VECTOR FOR TRAFFIC, ADVISE CLEAR OF WEATHER,

EXAMPLE–
"Unable requested deviation, turn thirty degrees right vector for traffic, advise clear of weather."

j. When forwarding weather deviation information, the transferring controller must clearly coordinate the nature of the route guidance service being provided. This coordination should include, but is not limited to: assigned headings, suggested headings, pilot–initiated deviations. Coordination can be accomplished by: verbal, automated, or predetermined procedures. Emphasis should be made between: controller assigned headings, suggested headings, or pilot initiated deviations.

EXAMPLE–
"(call sign) assigned heading three three zero for weather avoidance"
"(call sign) deviating west, pilot requested..."

REFERENCE–
FAA Order JO 7110.65, Para 2–1–14, Coordinate Use Of Airspace.
FAA Order JO 7110.65, Para 5–4–5, Transferring Controller Handoff.
FAA Order JO 7110.65, Para 5–4–6, Receiving Controller Handoff.
FAA Order JO 7110.65, Para 5–4–9, Prearranged Coordination.
FAA Order JO 7110.65, Para 5–4–10, En Route Fourth Line Data Block Usage.

k. En Route Fourth Line Data Transfer

1. The inclusion of /(NAVAID) or /(waypoint), when preceded by the designated characters for weather deviations, indicates that a pilot has been authorized to deviate for weather and rejoin the route at the specified NAVAID or waypoint. The use of /F, following the designated weather deviation characters, indicates that a pilot has been authorized to deviate and rejoin the route of flight at the next NAVAID or waypoint in the flight plan.

REFERENCE–
FAA Order JO 7110.65, Para 5–4–10, En Route Fourth Line Data Block Usage.

EXAMPLE–
"Deviation twenty degrees right approved, when able proceed direct O'Neill VORTAC and advise." In this case, the corresponding fourth line entry is "D20R/ONL," or "D20R/F" if O'Neill is the next NAVAID in the flight plan.

2. The absence of a NAVAID, waypoint, or /F in the fourth line indicates that:

(a) The pilot has been authorized to deviate for weather only, and the receiving controller must provide a clearance to rejoin the route in accordance with paragraph 2–1–15c.

EXAMPLE–
"Deviation twenty degrees right approved, advise clear of weather."

(b) The free text character limitation prevents the use of fourth line coordination. Verbal coordination is required.

EXAMPLE–
"Deviation 30 degrees left approved, when able fly heading zero niner zero, vector to join J324 and advise."

l. The supervisory traffic management coordinator–in–charge/operations supervisor/ controller–in–charge must verify the digitized radar weather information by the best means available (e.g., pilot reports, local tower personnel, etc.) if the weather data displayed by digitized radar is reported as questionable or erroneous. Errors in weather radar presentation must be reported to the technical operations technician and the air traffic supervisor must determine if the digitized radar derived weather data is to be displayed and a NOTAM distributed.

NOTE–
Anomalous propagation (AP) is a natural occurrence affecting radar and does not in itself constitute a weather circuit failure.

2–6–5. DISSEMINATING OFFICIAL WEATHER INFORMATION

TERMINAL. Observed elements of weather information must be disseminated as follows:

a. General weather information, such as "large breaks in the overcast," "visibility lowering to the south," or similar statements which do not include specific values, and any elements derived directly from instruments, pilots, or radar may be transmitted to pilots or other ATC facilities without consulting the weather reporting station.

b. Specific values, such as ceiling and visibility, may be transmitted if obtained by one of the following means:

1. You are properly certificated and acting as official weather observer for the elements being reported.

NOTE–
USAF controllers do not serve as official weather observers.

2. You have obtained the information from the official observer for the elements being reported.

3. The weather report was composed or verified by the weather station.

4. The information is obtained from a FAA approved automation surface weather system.

c. Differences between weather elements observed from the tower and those reported by the weather station must be reported to the official observer for the element concerned.

2–6–6. HAZARDOUS INFLIGHT WEATHER ADVISORY

Controllers must advise pilots of hazardous weather that may impact operations within 150 NM of their sector or area of jurisdiction. Hazardous weather information contained in the advisories includes Airmen's Meteorological Information (AIRMET) (except over the CONUS), Significant Meteorological Information (SIGMET), Convective SIGMET (WST), Urgent Pilot Weather Reports (UUA), and Center Weather Advisories (CWA). Facilities must review alert messages to determine the geographical area and operational impact of hazardous weather information. Advisories are not required if aircraft on your frequency(s) will not be affected.

NOTE–
In recognition that there are several uses/definitions for the acronym CONUS, references herein to CONUS are specific to the contiguous United States (i.e., "lower 48").

a. Controllers must broadcast a hazardous inflight weather advisory on all frequencies, except emergency frequency, upon receipt of hazardous weather information. Controllers are required to disseminate data based on the operational impact on the sector or area of control jurisdiction. Pilots requesting additional information must be directed to contact the nearest Flight Service.

PHRASEOLOGY−
ATTENTION ALL AIRCRAFT. HAZARDOUS WEATHER INFORMATION (SIGMET, Convective SIGMET, AIRMET, Urgent Pilot Weather Report (UUA), or Center Weather Advisory (CWA), Number or Numbers) FOR (specific weather phenomenon) WITHIN (geographical area), AVAILABLE ON FLIGHT SERVICE FREQUENCIES.

b. Terminal facilities have the option to limit hazardous weather information broadcasts as follows: Tower cab and approach control facilities may opt to broadcast hazardous weather information alerts only when any part of the area described is within 50 NM of the airspace under their jurisdiction.

REFERENCE−
AIM, Chapter 7, Section 1, Meteorology, Para 7−1−5 through Para 7−1−7.

c. *EN ROUTE.* ERAM. Controllers must electronically acknowledge hazardous weather information messages after appropriate action has been taken.

NOTE−
EN ROUTE. While hazardous weather information is commonly distributed via the SIGMET View, it is possible to receive the information via the GI View.

Section 7. Altimeter Settings

2–7–1. CURRENT SETTINGS

a. Current altimeter settings must be obtained from direct-reading instruments or directly from weather reporting stations.

REFERENCE–
FAA Order JO 7210.3, Chapter 2, Section 10, Wind/Altimeter Information.

b. If a pilot requests the altimeter setting in millibars, ask the nearest weather reporting station for the equivalent millibar setting.

c. USAF/USA. Use the term "Estimated Altimeter" for altimeter settings reported or received as estimated.

REFERENCE–
FAA Order JO 7110.65, Para 3–9–1, Departure Information.
FAA Order JO 7110.65, Para 3–10–1, Landing Information.
FAA Order JO 7110.65, Para 4–7–10, Approach Information.

2–7–2. ALTIMETER SETTING ISSUANCE BELOW LOWEST USABLE FL

a. *TERMINAL.* Identify the source of an altimeter setting when issued for a location other than the aircraft's departure or destination airport.

b. *EN ROUTE.* Identify the source of all altimeter settings when issued.

PHRASEOLOGY–
(If the altimeter is one hour old or less),
THE (facility name) ALTIMETER (setting).

or

(If the altimeter is more than one hour old),
THE (facility name) ALTIMETER (setting) MORE THAN ONE HOUR OLD.

c. Issue the altimeter setting:

1. To en route aircraft at least one time while operating in your area of jurisdiction. Issue the setting for the nearest reporting station along the aircraft's route of flight:

NOTE–
14 CFR Section 91.121(1) requires that the pilot set his/her altimeter to the setting of a station along his/her route of flight within 100 miles of the aircraft if one is available. However, issuance of the setting of an adjacent station during periods that a steep gradient exists will serve to inform the pilot of the difference between the setting he/she is using and the pressure in the local area and better enable him/her to choose a more advantageous setting within the limitations of 14 CFR Section 91.121.

2. *TERMINAL.* To all departures. Unless specifically requested by the pilot, the altimeter setting need not be issued to local aircraft operators who have requested this omission in writing or to scheduled air carriers.

REFERENCE–
FAA Order JO 7110.65, Para 3–9–1, Departure Information.

3. *TERMINAL.* To arriving aircraft on initial contact or as soon as possible thereafter. The tower may omit the altimeter if the aircraft is sequenced or vectored to the airport by the approach control having jurisdiction at that facility.

REFERENCE–
FAA Order JO 7110.65, Para 4–7–10, Approach Information.
FAA Order JO 7110.65, Para 5–10–2, Approach Information.

4. *EN ROUTE.* For the destination airport to arriving aircraft, approximately 50 miles from the destination, if an approach control facility does not serve the airport.

5. In addition to the altimeter setting provided on initial contact, issue changes in altimeter setting to aircraft executing a nonprecision instrument approach as frequently as practical when the official weather report includes the remarks "pressure falling rapidly."

d. If the altimeter setting must be obtained by the pilot of an arriving aircraft from another source, instruct the pilot to obtain the altimeter setting from that source.

NOTE–
1. *The destination altimeter setting, whether from a local or remote source, is the setting upon which the instrument approach is predicated.*

2. *Approach charts for many locations specify the source of altimeter settings as non–FAA facilities, such as UNICOMs.*

e. When issuing clearance to descend below the lowest usable flight level, advise the pilot of the altimeter setting of the weather reporting station nearest the point the aircraft will descend below that flight level. Local directives may delegate this responsibility to an alternate sector when Optimized Profile Descents (OPD) commence in sectors consisting entirely of Class A airspace.

f. Department of Defense (DoD) aircraft that are authorized to operate in restricted areas, MOAs, and ATC assigned airspace areas on "single altimeter settings" (CFR Exemption 2861A), must be issued altimeter settings in accordance with standard procedures while the aircraft are en route to and from the restricted areas, MOAs, and ATC assigned airspace areas.

NOTE–
The DoD is responsible for conducting all "single altimeter setting" operations within the boundaries of MOAs, restricted areas, and ATCAAs. Under an LOA, the DoD provides safe altitude clearance between DoD aircraft and other aircraft operating within, above, and below the MOAs, restricted areas, and ATCAAs with appropriate clearance of terrain.

REFERENCE–
FAA Order JO 7610.14, Appendix 4, Document 4, Grant of Exemption No. 2861A – Single Altimeter Setting For Frequent Transit of FL180.

g. When the barometric pressure is greater than 31.00 inches Hg., issue the altimeter setting and:

1. En Route/Arrivals. Advise pilots to remain set on altimeter 31.00 until reaching final approach segment.

2. Departures. Advise pilots to set altimeter 31.00 prior to reaching any mandatory/crossing altitude or 1,500 feet AGL, whichever is lower.

PHRASEOLOGY–
ALTIMETER (setting), SET THREE ONE ZERO ZERO UNTIL REACHING THE FINAL APPROACH FIX.

or

ALTIMETER (setting), SET THREE ONE ZERO ZERO PRIOR TO REACHING (mandatory/crossing altitude or 1,500 feet AGL, whichever is lower).

NOTE–
1. *Aircraft with Mode C altitude reporting will be displayed on the controller's radar scope with a uniform altitude offset above the assigned altitude. With an actual altimeter of 31.28 inches Hg, the Mode C equipped aircraft will show 3,300 feet when assigned 3,000 feet. This will occur unless local directives authorize entering the altimeter setting 31.00 into the computer system regardless of the actual barometric pressure.*

2. *Flight Standards will implement high barometric pressure procedures by NOTAM defining the geographic area affected.*

3. *Airports unable to accurately measure barometric pressures above 31.00 inches Hg. will report the barometric pressure as "missing" or "in excess of 31.00 inches of Hg." Flight operations to or from those airports are restricted to VFR weather conditions.*

REFERENCE–
AIM, Para 7–2–2, Procedures.
FAA Order JO 7110.65, Para 3–10–1, Landing Information.

Section 8. Runway Visibility Reporting– Terminal

2–8–1. FURNISH RVR VALUES

Where RVR equipment is operational, irrespective of subsequent operation or nonoperation of navigational or visual aids for the application of RVR as a takeoff or landing minima, furnish the values for the runway in use in accordance with paragraph 2–8–3, Terminology.

NOTE–
Readout capability of different type/model RVR equipment varies. For example, older equipment minimum readout value is 600 feet. Newer equipment may have minimum readout capability as low as 100 feet. Readout value increments also may differ. Older equipment have minimum readout increments of 200 feet. New equipment increments below 800 feet are 100 feet.

REFERENCE–
FAA Order 6560.10, Runway Visual Range (RVR).
FAA Order 6750.24, Instrument Landing System (ILS) and Ancillary Electronic Component Configuration & Perf. Req.

2–8–2. ARRIVAL/DEPARTURE RUNWAY VISIBILITY

a. Issue current touchdown RVR for the runway(s) in use:

1. When prevailing visibility is 1 mile or less regardless of the value indicated.

2. When RVR indicates a reportable value regardless of the prevailing visibility.

NOTE–
Reportable values are RVR 6,000 feet or less.

3. When it is determined from a reliable source that the indicated RVR value differs by more than 400 feet from the actual conditions within the area of the transmissometer, the RVR data is not acceptable and must not be reported.

NOTE–
A reliable source is considered to be a certified weather observer, automated weather observing system, air traffic controller, flight service specialist, or pilot.

4. When the observer has reliable reports, or has otherwise determined that the instrument values are not representative of the associated runway, the data must not be used.

b. Issue both mid-point and roll-out RVR when the value of either is less than 2,000 feet and the touchdown RVR is greater than the mid–point or roll–out RVR.

c. Local control must issue the current RVR to each aircraft prior to landing or departure in accordance with subparagraphs a and b.

2–8–3. TERMINOLOGY

a. Provide RVR information by stating the runway, the abbreviation RVR, and the indicated value. When issued along with other weather elements, transmit these values in the normal sequence used for weather reporting.

EXAMPLE–
"Runway One Four RVR Two Thousand Four Hundred."

b. When two or more RVR systems serve the runway in use, report the indicated values for the different systems in terms of touchdown, mid, and rollout as appropriate.

EXAMPLE–
"Runway Two Two Left RVR Two Thousand, rollout One Thousand Eight Hundred."

"Runway Two Seven Right RVR One Thousand, mid Eight Hundred, rollout Six Hundred."

c. When there is a requirement to issue an RVR value and a visibility condition greater or less than the reportable values of the equipment is indicated, state the condition as "MORE THAN" or "LESS THAN" the appropriate minimum or maximum readable value.

EXAMPLE–
"Runway Three Six RVR more than Six Thousand."

"Runway Niner RVR One Thousand, rollout less than Six Hundred."

d. When a readout indicates a rapidly varying visibility condition (1,000 feet or more for RVR), report the current value followed by the range of visibility variance.

EXAMPLE–
"Runway Two Four RVR Two Thousand, variable One Thousand Six Hundred to Three Thousand."

REFERENCE–
FAA Order JO 7110.65, Para 2–8–1, Furnish RVR Values.

Section 9. Automatic Terminal Information Service Procedures

2–9–1. APPLICATION

Use the ATIS, where available, to provide advance noncontrol airport/terminal area and meteorological information to aircraft.

a. Identify each ATIS message by a phonetic letter code word at both the beginning and the end of the message. Automated systems will have the phonetic letter code automatically appended. Exceptions may be made where omissions are required because of special programs or equipment.

1. Each alphabet letter phonetic word must be used sequentially, except as authorized in subparagraph a2, beginning with "Alpha," ending with "Zulu," and repeated without regard to the beginning of a new day. Identify the first resumed broadcast message with "Alpha" or the first assigned alphabet letter word in the event of a broadcast interruption of more than 12 hours.

2. Specific sequential portions of the alphabet may be assigned between facilities or an arrival and departure ATIS when designated by a letter of agreement or facility directive.

REFERENCE–
FAA Order JO 7210.3, Para 10–4–1, Automatic Terminal Information Service (ATIS).

b. The ATIS recording must be reviewed for completeness, accuracy, speech rate, and proper enunciation before being transmitted.

c. Arrival and departure messages, when broadcast separately, need only contain information appropriate for that operation.

2–9–2. OPERATING PROCEDURES

Maintain an ATIS message that reflects the most current arrival and departure information.

a. Make a new recording when any of the following occur:

1. Upon receipt of any new official weather regardless of whether there is or is not a change in values.

2. When runway braking action reports are received that indicate runway braking is worse than that which is included in the current ATIS broadcast.

3. When there is a change in any other pertinent data, such as runway change, instrument approach in use, new or canceled NOTAMs/PIREPs update, etc.

b. When a pilot acknowledges that he/she has received the ATIS broadcast, controllers may omit those items contained in the broadcasts if they are current. Rapidly changing conditions will be issued by ATC, and the ATIS will contain the following:

EXAMPLE–
"Latest ceiling/visibility/altimeter/wind/(other conditions) will be issued by approach control/tower."

c. Controllers must ensure that pilots receive the most current pertinent information by taking the following actions, as applicable:

1. When a pilot does not state the appropriate ATIS code on initial contact, ask the pilot to confirm receipt of the current ATIS information.

EXAMPLE–
"Verify you have information CHARLIE."
"Information CHARLIE current. Advise when you have CHARLIE."

2. When a pilot is unable to receive the ATIS, issue the current weather, runway in use, approach/departure information, pertinent NOTAMs, and airport conditions.

EXAMPLE–
"Wind two five zero at one zero. Visibility one zero. Ceiling four thousand five hundred broken. Temperature three four. Dew point two eight. Altimeter three zero one zero. ILS–DME Runway Two Seven Approach in use. Departing Runway Two Two Right. Hazardous Weather Information for (geographical area) available on Flight Service Frequencies. Braking Action advisories are in effect."

d. Advise aircraft of changes to the ATIS code by broadcasting the change on all appropriate frequencies. The broadcast must include changes to pertinent operational information, when known, that necessitated the ATIS change.

EXAMPLE–
"Attention all aircraft, information ALPHA current."

"Attention all aircraft, information BRAVO current. MICROBURST advisories in effect."

"Attention all aircraft, information CHARLIE current. Numerous flocks of ducks in the immediate vicinity of (name) airport, altitude unknown."

REFERENCE–
FAA Order JO 7110.65, Para 2–9–3, Content.

NOTE–
1. *No additional acknowledgement is required when a controller broadcasts information subsequent to the pilot's initial acknowledgement of the ATIS. Requiring each aircraft to acknowledge receipt of pertinent changes (broadcast) after initial confirmation of the ATIS could significantly impact workload.*

2. *Pertinent conditions are those that have a clear decisive relevance to the safety of air traffic. As noted in paragraph 2–1–2, Duty Priority, there are many variables involved that make it virtually impossible to develop a standard list of changes that are classified as relevant to every conceivable situation. Each set of circumstances must be evaluated on its own merit, and when more than one action is required, controllers must exercise their best judgment based on the facts and circumstances known to them.*

2–9–3. CONTENT

a. Include the following in ATIS broadcast as appropriate:

1. Airport/facility name.

2. Phonetic letter code.

3. Time of the latest weather sequence (UTC).

4. Weather information consisting of:

(a) Wind direction and velocity.

(b) Visibility.

(c) Obstructions to vision.

(d) Present weather consisting of: sky condition, temperature, dew point, altimeter, a density altitude advisory when appropriate, and other pertinent remarks included in the official weather observation. Always include weather observation remarks of lightning, cumulonimbus, and towering cumulus clouds.

NOTE–
ASOS/AWOS is to be considered the primary source of wind direction, velocity, and altimeter data for weather observation purposes at those locations that are so equipped. The ASOS Operator Interface Device (OID) displays the magnetic wind as "MAG WND" in the auxiliary data location in the lower left–hand portion of the screen. Other OID displayed winds are true and are not to be used for operational purposes.

REFERENCE–
FAA Order JO 7900.5, Surface Weather Observing Table 3–2.
FAA Order JO 7210.3, Para 10–2–1, Position Duties and Responsibilities.

5. Instrument approach and runway in use.

b. Man−Portable Air Defense Systems (MANPADS) alert and advisory. Specify the nature and location of threat or incident, whether reported or observed and by whom, time (if known), and notification to pilots to advise ATC if they need to divert.

EXAMPLE−
1. *"MANPADS alert. Exercise extreme caution. MANPADS threat reported by TSA, Chicago area." "Advise on initial contact if you want to divert."*

2. *"MANPADS alert. Exercise extreme caution. MANPADS attack observed by tower one−half mile northwest of airfield at one−two−five−zero Zulu." "Advise on initial contact if you want to divert."*

REFERENCE−
FAA Order JO 7110.65, Para 10−2−13, MANPADS Alert.
FAA Order JO 7210.3, Para 2−1−10, Handling MANPADS Incidents.

c. Terminal facilities must include reported unauthorized laser illumination events on the ATIS broadcast for one hour following the last report. Include the time, location, altitude, color, and direction of the laser as reported by the pilot.

PHRASEOLOGY−
UNAUTHORIZED LASER ILLUMINATION EVENT, (UTC time), (location), (altitude), (color), (direction).

EXAMPLE−
UNAUTHORIZED LASER ILLUMINATION EVENT, AT 0100z, 8 MILE FINAL RUNWAY 18R AT 3,000 FEET, GREEN LASER FROM THE SOUTHWEST.

REFERENCE−
FAA Order JO 7110.65, Para 10−2−14, Unauthorized Laser Illumination of Aircraft.
FAA Order JO 7210.3, Para 2−1−30, Reporting Unauthorized Laser Illumination of Aircraft.

d. The ceiling/sky condition, visibility, and obstructions to vision may be omitted if the ceiling is above 5,000 feet and the visibility is more than 5 miles.

EXAMPLE−
A remark may be made, "The weather is better than five thousand and five."

e. Instrument/visual approach/es in use. Specify landing runway/s unless the runway is that to which the instrument approach is made. Before advertising non-precision approaches, priority should be given to available precision, then APV approaches.

f. Departure runway/s (to be given only if different from landing runway/s or in the instance of a "departure only" ATIS).

g. Taxiway closures which affect the entrance or exit of active runways, other closures which impact airport operations, other NOTAMs and PIREPs pertinent to operations in the terminal area. Inform pilots of where hazardous weather is occurring and how the information may be obtained. Include available information of known bird activity.

REFERENCE−
FAA Order JO 7110.65, 2−1−23, Bird Activity Information.

h. When a runway length has been temporarily or permanently shortened, ensure that the word "WARNING" prefaces the runway number, and that the word "shortened" is also included in the text of the message.

1. Available runway length, as stated in the NOTAM, must be included in the ATIS broadcast. This information must be broadcast for the duration of the construction project.

2. For permanently shortened runways, facilities must continue to broadcast this information for a minimum of 30 days or until the Chart Supplement has been updated, whichever is longer.

PHRASEOLOGY−
WARNING, RUNWAY (number) HAS BEEN SHORTENED, (length in feet) FEET AVAILABLE.

EXAMPLE−
"Warning, Runway One-Zero has been shortened, niner-thousand eight hundred and fifty feet available."

i. Runway Condition Codes (RwyCC) when provided. Include the time of the report.

PHRASEOLOGY−
RUNWAY (number) condition codes (first value, second value, third value) AT (time),

EXAMPLE−
"Runway Two Seven, condition codes two, two, one at one zero one eight Zulu."

REFERENCE−
FAA Order JO 7110.65, Para 3−3−1, Landing Area Condition.

j. Runway Condition Codes "3/3/3" and the statement "Slippery When Wet."

EXAMPLE−
"Runway (number) condition codes three, three, three, Slippery When Wet at one two five five Zulu."

NOTE−
A Slippery When Wet FICON NOTAM indicates a runway has failed a friction survey, for example, due to excessive rubber build−up. Airport Operators will notify ATCT operational personnel of this concern and issue a FICON NOTAM prior to the expected arrival of rain. The FICON NOTAM will be canceled when the rain has ended and the runway environment is determined to be dry by the Airport Operator.

k. Runway Condition codes "X/X/X." When a FICON NOTAM indicates these values, the statement "Runway Condition Codes Missing" must be included on the ATIS broadcast.

EXAMPLE−
"Runway (number) condition codes missing at one three four seven Zulu."

NOTE−
A FICON NOTAM may be generated with "X/X/X" instead of Runway Condition Codes. This will occur when the NOTAM user interface is not functioning correctly; however, a FICON NOTAM is still present.

l. Other optional information as local conditions dictate in coordination with ATC. This may include such items as VFR arrival frequencies, temporary airport conditions, LAHSO operations being con−ducted, or other perishable items that may appear only for a matter of hours or a few days on the ATIS message.

m. When all 3 runway segments (touchdown, midpoint, and rollout) are reporting a code of 6, the Airport Operator will notify ATC that runway condition codes are no longer reportable.

n. Low level wind shear/microburst when reported by pilots or is detected on a wind shear detection system.

REFERENCE−
FAA Order JO 7110.65, Para 3−1−8, Low Level Wind Shear/Microburst Advisories.

o. A statement which advises the pilot to read back instructions to hold short of a runway. The air traffic manager may elect to remove this requirement 60 days after implementation provided that removing the statement from the ATIS does not result in increased requests from aircraft for read back of hold short instructions.

p. Instructions for the pilot to acknowledge receipt of the ATIS message by informing the controller on initial contact.

EXAMPLE−
"Boston Tower Information Delta. One four zero zero Zulu. Wind two five zero at one zero. Visibility one zero. Ceiling four thousand five hundred broken. Temperature three four. Dew point two eight. Altimeter three zero one zero. ILS−DME Runway Two Seven Approach in use. Departing Runway Two Two Right. Hazardous Weather Information for (geographical area) available on Flight Service Frequencies. Advise on initial contact you have Delta."

Section 10. Team Position Responsibilities

2-10-1. EN ROUTE OR OCEANIC SECTOR TEAM POSITION RESPONSIBILITIES

a. En Route or Oceanic Sector Team Concept and Intent: There are no absolute divisions of responsibilities regarding position operations. The tasks to be completed remain the same whether one, two, or three people are working positions within a sector. The team, as a whole, has responsibility for the safe and efficient operation of that sector.

b. *Terms.* The following terms will be used in en route facilities for the purpose of standardization:

1. *Sector.* The area of control responsibility (delegated airspace) of the en route sector team, and the team as a whole.

2. *Radar Position (R).* That position which is in direct communication with the aircraft and which uses radar information as the primary means of separation.

3. *Radar Associate (RA).* That position sometimes referred to as "D-Side" or "Manual Controller."

4. *Radar Coordinator Position (RC).* That position sometimes referred to as "Coordinator," "Tracker," or "Handoff Controller" (En Route).

5. *Radar Flight Data (FD).* That position commonly referred to as "Assistant Controller" or "A-Side" position.

6. *Nonradar Position (NR).* That position which is usually in direct communication with the aircraft and which uses nonradar procedures as the primary means of separation.

c. Primary responsibilities of the En Route Sector Team Positions:

1. ***Radar Position:***

(a) Ensure separation.

(b) Initiate control instructions.

(c) Monitor and operate radios.

(d) Accept and initiate automated handoffs.

(e) Assist the radar associate position with nonautomated handoff actions when needed.

(f) Assist the radar associate position in coordination when needed.

(g) Scan radar display. Correlate with flight progress strip information or EDST data, as applicable.

(h) Ensure computer entries are completed on instructions or clearances you issue or receive.

(i) Ensure strip marking and/or electronic flight data entries are completed on instructions or clearances you issue or receive.

(j) Adjust equipment at radar position to be usable by all members of the team.

(k) The radar controller must not be responsible for G/G communications when precluded by VSCS split functionality.

(l) At ERAM facilities, ensure the situation display accurately reflects the status of all SAAs that impact their area of control responsibility.

2. ***Radar Associate Position:***

(a) Ensure separation.

(b) Where available, use EDST to plan, organize, and expedite the flow of traffic.

(c) Initiate control instructions.

(d) Operate interphones.

(e) Accept and initiate nonautomated handoffs, and ensure radar position is made aware of the actions.

(f) Assist the radar position by accepting or initiating automated handoffs which are necessary for the continued smooth operation of the sector, and ensure that the radar position is made immediately aware of any action taken.

(g) Coordinate, including point outs.

(h) Monitor radios when not performing higher priority duties.

(i) Scan flight progress strips and/or EDST data. Correlate with radar data.

(j) Manage flight progress strips and/or electronic flight data.

(k) Ensure computer entries are completed on instructions issued or received. Enter instructions issued or received by the radar position when aware of those instructions.

(l) As appropriate, ensure strip marking and/or EDST data entries are completed on instructions issued or received, and record instructions issued or received by the radar position when aware of them.

(m) Adjust equipment at radar associate position to be usable by all members of the team.

(n) Where authorized, perform EDST data entries to keep the activation status of designated Airspace Configuration Elements current.

(o) At ERAM facilities, scan the radar associate display for electronically distributed information, evaluate the information, and take action as appropriate.

3. ***Radar Coordinator Position:***

(a) Perform interfacility/intrafacility/sector/position coordination of traffic actions.

(b) Advise the radar position and the radar associate position of sector actions required to accomplish overall objectives.

(c) Perform any of the functions of the en route sector team which will assist in meeting situation objectives.

(d) The RC controller must not be responsible for monitoring or operating radios when precluded by VSCS split functionality.

NOTE–
The Radar Position has the responsibility for managing the overall sector operations, including aircraft separation and traffic flows. The Radar Coordinator Position assumes responsibility for managing traffic flows and the Radar Position retains responsibility for aircraft separation when the Radar Coordinator Position is staffed.

4. ***Radar Flight Data:***

(a) Operate interphone.

(b) Assist Radar Associate Position in managing flight progress strips.

(c) Receive/process and distribute flight progress strips.

(d) Ensure flight data processing equipment is operational, except for EDST capabilities.

(e) Request/receive and disseminate weather, NOTAMs, NAS status, traffic management, and Special Use Airspace status messages.

(f) Manually prepare flight progress strips when automation systems are not available.

(g) Enter flight data into computer.

(h) Forward flight data via computer.

(i) Assist facility/sector in meeting situation objectives.

5. ***En Route Nonradar Position:***

(a) Ensure separation.

(b) Initiate control instructions.

(c) Monitor and operate radios.

(d) Accept and initiate transfer of control, communications, and flight data.

(e) Ensure computer entries are completed on instructions or clearances issued or received.

(f) Ensure strip marking is completed on instructions or clearances issued or received.

(g) Facilities utilizing nonradar positions may modify the standards contained in the radar associate, radar coordinator, and radar flight data sections to accommodate facility/sector needs, i.e., nonradar coordinator, nonradar data positions.

2–10–2. TERMINAL RADAR/NONRADAR TEAM POSITION RESPONSIBILITIES

a. *Terminal Radar Team Concept and Intent:* There are no absolute divisions of responsibilities regarding position operations. The tasks to be completed remain the same whether one, two, or three people are working positions within a facility/sector. The team, as a whole, has responsibility for the safe and efficient operation of that facility/sector.

b. *Terms.* The following terms will be used in terminal facilities for the purposes of standardization.

1. *Facility/Sector.* The area of control responsibility (delegated airspace) of the radar team, and the team as a whole.

2. *Radar Position (R).* That position which is in direct communication with the aircraft and which uses radar information as the primary means of separation.

3. *Radar Associate Position (RA).* That position commonly referred to as "Handoff Controller" or "Radar Data Controller."

4. *Radar Coordinator Position (RC).* That position commonly referred to as "Coordinator," "Tracker," "Sequencer," or "Overhead."

5. *Radar Flight Data (FD).* That position commonly referred to as "Flight Data."

6. *Nonradar Position (NR).* That position which is usually in direct communication with the aircraft and which uses nonradar procedures as the primary means of separation.

c. Primary Responsibilities of the Terminal Radar Team Positions:

1. ***Radar Position:***

(a) Ensure separation.

(b) Initiate control instructions.

(c) Monitor and operate radios.

(d) Accept and initiate automated handoffs.

(e) Assist the Radar Associate Position with nonautomated handoff actions when needed.

(f) Assist the Radar Associate Position in coordination when needed.

(g) Scan radar display. Correlate with flight progress strip information.

(h) Ensure computer entries are completed on instructions or clearances you issue or receive.

(i) Ensure strip marking is completed on instructions or clearances you issue or receive.

(j) Adjust equipment at Radar Position to be usable by all members of the team.

2. ***Radar Associate Position:***

(a) Ensure separation.

(b) Initiate control instructions.

(c) Operate interphones.

(d) Maintain awareness of facility/sector activities.

(e) Accept and initiate nonautomated handoffs.

(f) Assist the Radar Position by accepting or initiating automated handoffs which are necessary for the continued smooth operation of the facility/sector and ensure that the Radar Position is made immediately aware of any actions taken.

(g) Coordinate, including point outs.

(h) Scan flight progress strips. Correlate with radar data.

(i) Manage flight progress strips.

(j) Ensure computer entries are completed on instructions issued or received, and enter instructions issued or received by the Radar Position when aware of those instructions.

(k) Ensure strip marking is completed on instructions issued or received, and write instructions issued or received by the Radar Position when aware of them.

(l) Adjust equipment at Radar Associate Position to be usable by all members of the Radar Team.

3. ***Radar Coordinator Position:***

(a) Perform interfacility/sector/position coordination of traffic actions.

(b) Advise the Radar Position and the Radar Associate Position of facility/sector actions required to accomplish overall objectives.

(c) Perform any of the functions of the Radar Team which will assist in meeting situation objectives.

NOTE–
The Radar Position has the responsibility of managing the overall sector operations, including aircraft separation and traffic flows. The Radar Coordinator Position assumes responsibility for managing traffic flows and the Radar Position retains responsibility for aircraft separation when the Radar Coordinator Position is staffed.

4. ***Radar Flight Data:***

(a) Operate interphones.

(b) Process and forward flight plan information.

(c) Compile statistical data.

(d) Assist facility/sector in meeting situation objectives.

5. ***Terminal Nonradar Position:***

(a) Ensure separation.

(b) Initiate control instructions.

(c) Monitor and operate radios.

(d) Accept and initiate transfer of control, communications and flight data.

(e) Ensure computer entries are completed on instructions or clearances issued or received.

(f) Ensure strip marking is completed on instructions or clearances issued or received.

(g) Facilities utilizing nonradar positions may modify the standards contained in the radar associate, radar coordinator, and radar flight data sections to accommodate facility/sector needs, i.e., nonradar coordinator, nonradar data positions.

2–10–3. TOWER TEAM POSITION RESPONSIBILITIES

a. *Tower Team Concept and Intent:* There are no absolute divisions of responsibilities regarding position operations. The tasks to be completed remain the same whether one, two, or three people are working positions within a facility/sector. The team, as a whole, has responsibility for the safe and efficient operation of that facility/sector.

b. *Terms:* The following terms will be used in terminal facilities for the purpose of standardization.

1. *Tower Cab:* The area of control responsibility (delegated airspace and/or airport surface areas) of the tower team, and the team as a whole.

2. *Tower Position(s) (LC or GC):* That position which is in direct communications with the aircraft and ensures separation of aircraft in/on the area of jurisdiction.

3. *Tower Associate Position(s):* That position commonly referred to as "Local Assist," "Ground Assist," "Local Associate," or "Ground Associate."

4. *Tower Cab Coordinator Position (CC):* That position commonly referred to as "Coordinator."

5. *Flight Data (FD):* That position commonly referred to as "Flight Data."

6. *Clearance Delivery (CD):* That position commonly referred to as "Clearance."

c. Primary responsibilities of the Tower Team Positions:

1. ***Tower Position(s) (LC or GC):***

(a) Ensure separation.

(b) Initiate control instructions.

(c) Monitor and operate communications equipment.

(d) Utilize tower radar display(s).

(e) Utilize alphanumerics.

(f) Assist the Tower Associate Position with coordination.

(g) Scan tower cab environment.

(h) Ensure computer entries are completed for instructions or clearances issued or received.

(i) Ensure strip marking is completed for instructions or clearances issued or received.

(j) Process and forward flight plan information.

(k) Perform any functions of the Tower Team which will assist in meeting situation objectives.

2. ***Tower Associate Position(s):***

(a) Ensure separation.

(b) Operate interphones.

(c) Maintain awareness of tower cab activities.

(d) Utilize alphanumerics.

(e) Utilize tower radar display(s).

(f) Assist Tower Position by accepting/initiating coordination for the continued smooth operation of the tower cab and ensure that the Tower Position is made immediately aware of any actions taken.

(g) Manage flight plan information.

(h) Ensure computer entries are completed for instructions issued or received and enter instructions issued or received by a Tower Position.

(i) Ensure strip marking is completed for instructions issued or received and enter instructions issued or received by a Tower Position.

3. ***Tower Coordinator Position:***

(a) Perform interfacility/position coordination for traffic actions.

(b) Advise the tower and the Tower Associate Position(s) of tower cab actions required to accomplish overall objectives.

(c) Perform any of the functions of the Tower Team which will assist in meeting situation objectives.

NOTE–
The Tower Positions have the responsibility for aircraft separation and traffic flows. The Tower Coordinator Position assumes responsibility for managing traffic flows and the Tower Positions retain responsibility for aircraft separation when the Tower Coordinator Position is staffed.

4. ***Flight Data:***

(a) Operate interphones.

(b) Process and forward flight plan information.

(c) Compile statistical data.

(d) Assist tower cab in meeting situation objectives.

(e) Observe and report weather information.

(f) Utilize alphanumerics.

5. ***Clearance Delivery:***

(a) Operate communications equipment.

(b) Process and forward flight plan information.

(c) Issue clearances and ensure accuracy of pilot read back.

(d) Assist tower cab in meeting situation objectives.

(e) Operate tower equipment.

(f) Utilize alphanumerics.

NOTE–
The Tower Positions have the responsibility for aircraft separation and traffic flows. The Tower Coordinator Position assumes responsibility for managing traffic flows and the Tower Positions retain responsibility for aircraft separation when the Tower Coordinator Position is staffed.

Chapter 3. Airport Traffic Control– Terminal

Section 1. General

3–1–1. PROVIDE SERVICE

Provide airport traffic control service based only upon observed or known traffic and airport conditions.

NOTE–
When operating in accordance with CFRs, it is the responsibility of the pilot to avoid collision with other aircraft. However, due to the limited space around terminal locations, traffic information can aid pilots in avoiding collision between aircraft operating within Class B, Class C, or Class D surface areas and the terminal radar service areas, and transiting aircraft operating in proximity to terminal locations.

3–1–2. PREVENTIVE CONTROL

Provide preventive control service only to aircraft operating in accordance with a letter of agreement. When providing this service, issue advice or instructions only if a situation develops which requires corrective action.

NOTE–
1. *Preventive control differs from other airport traffic control in that repetitious, routine approval of pilot action is eliminated. Controllers intervene only when they observe a traffic conflict developing.*

2. *Airfield Operating instructions, Memorandums of Understanding, or other specific directives used exclusively by the Department of Defense (DoD) satisfies the criteria in paragraph 3–1–2 above.*

3–1–3. USE OF ACTIVE RUNWAYS

The local controller has primary responsibility for operations conducted on the active runway and must control the use of those runways. Positive coordination and control is required as follows:

NOTE–
Exceptions may be authorized only as provided in paragraph 1–1–11, Constraints Governing Supplements and Procedural Deviations, and FAA Order JO 7210.3, Facility Operation and Administration, paragraph 10–1–7, Use of Active Runways, where justified by extraordinary circumstances at specific locations.

REFERENCE–
FAA Order JO 7110.65, Para 1–1–11, Constraints Governing Supplements and Procedural Deviations.
FAA Order JO 7210.3, Para 10–1–7, Use of Active Runways.

a. Ground control must obtain approval from local control before authorizing an aircraft or a vehicle to cross or use any portion of an active runway. The coordination must include the point/intersection at the runway where the operation will occur.

PHRASEOLOGY–
CROSS (runway) AT (point/intersection).

b. When the local controller authorizes another controller to cross an active runway, the local controller must verbally specify the runway to be crossed and the point/intersection at the runway where the operation will occur preceded by the word "cross."

PHRASEOLOGY–
CROSS (runway) AT (point/intersection).

c. The ground controller must advise the local controller when the coordinated runway operation is complete. This may be accomplished verbally or through visual aids as specified by a facility directive.

d. *USA/USAF/USN NOT APPLICABLE.* Authorization for aircraft/vehicles to taxi/proceed on or along an active runway, for purposes other than crossing, must be provided via direct communications on the appropriate local control frequency. This authorization may be provided on the ground control frequency after coordination with local control is completed for those operations specifically described in a facility directive.

NOTE–
The USA, USAF, and USN establish local operating procedures in accordance with, respectively, USA, USAF, and USN directives.

e. The local controller must coordinate with the ground controller before using a runway not previously designated as active.

REFERENCE–
FAA Order JO 7110.65, Para 3–1–4, Coordination Between Local and Ground Controllers.

3–1–4. COORDINATION BETWEEN LOCAL AND GROUND CONTROLLERS

Local and ground controllers must exchange information as necessary for the safe and efficient use of airport runways and movement areas. This may be accomplished via verbal means, flight progress strips, other written information, or automation displays. As a minimum, provide aircraft identification and applicable runway/intersection/taxiway information as follows:

a. Ground control must notify local control when a departing aircraft has been taxied to a runway other than one previously designated as active.

REFERENCE–
FAA Order JO 7110.65, Para 3–1–3, Use of Active Runways.
FAA Order JO 7210.3, Para 10–1–6, Selecting Active Runways.

b. Ground control must notify local control of any aircraft taxied to an intersection for takeoff. This notification may be accomplished by verbal means or by flight progress strips.

REFERENCE–
FAA Order JO 7110.65, Para 3–9–7, Wake Turbulence Separation for Intersection Departures.

c. When the runways in use for landing/departing aircraft are not visible from the tower or the aircraft using them are not visible on radar, advise the local/ground controller of the aircraft's location before releasing the aircraft to the other controller.

3–1–5. VEHICLES/EQUIPMENT/PERSONNEL NEAR/ON RUNWAYS

a. When established in a letter of agreement (LOA), vehicles, equipment, and personnel in two–way communications with ATC may be authorized to operate in the runway safety area (RSA) up to the edge of the runway surface, which includes when aircraft are arriving, departing, or taxiing along the runway.

PHRASEOLOGY–
PROCEED AS REQUESTED; (and if necessary, additional instructions or information).

REFERENCE–
FAA Order JO 7210.3, Para 4–3–1, Letters of Agreement.

NOTE–
DoD–only airfields—See Service Manual and/or local operating procedures for guidance on aerodrome operations and LOA requirements.

b. Ensure that the runway to be used is free of all known ground vehicles, equipment, and personnel before a departing aircraft starts takeoff or a landing aircraft crosses the runway threshold.

NOTE–
"PROCEED AS REQUESTED" is not approved phraseology for instructing aircraft, vehicles, equipment, or personnel to cross or operate on a runway.

NOTE–
Establishing hold lines/signs is the responsibility of the airport manager. Standards for surface measurements, markings, and signs are contained in the following Advisory Circulars; AC 150/5300–13, Airport Design; AC 150/5340–1, Standards for Airport Markings, and AC 150/5340–18, Standards for Airport Sign Systems. The operator is responsible to properly position the aircraft, vehicle, or equipment at the appropriate hold line/sign or designated point. The requirements in paragraph 3–1–12, Visually Scanning Runways, remain valid as appropriate.

REFERENCE–
FAA Order JO 7110.65, Para 3–7–4, Runway Proximity.
FAA Order JO 7110.65, Para 3–8–2, Touch-and-Go or Stop-and-Go or Low Approach.
FAA Order JO 7110.65, Para 3–10–10, Altitude Restricted Low Approach.
AC 150/5300–13, Airport Design.
AC 150/5340–1G, Standards for Airport Markings.
14 CFR Section 91.129, Operations in Class D Airspace.
AIM, Para 2–2–3, Obstruction Lights.
P/CG Term – Runway in Use/Active Runway/Duty Runway.

3–1–6. TRAFFIC INFORMATION

a. Describe vehicles, equipment, or personnel on or near the movement area in a manner which will assist pilots in recognizing them.

EXAMPLE–
"Mower left of runway two seven."
"Trucks crossing approach end of runway two five."
"Workman on taxiway Bravo."
"Aircraft left of runway one eight."

b. Describe the relative position of traffic in an easy to understand manner, such as "to your right" or "ahead of you."

EXAMPLE–
1. *"Traffic, U.S. Air MD–Eighty on downwind leg to your left."*
2. *"King Air inbound from outer marker on straight-in approach to runway one seven."*
3. *"Traffic, Boeing 737 on 2–mile final to the parallel runway, runway two six right, cleared to land. Caution wake turbulence."*

c. When using a CTRD, you may issue traffic advisories using the standard radar phraseology prescribed in paragraph 2–1–21, Traffic Advisories.

REFERENCE–
FAA Order JO 7110.65, Para 3–10–10, Altitude Restricted Low Approach.

3–1–7. POSITION DETERMINATION

Determine the position of an aircraft, personnel or equipment before issuing taxi instructions, takeoff clearance, or authorizing personnel, and/or equipment to proceed onto the movement area.

NOTE–
When possible, positions of aircraft, vehicles, equipment and/or personnel may be determined visually or through use of a display system. When ATC is unable to determine position visually or via a display system, position reports may be used.

3–1–8. LOW LEVEL WIND SHEAR/MICROBURST ADVISORIES

a. When low level wind shear/microburst is reported by pilots, Integrated Terminal Weather System (ITWS), or detected on wind shear detection systems such as LLWAS NE++, LLWAS–RS, WSP, or TDWR, controllers must issue the alert to all arriving and departing aircraft. Continue the alert to aircraft until it is broadcast on the ATIS and pilots indicate they have received the appropriate ATIS code. A statement must be included on the ATIS for 20 minutes following the last report or indication of the wind shear/microburst.

PHRASEOLOGY–
LOW LEVEL WIND SHEAR (or MICROBURST, as appropriate) ADVISORIES IN EFFECT.

NOTE–
Some aircraft are equipped with Predictive Wind Shear (PWS) alert systems that warn the flight crew of a potential wind shear up to 3 miles ahead and 25 degrees either side of the aircraft heading at or below 1200' AGL. Pilot reports may include warnings received from PWS systems.

REFERENCE–
FAA Order JO 7110.65, Para 2–6–2, PIREP Solicitation and Dissemination.

FAA Order JO 7110.65, Para 2–9–3, Content.
FAA Order JO 7110.65, Para 3–10–1, Landing Information.

b. At facilities without ATIS, ensure that wind shear/microburst information is broadcast to all arriving and departing aircraft for 20 minutes following the last report or indication of wind shear/microburst.

c. Apply the following procedures and phraseology for the depicted wind shear detection system described below.

1. At locations equipped with LLWAS, the local controller must provide wind information as follows:

NOTE–
The LLWAS is designed to detect low level wind shear conditions around the periphery of an airport. It does not detect wind shear beyond that limitation.

REFERENCE–
FAA Order JO 7210.3, Para 10–3–3, Low Level Wind Shear/Microburst Detection Systems.

(a) If an alert is received, issue the airport wind and the displayed field boundary wind.

PHRASEOLOGY–
WIND SHEAR ALERT. AIRPORT WIND (direction) AT (velocity). (Location of sensor) BOUNDARY WIND (direction) AT (velocity).

(b) If multiple alerts are received, issue an advisory that there are wind shear alerts in two/several/all quadrants. After issuing the advisory, issue the airport wind in accordance with paragraph 3–9–1, Departure Information, followed by the field boundary wind most appropriate to the aircraft operation.

PHRASEOLOGY–
WIND SHEAR ALERTS TWO/SEVERAL/ALL QUADRANTS. AIRPORT WIND (direction) AT (velocity). (Location of sensor) BOUNDARY WIND (direction) AT (velocity).

(c) If requested by the pilot, issue specific field boundary wind information even though the LLWAS may not be in alert status.

NOTE–
The requirements for issuance of wind information remain valid as appropriate under this paragraph, paragraph 3–9–1, Departure Information, and paragraph 3–10–1, Landing Information.

2. Wind shear detection systems, including TDWR, WSP, LLWAS NE++ and LLWAS–RS provide the capability of displaying microburst alerts, wind shear alerts, and wind information oriented to the threshold or departure end of a runway. When detected, the associated ribbon display allows the controller to read the displayed alert without any need for interpretation.

(a) If a wind shear or microburst alert is received for the runway in use, issue the alert information for that runway to arriving and departing aircraft as it is displayed on the ribbon display.

PHRASEOLOGY–
(Runway) (arrival/departure) WIND SHEAR/MICROBURST ALERT, (windspeed) KNOT GAIN/LOSS, (location).

EXAMPLE–
17A MBA 40K – 3MF

PHRASEOLOGY–
RUNWAY 17 ARRIVAL MICROBURST ALERT 40 KNOT LOSS 3 MILE FINAL.

EXAMPLE–
17D WSA 25K+ 2MD

PHRASEOLOGY–
RUNWAY 17 DEPARTURE WIND SHEAR ALERT 25 KNOT GAIN 2 MILE DEPARTURE.

(b) If requested by the pilot or deemed appropriate by the controller, issue the displayed wind information oriented to the threshold or departure end of the runway.

PHRASEOLOGY–
(Runway) DEPARTURE/THRESHOLD WIND (direction) AT (velocity).

(c) LLWAS NE++ or LLWAS–RS may detect a possible wind shear/microburst at the edge of the system but may be unable to distinguish between a wind shear and a microburst. A wind shear alert message will be displayed, followed by an asterisk, advising of a possible wind shear outside of the system network.

NOTE–
LLWAS NE++ when associated with TDWR can detect wind shear/microbursts outside the network if the TDWR fails.

PHRASEOLOGY–
(Appropriate wind or alert information) POSSIBLE WIND SHEAR OUTSIDE THE NETWORK.

(d) If unstable conditions produce multiple alerts, issue an advisory of multiple wind shear/microburst alerts followed by specific alert or wind information most appropriate to the aircraft operation.

PHRASEOLOGY–
MULTIPLE WIND SHEAR/MICROBURST ALERTS (specific alert or wind information).

(e) The LLWAS NE++ and LLWAS–RS are designed to operate with as many as 50 percent of the total sensors inoperative. When all three remote sensors designated for a specific runway arrival or departure wind display line are inoperative then the LLWAS NE++ and LLWAS–RS for that runway arrival/departure must be considered out of service. When a specific runway arrival or departure wind display line is inoperative and wind shear/microburst activity is likely; (for example, frontal activity, convective storms, PIREPs), the following statement must be included on the ATIS, "WIND SHEAR AND MICROBURST INFORMATION FOR RUNWAY (runway number) ARRIVAL/DEPARTURE NOT AVAILABLE."

NOTE–
The geographic situation display (GSD) is a supervisory planning tool and is not intended to be a primary tool for microburst or wind shear.

d. Wind Shear Escape Procedures.

1. If an aircraft under your control informs you that it is performing a wind shear escape, do not issue control instructions that are contrary to pilot actions. ATC should continue to provide safety alerts regarding terrain or obstacles and traffic advisories for the escape aircraft, as appropriate.

EXAMPLE–
"Denver Tower, United 1154, wind shear escape."

NOTE–
Aircraft that execute a wind shear escape maneuver will usually conduct a full power climb straight ahead and will not accept any control instructions until onboard systems advise the crew or the pilot in command (PIC) advises ATC that the escape maneuver is no longer required.

REFERENCE–
P/CG Term – Wind Shear Escape.

2. Unless advised by additional aircraft that they are also performing an escape procedure, do not presume that other aircraft in the proximity of the escape aircraft are responding to wind shear alerts/events as well. Continue to provide control instructions, safety alerts, and traffic advisories, as appropriate.

3. Once the responding aircraft has initiated a wind shear escape maneuver, the controller is not responsible for providing approved separation between the aircraft that is responding to an escape and any other aircraft, airspace, terrain, or obstacle. Responsibility for approved separation resumes when one of the following conditions is met:

(a) Departures:

(1) A crew member informs ATC that the wind shear escape maneuver is complete and ATC observes that approved separation has been re-established, or

(2) A crew member informs ATC that the escape maneuver is complete and has resumed a previously assigned departure clearance/routing.

(b) Arrivals:

(1) A crew member informs ATC that the escape maneuver is complete, and

(2) The aircrew has executed an alternate clearance or requested further instructions.

NOTE–
When the escape procedure is complete, the flight crew must advise ATC they are returning to their previously assigned clearance or request further instructions.

EXAMPLE–
"Denver Tower, United 1154, wind shear escape complete, resuming last assigned heading/(name) DP/clearance."

Or

"Denver Tower, United 1154, wind shear escape complete, request further instructions."

3–1–9. USE OF TOWER RADAR DISPLAYS

a. Uncertified tower display workstations must be used only as an aid to assist controllers in visually locating aircraft or in determining their spatial relationship to known geographical points. Radar services and traffic advisories are not to be provided using uncertified tower display workstations. General information may be given in an easy to understand manner, such as "to your right" or "ahead of you."

EXAMPLE–
"Follow the aircraft ahead of you passing the river at the stacks." "King Air passing left to right."

REFERENCE–
FAA Order JO 7210.3, Para 10–5–3, Functional Use of Certified Tower Radar Displays.

b. Local controllers may use certified tower radar displays for the following purposes:

1. To determine an aircraft's identification, exact location, or spatial relationship to other aircraft.

NOTE–
This authorization does not alter visual separation procedures. When employing visual separation, the provisions of paragraph 7–2–1, Visual Separation, apply unless otherwise authorized by the Service Area Director of Air Traffic Operations.

REFERENCE–
FAA Order JO 7110.65, Para 5–3–2, Primary Radar Identification Methods.
FAA Order JO 7110.65, Para 5–3–3, Beacon/ADS–B Identification Methods.
FAA Order JO 7110.65, Para 5–3–4, Terminal Automation Systems Identification Methods.

2. To provide aircraft with radar traffic advisories.

3. To provide a direction or suggested headings to VFR aircraft as a method for radar identification or as an advisory aid to navigation.

PHRASEOLOGY–
(Identification), PROCEED (direction)–BOUND, (other instructions or information as necessary),

or

(identification), SUGGESTED HEADING (degrees), (other instructions as necessary).

NOTE–
It is important that the pilot be aware of the fact that the directions or headings being provided are suggestions or are advisory in nature. This is to keep the pilot from being inadvertently misled into assuming that radar vectors (and other associated radar services) are being provided when, in fact, they are not.

4. To provide information and instructions to aircraft operating within the surface area for which the tower has responsibility.

EXAMPLE–
"TURN BASE LEG NOW."

NOTE–
Unless otherwise authorized, tower radar displays are intended to be an aid to local controllers in meeting their responsibilities to the aircraft operating on the runways or within the surface area. They are not intended to provide radar benefits to pilots except for those accrued through a more efficient and effective local control position. In addition, local controllers at nonapproach control towers must devote the majority of their time to visually scanning the runways and local area; an assurance of continued positive radar identification could place distracting and operationally inefficient requirements upon the local controller. Therefore, since the requirements of paragraph 5–3–1, Application, cannot be assured, the radar functions prescribed above are not considered to be radar services and pilots should not be advised of being in "radar contact."

c. Additional functions may be performed provided the procedures have been reviewed and authorized by appropriate management levels.

REFERENCE–
FAA Order JO 7110.65, Para 5–5–4, Minima.

3–1–10. OBSERVED ABNORMALITIES

When requested by a pilot or when you deem it necessary, inform an aircraft of any observed abnormal aircraft condition.

PHRASEOLOGY–
(Item) APPEAR/S (observed condition).

EXAMPLE–
"Landing gear appears up."
"Landing gear appears down and in place."
"Rear baggage door appears open."

3–1–11. SURFACE AREA RESTRICTIONS

a. If traffic conditions permit, approve a pilot's request to cross Class C or Class D surface areas or exceed the Class C or Class D airspace speed limit. Do not, however, approve a speed in excess of 250 knots (288 mph) unless the pilot informs you a higher minimum speed is required.

NOTE–
14 CFR Section 91.117 permits speeds in excess of 250 knots (288 mph) when so required or recommended in the airplane flight manual or required by normal military operating procedures.

REFERENCE–
FAA Order JO 7110.65, Para 2–1–16, Surface Areas.

b. Do not approve a pilot's request or ask a pilot to conduct unusual maneuvers within surface areas of Class B, C, or D airspace if they are not essential to the performance of the flight.

EXCEPTION. A pilot's request to conduct aerobatic practice activities may be approved, when operating in accordance with a letter of agreement, and the activity will have no adverse effect on safety of the air traffic operation or result in a reduction of service to other users.

REFERENCE–
FAA Order JO 7210.3, Para 5–4–8, Aerobatic Practice Areas.

NOTE–
These unusual maneuvers include unnecessary low passes, unscheduled flybys, practice instrument approaches to altitudes below specified minima (unless a landing or touch-and-go is to be made), or any so-called "buzz jobs" wherein a flight is conducted at a low altitude and/or a high rate of speed for thrill purposes. Such maneuvers increase hazards to persons and property and contribute to noise complaints.

3–1–12. VISUALLY SCANNING RUNWAYS

a. Local controllers must visually scan runways to the maximum extent possible.

b. Ground control must assist local control in visually scanning runways, especially when runways are in close proximity to other movement areas.

3-1-13. ESTABLISHING TWO-WAY COMMUNICATIONS

Pilots are required to establish two-way radio communications before entering the Class D airspace. If the controller responds to a radio call with, "(a/c call sign) standby," radio communications have been established and the pilot can enter the Class D airspace. If workload or traffic conditions prevent immediate provision of airport traffic control services, inform the pilot to remain outside the Class D airspace until conditions permit the services to be provided.

PHRASEOLOGY-
(A/c call sign) REMAIN OUTSIDE DELTA AIRSPACE AND STANDBY.

REFERENCE-
FAA Order JO 7110.65, Para 7-2-1, Visual Separation.

3-1-14. GROUND OPERATIONS WHEN VOLCANIC ASH IS PRESENT

When volcanic ash is present on the airport surface, and to the extent possible:

a. Avoid requiring aircraft to come to a full stop while taxiing.

b. Provide for a rolling takeoff for all departures.

NOTE-
When aircraft begin a taxi or takeoff roll on ash contaminated surfaces, large amounts of volcanic ash will again become airborne. This newly airborne ash will significantly reduce visibility and will be ingested by the engines of following aircraft.

REFERENCE-
AIM, Para 7-5-9, Flight Operations in Volcanic Ash.

3-1-15. GROUND OPERATIONS RELATED TO THREE/FOUR-HOUR TARMAC RULE

When a request is made by the pilot-in-command of an aircraft to return to the ramp, gate, or alternate deplaning area due to the Three/Four-Hour Tarmac Rule:

a. Provide the requested services as soon as operationally practical, or

b. Advise the pilot-in-command that the requested service cannot be accommodated because it would create a significant disruption to air traffic operations.

NOTE-
Facility procedures, including actions that constitute a significant disruption, vary by airport and must be identified in the facility directive pertaining to the Three/Four-Hour Tarmac Rule.

PHRASEOLOGY-
(Identification) TAXI TO (ramp, gate, or alternate deplaning area) VIA (route).

or

(Identification) EXPECT A (number) MINUTE DELAY DUE TO (ground and/or landing and/or departing) TRAFFIC,

or

(Identification) UNABLE DUE TO OPERATIONAL DISRUPTION.

REFERENCE-
DOT Rule, Enhancing Airline Passenger Protections, 14 CFR, Part 259, commonly referred to as the Three/Four-Hour Tarmac Rule.

Section 2. Visual Signals

3-2-1. LIGHT SIGNALS

Use ATC light signals from TBL 3-2-1 to control aircraft and the movement of vehicles, equipment, and personnel on the movement area when radio communications cannot be employed.

REFERENCE-
FAA Order JO 7110.65, Para 3-10-10, Altitude Restricted Low Approach.
FAA Order JO 7210.3, Para 4-3-1, Letters of Agreement.

3-2-2. WARNING SIGNAL

Direct a general warning signal, alternating red and green, to aircraft or vehicle operators, as appropriate, when:

NOTE-
The warning signal is not a prohibitive signal and can be followed by any other light signal, as circumstances permit.

a. Aircraft are converging and a collision hazard exists.

b. Mechanical trouble exists of which the pilot might not be aware.

c. Other hazardous conditions are present which call for intensified pilot or operator alertness. These conditions may include obstructions, soft field, ice on the runway, etc.

3-2-3. RECEIVER-ONLY ACKNOWLEDGMENT

To obtain acknowledgment from an aircraft equipped with receiver only, request the aircraft to do the following:

a. *Fixed-wing aircraft:*

1. Between sunrise and sunset:

(a) Move ailerons or rudders while on the ground.

(b) Rock wings while in flight.

2. Between sunset and sunrise: Flash navigation or landing lights.

b. *Helicopters:*

1. Between sunrise and sunset:

(a) While hovering, either turn the helicopter toward the controlling facility and flash the landing light or rock the tip path plane.

(b) While in flight, either flash the landing light or rock the tip path plane.

2. Between sunset and sunrise: Flash landing light or search light.

TBL 3-2-1
ATC Light Signals

	Meaning		
Color and type of signal	**Aircraft on the ground**	**Aircraft in flight**	**Movement of vehicles, equipment and personnel**
Steady green	Cleared for takeoff	Cleared to land	Cleared to cross; proceed; go
Flashing green	Cleared to taxi	Return for landing (to be followed by steady green at the proper time)	Not applicable
Steady red	Stop	Give way to other aircraft and continue circling	Stop
Flashing red	Taxi clear of landing area or runway in use	Airport unsafe– Do not land	Clear the taxiway/runway
Flashing white	Return to starting point on airport	Not applicable	Return to starting point on airport
Alternating red and green	General Warning Signal– Exercise Extreme Caution	General Warning Signal– Exercise Extreme Caution	General Warning Signal– Exercise Extreme Caution

Section 3. Airport Conditions

3–3–1. LANDING AREA CONDITION

If you observe or are informed of any condition which affects the safe use of a landing area:

NOTE–
1. *The airport management/military operations office is responsible for observing and reporting the condition of the landing area.*

2. *It is the responsibility of the agency operating the airport to provide the tower with current information regarding airport conditions.*

3. *A disabled aircraft on a runway, after occupants are clear, is normally handled by flight standards and airport management/military operations office personnel in the same manner as any obstruction; e.g., construction equipment.*

a. Relay the information to the airport manager/military operations office concerned.

b. Copy verbatim any information received and record the name of the person submitting it.

c. Confirm information obtained from other than authorized airport or FAA personnel unless this function is the responsibility of the military operations office.

NOTE–
Civil airport managers are required to provide a list of airport employees who are authorized to issue information concerning conditions affecting the safe use of the airport.

d. If you are unable to contact the airport management or operator, issue a NOTAM publicizing an unsafe condition and inform the management or operator as soon as practicable.

EXAMPLE–
"DISABLED AIRCRAFT ON RUNWAY."

NOTE–
1. *Legally, only the airport management/military operations office can close a runway.*

2. *Military controllers are not authorized to issue NOTAMs. It is the responsibility of the military operations office.*

e. Runway Condition Codes (RwyCC).

1. Furnish RwyCC, as received from the Airport Operator, to aircraft via the ATIS.

(a) Use the runway number, followed by the RwyCC, for each of the three runway segments, and include the time of the report.

EXAMPLE–
"Runway Two–Seven, condition codes two, two, three at one zero one eight zulu."

(b) When an update to the RwyCC is provided, verbally issue to all aircraft until the ATIS broadcast can be updated.

EXAMPLE–
"Runway (number) condition codes two, three, one."

REFERENCE–
Advisory Circular AC 150/5200–30D, Airport Winter Safety and Operations

2. Issue FICON NOTAMs upon pilot request, workload permitting.

f. In the absence of RwyCC, issue to aircraft only factual information, as reported by the airport operator or pilots concerning the condition of the runway surface, describing the accumulation of precipitation.

EXAMPLE–
"All runways covered by compacted snow 6 inches deep."

REFERENCE–
FAA Order JO 7110.65, Para 4–7–12, Airport Conditions.

3-3-2. CLOSED/UNSAFE RUNWAY INFORMATION

If an aircraft requests to takeoff, land, or touch-and-go on a closed or unsafe runway, inform the pilot the runway is closed or unsafe, and

a. If the pilot persists in his/her request, quote him/her the appropriate parts of the NOTAM applying to the runway and inform him/her that a clearance cannot be issued.

b. Then, if the pilot insists and in your opinion the intended operation would not adversely affect other traffic, inform him/her that the operation will be at his/her own risk.

PHRASEOLOGY-
RUNWAY (runway number) CLOSED/UNSAFE.

If appropriate, (quote NOTAM information),

UNABLE TO ISSUE DEPARTURE/LANDING/TOUCH-AND-GO CLEARANCE.
DEPARTURE/LANDING/TOUCH-AND-GO WILL BE AT YOUR OWN RISK.

c. Except as permitted by paragraph 4-8-7, Side-Step Maneuver, where parallel runways are served by separate ILS systems and one of the runways is closed, the ILS associated with the closed runway should not be used for approaches unless not using the ILS would have an adverse impact on the operational efficiency of the airport.

REFERENCE-
FAA Order JO 7110.65, Para 3-10-5, Landing Clearance.
FAA Order JO 7110.65, Para 4-7-12, Airport Conditions.

3-3-3. TIMELY INFORMATION

Issue airport condition information necessary for an aircraft's safe operation in time for it to be useful to the pilot. Include the following, as appropriate:

a. Construction work on or immediately adjacent to the movement area.

b. Rough portions of the movement area.

c. Braking conditions caused by ice, snow, slush, or water.

d. Snowdrifts or piles of snow on or along the edges of the area and the extent of any plowed area.

e. Parked aircraft on the movement area.

f. Irregular operation of part or all of the airport lighting system.

g. Volcanic ash on any airport surface area and whether the ash is wet or dry (if known).

NOTE-
Braking action on wet ash may be degraded. Dry ash on the runway may necessitate minimum use of reverse thrust.

h. Other pertinent airport conditions.

REFERENCE-
FAA Order JO 7110.65, Para 4-7-12, Airport Conditions.
FAA Order JO 7110.65, Para 2-1-9, Reporting Essential Flight Information.
FAA Order JO 7110.65, Para 3-10-10, Altitude Restricted Low Approach.

3-3-4. BRAKING ACTION

Furnish quality of braking action, as received from pilots, to all aircraft as follows:

a. Describe the quality of braking action using the terms "good," "good to medium," "medium," "medium to poor," "poor," or "nil." If the pilot reports braking action in other than the approved terms, ask him/her to categorize braking action in these terms.

NOTE–
The term "nil" is used to indicate bad or no braking action.

b. Include type of aircraft from which the report is received.

EXAMPLE–
"Braking action medium, reported by a heavy Boeing Seven Sixty–Seven."
"Braking action poor, reported by a Boeing Seven Thirty–Seven."

c. If the braking action report affects only a portion of a runway, obtain enough information from the pilot to describe the braking action in terms easily understood by other pilots.

EXAMPLE–
"Braking action poor first half of runway, reported by a Boeing Seven Fifty–Seven."
"Braking action good to medium beyond the intersection of Runway Two Seven, reported by an Airbus Three Twenty–One."

NOTE–
Descriptive terms, such as the first or the last half of the runway, should normally be used rather than landmark descriptions, such as opposite the fire station, south of a taxiway, etc. Landmarks extraneous to the landing runway are difficult to distinguish during low visibility, at night, or anytime a pilot is busy landing an aircraft.

d. Issue the runway surface condition and/or the Runway Condition Reading (RCR), if provided, to all USAF and ANG aircraft. Issue the RCR to other aircraft upon pilot request.

EXAMPLE–
"Ice on runway, RCR zero five, patchy."

NOTE–
USAF offices furnish RCR information at airports serving USAF and ANG aircraft.

REFERENCE–
FAA Order JO 7110.65, Para 4–7–12, Airport Conditions.
FAA Order JO 7110.65, Para 3–3–5, Braking Action Advisories.

3–3–5. BRAKING ACTION ADVISORIES

a. When runway braking action reports are received from pilots which include the terms "medium," "poor," or "nil," or whenever weather conditions are conducive to deteriorating or rapidly changing runway conditions, include on the ATIS broadcast the statement "Braking Action Advisories are in effect."

REFERENCE–
FAA Order JO 7210.3, Para 10–4–1, Automatic Terminal Information Service (ATIS).

b. During the time Braking Action Advisories are in effect, take the following action:

1. Issue the latest braking action report for the runway in use to each arriving and departing aircraft early enough to be of benefit to the pilot. When possible, include reports from super or heavy aircraft when the arriving or departing aircraft is a super or_heavy.

2. If no report has been received for the runway of intended use, issue an advisory to that effect.

PHRASEOLOGY–
NO BRAKING ACTION REPORTS RECEIVED FOR RUNWAY (runway number).

3. Advise the Airport Operator that runway braking action reports of "good to medium," "medium," "medium to poor," "poor," or "nil" have been received.

REFERENCE–
FAA Order JO 7210.3, Para 4–3–1, Letters of Agreement.

4. Solicit PIREPs of runway braking action.

REFERENCE–
FAA Order JO 7110.65, Para, 2–9–3, Content.
FAA Order JO 7110.65, Para 3–9–1, Departure Information.
FAA Order JO 7110.65, Para 3–10–1, Landing Information.
FAA Order JO 7110.65, Para 4–7–12, Airport Conditions.
FAA Order JO 7110.65, Para 2–6–2, PIREP Solicitation and Dissemination.

3-3-6. ARRESTING SYSTEM OPERATION

a. For normal operations, arresting systems remotely controlled by ATC must remain in the retracted or down position.

NOTE–
1. *USN– Runway Arresting Gear– barriers are not operated by ATC personnel. Readiness/rigging of the equipment is the responsibility of the operations department.*

2. *A request to raise a barrier or hook cable means the barrier or cable on the departure end of the runway. If an approach end engagement is required, the pilot or military authority will specifically request that the approach end cable be raised.*

REFERENCE–
FAA Order JO 7610.14, Chapter 7, Section 1, Aircraft Arresting System, Single Frequency Approach (SFA), Simulated Flameout (SFO)/Emergency Landing Pattern (ELP) Operations, Celestial Navigation (CELNAV) Training.

b. Raise aircraft arresting systems whenever:

1. Requested by a pilot.

NOTE–
The standard emergency phraseology for a pilot requesting an arresting system to be raised for immediate engagement is:

"BARRIER – BARRIER – BARRIER"

or

"CABLE – CABLE – CABLE."

2. Requested by military authority; e.g., airfield manager, supervisor of flying, mobile control officer, etc.

NOTE–
USAF. Web barriers at the departure end of the runway may remain in the up position when requested by the senior operational commander. The IFR Enroute Supplement and AP-1 will describe specific barrier configuration. ATC will advise transient aircraft of the barrier configuration using the phraseology in subparagraph c, below.

3. A military jet aircraft is landing with known or suspected radio failure or conditions (drag chute/hydraulic/electrical failure, etc.) that indicate an arresting system may be needed. Exceptions are authorized for military aircraft which cannot engage an arresting system (C–9, C–141, C–5, T–39, etc.) and should be identified in a letter of agreement and/or appropriate military directive.

c. When requested by military authority due to freezing weather conditions or malfunction of the activating mechanism, the barrier/cable may remain in a raised position provided aircraft are advised.

PHRASEOLOGY–
YOUR DEPARTURE/LANDING WILL BE TOWARD/OVER A RAISED BARRIER/CABLE ON RUNWAY (number), (location, distance, as appropriate).

d. Inform civil and U.S. Army aircraft whenever rubber supported cables are in place at the approach end of the landing runway, and include the distance of the cables from the threshold. This information may be omitted if it is published in the Domestic Notices webpage, International Notices webpage, or the DoD FLIP.

EXAMPLE–
"Runway One Four arresting cable one thousand feet from threshold."

e. When arresting system operation has been requested, inform the pilot of the indicated barrier/cable position.

PHRASEOLOGY–
(Identification), BARRIER/CABLE INDICATES UP/DOWN. CLEARED FOR TAKEOFF/TO LAND.

f. Time permitting, advise pilots of the availability of all arresting systems on the runway in question when a pilot requests barrier information.

g. If an aircraft engages a raised barrier/cable, initiate crash alarm procedures immediately.

h. For preplanned practice engagements not associated with emergencies, crash alarm systems need not be activated if, in accordance with local military operating procedures, all required notifications are made before the practice engagement.

REFERENCE–
FAA Order JO 7110.65, Para 4–7–12, Airport Conditions.

3–3–7. FAR FIELD MONITOR (FFM) REMOTE STATUS UNIT

a. To meet the demand for more facilities capable of operating under CAT III weather, Type II equipment is being upgraded to Integrity Level 3. This integrity level will support operations which place a high degree of reliance on ILS guidance for positioning through touchdown.

b. Installation of the FFM remote status indicating units is necessary to attain the integrity necessary to meet internationally agreed upon reliability values in support of CAT III operations on Type II ILS equipment. The remote status indicating unit used in conjunction with Type II equipment adds a third integrity test; thereby, producing an approach aid which has integrity capable of providing Level 3 service.

c. The remote status sensing unit, when installed in the tower cab, will give immediate indications of localizer out-of-tolerance conditions. The alarm in the FFM remote status sensing unit indicates an inoperative or an out-of-tolerance localizer signal; e.g., the course may have shifted due to equipment malfunction or vehicle/aircraft encroachment into the critical area.

d. Operation of the FFM remote sensing unit will be based on the prevailing weather. The FFM remote sensing unit must be operational when the weather is below CAT II ILS minimums.

REFERENCE–
FAA Order 6750.24, Appendix A, Abnormal Checklist

e. When the remote status unit indicates that the localizer FFM is in alarm (aural warning following the preset delay) and:

1. The aircraft is outside the middle marker (MM) or in the absence of a MM, ½ mile final, check for encroachment of those portions of the critical area that can be seen from the tower. It is understood that the entire critical area may not be visible due to low ceilings and poor visibility. The check is strictly to determine possible causal factors for the out-of-tolerance situation. If the alarm has not cleared prior to the aircraft's arriving at the MM or in the absence of a MM, ½ mile final, immediately issue an advisory that the FFM remote status sensing unit indicates the localizer is unreliable.

2. The aircraft is between the MM or ½ mile final and the inner marker (IM), or if the IM is not installed, the CAT II Missed Approach Point (MAP), immediately issue an advisory that the FFM remote status sensing unit indicates the localizer is unreliable.

PHRASEOLOGY–
CAUTION, MONITOR INDICATES RUNWAY (number) LOCALIZER UNRELIABLE.

3. The aircraft has passed the IM or the CAT II MAP (if the IM is not installed) there is no action requirement. Although the FFM has been modified with filters which dampen the effect of false alarms, you may expect alarms when aircraft are located between the FFM and the localizer antenna either on landing or on takeoff.

REFERENCE–
FAA Order JO 7110.65, Para 4–7–12, Airport Conditions.

Section 4. Airport Lighting

3-4-1. EMERGENCY LIGHTING

Whenever you become aware that an emergency has or will occur, take action to provide for the operation of all appropriate airport lighting aids as required.

REFERENCE–
FAA Order JO 7110.65, Para 10–4–2, Lighting Requirements.

3-4-2. RUNWAY END IDENTIFIER LIGHTS (REIL)

When separate on–off controls are provided, operate runway end identifier lights:

a. When the associated runway lights are lighted. Turn the REIL off after:

1. An arriving aircraft has landed.

2. A departing aircraft has left the traffic pattern area.

3. It is determined that the lights are of no further use to the pilot.

b. As required by facility directives to meet local conditions.

c. As requested by the pilot.

d. Operate intensity setting in accordance with the values in TBL 3–4–1 except as prescribed in subparagraphs b and c above.

TBL 3–4–1
REIL Intensity Setting–Three Step System

Settings	Visibility	
	Day	Night
3	Less than 2 miles	Less than 1 mile
2	2 to 5 miles inclusive	1 to but not including 3 miles
1	When requested	3 miles or more

3-4-3. VISUAL APPROACH SLOPE INDICATORS (VASI)

VASI systems with remote on–off switching must be operated when they serve the runway in use and where intensities are controlled in accordance with TBL 3–4–2 and TBL 3–4–3 except:

a. As required by facility directives to meet local conditions.

b. As required by the pilot.

TBL 3–4–2
VASI Intensity Setting–Two Step System

Step	Period/Condition
High	Day–Sunrise to sunset.
Low	Night–Sunset to sunrise.

TBL 3-4-3
VASI Intensity Setting-Three Step System

Step	Period/Condition
High	Day-Sunrise to sunset.
Medium	Twilight-From sunset to 30 minutes after sunset and from 30 minutes before sunrise to sunrise,* and during twilight in Alaska.
Low	Night-Sunset to sunrise.
*During a 1 year period, twilight may vary 26 to 43 minutes between 25 and 49N latitude.	

NOTE-
The basic FAA standard for VASI systems permits independent operation by means of photoelectric device. This system has no on-off control feature and is intended for continuous operation. Other VASI systems in use include those that are operated remotely from the control tower. These systems may consist of either a photoelectric intensity control with only an on-off switch, a two step intensity system, or a three step intensity system.

REFERENCE-
FAA Order JO 7210.3, Para 10-6-5, Visual Approach Slope Indicator (VASI) Systems.
FAA Order 6850.2, Visual Guidance Lighting Systems.

3-4-4. PRECISION APPROACH PATH INDICATORS (PAPI)

PAPI systems with remote on-off switching shall be operated when they serve the runway in use and where intensities are controlled in accordance with TBL 3-4-4 except:

a. As required by local facility directives to meet local conditions.

b. As requested by the pilot.

NOTE-
The basic FAA standard for PAPI systems permits independent operation by means of photoelectric device. This system has no on-off control feature and is intended for continuous operation. Other PAPI systems in use include those that are operated remotely from the control tower. These systems may consist of either a photoelectric intensity control with only an on-off switch, or a five-step intensity system.

REFERENCE-
FAA Order 6850.2, Visual Guidance Lighting Systems.

TBL 3-4-4
PAPI Intensity Setting - Five Step System

Step	Period/Condition
5	On Pilot Request
4	Day - Sunrise to sunset
3	Night - Sunset to sunrise
2	On Pilot Request
1	On Pilot Request
*During a 1 year period, twilight may vary 26 to 43 minutes between 25 and 49N latitude.	

3-4-5. APPROACH LIGHTS

Operate approach lights:

a. Between sunset and sunrise when one of the following conditions exists:

1. They serve the landing runway.

2. They serve a runway to which an approach is being made but aircraft will land on another runway.

b. Between sunrise and sunset when the ceiling is less than 1,000 feet or the prevailing visibility is 5 miles or less and approaches are being made to:

1. A landing runway served by the lights.

2. A runway served by the lights but aircraft are landing on another runway.

3. The airport, but landing will be made on a runway served by the lights.

c. As requested by the pilot.

d. As you deem necessary, if not contrary to pilot's request.

NOTE−
In the interest of energy conservation, the ALS should be turned off when not needed for aircraft operations.

REFERENCE−
FAA Order JO 7110.65, Para 3−4−6, ALS Intensity Settings.

3−4−6. ALS INTENSITY SETTINGS

When operating ALS as prescribed in paragraph 3−4−5, Approach Lights, operate intensity controls in accordance with the values in TBL 3−4−5 except:

a. When facility directives specify other settings to meet local atmospheric, topographic, and twilight conditions.

b. As requested by the pilot.

c. As you deem necessary, if not contrary to pilot's request.

TBL 3−4−5

ALS Intensity Setting

Step	Visibility (Applicable to runway served by lights)	
	Day	**Night**
5	Less than 1 mile*	When requested
4	1 to but not including 3 miles	When requested
3	3 to but not including 5 miles	Less than 1 mile*
2	5 to but not including 7 miles	1 to 3 miles inclusive
1	When requested	Greater than 3 miles
*and/or 6,000 feet or less of the RVR on the runway served by the ALS and RVR.		

NOTE−
Daylight steps 2 and 3 provide recommended settings applicable to conditions in subparagraphs b and c. At night, use step 4 or 5 only when requested by a pilot.

3−4−7. SEQUENCED FLASHING LIGHTS (SFL)

Operate Sequenced Flashing Lights:

NOTE−
SFL are a component of the ALS and cannot be operated when the ALS is off.

a. When the visibility is less than 3 miles and instrument approaches are being made to the runway served by the associated ALS.

b. As requested by the pilot.

c. As you deem necessary, if not contrary to pilot's request.

3–4–8. MALSR/ODALS

Operate MALSR/ODALS that have separate on–off and intensity setting controls in accordance with TBL 3–4–6 and TBL 3–4–7 except:

a. When facility directives specify other settings to meet local atmospheric, topographic, and twilight conditions.

b. As requested by the pilot.

c. As you deem necessary, if not contrary to pilot's request.

TBL 3–4–6

Two Step MALS/One Step RAIL/Two Step ODALS

Settings		Visibility	
		Day	Night
MALS/ODALS RAIL	Hi On	Less than 3 miles	Less than 3 miles
MALS/ODALS RAIL	Low Off	When requested	3 miles or more
*At locations providing part–time control tower service, if duplicate controls are not provided in the associated FSS, the MALSR/ODALS must be set to low intensity during the hours of darkness when the tower is not staffed.			

TBL 3–4–7

Three Step MALS/Three Step RAIL/Three Step ODALS

Settings	Visibility	
	Day	Night
3	Less than 2 miles	Less than 1 mile
2	2 to 5 miles inclusive	1 to but not including 3 miles*
1	When requested	3 miles or more
*At locations providing part–time control tower service, if duplicate controls are not provided in the FSS on the airport, the air–to–ground radio link shall be activated during the hours of darkness when the tower is unmanned. If there is no radio air–to–ground control, the MALSR/ODALS shall be set on intensity setting 2 during the hours of darkness when the tower is not staffed.		

REFERENCE–
FAA Order JO 7210.3, Para 10–6–2, Operation of Lights When Tower is Closed.

3–4–9. ALSF–2/SSALR

a. When the prevailing visibility is $^3/_4$ mile or less or the RVR is 4,000 feet or less, operate the ALSF–2 system as follows:

1. As requested by the pilot.

2. As you deem necessary if not contrary to pilot request.

b. Operate the SSALR system when the conditions in subparagraph a are not a factor.

3–4–10. RUNWAY EDGE LIGHTS

Operate the runway edge light system/s serving the runway/s in use as follows:

a. Between sunset and sunrise, turn the lights on:

1. For departures. Before an aircraft taxies onto the runway and until it leaves the Class B, Class C, or Class D surface area.

2. For arrivals:

(a) IFR aircraft−Before the aircraft begins final approach, or

(b) VFR aircraft−Before the aircraft enters the Class B, Class C, or Class D surface area, and

(c) Until the aircraft has taxied off the landing runway.

b. Between sunrise and sunset, turn the lights on as shown in subparagraphs a1 and a2 when the surface visibility is less than 2 miles.

c. As required by facility directives to meet local conditions.

d. Different from subparagraphs a, b, or c above, when:

1. You consider it necessary, or

2. Requested by a pilot and no other known aircraft will be adversely affected.

NOTE−
Pilots may request lights to be turned on or off contrary to subparagraphs a, b, or c. However, 14 CFR Part 135 operators are required to land/takeoff on lighted runways/heliport landing areas at night.

e. Do not turn on the runway edge lights when a NOTAM closing the runway is in effect.

NOTE−
Application concerns use for takeoffs/landings/approaches and does not preclude turning lights on for use of unaffected portions of a runway for taxiing aircraft, surface vehicles, maintenance, repair, etc.

REFERENCE−
FAA Order JO 7210.3, Para 10−6−3, Incompatible Light System Operation.
FAA Order JO 7210.3, Para 10−6−9, Runway Edge Lights Associated With Medium Approach Light System/Runway Alignment Indicator Lights.

3−4−11. HIGH INTENSITY RUNWAY, RUNWAY CENTERLINE, AND TOUCHDOWN ZONE LIGHTS

Operate high intensity runway and associated runway centerline and touchdown zone lights in accordance with TBL 3−4−8, except:

a. Where a facility directive specifies other settings to meet local conditions.

b. As requested by the pilot.

c. As you deem necessary, if not contrary to pilot request.

TBL 3−4−8
HIRL, RCLS, TDZL Intensity Setting

Step	Visibility	
	Day	**Night**
5	Less than 1 mile*	When requested
4	1 to but not including 2 miles*	Less than 1 mile*
3	2 to but not including 3 miles	1 to but not including 3 miles*
2	When requested	3 to 5 miles inclusive
1	When requested	More than 5 miles
*and/or appropriate RVR equivalent.		

3–4–12. HIRL ASSOCIATED WITH MALSR

Operate HIRL which control the associated MALSR in accordance with TBL 3–4–9, except:

a. As requested by the pilot.

b. As you deem necessary, if not contrary to the pilot's request.

TBL 3–4–9
HIRL Associated with MALSR

Step	Visibility	
	Day	Night
5	Less than 1 mile	When requested
4	1 to but not including 2 miles	Less than 1 mile
3	2 to but not including 3 miles	1 to but not including 3 miles
2	When requested	3 to 5 miles inclusive
1	When requested	More than 5 miles

NOTE–
When going from a given brightness step setting to a lower setting, rotation of the brightness control to a point below the intended step setting and then back to the appropriate step setting will ensure that the MALSR will operate at the appropriate brightness.

REFERENCE–
FAA Order JO 7110.65, Para 3–4–14, Medium Intensity Runway Lights.

3–4–13. HIRL CHANGES AFFECTING RVR

Keep the appropriate approach controller or PAR controller informed, in advance if possible, of HIRL changes that affect RVR.

3–4–14. MEDIUM INTENSITY RUNWAY LIGHTS (MIRL)

Operate MIRL or MIRL which control the associated MALSR in accordance with TBL 3–4–10, except:

a. As requested by the pilot.

b. As you deem necessary, if not contrary to the pilot's request.

TBL 3–4–10
MIRL Intensity Setting

Step	Visibility	
	Day	Night
3	Less than 2 miles	Less than 1 mile
2	2 to 3 miles	1 to 3 miles
1	When requested	More than 3 miles

REFERENCE–
FAA Order JO 7110.65, Para 3–4–12, HIRL Associated With MALSR.

3–4–15. HIGH SPEED TURNOFF LIGHTS

Operate high speed turnoff lights:

a. Whenever the associated runway lights are used for arriving aircraft. Leave them on until the aircraft has either entered a taxiway or passed the last light.

b. As required by facility directives to meet local conditions.

c. As requested by the pilot.

3-4-16. TAXIWAY LIGHTS

Operate taxiway lights in accordance with TBL 3-4-11, TBL 3-4-12, or TBL 3-4-13 except:

a. Where a facility directive specifies other settings or times to meet local conditions.

b. As requested by the pilot.

c. As you deem necessary, if not contrary to pilot request.

TBL 3-4-11

Three Step Taxiway Lights

Step	Visibility	
	Day	Night
3	Less than 1 mile	When requested
2	When requested	Less than 1 mile
1	When requested	1 mile of more

TBL 3-4-12

Five Step Taxiway Lights

Step	Visibility	
	Day	Night
5	Less than 1 mile	When requested
4	When requested	Less than 1 mile
3	When requested	1 mile or more
1 & 2	When requested	When requested

TBL 3-4-13

One Step Taxiway Lights

Day	Night
Less than 1 mile	On

NOTE-
AC 150/5340-30, Design and Installation Details for Airport Visual Aides, contains recommended brightness levels for variable setting taxiway lights.

3-4-17. OBSTRUCTION LIGHTS

If controls are provided, turn the lights on between sunset and sunrise.

3-4-18. ROTATING BEACON

If controls are provided, turn the rotating beacon on:

a. Between sunset and sunrise.

b. Between sunrise and sunset when the reported ceiling or visibility is below basic VFR minima.

3-4-19. RUNWAY STATUS LIGHTS (RWSL)

TERMINAL

RWSL is equipped with automatic intensity settings and must be operated on a continuous basis except under the following conditions:

a. If a pilot or vehicle report indicates any portion of the RWSL system is on and is not able to accept an ATC clearance; then

1. ATC must visually scan the entire runway. If the runway is observed to be clear and the lights are still illuminated, then the lights must be turned off and clearance re-issued.

2. If a portion of the runway is not visible from the tower, ATC must visually scan the ASDE system. If the runway is observed to be clear and the lights are still illuminated, then the lights must be turned off and clearance re-issued.

b. When the RWSL Operational Status displays "Lost Comm with System," consider the RWSL system out of service until checked and confirmed to be operational by technical operations personnel.

c. Once RWSL systems are turned off, they must remain off until returned to service by technical operations personnel.

d. Upon pilot request, adjust the light intensity.

Section 5. Runway Selection

3–5–1. SELECTION

a. The ATCT supervisor/controller–in–charge (CIC) determines which runway/s are designated RUNWAY IN USE/ACTIVE RUNWAY/DUTY RUNWAY.

b. Assign the runway/s most nearly aligned with the wind when 5 knots or more, or the "calm wind" runway when less than 5 knots unless:

1. Use of another runway is operationally advantageous.

2. A Runway Use Program is in effect.

c. Tailwind and crosswind considerations take precedence over delay/capacity considerations, and noise abatement operations/procedures/agreements.

d. If a pilot prefers to use a runway different from that specified, the pilot is expected to advise ATC. ATC may honor such requests as soon as is operationally practicable. ATC will advise pilots when the requested runway is noise–sensitive.

3–5–2. STOL RUNWAYS

Use STOL runways as follows:

a. A designated STOL runway may be assigned only when requested by the pilot or as specified in a letter of agreement with an aircraft operator.

b. Issue the measured STOL runway length if the pilot requests it.

3–5–3. TAILWIND COMPONENTS

When authorizing use of runways and a tailwind component exists, always state both wind direction and velocity.

NOTE–
The wind may be described as "calm" when appropriate.

REFERENCE–
FAA Order JO 7110.65, Para 2–6–3, Reporting Weather Conditions.

Section 6. Airport Surface Detection Procedures

3–6–1. EQUIPMENT USAGE

a. The operational status of ASDE systems must be determined during the relief briefing, or as soon as possible after assuming responsibility for the associated position.

b. Use ASDE systems to augment visual observation of aircraft landing or departing, and aircraft or vehicular movements on runways and taxiways, or other parts of the movement area.

1. ASDE systems with safety logic must be operated continuously.

2. ASDE systems without safety logic must be operated:

(a) Continuously between sunset and sunrise.

(b) When visibility is less than the most distant point in the active movement area, or

(c) When, in your judgment, its use will assist you in the performance of your duties at any time.

3–6–2. IDENTIFICATION

a. To identify an observed target/track on an ASDE system display, correlate its position with one or more of the following:

1. Pilot/vehicle operator position report.

2. Controller's visual observation.

3. An identified target observed on the ASR or CTRD.

b. An observed target/track on an ASDE system display may be identified as a false target by visual observation. If the area containing a suspected false target is not visible from the tower, an airport operations vehicle or pilots of aircraft operating in the area may be used to conduct the visual observation.

c. After positive verification that a target is false, through pilot/vehicle operator position report or controller visual observation, the track may be temporarily dropped, which will remove the target from the display and safety logic processing. A notation must be made to FAA Form 7230–4, Daily Record of Facility Operation, when a track is temporarily dropped.

3–6–3. INFORMATION USAGE

a. ASDE system derived information may be used to:

1. Formulate clearances and control instructions to aircraft and vehicles on the movement area.

REFERENCE–
FAA Order JO 7210.3, Para 3–6–2, ATC Surveillance Source Use.

2. Position aircraft and vehicles using the movement area.

3. Determine the exact location of aircraft and vehicles, or spatial relationship to other aircraft/vehicles on the movement area.

4. Monitor compliance with control instructions by aircraft and vehicles on taxiways and runways.

5. Confirm pilot reported positions.

6. Provide directional taxi information, as appropriate.

PHRASEOLOGY–
TURN (left/right) ON THE TAXIWAY/RUNWAY YOU ARE APPROACHING.

b. Do not provide specific navigational guidance (exact headings to be followed) unless an emergency exists or by mutual agreement with the pilot.

NOTE–
It remains the pilot's responsibility to navigate visually via routes to the clearance limit specified by the controller and to avoid other parked or taxiing aircraft, vehicles, or persons in the movement area.

c. Do not allow an aircraft to begin departure roll or cross the landing threshold whenever there is an unidentified target/track displayed on the runway.

3–6–4. SAFETY LOGIC ALERT RESPONSES

When the system generates an alert, the controller must immediately assess the situation visually and as presented on the ASDE system display, then take appropriate action as follows:

a. When an arrival aircraft (still airborne, prior to the landing threshold) activates a warning alert, the controller must issue go–around instructions. (Exception: Alerts involving known formation flights, as they cross the landing threshold, may be disregarded if all other factors are acceptable.)

NOTE–
The intent of this paragraph is that an aircraft does not land on the runway, on that approach, when the safety logic system has generated a warning alert. A side–step maneuver or circle to land on another runway satisfies this requirement.

REFERENCE–
FAA Order JO 7110.65, Para 3–8–1, Sequence/Spacing Application.
FAA Order JO 7110.65, Para 3–9–6, Same Runway Separation.
FAA Order JO 7110.65, Para 3–10–3, Same Runway Separation.
P/CG Term– Go Around.

b. When an arrival aircraft activates a warning alert to a taxiway, the controller must issue go–around instructions.

c. When two arrival aircraft, or an arrival aircraft and a departing aircraft activate an alert, the controller will issue go–around instructions or take appropriate action to ensure intersecting runway separation is maintained.

REFERENCE–
FAA Order JO 7110.65, Para 3–9–8, Intersecting Runway/Intersecting Flight Path Operations.
FAA Order JO 7110.65, Para 3–10–4, Intersecting Runway/Intersecting Flight Path Separation.

d. For other safety logic system alerts, issue instructions/clearances based on good judgment and evaluation of the situation at hand.

3–6–5. RADAR–ONLY MODE

Radar–only mode is an enhancement of the ASDE–X and ASSC systems which allows the system to stay operational with safety logic processing, despite a critical fault in the Multilateration (MLAT) subsystem. The system stays in full core alert status under radar–only mode without data block capability.

Section 7. Taxi and Ground Movement Procedures

3–7–1. GROUND TRAFFIC MOVEMENT

Issue by radio or directional light signals specific instructions which approve or disapprove the movement of aircraft, vehicles, equipment, or personnel on the movement area except where permitted in an LOA.

REFERENCE–
FAA Order JO 7210.3, Para 4–3–1, Letters of Agreement.
FAA Order JO 7210.3, Para 4–3–2, Appropriate Subjects.

a. Do not issue *conditional* instructions that are dependent upon the movement of an arrival aircraft on or approaching the runway or a departure aircraft established on a takeoff roll. Do not say, "Line up and wait behind landing traffic," or "Taxi/proceed across Runway Three–Six behind departing/landing Citation." The above requirements do not preclude issuing instructions to follow an aircraft observed to be operating on the movement area in accordance with an ATC clearance/instruction and in such a manner that the instructions to follow are not ambiguous.

b. Do not issue unconditional instructions when authorizing movement on a runway/taxiway for the purpose of airfield checks or other airport operations. Instructions must ensure positive control with specific instructions to proceed on a runway or movement area, and as necessary, hold short instructions.

REFERENCE–
FAA Order JO 7110.65, Para 3–1–3, Use of Active Runways.
FAA Order JO 7110.65, Para 3–7–2, Taxi and Ground Movement Operations.

EXAMPLE–
"Airport 1, proceed on Runway 26R, hold short of Runway 18L."

"Airport 1 proceed on taxi way B, hold short of Runway18L."

"Airport 1 proceed on Runway 26R." (additional instructions as necessary.)

NOTE–
1. *The following are examples of unconditional instructions and are not approved for use: "THE FIELD IS YOURS," "CLEARED ON ALL SURFACES," "THE AIRPORT IS YOURS," and "PROCEED ON ALL RUNWAYS AND TAXIWAYS."*

2. *"PROCEED AS REQUESTED" is not approved phraseology for instructing aircraft, vehicles, equipment, or personnel to cross or operate on a runway.*

c. Do not use the word "cleared" in conjunction with authorization for aircraft to taxi or equipment/vehicle/personnel operations. Use the prefix "taxi," "proceed," or "hold," as appropriate, for aircraft instructions and "proceed" or "hold" for equipment/vehicles/personnel.

d. Intersection departures may be initiated by a controller or a controller may authorize an intersection departure if a pilot requests. Issue the measured distance from the intersection to the runway end rounded "down" to the nearest 50 feet to any pilot who requests and to all military aircraft, unless use of the intersection is covered in appropriate directives.

NOTE–
1. *Exceptions are authorized where specific military aircraft routinely make intersection takeoffs and procedures are defined in appropriate directives. The authority exercising operational control of such aircraft ensures that all pilots are thoroughly familiar with these procedures, including the usable runway length from the applicable intersection.*

2. *Some airports publish "declared distances" for a particular runway. These are published in the Chart Supplement or the Aeronautical Information Publication (AIP) and there is no requirement that facility personnel be aware of them. These distances are a means of satisfying airport design criteria and are intended to be used by pilots and/or operators for preflight performance planning only. There are no special markings, signing, or lighting associated with declared distances and they do not limit the actual runway available for use by an aircraft. Therefore, they cannot be used for any air traffic control purpose. If pilots inquire about the existence of declared distances, refer them to the Chart Supplement or AIP.*

PHRASEOLOGY–
RUNWAY (number) AT (taxiway designator) INTERSECTION DEPARTURE (remaining length) FEET AVAILABLE.

REFERENCE–
FAA Order JO 7110.65, Para 3–9–4, Line Up and Wait (LUAW).

e. Do not use the term "full length" when the runway length available for departures has been temporarily shortened. On permanently shortened runways, do not use the term "full length" until the Chart Supplement is updated to include the change(s).

REFERENCE–
FAA Order JO 7210.3, Para 10-3-12, Airport Construction.
FAA Order JO 7210.3, Para 10-3-13, Change in Runway Length Due to Construction.

3–7–2. TAXI AND GROUND MOVEMENT OPERATIONS

Issue the route for the aircraft/vehicle to follow on the movement area in concise and easy to understand terms. The taxi clearance/route must include the specific route to follow. When a taxi clearance to a runway is issued to an aircraft, confirm the aircraft has the correct runway assignment.

NOTE–
1. *A pilot's read back of taxi instructions with the runway assignment can be considered confirmation of runway assignment.*

2. *Movement of aircraft or vehicles on nonmovement areas is the responsibility of the pilot, the aircraft operator, or the airport management.*

a. When authorizing an aircraft to taxi or a vehicle to proceed on the movement area, specify the taxi instructions/route. If it is the intent to hold the aircraft/vehicle short of:

1. A runway: issue the route up to the runway hold short point. When issuing a runway crossing clearance, include specific instructions on where to cross the runway;

2. Any other point along the route, issue:

(a) the route up to the hold short point, or

(b) the entire route and then state the hold short instructions.

After issuing a crossing clearance, specify the taxi instructions/route an aircraft/vehicle is to follow, if not previously issued.

NOTE–
The absence of holding instructions authorizes an aircraft/vehicle to cross all taxiways that intersect the taxi route.

PHRASEOLOGY–
HOLD POSITION.

HOLD FOR (reason)

CROSS (runway), at (runway/taxiway)

or

TAXI/CONTINUE TAXIING/PROCEED VIA (route),

or

ON (runway number or taxiways, etc.),

or

TO (location),

or

(direction),

or

ACROSS RUNWAY (number), at (runway/taxiway).

or

VIA (route), HOLD SHORT OF (location)

or

FOLLOW (traffic) (restrictions as necessary)

or

BEHIND (traffic).

EXAMPLE–
"Cross Runway Two–Eight Left, at taxiway Alpha, hold short of Runway Two–Eight Right."

"Taxi/continue taxiing/proceed to the hangar."

"Taxi/continue taxiing/proceed straight ahead then via ramp to the hangar."

"Taxi/continue taxiing/proceed on Taxiway Charlie, hold short of Runway Two–Seven."

or

"Taxi/continue taxing/proceed on Charlie, hold short of Runway Two–Seven."

b. When authorizing an aircraft to taxi to an assigned takeoff runway, state the departure runway followed by the specific taxi route. Issue hold short instructions, in accordance with subparagraph a above, when an aircraft will be required to hold short of a runway or other points along the taxi route.

NOTE–
If the specific taxi route ends into a connecting taxiway with the same identifier (for example, taxiway "A" connects with Taxiway "A1") at the approach end of the runway, the connecting taxiway may be omitted from the clearance.

PHRASEOLOGY–
RUNWAY (number), TAXI VIA (route as necessary).

or

RUNWAY (number), TAXI VIA (route as necessary)(hold short instructions as necessary)."

EXAMPLE–
"Runway Three–Six Left, taxi via taxiway Alpha, hold short of taxiway Charlie."

or

"Runway Three–Six Left, taxi via Alpha, hold short of Charlie."

or

"Runway Three–Six Left, taxi via taxiway Alpha, hold short of Runway Two–Seven Right."

or

"Runway Three–Six Left, taxi via Charlie, cross Runway Two–Seven Left, hold short of Runway Two–Seven Right."

or

"Runway Three–Six Left, taxi via Alpha, Charlie, cross Runway One–Zero."

c. Issue a crossing clearance to aircraft for each runway their route crosses. An aircraft must have crossed a previous runway before another runway crossing clearance may be issued. At those airports where the taxi distance between runway centerlines is 1,300 feet or less, multiple runway crossings may be issued with a single clearance. The air traffic manager must submit a request to the appropriate Service Area Director of Air Traffic Operations and receive approval before authorizing multiple runway crossings.

NOTE–
Controllers should avoid crossing points that are not perpendicular or nearly perpendicular to the runway to be crossed, (for example, reverse high speed taxiways).

PHRASEOLOGY–
"Cross (runway) at(runway/taxiway), hold short of (runway)", or
Cross (runways) at (runway/taxiway).

EXAMPLE–
"Cross Runway One–Six Left at Taxiway Bravo, hold short of Runway One–Six Right."
"Cross Runway One–Six Left and Runway One–Six Right at Taxiway Bravo."

REFERENCE–
FAA Order JO 7210.3, Para 10–3–11 Multiple Runway Crossings.

d. When an aircraft/vehicle is instructed to "follow" traffic and requires a runway crossing, issue a runway crossing clearance in addition to the follow instructions and/or hold short instructions, as applicable.

EXAMPLE–
"Follow (traffic), cross Runway Two–Seven Right, at Taxiway Whiskey"

or

"Follow (traffic), cross Runway Two Seven–Right at Taxiway Whiskey, hold short of Runway Two–Seven Left."

e. Issue a crossing clearance to vehicles for each runway their route crosses. A vehicle must have crossed a previous runway before another runway crossing clearance may be issued.

NOTE–
A clearance is required for vehicles to operate on any active, inactive, or closed runway except for vehicles operating on closed runways in accordance with a Letter of Agreement (LOA).

f. Vehicles that have been issued a clearance onto a runway to conduct runway operations are authorized to cross intersecting runways, unless otherwise restricted. Issue hold short instructions as needed.

NOTE–
Vehicles should not normally use runways as transition routes to other parts of the airfield. These movements are not considered runway operations and the use of alternative routes is preferred.

g. Crossing of active runway(s) by aircraft/vehicle(s):

1. During departure operations, ensure that aircraft/vehicles intending to cross a runway do not cross the runway holding position markings until the controller visually observes the departure aircraft in a turn, or the departure aircraft has passed the point where the crossing aircraft/vehicle is located, regardless of altitude, unless authorized in FAA Order JO 7110.65, paragraph 3–10–10, Altitude Restricted Low Approach.

REFERENCE–
AIM, Runway Position Holding Markings, Subpara 2–3–5a.
FAA Order 7110.65, Para 3–10–10, Altitude Restricted Low Approach.

2. During arrival operations, ensure the following:

(a) An aircraft/vehicle has completed crossing prior to the arriving aircraft crossing the landing threshold, or

REFERENCE–
P/CG Term – Clear of the Runway.

(b) A crossing aircraft/vehicle will not cross the runway holding position markings until the arrival has landed and either:

(1) The controller has confirmed by verbal commitment from the pilot that the arriving aircraft will exit the runway prior to the point at which the crossing is intended, or

(2) The controller visually observes the aircraft exiting the runway prior to the point at which the crossing is intended, or

(3) The arriving aircraft has passed the point at which the crossing is intended.

REFERENCE–
FAA Order JO 7110.65, Para 3–10–4, Intersecting Runway/Intersecting Flight Path Separation.
FAA Order JO 7210.3, Para 10–3–7, Land and Hold Short Operations (LAHSO).

h. Request a read back of runway hold short instructions when it is not received from the pilot/vehicle operator.

PHRASEOLOGY–
READ BACK HOLD INSTRUCTIONS.

EXAMPLE–
1. *"American Four Ninety Two, Runway Three Six Left, taxi via taxiway Charlie, hold short of Runway Two Seven Right."*

or

"American Four Ninety Two, Runway Three Six Left, taxi via Charlie, hold short of Runway Two Seven Right."

"American Four Ninety Two, Roger."

"American Four Ninety Two, read back hold instructions."

2. *"Cleveland Tower, American Sixty Three is ready for departure."*

"American Sixty Three, hold short of Runway Two Three Left, traffic one mile final."

"American Sixty Three, Roger."

"American Sixty Three, read back hold instructions."

3. *"OPS Three proceed via taxiway Charlie hold short of Runway Two Seven."*

or

"OPS Three proceed via Charlie hold short of Runway Two Seven."

"OPS Three, Roger."

"OPS Three, read back hold instructions."

NOTE–
Read back hold instructions phraseology may be initiated for any point on a movement area when the controller believes the read back is necessary.

i. Issue progressive taxi/ground movement instructions when:

1. A pilot/operator requests.

2. The specialist deems it necessary due to traffic or field conditions, e.g., construction or closed taxiways.

3. Necessary during reduced visibility, especially when the taxi route is not visible from the tower.

NOTE–
Progressive instructions may include step–by–step directions and/or directional turns.

REFERENCE–
FAA Order JO 7110.65, Para 3–7–4, Runway Proximity.
FAA Order JO 7110.65, Para 3–11–1, Taxi and Ground Movement Operation.

j. Issue instructions to expedite a taxiing aircraft or a moving vehicle.

PHRASEOLOGY–
TAXI WITHOUT DELAY (traffic if necessary).

EXIT/PROCEED/CROSS (runway/taxiway) at (runway/taxiway) WITHOUT DELAY.

k. Issue instructions to aircraft/vehicle to hold short of an approach/departure hold area when required.

PHRASEOLOGY–
HOLD SHORT OF (runway) APPROACH

HOLD SHORT OF (runway)DEPARTURE

3–7–3. GROUND OPERATIONS

Avoid clearances which require:

a. Super or heavy aircraft to use greater than normal taxiing power.

b. Small aircraft or helicopters to taxi in close proximity to taxiing or hover-taxi helicopters.

NOTE–
Use caution when taxiing smaller aircraft/helicopters in the vicinity of larger aircraft/helicopters. Controllers may use the words rotor wash, jet blast, or prop wash when issuing cautionary advisories.

EXAMPLE–
"Follow Boeing 757, Runway Three–Six Left, taxi via Alpha, Caution jet blast."

or

When appropriate,

"Follow CH–53, Runway Two–One, taxi via Bravo, Caution rotor wash."

REFERENCE–
AC 90–23, Aircraft Wake Turbulence, Para 10 and Para 11.

3–7–4. RUNWAY PROXIMITY

Hold a taxiing aircraft or vehicle clear of the runway as follows:

a. Instruct aircraft or vehicle to hold short of a specific runway.

b. Instruct aircraft or vehicle to hold at a specified point.

c. Issue traffic information as necessary.

PHRASEOLOGY–
HOLD SHORT OF/AT (runway number or specific point), (traffic or other information).

NOTE–
Establishing hold lines/signs is the responsibility of the airport manager. The standards for surface measurements, markings, and signs are contained in AC 150/5300–13, Airport Design; AC 150/5340–1, Standards for Airport Markings, and AC 150/5340–18, Standards for Airport Sign Systems. The operator is responsible for properly positioning the aircraft, vehicle,

or equipment at the appropriate hold line/sign or designated point. The requirements in paragraph 3–1–12, Visually Scanning Runways, remain valid as appropriate.

REFERENCE–
FAA Order JO 7110.65, Para 3–7–2, Taxi and Ground Movement Operations.
FAA Order JO 7110.65, Para 3–10–10, Altitude Restricted Low Approach.
FAA Order JO 7110.65, Para 3–1–5, Vehicles/Equipment/Personnel on Runways.

3–7–5. PRECISION APPROACH CRITICAL AREA

a. Aircraft and vehicle access to the ILS critical area must be controlled to ensure the integrity of ILS course signals whenever the official weather observation is a ceiling of less than 800 feet or visibility less than 2 miles. Unless the arriving aircraft has reported the runway in sight or is circling to land to another runway, do not authorize vehicles/aircraft to operate in or over the critical area, except as specified in subparagraph a1, whenever an arriving aircraft is inside the ILS outer marker (OM) or the fix used in lieu of the OM.

PHRASEOLOGY–
HOLD SHORT OF (runway) ILS CRITICAL AREA.

NOTE–
When available weather sources such as METARs/SPECI/PIREPs/controller observations indicate weather conditions are changing from VFR to IFR and are deteriorating, actions are expected to be taken to update the official weather observation.

REFERENCE–
FAA Order JO 7110.65, Para 2–6–2 PIREP Solicitation and Dissemination.
FAA Order JO 7110.65, Para 2–6–3, Reporting Weather Conditions.
FAA Order JO 7110.65, Para 2–6–5, Disseminating Official Weather Information.
FAA Order JO 7210.3, Para 2–9–2, Receipt and Dissemination of Weather Observations.
FAA Order JO 7210.3, Para 10–3–1, SIGMENT and PIREP Handling.
FAA Order JO 7900.5, Para 6.4d, Equipment for Sky Condition.
FAA Order 6750.16, Siting Criteria for Instrument Landing Systems.

1. LOCALIZER CRITICAL AREA

(a) Do not authorize vehicle or aircraft operations in or over the area when an arriving aircraft is inside the ILS OM or the fix used in lieu of the OM when the official weather observation is a ceiling of less than 800 feet or visibility less than 2 miles, except:

(1) A preceding arriving aircraft on the same or another runway that passes over or through the area while landing or exiting the runway.

(2) A preceding departing aircraft or missed approach on the same or another runway that passes through or over the area.

(b) In addition to subparagraph a1(a), when the official weather observation indicates a ceiling of less than 200 feet or RVR 2,000 feet, do not authorize vehicles or aircraft operations in or over the area when an arriving aircraft is inside the middle marker, or in the absence of a middle marker, 1/2 mile final.

2. GLIDESLOPE CRITICAL AREA. Do not authorize vehicles or aircraft operations in or over the area when an arriving aircraft is inside the ILS OM or the fix used in lieu of the OM unless the arriving aircraft has reported the runway in sight or is circling to land on another runway when the official weather observation indicates a ceiling of less than 800 feet or visibility less than 2 miles.

b. Operators commonly conduct "coupled" or "autoland" approaches to satisfy maintenance, training, or reliability program requirements. Promptly issue an advisory if the critical area will not be protected when an arriving aircraft advises that a "coupled," "CATIII," "autoland," or similar type approach will be conducted and the official weather observation indicates a ceiling of 800 feet or more, or the visibility is 2 miles or more.

PHRASEOLOGY–
ILS CRITICAL AREA NOT PROTECTED.

c. The Department of Defense (DoD) is authorized to define criteria for protection of precision approach critical areas at military controlled airports. This protection is provided to all aircraft operating at that military controlled airport. Waiver authority for DoD precision approach critical area criteria rests with the appropriate military authority.

NOTE–
Signs and markings are installed by the airport operator to define the ILS critical area. No point along the longitudinal axis of the aircraft is permitted past the hold line for holding purposes. The operator is responsible to properly position the aircraft, vehicle, or equipment at the appropriate hold line/sign or designated point. The requirements in paragraph 3–1–12, Visually Scanning Runways, remain valid as appropriate.

REFERENCE–
AC150/5340–1, Standards for Airport Markings.

3–7–6. PRECISION OBSTACLE FREE ZONE (POFZ) AND FINAL APPROACH OBSTACLE CLEARANCE SURFACES (OCS)

a. Ensure the POFZ is clear of traffic (aircraft or vehicles) when an aircraft on a vertically–guided final approach is within 2 miles of the runway threshold and the official weather observation indicates the ceiling is below 300 feet or visibility is less than 3/4 SM to protect aircraft executing a missed approach**.**

NOTE–
Only horizontal surfaces (e.g., the wings) can penetrate the POFZ, but not the vertical surfaces (e.g., fuselage or tail). Three hundred feet (300) is used because ATC does not measure ceilings in fifty (50) foot increments.

b. Ensure the final approach OCS (e.g., ILS /LPV W, X, and Y surfaces) are clear of aircraft/vehicles when an aircraft on the vertically–guided approach is within 2 miles of the runway threshold and the official weather observation indicates the ceiling is below 800 feet or visibility is less than 2 SM to protect aircraft executing a missed approach.

NOTE–
1. *The POFZ and the close–in portion of the final approach obstacle clearance surfaces protect aircraft executing a missed approach.*

2. *Vehicles that are less than 10 feet in height, necessary for the maintenance of the airport and/or navigation facilities operating outside the movement area, are exempt.*

c. If it is not possible to clear the POFZ or OCS prior to an aircraft reaching a point 2 miles from the runway threshold and the weather is less than described in subparagraph a or b above, issue traffic to the landing aircraft.

NOTE–
The POFZ and/or OCS must be cleared as soon as practical.

PHRASEOLOGY–
(ACID), IN THE EVENT OF MISSED APPROACH (issue traffic).

TAXIING AIRCRAFT/VEHICLE LEFT/RIGHT OF RUNWAY.

EXAMPLE–
"United 623, in the event of missed approach, taxiing aircraft right of runway."

"Delta 1058, in the event of missed approach, vehicle left of runway."

REFERENCE–
FAA Order JO 7110.65, Para 3–1–6, Traffic Information.
AC 150/5300–13, Airport Design.

FIG 3−7−1

Precision Obstacle Free Zone (POFZ)

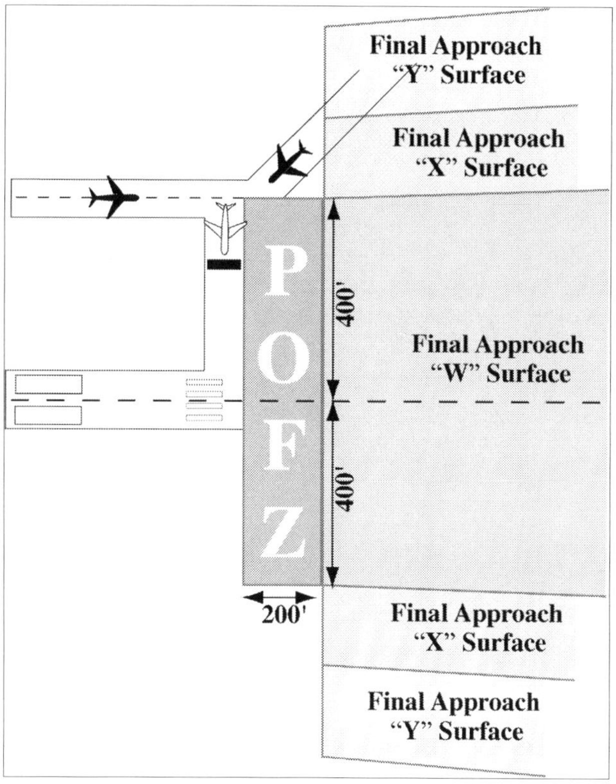

Section 8. Spacing and Sequencing

3–8–1. SEQUENCE/SPACING APPLICATION

Establish the sequence of arriving and departing aircraft by requiring them to adjust flight or ground operation, as necessary, to achieve proper spacing.

PHRASEOLOGY–
CLEARED FOR TAKEOFF.

CLEARED FOR TAKEOFF OR HOLD SHORT/HOLD IN POSITION/TAXI OFF THE RUNWAY (traffic).

EXTEND DOWNWIND.

MAKE SHORT APPROACH.

NUMBER (landing sequence number),

FOLLOW (description and location of traffic),

or if traffic is utilizing another runway,

TRAFFIC (description and location) LANDING RUNWAY (number of runway being used).

TRAFFIC (description and location) LANDING THE PARALLEL RUNWAY

CIRCLE THE AIRPORT.

MAKE LEFT/RIGHT THREE–SIXTY/TWO SEVENTY.

GO AROUND (additional instructions as necessary).

CLEARED TO LAND.

CLEARED:

TOUCH–AND–GO,
or

STOP–AND–GO,
or

LOW APPROACH.

CLEARED FOR THE OPTION,

or

OPTION APPROVED,

or

UNABLE OPTION, (alternate instructions).

or

UNABLE (type of option), OTHER OPTIONS APPROVED.

NOTE–

1. *The "Cleared for the Option" procedure will permit an instructor pilot/flight examiner/pilot the option to make a touch-and-go, low approach, missed approach, stop- and-go, or full stop landing. This procedure will only be used at those locations with an operational control tower and will be subject to ATC approval. After ATC approval of the option, the pilot should inform ATC as soon as possible of any delay on the runway during their stop-and-go or full stop landing.*

2. *For proper helicopter spacing, speed adjustments may be more practical than course changes.*

3. *Read back of hold short instructions apply when hold instructions are issued to a pilot in lieu of a takeoff clearance.*

REFERENCE–
FAA Order JO 7110.65, Para 3–7–2, Taxi and Ground Movement Operations.
AIM, Para 4–3–22, Option Approach.

3–8–2. TOUCH-AND-GO OR STOP-AND-GO OR LOW APPROACH

Consider an aircraft cleared for touch-and-go, stop-and-go, or low approach as an arriving aircraft until it touches down (for touch-and-go), or makes a complete stop (for stop-and-go), or crosses the landing threshold (for low approach), and thereafter as a departing aircraft.

REFERENCE–
FAA Order JO 7110.65, Para 3–1–5, Vehicles/Equipment/Personnel on Runways.
FAA Order JO 7110.65, Para 3–9–7, Wake Turbulence Separation for Intersection Departures.

3–8–3. SIMULTANEOUS SAME DIRECTION OPERATION

Authorize simultaneous, same direction operations on parallel runways, on parallel landing strips, or on a runway and a parallel landing strip only when the following conditions are met:

a. Operations are conducted in VFR conditions unless visual separation is applied.

b. Two-way radio communication is maintained with the aircraft involved and pertinent traffic information is issued.

c. The distance between the parallel runways or landing strips is in accordance with those specified in TBL 3–8–1.

TBL 3–8–1
Same Direction Distance Minima

Aircraft category	Minimum distance (feet) between parallel	
	Runway centerlines	Edges of adjacent strips or runway and strip
Category I or Category II	300	200
If either aircraft is a Category III	500	400
If either aircraft is a Heavy	700	600

NOTE–

1. *Aircraft Categories specified in TBL 3–8–1 are Same Runway Separation (SRS) categories as indicated in paragraph 3–9–6, Same Runway Separation.*

2. *When conducting Simultaneous Same Direction Operations (SSDO), applicable Wake Turbulence provisions apply.*

3–8–4. SIMULTANEOUS OPPOSITE DIRECTION OPERATION

Authorize simultaneous opposite direction operations on parallel runways, on parallel landing strips, or on a runway and a parallel landing strip only when the following conditions are met:

a. Operations are conducted in VFR conditions.

b. Two-way radio communication is maintained with the aircraft involved and pertinent traffic information is issued.

PHRASEOLOGY–
TRAFFIC (description) ARRIVING/DEPARTING/LOW APPROACH, OPPOSITE DIRECTION ON PARALLEL RUNWAY/LANDING STRIP.

c. The distance between the runways or landing strips is in accordance with the minima in TBL 3–8–2.

TBL 3–8–2
Opposite Direction Distance Minima

Type of Operation	Minimum distance (feet) between parallel	
	Runway centerlines	Edges of adjacent strips or runway and strip
Between sunrise and sunset	1,400	1,400
Between sunset and sunrise	2,800	Not authorized

Section 9. Departure Procedures and Separation

3–9–1. DEPARTURE INFORMATION

Provide current departure information, as appropriate, to departing aircraft.

a. Departure information contained in the ATIS broadcast may be omitted if the pilot states the appropriate ATIS code.

b. Issue departure information by including the following:

1. Runway in use. (May be omitted if pilot states "have the numbers.")

2. Surface wind from direct readout dial, wind shear detection system, or automated weather observing system information display. (May be omitted if pilot states "have the numbers.")

3. Altimeter setting. (May be omitted if pilot states "have the numbers.")

REFERENCE–
FAA Order JO 7110.65, Para 2–7–1, Current Settings.

c. Time, when requested.

d. Issue the official ceiling and visibility, when available, to a departing aircraft before takeoff as follows:

1. To a VFR aircraft when weather is below VFR conditions.

2. To an IFR aircraft when weather is below VFR conditions or highest takeoff minima, whichever is greater.

NOTE–
Standard takeoff minimums are published in 14 CFR Section 91.175(f). Takeoff minima other than standard are prescribed for specific airports/runways and published in a tabular form supplement to the FAA instrument approach procedures charts and appropriate FAA Forms 8260.

e. Issue the route for the aircraft/vehicle to follow on the movement area in concise and easy to understand terms. The taxi clearance must include the specific route to follow.

f. *USAF NOT APPLICABLE.* An advisory to "check density altitude" when appropriate.

REFERENCE–
FAA Order JO 7210.3, Para 2–10–6, Broadcast Density Altitude Advisory.

g. Issue braking action for the runway in use as received from pilots when braking action advisories are in effect.

REFERENCE–
FAA Order JO 7110.65, Para 2–7–2, Altimeter Setting Issuance Below Lowest Usable FL.
FAA Order JO 7110.65, Para 3–1–8, Low Level Wind Shear/Microburst Advisories.
FAA Order JO 7110.65, Para 3–3–5, Braking Action Advisories.
P/CG Term– Braking Action Advisories.

h. Runway Condition Codes. Furnish RwyCC, as received from the Airport Operator, to aircraft via the ATIS.

i. For opposite direction departure operations, controllers may verbally issue the RwyCC, as identified in the FICON NOTAM, in reverse order. Controllers must not include reversed RwyCC on the ATIS broadcast.

j. When the ATIS is unavailable, and when the runway length available for departure has been temporarily shortened, controllers must ensure that pilots receive the runway number combined with a shortened announcement for all departing aircraft.

PHRASEOLOGY–
RUNWAY (NUMBER) SHORTENED

EXAMPLE–
"Runway Two-Seven shortened."

3–9–2. DEPARTURE DELAY INFORMATION

USA/USAF/USN NOT APPLICABLE

When gate-hold procedures are in effect, issue the following departure delay information as appropriate:

REFERENCE–
FAA Order JO 7210.3, Para 10–4–3, Gate Hold Procedures.

a. Advise departing aircraft the time at which the pilot can expect to receive engine startup advisory.

PHRASEOLOGY–
GATE HOLD PROCEDURES ARE IN EFFECT. ALL AIRCRAFT CONTACT (position) ON (frequency) FOR ENGINE START TIME. EXPECT ENGINE START/TAXI (time).

b. Advise departing aircraft when to start engines and/or to advise when ready to taxi.

PHRASEOLOGY–
START ENGINES, ADVISE WHEN READY TO TAXI,

or

ADVISE WHEN READY TO TAXI.

c. If the pilot requests to hold in a delay absorbing area, the request must be approved if space and traffic conditions permit.

d. Advise all aircraft on GC/FD frequency upon termination of gate hold procedures.

PHRASEOLOGY–
GATE HOLD PROCEDURES NO LONGER IN EFFECT.

3–9–3. DEPARTURE CONTROL INSTRUCTIONS

Inform departing IFR, SVFR, VFR aircraft receiving radar service, and TRSA VFR aircraft of the following:

a. Before takeoff.

1. Issue the appropriate departure control frequency and beacon code. The departure control frequency may be omitted if a SID has been or will be assigned and the departure control frequency is published on the SID.

PHRASEOLOGY–
DEPARTURE FREQUENCY (frequency), SQUAWK (code).

2. Inform all departing IFR military turboprop/turbojet aircraft (except transport and cargo types) to change to departure control frequency. If the local controller has departure frequency override, transmit urgent instructions on this frequency. If the override capability does not exist, transmit urgent instructions on the emergency frequency.

PHRASEOLOGY–
CHANGE TO DEPARTURE.

3. *USAF.* USAF control towers are authorized to inform all departing IFR military transport/cargo type aircraft operating in formation flight to change to departure control frequency before takeoff.

b. After takeoff.

1. When the aircraft is about $^1/_2$ mile beyond the runway end, instruct civil aircraft, and military transport, and cargo types to contact departure control, provided further communication with you is not required.

2. Do not request departing military turboprop/turbojet aircraft (except transport and cargo types) to make radio frequency or radar beacon changes before the aircraft reaches 2,500 feet above the surface.

REFERENCE–
FAA Order JO 7110.65, Para 7–2–1, Visual Separation.

3–9–4. LINE UP AND WAIT (LUAW)

a. The intent of LUAW is to position aircraft for an imminent departure. Authorize an aircraft to line up and wait, except as restricted in subparagraph g, when takeoff clearances cannot be issued because of traffic. Issue traffic information to any aircraft so authorized. Traffic information may be omitted when the traffic is another aircraft which has landed on or is taking off the runway and is clearly visible to the holding aircraft. Do not use conditional phrases such as "behind landing traffic" or "after the departing aircraft."

b. First state the runway number followed by the line up and wait clearance.

PHRASEOLOGY–
RUNWAY (number), LINE UP AND WAIT.

NOTE–
When using LUAW, an imminent departure is one that will not be delayed beyond the time that is required to ensure a safe operation. An aircraft should not be in LUAW status for more than 90 seconds without additional instructions.

c. Procedures.

1. At facilities without a safety logic system or facilities with the safety logic system in limited configuration:

(a) Do not clear an aircraft for a full-stop, touch-and-go, stop-and-go, low approach, or option on the same runway with an aircraft holding in position or taxiing to LUAW until the aircraft in position has exited the runway or starts takeoff roll.

PHRASEOLOGY–
RUNWAY (number), CONTINUE, TRAFFIC HOLDING IN POSITION,

or

RUNWAY (number) (pattern instructions as appropriate) TRAFFIC HOLDING IN POSITION.

EXAMPLE–
"American 528, Runway Two–Three continue, traffic holding in position."

"Twin Cessna Four Four Golf, Runway One–Niner Right, base approved, traffic holding in position."

"Baron Two Five Foxtrot, Runway One–Niner, extend downwind, tower will call your base, traffic holding in position."

REFERENCE–
FAA Order JO 7110.65, Para 3–10–10, Altitude Restricted Low Approach.

(b) Do not authorize an aircraft to LUAW if an aircraft has been cleared for a full-stop, touch-and-go, stop-and-go, low approach, or option on the same runway.

2. Except when reported weather conditions are less than ceiling 800 feet or visibility less than 2 miles, facilities using the safety logic system in the full core alert mode:

(a) May issue clearance for a full-stop, touch-and-go, stop-and-go, low approach, or option on the same runway with an aircraft holding in position or taxiing to LUAW, or

(b) May authorize an aircraft to LUAW when an aircraft has been cleared for a full-stop, touch-and-go, stop-and-go, low approach, or option on the same runway.

REFERENCE–
FAA Order JO 7110.65, Para 3–10–5, Landing Clearance.

d. When an aircraft is authorized to LUAW, inform it of the closest traffic within 6 flying miles requesting a full-stop, touch-and-go, stop-and-go, low approach, or option to the same runway.

EXAMPLE–
"United Five, Runway One Eight, line up and wait. Traffic a Boeing Seven Thirty Seven, six mile final.

e. Do not authorize an aircraft to line up and wait when the departure point is not visible from the tower, unless the aircraft's position can be verified by ASDE or the runway is used for departures only.

f. An aircraft may be authorized to line up and wait at an intersection between sunset and sunrise under the following conditions:

1. The procedure must be approved by the appropriate Service Area Director of Air Traffic Operations.

2. The procedure must be contained in a facility directive.

3. The runway must be used as a departure–only runway.

4. Only one aircraft at a time is permitted to line up and wait on the same runway.

5. Document on FAA Form 7230–4, Daily Record of Facility Operation, the following: "LUAW at INT of RWY (number) and TWY (name) IN EFFECT" when using runway as a departure–only runway. "LUAW at INT of RWY (number) and TWY (name) SUSPENDED" when runway is not used as a departure–only runway.

g. Do not authorize an aircraft to line up and wait at anytime when the intersection is not visible from the tower.

h. Do not authorize aircraft to simultaneously line up and wait on the same runway, between sunrise and sunset, unless the local assist/local monitor position is staffed.

i. *USN.* Do not authorize aircraft to line up and wait simultaneously on intersecting runways.

PHRASEOLOGY–
CONTINUE HOLDING,

or

TAXI OFF THE RUNWAY.

REFERENCE–
FAA Order JO 7110.65, Para 3–10–10, Altitude Restricted Low Approach.

j. When aircraft are authorized to line up and wait on runways that intersect, traffic must be exchanged between that aircraft and the aircraft that is authorized to line up and wait, depart, or arrive to the intersecting runway(s).

EXAMPLE–
"United Five, Runway Four, line up and wait, traffic holding Runway Three–One."
"Delta One, Runway Three–One, line up and wait, traffic holding Runway Four."

Or, when issuing traffic information to an arrival aircraft and an aircraft that is holding on runway(s) that intersect(s):

"Delta One, Runway Four, line up and wait, traffic landing Runway Three–One."
"United Five, Runway Three–One, cleared to land. Traffic holding in position Runway Four."

Or, when issuing traffic information to a departing aircraft and an aircraft that is holding on runway(s) that intersect(s):

"Delta One, Runway Three–One, line up and wait, traffic departing Runway Four."
"United Five, Runway Four, cleared for takeoff, traffic holding in position Runway Three–One."

REFERENCE–
FAA Order JO 7110.65, Para 3–9–8, Intersecting Runway/Intersecting Flight Path Operations.
FAA Order JO 7110.65, Para 3–10–4, Intersecting Runway/Intersecting Flight Path Separation.

k. When a local controller delivers or amends an ATC clearance to an aircraft awaiting departure and that aircraft is holding short of a runway or is holding in position on a runway, an additional clearance must be issued to prevent the possibility of the aircraft inadvertently taxiing onto the runway and/or beginning takeoff roll. In such cases, append one of the following ATC instructions as appropriate:

1. HOLD SHORT OF RUNWAY, *or*

2. HOLD IN POSITION

l. *USAF/USN.* When issuing additional instructions or information to an aircraft holding in position, include instructions to continue holding or taxi off the runway, unless it is cleared for takeoff.

PHRASEOLOGY–
CONTINUE HOLDING,

or

TAXI OFF THE RUNWAY.

REFERENCE–
FAA Order JO 7110.65, Para 3–10–10, Altitude Restricted Low Approach.

m. When authorizing an aircraft to line up and wait at an intersection, state the runway intersection.

PHRASEOLOGY–
RUNWAY (number) AT (taxiway designator), LINE UP AND WAIT.

n. When two or more aircraft call the tower ready for departure, one or more at the full length of a runway and one or more at an intersection, state the location of the aircraft at the full length of the runway when authorizing that aircraft to line up and wait.

PHRASEOLOGY–
RUNWAY (number), FULL–LENGTH, LINE UP AND WAIT.

EXAMPLE–
"American Four Eighty Two, Runway Three–Zero full length, line up and wait."

NOTE–
The controller need not state the location of the aircraft departing the full length of the runway if there are no aircraft holding for departure at an intersection for that same runway.

o. Do not use the term "full length" when the runway length available for departure has been temporarily shortened. On permanently shortened runways, do not use the term "full length" until the Chart Supplement is updated to include the change(s).

NOTE–
The use of the term "full length" could be interpreted by the pilot(s) as the available runway length prior to the runway being shortened.

p. Whenever a runway length has been temporarily or permanently shortened, state the word "shortened" immediately following the runway number as part of the line up and wait clearance.

1. The addition of "shortened" must be included in the line up and wait clearance for the duration of the construction project when the runway is temporarily shortened.

2. The addition of "shortened" must be included in the line up and wait clearance until the Chart Supplement is updated to include the change(s) when the runway is permanently shortened.

PHRASEOLOGY–
RUNWAY (number) SHORTENED, LINE UP AND WAIT.

EXAMPLE–
"Runway Two-Seven shortened, line up and wait."

REFERENCE–
FAA Order JO 7210.3, Para 10-3-12, Airport Construction.
FAA Order JO 7210.3, Para 10-3-13, Change in Runway Length Due to Construction.

3–9–5. ANTICIPATING SEPARATION

Takeoff clearance need not be withheld until prescribed separation exists if there is a reasonable assurance it will exist when the aircraft starts takeoff roll.

REFERENCE–
P/CG Term – Clear of the Runway.

3–9–6. SAME RUNWAY SEPARATION

Separate a departing aircraft from a preceding departing or arriving aircraft using the same runway by ensuring that it does not begin takeoff roll until:

a. The other aircraft has departed and crossed the runway end or turned to avert any conflict. (See FIG 3–9–1.) If you can determine distances by reference to suitable landmarks, the other aircraft needs only be airborne if the following minimum distance exists between aircraft: (See FIG 3–9–2.)

1. When only Category I aircraft are involved– *3,000 feet.*

2. When a Category I aircraft is preceded by a Category II aircraft– *3,000 feet.*

3. When either the succeeding or both are Category II aircraft– *4,500 feet.*

4. When either is a Category III aircraft– *6,000 feet.*

5. When the succeeding aircraft is a helicopter, visual separation may be applied in lieu of using distance minima.

FIG 3–9–1
Same Runway Separation
[View 1]

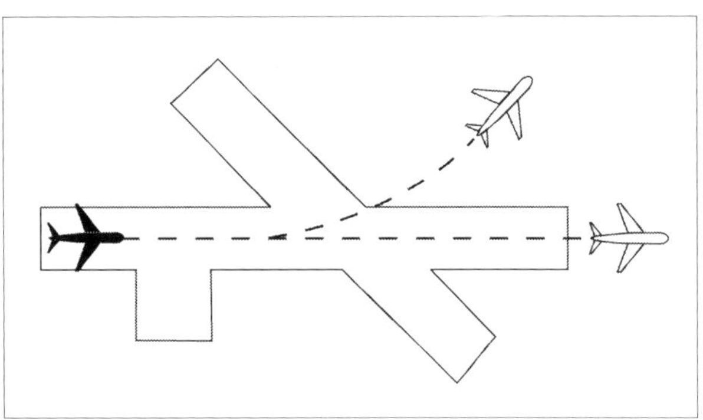

FIG 3–9–2
Same Runway Separation
[View 2]

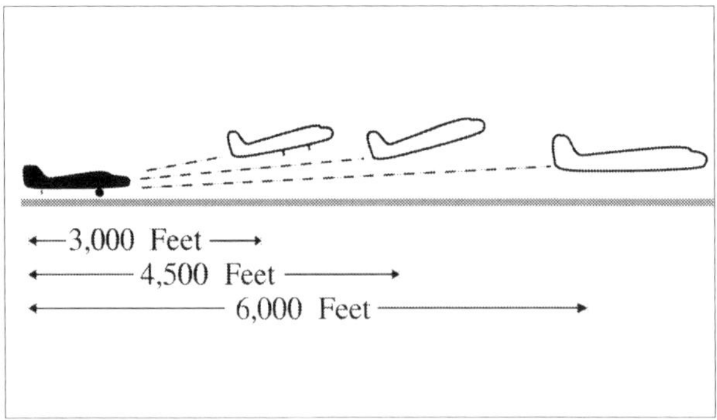

NOTE–
Aircraft same runway separation (SRS) categories are specified in FAA Order JO 7360.1, Aircraft Type Designators and based upon the following definitions:

CATEGORY I – small single–engine propeller driven aircraft weighing 12,500 lbs. or less, and all helicopters.

CATEGORY II – small twin–engine propeller driven aircraft weighing 12,500 lbs. or less.

CATEGORY III – all other aircraft.

b. A preceding landing aircraft is clear of the runway. (See FIG 3–9–3.)

FIG 3–9–3
Preceding Landing Aircraft Clear of Runway

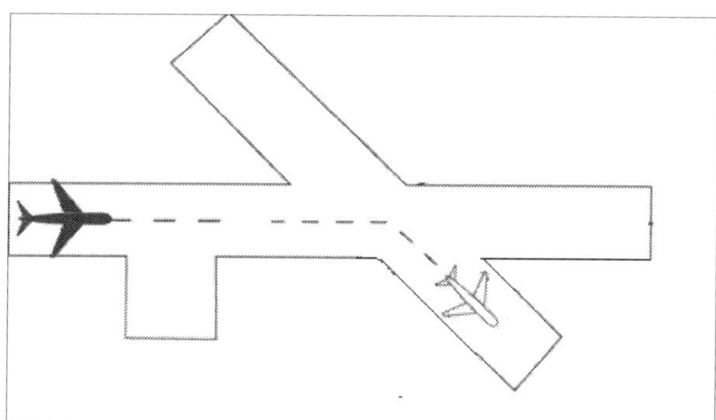

REFERENCE–
P/CG Term– Clear of the Runway.

WAKE TURBULENCE APPLICATION

c. Do not issue clearances which imply or indicate approval of rolling takeoffs by super or heavy aircraft except as provided in paragraph 3–1–14, Ground Operations When Volcanic Ash is Present.

d. Do not issue clearances to a small aircraft to line up and wait on the same runway behind a departing super or heavy aircraft to apply the necessary intervals.

REFERENCE–
AC 90–23, Aircraft Wake Turbulence.

e. The minima in paragraph 5–5–4, Minima, subparagraph f, may be applied in lieu of the time interval requirements in subparagraphs f, g, and h. When paragraph 5–5–4, Minima, is applied, ensure that the appropriate radar separation exists at or prior to the time an aircraft becomes airborne.

REFERENCE–
FAA Order JO 7210.3, Para 2–1–16, Authorization for Separation Services by Towers.
FAA Order JO 7210.3, Para 10–5–3, Functional Use of Certified Tower radar Displays.

NOTE–
1. *The pilot may request additional separation, but should make this request before taxiing on the runway.*

2. *Takeoff clearance to the following aircraft should not be issued until the time interval has passed after the preceding aircraft begins takeoff roll.*

f. Separate aircraft taking off from the same runway or a parallel runway separated by less than 2,500 feet (see FIG 3–9–4):

1. Heavy, large, or small behind super – *3 minutes.*

2. Heavy, large, or small behind heavy – *2 minutes.*

FIG 3–9–4
Same Runway Separation

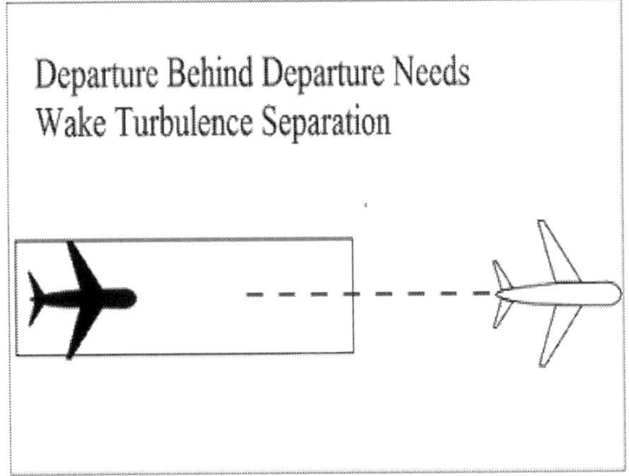

g. Separate a small behind a B757 aircraft by *2 minutes* when departing:

1. The same runway or a parallel runway separated by less than 700 feet. (See FIG 3–9–5 and FIG 3–9–6.)

FIG 3–9–5
Same Runway Separation

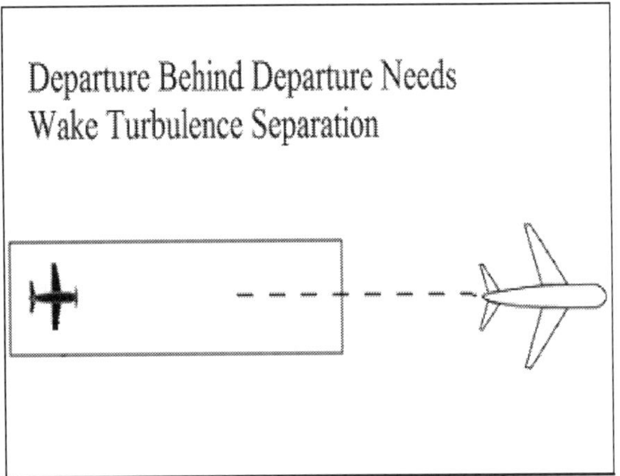

FIG 3–9–6
Parallel Runway Separated by Less than 700 Feet

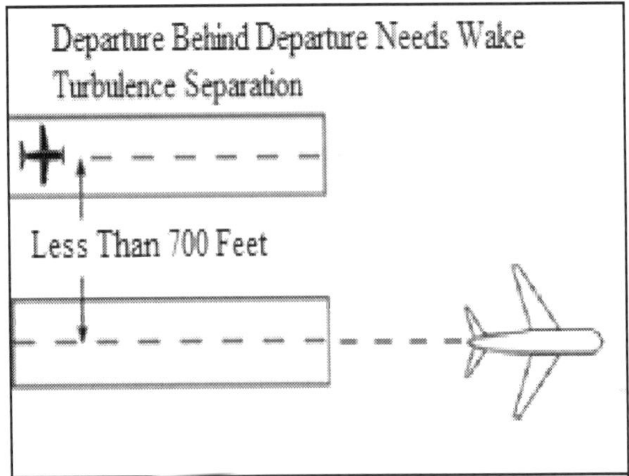

2. A parallel runway separated by 700 feet or more if projected flight paths will cross. (See FIG 3–9–7).

FIG 3–9–7
Parallel Runway Separated by 700 Feet or More Projected Flight Paths Cross

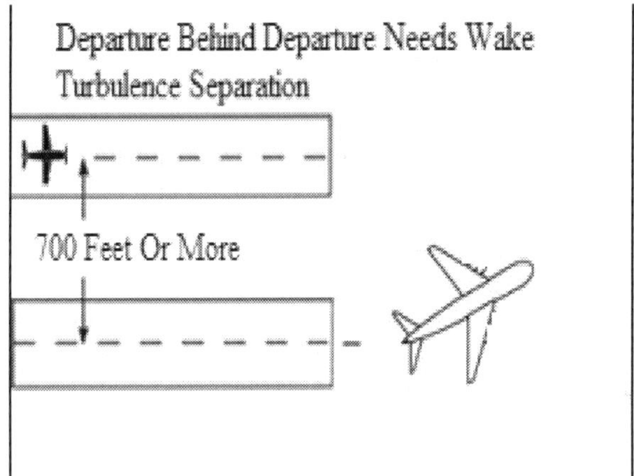

h. Separate aircraft departing from a parallel runway separated by 2,500 feet or more if projected flight paths will cross (See FIG 3–9–8):

1. Heavy, large, or small behind super – *3 minutes.*

2. Heavy, large, or small behind heavy – *2 minutes.*

FIG 3–9–8
Parallel Runways Separated by 2,500 feet or More

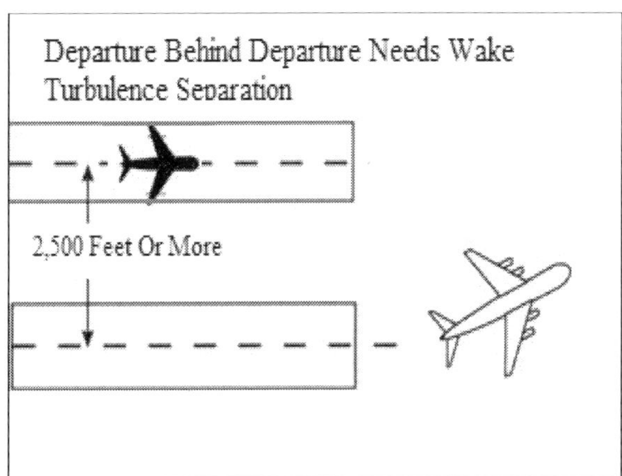

i. Separate aircraft when operating on a runway with a displaced landing threshold if projected flight paths will cross when either a departure follows an arrival or an arrival follows a departure by the following minima:

1. Heavy, large, or small behind super – *3 minutes.*

2. Heavy, large, or small behind heavy – *2 minutes.*

3. Small behind B757 – *2 minutes.*

j. Separate an aircraft behind another aircraft that has departed or made a low/missed approach when utilizing opposite direction takeoffs or landings on the same or parallel runways separated by less than 2,500 feet by the following minima:

1. Heavy, large, or small behind super – *4 minutes.*

2. Heavy, large, or small behind heavy – *3 minutes*

k. Separate a small aircraft behind a B757 that has departed or made a low/missed approach by *3 minutes* when utilizing opposite direction takeoffs or landings from:

1. The same runway or a parallel runway separated by less than 700 feet.

2. A parallel runway separated by 700 feet or more if projected flight paths will cross.

l. Do not approve pilot requests to deviate from the required intervals contained in subparagraphs f through k.

PHRASEOLOGY–
HOLD FOR WAKE TURBULENCE.

REFERENCE–
FAA Order JO 7110.65, Para 3–9–7, Wake Turbulence Separation for Intersection Departures.

m. Separate a small aircraft behind a large aircraft (except B757) that has departed or made a low/missed approach when utilizing opposite direction takeoffs on the same runway by *3 minutes* unless a pilot has initiated a request to deviate from the time interval. In the latter case, issue a wake turbulence cautionary advisory before clearing the aircraft for takeoff. Controllers must not initiate or suggest a waiver of the time interval.

NOTE–
A request for takeoff does not initiate a waiver request.

n. Inform aircraft when it is necessary to hold in order to provide the required time interval.

3–9–7. WAKE TURBULENCE SEPARATION FOR INTERSECTION DEPARTURES

a. Apply the following wake turbulence criteria for intersection departures:

1. Separate a small aircraft weighing 12,500 lbs. or less taking off from an intersection on the same runway (same or opposite direction takeoff) behind a departing small aircraft weighing more than 12,500 lbs. by ensuring that the aircraft does not start takeoff roll until at least *3 minutes* after the preceding aircraft has taken off.

2. Separate a small aircraft taking off from an intersection on the same runway (same or opposite direction takeoff) behind a departing large aircraft (except B757) by ensuring that the aircraft does not start takeoff roll until at least *3 minutes* after the preceding aircraft has taken off.

3. Separate a small aircraft taking off from an intersection (same or opposite direction takeoff) behind a preceding departing B757 aircraft by ensuring that the small aircraft does not start takeoff roll until at least *3 minutes* after the B757 has taken off from:

(a) The same runway or a parallel runway separated by less than 700 feet.

(b) Parallel runways separated by 700 feet or more, or parallel runways separated by 700 feet or more with the runway thresholds offset by 500 feet or more, if projected flight paths will cross.

4. Separate aircraft departing from an intersection on the same runway (same or opposite direction takeoff), parallel runways separated by less than 2,500 feet, and parallel runways separated by less than 2,500 feet with the runway thresholds offset by 500 feet or more, by ensuring that the aircraft does not start take-off roll until the following intervals exist after the preceding aircraft has taken off:

NOTE–
Apply paragraph 3–9–6, Same Runway Separation, subparagraph f to parallel runways separated by less than 2,500 feet with runway thresholds offset by less than 500 feet.

(a) Heavy, large, or small behind super - *4 minutes.*

(b) Heavy, large, or small behind heavy - *3 minutes.*

5. Inform aircraft when it is necessary to hold in order to provide the required time interval.

PHRASEOLOGY–
HOLD FOR WAKE TURBULENCE.

NOTE–
Aircraft conducting touch-and-go and stop-and-go operations are considered to be departing from an intersection.

REFERENCE–
FAA Order JO 7110.65, Para 3–8–2, Touch–and–Go or Stop–and–Go or Low Approach.

b. The time interval is not required when:

1. A pilot has initiated a request to deviate from the time intervals contained in subparagraph a1 or a2.

NOTE–
A request for takeoff does not initiate a waiver request; the request for takeoff must be accomplished by a request to deviate from the time interval.

2. USA NOT APPLICABLE. The intersection is 500 feet or less from the departure point of the preceding aircraft and both aircraft are taking off in the same direction.

3. Successive touch-and-go or stop-and-go operations are conducted with any aircraft following an aircraft in the pattern that requires wake turbulence separation, or an aircraft departing the same runway that requires wake turbulence separation in accordance with subparagraphs a1, a2, a3, or a4 (except for super aircraft), provided the pilot is maintaining visual separation/spacing behind the preceding aircraft. Issue a wake turbulence cautionary advisory and the position of the larger aircraft.

NOTE–
Not authorized with a Super as the lead or departure aircraft.

REFERENCE–
FAA Order JO 7110.65, Para 5–5–4, Minima, subpara g.
FAA Order JO 7110.65, Para 7–2–1, Visual Separation.

4. If action is initiated to reduce the separation between successive touch-and-go or stop-and-go operations, apply the appropriate separation contained in subparagraph a1, a2, a3, or a4.

c. When applying the provision of subparagraph b:

1. Issue a wake turbulence advisory before clearing the aircraft for takeoff.

2. Do not clear the intersection departure for an immediate takeoff.

3. Issue a clearance to permit the trailing aircraft to deviate from course enough to avoid the flight path of the preceding aircraft when applying subparagraph b1 or b2.

4. Separation requirements in accordance with paragraph 3–9–6, Same Runway Separation, must also apply.

REFERENCE–
FAA Order JO 7110.65, Para 3–9–6, Same Runway Separation.

3–9–8. INTERSECTING RUNWAY/INTERSECTING FLIGHT PATH OPERATIONS

a. Issue traffic information to each aircraft operating on intersecting runways.

b. Separate departing aircraft from another aircraft using an intersecting runway by ensuring that the departure does not begin takeoff roll until one of the following exists:

REFERENCE–
FAA Order JO 7110.65, Para 2–1–21, Traffic Advisories.

1. The preceding aircraft has departed and passed the intersection or is turning to avert any conflict. (See FIG 3–9–9).

FIG 3-9-9
Intersecting Runway Separation

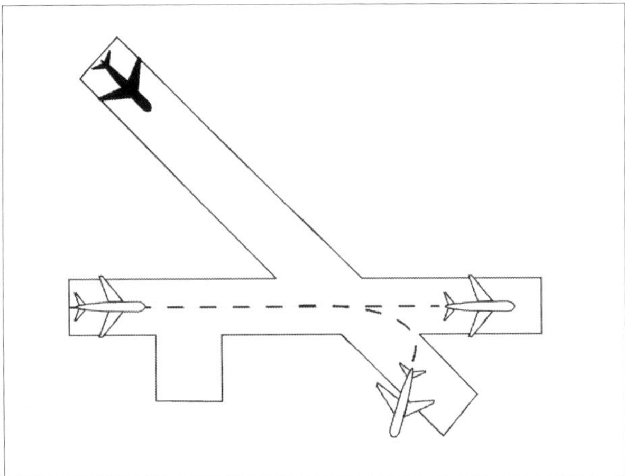

2. A preceding arriving aircraft (See FIG 3-9-10).

(a) Is clear of the landing runway, or

(b) Has completed the landing roll on the runway and will hold short of the intersection, or

(c) Has landed and will hold short of an intersecting runway, intersecting taxiway, intersecting approach/departure flight path, or other predetermined point in accordance with the Land and Hold Short Operations (LAHSO) directive, or

(d) Has completed the landing roll and is observed turning at an exit point prior to the intersection, or

(e) Has passed the intersection.

REFERENCE-
FAA Order 7110.118, Land and Hold Short Operations (LAHSO).
P/CG Term- Clear of the Runway.
P/CG Term - Landing Roll.

FIG 3-9-10
Intersecting Runway Separation

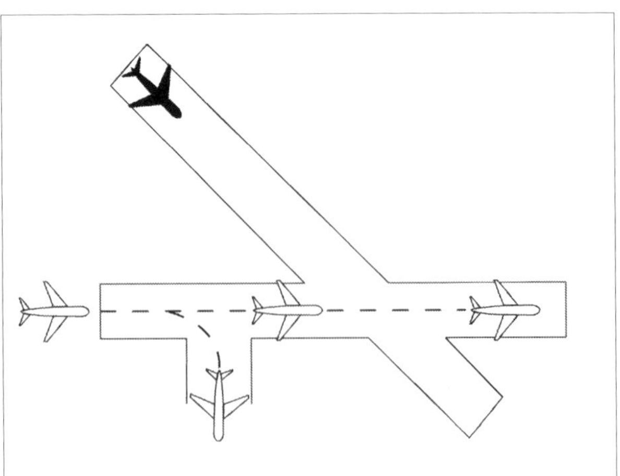

WAKE TURBULENCE APPLICATION

3. Separate aircraft taking off behind a departing or landing aircraft on an intersecting runway if flight paths will cross (see FIG 3-9-11 and FIG 3-9-12):

NOTE–
Takeoff clearance to the following aircraft should not be issued until the appropriate time interval has passed after the preceding aircraft began takeoff roll.

(a) Heavy, large, or small behind super – *3 minutes.*

(b) Heavy, large, or small behind heavy – *2 minutes.*

(c) Small behind B757 – *2 minutes.*

FIG 3–9–11
Departure Behind Departure on Intersecting Runway

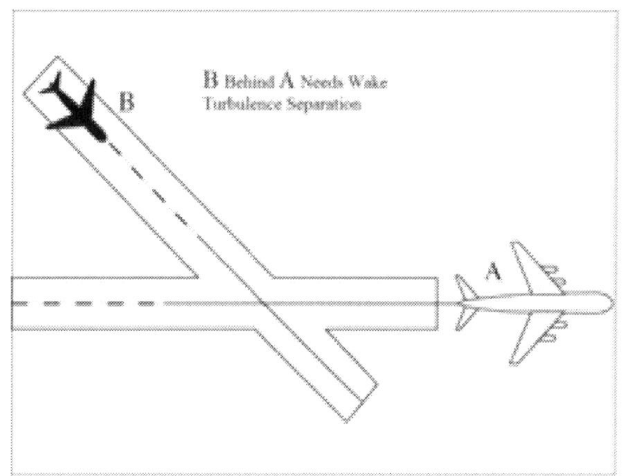

FIG 3–9–12
Departure Behind Arrival on Intersecting Runway

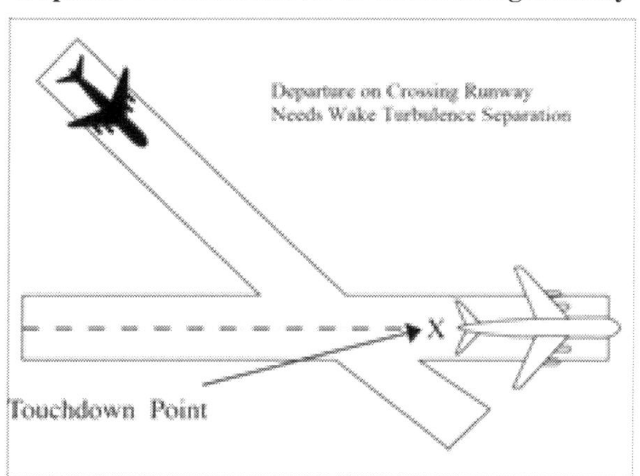

4. Pilot requests to deviate from the required time intervals must not be approved if the preceding aircraft requires wake turbulence separation.

REFERENCE–
FAA Order JO 7110.65, Para 5–5–4, Minima, Subpara g.

3–9–9. NONINTERSECTING CONVERGING RUNWAY OPERATIONS

a. Separate departing aircraft from an aircraft using a nonintersecting runway when the flight paths intersect by ensuring that the departure does not begin takeoff roll until one of the following exists:

REFERENCE–
FAA Order JO 7110.65, Para 2–1–21, Traffic Advisories.

1. The preceding aircraft has departed and crossed the departure runway, or is turning to avert any conflict (see FIG 3–9–13).

FIG 3–9–13
Intersecting Runway Separation

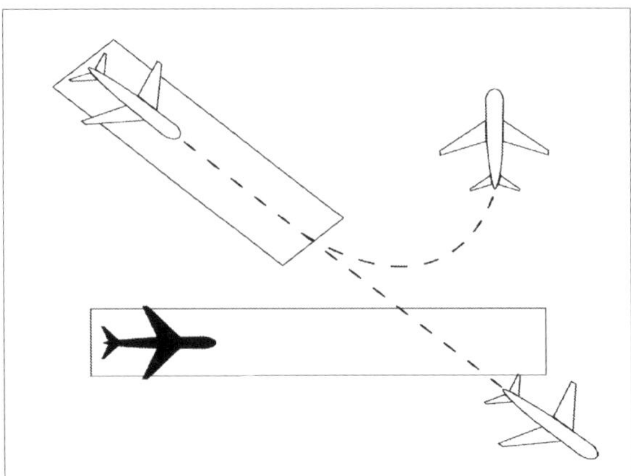

2. A preceding arriving aircraft has completed the landing roll and will hold short of the projected intersection, passed the projected intersection, or has crossed over the departure runway (see FIG 3–9–14 and FIG 3–9–15).

FIG 3–9–14
Intersecting Runway Separation

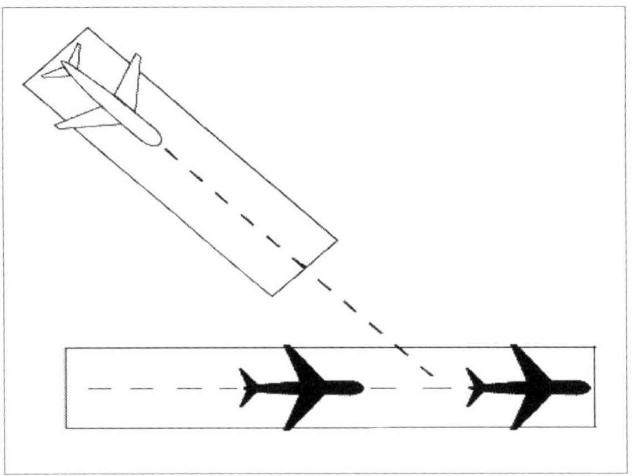

FIG 3–9–15
Intersecting Runway Separation

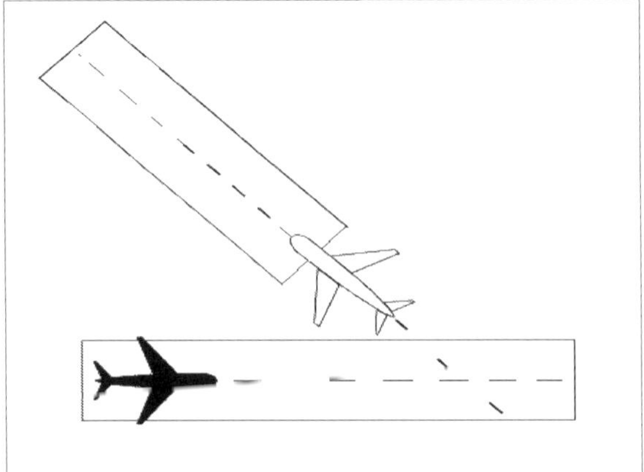

b. If the extended centerline of a runway crosses a converging runway or the extended centerline of a converging runway at a distance of 1 NM or less from either departure end, apply the provisions of paragraph

3–9–8, Intersecting Runway/ Intersecting Flight Path Operations, unless the facility is using aids specified in a facility directive, (may include but are not limited to, Arrival/Departure Window (ADW), ASDE–X Virtual Runway Intersection Point (VRIP), cut–off points or automation). (See FIG 3–9–16 and FIG 3–9–17.)

REFERENCE–
FAA Order JO 7210.3, Para 10-3-15, Go-Around/Missed Approach.

FIG 3–9–16
Intersecting Runway Separation

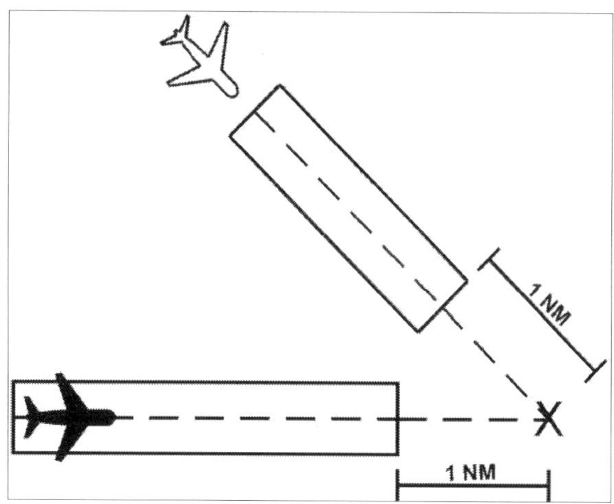

FIG 3–9–17
Intersecting Runway Separation

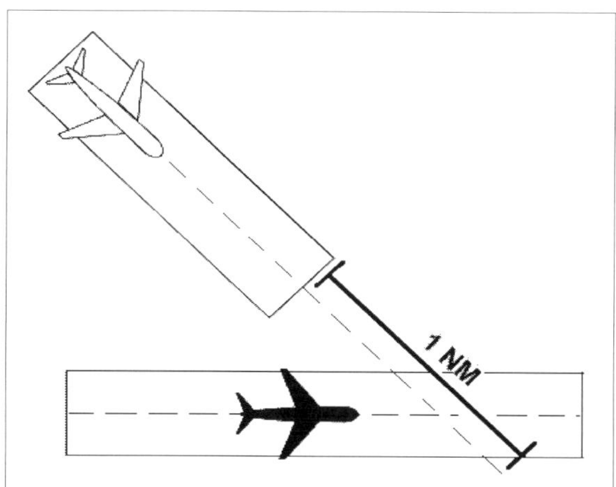

WAKE TURBULENCE APPLICATION

c. Separate aircraft taking off behind a departing aircraft on a crossing runway if projected flight paths will cross (See FIG 3–9–18):

1. Heavy, large, or small behind super – *3 minutes.*

2. Heavy, large, or small behind heavy – *2 minutes.*

3. Small behind B757 – *2 minutes.*

FIG 3-9-18
Intersecting Runway Separation

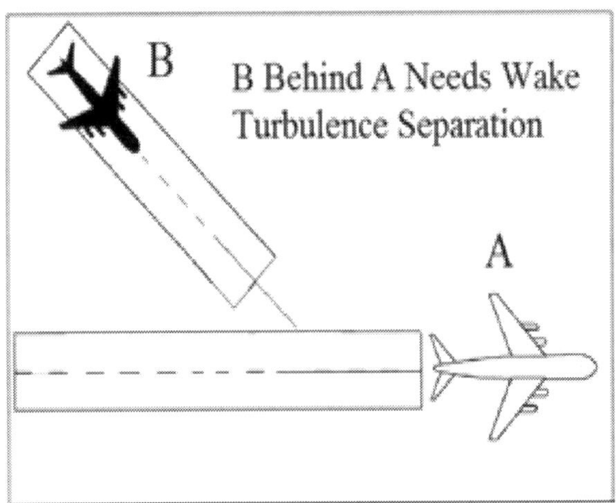

NOTE–
Takeoff clearance to the following aircraft should not be issued until the time interval has passed from when the preceding aircraft began takeoff roll.

d. Separate aircraft departing behind a landing aircraft on a crossing runway if the departure will fly through the airborne path of the arrival (See FIG 3-9-19):

1. Heavy, large, or small behind super – *3 minutes.*

2. Heavy, large, or small behind heavy – *2 minutes.*

3. Small behind B757 – *2 minutes.*

FIG 3-9-19
Intersecting Runway Separation

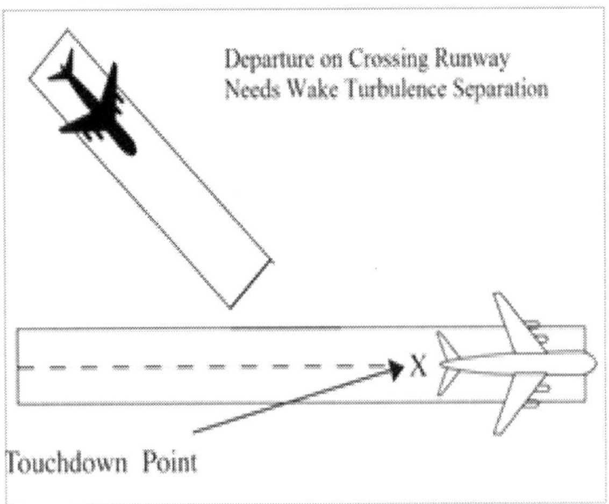

e. Do not approve pilot requests to deviate from the required time interval if the preceding aircraft requires wake turbulence separation.

REFERENCE–
FAA Order JO 7110.65, Para 5-8-3, Successive or Simultaneous Departures.
FAA Order JO 7110.65, Para 5-8-5, Departures and Arrivals on Parallel or Nonintersecting Diverging Runways.
FAA Order JO 7110.65, Para 5-5-4, Minima, Subpara g.

3-9-10. TAKEOFF CLEARANCE

a. When issuing a clearance for takeoff, first state the runway number followed by the takeoff clearance.

PHRASEOLOGY−
RUNWAY (number), CLEARED FOR TAKEOFF.

EXAMPLE−
"RUNWAY TWO SEVEN, CLEARED FOR TAKEOFF."

NOTE−
Turbine−powered aircraft may be considered ready for takeoff when they reach the runway unless they advise otherwise.

REFERENCE−
FAA Order JO 7110.65, Para 4−3−1, Departure Terminology.

b. When clearing an aircraft for takeoff from an intersection, state the runway intersection.

PHRASEOLOGY−
RUNWAY (number) AT (taxiway designator) CLEARED FOR TAKEOFF.

c. When two or more aircraft call the tower ready for departure, one or more at the full length of a runway and one or more at an intersection, state the location of the aircraft at the full length of the runway when clearing that aircraft for takeoff.

PHRASEOLOGY−
RUNWAY (number), FULL LENGTH, CLEARED FOR TAKEOFF.

EXAMPLE−
"American Four Eighty Two, Runway Three Zero full length, cleared for takeoff."

d. The controller must ensure that all runways along the taxi route that lead to the departure runway are crossed before the takeoff clearance is issued, except as stated in paragraph 3−9−10e.

FIG 3−9−20
Runway/Taxiway Proximity

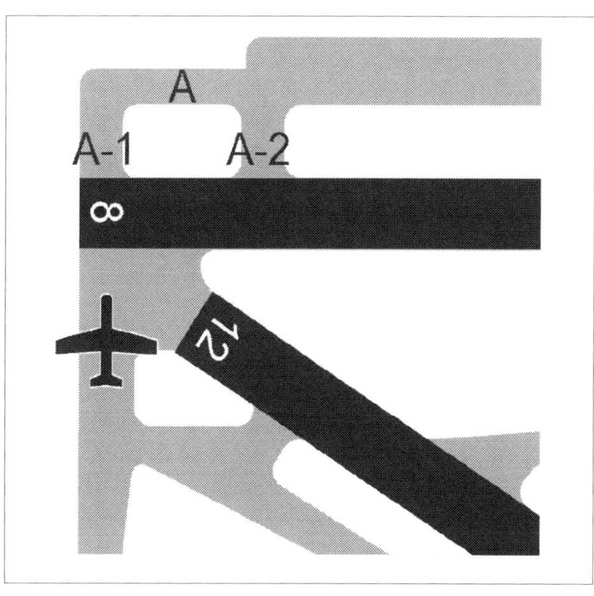

e. At those airports where the airport configuration does not allow for an aircraft to completely cross one runway and hold short of the departure runway and/or where airports do not have runway hold markings between runways, state the runway to be crossed with the takeoff clearance if the aircraft is not able to complete a runway crossing before reaching its departure runway.

PHRASEOLOGY−
CROSS RUNWAY (number), RUNWAY (number) CLEARED FOR TAKEOFF.

EXAMPLE−
"CROSS RUNWAY TWO FOUR LEFT, RUNWAY TWO FOUR RIGHT, CLEARED FOR TAKEOFF."

FIG 3-9-21
Runway/Taxiway Proximity

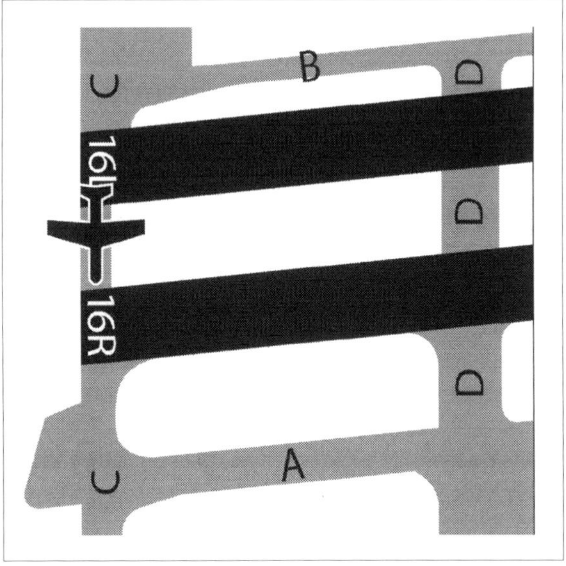

REFERENCE-
FAA Order JO 7210.3, Para 10-3-10, Takeoff Clearance.
P/CG Term - Clear of the Runway.

f. Do not use the term "full length" when the runway length available for departure has been temporarily shortened. On permanently shortened runways, do not use the term "full length" until the Chart Supplement is updated to include the change(s).

NOTE-
The use of the term "full length" could be interpreted by the pilot(s) as the available runway length prior to the runway being shortened.

g. Whenever a runway length has been temporarily or permanently shortened, state the word "shortened" immediately following the runway number as part of the takeoff clearance. This information must be issued in conjunction with the takeoff clearance.

1. The addition of "shortened" must be included in the takeoff clearance for the duration of the construction project when the runway is temporarily shortened.

2. The addition of "shortened" must be included in the takeoff clearance until the Chart Supplement is updated to include the change(s) when the runway is permanently shortened.

PHRASEOLOGY-
RUNWAY (number) SHORTENED, CLEARED FOR TAKEOFF.

EXAMPLE-
"Runway Two-Seven shortened, cleared for takeoff."

PHRASEOLOGY-
RUNWAY (number) AT (taxiway designator) INTERSECTION DEPARTURE SHORTENED, CLEARED FOR TAKEOFF.

EXAMPLE-
"Runway Two-Seven at Juliett, intersection departure shortened, cleared for takeoff."

REFERENCE-
FAA Order JO 7210.3, Para 10-3-12, Airport Construction.
FAA Order JO 7210.3, Para 10-3-13, Change in Runway Length Due to Construction.

h. *USAF.* When an aircraft is cleared for takeoff, inform it of the closest traffic within 6 miles on final approach to the same runway. If the approaching aircraft is on a different frequency, inform it of the departing aircraft.

i. *USA/USN/USAF.* Issue surface wind and takeoff clearance to aircraft.

PHRASEOLOGY–
RUNWAY (number), WIND (surface wind in direction and velocity). CLEARED FOR TAKEOFF.

3–9–11. CANCELLATION OF TAKEOFF CLEARANCE

Cancel a previously issued clearance for takeoff and inform the pilot of the reason if circumstances require. Once an aircraft has started takeoff roll, cancel the takeoff clearance only for the purpose of safety.

NOTE–
In no case should a takeoff clearance be canceled after an aircraft has started its takeoff roll solely for the purpose of meeting traffic management requirements/EDCT.

PHRASEOLOGY–
CANCEL TAKEOFF CLEARANCE (reason).

Section 10. Arrival Procedures and Separation

3–10–1. LANDING INFORMATION

Provide current landing information, as appropriate, to arriving aircraft. Landing information contained in the ATIS broadcast may be omitted if the pilot states the appropriate ATIS code. Runway, wind, and altimeter may be omitted if a pilot uses the phrase "have numbers." Issue landing information by including the following:

NOTE–
Pilot use of "have numbers" does not indicate receipt of the ATIS broadcast.

a. Specific traffic pattern information (may be omitted if the aircraft is to circle the airport to the left).

PHRASEOLOGY–
ENTER LEFT/RIGHT BASE.

STRAIGHT–IN.

MAKE STRAIGHT–IN.

STRAIGHT–IN APPROVED.

RIGHT TRAFFIC.

MAKE RIGHT TRAFFIC.

RIGHT TRAFFIC APPROVED.

CONTINUE.

NOTE–
Additional information should normally be issued with instructions to continue. Example: "continue, report one mile final"; "continue, expect landing clearance two mile final"; etc.

b. Runway in use.

c. Surface wind.

d. Altimeter setting.

REFERENCE–
FAA Order JO 7110.65, Para 2–7–1, Current Settings.

e. Any supplementary information.

f. Clearance to land.

g. Requests for additional position reports. Use prominent geographical fixes which can be easily recognized from the air, preferably those depicted on sectional charts. This does not preclude the use of the legs of the traffic pattern as reporting points.

NOTE–
At some locations, VFR checkpoints are depicted on sectional aeronautical and terminal area charts. In selecting geographical fixes, depicted VFR checkpoints are preferred unless the pilot exhibits a familiarity with the local area.

h. Ceiling and visibility if either is below basic VFR minima.

i. Low level wind shear or microburst advisories when available.

REFERENCE–
FAA Order JO 7110.65, Para 3–1–8, Low Level Wind Shear/Microburst Advisories.

j. Issue braking action for the runway in use as received from pilots when braking action advisories are in effect.

REFERENCE–
FAA Order JO 7110.65, Para 3–3–5 , Braking Action Advisories.

k. Runway Condition Codes. Furnish RwyCC, as received from the Airport Operator, to aircraft via the ATIS.

l. For opposite direction arrival operations, controllers may verbally issue the RwyCC, as identified in the FICON NOTAM, in reverse order. Controllers must not include reversed RwyCC on the ATIS broadcast.

m. If the pilot does not indicate the appropriate ATIS code, and when a runway has been shortened, controllers must ensure that pilots receive the runway number combined with a shortened announcement for all arriving aircraft.

3–10–2. FORWARDING APPROACH INFORMATION BY NONAPPROACH CONTROL FACILITIES

a. Forward the following, as appropriate, to the control facility having IFR jurisdiction in your area. You may eliminate those items that, because of local conditions or situations, are fully covered in a letter of agreement or a facility directive.

1. When you clear an arriving aircraft for a visual approach.

REFERENCE–
FAA Order JO 7110.65, Para 7–4–1 , Visual Approach.

2. Aircraft arrival time.

3. Cancellation of IFR flight plan.

4. Information on a missed approach, unreported, or overdue aircraft.

5. Runway in use.

6. Weather as required.

REFERENCE–
FAA Order JO 7110.65, Para 2–6–3, Reporting Weather Conditions.

b. When the weather is below 1,000 feet or 3 miles or the highest circling minimums, whichever is greater, issue current weather to aircraft executing an instrument approach if it changes from that on the ATIS or that previously forwarded to the center/approach control.

3–10–3. SAME RUNWAY SEPARATION

a. Separate an arriving aircraft from another aircraft using the same runway by ensuring that the arriving aircraft does not cross the landing threshold until one of the following conditions exists or unless authorized in paragraph 3–10–10, Altitude Restricted Low Approach.

1. The other aircraft has landed and is clear of the runway. (See FIG 3–10–1.) Between sunrise and sunset, if you can determine distances by reference to suitable landmarks and the other aircraft has landed, it need not be clear of the runway if the following minimum distance from the landing threshold exists:

REFERENCE–
P/CG Term – Clear of the Runway.

FIG 3–10–1
Same Runway Separation

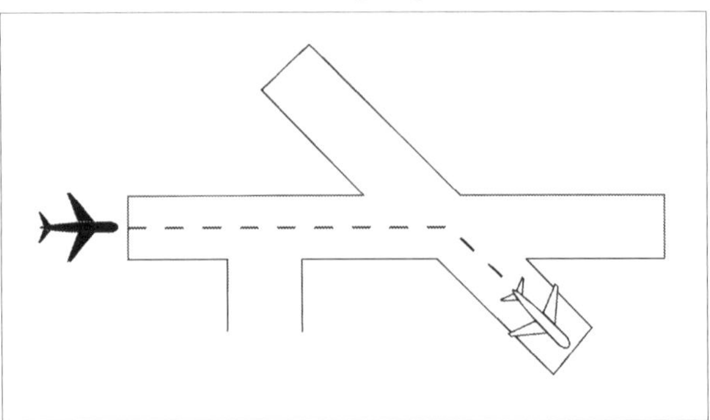

(a) When a Category I aircraft is landing behind a Category I or II– *3,000 feet.* (See FIG 3–10–2.)

FIG 3–10–2
Same Runway Separation

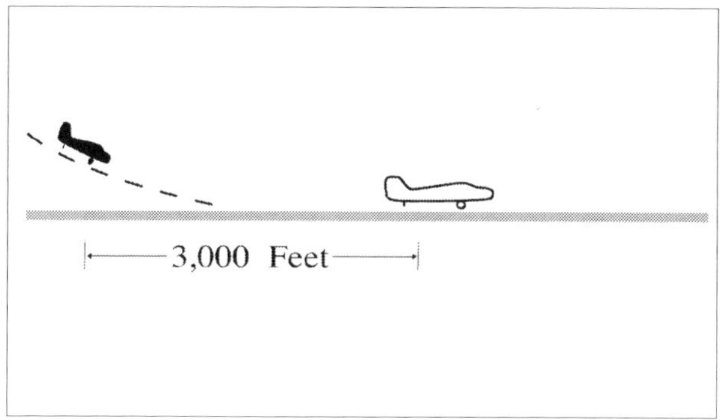

(b) When a Category II aircraft is landing behind a Category I or II– *4,500 feet.* (See FIG 3–10–3.)

FIG 3–10–3
Same Runway Separation

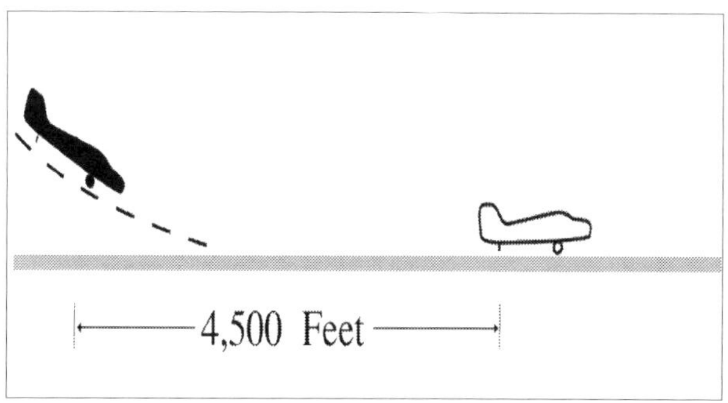

2. The other aircraft has departed and crossed the runway end. (See FIG 3–10–4). If you can determine distances by reference to suitable landmarks and the other aircraft is airborne, it need not have crossed the runway end if the following minimum distance from the landing threshold exists:

(a) Category I aircraft landing behind Category I or II– *3,000 feet.*

(b) Category II aircraft landing behind Category I or II– *4,500 feet.*

(c) When either is a category III aircraft– *6,000 feet.* (See FIG 3–10–5.)

FIG 3–10–4
Same Runway Separation

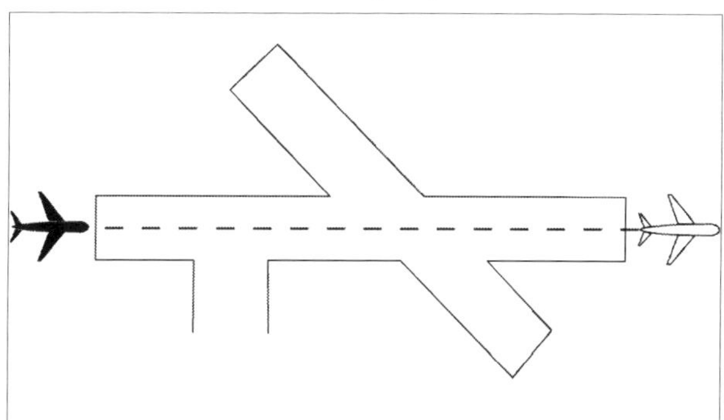

FIG 3-10-5
Same Runway Separation

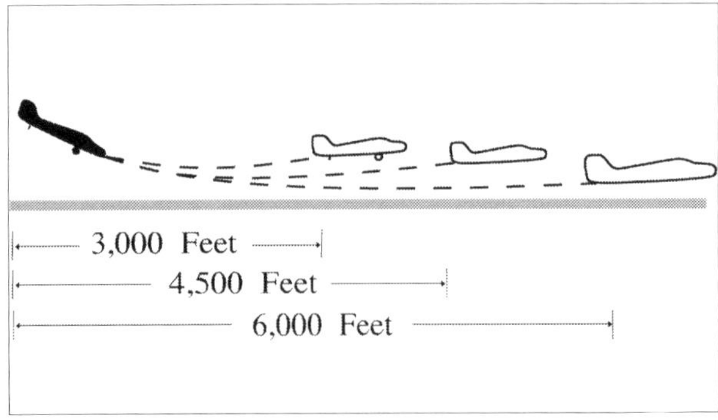

3. When the succeeding aircraft is a helicopter, visual separation may be applied in lieu of using distance minima.

WAKE TURBULENCE APPLICATION

b. Issue wake turbulence advisories, and the position, altitude if known, and the direction of flight of:

1. The super or heavy to aircraft landing behind a departing/arriving super or heavy on the same or parallel runways separated by less than 2,500 feet.

2. The B757/large aircraft to a small aircraft landing behind a departing/arriving B757/large aircraft on the same or parallel runways separated by less than 2,500 feet.

REFERENCE-
AC 90-23, Aircraft Wake Turbulence, Para 12, Pilot Responsibility.
FAA Order JO 7110.65, Para 3-10-10, Altitude Restricted Low Approach.

EXAMPLE-
1. *"Runway two seven left cleared to land, caution wake turbulence, heavy Boeing 747 departing runway two seven right."*

2. *"Number two follow Boeing 757 on 2-mile final. Caution wake turbulence."*

3. *"Traffic, Boeing 737 on 2-mile final to the parallel runway, runway two six right, cleared to land. Caution wake turbulence."*

3-10-4. INTERSECTING RUNWAY/INTERSECTING FLIGHT PATH OPERATIONS

Issue traffic information to each aircraft operating on intersecting runways.

a. Separate an arriving aircraft using one runway from another aircraft using an intersecting runway or a nonintersecting runway when the flight paths intersect by ensuring that the arriving aircraft does not cross the landing threshold or flight path of the other aircraft until one of the following conditions exists:

REFERENCE-
FAA Order JO 7110.65, Para 2-1-21, Traffic Advisories.

INTERPRETATION-
7110.65, 3-10-4, Intersecting Runway/Intersecting Flight Path Separation and 5-5-4, Minima (2021-06-09)

1. The preceding aircraft has departed and passed the intersection/flight path or is airborne and turning to avert any conflict. (See FIG 3-10-6 and FIG 3-10-7.)

FIG 3−10−6
Intersecting Runway Separation

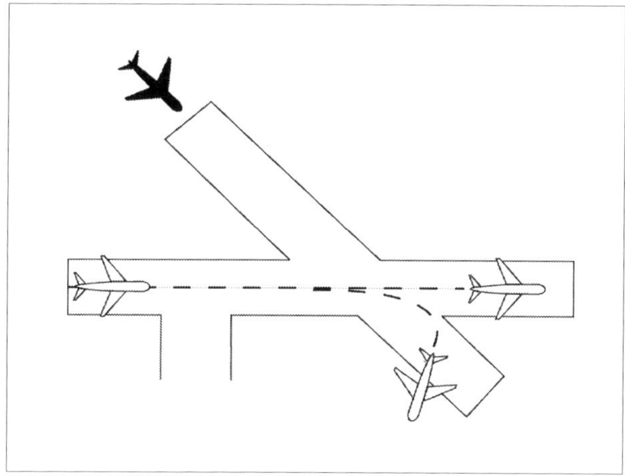

FIG 3−10−7
Intersecting Runway Separation

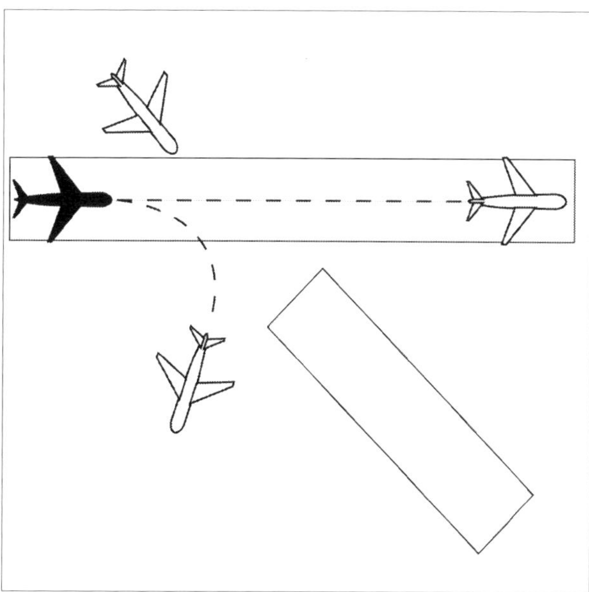

2. A preceding arriving aircraft is clear of the landing runway, completed landing roll and will hold short of the intersection/flight path, or has passed the intersection/flight path. (See FIG 3−10−8 and FIG 3−10−9.)

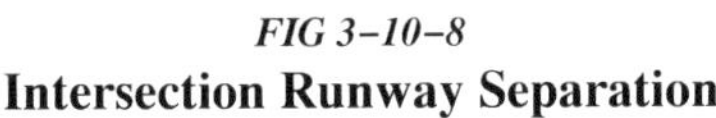

FIG 3-10-8
Intersection Runway Separation

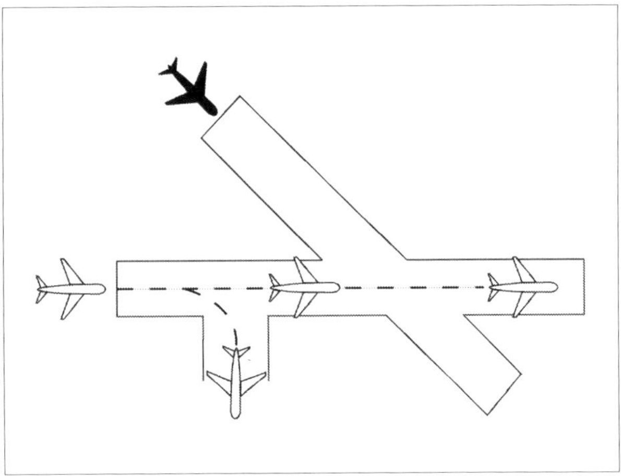

FIG 3-10-9
Intersection Runway Separation

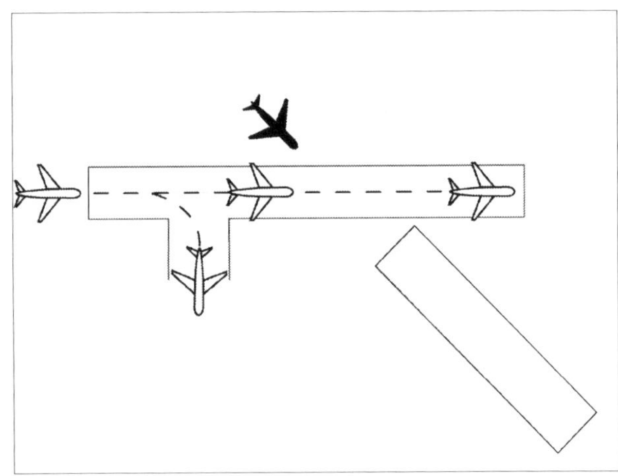

NOTE–
When visual separation is being applied by the tower, appropriate control instructions and traffic advisories must be issued to ensure go around or missed approaches avert any conflict with the flight path of traffic on the other runway.

REFERENCE–
FAA Order JO 7110.65, Para 7-2-1, Visual Separation, Subpara a2.

b. "USA/USAF/USN NOT APPLICABLE." An arriving aircraft may be authorized to land and hold short of an intersecting runway, an intersecting taxiway, an intersecting approach/departure flight path, or other predetermined point in accordance with procedures specified in the LAHSO directive. The following conditions apply:

NOTE–
Application of these procedures does not relieve controllers from the responsibility of providing other appropriate separation contained in this order.

REFERENCE–
FAA Order 7110.118, Land and Hold Short Operations (LAHSO).
FAA Order JO 7210.3, Para 10-3-7, Land and Hold Short Operations (LAHSO).

1. A simultaneous takeoff and landing operation must only be conducted in VFR conditions.

2. Instruct the landing aircraft to hold short of the intersecting runway being used by the aircraft taking off. In the case of simultaneous landings and no operational benefit is lost, restrict the aircraft of the lesser weight category (if known). LAHSO clearances must only be issued to aircraft that are listed in the current LAHSO directive, whose Available Landing Distance (ALD) does not exceed the landing distance requirement for the runway condition.

PHRASEOLOGY–
HOLD SHORT OF RUNWAY (runway number), (traffic, type aircraft or other information).

NOTE–
Pilots who prefer to use the full length of the runway or a runway different from that specified are expected to advise ATC prior to landing.

3. Issue traffic information to both aircraft involved and obtain an acknowledgment from each. Request a read back of hold short instructions when they are not received from the pilot of the restricted aircraft.

EXAMPLE–
1. *"Runway one eight cleared to land, hold short of runway one four left, traffic, (type aircraft) landing runway one four left."*

(When pilot of restricted aircraft responds with only acknowledgment):

"Runway one four left cleared to land, traffic, (type aircraft) landing runway one eight will hold short of the intersection."

"Read back hold short instructions."

2. *"Runway three six cleared to land, hold short of runway three three, traffic, (type aircraft) departing runway three three."*

"Traffic, (type aircraft) landing runway three six will hold short of the intersection, runway three three cleared for takeoff."

4. Issue the measured distance from the landing threshold to the hold short point rounded "down" to the nearest 50–foot increment if requested by either aircraft.

EXAMPLE–
"Five thousand fifty feet available."

5. The conditions in subparagraphs b2, 3, and 4 must be met in sufficient time for the pilots to take other action, if desired, and no later than the time landing clearance is issued.

6. Land and Hold Short runways must be free of any contamination as described in the current LAHSO directive, with no reports that braking action is less than good.

7. There is no tailwind for the landing aircraft restricted to hold short of the intersection. The wind may be described as "calm" when appropriate.

REFERENCE–
FAA Order JO 7110.65, Para 2–6–3, Reporting Weather Conditions.

8. The aircraft required landing distances are listed in the current LAHSO directive.

9. STOL aircraft operations are in accordance with a letter of agreement with the aircraft operator/pilot or the pilot confirms that it is a STOL aircraft.

WAKE TURBULENCE APPLICATION

c. Separate aircraft landing behind a departing aircraft on a crossing runway if the arrival will fly through the airborne path of the departure by the appropriate radar separation or the following interval: (See FIG 3–10–10):

1. Heavy, large, or small behind super – *3 minutes.*

2. Heavy, large, or small behind heavy – *2 minutes.*

3. Small behind B757 – *2 minutes.*

d. Issue wake turbulence cautionary advisories, the position, altitude if known, and direction of flight of the super, heavy, or B757 to:

REFERENCE–
AC 90–23, Aircraft Wake Turbulence, Para 11, Pilot Responsibility.

FIG 3–10–10
Intersecting Runway Separation

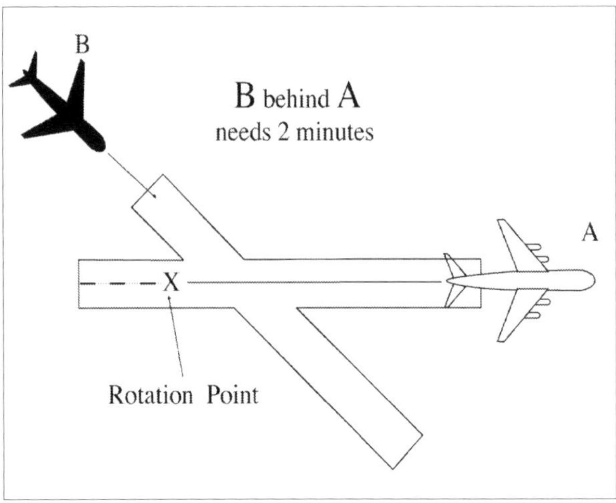

1. All aircraft landing on a crossing runway behind a departing super or heavy, or a small aircraft landing on a crossing runway behind a departing B757, if the arrival flight path will cross the takeoff path behind the departing aircraft rotation point. (See FIG 3–10–11.)

FIG 3–10–11
Intersecting Runway Separation

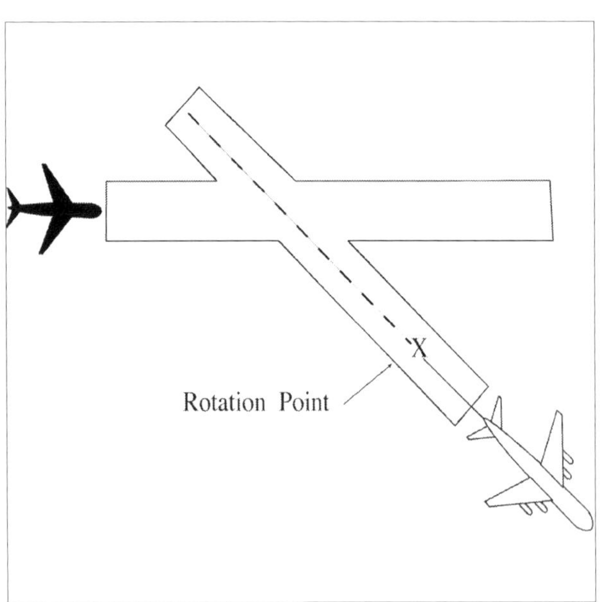

EXAMPLE–
"Runway niner cleared to land. Caution wake turbulence, heavy C–One Forty One departing runway one five."

2. All VFR aircraft landing on a crossing runway behind an arriving super or heavy, and VFR small aircraft landing on a crossing runway behind a B757, if the arrival flight paths will cross. (See FIG 3–10–12.)

FIG 3–10–12
Intersecting Runway Separation

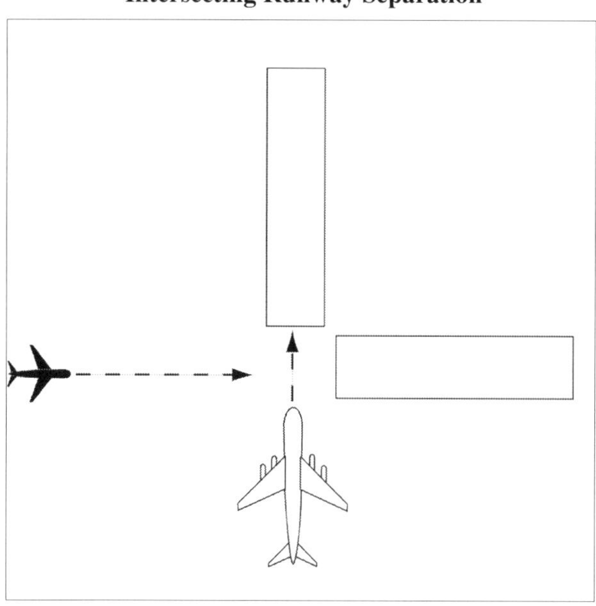

EXAMPLE–
"Runway niner cleared to land. Caution wake turbulence, Boeing Seven Fifty Seven landing runway three six."
REFERENCE–
FAA Order JO 7110.65, Para 7–4–4, Approaches to Multiple Runways.

3–10–5. LANDING CLEARANCE

a. When issuing a clearance to land, first state the runway number followed by the landing clearance. If the landing runway is changed, controllers must preface the landing clearance with "Change to runway" followed by the runway number. Controllers must then restate the runway number followed by the landing clearance.

PHRASEOLOGY–
RUNWAY (number) CLEARED TO LAND.

Or

CHANGE TO RUNWAY (number, RUNWAY (number) CLEARED TO LAND.

NOTE–
The purpose of the "change to runway" phraseology and restating the runway number is to emphasize to the pilot that they are being cleared to land on a runway other than what they were expecting.

b. When you become aware that an aircraft is aligned with the wrong surface, inform the pilot and:

1. Issue control instructions/clearances, or

EXAMPLE–
"United four twenty three, go–around, you appear to be aligned with the wrong runway."

"American sixty three, go–around, you appear to be aligned with a taxiway."

"Southwest two thirty nine, you appear to be aligned with Runway 27 Left (pertinent information), Runway 27 Left, cleared to land."

2. If time permits, verify the pilot is aligned with the correct runway. Issue control instructions/clearances as necessary.

EXAMPLE–
"Twin Cessna four one four lima bravo, verify you are aligned with Runway 27 Left."

REFERENCE–
FAA Order JO 7110.65, Para 3–6–4, Safety Logic Alert Responses.
FAA Order JO 7110.65, Para 3–10–8, Withholding Landing Clearance.

c. Procedures.

1. Facilities without a safety logic system or facilities with the safety logic system inoperative or in the limited configuration must not clear an aircraft for a full-stop, touch-and-go, stop-and-go, low approach, or option on the same runway with an aircraft holding in position or taxiing to LUAW until the aircraft in position has exited the runway or starts takeoff roll.

2. Facilities using safety logic in the full core alert runway configuration may clear an aircraft for a full-stop, touch-and-go, stop-and-go, low approach, or option on the same runway with an aircraft holding in position or taxiing to LUAW except when reported weather conditions are less than ceiling 800 feet or visibility less than 2 miles.

d. Inform the closest aircraft that is requesting a full-stop, touch-and-go, stop-and-go, low approach, or option when there is traffic authorized to LUAW on the same runway.

EXAMPLE–
"Delta One, Runway One–Eight, continue, traffic holding in position."

"Delta One, Runway One–Eight, cleared to land. Traffic holding in position."
"Twin Cessna Four Four Golf, Runway One-Niner base approved, traffic holding in position."
"Baron Two Five Foxtrot, Runway One-Niner Right extend downwind, tower will call your base, traffic holding in position."

e. USA/USN/USAF. Issue runway identifier along with surface wind when clearing an aircraft to land, touch and go, stop and go, low approach, or the option.

PHRASEOLOGY–
RUNWAY (number), WIND (surface wind direction and velocity), CLEARED TO LAND.

NOTE–
A clearance to land means that appropriate separation on the landing runway will be ensured. A landing clearance does not relieve the pilot from compliance with any previously issued restriction.

f. Whenever a runway length has been temporarily or permanently shortened, state the word "shortened" immediately following the runway number as part of the landing clearance. This information must be issued in conjunction with the landing clearance.

1. The addition of "shortened" must be included in the landing clearance for the duration of the construction project when the runway is temporarily shortened.

2. The addition of "shortened" must be included in the landing clearance until the Chart Supplement is updated to include the change(s) when the runway is permanently shortened.

PHRASEOLOGY–
RUNWAY (number) SHORTENED, CLEARED TO LAND.

EXAMPLE–
"Runway Two-Seven shortened, cleared to land."

g. If landing clearance is temporarily withheld, insert the word "shortened" immediately after the runway number to advise the pilot to continue.

PHRASEOLOGY–
RUNWAY (number) SHORTENED, CONTINUE.

EXAMPLE–
"Runway Two-Seven shortened, continue."

REFERENCE–
FAA Order JO 7210.3, Para 10-3-12, Airport Construction.
FAA Order JO 7210.3, Para 10-3-13, Change in Runway Length Due to Construction.

3–10–6. ANTICIPATING SEPARATION

a. Landing clearance to succeeding aircraft in a landing sequence need not be withheld if you observe the positions of the aircraft and determine that prescribed runway separation will exist when the aircraft crosses the landing threshold. Issue traffic information to the succeeding aircraft if a preceding arrival has not been previously reported and when traffic will be departing prior to their arrival.

EXAMPLE–
"American Two Forty–Five, Runway One–Eight, cleared to land, number two following a United Seven–Thirty–Seven two mile final. Traffic will depart prior to your arrival."

"American Two Forty–Five, Runway One–Eight, cleared to land. Traffic will depart prior to your arrival."

NOTE–
Landing sequence number is optional at tower facilities where the arrival sequence to the runway is established by the approach control.

b. Anticipating separation must not be applied when conducting LUAW operations, except as authorized in paragraph 3–10–5c2. Issue applicable traffic information when using this provision.

EXAMPLE–
"American Two Forty–Five, Runway One–Eight, cleared to land. Traffic will be a Boeing Seven–Fifty–Seven holding in position."

REFERENCE–
P/CG Term– Clear of the Runway.

3–10–7. LANDING CLEARANCE WITHOUT VISUAL OBSERVATION

When an arriving aircraft reports at a position where he/she should be seen but has not been visually observed, advise the aircraft as a part of the landing clearance that it is not in sight and restate the landing runway.

PHRASEOLOGY–
NOT IN SIGHT, RUNWAY (number) CLEARED TO LAND.

NOTE–
Aircraft observance on the CTRD satisfies the visually observed requirement.

3–10–8. WITHHOLDING LANDING CLEARANCE

Do not withhold a landing clearance indefinitely even though it appears a violation of Title 14 of the Code of Federal Regulations has been committed. The apparent violation might be the result of an emergency situation. In any event, assist the pilot to the extent possible.

3–10–9. RUNWAY EXITING

a. Instruct aircraft where to turn-off the runway after landing, when appropriate, and advise the aircraft to hold short of a runway or taxiway if required for traffic.

PHRASEOLOGY–
TURN LEFT/RIGHT (taxiway/runway),

or

IF ABLE, TURN LEFT/RIGHT (taxiway/runway)

and if required

HOLD SHORT OF (runway).

NOTE–
Runway exiting or taxi instructions should not normally be issued to an aircraft prior to, or immediately after, touchdown.

b. Taxi instructions must be provided to the aircraft by the local controller when:

1. Compliance with ATC instructions will be required before the aircraft can change to ground control, or

2. The aircraft will be required to enter an active runway in order to taxi clear of the landing runway.

EXAMPLE–
"U.S. Air Ten Forty Two, turn right next taxiway, cross runway two one, contact ground point seven."

"U.S. Air Ten Forty Two, turn right on Alfa/next taxiway, cross Bravo, hold short of Charlie, contact ground point seven."

NOTE–
1. *An aircraft is expected to taxi clear of the runway unless otherwise directed by ATC. Pilots must not exit the landing runway on to an intersecting runway unless authorized by ATC. In the absence of ATC instructions, an aircraft should taxi clear of the landing runway by clearing the hold position marking associated with the landing runway even if that requires the aircraft to protrude into or enter another taxiway/ramp area. This does not authorize an aircraft to cross a subsequent taxiway or ramp after clearing the landing runway.*

REFERENCE–
P/CG Term– Clear of the Runway.

2. *The pilot is responsible for ascertaining when the aircraft is clear of the runway by clearing the runway holding position marking associated with the landing runway.*

c. Ground control and local control must protect a taxiway/runway/ramp intersection if an aircraft is required to enter that intersection to clear the landing runway.

REFERENCE–
FAA Order JO 7210.3, Para 10–1–7, Use of Active Runways.

d. Request a read back of runway hold short instructions when not received from the pilot.

EXAMPLE–
"American Four Ninety–two, turn left at Taxiway Charlie, hold short of Runway 27 Right."

or

"American Four Ninety–two, turn left at Charlie, hold short of Runway 27 Right."

"American Four Ninety Two, Roger."

"American Four Ninety–two, read back hold instructions."

NOTE–
Read back hold instructions phraseology may be initiated for any point on a movement area when the controller believes the read back is necessary.

3–10–10. ALTITUDE RESTRICTED LOW APPROACH

A low approach with an altitude restriction of no less than 500 feet above the airport may be authorized except over an aircraft holding in position or a departing aircraft. Do not clear aircraft for restricted altitude low approaches over personnel unless airport authorities have advised these personnel that the approaches will be conducted. Advise the approaching aircraft of the location of applicable ground traffic, personnel, or equipment.

NOTE–
1. *The 500 feet restriction is a minimum. Higher altitudes should be used when warranted. For example, 1,000 feet is more appropriate for super or heavy aircraft operating over unprotected personnel or small aircraft on or near the runway.*

2. *This authorization includes altitude restricted low approaches over preceding landing or taxiing aircraft. Restricted low approaches are not authorized over aircraft holding in position or departing aircraft.*

PHRASEOLOGY–
CLEARED LOW APPROACH AT OR ABOVE (altitude). TRAFFIC (description and location).

REFERENCE–
FAA Order JO 7110.65, Para 3–1–5, Vehicles/Equipment/Personnel on Runways.
FAA Order JO 7110.65, Para 3–1–6, Traffic Information.
FAA Order JO 7110.65, Para 3–2–1, Light Signals.
FAA Order JO 7110.65, Para 3–3–3, Timely Information.
FAA Order JO 7110.65, Para 3–9–4, Line Up and Wait (LUAW).
FAA Order JO 7110.65, Para 3–10–3, Same Runway Separation.

3–10–11. CLOSED TRAFFIC

Approve/disapprove pilot requests to remain in closed traffic for successive operations subject to local traffic conditions.

PHRASEOLOGY–
LEFT/RIGHT (if required) CLOSED TRAFFIC APPROVED. REPORT (position if required),

or

UNABLE CLOSED TRAFFIC, (additional information as required).

NOTE–
Segregated traffic patterns for helicopters to runways and other areas may be established by letter of agreement or other local operating procedures.

REFERENCE–
FAA Order JO 7110.65, Para 3–7–4, Runway Proximity.
FAA Order JO 7110.65, Para 3–9–4, Line Up and Wait (LUAW).
FAA Order JO 7110.65, Para 3–10–3, Same Runway Separation.

3–10–12. OVERHEAD MANEUVER

Issue the following to arriving aircraft that will conduct an overhead maneuver:

a. Pattern altitude and direction of traffic. Omit either or both if standard or when you know the pilot is familiar with a nonstandard procedure.

PHRASEOLOGY–
PATTERN ALTITUDE (altitude). RIGHT TURNS.

b. Request for report on initial approach.

PHRASEOLOGY–
REPORT INITIAL.

c. "Break" information and request for pilot report. Specify the point of "break" only if nonstandard. Request the pilot to report "break" if required for traffic or other reasons.

PHRASEOLOGY–
BREAK AT (specified point).

REPORT BREAK.

d. Overhead maneuver patterns are developed at airports where aircraft have an operational need to conduct the maneuver. An aircraft conducting an overhead maneuver is VFR and the IFR flight plan is canceled when the aircraft reaches the "initial point" on the initial approach portion of the maneuver. The existence of a standard overhead maneuver pattern does not eliminate the possible requirement for an aircraft to conform to conventional rectangular patterns if an overhead maneuver cannot be approved.

NOTE–
Aircraft operating to an airport without a functioning control tower must initiate cancellation of the IFR flight plan prior to executing the overhead maneuver or after landing.

FIG 3-10-13
Overhead Maneuver

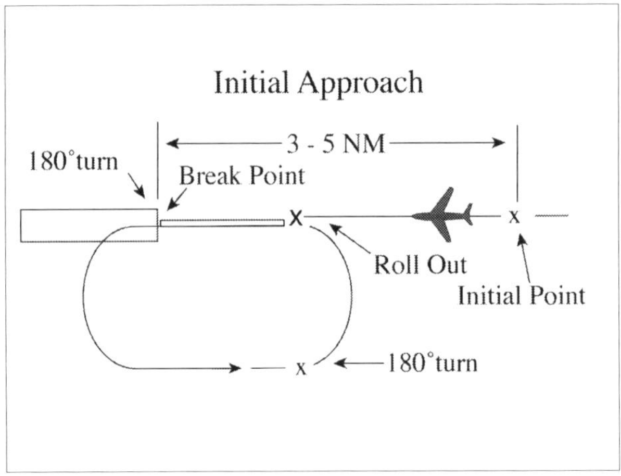

EXAMPLE-
"Air Force Three Six Eight, Runway Six, wind zero seven zero at eight, pattern altitude six thousand, report initial."

"Air Force Three Six Eight, break at midfield, report break."

"Air Force Three Six Eight, cleared to land."

"Alfa Kilo Two Two, Runway Three One, wind three three zero at one four, right turns, report initial."

"Alfa Kilo Two Two, report break."

"Alfa Kilo Two Two, cleared to land."

e. Timely and positive controller action is required to prevent a conflict when an overhead pattern could extend into the path of a departing or a missed approach aircraft. Local procedures and/or coordination requirements should be set forth in an appropriate letter of agreement, facility directive, base flying manual etc., when the frequency of occurrence warrants.

3-10-13. SIMULATED FLAMEOUT (SFO) APPROACHES/EMERGENCY LANDING PATTERN (ELP) OPERATIONS/PRACTICE PRECAUTIONARY APPROACHES

a. Authorize military aircraft to make SFO/ELP/practice precautionary approaches if the following conditions are met:

1. A letter of agreement or local operating procedure is in effect between the military flying organization and affected ATC facility.

(a) Include specific coordination, execution, and approval procedures for the operation.

(b) The exchange or issuance of traffic information as agreed to in any interfacility letter of agreement is accomplished.

(c) Include a statement in the procedure that clarifies at which points SFOs/ELPs may/may not be terminated. (See FIG 3-10-14 and FIG 3-10-16.)

2. Traffic information regarding aircraft in radio communication with or visible to tower controllers which are operating within or adjacent to the flameout maneuvering area is provided to the SFO/ELP aircraft and other concerned aircraft.

3. The high-key altitude or practice precautionary approach maneuvering altitudes of the aircraft concerned are obtained prior to approving the approach. (See FIG 3-10-14 and FIG 3-10-16.)

NOTE–
1. *Practice precautionary/SFO/ELP approaches are authorized only for specific aircraft. Any aircraft, however, might make precautionary approaches, when engine failure is considered possible. The practice precautionary approach maneuvering area/altitudes may not conform to the standard SFO/ELP maneuvering area/altitudes.*

2. *SFO/ELP approaches generally require high descent rates. Visibility ahead and beneath the aircraft is greatly restricted.*

3. *Pattern adjustments for aircraft conducting SFOs and ELPs may impact the effectiveness of SFO and ELP training.*

REFERENCE–
FAA Order JO 7110.65, Para 4–8–12, Low Approach and Touch-and-Go.
FAA Order JO 7610.14, Para 7–1–6, Simulated Flameout (SFO)/Emergency Landing Pattern (ELP) Operations.

b. For overhead SFO/ELP approaches:

1. Request a report at the entry point.

PHRASEOLOGY–
REPORT (high or low) KEY (as appropriate).

2. Request a report at low key.

PHRASEOLOGY–
REPORT LOW KEY.

3. At low key, issue low approach clearance or alternate instructions.

REFERENCE–
FAA Order JO 7110.65, Para 3–8–1, Sequence/Spacing Application.
FAA Order JO 7110.65, Para 10–1–7, Inflight Emergencies Involving Military Fighter-type Aircraft.
FAA Order JO 7610.14, Para 7–1–6, Simulated Flameout (SFO)/Emergency Landing Pattern (ELP) Operations.

c. For straight–in simulation flameout approaches:

1. Request a position report from aircraft conducting straight–in SFO approaches.

PHRASEOLOGY–
REPORT (distance) MILE SIMULATED FLAMEOUT FINAL.

2. At the appropriate position on final (normally no closer than 3 miles), issue low approach clearance or alternate instruction. (See FIG 3–10–15.)

FIG 3-10-14
Simulated Flameout [1]

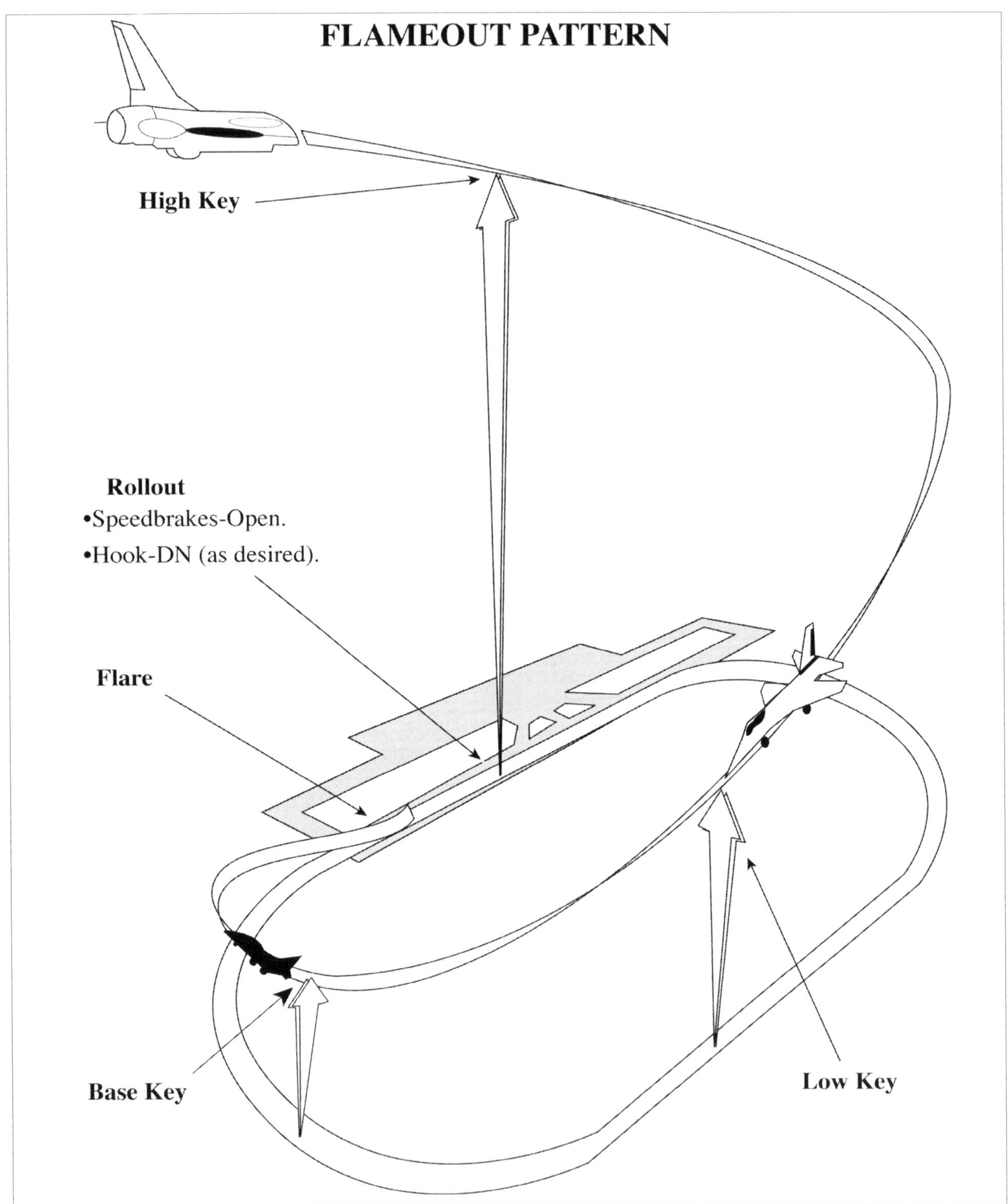

FIG 3-10-15
Simulated Flameout [2]

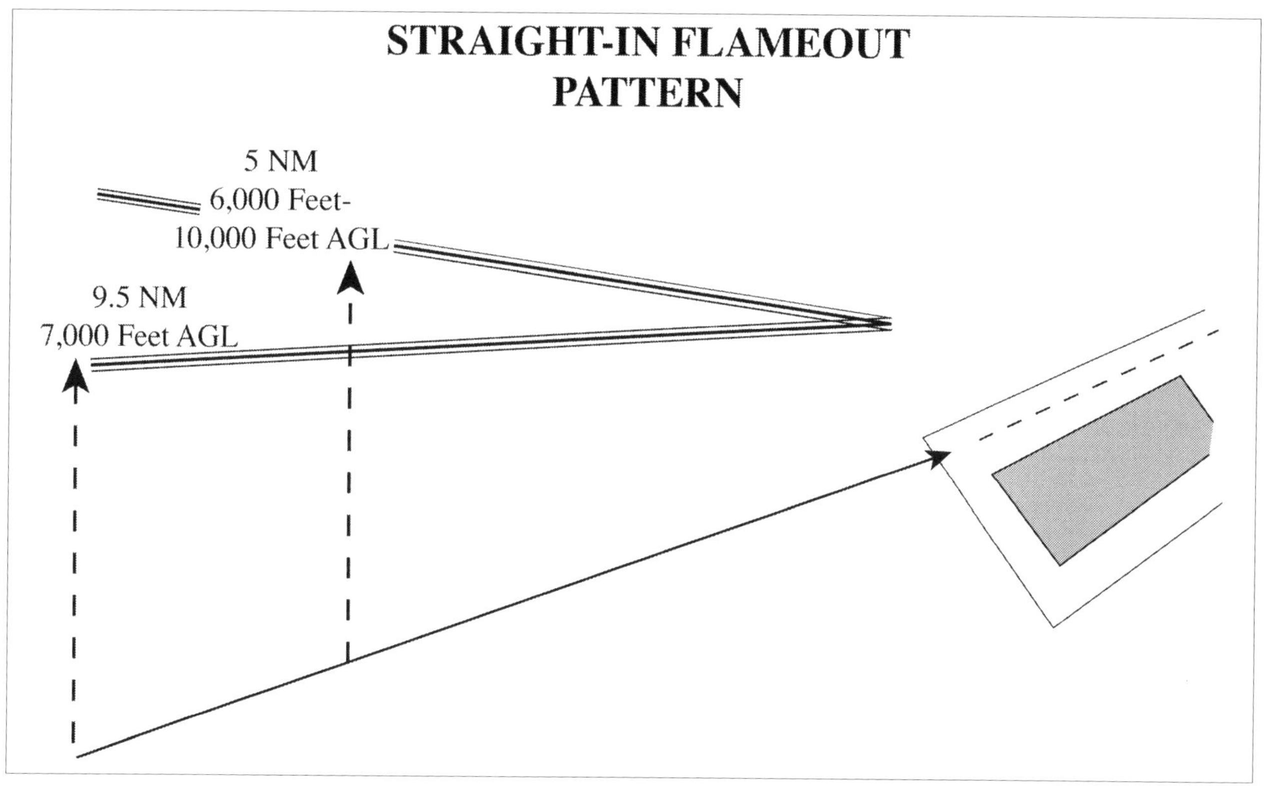

FIG 3-10-16
Emergency Landing Pattern

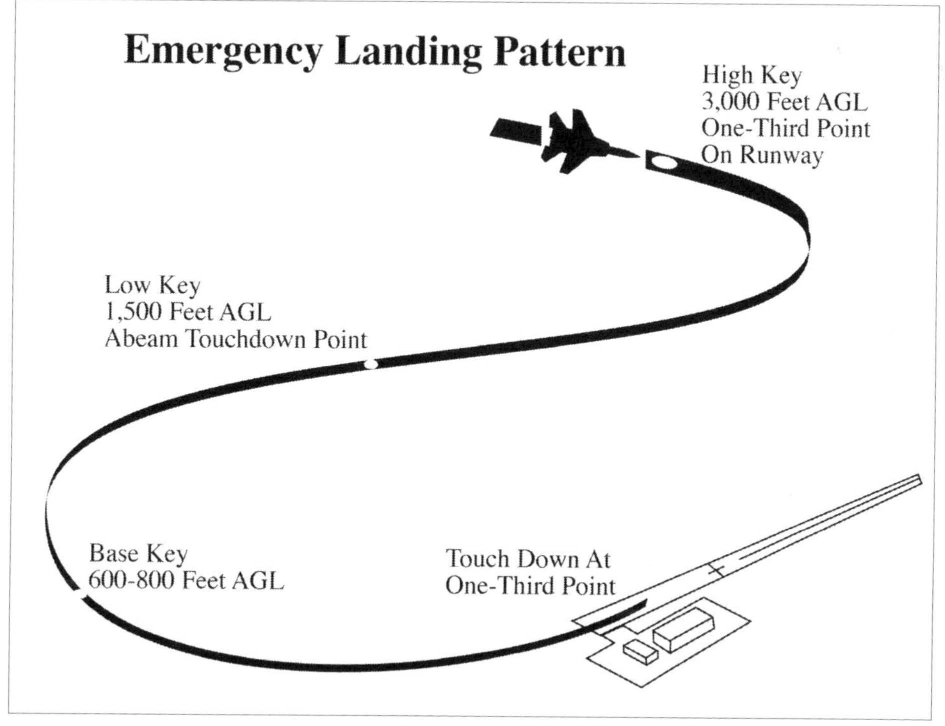

Section 11. Helicopter Operations

3–11–1. TAXI AND GROUND MOVEMENT OPERATION

a. When necessary for a wheeled helicopter to taxi on the surface, use the phraseology in paragraph 3–7–2, Taxi and Ground Movement Operations.

NOTE–
Ground taxiing uses less fuel than hover-taxiing and minimizes air turbulence. However, under certain conditions, such as rough, soft, or uneven terrain, it may become necessary to hover/air-taxi for safety considerations. Helicopters with articulating rotors (usually designs with three or more main rotor blades) are subject to "ground resonance" and may, on rare occasions, suddenly lift off the ground to avoid severe damage or destruction.

b. When requested or necessary for a helicopter/VTOL aircraft to proceed at a slow speed above the surface, normally below 20 knots and in ground effect, use the following phraseology, supplemented as appropriate with the phraseology in paragraph 3–7–2, Taxi and Ground Movement Operations.

PHRASEOLOGY–
HOVER-TAXI (supplemented, as appropriate, from paragraph 3–7–2, Taxi and Ground Movement Operations.)

CAUTION (dust, blowing snow, loose debris, taxiing light aircraft, personnel, etc.).

NOTE–
Hover-taxiing consumes fuel at a high burn rate, and helicopter downwash turbulence (produced in ground effect) increases significantly with larger and heavier helicopters.

REFERENCE–
P/CG Term– Hover Taxi.
AIM, Para 4–3–17, VFR Helicopter Operations at Controlled Airports.

c. When requested or necessary for a helicopter to proceed expeditiously from one point to another, normally below 100 feet AGL and at airspeeds above 20 knots, use the following phraseology, supplemented as appropriate with the phraseology in paragraph 3–7–2, Taxi and Ground Movement Operations.

PHRASEOLOGY–
AIR-TAXI:

VIA (direct, as requested, or specified route)

TO (location, heliport, helipad, operating/movement area, active/inactive runway).

AVOID (aircraft/vehicles/personnel).
If required,

REMAIN AT OR BELOW (altitude).

CAUTION (wake turbulence or other reasons above).

LAND AND CONTACT TOWER,

or

HOLD FOR (reason– takeoff clearance, release, landing/taxiing aircraft, etc.).

NOTE–
Air-taxi is the preferred method for helicopter movements on airports provided ground operations/conditions permit. Air-taxi authorizes the pilot to proceed above the surface either via hover-taxi or flight at speeds more than 20 knots. Unless otherwise requested or instructed, the pilot is expected to remain below 100 feet AGL. The pilot is solely responsible for selecting a safe airspeed for the altitude/operation being conducted.

REFERENCE–
P/CG Term – Air Taxi.
AIM, Para 4–3–17, VFR Helicopter Operations at Controlled Airports.

WAKE TURBULENCE APPLICATION

d. Avoid clearances which require small aircraft or helicopters to taxi in close proximity to taxiing or hover-taxi helicopters.

REFERENCE–
AC 90–23, Aircraft Wake Turbulence, Para 10 and Para 11.

3–11–2. HELICOPTER TAKEOFF CLEARANCE

a. Issue takeoff clearances from movement areas other than active runways or in diverse directions from active runways, with additional instructions as necessary. Whenever possible, issue takeoff clearance in lieu of extended hover–taxi or air–taxi operations.

PHRASEOLOGY–
(Present position, taxiway, helipad, numbers) MAKE RIGHT/LEFT TURN FOR (direction, points of compass, heading, NAVAID radial) DEPARTURE/DEPARTURE ROUTE (number, name, or code), AVOID (aircraft/vehicles/personnel),

or

REMAIN (direction) OF (active runways, parking areas, passenger terminals, etc.).

CAUTION (power lines, unlighted obstructions, trees, wake turbulence, etc.).

CLEARED FOR TAKEOFF.

b. If takeoff is requested from non–movement areas, an area not authorized for helicopter use, or an area off the airport, and, in your judgment, the operation appears to be reasonable, use the following phraseology instead of the takeoff clearance in subparagraph a.

PHRASEOLOGY–
DEPARTURE FROM (requested location) WILL BE AT YOUR OWN RISK (additional instructions, as necessary). USE CAUTION (if applicable).

c. Unless agreed to by the pilot, do not issue downwind takeoffs if the tailwind exceeds 5 knots.

NOTE–
A pilot request to takeoff from a given point in a given direction constitutes agreement.

3–11–3. HELICOPTER DEPARTURE SEPARATION

Separate a departing helicopter from other helicopters by ensuring that it does not takeoff until one of the following conditions exists:

NOTE–
Helicopters performing air-taxiing operations within the boundary of the airport are considered to be taxiing aircraft.

a. A preceding, departing helicopter has left the takeoff area. (See FIG 3–11–1.)

FIG 3-11-1
Helicopter Departure Separation

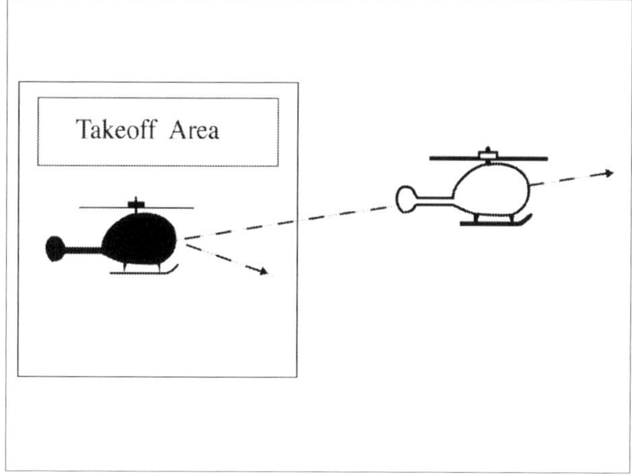

b. A preceding, arriving helicopter has taxied off the landing area. (See FIG 3-11-2.)

FIG 3-11-2
Helicopter Departure Separation

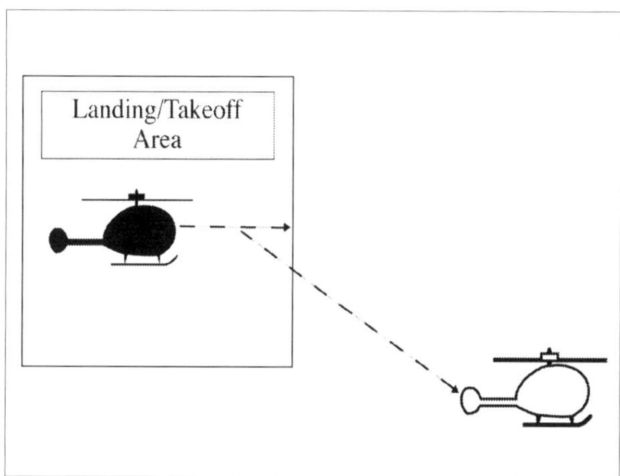

3-11-4. HELICOPTER ARRIVAL SEPARATION

Separate an arriving helicopter from other helicopters by ensuring that it does not land until one of the following conditions exists:

a. A preceding, arriving helicopter has come to a stop or taxied off the landing area. (See FIG 3-11-3 and FIG 3-11-4.)

FIG 3-11-3
Helicopter Arrival Separation

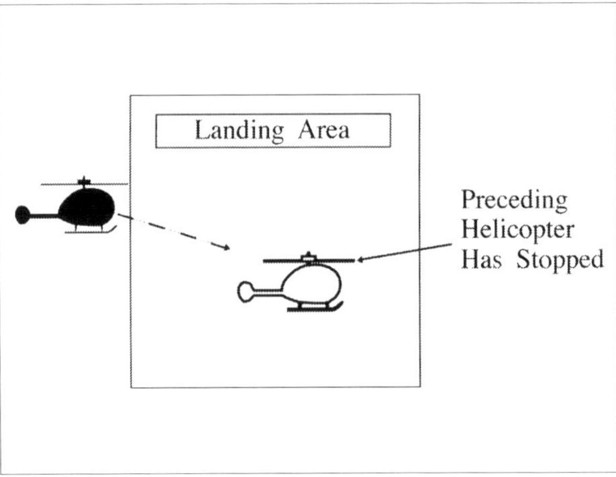

FIG 3-11-4
Helicopter Arrival Separation

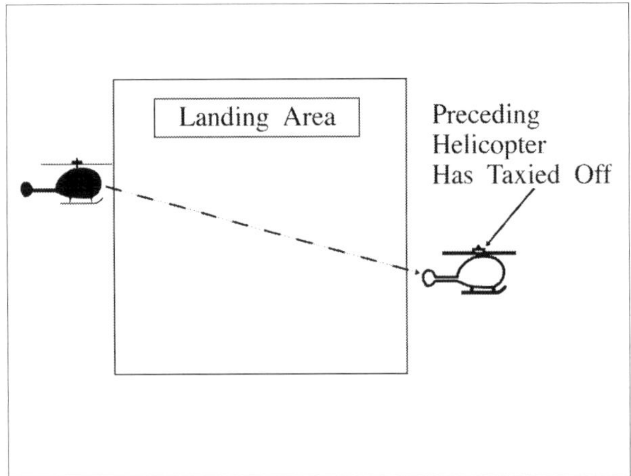

b. A preceding, departing helicopter has left the landing area. (See FIG 3-11-5.)

FIG 3-11-5
Helicopter Arrival Separation

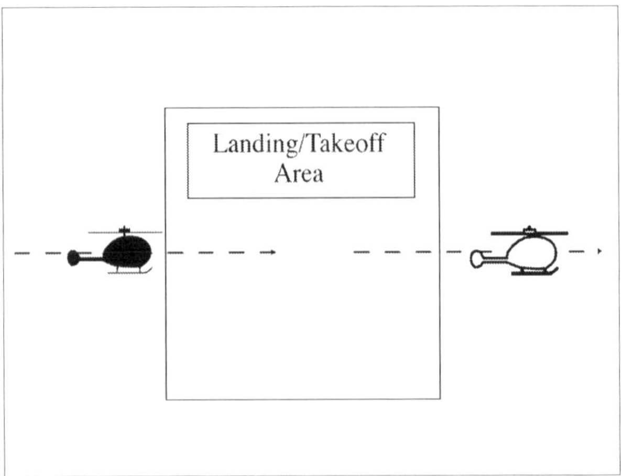

3-11-5. SIMULTANEOUS LANDINGS OR TAKEOFFS

Authorize helicopters to conduct simultaneous landings or takeoffs if the distance between the landing or takeoff points is at least 200 feet and the courses to be flown do not conflict. Refer to surface markings to determine the 200 foot minimum, or instruct a helicopter to remain at least 200 feet from another helicopter. (See FIG 3-11-6.)

FIG 3-11-6
Simultaneous Helicopter Landings or Takeoffs

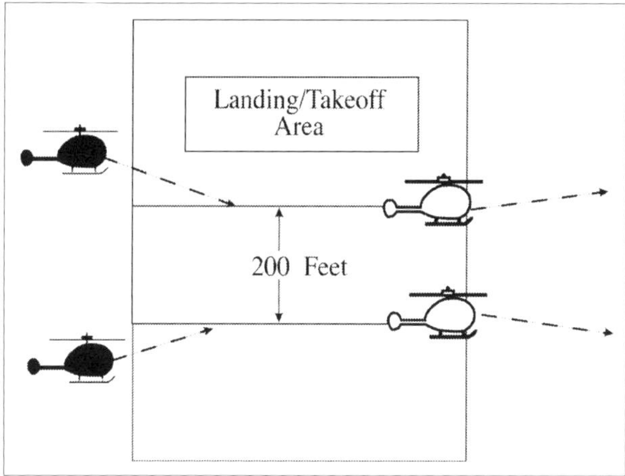

3-11-6. HELICOPTER LANDING CLEARANCE

a. Issue landing clearances to helicopters going to movement areas other than active runways or from diverse directions to points on active runways, with additional instructions as necessary. Whenever possible, issue a landing clearance in lieu of extended hover-taxi or air-taxi operations.

PHRASEOLOGY-
MAKE APPROACH STRAIGHT-IN/CIRCLING LEFT/RIGHT TURN TO (location, runway, taxiway, helipad, Maltese cross) ARRIVAL/ARRIVAL ROUTE (number, name, or code).

HOLD SHORT OF (active runway, extended runway centerline, other).

REMAIN (direction/distance; e.g., 700 feet, 1 1/2 miles) OF/FROM (runway, runway centerline, other helicopter/aircraft).

CAUTION (power lines, unlighted obstructions, wake turbulence, etc.).

CLEARED TO LAND.

b. If landing is requested to non-movement areas, an area not authorized for helicopter use, or an area off the airport, and, in your judgment, the operation appears to be reasonable, use the following phraseology instead of the landing clearance in subparagraph a.

PHRASEOLOGY-
LANDING AT (requested location) WILL BE AT YOUR OWN RISK (additional instructions, as necessary). USE CAUTION (if applicable).

c. Unless agreed to by the pilot, do not issue downwind landings if the tailwind exceeds 5 knots.

NOTE-
A pilot request to land at a given point from a given direction constitutes agreement.

Section 12. Sea Lane Operations

3–12–1. APPLICATION

Where sea lanes are established and controlled, apply the provisions of this section.

3–12–2. DEPARTURE SEPARATION

Separate a departing aircraft from a preceding departing or arriving aircraft using the same sea lane by ensuring that it does not commence takeoff until:

a. The other aircraft has departed and crossed the end of the sea lane or turned to avert any conflict. (See FIG 3–12–1). If you can determine distances by reference to suitable landmarks, the other aircraft need only be airborne if the following minimum distance exists between aircraft:

1. When only Category I aircraft are involved– *1,500 feet.*

2. When a Category I aircraft is preceded by a Category II aircraft– *3,000 feet.*

3. When either the succeeding or both are Category II aircraft– *3,000 feet.*

4. When either is a Category III aircraft– *6,000 feet.* (See FIG 3–12–2.)

FIG 3–12–1
Sea Lane Departure Operations

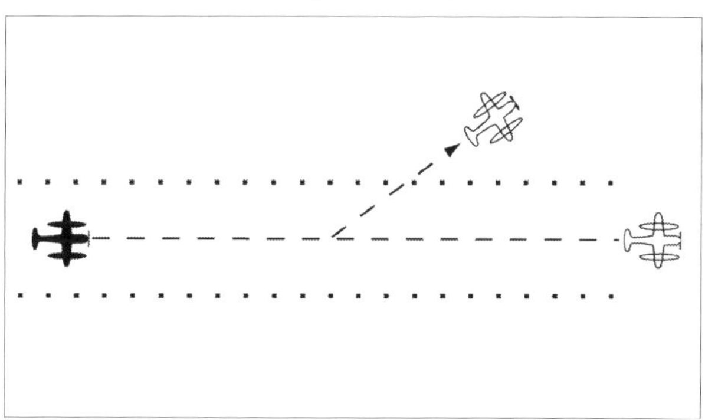

FIG 3–12–2
Sea Lane Departure Operations

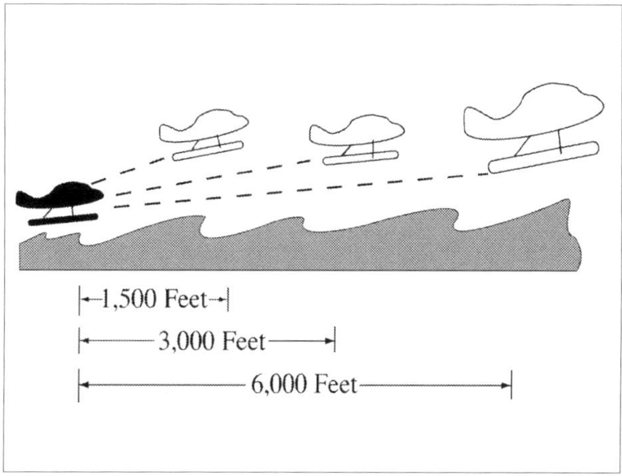

b. A preceding landing aircraft has taxied out of the sea lane.

NOTE–
Due to the absence of braking capability, caution should be exercised when instructing a float plane to hold a position as the aircraft will continue to move because of prop generated thrust. Therefore, clearance to line up and wait should be followed by takeoff or other clearance as soon as is practical.

3–12–3. ARRIVAL SEPARATION

Separate an arriving aircraft from another aircraft using the same sea lane by ensuring that the arriving aircraft does not cross the landing threshold until one of the following conditions exists:

a. The other aircraft has landed and taxied out of the sea lane. Between sunrise and sunset, if you can determine distances by reference to suitable landmarks and the other aircraft has landed, it need not be clear of the sea lane if the following minimum distance from the landing threshold exists:

1. When a Category I aircraft is landing behind a Category I or II– *2,000 feet.* (See FIG 3–12–3.)

FIG 3–12–3
Sea Lane Arrival Operations

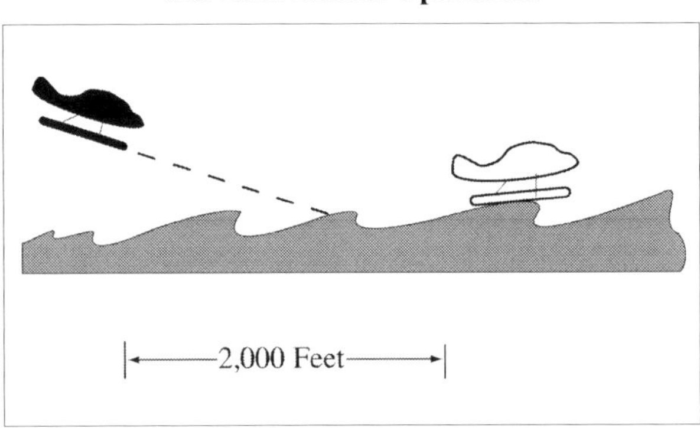

2. When a Category II aircraft is landing behind a Category I or II– *2,500 feet.* (See FIG 3–12–4.)

FIG 3–12–4
Sea Lane Arrival Operations
[View 2]

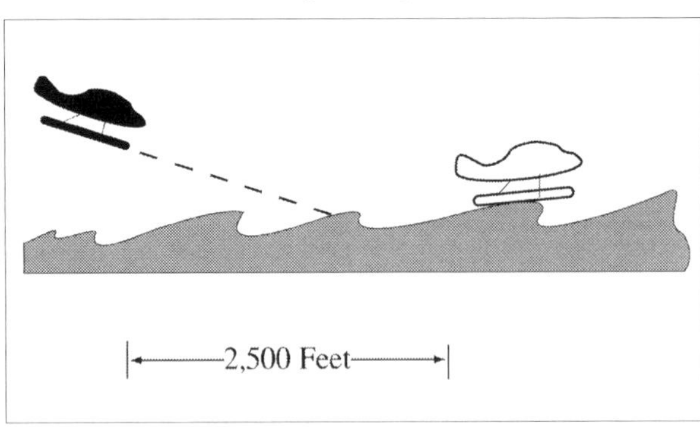

b. The other aircraft has departed and crossed the end of the sea lane or turned to avert any conflict. (See FIG 3–12–5.) If you can determine distances by reference to suitable landmarks and the other aircraft is airborne, it need not have crossed the end of the sea lane if the following minimum distance from the landing threshold exists:

1. When only Category I aircraft are involved– *1,500 feet.*

2. When either is a Category II aircraft– *3,000 feet.*

3. When either is a Category III aircraft– *6,000 feet.* (See FIG 3–12–6.)

FIG 3-12-5
Sea Lane Arrival Operations

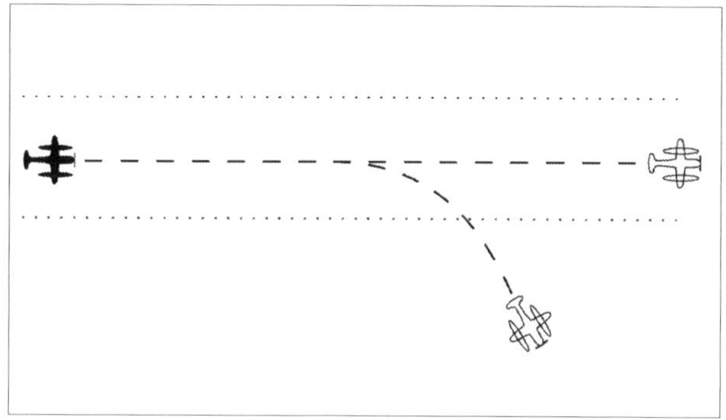

FIG 3-12-6
Sea Lane Arrival Operations

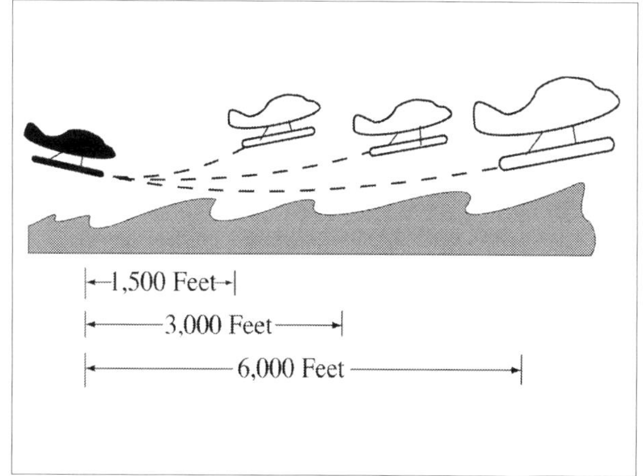

Chapter 4. IFR

Section 1. NAVAID Use Limitations

4-1-1. ALTITUDE AND DISTANCE LIMITATIONS

When specifying a route other than an established airway or route, do not exceed the limitations in the table on any portion of the route which lies within controlled airspace. (For altitude and distance limitations, see TBL 4-1-1, TBL 4-1-2, and TBL 4-1-3) (For correct application of altitude and distance limitations see FIG 4-1-1 and FIG 4-1-2.)

REFERENCE-
FAA Order JO 7110.65, Para 4-1-5, Fix Use.
FAA Order JO 7110.65, Para 5-6-2, Methods.

TBL 4-1-1
VOR/VORTAC/TACAN NAVAIDs
Normal Usable Altitudes and Radius Distances

Class	Altitude	Distance (miles)
T	12,000 and below	25
L	Below 18,000	40
H	Below 14,500	40
H	14,500 - 17,999	100
H	18,000 - FL 450	130
H	Above FL 450	100

TBL 4-1-2
L/MF Radio Beacon (RBN)
Usable Radius Distances for All Altitudes

Class	Power (watts)	Distance (miles)
CL	Under 25	15
MH	Under 50	25
H	50 - 1,999	50
HH	2,000 or more	75

TBL 4-1-3
ILS
Usable Height and Distance*

Height (feet) above transmitter	Distance (miles from transmitter)
4,500	10 (for glideslope)
4,500	18 (for localizer)
*Use the current flight check height/altitude limitations if different from the above minima.	

FIG 4-1-1
Application of Altitude and Distance Limitations
[Application 1]

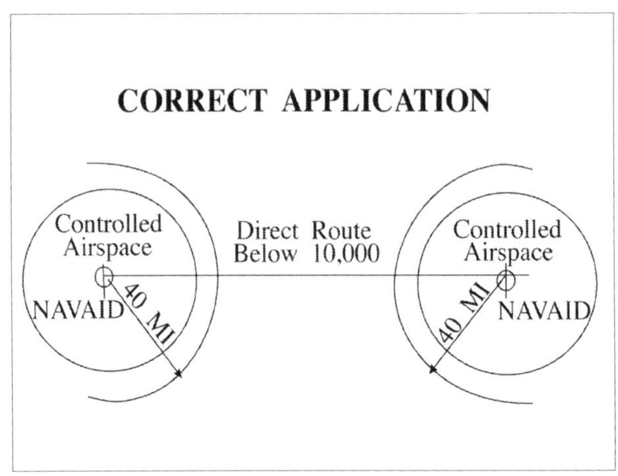

FIG 4-1-2
Application of Altitude and Distance Limitations
[Application 2]

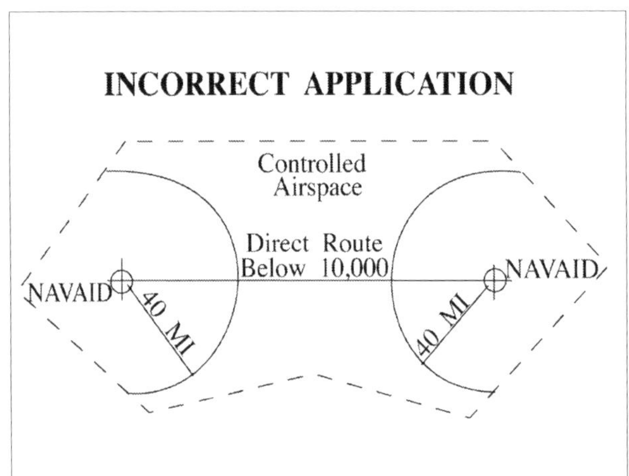

4-1-2. EXCEPTIONS

Altitude and distance limitations need not be applied when any of the following conditions are met:

a. Routing is initiated by ATC or requested by the pilot and radar monitoring is provided.

EXCEPTION-
GNSS equipped aircraft /G, /L, /S, and /V not on a random impromptu route.

NOTE-

1. *Except for GNSS-equipped aircraft /G, /L, /S, and /V, not on a random impromptu route, paragraph 5-5-1, Application, requires radar separation be provided to RNAV aircraft operating at and below FL450 on Q routes or random RNAV routes, excluding oceanic airspace.*

2. *When a clearance is issued beyond the altitude and/or distance limitations of a NAVAID, in addition to being responsible for maintaining separation from other aircraft and airspace, the controller is responsible for providing aircraft with information and advice related to significant deviations from the expected flight path.*

REFERENCE–
FAA Order JO 7110.65, Para 2–1–3, Procedural Preference.
FAA Order JO 7110.65, Para 4–4–2, Route Structure Transitions.
FAA Order JO 7110.65, Para 5–1–6, Deviation Advisories.
FAA Order JO 7110.65, Para 5–5–1, Application.
FAA Order JO 7110.65, Para 6–5–4, Minima Along Other Than Established Airways or Routes.
AIM, Para 5-1-8c, Direct Flights.
AIM, Para 5-1-8d, Area Navigation (RNAV).
P/CG Term - Global Navigation Satellite System (GNSS)[ICAO].

b. Operational necessity requires and approval has been obtained from the Frequency Management and Flight Inspection Offices to exceed them.

c. Requested routing is via an MTR.

REFERENCE–
FAA Order JO 7110.65, Para 5–6–2, Methods.

4–1–3. CROSSING ALTITUDE

Use an altitude consistent with the limitations of the aid when clearing an aircraft to cross or hold at a fix.

REFERENCE–
FAA Order JO 7110.65, Para 5–6–2, Methods.

4–1–4. VFR-ON-TOP

Use a route not meeting service volume limitations only if an aircraft requests to operate "VFR-on-top" on this route.

NOTE–
Aircraft equipped with TACAN only are expected to:

1. *Define route of flight between TACAN or VORTAC NAVAIDs in the same manner as VOR-equipped aircraft.*

2. *Except in Class A airspace, submit requests for "VFR-on-top" flight where insufficient TACAN or VORTAC NAVAIDs exist to define the route.*

REFERENCE–
FAA Order JO 7110.65, Para 5–6–2, Methods.

4–1–5. FIX USE

Request aircraft position reports only over fixes shown on charts used for the altitude being flown, except as follows:

NOTE–
Waypoints filed in random RNAV routes automatically become compulsory reporting points for the flight unless otherwise advised by ATC.

a. Unless the pilot requests otherwise, use only those fixes shown on high altitude en route charts, high altitude instrument approach procedures charts, and SID charts when clearing military turbojet single-piloted aircraft.

b. Except for military single-piloted turbojet aircraft, unpublished fixes may be used if the name of the NAVAID and, if appropriate, the radial/course/azimuth and frequency/channel are given to the pilot. An unpublished fix is defined as one approved and planned for publication which is not yet depicted on the charts or one which is used in accord with the following:

REFERENCE–
FAA Order 8260.3, United States Standard for Terminal Instrument Procedures (TERPS), Chapter 17, Basic Holding Criteria..

1. Unpublished fixes are formed by the en route radial and either a DME distance from the same NAVAID or an intersecting radial from an off-route VOR/VORTAC/TACAN. DME must be used in lieu of off-route radials, whenever possible.

2. Except where known signal coverage restrictions exist, an unpublished fix may be used for ATC purposes if its location does not exceed NAVAID altitude and distance limitation, and when off-route radials are used, the angle of divergence meets the criteria prescribed below.

NOTE–
Unpublished fixes should not negate the normal use of published intersections. Frequent routine use of an unpublished fix would justify establishing a fix.

REFERENCE–
FAA Order JO 7110.65, Para 4−1−1, Altitude and Distance Limitations.

3. Do not hold aircraft at unpublished fixes below the lowest assignable altitude dictated by terrain clearance for the appropriate holding pattern airspace area (template) regardless of the MEA for the route being flown.

4. When the unpublished fix is located on an off-route radial and the radial providing course guidance, it must be used consistent with the following divergence angles:

(a) When holding operations are involved with respect to subparagraphs (b) and (c) below, the angle of divergence must be at least 45 degrees.

(b) When both NAVAIDs involved are located within 30 NM of the unpublished fix, the minimum divergence angle is 30 degrees.

(c) When the unpublished fix is located over 30 NM from the NAVAID generating the off-course radial, the minimum divergence angle must increase 1 degree per NM up to 45 NM; e.g., 45 NM would require 45 degrees.

(d) When the unpublished fix is located beyond 45 NM from the NAVAID generating the off-course radial, the minimum divergence angle must increase ½ degree per NM; e.g., 130 NM would require 88 degrees.

c. Fixes contained in the route description of MTRs are considered filed fixes.

d. TACAN-only aircraft (type suffix M, N, or P) possess TACAN with DME, but no VOR or LF navigation system capability. Assign fixes based on TACAN or VORTAC facilities only.

NOTE–
TACAN-only aircraft can never be held overhead the NAVAID, be it TACAN or VORTAC.

e. DME fixes must not be established within the no-course signal zone of the NAVAID from which inbound holding course information would be derived.

REFERENCE–
FAA Order JO 7110.65, Para 2−5−3, NAVAID Fixes.
FAA Order JO 7110.65, Para 5−6−2, Methods.

Section 2. Clearances

4-2-1. CLEARANCE ITEMS

Issue the following clearance items, as appropriate, in the order listed below:

a. Aircraft identification.

b. Clearance limit.

1. When the clearance limit is an airport, the word "airport" must follow the airport name.

PHRASEOLOGY–
CLEARED TO (destination) AIRPORT.

2. When the clearance limit is a NAVAID, and the NAVAID type is known, the type of NAVAID must follow the NAVAID name.

PHRASEOLOGY–
CLEARED TO (NAVAID name and type).

3. When the clearance limit is an intersection or waypoint, and the type is known, the type must follow the intersection or waypoint name.

PHRASEOLOGY–
CLEARED TO (intersection or waypoint name and type).

c. Standard Instrument Departure (SID) or vectors, where applicable.

d. Route of flight including ADR/ADAR/AAR when applied.

e. Altitude data in the order flown.

f. Mach number, if applicable.

g. *USAF.* When issuing a clearance to an airborne aircraft containing an altitude assignment, do not include more than one of the following in the same transmission:

1. Frequency change.

2. Transponder change.

3. Heading.

4. Altimeter setting.

5. Traffic information containing an altitude.

h. Holding instructions.

i. Any special information.

j. Frequency and beacon code information.

REFERENCE–
FAA Order JO 7110.65, Para 4-2-8, IFR-VFR and VFR-IFR Flights.
FAA Order JO 7110.65, Para 4-5-7, Altitude Information.

4-2-2. CLEARANCE PREFIX

a. Prefix a clearance, information, or a request for information which will be relayed to an aircraft through a non-ATC facility by stating "A-T-C clears," "A-T-C advises," or "A-T-C requests."

b. Flight service stations and ARTCC Flight Data Units must prefix a clearance with the appropriate phrase: "ATC clears," "ATC advises," etc.

4-2-3. DELIVERY INSTRUCTIONS

Issue specific clearance delivery instructions, if appropriate.

4-2-4. CLEARANCE RELAY

Relay clearances verbatim.

REFERENCE-
FAA Order JO 7110.65, Para 10-4-4, Communications Failure.

4-2-5. ROUTE OR ALTITUDE AMENDMENTS

a. Amend route of flight in a previously issued clearance by one of the following:

1. State which portion of the route is being amended and then state the amendment.

PHRASEOLOGY-
CHANGE (portion of route) TO READ (new portion of route).

2. State the amendment to the route and then state that the rest of the route is unchanged.

PHRASEOLOGY-
(Amendment to route), REST OF ROUTE UNCHANGED.

3. Issue a clearance "direct" to a point on the previously issued route.

PHRASEOLOGY-
CLEARED DIRECT (fix, waypoint).
Or
CLEARED DIRECT (destination) AIRPORT.

NOTE-
Clearances authorizing "direct" to a point on a previously issued route do not require the phrase "rest of route unchanged." However, it must be understood where the previously cleared route is resumed. When necessary, "rest of route unchanged" may be used to clarify routing.

4. Issue the entire route by stating the amendment.

EXAMPLE-
(Cessna 21A has been cleared to the Airville Airport via V41 Delta VOR V174 Alfa VOR, direct Airville Airport, maintain 9000. After takeoff, the aircraft is rerouted via V41 Frank intersection, V71 Delta VOR, V174 Alfa VOR. The controller issues one of the following as an amended clearance):

1. *"Cessna Two One Alfa change Victor Forty-One Delta to read Victor Forty-One Frank, Victor Seventy-One Delta."*

2. *"Cessna Two One Alfa cleared via Victor Forty-One Frank, Victor Seventy-One Delta, rest of route unchanged."*

3. *"Cessna Two One Alfa cleared via Victor Forty-One Frank, Victor Seventy-One Delta, Victor One Seventy-Four Alfa V-O-R, direct Airville airport, maintain Niner Thousand."*

b. When route or altitude in a previously issued clearance is amended, restate all applicable altitude restrictions.

EXAMPLE-
1. *(A departing aircraft is cleared to cross Ollis intersection at or above 3,000; Gordonsville VOR at or above 12,000; maintain FL 200. Shortly after departure the altitude to be maintained is changed to FL 240. Because altitude restrictions remain in effect, the controller issues an amended clearance as follows):*

"Amend altitude. Cross Ollis intersection at or above Three Thousand; cross Gordonsville V-O-R at or above One Two Thousand; maintain Flight Level Two Four Zero."

(Shortly after departure, altitude restrictions are no longer applicable, the controller issues an amended clearance as follows):

"Climb and maintain Flight Level Two Four Zero."

2. *(An aircraft is cleared to climb via a SID with published altitude restrictions. Shortly after departure the top altitude is changed to FL 230 and compliance with the altitude restrictions is still required, the controller issues an amended clearance as follows):*

"Climb via SID except maintain Flight Level Two Three Zero."

NOTE−

1. *Restating previously issued altitude to "maintain" is an amended clearance. If altitude to "maintain" is changed or restated, whether prior to departure or while airborne and previously issued altitude restrictions are omitted, altitude restrictions are canceled, including SID/STAR altitude restrictions if any.*

2. *Crossing altitudes and speed restrictions on Obstacle Departure Procedure/s (ODP/s) cannot be canceled or amended by ATC.*

c. Issue an amended clearance if a speed restriction is declined because it cannot be complied with concurrently with a previously issued altitude restriction.

EXAMPLE−

(An aircraft is cleared to cross Gordonsville VOR at 11,000. Shortly thereafter he/she is cleared to reduce his/her airspeed to 300 knots. The pilot informs the controller he/she is unable to comply with both clearances simultaneously. The controller issues an amended clearance as follows):

"Cross Gordonsville VOR at One One Thousand. Then, reduce speed to Three Zero Zero."

NOTE−

The phrase "do the best you can" or comparable phrases are not valid substitutes for an amended clearance with altitude or speed restrictions.

REFERENCE−

FAA Order JO 7110.65, Para 2−1−18, Operational Requests.
FAA Order JO 7110.65, Section 6, Vectoring, Para 5−6−2, Methods.
FAA Order JO 7110.65, Section 7, Speed Adjustment, Para 5−7−2, Methods.

d. Air traffic control specialists should avoid route and/or altitude changes for aircraft participating in the North American Route Program (NRP) and that are displaying "NRP" in the remarks section of their flight plan.

NOTE−

Air traffic control specialists retain the latitude necessary to tactically resolve conflicts. Every effort should be made to ensure the aircraft is returned to the original filed flight plan/altitude as soon as conditions warrant.

REFERENCE−

FAA Order JO 7110.65, Para 2−1−4, Operational Priority.
FAA Order JO 7110.65, Para 2−2−15, North American Route Program (NRP) Information.
FAA Order JO 7110.65, Para 2−3−2, En Route Data Entries.
FAA Order JO 7210.3, Chapter 18, Section 17, North American Route Program.

4−2−6. THROUGH CLEARANCES

You may clear an aircraft through intermediate stops.

PHRASEOLOGY−

CLEARED THROUGH (airport) TO (fix).

4−2−7. ALTRV CLEARANCE

Use the phrase "via approved altitude reservation flight plan," if the aircraft will operate in an approved ALTRV.

PHRASEOLOGY−

VIA APPROVED ALTITUDE RESERVATION (mission name) FLIGHT PLAN.

NOTE−

An ALTRV normally includes the departure, climb, cruise, and arrival phases of flight up to and including holding pattern or point/time at which ATC provides separation between aircraft.

REFERENCE–
FAA Order JO 7110.65, Para 4–3–3, Abbreviated Departure Clearance.

4–2–8. IFR–VFR AND VFR–IFR FLIGHTS

a. Clear an aircraft planning IFR operations for the initial part of flight and VFR for the latter part to the fix at which the IFR part ends.

b. Treat an aircraft planning VFR for the initial part of flight and IFR for the latter part as a VFR departure. Issue a clearance to this aircraft when it requests IFR clearance approaching the fix where it proposes to start IFR operations. The phraseology CLEARED TO (destination) AIRPORT AS FILED may be used with abbreviated departure clearance procedures.

REFERENCE–
FAA Order JO 7110.65, Para 4–3–3, Abbreviated Departure Clearance.

c. When an aircraft changes from VFR to IFR, the controller must assign a beacon code to Mode-C equipped aircraft that will allow MSAW alarms.

d. When VFR aircraft operating below the minimum altitude for IFR operations requests an IFR clearance and the pilot informs you, or you are aware, that they are unable to climb in VFR conditions to the minimum IFR altitude:

1. Before issuing a clearance, ask if the pilot is able to maintain terrain and obstruction clearance during a climb to the minimum IFR altitude.

PHRASEOLOGY–
(Aircraft call sign), ARE YOU ABLE TO MAINTAIN YOUR OWN TERRAIN AND OBSTRUCTION CLEARANCE UNTIL REACHING (appropriate MVA/MIA/MEA/OROCA)

NOTE–
Pilots of pop–up aircraft are responsible for terrain and obstacle clearance until reaching minimum instrument altitude (MIA) or minimum en route altitude (MEA). Pilot compliance with an approved FAA procedure or an ATC instruction transfers that responsibility to the FAA; therefore, do not assign (or imply) specific course guidance that will (or could) be in effect below the MIA or MEA.

EXAMPLE–
"November Eight Seven Six, are you able to provide your own terrain and obstruction clearance between your present altitude and six thousand feet?"

2. If the pilot is able to maintain their own terrain and obstruction clearance, issue the appropriate IFR clearance as prescribed in paragraph 4–2–1, Clearance Items, and paragraph 4–5–6, Minimum En Route Altitudes.

3. If the pilot states that they are unable to maintain terrain and obstruction clearance, instruct the pilot to maintain VFR and to state intentions.

4. If appropriate, apply the provisions of paragraph 10–2–7, VFR Aircraft In Weather Difficulty, or paragraph 10–2–9, Radar Assistance Techniques, as necessary.

INTERPRETATION–
7110.65, 4–2–8, IFR–VFR and VFR–IFR Flights (11–03–2014)

4–2–9. CLEARANCE ITEMS

The following guidelines must be utilized to facilitate the processing of airfile aircraft:

a. Ensure the aircraft is within your area of jurisdiction unless otherwise coordinated.

b. Obtain necessary information needed to provide IFR service.

c. Issue clearance to destination, short range clearance, or an instruction to the pilot to contact an FSS if the flight plan cannot be processed. If clearance is to destination airport, the phraseology CLEARED TO (destination) AIRPORT must be used. If clearance is to a NAVAID, state the name of the NAVAID followed by the type of NAVAID, if the type is known. If clearance is to an intersection or waypoint and the type is known, the type must follow the intersection or waypoint name.

NOTE–
These procedures do not imply that the processing of airfiles has priority over another ATC duty to be performed.

REFERENCE–
FAA Order JO 7110.65, Para 2–2–1, Recording Information.

4–2–10. CANCELLATION OF IFR FLIGHT PLAN

a. If necessary, before instructing an IFR aircraft arriving at an airport not served by an air traffic control tower or flight service station to change to the common traffic advisory frequency, provide the pilot with instructions on how to cancel his/her IFR flight plan.

1. Airports with an air/ground communications station:

PHRASEOLOGY–
(Call sign) REPORT CANCELLATION OF IFR ON (frequency).

2. Airports without an air/ground communications station:

PHRASEOLOGY–
(Call sign) REPORT CANCELLATION OF IFR THIS FREQUENCY OR WITH FLIGHT SERVICE.

Or

(Call sign) REPORT CANCELLATION OF IFR THIS FREQUENCY OR WITH (FSS serving the area or the ATC controlling facility).

EXAMPLE–
"N13WA report cancellation of IFR this frequency or with McAlester Radio."

b. Respond to a pilot's cancellation of his/her IFR flight plan as follows:

PHRASEOLOGY–
(Call sign) IFR CANCELLATION RECEIVED.

Section 3. Departure Procedures

4-3-1. DEPARTURE TERMINOLOGY

Avoid using the term "takeoff" except to actually clear an aircraft for takeoff or to cancel a takeoff clearance. Use such terms as "depart," "departure," or "fly" in clearances when necessary.

REFERENCE-
FAA Order JO 7110.65, Para 3-9-9, Takeoff Clearance.
FAA Order JO 7110.65, Para 3-9-11, Cancellation of Takeoff Clearance.

4-3-2. DEPARTURE CLEARANCES

Include the following items in IFR departure clearances:

NOTE-
When considered necessary, controllers or pilots may initiate read backs of a clearance. Some pilots may be required by company rule to do so.

a. Always include the airport of departure when issuing a departure clearance for relay to an aircraft by an FSS, dispatcher, etc.

b. Clearance Limit.

1. Specify the destination airport when practicable, even though it is outside controlled airspace. Issue short range clearances as provided for in any procedures established for their use.

(a) When the clearance limit is an airport, the word "airport" must follow the airport name.

PHRASEOLOGY-
CLEARED TO (destination) AIRPORT

(b) When the clearance limit is a NAVAID and the NAVAID type is known, the type of NAVAID must follow the NAVAID name.

PHRASEOLOGY-
CLEARED TO (NAVAID name and type)

(c) When the clearance limit is an intersection or waypoint and the type is known, the type must follow the intersection or waypoint name.

PHRASEOLOGY-
CLEARED TO (intersection or waypoint name and type)

2. For Air Force One (AF1) operations, do not specify the destination airport.

NOTE-
Presidential detail is responsible for ensuring the accuracy of the destination airport.

PHRASEOLOGY-
DESTINATION AS FILED.

c. Departure Procedures.

1. Specify direction of takeoff/turn or initial heading to be flown after takeoff as follows:

(a) Locations with Airport Traffic Control Service-Specify direction of takeoff/turn or initial heading as necessary, consistent with published:

INTERPRETATION-
7110.65, 4-3-2 Departure Procedures (5-24-2011)

(1) Departure Procedures (DP). If an aircraft is vectored off a published Standard Instrument Departure (SID) or Obstacle Departure Procedure (ODP), that vector cancels the DP and ATC becomes responsible for separation from terrain and /or obstructions. IFR aircraft must be assigned an altitude.

(2) Diverse Vector Areas (DVA). The assignment of an initial heading using a DVA can be given to the pilot as part of the initial clearance, but must be given no later than with the takeoff clearance. Once airborne, an aircraft assigned headings within the DVA can be vectored below the MVA/MIA. Controllers cannot interrupt an aircraft's climb in the DVA until the aircraft is at or above the MVA/MIA.

NOTE–
1. *It is important for controllers to understand that there can be differences in published climb gradients applicable to individual departure procedures serving the same airport or runway. Assigning a different departure procedure without the pilot being able to re–brief may result in the pilot rejecting the new procedure.*

2. *When a departure clearance includes a SID, concurrent use of a diverse vector area (DVA) is not permitted.*

REFERENCE–
AIM, Para 5–2–7, Departure Control.
AIM, Para 5–2–9, Instrument Departure Procedures (DP) – Obstacle Departure Procedures (ODP) and Standard Instrument Departures (SID).

(b) Locations without Airport Traffic Control Service, but within a Class E surface area – specify direction of takeoff/turn or initial heading if necessary. Obtain/solicit the pilot's concurrence concerning a turn or heading before issuing them in a clearance.

NOTE–
Direction of takeoff and turn after takeoff can be obtained/solicited directly from the pilot, or relayed by an FSS, dispatcher, etc., as obtained/solicited from the pilot.

(c) At all other airports– Do not specify direction of takeoff/turn after takeoff. If necessary to specify an initial heading to be flown after takeoff, issue the initial heading so as to apply only within controlled airspace.

2. Where an ODP has been published for a location and pilot compliance is necessary to ensure separation, include the procedure as part of the ATC clearance. Additionally, when an ODP is included in the clearance and the Visual Climb over Airport (VCOA) is requested by the pilot or assigned by ATC when it is the only procedure published in the ODP, include an instruction to remain within the published visibility of the VCOA.

EXAMPLE–
"Depart via the (airport name)(runway number) obstacle departure procedure. Remain within (number of miles) miles of the (airport name) during visual climb" if applicable. Or,
"Depart via the (graphic ODP name) obstacle departure procedure. Remain within (number of miles) miles of the (airport name) during visual climb" if applicable.

NOTE–
1. *Pilots will advise ATC of their intent to use the VCOA option when requesting their IFR clearance.*

2. *Some aircraft are required by 14 CFR 91.175 to depart a runway under IFR using the ODP absent other instructions from ATC.*

3. *IFR takeoff minimums and obstacle departure procedures are prescribed for specific airports/runways and published in either a textual, or graphic form with the label (OBSTACLE) in the procedure title, and documented on an appropriate FAA Form 8260. To alert pilots of their existence, instrument approach procedure charts are annotated with a symbol:*

3. Compatibility with a procedure issued may be verified by asking the pilot if items obtained/ solicited will allow him/her to comply with local traffic pattern, terrain, or obstruction avoidance.

PHRASEOLOGY–
FLY RUNWAY HEADING.

DEPART (direction or runway).

TURN LEFT/RIGHT.

WHEN ENTERING CONTROLLED AIRSPACE (instruction), FLY HEADING (degrees) UNTIL REACHING (altitude, point, or fix) BEFORE PROCEEDING ON COURSE.

FLY A (degree) BEARING/AZIMUTH FROM/TO (fix) UNTIL (time),

or

UNTIL REACHING (fix or altitude),

and if required,

BEFORE PROCEEDING ON COURSE.

EXAMPLE−
"Verify right turn after departure will allow compliance with local traffic pattern," or "Verify this clearance will allow compliance with terrain or obstruction avoidance."

NOTE−
If a published IFR departure procedure is not included in an ATC clearance, compliance with such a procedure is the pilot's prerogative.

4. SIDs:

(a) Assign a SID (including transition if necessary). Assign an ADR/ADAR, when applicable or the route filed by the pilot, when a SID is not established for the departure route to be flown, or the pilot has indicated that he/she does not wish to use a SID.

NOTE−
Departure procedure descriptive text contained within parentheses (for example, "Jimmy One (RNAV) Departure") is not included in departure clearance phraseology.

PHRASEOLOGY−
(SID name and number) DEPARTURE.

(SID name and number) DEPARTURE, (transition name) TRANSITION.

EXAMPLE−
"Stroudsburg One Departure."
"Stroudsburg One Departure, Sparta Transition."

NOTE−
If a pilot does not wish to use a SID issued in an ATC clearance, or any other SID published for that location, he/she is expected to advise ATC.

(b) If it is necessary to assign a crossing altitude which differs from the SID altitude emphasize the change to the pilot.

PHRASEOLOGY−
(SID name and number) DEPARTURE, EXCEPT CROSS (revised altitude information).

EXAMPLE−
"Stroudsburg One Departure, except cross Quaker at five thousand."

"Astoria Two Departure, except cross Astor waypoint at six thousand."

(c) Specify altitudes when they are not included in the SID.

PHRASEOLOGY−
(SID name and number) DEPARTURE. CROSS (fix) AT (altitude).

EXAMPLE−
"Stroudsburg One Departure. Cross Jersey intersection at four thousand. Cross Range intersection at six thousand."

"Engle Two departure. Cross Pilim waypoint at or above five thousand. Cross Engle waypoint at or above seven thousand. Cross Gorge waypoint at niner thousand."

d. Route of flight. Specify one or more of the following:

1. Airway, route, course, heading, azimuth, arc, or vector.

2. The routing a pilot can expect if any part of the route beyond a short range clearance limit differs from that filed.

PHRASEOLOGY−
EXPECT FURTHER CLEARANCE VIA (airways, routes, or fixes.)

e. Altitude. Use one of the following in the order of preference listed.

NOTE−
Turbojet aircraft equipped with afterburner engines may occasionally be expected to use afterburning during their climb to the en route altitude. When so advised by the pilot, the controller may be able to plan his/her traffic to accommodate the high performance climb and allow the pilot to climb to his/her planned altitude without restriction.

REFERENCE−
P/CG, Climb Via, Top Altitude

1. To the maximum extent possible, Air Force One will be cleared unrestricted climb to:

(a) 9,000' AGL or higher.

(b) If unable 9,000' AGL or higher, then the highest available altitude below 9,000' AGL.

2. Assign the altitude requested by the pilot.

3. Assign an altitude, as near as possible to the altitude requested by the pilot, and

(a) Inform the pilot when to expect clearance to the requested altitude unless instructions are contained in the specified SID, or

(b) If the requested altitude is not expected to be available, inform the pilot what altitude can be expected and when/where to expect it.

4. Use one of the following when the SID contains published crossing restrictions:

(a) Instruct aircraft to "Climb via SID."

(b) Instruct the aircraft to "Climb via SID except maintain (altitude)" when a top altitude is not published or when it is necessary to issue an interim altitude.

EXAMPLE−
"Cleared to Johnston Airport, Scott One departure, Jonez transition, Q One Forty−five. Climb via SID."

"Cleared to Johnston Airport, Scott One departure, Jonez transition, Q One Forty−five, Climb via SID except maintain flight level one eight zero."

"Cleared to Johnston Airport, Scott One departure, Jonez transition, Q One Forty−five, Climb Via SID except maintain flight level one eight zero, expect flight level three five zero one zero minutes after departure."

NOTE−
1. *Use of "Climb via SID Except Maintain" to emphasize a published procedural constraint is an inappropriate use of this phraseology.*

2. *Considering the principle that the last ATC clearance issued has precedence over the previous, the phraseology "maintain (altitude)" alone cancels previously issued altitude restrictions, including SID/STAR altitude restrictions, unless they are restated or modified.*

REFERENCE−
FAA Order JO 7110.65, Para 4−2−5, Route or Altitude Amendments.
AIM, Para 4−4−10, Adherence to Clearance.

5. When a SID does not contain published crossing restrictions and/or is a SID with a Radar Vector segment or a Radar Vector SID; or a SID is constructed with a Radar Vector segment and contains published crossing restrictions after the vector segment, instruct aircraft to "MAINTAIN (altitude)."

NOTE−
1. *14 CFR Section 91.185, says that in the event of a two-way radio communication failure, in VFR conditions or if VFR*

conditions are encountered after the failure, the pilot must continue the flight under VFR and land as soon as practicable. That section also says that when the failure occurs in IFR conditions the pilot must continue flight at the highest of the following altitudes or flight levels for the route segment being flown:

a. *The altitude or flight level assigned in the last ATC clearance received.*

b. *The minimum altitude (converted, if appropriate, to minimum flight level as prescribed in 14 CFR Section 91.121(c)) for IFR operations. (This altitude should be consistent with MEAs, MOCAs, etc.)*

c. *The altitude or flight level ATC has advised may be expected in a further clearance.*

2. *If the expected altitude is the highest of the preceding choices, the pilot should begin to climb to that expected altitude at the time or fix specified in the clearance. The choice to climb to the expected altitude is not applicable if the pilot has proceeded beyond the specified fix or if the time designated in the clearance has expired.*

PHRASEOLOGY−

CLIMB AND MAINTAIN (the altitude as near as possible to the pilot's requested altitude). EXPECT (the requested altitude or an altitude different from the requested altitude) AT (time or fix),

and if applicable,

(pilot's requested altitude) IS NOT AVAILABLE.

EXAMPLE−

1. *A pilot has requested flight level 350. Flight level 230 is immediately available and flight level 350 will be available at the Appleton zero five zero radial 35 mile fix. The clearance will read:*
"Climb and maintain flight level two three zero. Expect flight level three five zero at Appleton zero five zero radial three five mile fix."

2. *A pilot has requested 9,000 feet. An altitude restriction is required because of facility procedures or requirements. Assign the altitude and advise the pilot at what fix/time the pilot may expect the requested altitude. The clearance could read:*
"Climb and maintain five thousand. Expect niner thousand one zero minutes after departure."

3. *A pilot has requested 17,000 feet which is unavailable. You plan 15,000 feet to be the pilot's highest altitude prior to descent to the pilot's destination but only 13,000 feet is available until San Jose VOR. Advise the pilot of the expected altitude change and at what fix/time to expect clearance to 15,000 feet. The clearance will read:*
"Climb and maintain one three thousand. Expect one five thousand at San Jose. One seven thousand is not available."

REFERENCE−
FAA Order JO 7110.65, Para 4−3−3, Abbreviated Departure Clearance.
FAA Order JO 7110.65, Para 5−8−2, Initial Heading.
FAA Order JO 7110.65 Para 4−2−5, Route or Altitude Amendments.
AIM, Para 4−4−10, Adherence to Clearance.

4−3−3. ABBREVIATED DEPARTURE CLEARANCE

a. Issue an abbreviated departure clearance if its use reduces verbiage and the following conditions are met:

REFERENCE−
FAA Order JO 7110.65, Para 4−2−8, IFR-VFR and VFR-IFR Flights.

1. The route of flight filed with ATC has not been changed by the pilot, company, operations officer, input operator, or in the stored flight plan program prior to departure.

NOTE−
A pilot will not accept an abbreviated clearance if the route of flight filed with ATC has been changed by him/her or the company or the operations officer before departure. He/she is expected to inform the control facility on initial radio contact if he/she cannot accept the clearance. It is the responsibility of the company or operations officer to inform the pilot when they make a change.

2. All ATC facilities concerned have sufficient route of flight information to exercise their control responsibilities.

NOTE−
The route of flight information to be provided may be covered in letters of agreement.

3. When the flight will depart IFR, destination airport information is relayed between the facilities concerned prior to departure.

EXAMPLE–
1. *A tower or flight service station relay of destination airport information to the center when requesting clearance: "Request clearance for United Four Sixty-One to O'Hare."*

2. *A center relay to the tower or flight service station when initiating a clearance: "Clearance for United Four Sixty-One to O'Hare."*

NOTE–
Pilots are expected to furnish the facility concerned with destination airport information on initial radio call-up. This will provide the information necessary for detecting any destination airport differences on facility relay.

4. The assigned altitude, according to the provisions in paragraph 4–3–2, Departure Clearances, subparagraph e, is stated in the clearance.

b. If it is necessary to modify a filed route of flight in order to achieve computer acceptance due, for example, to incorrect fix or airway identification, the contraction "FRC," meaning "Full Route Clearance Necessary," or "FRC/(fix)," will be added to the remarks. "FRC" or "FRC/(fix)" must always be the first item of intra-center remarks. When "FRC" or "FRC/(fix)" appears on a flight progress strip, the controller issuing the ATC clearance to the aircraft must issue a full route clearance to the specified fix, or, if no fix is specified, for the entire route.

EXAMPLE–
"Cleared to Missoula International Airport, Chief Two Departure to Angley; direct Salina; then as filed; maintain one seven thousand."

NOTE–
Changes, such as those made to conform with traffic flows and preferred routings, are only permitted to be made by the pilot (or his/her operations office) or the controller responsible for initiating the clearance to the aircraft.

c. Specify the destination airport in the clearance.

d. When no changes are required in the filed route, state the phrase: "Cleared to (destination) airport, ([SID name and number] and SID transition, as appropriate); then, as filed." If a SID is not assigned, follow with "As filed." If required, add any additional instructions or information, including requested altitude if different than assigned.

e. Use one of the following when the SID contains published crossing restrictions:

1. Instruct aircraft to "Climb via SID."

2. Instruct aircraft to "Climb via SID except maintain (altitude)" when a top altitude is not published or when it is necessary to issue an interim altitude.

NOTE–
Use of "Climb via SID Except Maintain" to emphasize a published procedural constraint is an inappropriate use of this phraseology.

f. Instruct aircraft to MAINTAIN (altitude) when:

1. No SID is assigned.

2. A SID does not contain published crossing restrictions and/or is a SID with a Radar Vector segment or is a Radar Vector SID.

3. A SID is constructed with a Radar Vector segment and contains published crossing restrictions after the vector segment.

PHRASEOLOGY–
CLEARED TO (destination) AIRPORT;

and as appropriate,

(SID name and number) DEPARTURE,
THEN AS FILED.

When the SID does not contain published crossing restrictions and/or is a SID with a Radar Vector segment or a Radar Vector SID; or is a SID with a radar vector segment and contains published crossing restrictions after the vector segment.

MAINTAIN (altitude); (additional instructions or information).

Or when a SID contains published crossing restrictions,

CLIMB VIA SID.

CLIMB VIA SID EXCEPT MAINTAIN (altitude); (additional instructions or information).

If a SID is not assigned,

CLEARED TO (destination) AIRPORT AS FILED.
MAINTAIN (altitude);

and if required,

(additional instructions or information).

EXAMPLE–
"Cleared to Reynolds Airport; David Two Departure, Kingham Transition; then, as filed. Maintain niner thousand. Expect flight level four one zero, one zero minutes after departure."

"Cleared to Reynolds Airport; David Two Departure, Kingham Transition; then, as filed. Climb via SID."

"Cleared to Reynolds Airport; David Two Departure, Kingham Transition; then, as filed. Climb via SID except maintain flight level two four zero. Expect flight level four one zero, one zero minutes after departure.

"Cleared to Reynolds Airport as filed. Maintain niner thousand. Expect flight level four one zero, one zero minutes after departure."

NOTE–
1. *SIDs are excluded from "cleared as filed" procedures.*

2. *If a pilot does not wish to accept an ATC clearance to fly a SID, he/she is expected to advise ATC or state "NO SID" in his/her flight plan remarks.*

REFERENCE–
P/CG, Climb Via, Top Altitude.

g. When a filed route will require revisions, the controller responsible for initiating the clearance to the aircraft must either:

1. Issue a FRC/FRC until a fix.

2. Specify the assigned altitude to maintain, or Climb Via SID, or Climb Via SID except maintain (altitude), as appropriate.

PHRASEOLOGY–
CLEARED TO (destination) AIRPORT.

Or when the SID does not contain published crossing restrictions and/ or is a SID with a Radar Vector segment or a Radar Vector SID

(SID name and number) DEPARTURE,
(transition name) TRANSITION; THEN, AS FILED, EXCEPT CHANGE ROUTE TO READ (amended route portion).
MAINTAIN (altitude);

Or when the SID contains published crossing restrictions,

CLIMB VIA SID

CLIMB VIA SID EXCEPT MAINTAIN (altitude).
and if required,

(additional instructions or information).

If a SID is not assigned,

CLEARED TO (destination) AIRPORT AS FILED,
EXCEPT CHANGE ROUTE TO READ (amended route portion). MAINTAIN (altitude);

and if required,

(additional instructions or information).

EXAMPLE–
"Cleared to Reynolds Airport; South Boston One Departure; then, as filed, except change route to read South Boston Victor Twenty Greensboro. Maintain eight thousand, report leaving four thousand."

"Cleared to Reynolds Airport; South Boston One Departure; then, as filed, except change route to read South Boston Victor Twenty Greensboro; climb via SID."

"Cleared to Reynolds Airport; South Boston One Departure; then, as filed, except change route to read South Boston Victor Twenty Greensboro; climb via SID except maintain flight level one eight zero, expect flight level three one zero one zero minutes after departure."

"Cleared to Reynolds Airport as filed, except change route to read South Boston Victor Twenty Greensboro. Maintain eight thousand, report leaving four thousand."

"Cleared to Reynolds Airport via Victor Ninety-one Albany, then as filed. Maintain six thousand."

h. In a nonradar environment specify one, two, or more fixes, as necessary, to identify the initial route of flight.

1. Specify the destination airport, when practicable, followed by the word "airport" even though it is outside controlled airspace.

PHRASEOLOGY–
CLEARED TO (destination) AIRPORT

2. When the clearance limit is a NAVAID, the type of NAVAID must follow the NAVAID name.

PHRASEOLOGY–
CLEARED TO (NAVAID name and type)

3. When the clearance limit is an intersection or waypoint and the type is known, the type must follow the intersection or waypoint name.

PHRASEOLOGY–
CLEARED TO (intersection or waypoint name and type)

EXAMPLE–
The filed route of flight is from Hutchinson V10 Emporia, thence V10N and V77 to St. Joseph. The clearance will read: "Cleared to Watson Airport as filed via Emporia, maintain Seven Thousand."

i. Do not apply these procedures when a pilot requests a detailed clearance or to military operations conducted within ALTRV, stereo routes, operations above FL 600, and other military operations requiring special handling.

NOTE–
Departure clearance procedures and phraseology for military operations within approved altitude reservations, military operations above FL 600, and other military operations requiring special handling are contained in separate procedures in this order or in a LOA, as appropriate.

REFERENCE–
FAA Order JO 7110.65, Para 4–2–7, ALTRV Clearance.
FAA Order JO 7110.65, Para 9–2–14, Military Operations Above FL 600.

4–3–4. DEPARTURE RELEASE, HOLD FOR RELEASE, RELEASE TIMES, DEPARTURE RESTRICTIONS, AND CLEARANCE VOID TIMES

Assign departure restrictions, clearance void times, or release times to separate departures from other traffic or to restrict or regulate the departure flow. Departures from an airport without an operating control tower must be issued either a departure release, a hold for release, or a release time.

REFERENCE–
FAA Order JO 7110.65, Para 10–3–1, Overdue Aircraft.
FAA Order JO 7110.65, Para 10–4–1, Traffic Restrictions.
FAA Order JO 7110.65, Para 10–4–3, Traffic Resumption.

a. Departure Release. When conditions allow, release the aircraft as soon as possible.

PHRASEOLOGY–
To another controller,
(aircraft identification) RELEASED.

To a flight service specialist, or Flight Data Communication Specialist (FDCS).

ADVISE (aircraft identification) RELEASED FOR DEPARTURE.

To a pilot at an airport without an operating control tower,
(aircraft identification) RELEASED FOR DEPARTURE.

b. Hold For Release (HFR).

1. "Hold for release" instructions must be used to inform a pilot or a controller that a departure clearance is not valid until additional instructions are received.

REFERENCE–
P/CG Term – Hold for Release.

2. When issuing hold for release instructions, include departure delay information.

PHRASEOLOGY–
(aircraft identification) HOLD FOR RELEASE, EXPECT (time in hours and/or minutes) DEPARTURE DELAY.

c. Release Times.

1. Release times must be issued to pilots when necessary to specify the earliest time an aircraft may depart.

NOTE–
A release time is a departure restriction issued to a pilot (either directly or through authorized relay) to separate a departing aircraft from other traffic.

2. The facility issuing a release time to a pilot _must issue a time check. A release time using a specified number of minutes does not require a time check.

PHRASEOLOGY–
(aircraft identification) RELEASED FOR DEPARTURE AT (time in hours and/or minutes),

and if required,

IF NOT OFF BY (time), ADVISE (facility) NOT LATER THAN (time) OF INTENTIONS.

TIME (time in hours, minutes, and nearest quarter minute).

(aircraft identification) RELEASED FOR DEPARTURE IN (number of minutes) MINUTES

and if required,

IF NOT OFF IN (number of minutes) MINUTES, ADVISE (facility) OF INTENTIONS WITHIN (number of minutes) MINUTES.

d. When expect departure clearance times (EDCT) are assigned through traffic management programs, excluding overriding call for release (CFR) operations as described in subparagraph e, the departure terminal must, to the extent possible, plan ground movement of aircraft destined to the affected airport(s) so that flights are sequenced to depart no earlier than 5 minutes before, and no later than 5 minutes after the EDCT. Do not release aircraft on their assigned EDCT if a ground stop (GS) applicable to that aircraft is in effect, unless approval has been received from the originator of the GS.

e. Call for Release (CFR). When CFR is in effect, release aircraft so they are airborne within a window that extends from 2 minutes prior and ends 1 minute after the assigned time, unless otherwise coordinated.

NOTE–
1. *Subparagraph e applies to all facilities.*

2. *Coordination may be verbal, electronic, or written.*

1. If an aircraft has begun to taxi or requests taxi in a manner consistent with meeting the EDCT, the aircraft must be released. Additional coordination is not required.

2. If an aircraft requests taxi or clearance for departure inconsistent with meeting the EDCT window, ask the pilot to verify the EDCT.

(a) If the pilot's EDCT is the same as the FAA EDCT, the aircraft is released consistent with the EDCT.

(b) If the pilot's EDCT is not the same as the FAA EDCT, refer to Trust and Verify note below.

3. If an aircraft requests taxi too late to meet the EDCT, contact the ATCSCC through the appropriate TMU.

NOTE–
(Trust & Verify) EDCTs are revised by Air Carriers and Traffic Management for changing conditions en route or at affected airport(s). Terminal controllers' use of aircraft reported EDCT for departure sequencing should be verified with the appropriate TMU prior to departure if this can be accomplished without the aircraft incurring delay beyond the EDCT reported by the aircraft. The preferred method for verification is the Flight Schedule Monitor (FSM). If the EDCT cannot be verified without incurring additional delay, the aircraft should be released based on the pilot reported EDCT. The aircraft operator is responsible for operating in a manner consistent to meet the EDCT.

f. Clearance Void Times.

1. When issuing clearance void times at airports without an operating control tower, provide alternative instructions requiring the pilots to advise ATC of their intentions no later than 30 minutes after the clearance void time if not airborne.

2. The facility delivering a clearance void time to a pilot must issue a time check. A void time issued using a specified number of minutes does not require a time check.

NOTE–
If the clearance void time expires, it does not cancel the departure clearance or IFR flight plan. It withdraws the pilot's authority to depart IFR until a new departure release/release time has been issued by ATC and acknowledged by the pilot.

PHRASEOLOGY–
CLEARANCE VOID IF NOT OFF BY (clearance void time),

and if required,
IF NOT OFF BY (clearance void time), ADVISE (facility) NOT LATER THAN (time) OF INTENTIONS.

TIME (time in hours, minutes, and the nearest quarter minute).

Or

CLEARANCE VOID IF NOT OFF IN (number of minutes) MINUTES

and if required,

IF NOT OFF IN (number of minutes) MINUTES, ADVISE (facility) OF INTENTIONS WITHIN (number of minutes) MINUTES.

4–3–5. GROUND STOP

Do not release an aircraft if a ground stop (GS) applicable to that aircraft is in effect, without the approval of the originator of the GS.

4–3–6. DELAY SEQUENCING

When aircraft elect to take delay on the ground before departure, issue departure clearances to them in the order in which the requests for clearance were originally made if practicable.

4–3–7. FORWARD DEPARTURE DELAY INFORMATION

Inform approach control facilities and/or towers of anticipated departure delays.

4–3–8. COORDINATION WITH RECEIVING FACILITY

a. Coordinate with the receiving facility before the departure of an aircraft if the departure point is less than 15 minutes flying time from the transferring facility's boundary unless an automatic transfer of data between automated systems will occur, in which case, the flying time requirement may be reduced to 5 minutes or replaced with a mileage from the boundary parameter when mutually agreeable to both facilities.

NOTE–
Agreements requiring additional time are encouraged between facilities that need earlier coordination. However, when agreements establish mandatory radar handoff procedures, coordination needs only be effected in a timely manner prior to transfer of control.

REFERENCE–
FAA Order JO 7110.65, Chapter 5, Section 4, Transfer of Radar Identification, Para 5–4–1, Application.

b. The actual departure time or a subsequent strip posting time must be forwarded to the receiving facility unless assumed departure times are agreed upon and that time is within 3 minutes of the actual departure time.

4–3–9. VFR RELEASE OF IFR DEPARTURE

When an aircraft which has filed an IFR flight plan requests a VFR departure through a terminal facility, FSS, ARTCC Flight Data Unit, or air/ground communications station:

a. After obtaining, if necessary, approval from the facility/sector responsible for issuing the IFR clearance, you may authorize an IFR flight planned aircraft to depart VFR. Inform the pilot of the proper frequency and, if appropriate, where or when to contact the facility responsible for issuing the clearance.

PHRASEOLOGY–
VFR DEPARTURE AUTHORIZED. CONTACT (facility) ON (frequency) AT (location or time if required) FOR CLEARANCE.

b. If the facility/sector responsible for issuing the clearance is unable to issue a clearance, inform the pilot, and suggest that the delay be taken on the ground. If the pilot insists upon taking off VFR and obtaining an IFR clearance in the air, inform the facility/sector holding the flight plan of the pilot's intentions and, if possible, the VFR departure time.

4-3-10. FORWARDING DEPARTURE TIMES

TERMINAL

Unless alternate procedures are prescribed in a letter of agreement or automatic departure messages are being transmitted between automated facilities, forward departure times to the facility from which you received the clearance and also to the terminal departure controller when that position is involved in the departure sequence.

NOTE-
1. *Letters of agreement prescribing assumed departure times or mandatory radar handoff procedures are alternatives for providing equivalent procedures.*

2. *The letters "DM" flashing in the data block signify unsuccessful transmission of a departure message.*

Section 4. Route Assignment

4–4–1. ROUTE USE

Clear aircraft via routes consistent with the altitude stratum in which the operation is to be conducted by one or more of the following:

NOTE–
Except for certain NAVAIDs/routes used by scheduled air carriers or authorized for specific uses in the control of IFR aircraft, Air Traffic Service (ATS) routes, and NAVAIDs established for use at specified altitudes are shown on U.S. government charts or DoD FLIP charts.

REFERENCE–
FAA Order JO 7110.65, Para 2–5–2, NAVAID Terms.
FAA Order JO 7110.65, Para 4–1–2, Exceptions.
FAA Order JO 7110.65, Para 4–5–6, Minimum En Route Altitudes.
FAA Order JO 7110.65, Para 5–6–1, Application.

a. Designated ATS routes.

PHRASEOLOGY–
VIA:

VICTOR (color) (airway number)(the word Romeo when RNAV for existing Alaska routes),

or

J (route number) (the word Romeo when RNAV for existing Alaska routes),

or

Q (route number)

or

Tango (route number)

or

SUBSTITUTE (ATS route) FROM (fix) to (fix),

or

IR (route number).

CROSS/JOIN VICTOR/(color) (airway number), (number of miles) MILES (direction) OF (fix).

b. Radials, courses, azimuths to or from NAVAIDs.

PHRASEOLOGY–
VIA;

(name of NAVAID) (specified) RADIAL/COURSE/AZIMUTH,

or

(fix) AND (fix),

or

RADIALS OF (ATS route) AND (ATS route).

c. Random routes.

1. When not being radar monitored, GNSS-equipped RNAV aircraft on random RNAV routes must be cleared via or reported to be established on a point–to–point route.

(a) The points must be published NAVAIDs, waypoints, fixes or airports recallable from the aircraft's navigation database. The points must be displayed on controller video maps or depicted on the controller chart displayed at the control position. When applying nonradar separation the maximum distance between points must not exceed 500 miles.

(b) Protect 4 miles either side of the route centerline.

(c) Assigned altitudes must be at or above the highest MIA along the projected route segment being flown, including the protected airspace of that route segment.

2. Impromptu.

PHRASEOLOGY–
DIRECT (name of NAVAID/waypoint/fix/airport).

NOTE–
A random impromptu routing is a direct course initiated by ATC or requested by the pilot during flight. Aircraft are cleared from their present position to a NAVAID, waypoint, fix, or airport.

3. Point-to-Point.

PHRASEOLOGY–
After (fix) proceed direct (fix)

NOTE–
A point-to-point route segment begins and ends with a published NAVAID, waypoint, fix, or airport.

d. DME arcs of NAVAIDs.

e. Radials, courses, azimuths, and headings of departure or arrival routes.

f. SIDs/STARs.

g. Vectors.

h. Fixes defined in terms of degree–distance from NAVAIDs for special military operations.

i. Courses, azimuths, bearings, quadrants, or radials within a radius of a NAVAID.

PHRASEOLOGY–
CLEARED TO FLY (general direction from NAVAID) OF (NAVAID name and type) BETWEEN (specified) COURSES TO/BEARINGS FROM/RADIALS (NAVAID name when a NDB) WITHIN (number of miles) MILE RADIUS,

or

CLEARED TO FLY (specified) QUADRANT OF (NAVAID name and type) WITHIN (number of miles) MILE RADIUS.

EXAMPLE–
1. *"Cleared to fly east of Allentown VORTAC between the zero four five and the one three five radials within four zero mile radius."*

2. *"Cleared to fly east of Crystal Lake radio beacon between the two two five and the three one five courses to Crystal Lake within three zero mile radius."*

3. *"Cleared to fly northeast quadrant of Philipsburg VORTAC within four zero mile radius."*

j. Fixes/waypoints defined in terms of:

1. Published name; or

2. Degree−distance from NAVAIDs; or

3. Latitude/longitude coordinates, state the latitude and longitude in degrees and minutes including the direction from the axis such as North or West; or

4. Offset from published or established ATS route at a specified distance and direction for random (impromptu) RNAV Routes.

PHRASEOLOGY−
DIRECT (fix/waypoint)

DIRECT TO THE (facility) (radial) (distance) FIX.

DIRECT (number degrees) DEGREES, (number minutes) MINUTES (north or south), (number degrees) DEGREES, (number minutes) MINUTES (east or west).

OFFSET (distance) RIGHT/LEFT OF (route).

EXAMPLE−
"Direct SUNOL."
"Direct to the Appleton three one zero radial two five mile fix."
"Direct 32 degrees, 45 minutes north, 105 degrees, 37 minutes west."
"Offset eight miles right of Victor six."

REFERENCE−
FAA Order JO 7110.65, Para 2−3−8, Aircraft Equipment Suffix.
FAA Order JO 7110.65, Para 2−5−3, NAVAID Fixes.
FAA Order JO 7110.65, Para 4−1−2, Exceptions.
FAA Order JO 7110.65, Para 5−5−1, Application.
FAA Order JO 7110.65, Para 6−5−4, Minima Along Other Than Established Airways or Routes.
P/CG Term - Global Navigation Satellite System (GNSS)[ICAO].

4−4−2. ROUTE STRUCTURE TRANSITIONS

To effect transition within or between route structures, clear an aircraft by one or more of the following methods, based on NAVAIDs or RNAV:

a. Vector aircraft to or from radials, courses, or azimuths of the ATS route assigned.

b. Assign a SID/STAR.

c. Clear departing or arriving aircraft to climb or descend via radials, courses, or azimuths of the ATS route assigned.

d. Clear departing or arriving aircraft directly to or between the NAVAIDs forming the ATS route assigned.

e. Clear aircraft to climb or descend via the ATS route on which flight will be conducted.

f. Clear aircraft to climb or descend on specified radials, courses, or azimuths of NAVAIDs.

g. Clear RNAV aircraft between designated or established ATS routes via random RNAV routes to a NAVAID, waypoint, airport or fix on the new route. Provide radar monitoring to aircraft transitioning via random RNAV routes.

EXCEPTION. GNSS−equipped aircraft /G, /L, /S, and /V on point−to−point routes, or transitioning between two point−to−point routes via an impromptu route.

REFERENCE−
FAA Order JO 7110.65, Para 4−1−2, Exceptions.
FAA Order JO 7110.65, Para 4−4−1, Route Use.
FAA Order JO 7110.65, Para 5−5−1, Application.
FAA Order JO 7110.65, Para 6−5−4, Minima Along Other Than Established Airways Or Routes.
P/CG Term − Global Navigation Satellite System (GNSS)[ICAO].

4-4-3. DEGREE-DISTANCE ROUTE DEFINITION FOR MILITARY OPERATIONS

EN ROUTE

a. Do not accept a military flight plan whose route or route segments do not coincide with designated Air Traffic Service routes or with a direct course between NAVAIDs unless it is authorized in subparagraph b and meets the following degree-distance route definition and procedural requirements:

1. The route or route segments must be defined in the flight plan by degree-distance fixes composed of:

(a) A location identifier;

(b) Azimuth in degrees magnetic; and

(c) Distance in miles from the NAVAID used.

EXAMPLE-
"MKE 030025."

2. The NAVAIDs selected to define the degree-distance fixes must be those authorized for use at the altitude being flown and at a distance within the published service volume area.

3. The distance between the fixes used to define the route must not exceed:

(a) Below FL 180- 80 miles;

(b) FL 180 and above- 260 miles; and

(c) For celestial navigation routes, all altitudes- 260 miles.

4. Degree-distance fixes used to define a route must be considered compulsory reporting points except that an aircraft may be authorized by ATC to omit reports when traffic conditions permit.

5. Military aircraft using degree-distance route definition procedures must conduct operations in accordance with the following:

(a) Unless prior coordination has been effected with the appropriate air traffic control facility, flight plan the departure and the arrival phases to conform with the routine flow of traffic when operating within 75 miles of the departure and the arrival airport. Use defined routes or airways or direct courses between NAVAIDs or as otherwise required to conform to the normal flow of traffic.

(b) Flight plans must be filed at least 2 hours before the estimated time of departure.

b. The following special military operations are authorized to define routes, or portions of routes, by degree-distance fixes:

1. Airborne radar navigation, radar bomb scoring (RBS), and airborne missile programming conducted by the USAF, USN, and RAF.

2. Celestial navigation conducted by the USAF, USN, and RAF.

3. Target aircraft operating in conjunction with air defense interceptors, and air defense interceptors while en route to and from assigned airspace.

4. Missions conducted above FL 450.

5. USN fighter and attack aircraft operating in positive control airspace.

6. USN/USMC aircraft, TACAN equipped, operating within the Honolulu FIR/Hawaiian airways area.

7. USAF/USN/USMC aircraft flight planned to operate on MTRs.

8. USAF Air Mobility Command (AMC) aircraft operating on approved station-keeping equipment (SKE) routes in accordance with the conditions and limitations listed in FAA Exemption No. 4371 to 14 CFR Section 91.177(a)(2) and 14 CFR Section 91.179(b)(1).

4-4-4. ALTERNATIVE ROUTES

When any part of an airway or route is unusable because of NAVAID status, clear aircraft that are not RNAV capable via one of the following alternative routes:

a. A route depicted on current U.S. Government charts/publications. Use the word "substitute" immediately preceding the alternative route in issuing the clearance.

b. A route defined by specifying NAVAID radials, courses, or azimuths.

c. A route defined as direct to or between NAVAIDs.

d. Vectors.

NOTE–
Inform area navigation aircraft that will proceed to the NAVAID location of the NAVAID outage.

4-4-5. CLASS G AIRSPACE

Include routes through Class G airspace only when requested by the pilot.

NOTE–
1. *Separation criteria are not applicable in Class G airspace. Traffic advisories and safety alerts are applicable within Class G airspace to aircraft that are in direct communication with ATC.*

2. *Flight plans filed for random RNAV routes through Class G airspace are considered a request by the pilot.*

3. *Flight plans containing MTR segments in/through Class G airspace are considered a request by the pilot.*

REFERENCE–
FAA Order JO 7110.65, Para 2-1-1, ATC Service.
P/CG – Class G Airspace.
P/CG – Uncontrolled Airspace.

4-4-6. DIRECT CLEARANCES

a. Unless operational necessity dictates, do not issue a routing clearance that will take an aircraft off of its flight plan route if:

1. The aircraft is part of a known traffic management initiative.

2. The part of the route under consideration for the direct routing is within a protected segment. If a flight routing within a protected segment is amended, coordination must be accomplished as follows:

(a) ATCS: with TMU.

(b) Terminal facility TMU: with overlying ARTCC TMU.

(c) ARTCC TMU (for amendments outside their facility): with ATCSCC.

b. *EN ROUTE.* Do not issue revised routing clearances that will take an aircraft off its flight plan route past the last fix in your facility's airspace, unless requested by the pilot or operational necessity dictates.

NOTE–
Nothing in this paragraph must preclude a controller from issuing a routing clearance that conforms to a letter of agreement or standard operating procedure within their own facility or between facilities, is required to maintain separation or comply with traffic flow management initiatives.

Section 5. Altitude Assignment and Verification

4–5–1. VERTICAL SEPARATION MINIMA

Separate instrument flight rules (IFR) aircraft using the following minima between altitudes:

a. Up to and including FL 410– 1,000 feet.

b. Apply 2,000 feet at or above FL 290 between non–RVSM aircraft and all other aircraft at or above FL 290.

c. Above FL 410– 2,000 feet, except:

1. In oceanic airspace, above FL 450 between a supersonic and any other aircraft– 4,000 feet.

2. Above FL 600 between military aircraft– 5,000 feet.

NOTE–
Oceanic separation procedures are supplemented in Chapter 8; Section 7, Section 8, Section 9 , and Section 10.

REFERENCE–
FAA Order JO 7110.65, Para 5–5–5, Vertical Application.
FAA Order JO 7110.65, Para 6–6–1, Application.
FAA Order JO 7110.65, Para 9–2–14, Military Operations Above FL 600.

4–5–2. FLIGHT DIRECTION

Clear aircraft at altitudes according to the TBL 4–5–1.

TBL 4–5–1
Altitude Assignment

Aircraft Operating	On course degrees magnetic	Assign	Examples
Below 3,000 feet above surface	Any course	Any altitude	
At and below FL 410	0 through 179	Odd cardinal altitude or flight levels at intervals of 2,000 feet	3,000, 5,000, FL 310, FL 330
	180 through 359	Even cardinal altitude or flight levels at intervals of 2,000 feet	4,000, 6,000, FL 320, FL 340
Above FL 410	0 through 179	Odd cardinal flight levels at intervals of 4,000 feet beginning with FL 450	FL 450, FL 490, FL 530
	180 through 359	Odd cardinal flight levels at intervals of 4,000 feet beginning with FL 430	FL 430, FL 470, FL 510
One way routes (except in composite systems)	Any course	Any cardinal altitude or flight level below FL 410 or any odd cardinal flight level above FL 410	FL 270, FL 280, FL 290, FL 300, FL 310, FL 410, FL 430, FL 450
Within an ALTRV	Any course	Any altitude or flight level	
In aerial refueling tracks and anchors	Any course	Altitude blocks as requested. Any altitude or flight level	050B080, FL 180B220, FL 280B310

REFERENCE–
FAA Order JO 7110.65, Para 4–5–3, Exceptions.
FAA Order JO 7110.65, Para 7–7–5, Altitude Assignments.
FAA Order JO 7110.65, Para 9–3–2, Separation Minima.

4-5-3. EXCEPTIONS

When traffic, meteorological conditions, or aircraft operational limitations prevent assignment of altitudes prescribed in paragraph 4-5-2, Flight Direction, assign any cardinal altitude or flight level below FL 410 or any odd cardinal flight level at or above FL 410 without regard to direction of flight as follows:

NOTE-
See paragraph 2-3-10, Control Symbology, for control abbreviations and symbols to be used in conjunction with this paragraph.

a. For traffic conditions, take this action only if one of the following conditions exists:

1. Aircraft remain within a facility's area and prior approval is obtained from other affected positions or sectors or the operations are covered in a Facility Directive.

2. Aircraft will proceed beyond the facility's area and specific operations and procedures permitting random altitude assignment are covered in a letter of agreement between the appropriate facilities.

b. Military aircraft are operating on random routes and prior approval is obtained from the facility concerned.

c. For meteorological conditions, take this action only if you obtain prior approval from other affected positions or sectors within your facility and, if necessary, from the adjacent facility concerned.

d. For aircraft operational limitations, take this action only if the pilot informs you the available appropriate altitude exceeds the operational limitations of his/her aircraft and only after you obtain prior approval from other affected positions or sectors within your facility and, if necessary, from the adjacent facility concerned.

e. For mission requirements, take this action only when the aircraft is operating on an MTR.

REFERENCE-
FAA Order JO 7110.65, Para 7-7-5, Altitude Assignments.
FAA Order JO 7110.65, Para 9-3-2, Separation Minima.

4-5-4. LOWEST USABLE FLIGHT LEVEL

If a change in atmospheric pressure affects a usable flight level in your area of jurisdiction, use TBL 4-5-2 to determine the lowest usable flight level to clear aircraft at or above 18,000 feet MSL.

TBL 4-5-2
Lowest Usable FL

Altimeter Setting	Lowest Usable FL
29.92" or higher	180
29.91" to 28.92"	190
28.91" to 27.92"	200

REFERENCE-
FAA Order JO 7110.65, Para 9-3-2, Separation Minima.

4-5-5. ADJUSTED MINIMUM FLIGHT LEVEL

When the prescribed minimum altitude for IFR operations is at or above 18,000 feet MSL and the atmospheric pressure is less than 29.92", add the appropriate adjustment factor from TBL 4-5-3 to the flight level equivalent of the minimum altitude in feet to determine the adjusted minimum flight level.

TBL 4-5-3
Minimum FL Adjustment

Altimeter Setting	Adjustment Factor
29.92" or higher	None
29.91" to 29.42"	500 feet
29.41" to 28.92"	1,000 feet
28.91" to 28.42"	1,500 feet
28.41" to 27.92"	2,000 feet

4-5-6. MINIMUM EN ROUTE ALTITUDES (MEA)

Except as provided in subparagraphs a and b below, assign altitudes at or above the MEA for the route segment being flown. When a lower MEA for subsequent segments of the route is applicable, issue the lower MEA only after the aircraft is over or past the Fix/NAVAID beyond which the lower MEA applies unless a crossing restriction at or above the higher MEA is issued.

a. An aircraft may be cleared below the MEA but not below the MOCA for the route segment being flown if the altitude assigned is at least 300 feet above the floor of controlled airspace and one of the following conditions is met:

NOTE-
Controllers must be aware that in the event of radio communications or GNSS failure, a pilot will climb to the MEA for the route segment being flown.

1. For aircraft using VOR, VORTAC or TACAN for navigation, this applies only within 22 miles of that NAVAID.

2. When radar procedures are used, the following actions are taken:

(a) In the absence of a published MOCA, assign altitudes at or above the MVA or MIA along the route of flight, and

(b) Lost communications instructions are issued.

3. The aircraft is GNSS equipped.

b. An aircraft may be cleared to operate on jet routes below the MEA (but not below the prescribed minimum altitude for IFR operations) or above the maximum authorized altitude if, in either case, radar service is provided.

NOTE-
Minimum en route and maximum authorized altitudes for certain jet route segments have been established above the floor of the jet route structure due to limitations on navigational signal coverage.

c. Where a higher altitude is required because of an MEA, the aircraft must be cleared to begin climb to the higher MEA as follows:

1. If no MCA is specified, prior to or immediately after passing the fix where the higher MEA is designated. (See FIG 4-5-1)

FIG 4–5–1
No MCA Specified

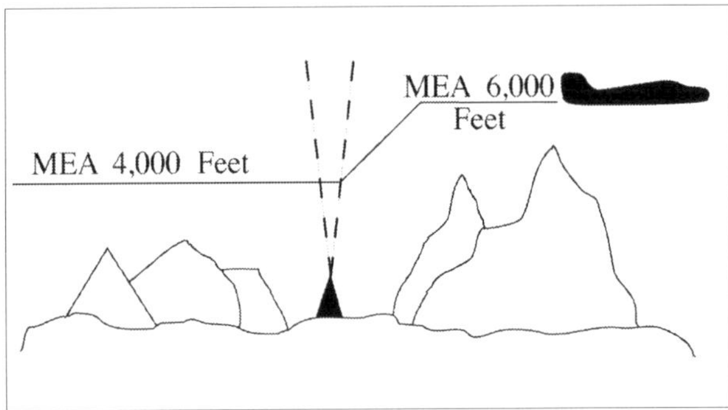

2. If a MCA is specified, prior to the fix so as to cross the fix at or above the MCA. (See FIG 4–5–2)

FIG 4–5–2
MCA Specified

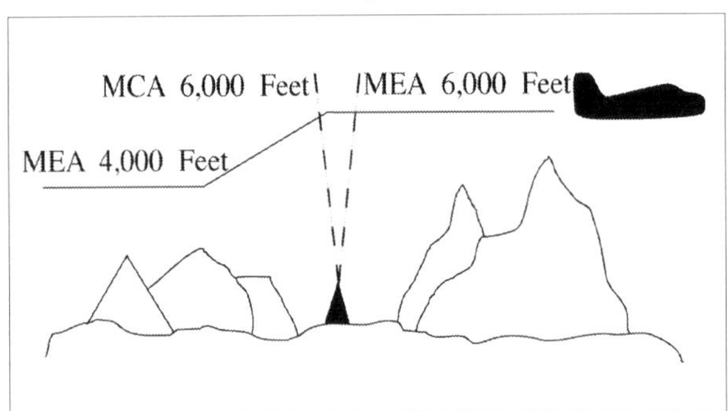

d. GNSS MEAs may be approved on published ATS routes. Air traffic may assign GNSS MEAs to GNSS–equipped aircraft where established.

NOTE–
On high altitude ATS routes, the GNSS MEA is FL180 unless published higher.

e. Where MEAs have not been established, clear an aircraft at or above the minimum altitude for IFR operations prescribed by 14 CFR Section 91.177.

REFERENCE–
FAA Order JO 7110.65, Para 4–2–8, IFR-VFR and VFR-IFR Flights.
FAA Order JO 7110.65, Para 4–4–1, Route Use.
FAA Order JO 7110.65, Chapter 5, Section 6, Para 5–6–1, Application.
FAA Order JO 7110.65, Para 7–7–5, Altitude Assignments.

4–5–7. ALTITUDE INFORMATION

Issue altitude instructions as follows:

REFERENCE–
FAA Order JO 7110.65, Para 4–2–1, Clearance Items.

a. Altitude to maintain or cruise. When issuing cruise in conjunction with an airport clearance limit and an unpublished route will be used, issue an appropriate crossing altitude to ensure terrain clearance until the aircraft reaches a fix, point, or route where the altitude information is available to the pilot. When issuing a cruise clearance to an airport which does not have a published instrument approach, a cruise clearance without a crossing restriction may be issued.

PHRASEOLOGY–
MAINTAIN/CRUISE (altitude). MAINTAIN (altitude) UNTIL (time, fix, waypoint),

or

(number of miles or minutes) MILES/MINUTES PAST (fix, waypoint).

CROSS (fix, point, waypoint),

or

INTERCEPT (route) AT OR ABOVE (altitude), CRUISE (altitude).

NOTE–

1. *The crossing altitude must assure IFR obstruction clearance to the point where the aircraft is established on a segment of a published route or instrument approach procedure.*

2. *When an aircraft is issued a cruise clearance to an airport which does not have a published instrument approach procedure, it is not possible to satisfy the requirement for a crossing altitude that will ensure terrain clearance until the aircraft reaches a fix, point, or route where altitude information is available to the pilot. Under those conditions, a cruise clearance without a crossing restriction authorizes a pilot to determine the minimum IFR altitude as prescribed in 14 CFR Section 91.177 and descend to it at pilot discretion if it is lower than the altitude specified in the cruise clearance.*

b. Instructions to climb or descend including restrictions, as required. Specify a time restriction reference the UTC clock reading with a time check. If you are relaying through an authorized communications provider, such as New York Radio, San Francisco Radio, FSS, etc., advise the radio operator to issue the current time to the aircraft when the clearance is relayed. The requirement to issue a time check must be disregarded if the clearance is issued via Controller Pilot Data Link Communications (CPDLC).

EXCEPTION. If you are in direct, two-way, VHF/UHF voice communication with the pilot and the aircraft is in radar contact, you may specify an elapsed time interval restriction, in full minute increments only, without any reference to the UTC clock. The time restriction begins once the clearance has been acknowledged by the pilot.

EXAMPLE–

1. *"United Four Seventeen, climb to reach one three thousand at two two one five."*
"Time two two one one and one–quarter."
The pilot is expected to be level at 13,000 feet at 2215 UTC.

2. Through Relay– *"Speedbird Five, climb to reach flight level three–five zero at one–two–one–five, time" (Issue a time check).*

3. *In radar contact and in direct controller to pilot, two-way, VHF/UHF voice communication - "United Four Seventeen, descend to reach flight level three five zero within two minutes." The time restriction begins once the clearance has been acknowledged by the pilot.*

4. *"United Four Seventeen climb to leave flight level three three zero within two minutes, maintain flight level three five zero."*

REFERENCE–
FAA Order JO 7110.65, Para 1–2–1, Word Meanings.
FAA Order JO 7110.65, Para 2–4–17, Numbers Usage.

PHRASEOLOGY–

CLIMB/DESCEND AND MAINTAIN (altitude).

If required,

AFTER PASSING (fix, waypoint),

or

AT (time) (time in hours, minutes, and nearest quarter minute).

CLIMB/DESCEND TO REACH (altitude)

AT (time (issue time check) or fix, waypoint),

or

AT (time). CLIMB/DESCEND AND MAINTAIN (altitude) WHEN ESTABLISHED AT LEAST (number of miles or minutes) MILES/MINUTES PAST (fix, waypoint) ON THE (NAVAID) (specified) RADIAL.
CLIMB/DESCEND TO REACH (altitude) AT (time or fix, waypoint),

or

A POINT (number of miles) MILES (direction) OF (name of DME NAVAID),

or

MAINTAIN (altitude) UNTIL (time (issue time check), fix, waypoint), THEN CLIMB/DESCEND AND MAINTAIN (altitude).

Through relay:

CLIMB TO REACH (altitude) AT (time) (issue a time check).

Or

Using a time interval while in radar contact and in direct controller to pilot, two-way, VHF/UHF voice communication:

CLIMB/DESCEND TO REACH/LEAVE (altitude) WITHIN (number) MINUTES, MAINTAIN (altitude).
Or

CLIMB/DESCEND TO REACH/LEAVE (altitude) IN (number) MINUTES OR LESS, MAINTAIN (altitude).

c. Specified altitude for crossing a specified fix or waypoint; or, specified altitude for crossing a distance (in miles) and direction from a specified fix or waypoint.

PHRASEOLOGY−
CROSS (fix, waypoint) AT (altitude).
CROSS (fix, waypoint) AT OR ABOVE/BELOW (altitude).
CROSS (number of miles) MILES (direction) OF (name of fix, waypoint) AT (altitude).
CROSS (number of miles) MILES (direction) OF (name of fix, waypoint) AT OR ABOVE/BELOW (altitude).

d. A specified altitude over a specified fix for that portion of a descent clearance where descent at pilot's discretion is permissible. At any other time it is practicable, authorize climb/descent at pilot's discretion.

PHRASEOLOGY−
CLIMB/DESCEND AT PILOT'S DISCRETION.

EXAMPLE−
"United Four Seventeen, descend and maintain six thousand."

NOTE−
The pilot is expected to commence descent upon receipt of the clearance and to descend at the suggested rates specified in the AIM, paragraph 4−4−10, Adherence to Clearance, until reaching the assigned altitude of 6,000 feet.

EXAMPLE−
"United Four Seventeen, descend at pilot's discretion, maintain six thousand."

NOTE−
The pilot is authorized to conduct descent within the context of the term "at pilot's discretion" as described in the AIM.

EXAMPLE−
"United Four Seventeen cross Lakeview V−O−R at or above flight level two zero zero, descend and maintain six thousand."

NOTE−
The pilot is authorized to conduct descent "at pilot's discretion" until reaching Lakeview VOR. The pilot must comply with

the clearance provision to cross the Lakeview VOR at or above FL 200, and after passing Lakeview VOR, the pilot is expected to descend at the rates specified in the AIM until reaching the assigned altitude of 6,000 feet.

EXAMPLE−
"United Four Seventeen, cross Lakeview V−O−R at and maintain six thousand."

NOTE−
The pilot is authorized to conduct descent "at pilot's discretion," but must comply with the clearance provision to cross Lakeview VOR at 6,000 feet.

EXAMPLE−
"United Four Seventeen, descend now to flight level two seven zero, cross Lakeview V−O−R at or below one zero thousand, descend and maintain six thousand."

NOTE−
The pilot is expected to promptly execute and complete descent to FL 270 upon receipt of the clearance. After reaching FL 270, the pilot is authorized to descend "at pilot's discretion" until reaching Lakeview VOR. The pilot must comply with the clearance provision to cross Lakeview VOR at or below 10,000 feet. After Lakeview VOR, the pilot is expected to descend at the rates specified in the AIM until reaching 6,000 feet.

NOTE−
1. *A descent clearance which specifies a crossing altitude authorizes descent at pilot's discretion for that portion of the flight to which the crossing altitude restriction applies.*

2. *Any other time that authorization to descend at pilot's discretion is intended, it must be specifically stated by the controller.*

3. *The pilot may need to know of any future restrictions that might affect the descent, including those that may be issued in another sector, in order to properly plan a descent at pilot's discretion.*

4. *Controllers need to be aware that the descent rates in the AIM are only suggested and aircraft will not always descend at those rates.*

REFERENCE−
P/CG Term− Pilot's Discretion.

e. When a portion of a climb/descent may be authorized at the pilot's discretion, specify the altitude the aircraft must climb/descend to followed by the altitude to maintain at the pilot's discretion.

PHRASEOLOGY−
CLIMB/DESCEND NOW TO (altitude), THEN CLIMB/DESCEND AT PILOT'S DISCRETION MAINTAIN (altitude).

EXAMPLE−
"United Three Ten, descend now to flight level two eight zero, then descend at pilot's discretion maintain flight level two four zero."

NOTE−
1. *The pilot is expected to commence descent upon receipt of the clearance and to descend as prescribed in the AIM, paragraph 4−4−10, Adherence to Clearance, until FL 280. At that point, the pilot is authorized to continue descent to FL 240 within context of the term "at pilot's discretion" as described in the AIM.*

2. *Controllers need to be aware that the descent rates are only suggested and aircraft will not always descend at those rates.*

f. When the "pilot's discretion" portion of a climb/descent clearance is being canceled by assigning a new altitude, inform the pilot that the new altitude is an "amended altitude."

EXAMPLE−
"American Eighty Three, amend altitude, descend and maintain Flight Level two six zero."

NOTE−
American Eighty Three, at FL 280, has been cleared to descend at pilot's discretion to FL 240. Subsequently, the altitude assignment is changed to FL 260. Therefore, pilot's discretion is no longer authorized.

g. Altitude assignments involving more than one altitude.

PHRASEOLOGY−
MAINTAIN BLOCK (altitude) THROUGH (altitude).

h. Instructions to vertically navigate SIDs/STARs with published crossing restrictions (Climb Via/Descend Via).

1. When established on the SID/STAR.

2. When navigating a published route inbound to the STAR.

3. When cleared direct to a waypoint/fix without a published altitude, assign a crossing altitude.

PHRASEOLOGY–
DESCEND VIA (STAR name and number).

DESCEND VIA (STAR name and number and runway transition number)

DESCEND VIA (STAR name and number and runway number).

CLIMB VIA (SID name and number).

PROCEED DIRECT (fix/waypoint),CROSS (waypoint/fix) at (altitude) THEN DESCEND VIA (STAR name and number)

EXAMPLE–
"Descend via the Eagul Five arrival."

"Descend via the Wynde Eight Arrival, Runway 28 right transition."

"Descend via the Lendy One Arrival, Runway 22 left."

"Climb via the Dawgs Four Departure."

"Proceed direct Denis, cross Denis at or above flight level two zero zero, then descend via the Mmell One arrival."

NOTE–
Pilots must comply with all published speed restrictions on SIDs/STARs, independent of a climb via or descend via clearance.

Clearance to "descent via" authorizes pilots:
1. To descend at pilot discretion to meet published restrictions on a STAR. Pilots navigating on a STAR must maintain the last assigned altitude until receiving clearance to descend via. Once leaving an altitude, the pilot may not return to that altitude without an ATC clearance.
2. When cleared direct to a waypoint, to descend at pilot discretion to meet restrictions on the procedure. ATC assumes obstacle clearance responsibility for aircraft not yet established or taken off of a procedure.
3. To adjust speeds prior to reaching waypoints with published speed restrictions.

NOTE–
When cleared for SIDs that contain published speed restrictions, the pilot must comply with those speed restrictions independent of any "climb via" clearance. Clearance to "climb via" authorizes pilots:
1. *When used in the IFR departure clearance, in a PDC, DCL or when subsequently cleared after departure to a waypoint depicted on a SID, to join a procedure after departure or resume a procedure.*
2. *When vertical navigation is interrupted and an altitude is assigned to maintain which is not contained on the published procedure, to climb from that previously-assigned altitude at pilot's discretion to the altitude depicted for the next waypoint. ATC must ensure obstacle clearance until the aircraft is established on the lateral and vertical path of the SID.*
3. *Once established on the depicted departure, to climb and to meet all published or assigned altitude and speed restrictions.*

REFERENCE–
FAA Order JO 7110.65, Para 4–4–2, Route Structure Transitions.
FAA Order JO 7110.65, Para 4–5–6, Minimum En Route Altitudes.
FAA Order JO 7110.65, Para 5–5–9, Separation From Obstructions.
P/CG – Climb Via, Descend Via.

NOTE–
Pilots cleared for vertical navigation using the phraseology "descend via" or "climb via" must inform ATC, upon initial contact, of the altitude leaving, the runway transition or landing direction if assigned (STARs), and any assigned restrictions not published on the procedure.

EXAMPLE–
"Delta One Twenty One leaving flight level one niner zero, descending via the Eagul Five arrival runway two-six transition."

"Delta One Twenty One leaving flight level one niner zero for one two thousand, descending via the Eagul Five arrival, runway two-six transition."

"JetBlue six zero two leaving flight level two one zero descending via the Ivane Two arrival landing south."

"Cactus Seven Eleven leaving two thousand climbing via the Laura Two departure."

"Cactus Seven Eleven leaving two thousand for one-six thousand, climbing via the Laura Two departure."

REFERENCE–
AIM, Para 5-2-8, Instrument Departure Procedures (DP) – Obstacle Departure Procedures (ODP) and Standard Instrument Departures (SID).
P/CG – Top Altitude, Bottom Altitude.
AIM, Para 5-4-1, Standard Terminal Arrival (STAR) Procedures.

INTERPRETATION–
7110.65, 4–5–7, Altitude Information (12–1–2015)

4. A "descend via" clearance must not be used where procedures contain only published "expect" altitude and/or speed restrictions.

NOTE–
Pilots are not expected to comply with published "expect" restrictions in the event of lost communications, unless ATC has specifically advised the pilot to expect these restrictions as part of a further clearance.

5. "Descend via" may be used on procedures that contain both "expect" and required altitude and speed restrictions only if altitude and/or speed restrictions or alternate restrictions are issued for the fix/waypoint associated with all expect restrictions.

6. "Descend via" clearances may also be issued if an aircraft is past all fixes/waypoints that have expect restrictions.

7. If it is necessary to assign a crossing altitude which differs from the STAR or SID altitude, emphasize the change to the pilot.

PHRASEOLOGY–
DESCEND VIA (STAR name and number) ARRIVAL, EXCEPT CROSS (fix, point, waypoint), (revised altitude information).

EXAMPLE–
"United 454 descend via the Haris One Arrival, except cross Haris at or above one six thousand."

NOTE–
The aircraft should track laterally and vertically on the Haris One Arrival and should descend so as to cross Haris at or above 16,000; remainder of the arrival must be flown as published.

PHRASEOLOGY–
CLIMB VIA SID, EXCEPT CROSS (fix, point, waypoint), (revised altitude information).

CLIMB VIA (SID name and number), EXCEPT CROSS (fix, point, waypoint), (revised altitude information).

EXAMPLE–
1. "Climb via SID except cross Mkala at or above seven thousand."

NOTE–
In Example 1, the aircraft will comply with the assigned SID departure lateral path and any published speed and altitude restrictions and climb so as to cross Mkala at or above 7,000; remainder of the departure must be flown as published.

EXAMPLE–
2. (There is a published altitude at Dvine WP): "Proceed direct Dvine, Climb via the Suzan Two departure except cross Mkala at or above seven thousand."

NOTE–
In Example 2, the aircraft will join the Suzan Two departure at Dvine, at the published altitude, and then comply with the published lateral path and any published speed or altitude restrictions. The aircraft will climb so as to cross Mkala at or above 7,000; remainder of the departure must be flown as published.

8. When an aircraft has been issued an interim altitude and after departure ATC can subsequently clear the aircraft to climb to the original top altitude published in a SID that contains published crossing restrictions, instruct aircraft to "climb via SID." When issuing a different altitude and compliance with published restrictions is still required, instruct aircraft to "climb via SID except maintain (altitude)."

PHRASEOLOGY–
CLIMB VIA SID.

CLIMB VIA SID EXCEPT MAINTAIN (altitude).

EXAMPLE–
1. (An aircraft was issued the Teddd One departure, "climb via SID" in the IFR departure clearance. An interim altitude of 10,000 was issued instead of the published top altitude of FL 230; after departure ATC is able to issue the published top altitude): "Climb via SID."

NOTE–
In Example 1, the aircraft will track laterally and vertically on the Teddd One departure and initially climb to 10,000; Once re-issued the "climb via" clearance the interim altitude is canceled aircraft will continue climb to FL230 while complying with published restrictions.

EXAMPLE–
2. (Using Example 1, after departure ATC is able to issue an altitude higher than the published top altitude): "Climb via SID except maintain flight level two six zero."

NOTE–
In Example 2, the aircraft will track laterally and vertically on the Teddd One departure and initially climb to 10,000; once issued "climb via" clearance to FL260 the aircraft will continue climb while complying with published restrictions.

9. If it is necessary to assign an interim altitude or assign a bottom or top altitude not contained on a STAR or SID, the provisions of subparagraph 4–5–7h may be used in conjunction with subparagraph 4–5–7a.

PHRASEOLOGY–
DESCEND VIA THE (STAR name and number) ARRIVAL EXCEPT AFTER (fix) MAINTAIN (revised altitude information).

EXAMPLE–
"United 454 descend via the Eagul Five Arrival, except after Geeno maintain one zero thousand."

NOTE–
The aircraft should track laterally and vertically on the Eagul Five Arrival and should descend so as to comply with all speed and altitude restrictions until reaching Geeno and then maintain 10,000. Upon reaching 10,000, aircraft should maintain 10,000 until cleared by ATC to continue to descend.

REFERENCE–
FAA Order JO 7110.65, Para 4–7–1, Clearance Information.
AIM, Para 5–4–1, Standard Terminal Arrival (STAR) Procedures.

PHRASEOLOGY–
CLIMB VIA SID EXCEPT AFTER (waypoint name), MAINTAIN (altitude).

EXAMPLE–
"Climb via SID except after Baret, maintain flight level one niner zero."

NOTE–
1. Considering the principle that the last ATC clearance issued has precedence over the previous, the phraseology "maintain (altitude)" alone cancels previously issued altitude restrictions, including SID/STAR altitude restrictions unless they are restated or modified, and authorizes an unrestricted climb or descent. Speed restrictions remain in effect unless the controller explicitly cancels the speed restrictions.

2. Restate "climb/descend via" and then use "except" or "except maintain" phraseology to modify published restrictions or assign a new top/bottom altitude. Use "resume" phraseology with "maintain" to rejoin a route and assign a new altitude where compliance with published altitude restrictions is not required.

REFERENCE–
FAA Order JO 7110.65, Para 4–2–5, Route or Altitude Amendments.
FAA Order JO 7110.65, Para 5–6–2, Methods.
AIM, Para 4–4–10 Adherence to Clearance.
AIM, Para 5–2–8. Instrument Departure Procedures (DP) – Obstacle Departure Procedures (ODP) and Standard Instrument Departures (SID).

i. When a pilot is unable to accept a clearance, issue revised instructions to ensure positive control and approved separation.

NOTE–

1. *14 CFR Section 91.123 states that a pilot is not allowed to deviate from an ATC clearance "that has been obtained...unless an amended clearance is obtained" (except when an emergency exists).*

2. *A pilot is therefore expected to advise the controller if a clearance cannot be accepted when the clearance is issued. "We will try" and other such acknowledgements do not constitute pilot acceptance of an ATC clearance.*

3. *Controllers are expected to issue ATC clearances which conform with normal aircraft operational capabilities and do not require "last minute" amendments to ensure approved separation.*

4. *"Expedite" is not to be used in lieu of appropriate restrictions to ensure separation.*

REFERENCE–
FAA Order JO 7110.65, Para 10–1–3, Providing Assistance.

4–5–8. ANTICIPATED ALTITUDE CHANGES

If practicable, inform an aircraft when to expect climb or descent clearance or to request altitude change from another facility.

PHRASEOLOGY–
EXPECT HIGHER/LOWER IN (number of miles or minutes) MILES/MINUTES,

or

AT (fix). REQUEST ALTITUDE/FLIGHT LEVEL CHANGE FROM (name of facility).

If required,

AT (time, fix, or altitude).

REFERENCE–
FAA Order JO 7110.65, Para 2–2–6, IFR Flight Progress Data.

4–5–9. ALTITUDE CONFIRMATION– NONRADAR

a. Request a pilot to confirm assigned altitude on initial contact and when position reports are received unless:

NOTE–
For the purpose of this paragraph, "initial contact" means a pilot's first radio contact with each sector/position.

1. The pilot states the assigned altitude, or

2. You assign a new altitude to a climbing or descending aircraft, or

3. *TERMINAL.* The aircraft was transferred to you from another sector/position within your facility (intrafacility).

PHRASEOLOGY–
(In level flight situations),

VERIFY AT (altitude/flight level).

(In climbing/descending situations),

(if aircraft has been assigned an altitude below the lowest useable flight level),

VERIFY ASSIGNED ALTITUDE (altitude).

(If aircraft has been assigned a flight level at or above the lowest useable flight level),

VERIFY ASSIGNED FLIGHT LEVEL (flight level).

b. *USA.* Reconfirm all pilot altitude read backs.

PHRASEOLOGY−
(If altitude read back is correct),
AFFIRMATIVE (altitude).

(If altitude read back is not correct),
NEGATIVE. CLIMB/DESCEND AND MAINTAIN (altitude),

or

NEGATIVE. MAINTAIN (altitude).

Section 6. Holding Aircraft

4–6–1. CLEARANCE TO HOLDING FIX

Consider operational factors such as length of delay, holding airspace limitations, navigational aids, altitude, meteorological conditions when necessary to clear an aircraft to a fix other than the destination airport. Issue the following:

a. Clearance limit (if any part of the route beyond a clearance limit differs from the last routing cleared, issue the route the pilot can expect beyond the clearance limit).

PHRASEOLOGY–
EXPECT FURTHER CLEARANCE VIA (routing).

EXAMPLE–
"Expect further clearance via direct Stillwater V–O–R, Victor Two Twenty-Six Snapy intersection, direct Newark."

b. Holding instructions.

1. Holding instructions may be eliminated when you inform the pilot that no delay is expected.

2. When the assigned procedure or route being flown includes a charted pattern, you may omit all holding instructions except the charted holding direction and the statement "as published." Always issue complete holding instructions when the pilot requests them.

NOTE–
The most generally used holding patterns are depicted on U.S. Government or commercially produced low/high altitude en route, area, and STAR Charts.

PHRASEOLOGY–
CLEARED TO (fix), HOLD (direction), AS PUBLISHED,

or

CLEARED TO (fix), NO DELAY EXPECTED.

c. EFC. Do not specify this item if no delay is expected.

1. When additional holding is expected at any other fix in your facility's area, state the fix and your best estimate of the additional delay. When more than one fix is involved, state the total additional en route delay (omit specific fixes).

NOTE–
Additional delay information is not used to determine pilot action in the event of two-way communications failure. Pilots are expected to predicate their actions solely on the provisions of 14 CFR Section 91.185.

PHRASEOLOGY–
EXPECT FURTHER CLEARANCE (time),

and if required,

ANTICIPATE ADDITIONAL (time in minutes/hours) MINUTE/HOUR DELAY AT (fix),

or

ANTICIPATE ADDITIONAL (time in minutes/hours) MINUTE/HOUR EN ROUTE DELAY.

EXAMPLE–
1. *"Expect further clearance one niner two zero, anticipate additional three zero minute delay at Sweet."*

2. *"Expect further clearance one five one zero, anticipate additional three zero minute en route delay."*

2. When additional holding is expected in an approach control area, state the total additional terminal delay.

PHRASEOLOGY–
EXPECT FURTHER CLEARANCE (time),

and if required,

ANTICIPATE ADDITIONAL (time in minutes/hours) MINUTE/HOUR TERMINAL DELAY.

3. *TERMINAL.* When terminal delays exist or are expected, inform the appropriate center or approach control facility so that the information can be forwarded to arrival aircraft.

4. When delay is expected, issue items in subparagraphs a and b at least 5 minutes before the aircraft is estimated to reach the clearance limit. If the traffic situation requires holding an aircraft that is less than 5 minutes from the holding fix, issue these items immediately.

NOTE–
1. *The AIM indicates that pilots should start speed reduction when 3 minutes or less from the holding fix. The additional 2 minutes contained in the 5–minute requirement are necessary to compensate for different pilot/controller ETAS at the holding fix, minor differences in clock times, and provision for sufficient planning and reaction times.*

2. *When holding is necessary, the phrase "delay indefinite" should be used when an accurate estimate of the delay time and the reason for the delay cannot immediately be determined; i.e., disabled aircraft on the runway, terminal or center sector saturation, weather below landing minimums, etc. In any event, every attempt should be made to provide the pilot with the best possible estimate of his/her delay time and the reason for the delay. Controllers/supervisors should consult, as appropriate, with personnel (other sectors, weather forecasters, the airport management, other facilities, etc.) who can best provide this information.*

PHRASEOLOGY–
DELAY INDEFINITE, (reason if known), EXPECT FURTHER CLEARANCE (time). (After determining the reason for the delay, advise the pilot as soon as possible.)

EXAMPLE–
"Cleared to Drewe, hold west, as published, expect further clearance via direct Sidney V–O–R one three one five, anticipate additional two zero minute delay at Woody."

"Cleared to Aston, hold west on Victor two twenty-five, seven mile leg, left turns, expect further clearance one niner two zero, anticipate additional one five minute terminal delay."

"Cleared to Wayne, no delay expected."

"Cleared to Wally, hold north, as published, delay indefinite, snow removal in progress, expect further clearance one one three zero."

4–6–2. CLEARANCE BEYOND FIX

a. If no delay is expected, issue a clearance beyond the clearance limit as soon as possible and, whenever possible, at least 5 minutes before the aircraft reaches the fix.

b. Include the following items when issuing clearance beyond a clearance limit:

1. Clearance limit or approach clearance.

2. Route of flight. Specify one of the following:

(a) Complete details of the route (airway, route, course, fix(es), azimuth course, heading, arc, or vector.)

(b) The phrase "via last routing cleared." Use this phrase only when the most recently issued routing to the new clearance limit is valid and verbiage will be reduced.

PHRASEOLOGY–
VIA LAST ROUTING CLEARED.

3. Assigned altitude if different from present altitude.

NOTE–
Except in the event of a two-way communications failure, when a clearance beyond a fix has not been received, pilots are expected to hold as depicted on U.S. Government or commercially produced (meeting FAA requirements) low/high altitude en route and area or STAR charts. If no holding pattern is charted and holding instructions have not been issued, pilots should ask ATC for holding instructions prior to reaching the fix. If a pilot is unable to obtain holding instructions prior to reaching the fix, the pilot is expected to hold in a standard pattern on the course on which the aircraft approached the fix and request further clearance as soon as possible.

4-6-3. DELAYS

a. Advise your supervisor or flow controller as soon as possible when you delay or expect to delay aircraft.

b. When arrival delays reach or are anticipated to reach 30 minutes, take the following action:

1. *EN ROUTE.* The center responsible for transferring control to an approach control facility or, for a nonapproach control destination, the center in whose area the aircraft will land must issue total delay information as soon as possible after the aircraft enters the center's area. Whenever possible, the delay information must be issued by the first center controller to communicate with the aircraft.

REFERENCE–
FAA Order JO 7110.65, Para 5-13-9, ERAM Computer Entry of Hold Information.

2. *TERMINAL.* When tower en route control service is being provided, the approach control facility whose area contains the destination airport must issue total delay information as soon as possible after the aircraft enters its approach control area. Whenever possible, the delay information must be issued by the first terminal controller to communicate with the aircraft.

3. Unless a pilot requests delay information, the actions specified in subparagraphs 1 and 2 above may be omitted when total delay information is available to pilots via ATIS.

PHRASEOLOGY–
(Airport) ARRIVAL DELAYS (time in minutes/hours).

4-6-4. HOLDING INSTRUCTIONS

When issuing holding instructions, specify:

a. Direction of holding from the fix/waypoint.

b. Holding fix or waypoint.

NOTE–
The holding fix may be omitted if included at the beginning of the transmission as the clearance limit.

c. Radial, course, bearing, track, azimuth, airway, or route on which the aircraft is to hold.

d. Leg length in miles if DME or RNAV is to be used. Specify leg length in minutes if the pilot requests it or you consider it necessary.

e. Direction of holding pattern turns only if left turns are to be made, the pilot requests it, or you consider it necessary.

PHRASEOLOGY–
HOLD (direction) OF (fix/waypoint) ON (specified radial, course, bearing, track, airway, azimuth(s), or route.)

If leg length is specified,

(number of minutes/miles) MINUTE/MILE LEG.

If direction of turn is specified,

LEFT/RIGHT TURNS.

f. Issue maximum holding airspeed advisories when an aircraft is:

1. Approved to exceed the maximum airspeed of a pattern, and is cleared into a holding pattern that will protect for the greater speed; or

2. Observed deviating from the holding pattern airspace area; or

3. Cleared into an airspeed restricted holding pattern in which the icon has not been published.

EXAMPLE–
Due to turbulence, a turboprop requests to exceed the recommended maximum holding airspeed. ATCS may clear the aircraft into a pattern that protects for the airspeed request, and must advise the pilot of the maximum holding airspeed for the holding pattern airspace area.

PHRASEOLOGY–
"MAXIMUM HOLDING AIRSPEED IS TWO ONE ZERO KNOTS."

4–6–5. VISUAL HOLDING POINTS

You may use as a holding fix a location which the pilot can determine by visual reference to the surface if he/she is familiar with it.

PHRASEOLOGY–
HOLD AT (location) UNTIL (time or other condition.)

REFERENCE–
FAA Order JO 7110.65, Para 7–1–4, Visual Holding of VFR Aircraft.

4–6–6. HOLDING FLIGHT PATH DEVIATION

Approve a pilot's request to deviate from the prescribed holding flight path if obstacles and traffic conditions permit.

4–6–7. UNMONITORED NAVAIDs

Separate an aircraft holding at an unmonitored NAVAID from any other aircraft occupying the course which the holding aircraft will follow if it does not receive signals from the NAVAID.

4–6–8. ILS PROTECTION/CRITICAL AREAS

When the official weather observation indicates a ceiling of less than 800 feet or visibility of 2 miles, do not authorize aircraft to hold below 5,000 feet AGL inbound toward the airport on or within 1 statute mile of the localizer between the ILS OM or the fix used in lieu of the OM and the airport. *USAF.* The holding restriction applies only when an arriving aircraft is between the ILS OM or the fix used in lieu of the OM and the runway.

REFERENCE–
FAA Order 8260.3, United States Standard for Terminal Instrument Procedures (TERPS), Chapter 17, Basic Holding Criteria.

Section 7. Arrival Procedures

4-7-1. CLEARANCE INFORMATION

Clear an arriving aircraft to a clearance limit by specifying the following:

a. Name of fix or airport.

PHRASEOLOGY-
CLEARED TO (destination) AIRPORT.
Or
CLEARED TO (NAVAID name and type if known).
Or
CLEARED TO (intersection or waypoint name and type if known).

b. Route of flight including a STAR/RNAV STAR and STAR/RNAV STAR transition, if appropriate. Assign a STAR/RNAV STAR and STAR/RNAV STAR transition to any aircraft in lieu of other routes; e.g., airways or preferential arrival routes when the routings are the same. The clearance must include the name and transition, if necessary, of the STAR/RNAV STAR to be flown.

TERMINAL: When the STAR/RNAV STAR transition is designed to provide course guidance to multiple runways, the facility must state intended runway number on initial contact, or as soon as practical. If the runway assignment, or any subsequent runway change, is not issued prior to 10 NM from the runway transition waypoint, radar vectors to final must be provided.

PHRASEOLOGY-
(STAR/RNAV STAR name and number) ARRIVAL.
(STAR/RNAV STAR name and number) ARRIVAL, (transition name) TRANSITION.
CHANGE/AMEND TRANSITION TO (runway number).
CHANGE/AMEND TRANSITION TO (runway number) TURN LEFT/RIGHT or HEADING (heading) FOR VECTOR TO FINAL APPROACH COURSE.

EXAMPLE-
"Rosewood One arrival."
"Rosewood One arrival, Delta transition."
"Change transition to Runway 09 right."
"Amend transition to Runway 22 left, turn right heading 180 for vector to final approach course."

NOTE-
1. *If a civil pilot does not wish to use a STAR issued in an ATC clearance or any other STAR published for that location, the pilot is expected to advise ATC.*

2. *Arrival procedure descriptive text contained within parentheses (for example, "Devine One (RNAV) Arrival") are not included in arrival clearance phraseology.*

c. Altitude instructions, as follows:

1. Assigned altitude; or

2. Instructions to vertically navigate on the STAR or STAR transition.

EXAMPLE-
"Bayview Three Arrival, Helen Transition, maintain Flight Level Three Three Zero."
"Descend via the Civit One Arrival."
"Descend via the Lendy One Arrival, Runway 22 left."

"Cross JCT at Flight Level Two Four Zero."
"Descend via the Coast Two Arrival."
"Civit One Arrival, Descend and Maintain Flight Level Two Four Zero."

REFERENCE-
FAA Order JO 7110.65, Para 4-5-7, Altitude Information.
AIM, Para 5-4-1, Standard Terminal Arrival (STAR) Procedures.

d. Issue holding instructions, EFC, and additional delay information as required.

e. Instructions regarding further communications as appropriate.

REFERENCE–
FAA Order JO 7110.65, Para 2–1–17, Radio Communications.

4–7–2. ADVANCE DESCENT CLEARANCE

EN ROUTE

Take the following action when exercising control of aircraft landing at an airport located in an adjacent center's control area near the common boundary:

a. Coordinate with the receiving facility for a lower altitude and issue a clearance to the aircraft as appropriate.

b. Initiate this action at a distance sufficient from destination to allow for normal descent and speed reduction.

4–7–3. SINGLE FREQUENCY APPROACHES (SFA)

TERMINAL

Where SFA procedures for military single-piloted turbojet aircraft on an IFR flight plan are contained in a letter of agreement, do not require a radio frequency change after the aircraft begins approach or after initial contact during an en route descent until a landing or low approach has been completed except under the following conditions:

REFERENCE–
FAA Order JO 7610.14, Para 7–1–5, Single Frequency Approach (SFA).
P/CG Term – Single-Piloted Aircraft.

a. During daylight hours while the aircraft is in VFR conditions.

b. On pilot request.

c. When pilot cancels IFR flight plan.

d. In an emergency situation.

e. When aircraft is cleared for visual approach.

4–7–4. RADIO FREQUENCY AND RADAR BEACON CHANGES FOR MILITARY AIRCRAFT

When military single-piloted turbojet aircraft will conduct an approach wholly or partly in IFR conditions or at night, take the following action:

NOTE–
It is known that the mental distraction and the inadvertent movement of aircraft controls resulting from the pilot's turning, reaching, or leaning to change frequencies can induce spatial disorientation (vertigo).

a. Avoid radio frequency and radar beacon changes to the maximum extent that communications capabilities and traffic will permit. However, when changes are required:

1. Give instructions early enough to allow the change before the aircraft reaches the approach fix or handoff point.

2. Keep frequency/radar beacon changes to a minimum below 2,500 feet above the surface.

3. Avoid requiring frequency/radar beacon changes during the time the aircraft is making a turn.

b. When traffic volume requires, a frequency other than the one used by aircraft making approaches may be assigned for use in transferring control to the approach control facility.

TERMINAL

c. If practicable, use a frequency common to both the GCA unit and approach control to minimize frequency changes.

d. When a GCA unit is not able to communicate on a common frequency, a change to a GCA frequency may be authorized.

e. When a nonradar approach will be made, aircraft may be instructed to change to tower frequency when:

1. The reported ceiling is at or above 1,500 feet and visibility is 5 statute miles or more.

2. The aircraft reports able to proceed by visual reference to the surface.

3. The aircraft requests and is cleared for a contact approach.

4. The aircraft is cleared for a visual approach.

f. Avoid making frequency/radar beacon changes after an aircraft begins a high altitude approach.

g. In the event of a missed approach, do not require a frequency/radar beacon change before the aircraft reaches the missed approach altitude, the MEA, or the MVA.

4-7-5. MILITARY TURBOJET EN ROUTE DESCENT

Provide military turbojet aircraft the same arrival procedures that are provided for nonmilitary turbojet aircraft except:

NOTE-
It is the responsibility of the pilot to request a high altitude approach if he/she does not want normal arrival handling.

a. An en route descent may be used in a nonradar environment; however, radar capability should exist which will permit the aircraft to be vectored to the final approach course of a published high altitude instrument approach procedure or PAR/ASR approach. Do not use this procedure if other than normal vectoring delays are anticipated.

b. Prior to issuance of a descent clearance below the highest initial approach fix altitude established for any high altitude instrument approach procedure for the destination airport inform the aircraft:

1. Type of approach to expect.

EXAMPLE-
"Expect V-O-R approach to runway three two."

2. Radar vectors will be provided to the final approach course.

EXAMPLE-
"Expect surveillance/precision approach to runway one seven; radar vectors to final approach course."

3. Current weather whenever the ceiling is below 1,000 feet (**USAF:** 1,500 feet) or the highest circling minimum whichever is greater, or when the visibility is less than 3 miles.

EXAMPLE-
"Expect ILS approach to runway eight; radar vectors to localizer course. Weather (reported weather)."

c. If ATIS is provided and the pilot advises he/she has received the current ATIS broadcast before the descent clearance in subparagraph b is issued, omit those items in subparagraph b that are contained in the broadcast.

d. To avoid requiring an aircraft to fly at low altitudes for an excessive distance, descent clearance should be issued at a point determined by adding 10 to the first two digits of the flight level.

EXAMPLE-
For FL 370, 37 + 10 = 47 miles.

NOTE-
Turbojet en route descents are based on a rate of descent of 4,000 to 6,000 feet per minute.

e. Do not terminate the en route descent of an aircraft without the consent of the pilot except as required by radar outage or an emergency situation.

REFERENCE–
FAA Order JO 7110.65, Para 4–8–4, Altitude Assignment for Military High Altitude Instrument Approaches.

4–7–6. ARRIVAL INFORMATION

EN ROUTE

a. Forward the following information to nonapproach control towers soon enough to permit adjustment of the traffic flow or to FSSs (Alaska Only) soon enough to provide local airport advisory where applicable:

1. Aircraft identification.

2. Type of aircraft.

3. ETA.

4. Type of instrument approach procedure the aircraft will execute; or

5. For SVFR, the direction from which the aircraft will enter Class B, Class C, Class D, or Class E surface area and any altitude restrictions that were issued; or

6. For aircraft executing a contact approach the position of the aircraft.

NOTE–
Specific time requirements are usually stated in a letter of agreement.

b. Forward the following information to approach control facilities before transfer of control jurisdiction:

NOTE–
Transfer points are usually specified in a letter of agreement.

1. Aircraft identification.

2. Type of aircraft and appropriate aircraft equipment suffix.

3. ETA or actual time, and proposed or actual altitude over clearance limit. The ETA need not be given if the arrival information is being forwarded during a radar handoff.

4. Clearance limit (when other than the destination airport) and EFC issued to the aircraft. Clearance limit may be omitted when provided for in a letter of agreement.

5. Time, fix, or altitude when control responsibility is transferred to the approach control facility. This information may be omitted when provided for in a letter of agreement.

PHRASEOLOGY–
(Identification), (type of aircraft), ESTIMATED/OVER (clearance limit), (time), (altitude), EFC (time).

If required,

YOUR CONTROL,

or

YOUR CONTROL AT (time, fix or altitude).

4–7–7. WEATHER INFORMATION

EN ROUTE

When an available official weather report indicates weather conditions are below a 1,000–foot (*USAF:* 1,500–foot) ceiling or below the highest circling minimum, whichever is higher, or less than three-miles visibility for the airport concerned, transmit the weather report and changes classified as special weather observations to an arriving aircraft prior to or as part of the approach clearance when:

a. It is transmitted directly to the pilot via center controller-to-pilot communications.

b. It is relayed through a communications station other than an air carrier company radio or through a nonapproach control facility. You may do this by telling the station or nonapproach control facility to issue current weather.

4-7-8. BELOW MINIMA REPORT BY PILOT

If an arriving aircraft reports weather conditions are below his/her landing minima:

NOTE-
Determination that existing weather/visibility is adequate for approach/landing is the responsibility of the pilot/aircraft operator.

a. Issue appropriate instructions to the aircraft to hold or proceed to another airport.

b. Adjust, as necessary, the position in the landing sequence of any other aircraft desiring to make approaches and issue approach clearances accordingly.

4-7-9. TRANSFER OF JURISDICTION

Transfer radio communications and control responsibility early enough to allow the receiving facility to clear an aircraft beyond the clearance limit before the aircraft reaches it.

4-7-10. APPROACH INFORMATION

a. Both en route and terminal approach control sectors must provide current approach information to aircraft destined to airports for which they provide approach control services. This information must be provided on initial contact or as soon as possible thereafter. Approach information contained in the ATIS broadcast may be omitted if the pilot states the appropriate ATIS code. For pilots destined to an airport without ATIS, items 3-5 below may be omitted after the pilot advises receipt of the automated weather; otherwise, issue approach information by including the following:

1. Approach clearance or type approach to be expected if two or more approaches are published and the clearance limit does not indicate which will be used.

2. Runway if different from that to which the instrument approach is made.

3. Surface wind.

4. Ceiling and visibility if the reported ceiling at the airport of intended landing is below 1,000 feet or below the highest circling minimum, whichever is greater, or the visibility is less than 3 miles.

5. Altimeter setting for the airport of intended landing.

REFERENCE-
FAA Order JO 7110.65, Chapter 2, Section 7, Altimeter Settings.

b. Upon pilot request, controllers must inform pilots of the frequency where automated weather data may be obtained and, if appropriate, that airport weather is not available.

PHRASEOLOGY-
(Airport) AWOS/ASOS WEATHER AVAILABLE ON (frequency).

1. ASOS/AWOS must be set to provide one minute weather at uncontrolled airports that are without ground-to-air weather broadcast capability by a CWO, NWS or FSS observer.

2. Controllers will consider the long-line disseminated weather from an automated weather system at an uncontrolled airport as trend information only and must rely on the pilot for the current weather information for that airport.

3. Controllers must issue the last long-line disseminated weather to the pilot if the pilot is unable to receive the ASOS/AWOS broadcast.

NOTE–
Aircraft destined to uncontrolled airports, which have automated weather data with broadcast capability, should monitor the ASOS/AWOS frequency to ascertain the current weather at the airport. The pilot should advise the controller when he/she has received the broadcast weather and state his/her intentions.

c. Issue any known changes classified as special weather observations as soon as possible. Special weather observations need not be issued after they are included in the ATIS broadcast and the pilot states the appropriate ATIS code.

d. Advise pilots when the ILS on the runway in use is not operational if that ILS is on the same frequency as an operational ILS serving another runway.

EXAMPLE–
"Expect visual approach runway two five right, runway two five right I–L–S not operational."

REFERENCE–
FAA Order JO 7110.65, Para 2–7–2, Altimeter Setting Issuance Below Lowest Usable FL.
FAA Order JO 7110.65, Para 5–10–2, Approach Information.
14 CFR Section 91.129 Operations in Class D Airspace, Subpara (d)(2).

e. *TERMINAL*: If multiple runway transitions are depicted on a STAR procedure, advise pilots of the runway assignment on initial contact or as soon as possible thereafter.

4–7–11. ARRIVAL INFORMATION BY APPROACH CONTROL FACILITIES

TERMINAL

a. Forward the following information to nonapproach control towers soon enough to permit adjustment of the traffic flow or to FSSs soon enough to provide local airport advisory where applicable:

1. Aircraft identification.

2. Type of aircraft.

3. ETA.

4. Type of instrument approach procedure the aircraft will execute; or

5. For SVFR, the direction from which the aircraft will enter Class B, Class C, Class D, or Class E surface area and any altitude restrictions that were issued; or

6. For aircraft executing a contact approach, the position of the aircraft.

NOTE–
Specific time requirements are usually stated in a letter of agreement.

b. Forward the following information to the tower when the tower and TRACON are part of the same facility:

1. Aircraft identification.

2. Type aircraft if required for separation purposes.

3. Type of instrument approach procedure and/or runway if differing from that in use.

NOTE–
The local controller has the responsibility to determine whether or not conditions are adequate for the use of STARS data on the CTRD where a facility directive authorizes its use for the transfer of arrival data.

REFERENCE–
FAA Order JO 7210.3, Para 12–6–4, Use of STARS Quick Look Functions.

c. Where the collocated or satellite tower has STARS data displayed on its CTRD, the STARS modify or quick look functions may be used to forward arrival data provided that a facility directive at the collocated tower or a letter of agreement with the satellite tower exists which outlines procedures for using STARS for transferring this data.

d. Forward the following information to centers:

1. Where two or more instrument approach procedures are published for the airport, the particular procedure which an aircraft can expect or that it will be vectored toward the airport for a visual approach.

2. Highest altitude being used by the approach control facility at the holding fix.

3. Average time interval between successive approaches.

4. Arrival time of aircraft over the holding fix or, if control has been transferred to you before an aircraft has reached the fix, a statement or other indication acknowledging receipt of control responsibility.

5. Revised EFC if different by 10 minutes or more from that issued by the center.

6. Missed approaches if they affect center operations.

7. Information relating to an unreported or overdue aircraft.

4−7−12. AIRPORT CONDITIONS

a. *EN ROUTE.* Before issuing an approach clearance, and subsequently as changes occur, inform an aircraft of any abnormal operation of approach and landing aids and of destination airport conditions that you know of which might restrict an approach or landing. This information may be omitted if it is contained in the ATIS broadcast and the pilot states that he/she has received the appropriate ATIS code.

NOTE−

1. *Airport conditions information, in the provision of en route approach control service, does not include the following:*

a. *The airport surface environment other than the landing area(s) (e.g. TAXIWAY, APRON or SERVICE keyword NOTAMs).*

b. *Obstruction information (e.g. OBST NOTAMs) for aircraft that will be cleared for an instrument approach.*

c. *Information pertaining to cold temperature compensation.*

2. *When advised of special use airspace (SUA) or military training route (MTR) activation, appropriate action is taken to separate nonparticipating IFR aircraft from those activities when required, and/or to issue applicable advisories as warranted. When meeting this requirement, there is no requirement for controllers to additionally issue the associated D NOTAM activating that SUA or MTR to the pilot. Accordingly, D NOTAMs for SUA that contain the accountability codes SUAE, SUAC, and SUAW are not required to be issued.*

3. *Although a pilot may have obtained NOTAM information during pre−flight briefings, airport conditions may have changed in flight. Therefore a pilot stating, or a controller asking, if they "have the NOTAMS" does not relieve the controller of the responsibility of issuing airport conditions that might restrict an approach or landing. Additionally, controller instructions to contact FSS to obtain the NOTAMs does not relieve the controller of their responsibilities specified in this paragraph.*

b. *TERMINAL.* On first contact or as soon as possible thereafter, and subsequently as changes occur, inform an aircraft of any abnormal operation of approach and landing aids and of destination airport conditions that you know of which might restrict an approach or landing. This information may be omitted if it is contained in the ATIS broadcast and the pilot states the appropriate ATIS code.

REFERENCE−
FAA Order JO 7110.65, Chapter 3, Section 3, Airport Conditions.

c. Issue RwyCC contained in a FICON NOTAM to aircraft in accordance with one of the following:

1. Before or when an approach clearance is issued.

2. Before an en route descent clearance is issued.

3. *TERMINAL.* Prior to departure.

4. As soon as possible after receipt of any subsequent changes in previously issued RwyCC information.

d. RwyCC may be issued in lieu of the complete FICON NOTAM. Issue the complete FICON NOTAM upon pilot request, workload permitting.

EXAMPLE–
Boston Runway Two Seven, field condition, three, three, three, one hundred percent, two inches dry snow over compacted snow. Observed at one five three zero zulu.

NOTE–
RwyCC may be transmitted via the ATIS as prescribed in paragraphs 2–9–3, Content; 3–3–1, Landing Area Condition; 3–9–1, Departure Information; and 3–10–1, Landing Information.

e. *TERMINAL.* Where RCRs are provided, transmit this information to USAF and ANG aircraft. Issue the RCR to other aircraft upon pilot request.

NOTE–
USAF offices furnish RCR information at airports serving USAF and ANG aircraft.

REFERENCE–
FAA Order JO 7110.65, Para 2–9–3, Content.
FAA Order JO 7110.65, Para 3–3–1, Landing Area Condition.
FAA Order JO 7110.65, Para 3–9–1, Departure Information.
FAA Order JO 7110.65, Para 3–10–1, Landing Information.

4–7–13. SWITCHING ILS RUNWAYS

TERMINAL

When a change is made from one ILS to another at airports equipped with multiple systems which are not used simultaneously, coordinate with the facilities which use the fixes formed by reference to these NAVAIDs.

Section 8. Approach Clearance Procedures

4-8-1. APPROACH CLEARANCE

a. Clear aircraft for "standard" or "special" instrument approach procedures only.

1. To require an aircraft to execute a particular instrument approach procedure, specify in the approach clearance the name of the approach as published on the approach chart. Where more than one procedure is published on a single chart and a specific procedure is to be flown, amend the approach clearance to specify execution of the specific approach to be flown. If only one instrument approach of a particular type is published, the approach needs not be identified by the runway reference.

2. An aircraft conducting an ILS or LDA approach must be advised at the time an approach clearance is issued when the glideslope is reported out of service, unless the title of the published approach procedure allows (for example, ILS or LOC Rwy 05).

3. Standard instrument approach procedures (SIAP) must begin at an initial approach fix (IAF) or an intermediate fix (IF) if there is not an IAF.

4. Where adequate radar coverage exists, radar facilities may vector aircraft to the final approach course in accordance with paragraph 5-9-1, Vectors to Final Approach Course, and paragraph 5-9-2, Final Approach Course Interception.

5. Where adequate radar coverage exists, radar facilities may clear an aircraft to any fix 3 NM or more prior to the FAF, along the final approach course, at an intercept angle not greater than 30 degrees.

6. Controllers must not disapprove a pilot request to cold temperature compensate in conjunction with the issuance of an approach clearance.

PHRASEOLOGY–
CLEARED (type) APPROACH.

CLEARED APPROACH.

(To authorize a pilot to execute his/her choice of instrument approach),

CLEARED (specific procedure to be flown) APPROACH.

(Where more than one procedure is published on a single chart and a specific procedure is to be flown),

CLEARED (ILS/LDA) APPROACH, GLIDESLOPE UNUSABLE.

(To authorize a pilot to execute an ILS or an LDA approach when the glideslope is out of service)

CLEARED LOCALIZER APPROACH

(When the title of the approach procedure contains "or LOC")

CANCEL APPROACH CLEARANCE (additional instructions as necessary)

(When it is necessary to cancel a previously issued approach clearance)

EXAMPLE–
"Cleared Approach."
"Cleared (V-O-R/I-L-S/Localizer) Approach."
"Cleared L-D-A Runway Three-Six Approach."

"Cleared Localizer Back Course Runway One-Three Approach."
"Cleared (GPS/RNAV Z) Runway Two-Two Approach."
"Cleared BRANCH ONE Arrival and (ILS/RNAV) Runway One-Three Approach."
"Cleared I-L-S Runway Three-Six Approach, glideslope unusable."
"Cleared S-D-F Approach."
"Cleared G-L-S Approach."

NOTE–

1. *Clearances authorizing instrument approaches are issued on the basis that, if visual contact with the ground is made before the approach is completed, the entire approach procedure will be followed unless the pilot receives approval for a contact approach, is cleared for a visual approach, or cancels their IFR flight plan.*

2. *Approach clearances are issued based on known traffic. The receipt of an approach clearance does not relieve the pilot of his/her responsibility to comply with applicable Parts of Title 14 of the Code of Federal Regulations and the notations on instrument approach charts which levy on the pilot the responsibility to comply with or act on an instruction; for example, "Straight-in minima not authorized at night," "Procedure not authorized when glideslope/glidepath not used," "Use of procedure limited to aircraft authorized to use airport," or "Procedure not authorized at night" or Snowflake icon with associated temperature.*

3. *In some cases, the name of the approach, as published, is used to identify the approach, even though a component of the approach aid, other than the localizer on an ILS is inoperative.*

4. *Where more than one procedure to the same runway is published on a single chart, each must adhere to all final approach guidance contained on that chart, even though each procedure will be treated as a separate entity when authorized by ATC.*

5. *The use of alphabetical identifiers in the approach name with a letter from the end of the alphabet; for example, X, Y, Z, such as "HI TACAN Z Rwy 6L or RNAV(GPS) Y Rwy 04", denotes multiple straight-in approaches to the same runway that use the same approach aid.*

6. *Alphabetical suffixes with a letter from the beginning of the alphabet; for example, A, B, C, denote a procedure that does not meet the criteria for straight-in landing minimums authorization.*

7. *14 CFR Section 91.175(j) requires a pilot to receive a clearance to conduct a procedure turn when vectored to a final approach course or fix, conducting a timed approach, or when the procedure specifies "NO PT."*

8. *An aircraft which has been cleared to a holding fix and prior to reaching that fix is issued a clearance for an approach, but not issued a revised routing; that is, "proceed direct to...." may be expected to proceed via the last assigned route, a feeder route (if one is published on the approach chart), and then to commence the approach as published. If, by following the route of flight to the holding fix, the aircraft would overfly an IAF or the fix associated\ with the beginning of a feeder route to be used, the aircraft is expected to commence the approach using the published feeder route to the IAF or from the IAF as appropriate; that is, the aircraft would not be expected to overfly and return to the IAF or feeder route.*

9. *Approach name items contained within parenthesis; for example, RNAV (GPS) Rwy 04, are not included in approach clearance phraseology.*

10. *Pilots are required to advise ATC when intending to apply cold temperature compensation to instrument approach segments. Pilots must advise ATC of the amount of compensation required for each affected segment on initial contact or as soon as possible. Pilots are not required to advise ATC when correcting on the final segment only. Controllers may delay the issuance of an approach clearance to comply with approved separation requirements when informed that a pilot will apply cold temperature compensation (CTC). Pilots will not apply altitude compensation, unless authorized, when assigned an altitude prior to an approach clearance. Consideration should be given to vectoring aircraft at or above the requested compensating altitude if possible. This eliminates pilots having to climb once on the approach.*

REFERENCE–
FAA Order 8260.3, United States Standard for Terminal Instrument Procedures (TERPS).
P/CG Term – Cold Temperature Compensation.
AIM, Para 5-1-17, Cold Temperature Operations.
AIM, Para 5-5-4, Instrument Approach.

11. *There are some systems, for example, Enhanced Flight Vision System (EFVS), which allow pilots to conduct Instrument Approach Procedures (IAP) when the reported weather is below minimums prescribed on the IAP to be flown.*

REFERENCE–
14 CFR § 91.175(l).
P/CG Term – EFVS.

b. For aircraft operating on unpublished routes, issue the approach clearance only after the aircraft is:

1. Established on a segment of a published route or instrument approach procedure, or (See FIG 4–8–1)

EXAMPLE–
The aircraft is established on a segment of a published route at 5,000 feet. "Cleared V-O-R Runway Three Four Approach."

FIG 4–8–1
Approach Clearance Example

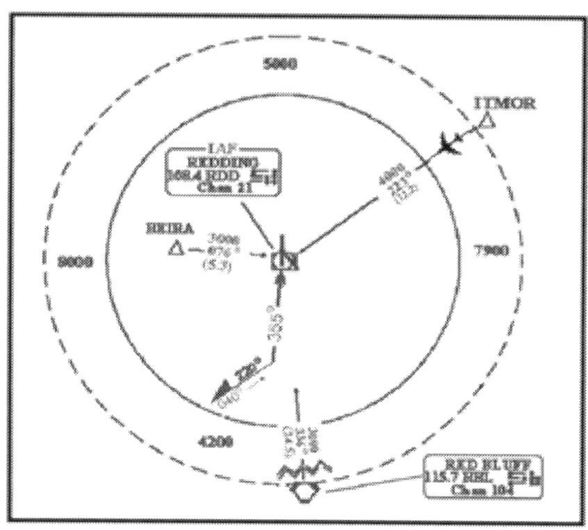

2. Assigned an altitude to maintain until the aircraft is established on a segment of a published route or instrument approach procedure. (See FIG 4-8-2.)

EXAMPLE–
Aircraft 1 is cleared direct LEFTT. The MVA in the area is 3,000 feet, and the aircraft is at 4,000 feet. "Cross LEFTT at or above three thousand five hundred, cleared RNAV Runway One Eight Approach."

The MVA in the area is 3,000 feet and Aircraft 2 is at 3,000 feet. "Cleared direct LEFTT direct CENTR, maintain three thousand until CENTR, cleared straight-in RNAV Runway One Eight Approach."

FIG 4–8–2
Approach Clearance Example

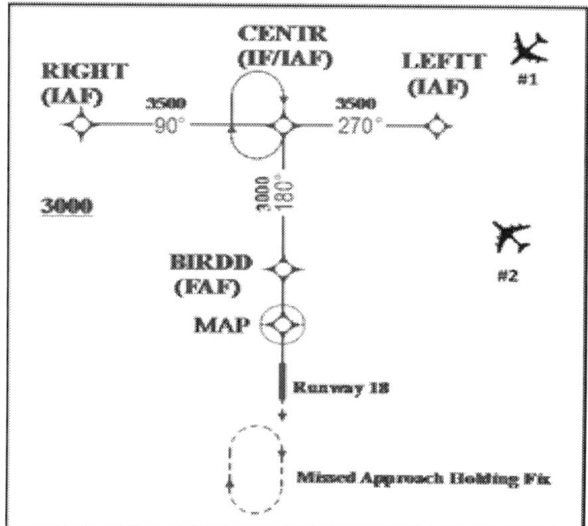

NOTE–
1. *The altitude assigned must assure IFR obstruction clearance from the point at which the approach clearance is issued until established on a segment of a published route or instrument approach procedure.*

2. *If the altitude assignment is VFR-on-top, it is conceivable that the pilot may elect to remain high until arrival over the final approach fix which may require the pilot to circle to descend so as to cross the final approach fix at an altitude that would permit landing.*

3. *An aircraft is not established on an approach until at or above an altitude published on that segment of the approach.*

REFERENCE–
FAA Order 8260.3 United States Standard for Terminal Instrument Procedures (TERPS), Para 11-3.

c. Except for visual approaches, do not clear an aircraft direct to the FAF unless it is also an IAF, wherein the aircraft is expected to execute the depicted procedure turn or hold-in-lieu of procedure turn.

d. Intercept angles greater than 90 degrees may be used when a procedure turn, a hold-in-lieu of procedure turn pattern, or arrival holding is depicted and the pilot will execute the procedure.

e. If a procedure turn, hold-in-lieu of procedure turn, or arrival holding pattern is depicted and the angle of intercept is 90 degrees or less, the aircraft must be instructed to conduct a straight-in approach if ATC does not want the pilot to execute a procedure turn or hold-in-lieu of procedure turn. (See FIG 4–8–3)

PHRASEOLOGY–
CLEARED STRAIGHT-IN (type) APPROACH

NOTE–
1. *Restate "cleared straight-in" in the approach clearance even if the pilot was advised earlier to expect a straight-in approach.*

2. *Some approach charts have an arrival holding pattern depicted at the IAF using a "thin line" holding symbol. It is charted where holding is frequently required prior to starting the approach procedure so that detailed holding instructions are not required. The arrival holding pattern is not authorized unless assigned by ATC.*

EXAMPLE–
"Cleared direct SECND, maintain at or above three thousand until SECND, cleared straight-in ILS Runway One-Eight approach."

REFERENCE–
AIM, Para 5-4-5, Instrument Approach Procedure Charts.
AIM, Para 5-4-9, Procedure Turn and Hold-in-lieu of Procedure Turn.

FIG 4-8-3
Approach Clearance Example
For Aircraft On a Conventional Approach

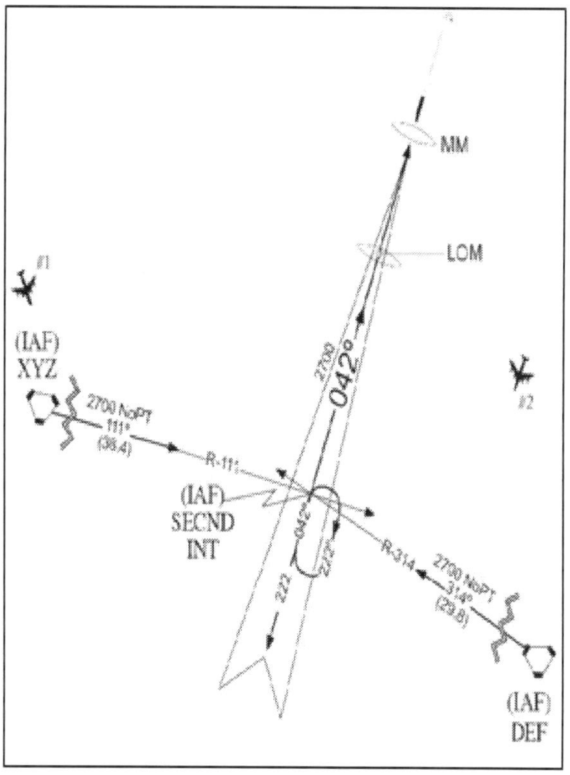

EXAMPLE–
Aircraft 1 can be cleared direct to XYZ VORTAC, or SECND because the intercept angle is 90 degrees or less.

Aircraft 2 cannot be cleared to XYZ VORTAC because the intercept angle is greater than 90 degrees.

Aircraft 2 can be cleared to SECND if allowed to execute the hold-in-lieu of procedure turn pattern.

f. Except when applying radar procedures, timed or visual approaches, clear an aircraft for an approach to an airport when the preceding aircraft has landed or canceled IFR flight plan.

g. Where instrument approaches require radar monitoring and radar services are not available, do not use the phraseology "cleared approach," which allows the pilot his/her choice of instrument approaches.

RNAV APPLICATION

h. For RNAV–equipped aircraft operating on unpublished routes, issue approach clearance for conventional or RNAV SIAP including approaches with RF legs only after the aircraft is: (See FIG 4–8–4).

1. Established on a heading or course direct to the IAF at an intercept angle not greater than 90 degrees and is assigned an altitude in accordance with b2. Radar monitoring is required to the IAF for RNAV (RNP) approaches when no hold–in–lieu of procedure turn is executed.

EXAMPLE–
Aircraft 1 can be cleared direct to CENTR. The intercept angle at that IAF is 90 degrees or less. The minimum altitude for IFR operations (14 CFR, section 91.177) along the flight path to the IAF is 3,000 feet. If a hold in lieu of procedure turn pattern is depicted at an IAF and a TAA is not defined, the aircraft must be instructed to conduct a straight-in approach if ATC does not want the pilot to execute a hold-in-lieu procedure turn. "Cleared direct CENTR, maintain at or above three thousand until CENTR, cleared straight-in RNAV Runway One-Eight Approach."

2. Established on a heading or course direct to the IF at an angle not greater than 90 degrees, provided the following conditions are met:

(a) Assign an altitude in accordance with b2 that will permit a normal descent to the FAF.

NOTE–
Controllers should expect aircraft to descend at approximately 150-300 feet per nautical mile when applying guidance in subparagraph h2(a).

(b) Radar monitoring is provided to the IF.

(c) The SIAP must identify the intermediate fix *with the letters "IF."*

(d) For procedures where an IAF is published, the pilot is advised to expect clearance to the IF at least 5 miles from the fix.

EXAMPLE–
"Expect direct CENTR for RNAV Runway One-Eight Approach."

3. Established on a heading or course direct to a fix between the IF and FAF, at an intercept angle not greater than 30 degrees, and assigned an altitude in accordance with b2.

EXAMPLE–
Aircraft 1 is more than 5 miles from SHANN. The minimum altitude for IFR operations (14 CFR Section 91.177) along the flight path to SHANN is 3,000 feet. SHANN is a step down fix between the IF/IAF (CENTR) and the FAF. To clear Aircraft 1 to SHANN, ATC must ensure the intercept angle for the intermediate segment at SHANN is not greater than 30 degrees and must be cleared to an altitude that will allow a normal descent to the FAF. "Cleared direct SHANN, cross SHANN at or above three thousand, cleared RNAV Runway One-Eight Approach."

REFERENCE–
FAA Order JO 7110.65, Para 5–6–2, Methods.
FAA Order JO 7110.65, Chapter 5, Section 9, Radar Arrivals.

FIG 4–8–4
Approach Clearance Example
For RNAV Aircraft

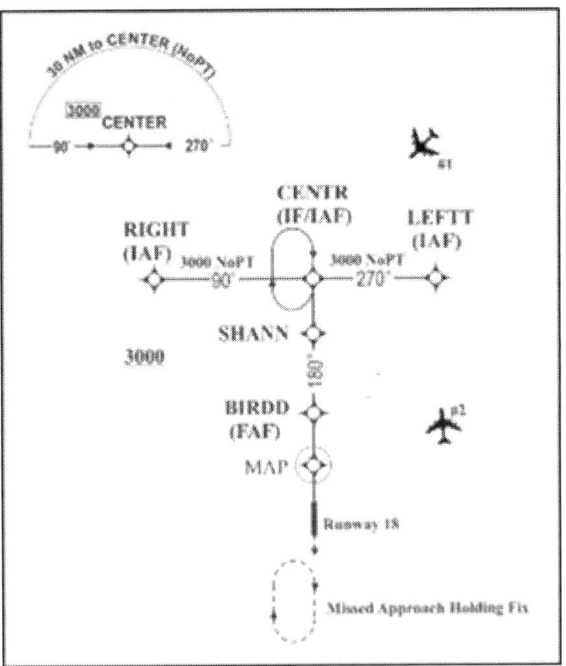

EXAMPLE–
Aircraft 2 cannot be cleared direct to CENTR unless the aircraft is allowed to execute the hold-in-lieu of procedure turn. The intercept angle at that IF/IAF is greater than 90 degrees. The minimum altitude for IFR operations (14 CFR Section

91.177) along the flight path to the IAF is 3,000 feet. "Cleared direct CENTR, maintain at or above three thousand until CENTR, cleared RNAV Runway One-Eight approach." The pilot is expected to proceed direct CENTR and execute the hold-in-lieu of procedure turn.

Aircraft 2 can be cleared direct LEFTT. The intercept angle at that IAF is 90 degrees or less. The minimum altitude for IFR operations (14 CFR Section 91.177) along the flight path to the IAF is 3,000 feet. "Cleared direct LEFTT, maintain at or above three thousand until LEFTT, cleared RNAV Runway One-Eight Approach." The pilot does not have to be cleared for a straight-in approach since no hold-in-lieu of procedure turn pattern is depicted at LEFTT.

REFERENCE–
FAA Order JO 7110.65, Chapter 5, Section 9, Radar Arrivals.

i. Clear RNAV–equipped aircraft conducting RNAV instrument approach procedures that contain radius to fix (RF) legs:

1. Via published transitions, or

2. In accordance with subparagraph h.

3. Do not clear aircraft direct to any waypoint beginning or within an RF leg.

4. Do not assign fix/waypoint crossing speeds in excess of charted speed restrictions.

NOTE–
1. *RNAV approaches (containing RF legs) that commence at 10,000 feet or above require special procedures that will be site specific and specified in a facility directive.*

2. *An RF leg is defined as a curved segment indicating a constant radius circular path about a defined turn center that begins at a waypoint. RF legs may have maximum airspeeds charted for procedural containment that must be followed.*

3. *If an aircraft is vectored off the procedure, expect the aircraft to request a return to an IAF.*

FIG 4–8–5
Radius to Fix (RF) and Track to Fix (TF)

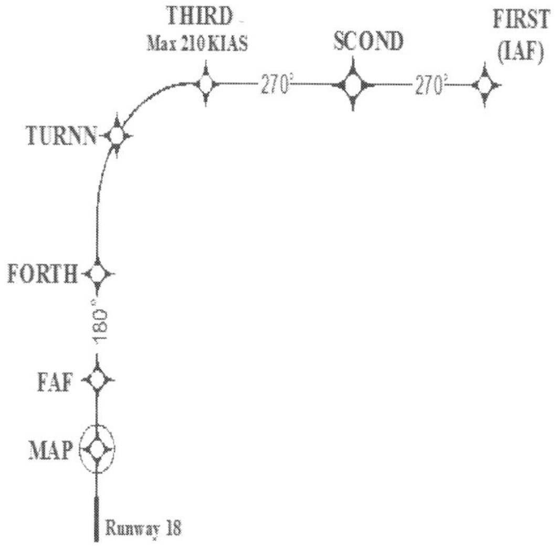

NOTE–
1. *The segment between THIRD and FORTH in FIG 4–8–5 is an RF leg.*

2. *The straight segments between waypoints in FIG 4–8–5 are TF legs.*

j. Where a terminal arrival area (TAA) has been established to support RNAV approaches, use the procedures under subparagraph b above. (See FIG 4–8–6.)

NOTE–
1. *Aircraft that are within the lateral boundary of a TAA, and at or above the TAA minimum altitude, are established on the approach and may be issued an approach clearance without an altitude restriction.*

2. *The TAA minimum altitude may be higher than the MVA/MIA. If an aircraft is below the TAA minimum altitude, it must either be assigned an altitude to maintain until established on a segment of a published route or instrument approach procedure, or climbed to the TAA altitude.*

EXAMPLE–
Aircraft 1: The aircraft is at or above the minimum TAA altitude and within the lateral boundary of the TAA. "Cleared R–NAV Runway One Eight Approach."
Aircraft 2: The MVA is 3000 feet and the aircraft is level at 4000 feet. The TAA minimum altitude is 4200 feet. The aircraft must be assigned an altitude to maintain until established on a segment of the approach. "Cross RIGHT at or above three thousand, cleared R–NAV Runway One Eight Approach."
Aircraft 3: The aircraft is inbound to the CHARR IAF on an unpublished direct route at 7,000 feet. The minimum IFR altitude for IFR operations (14 CFR Section 91.177) along this flight path to the IAF is 5,000 feet. "Cleared direct CHARR, maintain at or above five thousand until entering the TAA, cleared RNAV Runway One–Eight Approach."

FIG 4–8–6
Basic "T" and TAA Design

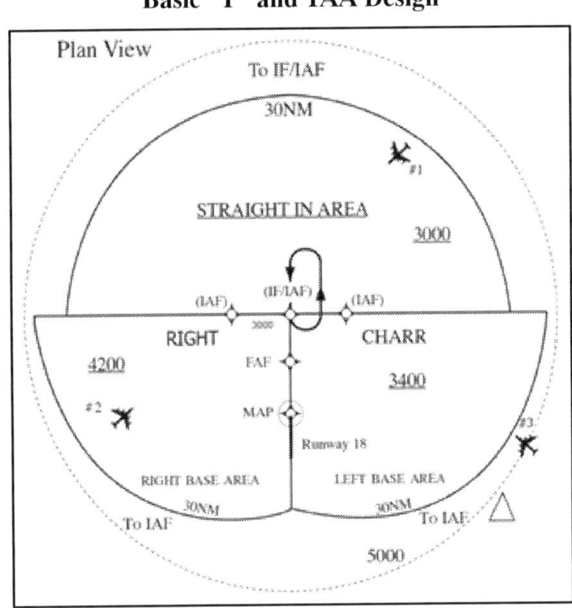

k. When GPS TESTING NOTAMs are published and testing is actually occurring, inform pilots requesting or cleared for a RNAV approach that GPS may not be available and request intentions. Do not resume RNAV approach operations until certain that GPS interference is no longer a factor or such GPS testing exercise has ceased.

INTERPRETATION–
7110.65, 4–8–1, Approach Clearance (ZAB) (7–17–2015)
7110.65, 4–8–1, Approach Clearance (ZKC) (7–17–2015)

l. During times when pilots report GPS anomalies, request the pilot's intentions and/or clear that aircraft for an alternative approach, if available and operational. Announce to other aircraft requesting an RNAV approach that GPS is reported unavailable and request intentions.

REFERENCE–
FAA Order JO 7110.65, Para 2–1–10, NAVAID Malfunctions.
FAA Order JO 7110.65, Para 4–7–12, Airport Conditions.

m. When clearing an aircraft for an RNAV approach, and a GPS NOTAM is published (a WAAS NOTAM is not issued), both GPS and WAAS may become unavailable. Therefore, when a GPS anomaly is reported, request the pilot's intentions.

NOTE–
WAAS UNAVAILABLE NOTAMs are published to indicate a failure of a WAAS system component. Airborne GPS/WAAS equipment may revert to GPS-only operation which satisfies the requirements for basic RNAV (GPS) approaches to the airport of intended landing or filed alternate airport, if airborne equipment is approved for such operations.

4–8–2. CLEARANCE LIMIT

Issue approach or other clearances, as required, specifying the destination airport as the clearance limit if airport traffic control service is not provided even though this is a repetition of the initial clearance.

PHRASEOLOGY–
CLEARED TO (destination) AIRPORT

4–8–3. RELAYED APPROACH CLEARANCE

TERMINAL

Include the weather report, when it is required and available, when an approach clearance is relayed through a communication station other than an air carrier company radio. You may do this by telling the station to issue current weather.

4–8–4. ALTITUDE ASSIGNMENT FOR MILITARY HIGH ALTITUDE INSTRUMENT APPROACHES

Altitudes above those shown on the high altitude instrument approach procedures chart may be specified when required for separation.

NOTE–
To preclude the possibility of aircraft exceeding rate-of-descent or airspeed limitations, the maximum altitudes which may be assigned for any portion of the high altitude instrument approach procedure will be determined through coordination between the ATC facility concerned and the military authority which originated the high altitude instrument approach procedure.

REFERENCE–
FAA Order JO 7110.65, Para 4–7–5, Military Turbojet En Route Descent.

4–8–5. SPECIFYING ALTITUDE

Specify in the approach clearance the altitude shown in the approach procedures when adherence to that altitude is required for separation. When vertical separation will be provided from other aircraft by pilot adherence to the prescribed maximum, minimum, or mandatory altitudes, the controller may omit specifying the altitude in the approach clearance.

NOTE–
Use FAA or NGA instrument approach procedures charts appropriate for the aircraft executing the approach.

4–8–6. CIRCLING APPROACH

a. Circling approach instructions may only be given for aircraft landing at airports with operational control towers.

b. Include in the approach clearance instructions to circle to the runway in use if landing will be made on a runway other than that aligned with the direction of instrument approach. When the direction of the circling maneuver in relation to the airport/runway is required, state the direction (eight cardinal compass points) and specify a left or right base/downwind leg as appropriate.

PHRASEOLOGY–
CIRCLE TO RUNWAY (number),

or

CIRCLE (direction using eight cardinal compass points) OF THE AIRPORT/RUNWAY FOR A LEFT/RIGHT BASE/DOWNWIND TO RUNWAY (number).

NOTE−
Where standard instrument approach procedures (SIAPs) authorize circling approaches, they provide a basic minimum of 300 feet of obstacle clearance at the MDA within the circling area considered. The dimensions of these areas, expressed in distances from the runways, vary for the different approach categories of aircraft. In some cases a SIAP may otherwise restrict circling approach maneuvers.

c. Do not issue clearances, such as "extend downwind leg," which might cause an aircraft to exceed the circling approach area distance from the runways within which required circling approach obstacle clearance is assured.

4−8−7. SIDE−STEP MANEUVER

TERMINAL

Side-step Maneuver. When authorized by an instrument approach procedure, you may clear an aircraft for an approach to one runway and inform the aircraft that landing will be made on a parallel runway.

EXAMPLE−
"Cleared I−L−S Runway seven left approach. Side-step to runway seven right."

NOTE−
Side-step maneuvers require higher weather minima/MDA. These higher minima/MDA are published on the instrument approach charts.

REFERENCE−
FAA Order JO 7110.65, Para 3−3−2, Closed/Unsafe Runway Information.
P/CG Term − Side−step Maneuver.

4−8−8. COMMUNICATIONS RELEASE

If an IFR aircraft intends to land at an airport not served by a tower or FSS, approve a change to the advisory service frequency when you no longer require direct communications.

PHRASEOLOGY−
CHANGE TO ADVISORY FREQUENCY APPROVED.

NOTE−
An expeditious frequency change permits the aircraft to receive timely local airport traffic information in accordance with AC 90−66, Non-Towered Airport Flight Operations.

INTERPRETATION−
7110.65, 4−8−8, Communication Release and Applicability to Special VFR Aircraft (9−24−2014)

4−8−9. MISSED APPROACH

Except in the case of a VFR aircraft practicing an instrument approach, an approach clearance automatically authorizes the aircraft to execute the missed approach procedure depicted for the instrument approach being flown. An alternate missed approach procedure as published on the appropriate FAA Form 8260 or appropriate military form may be assigned when necessary. After an aircraft commences a missed approach, it may be vectored at or above the MVA/MIA, or follow the provisions of paragraph 5−6−3, Vectors Below Minimum Altitude.

NOTE−
1. *Alternate missed approach procedures are published on the appropriate FAA Form 8260 or appropriate military form and require a detailed clearance when they are issued to the pilot.*

2. *In the event of a missed approach involving a turn, unless otherwise cleared, the pilot will proceed to the missed approach point before starting that turn.*

3. *Pilots must advise ATC when intending to apply cold temperature compensation and of the amount of compensation required. Pilots will not apply altitude compensation, unless authorized, when assigned an altitude if provided an initial heading to fly or radar vectors in lieu of published missed approach procedures. Consideration should be given to vectoring aircraft at or above the requested compensating altitude if possible.*

REFERENCE–
FAA Order JO 7110.65, Para 4–8–11, Practice Approaches.
FAA Order JO 7110.65, Para 5–6–3, Vectors Below Minimum Altitude.
FAA Order JO 7110.65, Para 5–8–3, Successive or Simultaneous Departures.
FAA Order 8260.19, Flight Procedures and Airspace, Para 8–6–6
FAA Order 8260.3, United States Standard for Terminal Instrument Procedures (TERPS), Para 2–8–1 and Chapter 16.
AIM, Para 5–5–5, Missed Approach.

4–8–10. APPROACH INFORMATION

Specify the following in the approach clearance when the pilot says he/she is unfamiliar with the procedure:

a. Initial approach altitude.

b. Direction and distance from the holding fix within which procedure turn is to be completed.

c. Altitude at which the procedure turn is to be made.

d. Final approach course and altitude.

e. Missed approach procedures if considered necessary.

PHRASEOLOGY–
INITIAL APPROACH AT (altitude), PROCEDURE TURN AT (altitude), (number) MINUTES/MILES (direction), FINAL APPROACH ON (name of NAVAID) (specified) COURSE/RADIAL/AZIMUTH AT (altitude).

f. Applicable notations on instrument approach charts which levy on the pilot the responsibility to comply with or act on an instruction; for example, "Straight-in minima not authorized at night," "Procedure not authorized when glideslope/glidepath not used," "Use of procedure limited to aircraft authorized to use airport," "Procedure not authorized at night," or a Snowflake icon indicating mandatory cold temperature compensation.

REFERENCE–
AIM, Para 5–1–17, Cold Temperature Operations.
AIM, Para 5–5–4, Instrument Approach.
AIM, Para 5–5–5, Missed Approach.

4–8–11. PRACTICE APPROACHES

Except for military aircraft operating at military airfields, ensure that neither VFR nor IFR practice approaches disrupt the flow of other arriving and departing IFR or VFR aircraft. Authorize, withdraw authorization, or refuse to authorize practice approaches as traffic conditions require. Normally, approaches in progress should not be terminated.

NOTE–
The priority afforded other aircraft over practice instrument approaches is not intended to be so rigidly applied that it causes grossly inefficient application of services.

a. Separation.

1. IFR aircraft practicing instrument approaches must be afforded approved separation in accordance with Chapter 3, Chapter 4, Chapter 5, Chapter 6, and Chapter 7 minima until:

(a) The aircraft lands, and the flight is terminated, or

(b) The pilot cancels the flight plan.

2. Where procedures require application of IFR separation to VFR aircraft practicing instrument approaches, IFR separation in accordance with Chapter 3, Chapter 4, Chapter 5, Chapter 6, and Chapter 7 must be provided. Controller responsibility for separation begins at the point where the approach clearance becomes effective. Except for super or heavy aircraft, 500 feet vertical separation may be applied between VFR aircraft and between a VFR and an IFR aircraft.

REFERENCE–
FAA Order JO 7210.3, Para 6–4–4, Practice Instrument Approaches.
FAA Order JO 7210.3, Para 10–4–5, Practice Instrument Approaches.

3. Where separation services are not provided to VFR aircraft practicing instrument approaches, the controller must;

(a) Instruct the pilot to maintain VFR.

(b) Advise the pilot that separation services are not provided.

PHRASEOLOGY–
"(Aircraft identification) MAINTAIN VFR, PRACTICE APPROACH APPROVED, NO SEPARATION SERVICES PROVIDED."

(c) Provide traffic information or advise the pilot to contact the appropriate facility.

4. If an altitude is assigned, including at or above/below altitudes, the altitude specified must meet MVA, minimum safe altitude, or minimum IFR altitude criteria.

REFERENCE–
FAA Order JO 7110.65, Para 7–7–5, Altitude Assignments.

5. All VFR aircraft must be instructed to maintain VFR on initial contact or as soon as possible thereafter.

NOTE–
This advisory is intended to remind the pilot that even though ATC is providing IFR-type instructions, the pilot is responsible for compliance with the applicable parts of the CFR governing VFR flight.

b. Missed Approaches.

1. Unless alternate instructions have been issued, IFR aircraft are automatically authorized to execute the missed approach depicted for the instrument approach being flown.

REFERENCE–
FAA Order JO 7110.65, Para 4–8–9, Missed Approach.

2. VFR aircraft are not automatically authorized to execute the missed approach procedure. This authorization must be specifically requested by the pilot and approved by the controller. When a missed approach has been approved and the practice approach is conducted in accordance with paragraph 4–8–11 a2, separation must be provided throughout the procedure including the missed approach. If the practice approach is conducted in accordance with paragraph 4–8–11 a3, separation services are not required during the missed approach.

REFERENCE–
FAA Order JO 7110.65, Para 7–2–1, Visual Separation.

4–8–12. LOW APPROACH AND TOUCH-AND-GO

Consider an aircraft cleared for a touch-and-go, low approach, or practice approach as an arriving aircraft until that aircraft touches down or crosses the landing threshold; thereafter, consider the aircraft as a departing aircraft. Before the aircraft begins its final descent, issue the appropriate departure instructions the pilot is to follow upon completion of the approach (in accordance with paragraph 4–3–2, Departure Clearances). Climb-out instructions must include a specific heading or a route of flight and altitude, except when the aircraft will maintain VFR and contact the tower.

EXAMPLE–
"After completing low approach, climb and maintain six thousand. Turn right, heading three six zero."

"Maintain VFR, contact tower."

(Issue other instructions as appropriate.)

NOTE–
Climb-out instructions may be omitted after the first approach if instructions remain the same.

Chapter 5. Radar

Section 1. General

5–1–1. PRESENTATION AND EQUIPMENT PERFORMANCE

a. Provide radar services only if you are personally satisfied that the radar presentation and equipment performance is adequate for the service being provided.

NOTE–
The provision of radar services is not limited to the distance and altitude parameters obtained during the commissioning flight check. FAA Order 8200.1, United States Standard Flight Inspection Manual, Chapter 14, Surveillance, describes the surveillance flight inspection procedures.

b. Notify the OS/CIC of any radar malfunctions or unexpected outages. Advise adjacent facilities when appropriate.

REFERENCE–
FAA Order JO 7110.65, Para 2–1–9, Reporting Essential Flight Information.
FAA Order JO 7210.3, Chapter 3, Chapter 7, Chapter 10 Section 5, and Chapter 12 Section 6.

5–1–2. ATC SURVEILLANCE SOURCE USE

Use approved ATC surveillance sources. TERMINAL. When operating in FUSION mode, the provisions of 5–1–2a are not applicable, unless required by facility directive.

REFERENCE–
FAA Order JO 7110.65, Para 5–2–13, Inoperative or Malfunctioning Interrogator.

a. Secondary radar may be used as the sole display source as follows:

1. In Class A airspace.

REFERENCE–
FAA Order JO 7110.65, Para 5–2–14, Failed Transponder or ADS–B Out Transmitter.
14 CFR Section 91.135, Operations in Class A Airspace.

2. Outside Class A airspace, or where mix of Class A airspace/non–Class A airspace exists, only when:

(a) Additional coverage is provided by secondary radar beyond that of the primary radar, or

(b) The primary radar is temporarily unusable or out of service. Advise pilots when these conditions exist, or

PHRASEOLOGY–
PRIMARY RADAR UNAVAILABLE (describe location). RADAR SERVICES AVAILABLE ON TRANSPONDER OR ADS–B EQUIPPED AIRCRAFT ONLY.

NOTE–
1. *Advisory may be omitted when provided on ATIS and pilot indicates having ATIS information.*

2. *This provision is to authorize secondary radar only operations where there is no primary radar available and the condition is temporary.*

(c) A secondary radar system is the only source of radar data for the area of service. *TERMINAL*. Advise pilots when these conditions exist.

NOTE–
Advisory may be omitted when provided on ATIS or by other appropriate notice to pilots.

b. *TERMINAL.* Do not use secondary radar only to conduct surveillance (ASR) final approaches unless an emergency exists and the pilot concurs.

c. Targets derived from ADS–B and WAM may be used for the provision of all terminal services when operating in STARS Fusion, STARS FMA, and STARS Multi-Sensor Mode, including those associated with any published instrument procedure annotated "radar required."

NOTE–
Targets derived from WAM cannot be used to provide 3 NM separation in the EAS. 3 NM targets are not derived from WAM within the EAS.

REFERENCE–
FAA Order JO 7110.65, Para 4–1–2, Exceptions.
FAA Order JO 7110.65, Para 4–4–2, Route Structure Transitions.
FAA Order JO 7110.65, Para 5–5–1, Application.
FAA Order JO 7110.65, Para 6–5–4, Minima Along Other Than Established Airways or Routes.
FAA Order JO 7110.65, Chapter 6, Nonradar.
FAA Order JO 7110.65, Para 5–5–4, Minima.
FAA Order JO 7210.3, Para 3–6–2, ATC Surveillance Source Use.

5–1–3. ELECTRONIC ATTACK (EA) ACTIVITY

a. Refer all EA activity requests to the appropriate center supervisor.

REFERENCE–
FAA Order JO 7610.4, Chapter 2, Section 3, Electronic Attack (EA) Mission Coordination.

NOTE–
EA activity can subsequently result in a request to apply EA videos to the radar system which may necessitate the decertification of the narrowband search radar. The Systems Engineer should be consulted concerning the effect of EA on the operational use of the narrowband radar prior to approving/disapproving requests to conduct EA activity.

b. When EA activity interferes with the operational use of radar:

1. *EN ROUTE.* Request the responsible military unit or aircraft, if initial request was received directly from pilot, to suspend the activity.

2. *TERMINAL.* Request suspension of the activity through the ARTCC. If immediate cessation of the activity is required, broadcast the request directly to the EA aircraft on the emergency frequency. Notify the ARTCC of direct broadcast as soon as possible.

c. When previously suspended activity will no longer interfere:

1. *EN ROUTE.* Inform the NORAD unit or aircraft that it may be resumed.

2. *TERMINAL.* Inform the ARTCC or aircraft that it may be resumed. Obtain approval from the ARTCC prior to broadcasting a resume clearance directly to the aircraft.

d. In each stop request, include your facility name, type of EA activity (chaff dispensing– "stream"/"burst" or electronic jamming– "buzzer"), radar band affected and, when feasible, expected duration of suspension.

PHRASEOLOGY–
BIG PHOTO (identification, if known) (name) CENTER/TOWER/APPROACH CONTROL.

To stop EA activity:

STOP STREAM/BURST IN AREA (area name) (degree and distance from facility),

or

STOP BUZZER ON (frequency band or channel).

To resume EA activity:

RESUME STREAM/BURST,

or

RESUME BUZZER ON (frequency band or channel).

5-1-4. MERGING TARGET PROCEDURES

a. Except while they are established in a holding pattern, apply merging target procedures to all radar identified:

1. Aircraft at 10,000 feet and above.

2. Turbojet aircraft regardless of altitude.

REFERENCE-
P/CG Term - Turbojet Aircraft.

3. Presidential aircraft regardless of altitude.

b. Issue traffic information to the aircraft listed in subparagraph a whose targets appear likely to merge unless the aircraft are separated by more than the appropriate vertical separation minima.

EXAMPLE-
"Traffic twelve o'clock, seven miles, eastbound, Gulfstream 650, one seven thousand."

"United Sixteen and American Twenty-Five, traffic twelve o'clock, one zero miles, opposite direction, eastbound Seven Thirty-Seven at flight level three three zero, westbound Airbus Three Twenty at flight level three two zero."

REFERENCE-
FAA Order JO 7110.65, Para 2-4-21, Description of Aircraft Types.

c. When both aircraft in subparagraph b are in RVSM airspace and vertically separated by 1,000 feet, and either pilot reports they are unable to maintain RVSM due to turbulence or mountain wave, use vectors to prevent the targets from merging.

EXAMPLE-
"Delta One Twenty-Three, fly heading two niner zero, vector for traffic. Traffic twelve o'clock, one zero miles, opposite direction, Seven Thirty-Seven, eastbound at flight level three one zero."

d. If the pilot requests, vector their aircraft to avoid merging targets with the previously issued traffic.

NOTE-
Because aircraft closure rates can be rapid, issue traffic with enough time for the pilot to decide if a vector is necessary.

e. If unable to provide vector service, inform the pilot.

NOTE-
The phraseology "Unable RVSM due to turbulence (or mountain wave)" is only intended for severe turbulence or other weather encounters with altitude deviations of approximately 200 feet or more.

5-1-5. HOLDING PATTERN SURVEILLANCE

Provide radar surveillance of outer fix holding pattern airspace areas, or any portions thereof, shown on your radar scope (displayed on the video map or scribed on the map overlay) whenever aircraft are holding there. Attempt to detect any aircraft that stray outside the area. If you detect an aircraft straying outside the area, assist it to return to the assigned airspace.

5-1-6. DEVIATION ADVISORIES

Inform an aircraft when it is observed in a position and on a track which will obviously cause the aircraft to deviate from its protected airspace area. If necessary, help the aircraft to return to the assigned protected airspace.

NOTE-
1. *RNAV ATS routes have a width of 8 miles and laterally protected airspace of 4 miles on each side of the route centerline*

2. *Navigation system performance requirements for operations on RNAV ATS routes require the aircraft system be capable of remaining within 2 miles of the route centerline. Aircraft approaching this limit may be experiencing a navigation system error or failure.*

REFERENCE–
FAA Order JO 7110.65, Para 4–2–5, Route or Altitude Amendments.
FAA Order JO 7110.65, Para 7–9–3, Methods.
FAA Order JO 7400.2, Para 20–5–2, RNAV Route Criteria.
AC 90-100A, U.S. Terminal and En Route Area Navigation (RNAV) Operations, Para 8a. Navigation System Accuracy.

5–1–7. MANUAL FIX POSTING

EN ROUTE

Manually record the observed or reported time over a fix at least once for each controlled aircraft in your sector of responsibility when the flight progress recording components of the EAS FDP are not operational.

REFERENCE–
FAA Order JO 7210.3, Para 6–1–6, Flight Progress Strip Usage.

5–1–8. POSITION REPORTING

If necessary, you may request an aircraft to provide an estimate or report over a specific fix. After an aircraft receives the statement "radar contact" from ATC, it discontinues reporting over compulsory reporting points. It resumes normal position reporting when ATC informs it "radar contact lost" or "radar service terminated."

REFERENCE–
P/CG Term– Radar Contact.

a. When required, inform an aircraft of its position with respect to a fix or airway.

PHRASEOLOGY–
OVER/PASSING (fix).

(Number of miles) MILES FROM (fix).

(Number of miles) MILES (direction) OF (fix, airway, or location).

CROSSING/JOINING/DEPARTING (airway or route).

INTERCEPTING/CROSSING (name of NAVAID) (specified) RADIAL.

5–1–9. RADAR SERVICE TERMINATION

a. Inform aircraft when radar service is terminated.

PHRASEOLOGY–
RADAR SERVICE TERMINATED (nonradar routing if required).

b. Radar service is automatically terminated and the aircraft needs not be advised of termination when:

NOTE–
Termination of radar monitoring when conducting simultaneous ILS approaches is prescribed in paragraph 5–9–7, Simultaneous Independent Approaches– Dual & Triple.

1. An aircraft cancels its IFR flight plan, except within Class B airspace, Class C airspace, TRSA, or where basic radar service is provided.

2. An aircraft conducting an instrument, visual, or contact approach has landed or has been instructed to change to advisory frequency.

3. At tower-controlled airports where radar coverage does not exist to within $^{1}/_{2}$ mile of the end of the runway, arriving aircraft must be informed when radar service is terminated.

REFERENCE–
FAA Order JO 7210.3, Para 10–5–6, Radar Tolerances.

4. *TERMINAL.* An arriving VFR aircraft receiving radar service to a tower-controlled airport within Class B airspace, Class C airspace, TRSA, or where basic radar service is provided has landed, or to all other airports, is instructed to change to tower or advisory frequency.

5. *TERMINAL.* An aircraft completes a radar approach.

REFERENCE–
FAA Order JO 7110.65, Para 7–6–12, Service Provided When Tower is Inoperative.

Section 2. Beacon/ADS–B Systems

5–2–1. ASSIGNMENT CRITERIA

a. General.

1. Mode 3/A is designated as the common military/civil mode for air traffic control use.

2. Make beacon code assignments to only ADS–B and/or transponder–equipped aircraft.

NOTE–
Aircraft equipped with ADS–B are also still required to have an operable transponder. The ATC–assigned beacon code is one of the required message elements of ADS–B Out.

b. Unless otherwise specified in this section, a facility directive, or a letter of agreement, issue beacon codes assigned by the computer. Computer–assigned codes may be modified as required.

NOTE–
The computer will assign only discrete beacon codes unless all the discrete codes allocated to a facility are in use.

1. *TERMINAL.* Aircraft that will remain within the terminal facility's delegated airspace must be assigned a code from the code subset allocated to the terminal facility.

2. *TERMINAL.* Unless otherwise specified in a facility directive or a letter of agreement, aircraft that will enter an adjacent facility's delegated airspace must be assigned a beacon code assigned by the ARTCC computer.

NOTE–
This will provide the adjacent facility advance information on the aircraft and will cause auto–acquisition of the aircraft prior to handoff. When an airborne aircraft that has been assigned a beacon code by the ARTCC computer and whose flight plan will terminate in another facility's area cancels ATC service, appropriate action should be taken to remove flight plan information on that aircraft.

PHRASEOLOGY–
SQUAWK THREE/ALFA (code),

or

SQUAWK (code).

REFERENCE–
FAA Order JO 7110.65, Para 5–3–3, Beacon/ADS–B Identification Methods.
FAA Order JO 7110.65, Para 5–3–4, Terminal Automation Systems Identification Methods.

c. Code 4000 should be assigned when aircraft are operating on a flight plan specifying frequent or rapid changes in assigned altitude in more than one stratum or other category of flight not compatible with a discrete code assignment.

NOTE–
1. *Categories of flight that can be assigned Code 4000 include certain flight test aircraft, MTR missions, aerial refueling operation requiring descent involving more than one stratum, ALTRVs where continuous monitoring of ATC frequencies is not required and frequent altitude changes are approved, and other flights requiring special handling by ATC.*

2. *Military aircraft operating in restricted/warning areas or on VR routes will squawk 4000 unless another code has been assigned or coordinated with ATC.*

5–2–2. RADAR BEACON CODE CHANGES

Unless otherwise specified in a directive or a letter of agreement or coordinated at the time of handoff, do not request an aircraft to change from the code it was squawking in the transferring facility's area until the aircraft is within your area of responsibility.

REFERENCE–
FAA Order JO 7110.65, Para 4–2–8, IFR-VFR and VFR-IFR Flights.
FAA Order JO 7110.65, Para 5–3–3, Beacon/ADS–B Identification Methods.

5-2-3. EMERGENCY CODE ASSIGNMENT

Assign codes to emergency aircraft as follows:

a. Code 7700 when the pilot declares an emergency and the aircraft is not radar identified.

PHRASEOLOGY-
SQUAWK MAYDAY ON 7700.

NOTE-
Instead of displaying "7700" in the data block, ERAM will display "EMRG," and STARS/MEARTS will display "EM."

b. After radio and radar contact have been established, you may request other than single-piloted helicopters and single-piloted turbojet aircraft to change from **Code 7700** to a computer-assigned discrete code.

NOTE-
1. *The code change, based on pilot concurrence, the nature of the emergency, and current flight conditions, will signify to other ATC facilities that the aircraft in distress is identified and under ATC control.*

2. *Pilots of single-piloted helicopters and single-piloted turbojet aircraft may be unable to change transponder settings during an emergency.*

PHRASEOLOGY-
RADAR CONTACT (position). IF FEASIBLE, SQUAWK (code).

REFERENCE-
FAA Order JO 7110.65, Para 5-3-3, Beacon/ADS-B Identification Methods.

c. The following must be accomplished on a Mode C equipped VFR aircraft which is in emergency but no longer requires the assignment of **Code 7700**:

1. *TERMINAL.* Assign a beacon code that will permit terminal minimum safe altitude warning (MSAW) alarm processing.

2. *EN ROUTE.* An appropriate keyboard entry must be made to ensure en route MSAW (EMSAW) alarm processing.

5-2-4. RADIO FAILURE

When you observe a **Code 7600** display, apply the procedures in paragraph 10-4-4, Communications Failure.

NOTE-
1. *An aircraft experiencing a loss of two-way radio communications capability can be expected to squawk* ***Code 7600.***

2. *Instead of displaying "7600" in the data block, ERAM will display "RDOF," and STARS/MEARTS will display "RF."*

REFERENCE-
FAA Order JO 7110.65, Para 5-3-3, Beacon/ADS-B Identification Methods.

5-2-5. HIJACK/UNLAWFUL INTERFERENCE

When you observe a Code 7500 display, apply the procedures in paragraph 10-2-6, Hijacked Aircraft.

NOTE-
Instead of displaying "7500" in the data block, ERAM will display "HIJK," and STARS/MEARTS will display "HJ."

REFERENCE-
FAA Order JO 7110.65, Para 5-3-3, Beacon/ADS-B Identification Methods.

5-2-6. UNMANNED AIRCRAFT SYSTEMS (UAS) LOST LINK

Code 7400 may be transmitted by unmanned aircraft systems (UAS) when the control link between the aircraft and the pilot is lost. Lost link procedures are programmed into the flight management system and associated with the flight plan being flown.

When you observe a **Code 7400** display, do the following:

NOTE–
Instead of displaying "7400" in the data block, ERAM will display "LLNK," and STARS/MEARTS will display "LL."

a. Determine the lost link procedure, as outlined in the Special Airworthiness Certificate or Certificate of Waiver or Authorization (COA).

b. Coordinate, as required, to allow UAS to execute the lost link procedure.

c. Advise the OS/CIC, when feasible, so the event can be documented.

d. If you observe or are informed by the PIC that the UAS is deviating from the programmed Lost Link procedure, or is encountering another anomaly, treat the situation in accordance with FAA Order JO 7110.65 Chapter 10, Section 1, paragraph 10–1–1c.

NOTE–
1. *The available lost link procedure should, at a minimum, include lost link route of flight, lost link orbit points, lost link altitudes, communications procedures and preplanned flight termination points if the event recovery of the UAS is deemed unfeasible.*

2. *Each lost link procedure may differ and is dependent upon airframe and operation. These items are contained in the flight's Certificate of Authorization or Waiver (COA) and must be made available to ATC personnel in their simplest form at positions responsible for Unmanned Aircraft (UAs).*

3. *Some UA airframes (Global Hawk) will not be programmed upon the NAS Automation roll out to squawk **7400**. These airframes will continue to squawk **7600** should a lost link occur. The ATC Specialist must apply the same procedures described above.*

5–2–7. VFR CODE ASSIGNMENTS

a. For VFR aircraft receiving radar advisories, issue a computer–assigned beacon code.

1. If the aircraft is outside of your area of responsibility and an operational benefit will be gained by retaining the aircraft on your frequency for the purpose of providing services, ensure that coordination has been effected:

(a) As soon as possible after positive identification, and

(b) Prior to issuing a control instruction or providing a service other than a safety alert/traffic advisory.

NOTE–
Safety alerts/traffic advisories may be issued to an aircraft prior to coordination if an imminent situation may be averted by such action. Coordination should be effected as soon as possible thereafter.

b. Instruct an IFR aircraft that cancels its IFR flight plan and is not requesting radar advisory service, or a VFR aircraft for which radar advisory service is being terminated, to squawk VFR.

PHRASEOLOGY–
SQUAWK VFR.

or

SQUAWK 1200.

NOTE–
1. *Aircraft not in contact with ATC may squawk **1255** in lieu of **1200** while en route to/from or within designated firefighting areas.*

2. *VFR aircraft that fly authorized SAR missions for the USAF or USCG may be advised to squawk **1277** in lieu of **1200** while en route to/from or within the designated search area.*

3. *VFR gliders should squawk **1202** in lieu of **1200**. Gliders operate under some flight and maneuvering limitations. They may go from essentially stationary targets while climbing and thermaling to moving targets very quickly. They can be expected to make radical changes in flight direction to find lift and cannot hold altitude in a response to an ATC request. Gliders may congregate together for short periods of time to climb together in thermals and may cruise together in loose formations while traveling between thermals.*

4. *The lead aircraft in a standard VFR formation flight not in contact with ATC should squawk 1203 in lieu of 1200. All other aircraft in the formation should squawk standby.*

REFERENCE–
FAA Order JO 7110.66, National Beacon Code Allocation Plan.

c. When an aircraft changes from VFR to IFR, assign a beacon code to Mode C equipped aircraft that will allow MSAW alarms.

REFERENCE–
FAA Order JO 7110.65, Para 5–3–3, Beacon/ADS–B Identification Methods.

5–2–8. BEACON CODES FOR PRESSURE SUIT FLIGHTS AND FLIGHTS ABOVE FL 600

Special use Mode 3/A codes are reserved for certain pressure suit flights and aircraft operations above FL 600 in accordance with FAA Order JO 7610.4, Sensitive Procedures and Requirements for Special Operations, Appendix 4, Document 2.

a. Ensure that these flights remain on one of the special use codes if filed in the flight plan, except:

b. When unforeseen events cause more than one aircraft to be in the same or adjacent ARTCC's airspace at the same time on the same special use discrete code, if necessary, you may request the pilot to make a code change, squawk standby, or stop squawk as appropriate.

NOTE–
1. *Current FAA automation systems track multiple targets on the same beacon code with much greater reliability than their predecessors, and a code change may not be necessary for such flights.*

2. *The beacon code is often preset on the ground for such flights and is used throughout the flight profile, including operations below FL 600. Due to equipment inaccessibility, the flight crew may not be able to accept transponder changes identified in this subparagraph.*

3. *In case of emergency, Code 7700 can still be activated. Instead of displaying "7700" in the data block, ERAM will display "EMRG," and STARS/MEARTS will display "EM."*

REFERENCE–
FAA Order JO 7110.65, Para 5–3–3, Beacon/ADS–B Identification Methods.

5–2–9. AIR DEFENSE EXERCISE BEACON CODE ASSIGNMENT

EN ROUTE

Ensure exercise FAKER aircraft remain on the exercise flight plan filed discrete beacon code.

NOTE–
1. *NORAD will ensure exercise FAKER aircraft flight plans are filed containing discrete beacon codes from the Department of Defense code allocation specified in FAA Order JO 7610.4, Sensitive Procedures and Requirements for Special Operations, Appendix 6.*

2. *NORAD will ensure that those FAKER aircraft assigned the same discrete beacon code are not flight planned in the same or any adjacent ARTCC's airspace at the same time. (Simultaneous assignment of codes will only occur when operational requirements necessitate.)*

REFERENCE–
FAA Order JO 7110.65, Para 5–3–3, Beacon/ADS–B Identification Methods.

5–2–10. STANDBY OPERATION

You may instruct an aircraft operating on an assigned code to change the transponder/ADS–B to "standby" position:

a. When approximately 15 miles from its destination and you no longer desire operation of the transponder/ADS–B; or

b. When necessary to reduce clutter in a multi–target area, provided you instruct the pilot to return the transponder/ADS–B to "normal" position as soon as possible thereafter.

PHRASEOLOGY–
SQUAWK STANDBY,

or

SQUAWK NORMAL.

REFERENCE–
FAA Order JO 7110.65, Para 5–3–3, Beacon/ADS–B Identification Methods.

5–2–11. CODE MONITOR

a. Continuously monitor the codes assigned to aircraft operating within your area of responsibility. Additionally, monitor Code 1200, Code 1202, Code 1203, Code 1255, and Code 1277 unless your area of responsibility includes only Class A airspace. During periods when excessive VFR target presentations derogate the separation of IFR traffic, monitoring of the aforementioned codes may be temporarily discontinued.

b. When your area of responsibility contains or is immediately adjacent to a restricted area, warning area, VR route, or other category where Code 4000 is appropriate, monitor Code 4000 and any other code used in lieu of 4000.

REFERENCE–
FAA Order JO 7210.3, Para 3–6–3, Monitoring of Mode 3/A Radar Beacon Codes.

5–2–12. FAILURE TO DISPLAY ASSIGNED BEACON CODE OR INOPERATIVE/MALFUNCTIONING TRANSPONDER

a. Inform an aircraft with an operable transponder that the assigned beacon code is not being displayed.

PHRASEOLOGY–
(Identification) RESET TRANSPONDER, SQUAWK (appropriate code).

b. Inform an aircraft when its transponder appears to be inoperative or malfunctioning.

PHRASEOLOGY–
(Identification) YOUR TRANSPONDER APPEARS INOPERATIVE/MALFUNCTIONING, RESET, SQUAWK (appropriate code).

c. Ensure that the subsequent control position in the facility or the next facility, as applicable, is notified when an aircraft transponder is malfunctioning/inoperative.

REFERENCE–
FAA Order JO 7110.65, Para 5–3–3, Beacon/ADS–B Identification Methods.

5–2–13. INOPERATIVE OR MALFUNCTIONING INTERROGATOR

Inform aircraft concerned when the ground interrogator appears to be inoperative or malfunctioning.

PHRASEOLOGY–
(Name of facility or control function) BEACON INTERROGATOR INOPERATIVE/MALFUNCTIONING.

REFERENCE–
FAA Order JO 7110.65, Para 5–1–2, ATC Surveillance Source Use.
FAA Order JO 7110.65, Para 5–3–3, Beacon/ADS–B Identification Methods.

5–2–14. FAILED TRANSPONDER OR ADS–B OUT TRANSMITTER

Disapprove a request or withdraw a previously issued approval to operate with a failed transponder or ADS–B Out solely on the basis of traffic conditions or other operational factors.

REFERENCE–
FAA Order JO 7110.65, Para 5–1–2, ATC Surveillance Source Use.
FAA Order JO 7110.65, Para 5–3–3, Beacon/ADS–B Identification Methods.

5–2–15. VALIDATION OF MODE C ALTITUDE READOUT

a. Ensure that Mode C altitude readouts are valid after:

1. Initial track start.

2. Track start from coast/frozen status.

3. During and after an unreliable Mode C readout.

4. Accepting an interfacility handoff, except:

(a) CTRD-equipped tower cabs are not required to validate Mode C altitude readouts after accepting interfacility handoffs from TRACONs according to the procedures in paragraph 5−4−3, Methods, subparagraph a4.

(b) ERAM facilities are not required to validate Mode C altitude readouts after accepting interfacility handoffs from other ERAM facilities, except:

(1) After initial track start or track start from coast is required, or

(2) During and after the display of a missing, unreasonable, exceptional, or otherwise unreliable Mode C readout indicator.

NOTE−
Consider a Mode C readout unreliable when any condition exists that indicates the Mode C may be in error, not just those that display an indicator in the Data Block.

b. Consider an altitude readout valid when:

1. It varies less than 300 feet from the pilot reported altitude, or

PHRASEOLOGY−
(If aircraft is known to be operating below the lowest useable flight level),

SAY ALTITUDE.

or

(If aircraft is known to be operating at or above the lowest useable flight level),

SAY FLIGHT LEVEL.

2. You receive a continuous readout from an aircraft on the airport and the readout varies by less than 300 feet from the field elevation, or

NOTE−
A continuous readout exists only when the altitude filter limits are set to include the field elevation.

REFERENCE−
FAA Order JO 7110.65, Para 5−2−21, Altitude Filters.
FAA Order JO 7110.65, Para 5−13−5, Selected Altitude Limits.

3. You have correlated the altitude information in your data block with the validated information in a data block generated in another facility (by verbally coordinating with the other controller) and your readout is exactly the same as the readout in the other data block.

c. When unable to validate the readout, do not use the Mode C altitude information for separation.

d. Whenever you observe an aircraft below FL 180 with an invalid Mode C readout:

1. Issue the correct altimeter setting and confirm the pilot has accurately reported the altitude.

PHRASEOLOGY−
(Location) ALTIMETER (appropriate altimeter), VERIFY ALTITUDE.

2. If the altitude readout continues to be invalid:

(a) Instruct the pilot to turn off the altitude- reporting part of his/her transponder and include the reason; and

(b) Notify the operations supervisor-in-charge of the aircraft call sign.

PHRASEOLOGY–
STOP ALTITUDE SQUAWK. ALTITUDE DIFFERS BY (number of feet) FEET.

e. Whenever you observe an aircraft at or above FL 180 with an invalid Mode C readout, unless the aircraft is descending below Class A airspace:

1. Verify that the pilot is using 29.92 inches of mercury as the altimeter setting and has accurately reported the altitude.

PHRASEOLOGY–
VERIFY USING TWO NINER NINER TWO AS YOUR ALTIMETER SETTING.

(If aircraft is known to be operating at or above the lowest useable flight level),

VERIFY FLIGHT LEVEL.

2. If the Mode C readout continues to be invalid:

(a) Instruct the pilot to turn off the altitude- reporting part of his/her transponder and include the reason; and

(b) Notify the operations supervisor-in-charge of the aircraft call sign.

PHRASEOLOGY–
STOP ALTITUDE SQUAWK. ALTITUDE DIFFERS BY (number of feet) FEET.

f. Whenever possible, inhibit altitude readouts on all consoles when a malfunction of the ground equipment causes repeated invalid readouts.

5–2–16. ALTITUDE CONFIRMATION– MODE C

Request a pilot to confirm assigned altitude on initial contact unless:

NOTE–
For the purpose of this paragraph, "initial contact" means a pilot's first radio contact with each sector/position.

a. The pilot states the assigned altitude, or

b. You assign a new altitude to a climbing or a descending aircraft, or

c. The Mode C readout is valid and indicates that the aircraft is established at the assigned altitude, or

d. *TERMINAL.* The aircraft was transferred to you from another sector/position within your facility (intrafacility).

PHRASEOLOGY–
(In level flight situations), VERIFY AT (altitude/flight level).

(In climbing/descending situations),

(if aircraft has been assigned an altitude below the lowest useable flight level),

VERIFY ASSIGNED ALTITUDE (altitude).

or

(If aircraft has been assigned a flight level at or above the lowest useable flight level),

VERIFY ASSIGNED FLIGHT LEVEL (flight level).

REFERENCE–
FAA Order JO 7110.65, Para 5–3–3, Beacon/ADS–B Identification Methods.

5-2-17. ALTITUDE CONFIRMATION- NON-MODE C

a. Request a pilot to confirm assigned altitude on initial contact unless:

NOTE-
For the purpose of this paragraph, "initial contact" means a pilot's first radio contact with each sector/position.

1. The pilot states the assigned altitude, or

2. You assign a new altitude to a climbing or a descending aircraft, or

3. *TERMINAL.* The aircraft was transferred to you from another sector/position within your facility (intrafacility).

PHRASEOLOGY-
(In level flight situations), VERIFY AT (altitude/flight level).

(In climbing/descending situations), VERIFY ASSIGNED ALTITUDE/FLIGHT LEVEL (altitude/flight level).

b. USA. Reconfirm all pilot altitude read backs.

PHRASEOLOGY-
(If the altitude read back is correct),

AFFIRMATIVE (altitude).

(If the altitude read back is not correct),

NEGATIVE. CLIMB/DESCEND AND MAINTAIN (altitude),

or

NEGATIVE. MAINTAIN (altitude).

REFERENCE-
FAA Order JO 7110.65, Para 5-3-3, Beacon/ADS-B Identification Methods.

5-2-18. AUTOMATIC ALTITUDE REPORTING

Inform an aircraft when you want it to turn on/off the automatic altitude reporting feature of its transponder.

PHRASEOLOGY-
SQUAWK ALTITUDE,

or

STOP ALTITUDE SQUAWK.

NOTE-
Controllers should be aware that not all aircraft have a capability to disengage the altitude squawk independently from the beacon code squawk. On some aircraft both functions are controlled by the same switch.

REFERENCE-
FAA Order JO 7110.65, Para 5-2-15, Validation of Mode C Altitude Readout.
FAA Order JO 7110.65, Para 5-3-3, Beacon/ADS-B Identification Methods.
P/CG Term - Automatic Altitude Report.

5-2-19. INFLIGHT DEVIATIONS FROM TRANSPONDER/MODE C REQUIREMENTS BETWEEN 10,000 FEET AND 18,000 FEET

Apply the following procedures to requests to deviate from the Mode C transponder requirement by aircraft operating in the airspace of the 48 contiguous states and the District of Columbia at and above 10,000 feet MSL and below 18,000 feet MSL, excluding the airspace at and below 2,500 feet AGL.

NOTE–
1. *14 CFR Section 91.215(b) provides, in part, that all U.S. registered civil aircraft must be equipped with an operable, coded radar beacon transponder when operating in the altitude stratum listed above. Such transponders must have a Mode 3/A 4096 code capability, replying to Mode 3/A interrogation with the code specified by ATC, or a Mode S capability, replying to Mode 3/A interrogations with the code specified by ATC. The aircraft must also be equipped with automatic pressure altitude reporting equipment having a Mode C capability that automatically replies to Mode C interrogations by transmitting pressure altitude information in 100–foot increments.*

2. *The exception to 14 CFR Section 91.215 (b) is 14 CFR Section 91.215(b)(5) which states: except balloons, gliders, and aircraft without engine–driven electrical systems.*

REFERENCE–
FAA Order JO 7210.3, Chapter 20, Temporary Flight Restrictions.

a. Except in an emergency, do not approve inflight requests for authorization to deviate from 14 CFR Section 91.215(b)(5)(i) requirements originated by aircraft without transponder equipment installed.

b. Approve or disapprove other inflight deviation requests, or withdraw approval previously issued to such flights, solely on the basis of traffic conditions and other operational factors.

c. Adhere to the following sequence of action when an inflight VFR deviation request is received from an aircraft with an inoperative transponder or Mode C, or is not Mode C equipped:

1. Suggest that the aircraft conduct its flight in airspace unaffected by the CFRs.

2. Suggest that the aircraft file an IFR flight plan.

3. Suggest that the aircraft provide a VFR route of flight and maintain radio contact with ATC.

d. Do not approve an inflight deviation unless the aircraft has filed an IFR flight plan or a VFR route of flight is provided and radio contact with ATC is maintained.

e. You may approve an inflight deviation request which includes airspace outside your jurisdiction without the prior approval of the adjacent ATC sector/facility providing a transponder/Mode C status report is forwarded prior to control transfer.

f. Approve or disapprove inflight deviation requests within a reasonable period of time or advise when approval/disapproval can be expected.

REFERENCE–
FAA Order JO 7110.65, Para 5–3–3, Beacon/ADS–B Identification Methods.

5–2–20. BEACON TERMINATION

Inform the pilot when you want their aircraft's transponder and ADS–B Out turned off.

PHRASEOLOGY–

STOP SQUAWK.

(For a military aircraft when you do not know if the military service requires that it continue operating on another mode),

STOP SQUAWK (mode in use).

REFERENCE–
FAA Order JO 7110.65, Para 5–3–3, Beacon/ADS–B Identification Methods.

5–2–21. ALTITUDE FILTERS

TERMINAL

Set altitude filters to display Mode C altitude readouts to encompass all altitudes within the controller's jurisdiction. Set the upper limits no lower than 1,000 feet above the highest altitude for which the controller is responsible. In those stratified positions, set the lower limit to 1,000 feet or more below the lowest altitude for which the controller is responsible. When the position's area of responsibility includes down to an airport field elevation, the facility will normally set the lower altitude filter limit to encompass the field elevation so that provisions of paragraph 2–1–6, Safety Alert, and paragraph 5–2–15, Validation of Mode C Altitude Readout, subparagraph b2 may be applied. Air traffic managers may authorize temporary suspension of this requirement when target clutter is excessive.

5–2–22. INOPERATIVE OR MALFUNCTIONING ADS-B TRANSMITTER

a. When an aircraft's ADS–B transmitter appears to be inoperative or malfunctioning, notify the OS/CIC of the aircraft call sign, location, and time of the occurrence (UTC). Except for DoD aircraft or those provided for in paragraph 5–2–24, inform the pilot.

PHRASEOLOGY–
YOUR ADS–B TRANSMITTER APPEARS TO BE INOPERATIVE / MALFUNCTIONING.

NOTE–
FAA Flight Standards Service, Safety Standards Division (AFS) is responsible for working with aircraft operators to correct ADS–B malfunctions. The intent of this paragraph is to capture ADS–B anomalies observed by ATC, such as errors in the data (other than Call Sign Mis-Match events, which are detected and reported to AFS automatically) or instances when civil ADS–B transmissions would normally be expected but are not received (e.g., ADS–B transmissions were observed on a previous flight leg).

b. If a malfunctioning ADS–B transmitter is jeopardizing the safe execution of air traffic control functions, instruct the aircraft to stop ADS–B transmissions, and notify the OS/CIC.

PHRASEOLOGY–
STOP ADS–B TRANSMISSIONS, AND IF ABLE, SQUAWK THREE/ALFA (code).

NOTE–
Not all aircraft have a capability to disengage the ADS–B transmitter independently from the beacon code squawk.

REFERENCE–
FAA Order JO 7110.65, Para 5–2–23, ADS–B Alerts.
FAA Order JO 7210.3, Para 2–1–33, Reporting Inoperative or Malfunctioning ADS–B Transmitters.
FAA Order JO 7210.3, Para 5–4–9, ADS–B Out OFF Operations.
FAA Order JO 7110.67, Para 19, ATC Security Procedures for ADS–B Out OFF Operations.

5–2–23. ADS–B ALERTS

a. Call Sign Mis–Match (CSMM). A CSMM alert will occur when the transmitted ADS–B Flight Identification (FLT ID) does not match the flight plan aircraft identification. Inform the aircraft of the CSMM.

PHRASEOLOGY–
YOUR ADS–B FLIGHT ID DOES NOT MATCH YOUR FLIGHT PLAN AIRCRAFT IDENTIFICATION.

b. Duplicate ICAO Address. If the broadcast ICAO address is shared with one or more flights in the same ADS–B Service Area (regardless of altitude), and radar reinforcement is not available, target resolution may be lost on one or both targets.

NOTE–
Duplicate ICAO Address Alerts appear as "DA" and are associated with the Data Block (DB) on STARS systems. Duplicate ICAO Address Alerts appear as "DUP" and are associated with the DB on MEARTS systems. Duplicate ICAO Address Alerts appear as "Duplicate 24–bit Address" at the AT Specialist Workstation on ERAM systems.

c. If a CSMM or Duplicate ICAO address is jeopardizing the safe execution of air traffic control functions, instruct the aircraft to stop ADS–B transmissions, and notify the OS/CIC.

PHRASEOLOGY–
STOP ADS–B TRANSMISSIONS, AND IF ABLE, SQUAWK THREE/ALFA (code).

NOTE–
Not all aircraft are capable of disengaging the ADS–B transmitter independently from the transponder.

5-2-24. ADS-B OUT OFF OPERATIONS

Operators of aircraft with functional ADS-B Out avionics installed and requesting an exception from the requirement to transmit at all times must obtain authorization from FAA System Operations Security. The OS/CIC should inform you of any ADS-B Out OFF operations in your area of jurisdiction.

a. Do not inform such aircraft that their ADS-B transmitter appears to be inoperative.

b. Do not approve any pilot request for ADS-B Out OFF operations. Notify the OS/CIC of the request, including the aircraft call sign and location.

NOTE-
14 CFR Section 91.225(f) requires, in part, that "each person operating an aircraft equipped with ADS-B Out must operate this equipment in the transmit mode at all times unless otherwise authorized by the FAA when that aircraft is performing a sensitive government mission for national defense, homeland security, intelligence or law enforcement purposes, and transmitting would compromise the operations security of the mission or pose a safety risk to the aircraft, crew, or people and property in the air or on the ground."

REFERENCE-
FAA Order JO 7110.65, Para 5-2-22, Inoperative or Malfunctioning ADS-B Transmitter.
FAA Order JO 7210.3, Para 5-4-9, ADS-B Out OFF Operations.
FAA Order JO 7110.67, Para 11, Responsibilities.

Section 3. Radar Identification

5–3–1. APPLICATION

Before you provide radar service, establish and maintain radar identification of the aircraft involved, except as provided in paragraph 5–5–1, Application, subparagraphs b2, b3 and in paragraph 8–5–5, Radar Identification Application.

REFERENCE–
FAA Order JO 7110.65, Para 3–1–9, Use of Tower Radar Displays.
FAA Order JO 7110.65, Para 5–1–1, Presentation and Equipment Performance.

5–3–2. PRIMARY RADAR IDENTIFICATION METHODS

Identify a primary, radar beacon, or ADS–B target by using one of the following methods:

a. Observing a departing aircraft target within 1 mile of the takeoff runway end at airports with an operating control tower, provided one of the following methods of coordination is accomplished.

1. A verbal rolling/boundary notification is issued for each departure, or

2. A nonverbal rolling/boundary notification is used for each departure aircraft.

NOTE–
Nonverbal notification can be accomplished via the use of a manual or electronic "drop tube" or automation.

b. Observing a target whose position with respect to a fix (displayed on the video map, scribed on the map overlay, or displayed as a permanent echo) or a visual reporting point (whose range and azimuth from the radar antenna has been accurately determined and made available to the controller) corresponds with a direct position report received from an aircraft, and the observed track is consistent with the reported heading or route of flight. If a TACAN/VORTAC is located within 6,000 feet of the radar antenna, the TACAN/VORTAC may be used as a reference fix for radar identification without being displayed on the video map or map overlay.

NOTE–
1. *Establishment of radar identification through use of DME position information can be complicated by the fact that some military TACANs are not collocated with frequency–paired VORs and might be separated from them by as much as 31 miles.*

2. *Visual reporting points used for RADAR identification are limited to those most used by pilots and whose range and azimuth have been determined by supervisory personnel.*

c. Observing a target make an identifying turn or turns of 30 degrees or more, provided the following conditions are met:

NOTE–
Use of identifying turns or headings which would cause the aircraft to follow normal IFR routes or known VFR flight paths might result in misidentification. When these circumstances cannot be avoided, additional methods of identification may be necessary.

1. Except in the case of a lost aircraft, a pilot position report is received which assures you that the aircraft is within radar coverage and within the area being displayed.

2. Only one aircraft is observed making these turns.

3. For aircraft operating in accordance with an IFR clearance, you either issue a heading away from an area which will require an increased minimum IFR altitude or have the aircraft climb to the highest minimum altitude in your area of jurisdiction before you issue a heading.

REFERENCE–
FAA Order JO 7110.65, Para 3–1–9, Use of Tower Radar Displays.
FAA Order JO 7110.65, Para 5–12–11, Surveillance Unusable.

5–3–3. BEACON/ADS–B IDENTIFICATION METHODS

When using only Mode 3/A radar beacon or ADS–B to identify a target, use one of the following methods:

a. Request the pilot to activate the "IDENT" feature of the transponder/ADS–B and then observe the identification display.

PHRASEOLOGY–
IDENT.
SQUAWK (code) AND IDENT.

b. Request the pilot to change to a specific discrete or nondiscrete code, as appropriate, and then observe the target or code display change. If a code change is required in accordance with Section 2, Beacon/ADS–B Systems, of this chapter, use the codes specified therein.

c. Request the pilot to change their transponder/ADS–B to "standby." After you observe the target disappear for sufficient scans to assure that loss of target resulted from placing the transponder/ADS–B in "standby" position, request the pilot to return the transponder to normal operation and then observe the reappearance of the target.

PHRASEOLOGY–
SQUAWK STANDBY,

then

SQUAWK NORMAL.

d. *EN ROUTE.* An aircraft may be considered identified when the full data block is automatically associated with the target symbol of an aircraft that is squawking a discrete code assigned by the computer.

NOTE–
Paired LDBs in ERAM do not display a beacon code.

PHRASEOLOGY–
SQUAWK (4 digit discrete code),

or, if aircraft's altitude reporting capability is turned off,

SQUAWK (4 digit discrete code), SQUAWK ALTITUDE.

NOTE–
The AIM informs pilots to adjust Mode C transponders and ADS–B with altitude reporting capability activated unless deactivation is requested by ATC. "Squawk altitude" is included here to provide applicable phraseology.

REFERENCE–
FAA Order JO 7110.65, Para 3–1–9, Use of Tower Radar Displays.
FAA Order JO 7110.65, Para 5–3–6, Position Information.

5–3–4. TERMINAL AUTOMATION SYSTEMS IDENTIFICATION METHODS

TERMINAL

a. Consider an auto-acquired aircraft as identified when the data block is displayed and is visible to you, and one of the following conditions exist:

1. The radar or beacon identification procedures have been used to confirm the identity of the tagged target.

2. The aircraft is being handed off using a NAS automated system and one of the following does not appear in the data block: "CST", "NAT", "NT", "AMB", "OLD", "AM", or "TRK".

b. Use the data block to maintain target identity unless it is in a coast status or displaced from the appropriate target.

c. A displaced data block must be updated at all times.

REFERENCE–
FAA Order JO 7110.65, Para 3–1–9, Use of Tower Radar Displays.

5–3–5. QUESTIONABLE IDENTIFICATION

a. Use more than one method of identification when proximity of targets, duplication of observed action, or any other circumstances cause doubt as to target identification.

b. If identification is questionable for any reason, take immediate action to re–identify the aircraft or terminate radar service. Identify the aircraft as follows:

1. As described in paragraph 5–3–2, Primary Radar Identification Methods, or paragraph 5–3–3, Beacon/ADS–B Identification Methods.

2. En route. Ensure that all primary targets are displayed when radar identification is lost or is questionable.

REFERENCE–
FAA Order JO 7110.65, Para 5–4–3, Methods.

5–3–6. POSITION INFORMATION

Inform an aircraft of its position whenever radar identification is established by means of identifying turns or by any of the beacon identification methods outlined in paragraph 5–3–3, Beacon/ADS–B Identification Methods. Position information need not be given when identification is established by position correlation or when a departing aircraft is identified within 1 mile of the takeoff runway end.

5–3–7. IDENTIFICATION STATUS

a. Inform an aircraft of radar contact when:

1. Initial radar identification in the ATC system is established.

2. Subsequent to loss of radar contact or terminating radar service, radar identification is reestablished.

PHRASEOLOGY–
RADAR CONTACT (position if required).

b. Inform an aircraft when radar contact is lost.

PHRASEOLOGY–
RADAR CONTACT LOST (alternative instructions when required).

5–3–8. DATA BLOCKS

EN ROUTE

Retain data blocks that are associated with the appropriate target symbol in order to maintain continuous identity of aircraft. Retain the data block until the aircraft has exited the sector or delegated airspace, and all potential conflicts have been resolved; including an aircraft that is a point out. The data block must display flight identification and altitude information, as a minimum. The displayed altitude may be assigned, interim, or reported.

ERAM: When you have separation responsibility for an aircraft and a paired track exists, display a full data block (FDB).

5–3–9. DATA BLOCKS

TERMINAL

a. Retain data blocks that are associated with the appropriate target symbol in order to maintain continuous identity of aircraft. Retain the data block until the aircraft has exited the sector or delegated airspace, and all potential conflicts have been resolved; including an aircraft that is a point out. The data block must display flight identification and altitude information, as a minimum.

NOTE–
Where delegated airspace extends beyond Class B and/or Class C airspace, the following will apply: If a VFR aircraft is clear of Class B and Class C airspace and radar services have been terminated then retention of the data block is no longer required.

b. During prearranged coordination procedures, the controllers who penetrate another controller's airspace must display data block information of that controller's aircraft which must contain, at a minimum, the position symbol and altitude information.

REFERENCE–
FAA Order JO 7110.65, Para 2–1–14, Coordinate Use of Airspace.
FAA Order JO 7110.65, Para 5–4–3, Methods.
FAA Order JO 7110.65, Para 5–4–8, Automated Information Transfer (AIT).
FAA Order JO 7110.65, Para 5–4–9, Prearranged Coordination.
FAA Order JO 7210.3, Para 3–6–6, Prearranged Coordination.

Section 4. Transfer of Radar Identification

5–4–1. APPLICATION

To provide continuous radar service to an aircraft and facilitate a safe, orderly, and expeditious flow of traffic, it is often necessary to transfer radar identification of an aircraft from one controller to another. This section describes the terms, methods, and responsibilities associated with this task. Interfacility and intrafacility transfers of radar identification must be accomplished in all areas of radar surveillance except where it is not operationally feasible. Where such constraints exist, they must be:

a. Covered in letters of agreement which clearly state that control will not be based upon a radar handoff, or

b. Coordinated by the transferring and receiving controllers for a specified period of time.

REFERENCE–
FAA Order JO 7110.65, Para 4–3–8, Coordination with Receiving Facility.

5–4–2. TERMS

a. *Handoff.* An action taken to transfer the radar identification of an aircraft from one controller to another controller if the aircraft will enter the receiving controller's airspace and radio communications with the aircraft will be transferred.

b. *Radar Contact.* The term used to inform the controller initiating a handoff that the aircraft is identified and approval is granted for the aircraft to enter the receiving controller's airspace.

c. *Point Out.* An action taken by a controller to transfer the radar identification of an aircraft to another controller and radio communications will not be transferred.

d. *Point Out Approved.* The term used to inform the controller initiating a point out that the aircraft is identified and that approval is granted for the aircraft to enter the receiving controller's airspace, as coordinated, without a communications transfer or the appropriate automated system response.

e. *Traffic.* A term used to transfer radar identification of an aircraft to another controller for the purpose of coordinating separation action. Traffic is normally issued:

1. In response to a handoff or point out;

2. In anticipation of a handoff or point out; or

3. In conjunction with a request for control of an aircraft.

f. *Traffic Observed.* The term used to inform the controller issuing the traffic restrictions that the traffic is identified and that the restrictions issued are understood and will be complied with.

5–4–3. METHODS

a. Transfer the radar identification of an aircraft by at least one of the following methods:

1. Physically point to the target on the receiving controller's display.

2. Use landline voice communications.

3. Use automation capabilities.

NOTE–
Automated handoff capabilities are only available when FDP is operational.

4. *TERMINAL.* Use the "Modify" or "Quick Look" functions for data transfer between the TRACON and tower cab only if specific procedures are established in a facility directive. The local controller has the responsibility to determine whether or not conditions are adequate for the use of STARS data on the TDW.

REFERENCE–
FAA Order JO 7210.3, Para 12–6–4, Use of Stars Quick Look Functions.

b. When making a handoff, point out, or issuing traffic restrictions, relay information to the receiving controller in the following order:

1. The position of the target relative to a fix, map symbol, or radar target known and displayed by both the receiving and transferring controller. Mileage from the reference point may be omitted when relaying the position of a target if a full data block associated with the target has been forced on the receiving controller's radar display.

EXAMPLE–
"Point out, Southwest of Richmond VOR . . .."

2. The aircraft identification, as follows:

(a) The aircraft call sign, or

(b) The discrete beacon code of the aircraft during interfacility point outs only, if both the receiving and the transferring controllers agree.

NOTE–
Acceptance of a point out using the discrete beacon code as the aircraft's identification constitutes agreement.

(c) EN ROUTE. The Computer Identification Number (CID) during intrafacility point outs.

EXAMPLE–
"Point Out, Southwest of Richmond VOR, C-I-D 123…"

3. The assigned altitude, appropriate restrictions, and information that the aircraft is climbing or descending, if applicable, except when inter/intrafacility directives ensure that the altitude information will be known by the receiving controller.

NOTE–
When physically pointing to the target, you do not have to state the aircraft position.

4. Advise the receiving controller of pertinent information not contained in the data block or available flight data unless covered in an LOA or facility directive. Pertinent information may include:

(a) Assigned heading.

(b) Speed/altitude restrictions.

(c) Observed track or deviation from the last route clearance.

(d) Any other pertinent information.

PHRASEOLOGY–
HANDOFF/POINT–OUT/TRAFFIC (aircraft position), (aircraft ID or discrete beacon code), (altitude, restrictions, and other pertinent information, if applicable).

c. When receiving a handoff, point out, or traffic restrictions, respond to the transferring controller as follows:

PHRASEOLOGY–
(Aircraft ID) (restrictions, if applicable) RADAR CONTACT,

or

(aircraft ID or discrete beacon code) (restrictions, if applicable) POINT OUT APPROVED,

or

TRAFFIC OBSERVED,

or

UNABLE (appropriate information, as required).

d. If any doubt as to target identification exists after attempting confirmation in accordance with this section, apply the provisions of paragraph 5–3–5, Questionable Identification.

REFERENCE–
FAA Order JO 7110.65, Para 5–2–15, Validation of Mode C Altitude Readout.

5–4–4. TRAFFIC

a. When using the term "traffic" for coordinating separation, the controller issuing traffic must issue appropriate restrictions.

b. The controller accepting the restrictions must be responsible to ensure that approved separation is maintained between the involved aircraft.

5–4–5. TRANSFERRING CONTROLLER HANDOFF

Unless otherwise coordinated or specified in an LOA or facility directive, the transferring controller must:

a. Complete a handoff prior to an aircraft entering the airspace delegated to the receiving controller.

b. Verbally obtain the receiving controller's approval prior to making any changes to an aircraft's flight path, altitude, speed, or data block information while the handoff is being initiated or after acceptance.

c. Advise the receiving controller of pertinent information not contained in the data block or flight progress strip, including:

1. Assigned heading.

2. Airspeed restrictions.

3. Altitude information issued.

4. Observed track or deviation from the last route clearance.

5. The beacon code, if different from that normally used or previously coordinated.

6. Any other pertinent information.

d. Initiate verbal coordination to verify the position of primary or nondiscrete targets, except for intrafacility automated handoffs in STARS, ERAM, or MEARTS in Fused Display Mode.

e. Initiate verbal coordination before transferring control of a track when "CST," "FAIL," "NONE," "IF," "NT," or "TRK" is displayed in the data block.

f. Advise the receiving controller if radar monitoring is required.

REFERENCE–
FAA Order JO 7110.65, Para 4–1–2, Exceptions.
FAA Order JO 7110.65, Para 4–4–2, Route Structure Transitions.

g. Consider the target being transferred as identified on the receiving controller's display when the receiving controller acknowledges receipt verbally or accepts the automated handoff.

h. Prior to transferring communications:

1. Resolve any potential violations of adjacent airspace and potential conflicts with other aircraft in your area of jurisdiction.

2. Coordinate with any controller whose area of jurisdiction the aircraft will transit prior to entering the receiving controller's area of jurisdiction.

3. Forward to the receiving controller any restrictions issued to ensure separation.

4. Comply with restrictions issued by the receiving controller.

i. Comply with the provisions of paragraph 2–1–17, Radio Communications. To the extent possible, transfer communications when the handoff has been accepted.

NOTE–
Before the STARS "modify/quick look" function is used to effect a handoff, a facility directive that specifies communication transfer points is required.

j. After transferring communications, continue to comply with the requirements of subparagraphs h1 and h2.

k. Before releasing control of the aircraft, issue restrictions to the receiving controller that are necessary to maintain separation from other aircraft within your area of jurisdiction.

REFERENCE–
FAA Order JO 7110.65, Para 2–1–14, Coordinate Use of Airspace.
FAA Order JO 7110.65, Para 2–1–15, Control Transfer.
FAA Order JO 7110.65, Para 5–4–6, Receiving Controller Handoff.
FAA Order JO 7110.65, Para 5–4–8, Automated Information Transfer (AIT).
FAA Order JO 7210.3, Para 4–3–10, Automated Information Transfer (AIT).

5–4–6. RECEIVING CONTROLLER HANDOFF

The receiving controller must:

a. Ensure that the target position corresponds with the position given by the transferring controller or that there is an appropriate association between an automated data block and the target being transferred before accepting a handoff.

REFERENCE–
FAA Order JO 7110.65, Para 2–1–14, Coordinate Use of Airspace.
FAA Order JO 7110.65, Para 2–1–15, Control Transfer.
FAA Order JO 7110.65, Para 5–4–5, Transferring Controller Handoff.

b. Issue restrictions that are needed for the aircraft to enter your sector safely before accepting the handoff.

c. Comply with restrictions issued by the transferring controller unless otherwise coordinated.

d. After accepting a handoff from another facility, confirm the identification of a primary target by advising the aircraft of its position, and of a nondiscrete beacon target by observing a code change, an "ident" reply, or a "standby" squawk unless one of these was used during handoff. These provisions do not apply at those towers and GCAs that have been delegated the responsibility for providing radar separation within designated areas by the overlying approach control facility and the aircraft identification is assured by sequencing or positioning prior to the handoff.

REFERENCE–
FAA Order JO 7110.65, Para 5–9–5, Approach Separation Responsibility.

e. Consider a beacon target's identity to be confirmed when:

1. The data block associated with the target being handed off indicates the computer assigned discrete beacon code is being received; or

2. You observe the deletion of a discrete code that was displayed in the data block; or

NOTE–
When the beacon code received from the aircraft does not match the computer assigned beacon code, the code received (ERAM, MEARTS) or the site–adapted code (received, computer–assigned, or both for STARS) will be displayed in the data block. When the aircraft changes to the computer assigned code, the code is automatically removed from the data block. In this instance, the observance of code removal from the data block satisfies confirmation requirements.

3. You observe the numeric display of a discrete code that an aircraft has been instructed to squawk or reports squawking.

f. Take the identified action prior to accepting control of a track when the following indicators are displayed in the data block:

1. "AMB" or "AM": advise the other facility that a disparity exists between the position declared by their computer and the position declared by your STARS/MEARTS system.

2. "NAT" or "NT": advise the other facility if a disparity exists between the position declared by their computer and the actual target position.

3. "DATA," "CST," "NONE," or "OLD": initiate verbal coordination.

g. ERAM: Notify the OS/CIC when a MISM is displayed in the data block.

h. Advise the transferring controller as soon as possible if you will delay the climb or descent of the aircraft through the vertical limits of that controller's area of jurisdiction, unless otherwise specified in an LOA or a facility directive.

5-4-7. POINT OUT

a. The transferring controller must:

1. Obtain approval before permitting an aircraft to enter the receiving controller's delegated airspace.

(a) EN ROUTE: Automated approval may be utilized in lieu of verbal approval. If the receiving controller takes no action, revert to verbal procedures.

NOTE–

1. *Use fourth line data for aircraft not on their flight plan route.*

2. *Where specified in a letter of agreement, some facilities may restrict interfacility automated point outs.*

REFERENCE–

FAA Order JO 7110.65, Para 2-10-1, En Route Or Oceanic Sector Team Responsibilities.
FAA Order JO 7110.65, Para 5-4-3, Methods.
FAA Order JO 7110.65, Para 5-4-10, En Route Fourth Line Data Block Usage.
FAA Order JO 7110.65, Para 5-13-3, Computer Entry of Flight Plan Information.

(b) TERMINAL: Automated point out approval may be utilized in lieu of verbal provided the procedures are contained in a facility directive/LOA.

2. Obtain the receiving controller's approval before making any changes to an aircraft's flight path, altitude, speed, or data block information after the point out has been approved.

3. Comply with restrictions issued by the receiving controller unless otherwise coordinated.

4. Be responsible for subsequent radar handoffs and communications transfer, including flight data revisions and coordination, unless otherwise agreed to by the receiving controller or as specified in a LOA.

b. The receiving controller must:

1. Ensure that the target position corresponds with the position given by the transferring controller or that there is an association between a computer data block and the target being transferred prior to approving a point out.

2. Be responsible for separation between point out aircraft and other aircraft for which he/she has separation responsibility.

3. Issue restrictions necessary to provide separation from other aircraft within his/her area of jurisdiction.

5-4-8. AUTOMATED INFORMATION TRANSFER (AIT)

Transfer radar identification, altitude control, and/or en route fourth line control information, without verbal coordination under the following conditions:

a. During radar handoff; and

b. Via information displayed in full data blocks; and

c. When following procedures specified in your facility AIT directive and/or LOA.

NOTE–
Information transferred using AIT procedures may be bi–directional, and may involve more than two sectors. Complete coordination, awareness of traffic flow, and understanding of each position's responsibilities concerning AIT procedures cannot be overemphasized.

REFERENCE–
FAA Order JO 7110.65, Para 5–4–10, En Route Fourth Line Data Block Usage.
FAA Order JO 7210.3, Para 4–3–10, Automated Information Transfer (AIT).

5–4–9. PREARRANGED COORDINATION

Prearranged coordination allowing aircraft under your control to enter another controller's area of jurisdiction may only be approved provided procedures are established and published in a facility directive in accordance with FAA Order JO 7210.3, paragraph 3–6–6, Prearranged Coordination.

NOTE–
Under no circumstances may one controller permit an aircraft to enter another's airspace without proper coordination. Coordination can be accomplished by several means; i.e., radar handoff, automated information transfer, verbal, point–out, and by prearranged coordination procedures identified in a facility directive that clearly describe the correct application. Airspace boundaries should not be permitted to become barriers to the efficient movement of traffic. In addition, complete coordination, awareness of traffic flow, and understanding of each position's responsibility concerning penetration of another's airspace cannot be overemphasized.

REFERENCE–
FAA Order JO 7110.65, Para 2–1–14, Coordinate Use of Airspace.
FAA Order JO 7110.65, Para 5–4–3, Methods.
FAA Order JO 7110.65, Para 5–4–8, Automated Information Transfer (AIT).
FAA Order JO 7210.3, Para 3–6–6, Prearranged Coordination.

5–4–10. EN ROUTE FOURTH LINE DATA BLOCK USAGE

a. The fourth line of the data block must be displayed. When used for forwarding control information, only the specified messages listed in this section may be used. Any additional control information must be forwarded via other communications methods. Free text may be used by individual sector teams for recording information the team deems appropriate for managing the sector, but must be removed prior to initiation of identification transfer.

REFERENCE–
FAA Order JO 7110.65, Para 5–4–5, Transferring Controller Handoff, subpara b.
FAA Order JO 7110.65, Para 5–4–8, Automated Information Transfer (AIT).

b. The en route fourth line data block area must be used for coordination purposes only in association with radar identified aircraft.

c. When automated information transfer (AIT) procedures are applied, en route fourth line usage for transfer of control information must be specifically defined within facility AIT directive.

REFERENCE–
FAA Order JO 7110.65, Para 5–4–8, Automated Information Transfer (AIT).
FAA Order JO 7210.3, Para 4–3–10, Automated Information Transfer (AIT).

d. Coordination format for assigned headings must use the designation character "H" preceding a three–digit number.

EXAMPLE–
H080, H270

e. Aircraft assigned a heading until receiving a fix or joining a published route must be designated with assigned heading format followed by the fix or route.

NOTE–
1. *The notation "PH" may be used to denote present heading.*

2. *The character "H" may be omitted as a prefix to the heading assignment only if necessary due to character field limitations, and it does not impede understanding.*

EXAMPLE–
H080/ALB, 080/J121, PH/ALB

f. Coordination format for weather deviations must use the designated characters:
D–deviation
L–left
R–right
N–north
E–east
S–south
W–west
/F–direct next NAVAID/waypoint in the flight plan
D(heading)–(heading)–deviate between two specified headings.

NOTE–
1. *Two digits specify turns in degrees and must include direction character(s). Three digits specify heading(s).*

2. *The inclusion of /(NAVAID) or /(waypoint), when preceded by the designated characters for weather deviations, indicates that a pilot has been authorized to deviate for weather and rejoin the route at the specified NAVAID or waypoint. The use of /F, following the designated weather deviation characters, indicates that a pilot has been authorized to deviate and rejoin the route of flight at the next fix in the route in accordance with paragraph 2–6–4.*

EXAMPLE–
D90L/ATL, DL/KD75U, D090/F

3. *The absence of /NAVAID, /waypoint, or /F after the weather deviation designated characters indicates that the pilot has been authorized to deviate for weather, and the receiving controller must provide a clearance to rejoin the route of flight in accordance with subparagraph 2–1–15c.*

EXAMPLE–
DN, D20L, D30R, D180–210

g. Coordination format for specific assigned airspeeds must use the designation character "S" preceding a three–digit number. A three–digit number followed by a "+" must be used to denote an assigned speed at or greater than the displayed value, or followed by a "–" to denote an assigned speed at or less than the displayed value.

EXAMPLE–
S210, 250+, 280–

h. Aircraft assigned a Mach number must use the designation "M", "M.", or "." preceding the two–digit assigned value. The displayed Mach number shall also be followed by a "+" to denote an assigned speed at or greater than the displayed value, or a "–" to denote an assigned speed at or less than the displayed value.

EXAMPLE–
M80, M80+, M80–, M.80, .80, .80–

i. Aircraft authorized to conduct celestial navigation training within 30 NM of the route centerline specified within the en route clearance.

EXAMPLE–
CELNAV

j. Coordination format for aircraft requesting an altitude change must use the designation characters "RQ" preceding a three–digit number.

EXAMPLE–
RQ170, RQ410

k. Coordination format for aircraft requesting a route change must use the designation "RQ/" preceding a specific fix identifier.

EXAMPLE–
RQ/LAX, RQ/NEUTO

l. The acceptance of a handoff by the receiving controller must constitute receipt of the information contained within the en route fourth line data block. This information must not be modified outside of the controller's area of jurisdiction unless verbally coordinated or specified in a Letter of Agreement or Facility Directive. It is the responsibility of the receiving controller to advise the transferring controller if any information is not understood, or needs to be revised.

NOTE–
Due to system and character limitations the usage of these standardized entries may require additional support via facility directive in order to provide complete coordination.

m. All other control information must be coordinated via other methods.

Section 5. Radar Separation

5–5–1. APPLICATION

a. Radar separation must be applied to all RNAV aircraft operating at and below FL450 on Q routes or random RNAV routes, excluding oceanic airspace.

EXCEPTION. GNSS-equipped aircraft /G, /L, /S, and /V on point-to-point routes, or transitioning between two point–to–point routes via an impromptu route.

REFERENCE–
FAA Order JO 7110.65, Para 2–3–8, Aircraft Equipment Suffixes.
FAA Order JO 7110.65, TBL 2–3–10, Aircraft Equipment Suffixes.
FAA Order JO 7110.65, Para 4–4–1, Route Use.
AIM, Para 5–1–8, Area Navigation (RNAV).
AIM, Para 5–3–4, Area Navigation (RNAV) Routes.
P/CG Term – Global Navigation Satellite System (GNSS)[ICAO].
P/CG Term – Global Positioning Satellite/ Wide Area Augmentation Minimum En Route IFR Altitude (GPS/WAAS MEA).
P/CG Term – Parallel Offset Route.

b. Radar separation may be applied between:

1. Radar identified aircraft.

2. An aircraft taking off and another radar identified aircraft when the aircraft taking off will be radar-identified within 1 mile of the runway end.

3. A radar-identified aircraft and one not radar-identified when either is cleared to climb/descend through the altitude of the other provided:

(a) The performance of the radar system is adequate and, as a minimum, primary radar targets or ASR–9/Full Digital Radar Primary Symbol targets are being displayed on the display being used within the airspace within which radar separation is being applied; and

(b) Flight data on the aircraft not radar-identified indicate it is a type which can be expected to give adequate primary/ASR–9/Full Digital Radar Primary Symbol return in the area where separation is applied; and

(c) The airspace within which radar separation is applied is not less than the following number of miles from the edge of the radar display:

(1) When less than 40 miles from the antenna– *6 miles;*

(2) When 40 miles or more from the antenna– *10 miles*;

(3) Narrowband radar operations– *10 miles;* and

(d) Radar separation is maintained between the radar-identified aircraft and all observed primary, ASR–9/Full Digital Radar Primary Symbol, and secondary radar targets until nonradar separation is established from the aircraft not radar identified; and

(e) When the aircraft involved are on the same relative heading, the radar-identified aircraft is vectored a sufficient distance from the route of the aircraft not radar identified to assure the targets are not superimposed prior to issuing the clearance to climb/descend.

REFERENCE–
FAA Order JO 7110.65, Para 4–1–2, Exceptions.
FAA Order JO 7110.65, Para 4–4–1, Route Use.
FAA Order JO 7110.65, Para 5–3–1, Application.
FAA Order JO 7110.65, Para 5–5–8, Additional Separation for Formation Flights.
FAA Order JO 7110.65, Para 5–9–5, Approach Separation Responsibility.

4. A radar-identified aircraft and one not radar-identified that is in transit from oceanic airspace or nonradar offshore airspace into an area of known radar coverage where radar separation is applied as specified in paragraph 8−5−5, Radar Identification Application, until the transiting aircraft is radar-identified or the controller establishes other approved separation in the event of a delay or inability to establish radar identification of the transiting aircraft.

REFERENCE−
FAA Order JO 7110.65, Para 2−2−6, IFR Flight Progress Data.
FAA Order JO 7110.65, Para 5−1−1, Presentation and Equipment Performance.
FAA Order JO 7110.65, Para 5−3−1, Application.
FAA Order JO 7110.65, Para 8−1−8, Use of Control Estimates.
FAA Order JO 7110.65, Para 8−5−5, Radar Separation.

5−5−2. TARGET SEPARATION

Apply radar separation:

a. Between the centers of primary radar targets; however, do not allow a primary target to touch another primary target or a beacon control slash.

b. Between the ends of beacon control slashes.

c. Between the end of a beacon control slash and the center of a primary target.

d. All−digital displays. Between the centers of digital targets; do not allow digital targets to touch.

REFERENCE−
FAA Order JO 7110.65, Para 5−9−7, Simultaneous Independent Approaches− Dual & Triple.

5−5−3. TARGET RESOLUTION

a. A process to ensure that correlated radar targets or digitized targets do not touch.

b. Mandatory traffic advisories and safety alerts must be issued when this procedure is used.

NOTE−
This procedure must not be provided utilizing mosaic radar systems.

c. Target resolution must be applied as follows:

1. Between the edges of two primary targets or the edges of primary digitized targets.

2. Between the end of the beacon control slash and the edge of a primary target or primary digitized target.

3. Between the ends of two beacon control slashes.

5−5−4. MINIMA

Separate aircraft by the following minima:

a. *TERMINAL*. Single Sensor ASR or Digital Terminal Automation System (DTAS):

NOTE−
1. *Includes single sensor long range radar mode.*
2. *ADS−B and WAM are not selectable sources when in Single Sensor Mode.*

1. When less than 40 miles from the antenna− *3 miles.*

2. When 40 miles or more from the antenna− *5 miles.*

3. For single sensor monopulse secondary surveillance radar (MSSR), when less than 60 miles from the antenna− *3 miles.*

NOTE−
Wake turbulence procedures specify increased separation minima required for certain classes of aircraft because of the possible effects of wake turbulence.

4. If TRK appears in the data block, handle in accordance with paragraph 5−3−7, Identification Status, subparagraph b, and take appropriate steps to establish nonradar separation.

NOTE–
TRK appears in the data block whenever the aircraft is being tracked by a radar site other than the radar currently selected. Current equipment limitations preclude a target from being displayed in the single sensor mode; however, a position symbol and data block, including altitude information, will still be displayed. Therefore, low altitude alerts must be provided in accordance with paragraph 2–1–6, Safety Alert.

b. *TERMINAL.* FUSION:

1. Fusion target symbol – *3 miles.*

2. When displaying ISR in the data block- *5 miles.*

NOTE–
In the event of an unexpected ISR on one or more aircraft, the ATCS working that aircraft must transition from 3-mile to 5-mile separation, or establish some other form of approved separation as soon as feasible. This action must be timely, but taken in a reasonable fashion, using the controller's best judgment, as not to reduce safety or the integrity of the traffic situation. For example, if ISR appears when an aircraft is established on final with another aircraft on short final, it would be beneficial from a safety perspective to allow the trailing aircraft to continue the approach and land rather than terminate a stabilized approach.

3. If TRK appears in the data block, handle in accordance with paragraph 5–3–7, Identification Status, subparagraph b, and take appropriate steps to establish nonradar separation.

4. The ADS-B Computer Human Interface (CHI) may be implemented by facilities on a sector by sector or facility wide basis when the determination is made that utilization of the ADS-B CHI provides an operational advantage to the controller.

c. STARS Multi–Sensor Mode – 5 miles.

NOTE–
STARS Multi–Sensor Mode displays target symbols derived from radar, ADS–B, and WAM.

d. ERAM:

1. Below FL 600- *5 miles.*

2. At or above FL 600- *10 miles.*

3. Up to and including FL 230 where all the following conditions are met – *3 miles:*

(a) Within the 3 NM separation area, and:

(1) Within 40 NM of the preferred radar; or

(2) Within 60 NM of the preferred radar when using an MSSR; or

(3) When operating in track–based display mode.

(b) The preferred sensor and/or ADS–B is providing reliable targets.

(c) Facility directives specifically define the 3 NM separation area.

(d) The 3 NM separation area is displayable on the video map.

(e) Involved aircraft are displayed using the 3 NM target symbol.

NOTE–
ADS–B allows the expanded use of 3 NM separation in approved areas. It is not required for and does not affect the use of radar for 3 NM separation.

4. When transitioning from terminal to en route control, 3 miles increasing to 5 miles or greater, provided:

(a) The aircraft are on diverging routes/courses, and/or

(b) The leading aircraft is and will remain faster than the following aircraft; and

(c) Separation constantly increasing and the first center controller will establish 5 NM or other appropriate form of separation prior to the aircraft departing the first center sector; and

(d) The procedure is covered by a letter of agreement between the facilities involved and limited to specified routes and/or sectors/positions.

REFERENCE–
FAA Order JO 7210.3, Para 8–2–1, Three Mile Airspace Operations.

e. MEARTS Mosaic Mode:

1. Below FL 600- *5 miles.*

2. At or above FL 600- *10 miles.*

3. For areas meeting all of the following conditions – *3 miles*:

(a) Radar site adaptation is set to single sensor mode.

NOTE–
1. *Single Sensor Mode displays information from the radar input of a single site.*

2. *Procedures to convert MEARTS Mosaic Mode to MEARTS Single Sensor Mode at each PVD/MDM will be established by facility directive.*

(b) Significant operational advantages can be obtained.

(c) Within 40 NM of the sensor or within 60 NM of the sensor when using an MSSR and within the 3 NM separation area.

(d) Up to and including FL230.

(e) Facility directives specifically define the area where the separation can be applied and define_the requirements for displaying the area on the controller's PVD/MDM.

4. MEARTS Mosaic Mode Utilizing Single Source Polygon (San Juan CERAP and Honolulu Control Facility only) when meeting all of the following conditions– *3 miles*:

(a) Up to and including FL230 within 40 miles from the antenna or within 60 NM when using an MSSR and targets are from the adapted sensor.

(b) The single source polygon must be displayed on the controller's PVD/MDM.

(c) Significant operational advantages can be obtained.

(d) Facility directives specifically define the single source polygon area where the separation can be applied and specify procedures to be used.

(e) Controller must commence a transition to achieve either vertical separation or 5 mile lateral separation in the event that either target is not from the adapted sensor.

WAKE TURBULENCE APPLICATION

f. Separate aircraft operating directly behind or following an aircraft conducting an instrument approach by the minima specified and in accordance with the following:

NOTE–
Consider parallel runways less than 2,500 feet apart as a single runway because of the possible effects of wake turbulence.

1. When operating within 2,500 feet of the flight path of the leading aircraft over the surface of the earth and less than 1,000 feet below:

(a) *TERMINAL.* Behind super:

(1) Heavy - *6 miles.*

(2) Large - *7 miles.*

(3) Small - *8 miles.*

(b) *EN ROUTE.* Behind super - *5 miles,* unless the super is operating at or below FL240 and below 250 knots, then:

(1) Heavy - *6 miles.*

(2) Large - *7 miles.*

(3) Small - *8 miles.*

(c) Behind heavy:

(1) Heavy - *4 miles.*

(2) Large or small - *5 miles.*

2. Separate small aircraft behind a B757 by *4 miles* when operating within 2,500 feet of the flight path of the leading aircraft over the surface of the earth and/or less than 500 feet below.

3. *TERMINAL.* When departing parallel runways separated by less than 2,500 feet, the 2,500 feet requirement in subparagraph 2 is not required when a small departs the parallel runway behind a B757. Issue a wake turbulence cautionary advisory and instructions that will establish lateral separation in accordance with subparagraph 2. Do not issue instructions that will allow the small to pass behind the B757.

NOTE−

1. *The application of paragraph 5−8−3, Successive or Simultaneous Departures, satisfies this requirement.*

2. *Consider runways separated by less than 700 feet as a single runway because of the possible effects of wake turbulence.*

WAKE TURBULENCE APPLICATION

g. In addition to subparagraph f, separate an aircraft landing behind another aircraft on the same runway, or one making a touch-and-go, stop-and-go, or low approach by ensuring the following minima will exist at the time the preceding aircraft is over the landing threshold:

NOTE−

Consider parallel runways less than 2,500 feet apart as a single runway because of the possible effects of wake turbulence.

1. Small behind large− *4 miles.*

2. Small behind heavy− *6 miles.*

If the landing threshold cannot be determined, apply the above minima as constant or increasing at the closest point that can be determined prior to the landing threshold.

h. *TERMINAL.* When NOWGT is displayed in an aircraft data block, provide *10 miles* separation behind the preceding aircraft and *10 miles* separation to the succeeding aircraft.

INTERPRETATION−

7110.65, 5−5−4, Minima, Wake Turbulence Minima Application (2−23−2023)

7110.65, 5−5−4h, Minima (2−21−2023)

i. *TERMINAL.* 2.5 nautical miles (NM) separation is authorized between aircraft established on the final approach course within 10 NM of the landing runway when operating in FUSION, or single sensor slant range mode if the aircraft remains within 40 miles of the antenna and:

1. The leading aircraft's weight class is the same or less than the trailing aircraft;

2. Super and heavy aircraft are permitted to participate in the separation reduction as the trailing aircraft only;

3. An average runway occupancy time of 50 seconds or less is documented;

4. CTRDs are operational and used for quick glance references;

REFERENCE−

FAA Order JO 7110.65, Para 3−1−9, Use of Tower Radar Displays.

5. Turnoff points are visible from the control tower.

REFERENCE–
FAA Order JO 7110.65, Para 2–1–19, Wake Turbulence.
FAA Order JO 7110.65, Para 3–9–6, Same Runway Separation.
FAA Order JO 7110.65, Para 5–5–7, Passing or Diverging.
FAA Order JO 7110.65, Para 5–5–9, Separation from Obstructions.
FAA Order JO 7110.65, Para 5–8–3, Successive or Simultaneous Departures.
FAA Order JO 7110.65, Para 5–9–5, Approach Separation Responsibility.
FAA Order JO 7110.65, Para 7–6–7, Sequencing.
FAA Order JO 7110.65, Para 7–7–3, Separation.
FAA Order JO 7110.65 Para 7–8–3, Separation.
FAA Order JO 7210.3, Para 10–4–10, Reduced Separation on Final.

5–5–5. VERTICAL APPLICATION

Aircraft not laterally separated, may be vertically separated by one of the following methods:

a. Assign altitudes to aircraft, provided valid Mode C altitude information is monitored and the applicable separation minima is maintained at all times.

REFERENCE–
FAA Order JO 7110.65, Para 4–5–1, Vertical Separation Minima.
FAA Order JO 7110.65, Para 5–2–15, Validation of Mode C Altitude Readout.
FAA Order JO 7110.65, Para 7–7–3, Separation.
FAA Order JO 7110.65, Para 7–8–3, Separation.
FAA Order JO 7110.65, Para 7–9–4, Separation.

b. Assign an altitude to an aircraft after the aircraft previously at that altitude has been issued a climb/descent clearance and is observed (valid Mode C), or reports leaving the altitude.

NOTE–
1. *Consider known aircraft performance characteristics, pilot furnished and/or Mode C detected information which indicate that climb/descent will not be consistent with the rates recommended in the AIM.*

2. *It is possible that the separation minima described in paragraph 4–5–1, Vertical Separation Minima, paragraph 7–7–3, Separation, paragraph 7–8–3, Separation, or paragraph 7–9–4, Separation, might not always be maintained using subparagraph b. However, correct application of this procedure will ensure that aircraft are safely separated because the first aircraft must have already vacated the altitude prior to the assignment of that altitude to the second aircraft.*

REFERENCE–
FAA Order JO 7110.65, Para 2–1–3, Procedural Preference.
FAA Order JO 7110.65, Para 4–5–1, Vertical Separation Minima.
FAA Order JO 7110.65, Para 5–2–15, Validation of Mode C Altitude Readout.
FAA Order JO 7110.65, Para 6–6–1, Application.

5–5–6. EXCEPTIONS

a. Do not use Mode C to effect vertical separation with an aircraft on a cruise clearance, contact approach, or as specified in paragraph 5–14–4, System Requirements, subparagraph f3.

REFERENCE–
FAA Order JO 7110.65, Para 6–6–2, Exceptions.
FAA Order JO 7110.65, Para 7–4–7, Contact Approach.
P/CG Term – Cruise.

b. Assign an altitude to an aircraft only after the aircraft previously at that altitude is observed at or passing through another altitude separated from the first by the appropriate minima when:

1. Severe turbulence is reported.

2. Aircraft are conducting military aerial refueling.

REFERENCE–
FAA Order JO 7110.65, Para 9–2–13, Military Aerial Refueling.

3. The aircraft previously at that altitude has been issued a climb/descent at pilot's discretion.

c. *EN ROUTE.* When the position symbol associated with the data block falls more than one history behind the actual aircraft target or there is no target symbol displayed, the Mode C information in the data block must not be used for the purpose of determining separation.

5-5-7. PASSING OR DIVERGING

a. *TERMINAL.* In accordance with the following criteria, all other approved separation may be discontinued and passing or diverging separation applied when:

1. Single Site ASR or FUSION Mode

(a) Aircraft are on opposite/reciprocal courses and you have observed that they have passed each other; or aircraft are on same or crossing courses/assigned radar vectors and one aircraft has crossed the projected course of the other, and the angular difference between their courses/assigned radar vectors is at least 15 degrees.

NOTE–
Two aircraft, both assigned courses and/or radar vectors with an angular difference of at least 15 degrees, is considered a correct application of this paragraph.

(b) The tracks are monitored to ensure that the primary targets, beacon control slashes, FUSION target symbols, or full digital terminal system primary and/or beacon target symbols will not touch.

REFERENCE–
FAA Order JO 7110.65, Para 1-2-2, Course Definitions.

2. Single Site ARSR or FUSION Mode when target refresh is only from an ARSR or when in FUSION Mode – ISR is displayed.

(a) Aircraft are on opposite/reciprocal courses and you have observed that they have passed each other; or aircraft are on same or crossing courses/assigned radar vectors and one aircraft has crossed the projected course of the other, and the angular difference between their courses/assigned radar vectors is at least 45 degrees.

NOTE–
Two aircraft, both assigned courses and/or radar vectors with an angular difference of at least 45 degrees, is considered a correct application of this paragraph.

(b) The tracks are monitored to ensure that the primary targets, beacon control slashes, FUSION target symbols, or full digital terminal system primary and/or beacon target symbols will not touch.

3. Although approved separation may be discontinued, the requirements of paragraph 5-5-4, Minima, subparagraph g must be applied when wake turbulence separation is required.

REFERENCE–
FAA Order JO 7110.65, Para 1-2-2, Course Definitions.

b. *EN ROUTE, TERMINAL (when STARS Multi-Sensor Mode is selected).* Vertical separation between aircraft may be discontinued when they are on opposite courses as defined in paragraph 1-2-2, Course Definitions; and

1. You are in communications with both aircraft involved; and

2. You tell the pilot of one aircraft about the other aircraft, including position, direction, type; and

3. One pilot reports having seen the other aircraft and that the aircraft have passed each other; and

4. You have observed that the radar targets have passed each other; and

5. You have advised the pilots if either aircraft is classified as a super or heavy aircraft.

6. Although vertical separation may be discontinued, the requirements of paragraph 5-5-4, Minima, subparagraph g must be applied when wake turbulence separation is required.

EXAMPLE–
"Traffic, twelve o'clock, Boeing Seven Twenty Seven, opposite direction. Do you have it in sight?"

(If the answer is in the affirmative):

"Report passing the traffic."

(When pilot reports passing the traffic and the radar targets confirm that the traffic has passed, issue appropriate control instructions.)

5–5–8. ADDITIONAL SEPARATION FOR FORMATION FLIGHTS

Because of the distance allowed between formation aircraft and lead aircraft, additional separation is necessary to ensure the periphery of the formation is adequately separated from other aircraft, adjacent airspace, or obstructions. Provide supplemental separation for formation flights as follows:

a. Separate a standard formation flight by adding 1 mile to the appropriate radar separation minima.

REFERENCE–
FAA Order JO 7110.65, Para 2–1–13, Formation Flights.
FAA Order JO 7110.65, Para 5–5–1, Application.
FAA Order JO 7110.65, Para 7–7–3, Separation.
P/CG Term – Formation Flight.

b. Separate two standard formation flights from each other by adding 2 miles to the appropriate separation minima.

c. Separate a nonstandard formation flight by applying the appropriate separation minima to the perimeter of the airspace encompassing the nonstandard formation or from the outermost aircraft of the nonstandard formation whichever applies.

d. If necessary for separation between a nonstandard formation and other aircraft, assign an appropriate beacon code to each aircraft in the formation or to the first and last aircraft in-trail.

NOTE–
The additional separation provided in paragraph 5–5–8, Additional Separation for Formation Flights, is not normally added to wake turbulence separation when a formation is following a heavier aircraft since none of the formation aircraft are likely to be closer to the heavier aircraft than the lead aircraft (to which the prescribed wake turbulence separation has been applied).

REFERENCE–
FAA Order JO 7110.65, Para 9–2–13 , Military Aerial Refueling.

5–5–9. SEPARATION FROM OBSTRUCTIONS

a. TERMINAL. Separate aircraft from prominent obstructions depicted on the radar display by the following minima:

1. When less than 40 miles from the antenna– *3 miles.*

2. When 40 miles or more from the antenna– *5 miles.*

3. For single sensor MSSR, when less than 60 miles from the antenna – *3 miles.*

4. FUSION:

(a) Fusion target symbol – *3 miles.*

(b) When ISR is displayed – *5 miles.*

NOTE–
When operating in FUSION, distances from the antenna listed in paragraph 5–5–9, a1 through a3, do not apply.

5. STARS Multi–Sensor Mode – *5 miles.*

b. TERMINAL. Vertical separation of aircraft above a prominent obstruction depicted on the radar display and contained within a buffer area may be discontinued after the aircraft has passed the obstruction.

c. EAS. Apply the radar separation minima specified in paragraph 5–5–4, Minima.

5–5–10. ADJACENT AIRSPACE

a. If coordination between the controllers concerned has not been effected, separate radar-controlled aircraft from the boundary of adjacent airspace in which radar separation is also being used by the following minima:

REFERENCE–
FAA Order JO 7110.65, Para 2–1–14, Coordinate Use of Airspace.

1. When less than 40 miles from the antenna– *1 1/2 miles.*

2. When 40 miles or more from the antenna– *2 1/2 miles.*

3. *EAS:*

(a) Below Flight Level 600– *2 1/2 miles.*

(b) Flight Level 600 and above– *5 miles.*

b. Separate radar-controlled aircraft from the boundary of airspace in which nonradar separation is being used by the following minima:

1. When less than 40 miles from the antenna– *3 miles.*

2. When 40 miles or more from the antenna– *5 miles.*

3. *EAS:*

(a) Below Flight Level 600– *5 miles.*

(b) Flight Level 600 and above– *10 miles.*

c. The provisions of subparagraphs a and b do not apply to VFR aircraft being provided Class B, Class C, or TRSA services. Ensure that the targets of these aircraft do not touch the boundary of adjacent airspace.

d. VFR aircraft approaching Class B, Class C, Class D, or TRSA airspace which is under the control jurisdiction of another air traffic control facility should either be provided with a radar handoff or be advised that radar service is terminated, given their position in relation to the Class B, Class C, Class D, or TRSA airspace, and the ATC frequency, if known, for the airspace to be entered. These actions should be accomplished in sufficient time for the pilot to obtain the required ATC approval prior to entering the airspace involved, or to avoid the airspace.

5–5–11. EDGE OF SCOPE

Separate a radar-controlled aircraft climbing or descending through the altitude of an aircraft that has been tracked to the edge of the scope/display by the following minima until nonradar separation has been established:

a. When less than 40 miles from the antenna– *3 miles* from edge of scope.

b. When 40 miles or more from the antenna– *5 miles* from edge of scope.

c. *EAS:*

1. Below Flight Level 600– *5 miles.*

2. Flight Level 600 and above– *10 miles.*

5–5–12. BEACON TARGET DISPLACEMENT

When using a radar target display with a previously specified beacon target displacement to separate a beacon target from a primary target, adjacent airspace, obstructions, or terrain, add a 1 mile correction factor to the applicable minima. The maximum allowable beacon target displacement which may be specified by the facility air traffic manager is 1/2 mile.

REFERENCE–
FAA Order JO 7210.3, Para 3–6–4, Monitoring of Mode 3/A Radar Beacon Codes.

Section 6. Vectoring

5–6–1. APPLICATION

Vector aircraft:

a. In controlled airspace for separation, safety, noise abatement, operational advantage, confidence maneuver, or when a pilot requests.

b. In Class G airspace only upon pilot request and as an additional service.

c. At or above the MVA or the minimum IFR altitude except as authorized for radar approaches, radar departures, special VFR, VFR operations, or by paragraph 5–6–3, Vectors Below Minimum Altitude.

NOTE–
VFR aircraft not at an altitude assigned by ATC may be vectored at any altitude. It is the responsibility of the pilot to comply with the applicable parts of CFR Title 14.

REFERENCE–
FAA Order JO 7110.65, Para 4–5–6, Minimum En Route Altitudes.
FAA Order JO 7110.65, Para 7–5–2, Priority.
FAA Order JO 7110.65, Para 7–5–4, Altitude Assignment.
FAA Order JO 7110.65, Para 7–7–5, Altitude Assignments.
14 CFR Section 91.119, Minimum Safe Altitudes: General.

d. In airspace for which you have control jurisdiction, unless otherwise coordinated.

e. So as to permit it to resume its own navigation within radar coverage.

f. Operating special VFR only within Class B, Class C, Class D, or Class E surface areas.

g. Operating VFR at those locations where a special program is established, or when a pilot requests, or you suggest and the pilot concurs.

REFERENCE–
FAA Order JO 7110.65, Para 4–4–1, Route Use.
FAA Order JO 7110.65, Para 7–2–1, Visual Separation.
FAA Order JO 7110.65, Para 7–5–3, Separation.
FAA Order JO 7110.65, Para 7–6–1, Application.
FAA Order JO 7110.65, Para 9–4–4, Separation Minima.
FAA Order JO 7210.3, Chapter 12, Section 1, Terminal VFR Radar Services.

5–6–2. METHODS

a. Vector aircraft by specifying:

1. Direction of turn, if appropriate, and magnetic heading to be flown, or

PHRASEOLOGY–
TURN LEFT/RIGHT HEADING (degrees).

FLY HEADING (degrees).

FLY PRESENT HEADING.

DEPART (fix) HEADING (degrees).

2. The number of degrees, in group form, to turn and the direction of turn, or

PHRASEOLOGY–
TURN (number of degrees) DEGREES LEFT/RIGHT.

3. For NO-GYRO procedures, the type of vector, direction of turn, and when to stop turn.

PHRASEOLOGY–
THIS WILL BE A NO-GYRO VECTOR,

TURN LEFT/RIGHT.

STOP TURN.

b. When initiating a vector, advise the pilot of the purpose, and if appropriate, what to expect when radar navigational guidance is terminated.

PHRASEOLOGY–
VECTOR TO (fix or airway).

VECTOR TO INTERCEPT (name of NAVAID) (specified) RADIAL.

VECTOR FOR SPACING.

(if appropriate) EXPECT DIRECT (NAVAID, waypoint, fix)

VECTOR TO FINAL APPROACH COURSE,

or if the pilot does not have knowledge of the type of approach,

VECTOR TO (approach name) FINAL APPROACH COURSE.

NOTE–
Determine optimum routing based on factors such as wind, weather, traffic, pilot requests, noise abatement, adjacent sector requirement, and letters of agreement.

c. When vectoring or approving course deviations, assign an altitude to maintain and, if necessary, a speed, when:

1. The vector or approved deviation is off an assigned procedure which contains altitude or speed restrictions, i.e., instrument approach, etc.

2. The previously issued clearance included crossing restrictions.

REFERENCE–
FAA Order JO 7110.65, Para 4–2–5, Route or Altitude Amendments.

3. The vector or approved deviation is off an assigned procedure that contains published altitude or speed restrictions, i.e., SID, STAR, and a clearance to Climb Via/Descend Via has been issued.

d. When vectoring or approving an aircraft to deviate off of a procedure, advise the pilot if you intend on clearing the aircraft to resume the procedure.

PHRASEOLOGY–
FLY HEADING (degrees), MAINTAIN (altitude), (if necessary, MAINTAIN (speed)), EXPECT TO RESUME (SID, STAR, etc.).

DEVIATION (restrictions if necessary) APPROVED, MAINTAIN (altitude), (if necessary, MAINTAIN (speed)), EXPECT TO RESUME (SID, STAR, etc.) AT (NAVAID, fix, waypoint).

NOTE–
After a climb via or descend via clearance has been issued, a vector/deviation off of a SID/STAR cancels all published altitude and speed restrictions on the procedure. The aircraft's Flight Management System (FMS) may be unable to process crossing altitude restrictions once the aircraft leaves the SID/STAR lateral path. Without an assigned altitude, the aircraft's FMS may revert to leveling off at the altitude set by the pilot, which may be the SID/STAR published top or bottom altitude.

e. Provide radar navigational guidance until the aircraft is:

1. Established within the airspace to be protected for the nonradar route to be flown, or

2. On a heading that will, within a reasonable distance, intercept the nonradar route to be flown, and

3. Informed of its position unless the aircraft is RNAV, FMS, or DME equipped and being vectored toward a VORTAC/TACAN or waypoint and within the service volume of the NAVAID.

PHRASEOLOGY–

(Position with respect to course/fix along route),
RESUME OWN NAVIGATION,

or

FLY HEADING (degrees). WHEN ABLE, PROCEED DIRECT (name of fix),

or
RESUME (SID/STAR/transition/procedure).

REFERENCE–
FAA Order JO 7110.65, Chapter 4, Section 1, NAVAID Use Limitations.
FAA Order JO 7110.65, Para 4–5–7, Altitude Information.

f. Aircraft instructed to resume a procedure which contains published crossing restrictions (SID/STAR) must be issued/reissued all applicable restrictions or be instructed to Climb Via/Descend Via.

PHRASEOLOGY–

CLEARED DIRECT (NAVAID, fix, waypoint) CROSS (NAVAID, fix, waypoint) AT/AT OR ABOVE/AT OR BELOW (altitude), then CLIMB VIA/DESCEND VIA (SID/STAR)

EXAMPLE–

"Cleared direct Luxor, then descend via the Ksino One arrival."
"Cleared direct HITME, cross HITME at or above one one thousand, then climb via the Boach Five departure."

g. Aircraft may not be vectored off an Obstacle Departure Procedure (ODP), or issued an altitude lower than published altitude on an ODP, until at or above the MVA/MIA, at which time the ODP is canceled.

NOTE–

Once an aircraft has been vectored off an Obstacle Departure Procedure, the procedure is canceled and ATC cannot clear the aircraft to resume the ODP.

REFERENCE–
P/CG – Obstacle Departure Procedure.

h. Aircraft vectored off an RNAV route must be recleared to the next waypoint or as requested by the pilot.

i. When flight data processing is available, update the route of flight in the computer unless an operational advantage is gained and coordination is accomplished.

j. Inform the pilot when a vector will take the aircraft across a previously assigned nonradar route.

PHRASEOLOGY–

EXPECT VECTOR ACROSS (NAVAID radial) (airway/route/course) FOR (purpose).

REFERENCE–
FAA Order JO 7110.65, Para 7–6–1, Application.

5–6–3. VECTORS BELOW MINIMUM ALTITUDE

a. TERMINAL. As described in facility directives, when vectoring a departing IFR aircraft, or one executing a missed approach, when ISR is not displayed in the full data block and before it reaches the minimum altitude for IFR operations if separation from prominent obstacles shown on the radar scope is applied in accordance with one of the following:

1. The flight path is 3 miles or more from the obstacle and the aircraft is climbing to an altitude at least 1,000 feet above the obstacle, vector the aircraft to maintain at least 3 miles separation from the obstacle until the aircraft reports leaving an altitude above the obstacle, or;

2. The flight path is less than 3 miles from the obstacle and the aircraft is climbing to an altitude at least 1,000 feet above the obstacle, vector the aircraft to increase lateral separation from the obstacle until the 3 mile minimum is achieved or until the aircraft reports leaving an altitude above the obstacle, or;

3. Radar facilities may vector aircraft below the MVA/MIA, provided:

(a) No prominent obstacles are within 10 NM of the departure end of runway (DER).

(b) Aircraft must be allowed an uninterrupted climb to meet the MVA/MIA within 10 NM of the DER.

NOTE–
ATC assumes responsibility for terrain and obstacle avoidance when IFR aircraft are below the minimum IFR altitude (MVA, MIA, MEA) and are taken off departure/missed approach procedures, or if issued go–around instructions, except after conducting a visual approach. ATC does not assume this responsibility when utilizing a Diverse Vector Area (DVA) or when operating on SIDs with or without a published range of headings in the departure route description.

b. After reaching the first MVA/MIA sector, all subsequent MVA/MIA sectors encountered must be met.

REFERENCE–
P/CG Term – Obstacle.
P/CG Term – Obstruction.
P/CG Term – Prominent Obstacle.

c. At those locations where diverse vector areas (DVA) have been established, radar facilities may vector aircraft below the MVA/MIA within the DVA described in facility directives.

d. At those locations using radar SIDs, radar facilities may vector aircraft below the MVA/MIA, in accordance with facility directives.

e. At locations that vector aircraft conducting a go–around or missed approach, use authorized headings and display those prominent obstacles stipulated in facility directives until reaching the MVA/MIA.

REFERENCE–
FAA Order JO 7110.65, Para 5–8–1, Procedures.
FAA Order JO 7210.3, Para 3–8–5, Establishing Diverse Vector Area/s (DVA).
FAA Order JO 7210.3, Para 10–3–15, Go–Around/Missed Approach.

Section 7. Speed Adjustment

5-7-1. APPLICATION

Keep speed adjustments to the minimum necessary to achieve or maintain required or desired spacing. Avoid adjustments requiring alternate decreases and increases. Terminate speed adjustments when no longer needed.

NOTE–
It is the pilot's responsibility and prerogative to refuse speed adjustment that he/she considers excessive or contrary to the aircraft's operating specifications.

a. Consider the following when applying speed control:

1. Determine the interval required and the point at which the interval is to be accomplished.

2. Implement speed adjustment based on the following principles.

(a) Priority of speed adjustment instructions is determined by the relative speed and position of the aircraft involved and the spacing requirement.

(b) Speed adjustments are not achieved instantaneously. Aircraft configuration, altitudes, and speed determine the time and distance required to accomplish the adjustment.

3. Use the following techniques in speed control situations:

(a) Compensate for compression when assigning air speed adjustment in an in-trail situation by using one of the following techniques:

(1) Reduce the trailing aircraft first.

(2) Increase the leading aircraft first.

(b) Assign a specific airspeed if required to maintain spacing.

(c) Allow increased time and distance to achieve speed adjustments in the following situations:

(1) Higher altitudes.

(2) Greater speed.

(3) Clean configurations.

(d) Ensure that aircraft are allowed to operate in a clean configuration as long as circumstances permit.

(e) Keep the number of speed adjustments per aircraft to the minimum required to achieve and maintain spacing.

b. Do not assign speed adjustment to aircraft:

1. At or above FL 390 without pilot consent.

2. Executing a published high altitude instrument approach procedure.

3. In a holding pattern.

REFERENCE–
FAA Order JO 7110.65, Para 4-6-4, Holding Instructions.

4. Inside the final approach fix on final or a point 5 miles from the runway, whichever is closer to the runway.

c. At the time approach clearance or a climb via/descend via clearance is issued, previously assigned speeds must be restated if required.

d. Approach clearances or climb via/descend via clearances cancel any previously assigned speeds. Pilots are expected to make their own speed adjustments to fly the approach, SID, or STAR unless assigned speeds are restated.

NOTE–
Pilots are required to comply with published speed restrictions.

e. A speed restriction published as part of a SID/STAR is canceled when an aircraft is vectored off, or a deviation from the SID/STAR is approved. If necessary, assign a speed in conjunction with the vector or approval to deviate.

NOTE–
The last published speed on a STAR will be maintained by the aircraft until ATC deletes it, assigns a new speed, issues a vector, assigns a direct route or issues an approach clearance.

f. When issuing speed adjustments to aircraft cleared along a route or procedure that has published speed restrictions, if feasible, advise the pilot where you intend on allowing the aircraft to resume the published speed.

NOTE–
If it is anticipated that an aircraft will be allowed to resume the published speeds on a procedure, advising the pilot where that may occur avoids flight crews from unnecessarily deleting speeds from the Flight Management System.

g. Express speed adjustments in terms of knots based on indicated airspeed (IAS) in 5–knot increments. At or above FL 240, speeds may be expressed in terms of Mach numbers in 0.01 increments for turbojet aircraft with Mach meters (i.e., Mach 0.69, 0.70, 0.71, etc.).

NOTE–
1. *Pilots complying with speed adjustment instructions (published or assigned) should maintain a speed within plus or minus 10 knots or 0.02 Mach number of the specified speed.*

2. *When assigning speeds to achieve spacing between aircraft at different altitudes, consider that ground speed may vary with altitude. Further speed adjustment may be necessary to attain the desired spacing.*

3. *Controllers should anticipate pilots will begin adjusting speed at the minimum distance necessary prior to a published speed restriction so as to cross the waypoint/fix at the published speed. Once at the published speed, controllers should expect pilots will maintain the published speed until additional adjustment is required to comply with further published restrictions or ATC assigned speed restrictions.*

REFERENCE–
FAA Order JO 7110.65, Para 5–6–1, Application.
FAA Order JO 7110.65, Para 5–7–2, Methods.

5–7–2. METHODS

a. Instruct aircraft to:

1. Maintain present/specific speed.

2. Maintain specified speed or greater/less.

3. Maintain the highest/lowest practical speed.

4. Increase or reduce to a specified speed in single-digit form or by a specified number of knots in group form.

PHRASEOLOGY–
SAY AIRSPEED.

SAY MACH NUMBER.

MAINTAIN PRESENT SPEED.

MAINTAIN (specific speed) KNOTS.

MAINTAIN (specific speed) KNOTS OR GREATER.

DO NOT EXCEED (speed) KNOTS.

MAINTAIN MAXIMUM FORWARD SPEED.

MAINTAIN SLOWEST PRACTICAL SPEED.

INCREASE/REDUCE SPEED:

TO (specified speed in knots),

or

TO MACH (Mach number),

or

(number of knots) KNOTS.

EXAMPLE–

"Increase speed to Mach point seven two."
"Reduce speed to two five zero."
"Reduce speed twenty knots."
"Maintain two eight zero knots."
"Maintain maximum forward speed."

NOTE–

1. *A pilot operating at or above 10,000 feet MSL on an assigned speed adjustment greater than 250 knots is expected to comply with 14 CFR Section 91.117(a) when cleared below 10,000 feet MSL, within domestic airspace, without notifying ATC. Pilots are expected to comply with the other provisions of 14 CFR Section 91.117 without notification.*

2. *Speed restrictions of 250 knots do not apply to aircraft operating beyond 12 NM from the coastline within the U.S. Flight Information Region, in offshore Class E airspace below 10,000 feet MSL. However, in airspace underlying a Class B airspace area designated for an airport, or in a VFR corridor designated through such a Class B airspace area, pilots are expected to comply with the 200 knot speed limit specified in 14 CFR Section 91.117(c). (See 14 CFR Sections 91.117(c) and 91.703.)*

3. *The phrases "maintain maximum forward speed" and "maintain slowest practical speed" are primarily intended for use when sequencing a group of aircraft. As the sequencing plan develops, it may be necessary to determine the specific speed and/or make specific speed assignments.*

b. To obtain pilot concurrence for a speed adjustment at or above FL 390, as required by paragraph 5–7–1, Application, use the following phraseology.

PHRASEOLOGY–

(Speed adjustment), IF UNABLE ADVISE.

EXAMPLE–

"Reduce speed to one niner zero, if unable advise."

c. Simultaneous speed reduction and descent can be extremely difficult, particularly for turbojet aircraft. Specifying which action is to be accomplished first removes any doubt the pilot may have as to controller intent or priority. Specify which action is expected first when combining speed reduction with a descent clearance.

1. Speed reductions prior to descent.

PHRASEOLOGY–

REDUCE SPEED:

TO (specified speed),

or

(number of knots) KNOTS.

THEN, DESCEND AND MAINTAIN (altitude).

2. Speed reduction following descent.

PHRASEOLOGY−
DESCEND AND MAINTAIN (altitude).

THEN, REDUCE SPEED:

TO (specified speed in knots),

or

TO MACH (Mach number),

or

(number of knots) KNOTS.

NOTE−
When specifying descent prior to speed reduction, consider the maximum speed requirements specified in 14 CFR Section 91.117. It may be necessary for the pilot to level off temporarily and reduce speed prior to descending below 10,000 feet MSL.

d. Specify combined speed/altitude fix crossing restrictions.

PHRASEOLOGY−
CROSS (fix) AT AND MAINTAIN (altitude) AT (specified speed) KNOTS.

EXAMPLE−
"Cross Robinsville at and maintain six thousand at two three zero knots."

REFERENCE−
FAA Order JO 7110.65, Para 2−4−17, Numbers Usage.
FAA Order JO 7110.65, Para 4−5−7, Altitude Information.

e. When issuing speed adjustments to aircraft cleared on procedures with published speed restrictions, specify the point at which the issued restriction begins, ends, or changes the published restrictions.

PHRASEOLOGY−
CROSS (fix/waypoint) AT (speed).

MAINTAIN (speed) UNTIL (fix/waypoint),

THEN (additional instructions).

RESUME PUBLISHED SPEED.

COMPLY WITH SPEED RESTRICTIONS.

(if required) EXCEPT (alternate instructions).

DELETE SPEED RESTRICTIONS.

CLIMB/DESCEND VIA (SID/STAR name and number) (transition if required.)

NOTE−
1. *Aircraft will meet all published speed restrictions when on any route or procedure with published speed restrictions regardless of climb via or descend via clearance.*

2. *Due to variations of aircraft types, Flight Management Systems, and environmental conditions, ATC should anticipate that aircraft will begin speed adjustments at varying locations along cleared routes or procedures that contain published speed restrictions.*

3. *Issuing speed adjustments to aircraft flying procedures with published speed restrictions may impact the pilot's ability to fly the intended flight profile of the procedure.*

EXAMPLE–
1. *"Cross Alisa at two two zero knots, then climb via the TIMMY One departure."*

NOTE–
The aircraft will maintain the ATC assigned speed until Alisa waypoint and will then comply with the speed restrictions on the TIMMY One departure.

EXAMPLE–
2. *"Cross Alisa at one zero thousand, then climb via the TIMMY One departure, except maintain two two zero knots."*

NOTE–
The aircraft will maintain the ATC assigned speed of two two zero knots and will not meet any published speed restrictions. Aircraft will meet all published altitude restrictions after Alisa.

EXAMPLE–
3. *"Maintain two two zero knots until BALTR then resume published speed."*

NOTE–
The ATC assigned speed assignment of two two zero knots would apply until BALTR. The aircraft would then comply with the published speed restrictions.

EXAMPLE–
4. *"Descend via the KEPEC Two arrival, except after NIPZO maintain one eight zero knots."*

NOTE–
The aircraft will comply with all published restrictions. After NIPZO, the aircraft will continue to comply with altitude restrictions, but will comply with the ATC assigned speed adjustment.

REFERENCE–
FAA Order JO 7110.65, Para 2–4–17, Numbers Usage.
FAA Order JO 7110.65, Para 4–5–7, Altitude Information.
FAA Order JO 7110.65, Para 5–7–1, Application.

5–7–3. SPEED ASSIGNMENTS

When assigning airspeeds, use the following:

a. To aircraft operating between FL 280 and 10,000 feet, a speed not less than 250 knots or the equivalent Mach number.

NOTE–
1. *On a standard day the Mach numbers equivalent to 250 knots calibrated airspeed (CAS) (subject to minor variations) are:*
FL 240–0.6
FL 250–0.61
FL 260–0.62
FL 270–0.64
FL 280–0.65
FL 290–0.66.

2. *A pilot will advise if unable to comply with the speed assignment.*

b. To aircraft operating beneath Class B airspace or in a VFR corridor designated through Class B airspace: assign a speed not more than 200 knots.

c. To arrival aircraft operating below 10,000 feet:

1. Turbojet aircraft:

(a) Assign a speed not less than 210 knots, except for the aircraft as specified in subparagraph b above, or

(b) Assign a speed not less than 170 knots when the aircraft is within 20 flying miles of the runway threshold.

2. Reciprocating and turboprop aircraft:

(a) Assign a speed not less than 200 knots, or

(b) Assign a speed not less than 150 knots when the aircraft is within 20 flying miles of the runway threshold.

d. To departures:

1. Turbojet aircraft: assign a speed not less than 230 knots.

2. Reciprocating and turboprop aircraft: assign a speed not less than 150 knots.

e. To helicopters: Assign a speed not less than 60 knots.

REFERENCE–
FAA Order JO 7110.65, Para 5–7–2, Methods.

f. Lower speeds may be assigned when operationally advantageous.

NOTE–
1. *A pilot operating at or above 10,000 feet MSL on an assigned speed adjustment greater than 250 knots is expected to comply with 14 CFR Section 91.117(a) when cleared below 10,000 feet MSL, within domestic airspace, without notifying ATC. Pilots are expected to comply with the other provisions of 14 CFR Section 91.117 without notification.*

2. *Speed restrictions of 250 knots do not apply to aircraft operating beyond 12 NM from the coastline within the U.S. Flight Information Region, in offshore Class E airspace below 10,000 feet MSL. However, in airspace underlying a Class B airspace area designated for an airport, or in a VFR corridor designated through such a Class B airspace area, pilots are expected to comply with the 200 knot speed limit specified in 14 CFR Section 91.117(c). (See 14 CFR Sections 91.117(c) and 91.70).*

3. *The phrases "maintain maximum forward speed" and "maintain slowest practical speed" are primarily intended for use when sequencing a group of aircraft. As the sequencing plan develops, it may be necessary to determine the specific speed and/or make specific speed assignments.*

REFERENCE–
FAA Order JO 7110.65, Para 5–7–2, Methods.
14 CFR Sections 91.117(c) and 91.703.

5–7–4. TERMINATION

Advise aircraft when speed adjustments are no longer needed.

a. Advise aircraft to "resume normal speed" when ATC-assigned speed adjustments are no longer required and no published speed restrictions apply.

PHRASEOLOGY–
RESUME NORMAL SPEED.

NOTE–
"Resume normal speed" is only used where there is no underlying published speed restriction. It does not delete speed restrictions on upcoming segments of flight and does not relieve the pilot of those speed restrictions which are applicable to 14 CFR Section 91.117.

b. Instruct aircraft to "comply with speed restrictions" applicable to the charted procedure or route being flown.

PHRASEOLOGY–
COMPLY WITH SPEED RESTRICTIONS

NOTE–
The phraseology "comply with restrictions" requires compliance with all altitude and/or speed restrictions depicted on the procedure.

REFERENCE–
FAA Order JO 7110.65, Para 5–6–2, Methods.

c. Advise aircraft to "resume published speed" when aircraft have been assigned an unpublished speed and ATC wants aircraft to meet subsequent published speed restrictions on the route or procedure.

PHRASEOLOGY–
RESUME PUBLISHED SPEED

REFERENCE–
FAA Order JO 7110.65, Para 4–5–7, Altitude Information.

d. Advise aircraft when either ATC assigned speed adjustments or published speed restrictions are no longer required.

PHRASEOLOGY–
DELETE SPEED RESTRICTIONS

NOTE–
When deleting published restrictions, ATC must ensure obstacle clearance until aircraft are established on a route where no published restrictions apply. This does not relieve the pilot of those speed restrictions which are applicable to 14 CFR Section 91.117.

REFERENCE–
FAA Order JO 7110.65, Para 5–7–1, Application.

INTERPRETATION–
7110.65, 5–7–4, Termination of Speed Adjustment (10–21–2015)

Section 8. Radar Departures

5-8-1. PROCEDURES

a. When vectoring a departing aircraft on a radar SID, concurrent use of a diverse vector area (DVA) is not permitted.

b. When the departure route description on a radar SID contains the phrase, "Fly assigned heading," "as assigned by ATC," or similar phrases, with a published range of headings in the route description, assign headings or vectors as needed not to exceed those headings in the published range until reaching the MVA/MIA.

REFERENCE–
FAA Order JO 7110.65, Para 5–6–3, Vectors Below Minimum Altitude.

5-8-2. INITIAL HEADING

a. Before departure, assign the initial heading consistent with either a SID being flown or DVA, if applicable, when a departing aircraft is to be vectored immediately after takeoff. At locations that have a DVA, concurrent use of both a SID and DVA is not permitted.

PHRASEOLOGY–
FLY RUNWAY HEADING.
TURN LEFT/RIGHT, HEADING (degrees).

NOTE–
1. *TERMINAL. A purpose for the heading is not necessary, since pilots operating in a radar environment associate assigned headings with vectors to their planned route of flight.*

2. *ATC assumes responsibility for terrain and obstacle avoidance when IFR aircraft are below the minimum IFR altitude (MVA, MIA, MEA) and are taken off departure/missed approach procedures, or if issued go–around instructions, except after conducting a visual approach. ATC does not assume this responsibility when utilizing a Diverse Vector Area (DVA) or when operating on SIDs with or without a published range of headings in the departure route description.*

REFERENCE–
FAA Order JO 7110.65, Para 4–3–2, Departure Clearances.
FAA Order JO 7110.65, Para 5–6–3, Vectors Below Minimum Altitude.

b. At locations with both SIDs and DVAs, an amended departure clearance is required to cancel a previously assigned SID and subsequently utilize a DVA or vice versa. The amended clearance must be provided to the pilot in a timely manner so that the pilot may brief the changes in advance of entering the runway.

c. Issue an altitude to maintain with the initial heading when the heading will take the aircraft off a departure procedure that contains both a published lateral path to a waypoint and crossing restrictions.

d. When conducting simultaneous parallel runway departures utilizing RNAV SIDs, advise aircraft of the initial fix/waypoint on the RNAV route.

PHRASEOLOGY–
RNAV to (fix/waypoint), RUNWAY (number), CLEARED FOR TAKEOFF.

EXAMPLE–
"RNAV to MPASS, Runway Two–Six Left, cleared for takeoff."

NOTE–
1. *TERMINAL. A purpose for an initial waypoint advisory is not necessary since pilots associate this advisory with the flight path to their planned route of flight. Pilots must immediately advise ATC if a different RNAV SID is entered in the aircraft FMS.*

2. *The SID transition is not restated as it is contained in the ATC clearance.*

3. *Aircraft cleared via RNAV SIDs designed to begin with a vector to the initial waypoint are assigned a heading before departure.*

REFERENCE–
FAA Order JO 7110.65, Para 3–9–9, Nonintersecting Converging Runway Operations.
FAA Order JO 7110.65, Para 4–3–2, Departure Clearances.
AIM, Para 5–2–7, Departure Control.

5–8–3. SUCCESSIVE OR SIMULTANEOUS DEPARTURES

TERMINAL

Separate aircraft departing from the same airport/heliport or adjacent airports/heliports in accordance with the following minima provided radar identification with the aircraft will be established within 1 mile of the takeoff runway end/helipad and courses will diverge by at least the minimum required, as stated below.

NOTE–
1. *FAA Order 8260.46, Departure Procedure (DP) Program, and FAA Order 8260.3, United States Standard for Terminal Instrument Procedures (TERPS), Volume 4, establishes guidelines for IFR departure turning procedures which assumes a climb to 400 feet above the departure end of runway (DER) elevation before a turn is commenced. TERPS criteria ensures obstacle clearance with a climb gradient of 200 feet per nautical mile from the DER. "Immediately after departure" is considered to be any turn that provides at least the minimum required divergence that commences no later than 2 miles from the DER.*

2. *Consider known aircraft performance characteristics when applying initial separation to successive departing aircraft.*

3. *When one or both of the departure surfaces is a helipad, use the takeoff course of the helicopter as a reference, comparable to the centerline of a runway and the helipad center as the threshold.*

a. Between successive departures from the same runway/helipad or parallel runways/helicopter takeoff courses separated by less than 2,500 feet– *1 mile* if courses diverge by 15 degrees or more immediately after departure. (See FIG 5–8–1, FIG 5–8–2, and FIG 5–8–3.)

FIG 5–8–1
Successive Departures

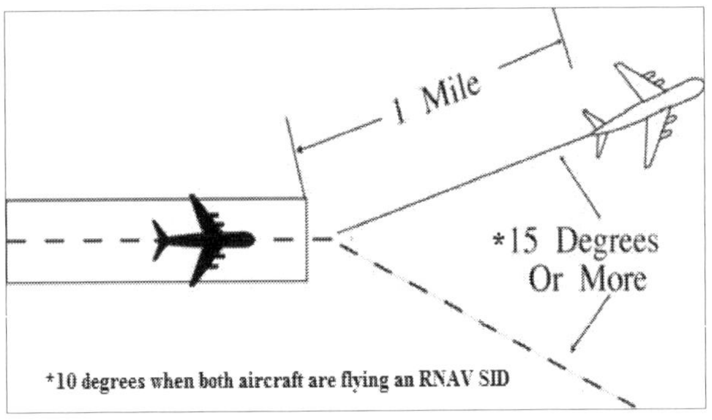

FIG 5–8–2
Simultaneous Departures

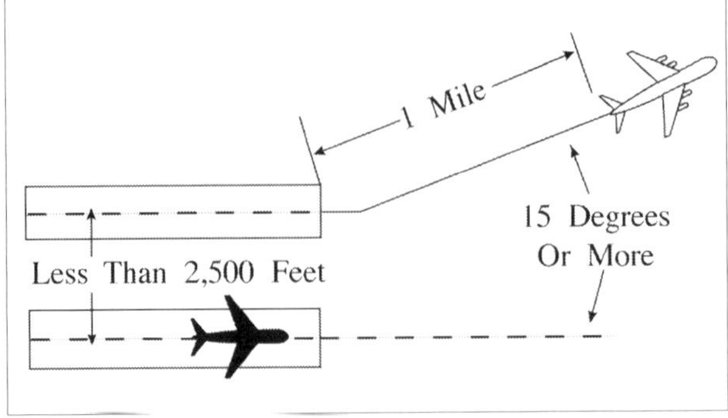

FIG 5-8-3
Simultaneous Departures

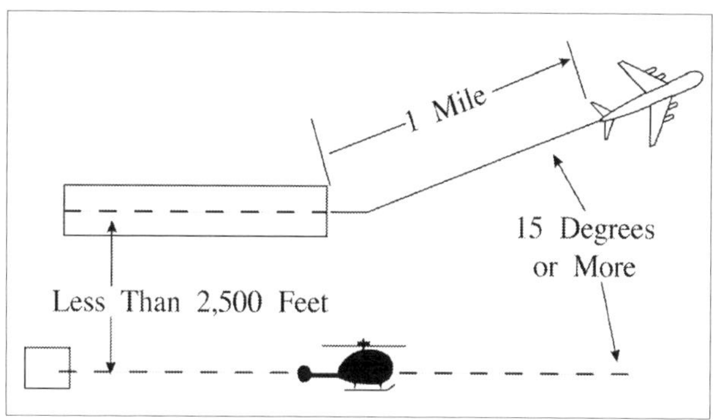

NOTE-
This procedure does not apply when wake turbulence separation is required.

REFERENCE-
FAA Order JO 7110.65, Para 3-9-7, Wake Turbulence Separation for Intersection Departures.
FAA Order JO 7110.65, Para 3-9-8, Intersecting Runway/Intersecting Flight Path Operations.
FAA Order JO 7110.65, Para 5-5-4, Minima.
FAA Order JO 7110.65, Para 5-5-4, Minima, Subparagraph g.

b. Between simultaneous departures departing in the same direction from parallel runways/helicopter takeoff courses, authorize simultaneous takeoffs if the centerlines/takeoff courses are separated by at least 2,500 feet and courses diverge by 15 degrees or more immediately after departure. (See FIG 5-8-5, and FIG 5-8-6.)

REFERENCE-
FAA Order JO 7110.65, Para 5-5-4, Minima, Subparagraph f.

c. When both aircraft are flying an RNAV SID:

1. Between successive departures from the same runway- *1 mile* if courses diverge by 10 degrees or more immediately after departure. (See FIG 5-8-1.)

NOTE-
This procedure does not apply when wake turbulence separation is required.

2. Between simultaneous departures from parallel runways/helicopter takeoff courses, authorize simultaneous takeoffs if the centerlines/takeoff courses are separated by at least 700 feet and less than 2,500 feet, courses diverge by 15 degrees or more, and departures are released in accordance with the release distance stagger stated in TBL 5-8-1 below.

TBL 5-8-1
Departure Release Distances

Distance to Divergence (Measured from the further DER)	Minimum Centerline Separation	Release Distance Stagger
Immediately	700	1000 feet
No later than 5 NM	1020	2000 feet
No later than 8 NM	1130	3000 feet
No later than 11 NM	1360	4000 feet

NOTE-
This procedure does not apply when wake turbulence separation is required.

FIG 5–8–4
Simultaneous Dependent Departures

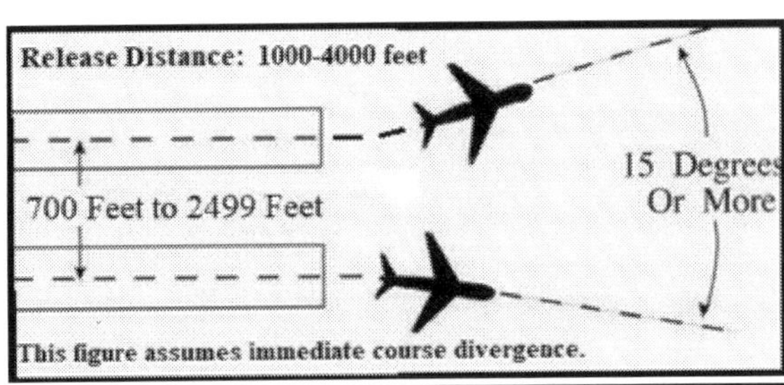

3. Between simultaneous departures from parallel runways/helicopter takeoff courses, authorize simultaneous takeoffs if the centerlines/takeoff courses are separated by at least 2,500 feet and courses diverge by 10 degrees or more immediately after departure. (See FIG 5–8–5, and FIG 5–8–6.)

NOTE–
RNAV SIDs specific to this paragraph are those SIDs constructed with a specific lateral path that begins at the DER.

FIG 5–8–5
Parallel Runway Departures

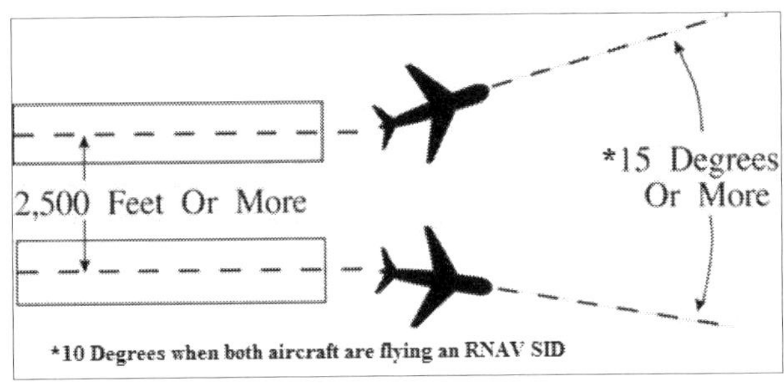

FIG 5–8–6
Parallel Helicopter Course Departures

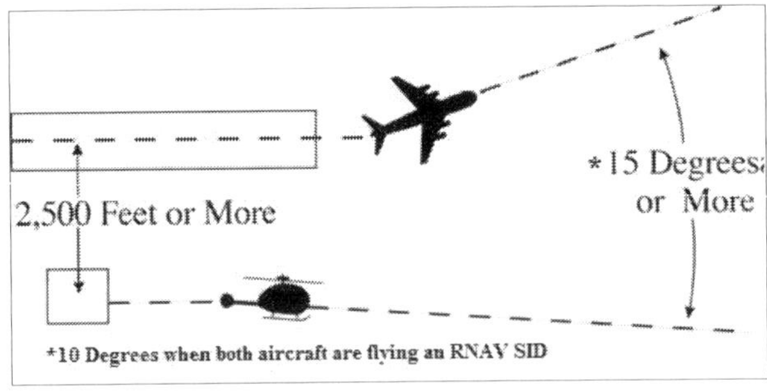

d. Between aircraft departing from diverging runways:

1. Nonintersecting runways. Authorize simultaneous takeoffs if runways diverge by 15 degrees or more. (See FIG 5–8–7.)

FIG 5-8-7
Nonintersecting Runway Departures

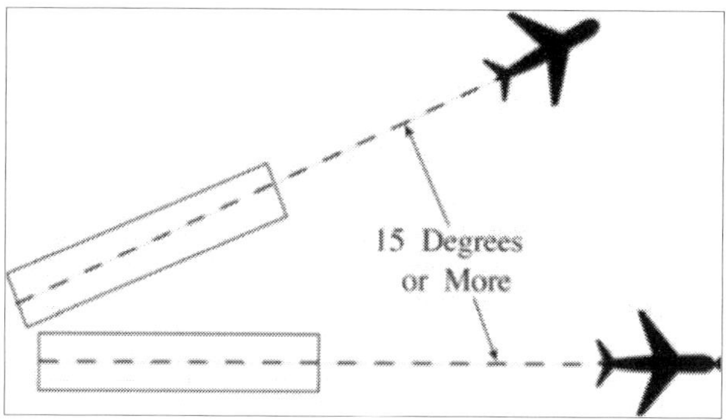

2. Intersecting runways and/or helicopter takeoff courses which diverge by 15 degrees or more. Authorize takeoff of a succeeding aircraft when the preceding aircraft has passed the point of runway and/or takeoff course intersection. When applicable, apply the procedure in paragraph 3-9-5, Anticipating Separation. (See FIG 5-8-8 and FIG 5-8-9.)

FIG 5-8-8
Intersecting Runway Departures

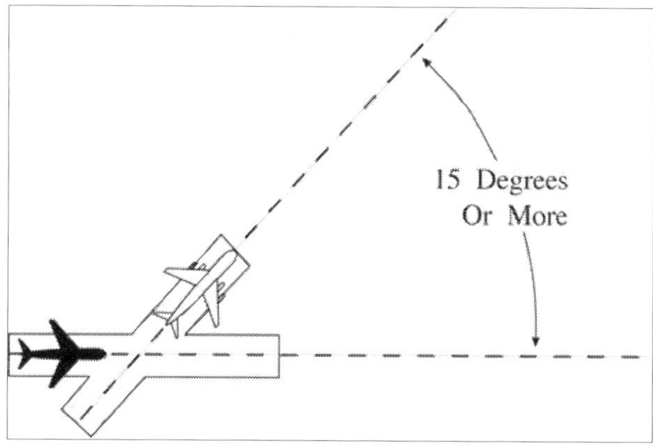

FIG 5-8-9
Intersecting Helicopter Course Departures

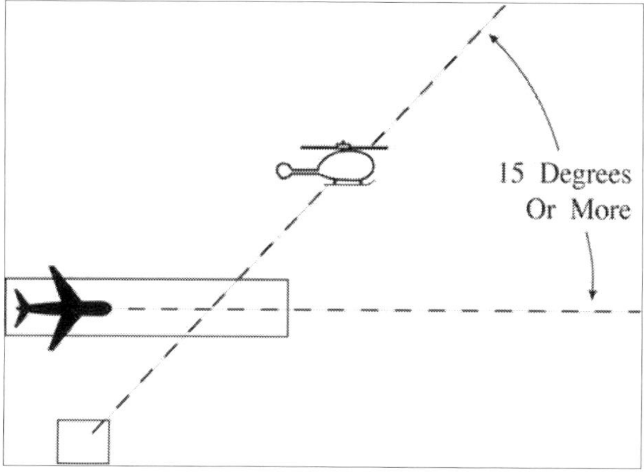

NOTE-
This procedure does not apply when wake turbulence separation is required.

REFERENCE-
FAA Order JO 7110.65, Para 5-5-4, Minima, Subparagraph f.

5-8-4. DEPARTURE AND ARRIVAL

TERMINAL. Except as provided in paragraph 5-8-5, Departures and Arrivals on Parallel or Nonintersecting Diverging Runways, separate a departing aircraft from an arriving aircraft on final approach by a minimum of *2 miles* if separation will increase to a minimum of 3 miles (5 miles when 40 miles or more from the antenna) within 1 minute after takeoff.

NOTE-
1. *This procedure permits a departing aircraft to be released so long as an arriving aircraft is no closer than 2 miles from the runway at the time. This separation is determined at the time the departing aircraft commences takeoff roll.*

2. *Consider the effect surface conditions, such as ice, snow, and other precipitation, may have on known aircraft performance characteristics, and the influence these conditions may have on the pilot's ability to commence takeoff roll in a timely manner.*

5-8-5. DEPARTURES AND ARRIVALS ON PARALLEL OR NONINTERSECTING DIVERGING RUNWAYS

TERMINAL. Authorize simultaneous operations between an aircraft departing on a runway and an aircraft on final approach to another parallel or nonintersecting diverging runway if the departure course diverges immediately by at least 30 degrees from the missed approach course until separation is applied and provided one of the following conditions is met:

NOTE-
When one or both of the takeoff/landing surfaces is a helipad, consider the helicopter takeoff course as the runway centerline and the helipad center as the threshold.

a. When parallel runway thresholds are even, the runway centerlines are at least 2,500 feet apart. (See FIG 5-8-10 and FIG 5-8-11.)

FIG 5-8-10
Parallel Thresholds are Even

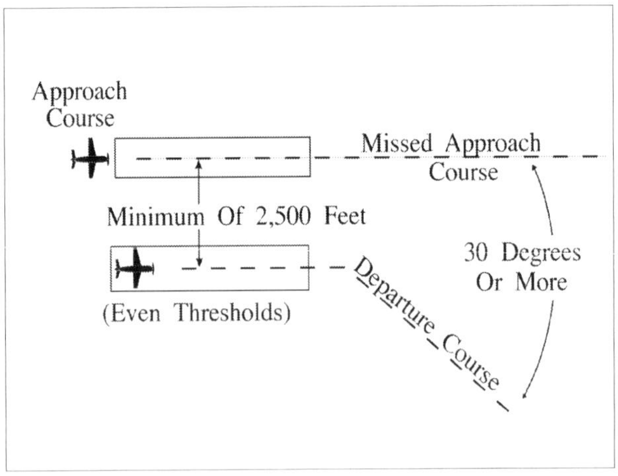

FIG 5-8-11
Parallel Thresholds are Even

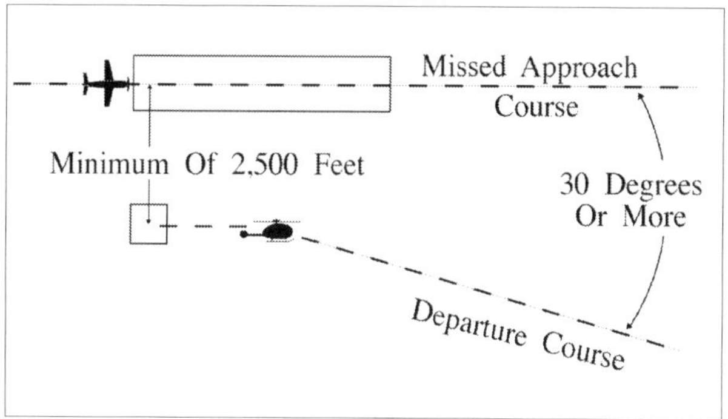

b. When parallel runway thresholds are staggered and:

1. The arriving aircraft is approaching the nearer runway: the centerlines are at least 1,000 feet apart and the landing thresholds are staggered at least 500 feet for each 100 feet less than 2,500 the centerlines are separated. (See FIG 5-8-12 and FIG 5-8-13.)

FIG 5-8-12
Parallel Thresholds are Staggered

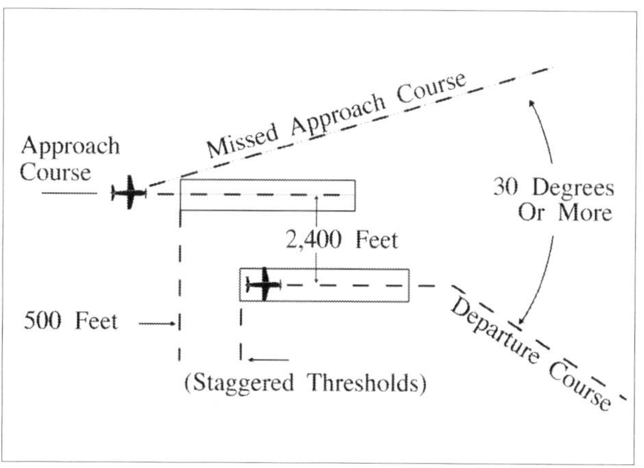

FIG 5-8-13
Parallel Thresholds are Staggered

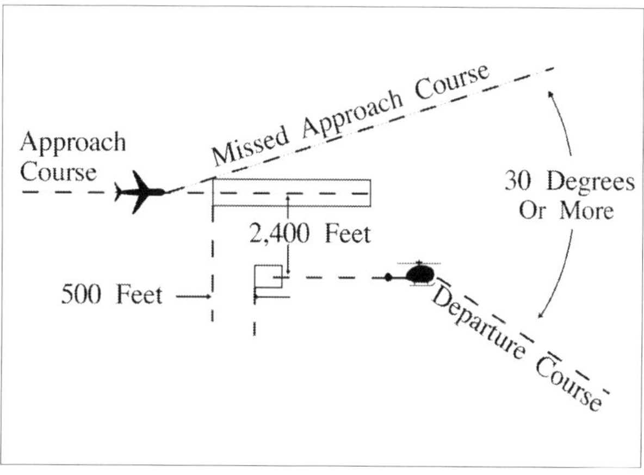

NOTE-
In the event of a missed approach by an aircraft requiring wake turbulence separation behind it, apply the procedures in

paragraph 3–9–6, Same Runway Separation and/or paragraph 3–9–8, Intersecting Runway/Intersecting Flight Path Operations to ensure that the larger aircraft does not overtake or cross in front of an aircraft departing from the adjacent parallel runway.

REFERENCE–
FAA Order JO 7110.65, Para 5–5–4, Minima, Subpara f.

INTERPRETATION–
7110.65, 5–8–5, Departure and Arrivals on Parallel or Nonintersecting Diverging Runways (6–14–2017)

2. The arriving aircraft is approaching the farther runway: the runway centerlines separation exceeds 2,500 feet by at least 100 feet for each 500 feet the landing thresholds are staggered. (See FIG 5–8–14.)

FIG 5–8–14
Parallel Thresholds are Staggered

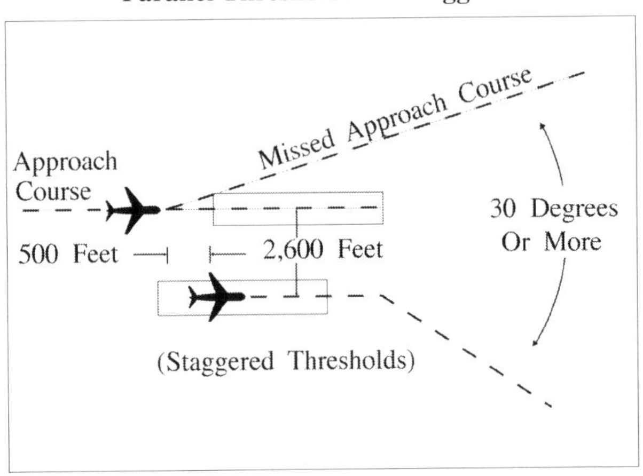

c. When nonintersecting runways diverge by 15 degrees or more and runway edges do not touch. (See FIG 5–8–15.)

FIG 5–8–15
Diverging Nonintersecting Runways

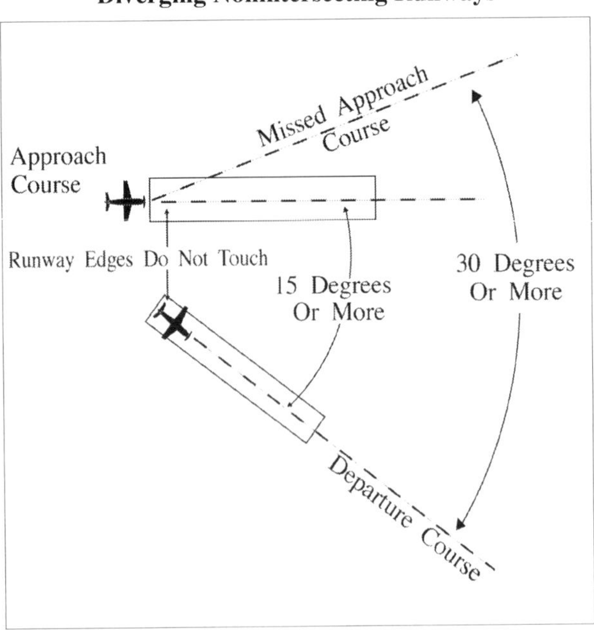

d. When the aircraft on takeoff is a helicopter, hold the helicopter until visual separation is possible or apply the separation criteria in subparagraphs a, b, or c.

REFERENCE–
FAA Order JO 7110.65, Para 5–8–4, Departure and Arrival.

Section 9. Radar Arrivals

5–9–1. VECTORS TO FINAL APPROACH COURSE

Except as provided in paragraph 7–4–2, Vectors for Visual Approach, vector arriving aircraft to intercept the final approach course:

a. At least 2 miles outside the approach gate unless one of the following exists:

1. When the reported ceiling is at least 500 feet above the MVA/MIA and the visibility is at least 3 miles (report may be a PIREP if no weather is reported for the airport), aircraft may be vectored to intercept the final approach course closer than 2 miles outside the approach gate but no closer than the approach gate.

2. If specifically requested by the pilot, aircraft may be vectored to intercept the final approach course inside the approach gate but no closer than the final approach fix.

EXCEPTION. Conditions 1 and 2 above do not apply to RNAV aircraft being vectored for a GPS or RNAV approach.

b. Provide a minimum of 1,000 feet vertical separation between aircraft on opposite base legs unless another form of approved separation is established during turn-on to final approach.

c. For a precision approach, at an altitude not above the glideslope/glidepath or below the minimum glideslope intercept altitude specified on the approach procedure chart.

d. For a nonprecision approach, at an altitude which will allow descent in accordance with the published procedure.

NOTE–
A pilot request for an "evaluation approach," or a "coupled approach," or use of a similar term, indicates the pilot desires the application of subparagraphs a and b.

e. *EN ROUTE.* The following provisions are required before an aircraft may be vectored to the final approach course:

1. The approach gate and a line (solid or broken), depicting the final approach course starting at or passing through the approach gate and extending away from the airport, be displayed on the radar scope; for a precision approach, the line length must extend at least the maximum range of the localizer; for a nonprecision approach, the line length must extend at least 10 NM outside the approach gate; and

2. The maximum range selected on the radar display is 150 NM; or

3. An adjacent radar display is set at 125 NM or less, configured for the approach in use, and is utilized for the vector to the final approach course.

4. If unable to comply with subparagraphs 1, 2, or 3 above, issue the clearance in accordance with paragraph 4–8–1, Approach Clearance.

REFERENCE–
FAA Order JO 7110.65, Para 4–8–1, Approach Clearance.
FAA Order JO 7110.65, Para 5–9–2, Final Approach Course Interception.

5–9–2. FINAL APPROACH COURSE INTERCEPTION

a. Assign headings that will permit final approach course interception on a track that does not exceed the interception angles specified in TBL 5–9–1.

TBL 5–9–1
Approach Course Interception Angle

Distance from interception point to approach gate	Maximum interception angle
Less than 2 miles or triple simultaneous approaches in use	20 degrees
2 miles or more	30 degrees (45 degrees for helicopters)

b. If deviations from the final approach course are observed after initial course interception, apply the following:

1. Outside the approach gate: apply procedures in accordance with subparagraph a, if necessary, vector the aircraft for another approach.

2. Inside the approach gate: inform the pilot of the aircraft's position and ask intentions.

PHRASEOLOGY–
(Ident) (distance) MILE(S) FROM THE AIRPORT, (distance) MILE(S) RIGHT/LEFT OF COURSE, SAY INTENTIONS.

NOTE–
The intent is to provide for a track course intercept angle judged by the controller to be no greater than specified by this procedure.

REFERENCE–
FAA Order JO 7110.65, Chapter 5, Section 9, Radar Arrivals, and Section 10, Radar Approaches– Terminal.

c. *EN ROUTE.* When using a radar scope range above 125 NM, the controller must solicit and receive a pilot report that the aircraft is established on the final approach course. If the pilot has not reported established by the final approach gate, inform the pilot of his/her observed position and ask intentions.

NOTE–
It may be difficult to accurately determine small distances when using very large range settings.

5–9–3. VECTORS ACROSS FINAL APPROACH COURSE

Inform the aircraft whenever a vector will take it across the final approach course and state the reason for such action.

NOTE–
In the event you are unable to so inform the aircraft, the pilot is not expected to turn inbound on the final approach course unless approach clearance has been issued.

PHRASEOLOGY–
EXPECT VECTORS ACROSS FINAL FOR (purpose).

EXAMPLE–
"EXPECT VECTORS ACROSS FINAL FOR SPACING."

REFERENCE–
FAA Order JO 7110.65, Para 5–9–2, Final Approach Course Interception.

5–9–4. ARRIVAL INSTRUCTIONS

Issue all of the following to an aircraft before it reaches the approach gate:

a. Position relative to a fix on the final approach course. If none is portrayed on the radar display or if none is prescribed in the procedure, issue position information relative to the navigation aid which provides final approach guidance or relative to the airport.

b. Vector to intercept the final approach course if required.

c. Approach clearance except when conducting a radar approach. Issue approach clearance only after the aircraft is:

1. Established on a segment of a published route or instrument approach procedure, or see FIG 5–9–1 Example 1.

FIG 5–9–1
Arrival Instructions

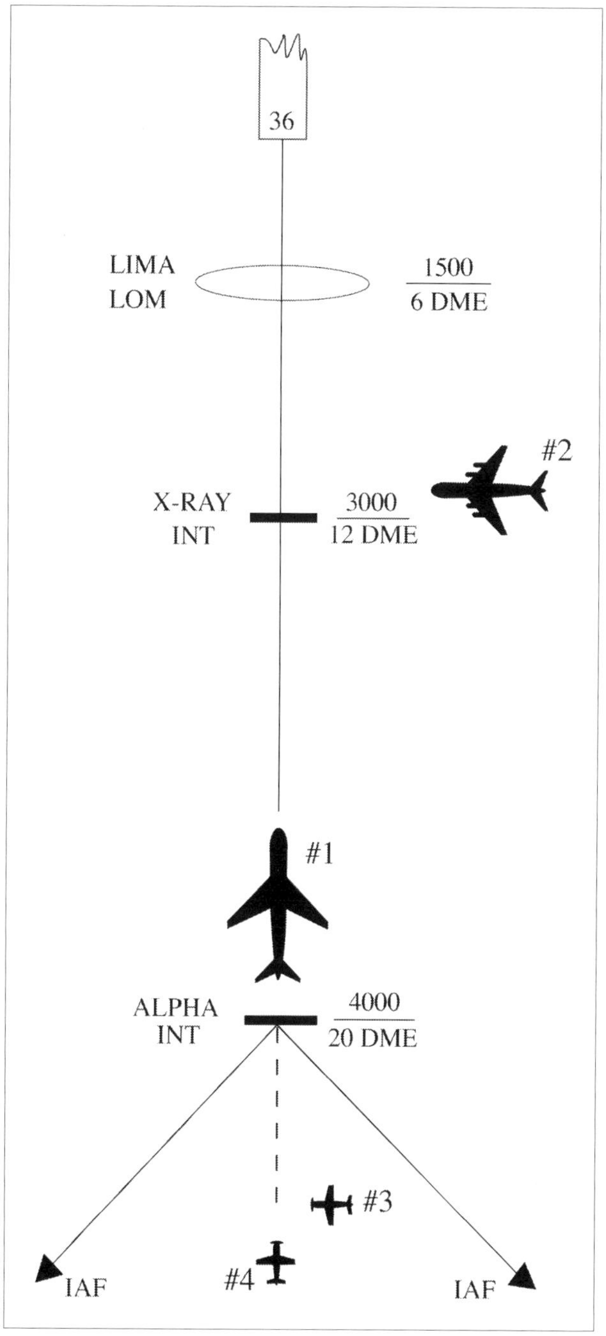

36
LIMA
LOM
1500
6 DME
#2
X-RAY
INT
3000
12 DME
#1
ALPHA
INT
4000
20 DME
#3
IAF
#4
IAF

EXAMPLE–
1. *Aircraft 1 was vectored to the final approach course but clearance was withheld. It is now at 4,000 feet and established on a segment of the instrument approach procedure. "Seven miles from X-RAY. Cleared I–L–S runway three six approach." (See FIG 5–9–1.)*

2. *Aircraft 2 is being vectored to a published segment of the final approach course, 4 miles from LIMA at 2,000 feet. The MVA for this area is 2,000 feet. "Four miles from LIMA. Turn right heading three four zero. Maintain two thousand until established on the localizer. Cleared I–L–S runway three six approach." (See FIG 5–9–1.)*

3. *Aircraft 3 is being vectored to intercept the final approach course beyond the approach segments, 5 miles from Alpha at 5,000 feet. the MVA for this area is 4,000 feet. "Five miles from Alpha. Turn right heading three three zero. Cross Alpha at or above four thousand. Cleared I−L−S runway three six approach." (See FIG 5−9−1.)*

4. *Aircraft 4 is established on the final approach course beyond the approach segments, 8 miles from Alpha at 6,000 feet. The MVA for this area is 4,000 feet. "Eight miles from Alpha. Cross Alpha at or above four thousand. Cleared I−L−S runway three six approach." (See FIG 5−9−1.)*

2. Assigned an altitude to maintain until the aircraft is established on a segment of a published route or instrument approach procedure.

FIG 5−9−2
Arrival Instructions

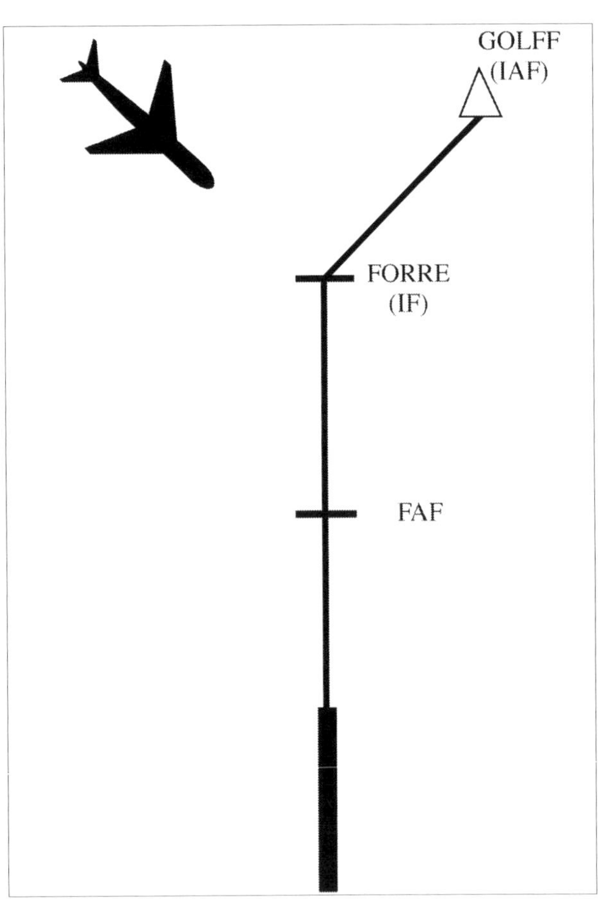

EXAMPLE−
The aircraft is being vectored to the intermediate fix FORRE for an RNAV approach. "Seven miles from FORRE, cleared direct FORRE, cross FORRE at or above four thousand, cleared RNAV runway one eight approach."

NOTE−
1. *The altitude assigned must assure IFR obstruction clearance from the point at which the approach clearance is issued until established on a segment of a published route or instrument approach procedure.*

2. *If the altitude assignment is VFR-on-top, it is conceivable that the pilot may elect to remain high until arrival over the final approach fix which may require the pilot to circle to descend so as to cross the final approach fix at an altitude that would permit landing.*

3. *Aircraft being vectored to the intermediate fix in FIG 5−9−2 must meet all the provisions described in subparagraph 4−8−1h2.*

d. Instructions to do one of the following:

NOTE–
The principal purpose of this paragraph is to ensure that frequency changes are made prior to passing the final approach fix. However, at times it will be desirable to retain an aircraft on the approach control frequency to provide a single-frequency approach or other radar services. When this occurs, it will be necessary to relay tower clearances or instructions to preclude changing frequencies prior to landing or approach termination.

1. Monitor local control frequency, reporting to the tower when over the approach fix.

2. Contact the tower on local control frequency.

REFERENCE–
FAA Order JO 7110.65, Para 4–8–8, Communications Release.

3. Contact the final controller on the appropriate frequency if radar service will be provided on final on a different frequency.

REFERENCE–
FAA Order JO 7110.65, Para 5–10–8, Final Controller Changeover.

4. When radar is used to establish the final approach fix, inform the pilot that after being advised that he/she is over the fix he/she is to contact the tower on local control frequency.

EXAMPLE–
"Three miles from final approach fix. Turn left heading zero one zero. Maintain two thousand until established on the localizer. Cleared I–L–S runway three six approach. I will advise when over the fix."

"Over final approach fix. Contact tower one one eight point one."

NOTE–
ARSR may be used for establishment of initial approach and intermediate approach fixes only. ASR must be used to establish the final approach fix.

REFERENCE–
FAA Order JO 7110.65, Para 5–9–2, Final Approach Course Interception.
FAA Order JO 7110.65, Para 5–9–7, Simultaneous Independent Approaches– Dual & Triple.

e. Where a Terminal Arrival Area (TAA) has been established to support RNAV approaches, inform the aircraft of its position relative to the appropriate IAF and issue the approach clearance. (See FIG 5–9–3.)

EXAMPLE–
1. *Aircraft 1: The aircraft is in the straight in area of the TAA. "Seven miles from CENTR, Cleared R–NAV Runway One Eight Approach."*

2. *Aircraft 2: The aircraft is in the left base area of the TAA. "One five miles from LEFTT, Cleared R-NAV Runway One Eight Approach."*

3. *Aircraft 3: The aircraft is in the right base area of the TAA. "Four miles from RIGHT, Cleared R-NAV Runway One Eight Approach."*

FIG 5-9-3
Basic "T" Design

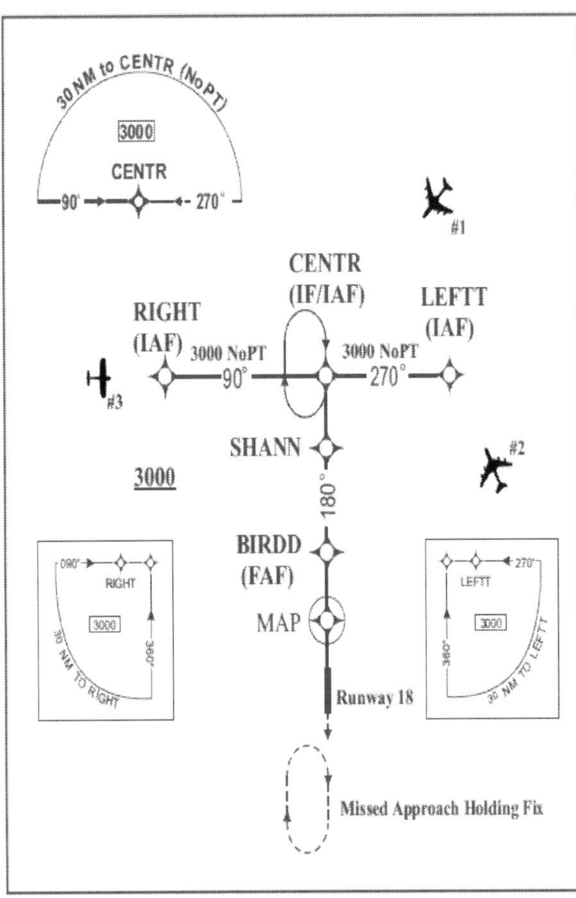

5-9-5. APPROACH SEPARATION RESPONSIBILITY

a. The radar controller performing the approach control function is responsible for separation of radar arrivals unless visual separation is provided by the tower, or a letter of agreement/facility directive authorizes otherwise. Radar final controllers ensure that established separation is maintained between aircraft under their control and other aircraft established on the same final approach course.

NOTE-
The radar controller may be a controller in an ARTCC, a terminal facility, or a tower controller when authorized to perform the approach control function in a terminal area.

REFERENCE-
FAA Order JO 7110.65, Para 2-1-19, Wake Turbulence.
FAA Order JO 7110.65, Section 5, Radar Separation, Para 5-5-1, Application.
FAA Order JO 7110.65, Para 7-2-1, Visual Separation.
FAA Order JO 7110.65, Para 5-5-4, Minima.
FAA Order JO 7210.3, Para 2-1-16, Authorization for Separation Services by Towers.

b. When timed approaches are being conducted, the radar controller must maintain the radar separation specified in paragraph 6-7-5, Interval Minima, until the aircraft is observed to have passed the final approach fix inbound (nonprecision approaches) or the OM or the fix used in lieu of the outer marker (precision approaches) and is within 5 miles of the runway on the final approach course or until visual separation can be provided by the tower.

REFERENCE-
FAA Order JO 7110.65, Para 5-4-6, Receiving Controller Handoff.
FAA Order JO 7110.65, Para 5-9-2, Final Approach Course Interception.

FAA Order JO 7110.65, Para 5–9–6, Parallel Dependent Approaches.
FAA Order JO 7110.65, Para 6–7–2, Approach Sequence.

INTERPRETATION–
7110.65, 5–9–5b, Approach Separation Responsibility and Chapter 6, Section 7, Timed Approaches (6–19–2015)

5–9–6. SIMULTANEOUS DEPENDENT APPROACHES

TERMINAL

a. Apply the following minimum separation when conducting simultaneous dependent approaches:

1. Provide a minimum of 1,000 feet vertical or a minimum of 3 miles radar separation between aircraft during turn on.

2. Provide a minimum of 1 mile radar separation diagonally between successive aircraft on adjacent final approach courses when runway centerlines are at least 2,500 feet but no more than 3,600 feet apart.

FIG 5–9–4
Simultaneous Dependent Approaches

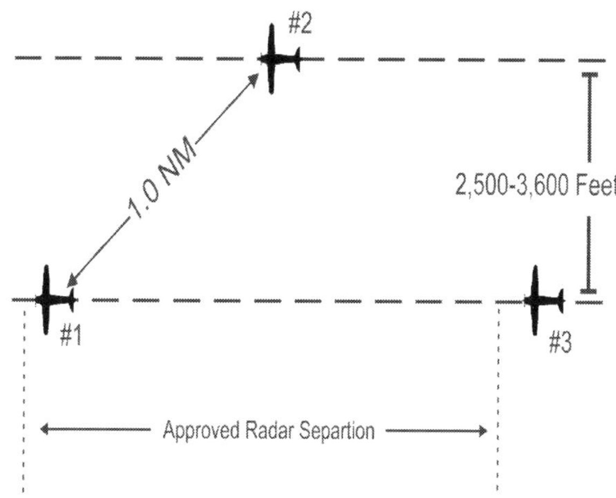

EXAMPLE–
In FIG 5–9–4, Aircraft 2 is 1.0 mile from Aircraft 1. Approved radar separation must be maintained between Aircraft 1 and Aircraft 3.

3. Provide a minimum of 1.5 miles radar separation diagonally between successive aircraft on adjacent final approach courses when runway centerlines are more than 3,600 feet but no more than 8,300 feet apart.

FIG 5-9-5
Simultaneous Dependent Approaches

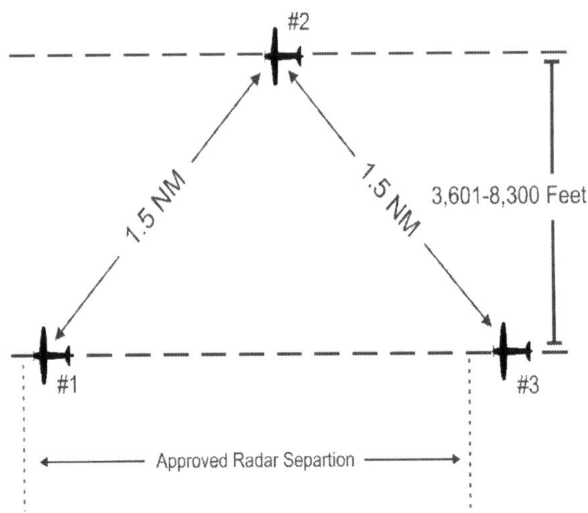

EXAMPLE-
In FIG 5-9-5, Aircraft 2 is 1.5 miles from Aircraft 1, and Aircraft 3 is 1.5 miles or more from Aircraft 2. Approved radar separation must be maintained between aircraft on the same final.

4. Provide a minimum of 2 miles radar separation diagonally between successive aircraft on adjacent final approach courses where runway centerlines are more than 8,300 feet but no more than 9,000 feet apart.

FIG 5-9-6
Simultaneous Dependent Approaches

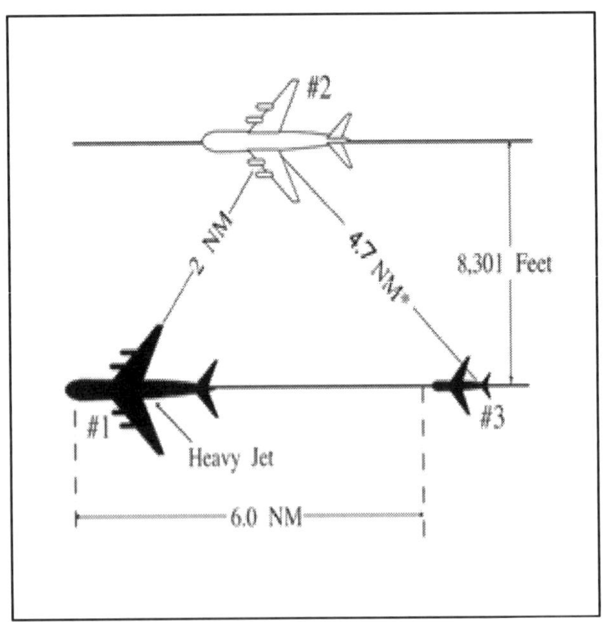

EXAMPLE-
*In FIG 5-9-6, Aircraft 2 is 2 miles from heavy Aircraft 1. Aircraft 3 is a small aircraft and is 6 miles from Aircraft 1. *The resultant separation between Aircraft 2 and 3 is at least 4.7 miles.*

5. Provide the minimum approved radar separation between aircraft on the same final approach course.

REFERENCE-
FAA Order JO 7110.65, Section 5, Radar Separation, Para 5-5-4, Minima.

b. The following conditions are required when applying the minimum radar separation on adjacent final approach courses allowed in subparagraph a:

NOTE–
1. *Established on RNP (EoR) operations are not authorized in conjunction with simultaneous dependent approaches.*
2. *Simultaneous dependent approaches may only be conducted where instrument approach charts specifically authorize simultaneous approaches.*

1. Apply this separation standard only after aircraft are established on the parallel final approach course.

2. Straight-in landings will be made.

3. Missed approach procedures do not conflict.

4. Aircraft are informed that approaches to both runways are in use. This information may be provided through the ATIS.

5. Approach control must have the interphone capability of communicating directly with the local controller at locations where separation responsibility has not been delegated to the tower.

NOTE–
The interphone capability is an integral part of this procedure when approach control has the sole separation responsibility.

REFERENCE–
FAA Order JO 7110.65, Para 5–9–5, Approach Separation Responsibility.
FAA Order JO 7210.3, Para 2–1–16, Authorization for Separation Services by Towers.

c. Consideration should be given to known factors that may in any way affect the safety of the instrument approach phase of flight, such as surface wind direction and velocity, wind shear alerts/reports, severe weather activity, etc. Closely monitor weather activity that could impact the final approach course. Weather conditions in the vicinity of the final approach course may dictate a change of approach in use.

REFERENCE–
FAA Order JO 7110.65, Para 5–9–2, Final Approach Course Interception.

5–9–7. SIMULTANEOUS INDEPENDENT APPROACHES– DUAL & TRIPLE

TERMINAL

a. Apply the following minimum separation when conducting simultaneous independent approaches:

1. Provide a minimum of 1,000 feet vertical or a minimum of 3 miles radar separation between aircraft :

(a) during turn–on to parallel final approach, or

(b) until aircraft are established on a published segment of an approach authorized for Established on RNP (EoR) operations.

NOTE–
Aircraft are considered EoR on an initial or intermediate segment of an instrument approach authorized for EoR operations after the approach clearance has been issued, read back by the pilot and the aircraft is observed on the published procedure (lateral and vertical path, and within any procedure specified speed restriction), and is conducting a simultaneous independent parallel approach with an authorized simultaneous instrument approach to a parallel runway.

REFERENCE–
FAA Order JO 7210.3, Para 10–4–6, Simultaneous Independent Approaches.
P/CG Term – Required Navigation Performance (RNP).
P/CG Term – Established on RNP Concept.

2. Dual parallel runway centerlines are at least 3,600 feet apart, or dual parallel runway centerlines are at least 3,000 feet apart with a 2.5° to 3.0° offset approach to either runway.

3. Triple parallel approaches may be conducted when:

(a) Parallel runway centerlines are at least 3,900 feet apart; or

(b) Parallel runway centerlines are at least 3,000 feet apart, a 2.5° to 3.0° offset approach to both outside runways; or

(c) Parallel runway centerlines are at least 3,000 feet apart, a single 2.5° to 3.0° offset approach to either outside runway while parallel approaches to the remaining two runways are separated by at least 3,900 feet.

(d) Parallel approaches to airports where the airport field elevation is more than 2,000 feet MSL require the use of the final monitor aid (FMA) system.

4. Provide the minimum applicable radar separation between aircraft on the same final approach course.

NOTE–
Except when conducting an EoR operation, no two aircraft will be assigned the same altitude during turn–on to final. All three aircraft will be assigned altitudes which differ by a minimum of 1,000 feet. Example: 3,000, 4,000, 5,000; 7,000, 8,000, 9,000.

HIGH UPDATE RATE SURVEILLANCE

b. At locations with high update rate surveillance capable of update rates of 1.2 seconds or faster, and where fusion display mode is utilized, simultaneous independent approaches may be conducted under the following conditions:

1. Dual parallel runway centerlines are at least 3,100 feet apart, or dual parallel runway centerlines are at least 2,500 feet apart with a 2.5° to 3.0° offset approach to either runway.

2. Triple parallel runway centerlines are at least 3,100 feet apart, or triple parallel runway centerlines are at least 2,500 feet apart with a 2.5° to 3.0° offset approach to both outside runways, or triple parallel runway centerlines are at least 2,500 feet apart, and a single 2.5° to 3.0° offset approach to either outside runway while parallel approaches to the remaining two runways are separated by at least 3,100 feet.

NOTE–
Aircraft without functioning ADS–B Out are restricted from utilizing these high update rate (HUR) procedures unless an alternative HUR surveillance source providing one–second or faster target report updating is utilized.

3. A surveillance update rate of at least 1.2 seconds is required for monitoring the no transgression zone (NTZ) when conducting simultaneous independent approaches to the runway centerline spacing (RCLS) provided in this paragraph.

NOTE–
1. *HUR procedures cannot be conducted if notified that a 1.2-second update rate is not being provided.*

2. *Where RCLS is ≤3400 feet, the normal operating zone (NOZ) is constant at 700 feet; and for RCLS ≥3400 feet, the no transgression zone (NTZ) remains constant at 2000 feet.*

4. Provide the minimum applicable radar separation between aircraft on the same final approach course.

c. A color digital display set to a 4 to 1 (4:1) aspect ratio (AR) with visual and aural alerts, such as the STARS final monitor aid (FMA), and a surveillance update rate at 4.8 seconds or faster must be used to monitor approaches where:

1. Dual parallel runway centerlines are at least 2,500 and less than 4,300 feet apart.

2. Triple parallel runway centerlines are at least 2,500 but less than 5,000 feet apart.

3. Triple parallel approaches to airports where the airport field elevation is more than 2,000 feet MSL require use of the FMA system.

NOTE–
At locations where the airfield elevation is 2000 feet or less, FMA is not required to monitor the NTZ for runway centerlines 4,300 feet or greater for dual runways, and 5,000 feet or greater for triple operations.

d. The following conditions must be met when conducting dual or triple simultaneous independent approaches:

NOTE–
Simultaneous independent approaches may only be conducted where instrument approach charts specifically authorize simultaneous approaches.

REFERENCE–
FAA Order JO 7210.3, Para 10-4-6, Simultaneous Approaches (Dependent/Independent).

1. Straight-in landings will be made.

2. All appropriate communication, navigation, and surveillance systems are operating normally.

3. Inform aircraft that simultaneous independent approaches are in use, or when runway centerlines are less than 4,300 feet, PRM approaches are in use, prior to aircraft departing an outer fix. This information may be provided through the ATIS.

REFERENCE–
P/CG Term – Precision Runway Monitor (PRM) System.

4. Clear the aircraft to descend to the appropriate glideslope/glidepath intercept altitude soon enough to provide a period of level flight to dissipate excess speed. Provide at least 1 mile of straight flight prior to the final approach course intercept.

NOTE–
Not applicable to approaches with RF legs.

5. An NTZ is established an equal distance between extended runway final approach courses and must be depicted on the monitor display. The primary responsibility for navigation on the final approach course rests with the pilot. Control instructions and information are issued only to ensure separation between aircraft and to prevent aircraft from penetrating the NTZ.

NOTE–
Where RCLS is $\leq$3400 feet, the normal operating zone (NOZ) is constant at 700 feet; and for RCLS $\geq$3400 feet, the no transgression zone (NTZ) remains constant at 2000 feet.

6. Monitor all approaches regardless of weather. Monitor local control frequency to receive any aircraft transmission. Issue control instructions as necessary to ensure aircraft do not enter the NTZ.

NOTE–
1. *Separate monitor controllers, each with transmit/receive and override capability on the local control frequency, must ensure aircraft do not penetrate the depicted NTZ. For PRM approaches, a transmit–only secondary "PRM frequency" is also used. Facility directives must define responsibility for providing the minimum applicable longitudinal separation between aircraft on the same final approach course.*

2. *The aircraft is considered the center of the primary radar return for that aircraft, or, if an FMA or other color final monitor aid is used, the center of the digitized target of that aircraft, for the purposes of ensuring an aircraft does not penetrate the NTZ. The provisions of paragraph 5–5–2, Target Separation, apply also.*

7. Communications transfer to the tower controller's frequency must be completed prior to losing 1,000 feet vertical or 3 miles radar separation between aircraft.

e. The following procedures must be used by the final monitor controllers:

1. For PRM approaches, provide position information to an aircraft that is left/right of the depicted final approach course centerline, and in your judgment is continuing on a track that may penetrate the NTZ.

PHRASEOLOGY–
(Aircraft call sign) I SHOW YOU (left/right) OF THE FINAL APPROACH COURSE.

2. Instruct the aircraft to return to the correct final approach course when aircraft are observed to overshoot the turn-on or to continue on a track which will penetrate the NTZ.

PHRASEOLOGY–
YOU HAVE CROSSED THE FINAL APPROACH COURSE. TURN (left/right) IMMEDIATELY AND RETURN TO THE FINAL APPROACH COURSE,

or

TURN (left/right) AND RETURN TO THE FINAL APPROACH COURSE.

3. Instruct aircraft on the adjacent final approach course to alter course to avoid the deviating aircraft when an aircraft is observed penetrating or in your judgment will penetrate the NTZ.

NOTE–
For PRM approaches, an instruction that may include a descent to avoid the deviating aircraft should only be used when there is no other reasonable option available to the controller. In such a case, the descent must not put the aircraft below the MVA.

PHRASEOLOGY–
TRAFFIC ALERT, (call sign), TURN (right/left) IMMEDIATELY HEADING (degrees), CLIMB/DESCEND AND MAINTAIN (altitude).

4. Terminate radar monitoring when one of the following occurs:

(a) Visual separation is applied.

(b) The aircraft reports the approach lights or runway in sight.

(c) The aircraft is 1 mile or less from the runway threshold, if procedurally required and contained in facility directives.

5. Do not inform the aircraft when radar monitoring is terminated.

f. Consideration should be given to known factors that may in any way affect the safety of the instrument approach phase of flight when simultaneous independent approaches, or PRM approaches, if applicable, are being conducted to parallel runways. Factors include, but are not limited to, wind direction/velocity, windshear alerts/reports, severe weather activity, etc. Closely monitor weather activity that could impact the final approach course. Weather conditions in the vicinity of the final approach course may dictate a change of approach in use.

REFERENCE–
FAA Order JO 7110.65, Para 5–1–9, Radar Service Termination.
FAA Order JO 7110.65, Para 5–9–2, Final Approach Course Interception.

5–9–8. SIMULTANEOUS INDEPENDENT CLOSE PARALLEL APPROACHES –PRECISION RUNWAY MONITOR (PRM) APPROACHES

TERMINAL

When conducting PRM approaches, apply all pertinent provisions of paragraph 5–9–7 and the following:

a. PRM approaches may only be conducted when charted in the approach title, and where instrument approach charts specifically authorize simultaneous approaches.

REFERENCE–
P/CG – Precision Runway Monitor (PRM) System.
P/CG – Simultaneous Close Parallel Approaches.
P/CG – PRM Approach.

b. PRM approaches must be assigned when conducting instrument approaches to dual and triple parallel runways with runway centerlines separated by less than 4,300 feet.

5–9–9. SIMULTANEOUS OFFSET INSTRUMENT APPROACHES (SOIA)

TERMINAL

a. Simultaneous offset instrument approaches (SOIA) may be conducted at FAA designated airports that have an authorization issued by the Director, Operational Policy and Implementation, AJT–2, in coordination with AFS with parallel runways that have centerlines separated by at least 750 feet and less than 3,000 feet with one final approach course offset by 2.5 to 3.0 degrees; and

1. Provide a minimum of 1,000 feet vertical or a minimum of 3 miles radar separation between aircraft during turn–on to final approaches.

NOTE–
Communications transfer to the tower controller's frequency must be completed prior to losing vertical separation between aircraft.

2. Provide the minimum applicable radar separation between aircraft on the same final approach course.

3. Provide the minimum applicable radar separation between the trailing offset aircraft of a leading SOIA pair and the lead straight-in aircraft in the subsequent SOIA pair when the parallel runways have centerlines separated by less than 2,500 feet.

REFERENCE–
FAA Order JO 7110.65, Para 5–5–4, Minima.

b. The following conditions are required when applying the minimum separation between lead straight-in and offset trailing approaches with glideslope courses or vertical navigation authorized in subparagraph a above:

1. Straight–in landings will be made.

2. All appropriate communication, navigation, and surveillance systems are operating normally.

3. Inform aircraft that PRM approaches are in use prior to aircraft departing an outer fix. This information may be provided through the ATIS.

4. Clear the aircraft to descend to the appropriate glideslope/glidepath intercept altitude soon enough to provide a period of level flight to dissipate excess speed. Provide at least 1 mile of straight flight prior to the final approach course intercept.

NOTE–
Not applicable to approaches with RF legs.

5. A no transgression zone (NTZ) is established an equal distance between extended runway final approach courses and must be depicted on the monitor display. The NTZ begins prior to the point where adjacent inbound aircraft first lose vertical separation and extends to a point coincident with the location of the offset approach MAP. The primary responsibility for navigation on the final approach course rests with the pilot. Control instructions and information are issued only to ensure separation between aircraft and to prevent aircraft from penetrating the NTZ.

NOTE–
Where RCLS is ≤3400 feet, the normal operating zone (NOZ) is constant at 700 feet; and for RCLS ≥3400 feet, the no transgression zone (NTZ) remains constant at 2000 feet.

6. Monitor all approaches regardless of weather. Monitor local control frequency to receive any aircraft transmission. Issue control instructions as necessary to ensure aircraft do not enter the NTZ.

7. Separate monitor controllers, each with transmit/receive and override capability on the local control frequency, must ensure aircraft do not penetrate the depicted NTZ. Facility directives must define the responsibility for providing the minimum applicable longitudinal separation between aircraft on the same final approach course and the minimum applicable longitudinal separation between the trailing offset aircraft of a leading SOIA pair and the lead straight in aircraft in the subsequent SOIA pair when the parallel runways have centerlines separated by less than 2,500 feet.

NOTE–
The aircraft is considered the center of the digitized target for that aircraft for the purposes of ensuring an aircraft does not penetrate the NTZ.

c. The following procedures must be used by the final monitor controllers:

1. Provide position information to an aircraft that is (left/right) of the depicted final approach course centerline, and in your judgment is continuing on a track that may penetrate the NTZ.

PHRASEOLOGY–
(Aircraft call sign) I SHOW YOU (left/right) OF THE FINAL APPROACH COURSE.

2. Instruct the aircraft to return immediately to the correct final approach course when aircraft are observed to overshoot the turn–on or continue on a track which will penetrate the NTZ.

PHRASEOLOGY–
YOU HAVE CROSSED THE FINAL APPROACH COURSE. TURN (left/right) IMMEDIATELY AND RETURN TO FINAL

APPROACH COURSE.

or

TURN (left/right) AND RETURN TO THE FINAL APPROACH COURSE.

3. Instruct aircraft on the adjacent final approach course to alter course to avoid the deviating aircraft when an aircraft is observed penetrating or in your judgment will penetrate the NTZ.

NOTE–
An instruction that may include a descent to avoid the deviating aircraft should only be used when there is no other reasonable option available to the controller. In such a case, the descent must not put the aircraft below the MVA.

PHRASEOLOGY–
TRAFFIC ALERT, (call sign), TURN (left/right) IMMEDIATELY HEADING (DEGREES), CLIMB AND MAINTAIN (altitude).

4. Terminate radar monitoring when one of the following occurs:

(a) The lead straight in aircraft passes the end of the NTZ nearest the runway threshold.

(b) The trailing offset aircraft passes the end of the NTZ nearest the runway threshold and has reported the lead straight in aircraft in sight.

(c) The aircraft begins the visual segment of the approach.

5. Do not inform the aircraft when radar monitoring is terminated.

d. Advise the pilot of the trailing offset aircraft of traffic on the adjacent lead straight–in approach course, if that traffic will be a factor in the visual segment of the approach. The provisions of paragraph 7–2–1, Visual Separation, subparagraph a1, concerning visual separation between aircraft being provided by the tower must not be applied to aircraft conducting SOIAs.

NOTE–
Once advised, the pilot is authorized to continue past the offset approach MAP if all of the following conditions are met: The pilot has the straight-in approach traffic in sight and expects the traffic to remain in sight; the pilot advises ATC that the traffic is in sight; and the pilot has the runway environment in sight. Otherwise, it is the pilot's responsibility to execute a missed approach at the offset approach MAP.

e. Ensure that the trailing offset aircraft is positioned to facilitate the flight crew's ability to see the lead straight in traffic from the nominal clear-of-clouds point to the offset approach MAP so that the flight crew can remain separated from that traffic visually from the offset approach MAP to the runway threshold.

NOTE–
After accepting a clearance for an offset PRM approach, pilots must remain on the offset approach course until passing the offset approach MAP prior to alignment with the runway centerline. Between the offset approach MAP and the runway threshold, the pilot of the offset approach aircraft assumes visual separation responsibility from the aircraft on the straight-in approach, which means maneuvering the aircraft as necessary to avoid the straight in approach traffic until landing, and providing wake turbulence avoidance, if necessary.

f. In the visual segment between the offset approach MAP and the runway threshold, if the pilot of the trailing offset aircraft loses visual contact with the lead straight-in traffic, the pilot must advise ATC as soon as practical and follow the published missed approach procedure. If necessary, issue alternate missed approach instructions.

g. Wake turbulence requirements between aircraft on adjacent final approach courses inside the offset approach MAP are as follows (standard in-trail wake separation must be applied between aircraft on the same approach course):

1. When runways are at least 2,500 feet apart, there are no wake turbulence requirements between aircraft on adjacent final approach courses.

2. For runways less than 2,500 feet apart, whenever the ceiling is greater than or equal to 500 feet above the MVA, wake vortex spacing between aircraft on adjacent final approach courses need not be applied.

3. For runways less than 2,500 feet apart, whenever the ceiling is less than 500 feet above the MVA, wake vortex spacing between aircraft on adjacent final approach courses, as described in paragraph 5–5–4, Minima, must be applied unless acceptable mitigating techniques and operational procedures have been documented and verified by an AFS safety assessment and authorized by the Director, Operational Policy and Implementation, AJT–2. The wake turbulence mitigation techniques employed will be based on each airport's specific runway geometry and meteorological conditions and implemented through local facility directives.

4. Issue all applicable wake turbulence advisories.

REFERENCE–
FAA Order JO 8260.49, Para 13.0, Wake Turbulence Requirements.
FAA Order JO 7210.3, Para 10–4–6, Simultaneous Independent Approaches.
FAA Order JO 7110.65, Para 2–1–20, Wake Turbulence Cautionary Advisories.
FAA Order JO 7110.65, Para 5–5–4, Minima.

h. Consideration should be given to known factors that may in any way affect the safety of the instrument approach phase of flight when conducting SOIA to parallel runways. Factors include but are not limited to wind direction/velocity, wind–shear alerts/reports, severe weather activity, etc. Closely monitor weather activity that could impact the final approach course. Weather conditions in the vicinity of the final approach course may dictate a change of the approach in use.

REFERENCE–
FAA Order JO 7110.65, Para 5–1–9, Radar Service Termination.
FAA Order JO 7110.65, Para 5–9–2, Final Approach Course Interception.

5–9–10. SIMULTANEOUS INDEPENDENT APPROACHES TO WIDELY-SPACED PARALLEL RUNWAYS WITHOUT FINAL MONITORS

TERMINAL

a. Simultaneous independent approaches to widely-spaced parallel runways may only be conducted where instrument approach charts specifically authorize simultaneous approaches.

b. Apply the following minimum separation when conducting simultaneous independent approaches to runway centerlines that are separated by more than 9,000 feet with a field elevation at or below 5,000 feet MSL, or 9,200 feet between runway centerlines with a field elevation above 5,000 feet MSL:

1. Provide a minimum of 1,000 feet vertical or a minimum of 3 miles radar separation between aircraft:

(a) during turn-on to parallel final approach, or

(b) conducting EoR operations, until aircraft are established on a published segment of an approach authorized for EoR operations.

NOTE–
Aircraft are considered EoR on an initial or intermediate segment of an instrument approach authorized for EoR operations after the approach clearance has been issued, read back by the pilot and the aircraft is observed on the published procedure (lateral and vertical path, and within any procedure specified speed restriction), and is conducting a simultaneous independent parallel approach with an authorized simultaneous instrument approach to a parallel runway.

REFERENCE–
FAA Order JO 7210.3, Para 10-4-7, Simultaneous Widely-Spaced Parallel Operations.
P/CG Term – Required Navigation Performance (RNP).
P/CG Term – Established on RNP Concept.

2. Provide the minimum applicable radar separation between aircraft on the same final approach course.

REFERENCE–
FAA Order JO 7110.65, Para 5–5–4, Minima.

c. The following conditions are required when applying the minimum separation on widely–spaced parallel courses allowed in subparagraph b:

1. Straight-in landings will be made.

2. The approach system, radar, and appropriate frequencies are operating normally.

3. Inform aircraft that simultaneous approaches are in use prior to aircraft departing an outer fix. This information may be provided through the ATIS.

4. Clear an aircraft to descend to the appropriate glideslope/glidepath intercept altitude soon enough to provide a period of level flight to dissipate excess speed. Provide at least 1 mile of straight flight prior to the final approach course intercept.

NOTE–
Not applicable to approaches with RF legs.

5. Separate final and local controllers are required for each final. Aircraft on the final must be on the appropriate final controller frequency for that runway.

6. Transfer of communication to the tower controller's frequency must be specified in a facility directive and/or Letter of Agreement.

d. The following procedures must be used by the final approach controllers:

NOTE–
There is no requirement for establishment of a NTZ.

1. Instruct the aircraft to return to the correct final approach course when that aircraft is observed to overshoot the turn-on or continue on a track which deviates from the final approach course in the direction of the adjacent approach course.

PHRASEOLOGY–
YOU HAVE CROSSED THE FINAL APPROACH COURSE. TURN (left/right) IMMEDIATELY AND RETURN TO THE FINAL APPROACH COURSE,

or

TURN (left/right) AND RETURN TO THE FINAL APPROACH COURSE.

2. Instruct aircraft on adjacent final approach course to alter course to avoid the deviating aircraft when an aircraft is observed, or in the controller's judgment, has deviated from the final approach course in the direction of the adjacent approach course.

PHRASEOLOGY–
TRAFFIC ALERT, (call sign), TURN (left/right) IMMEDIATELY HEADING (degrees), CLIMB AND MAINTAIN (altitude)

e. Consideration should be given to known factors that may in any way affect the safety of the instrument approach phase of flight when simultaneous approaches are being conducted to parallel runways. Factors include, but are not limited to, wind direction/velocity, wind-shear alerts/reports, severe weather activity, etc. Closely monitor weather activity that could impact the final approach course. Weather conditions in the vicinity of the final approach course may dictate a change of approach in use.

REFERENCE–
FAA Order JO 7110.65, Para 5–9–2, Final Approach Course Interception.

5–9–11. TRANSITIONAL PROCEDURE

When aircraft are conducting simultaneous dependent, independent, or any approaches allowing for reduced separation, and one of the aircraft executes a go-around or has its approach clearance terminated and prior to losing the approved reduced separation, control instructions must be expeditiously issued to increase separation between the applicable aircraft. These control instructions must establish approved separation (for example, altitude and/or lateral separation via divergence). In addition, wake turbulence cautionary advisories must be issued in accordance with paragraph 2–1–20, Wake Turbulence Cautionary Advisories.

Section 10. Radar Approaches− Terminal

5−10−1. APPLICATION

a. Provide radar approaches in accordance with standard or special instrument approach procedures.

b. A radar approach may be given to any aircraft upon request and may be offered to aircraft in distress regardless of weather conditions or to expedite traffic.

NOTE−
Acceptance of a radar approach by a pilot does not waive the prescribed weather minima for the airport or for the particular aircraft operator concerned. The pilot is responsible for determining if the approach and landing are authorized under the existing weather minima.

REFERENCE−
FAA Order JO 7110.65, Para 5−9−2, Final Approach Course Interception.
FAA Order JO 7110.65, Para 5−12−10, Elevation Failure.
FAA Order JO 7110.65, Para 4−8−1a, Approach Clearance.
P/CG Term − EFVS.

5−10−2. APPROACH INFORMATION

a. Issue the following information to an aircraft that will conduct a radar approach. Current approach information contained in the ATIS broadcast may be omitted if the pilot states the appropriate ATIS broadcast code. All items listed below, except for subparagraph 3 may be omitted after the first approach if repeated approaches are made and no change has occurred. Transmissions with aircraft in this phase of the approach should occur approximately every minute.

REFERENCE−
FAA Order JO 7110.65, Para 4−7−10, Approach Information.

1. Altimeter setting.

2. If available, ceiling and visibility if the ceiling at the airport of intended landing is reported below 1,000 feet or below the highest circling minimum, whichever is greater, or if the visibility is less than 3 miles. Advise pilots when weather information is available via the Automated Weather Observing System (AWOS)/Automated Surface Observing System (ASOS) and, if requested, issue the appropriate frequency.

NOTE−
Automated weather observing systems may be set to provide one minute updates. This one minute data may be useful to the pilot for possible weather trends. Controllers provide service based solely on official weather, i.e., hourly and special observations.

3. Issue any known changes classified as special weather observations as soon as possible. Special weather observations need not be issued after they are included in the ATIS broadcast and the pilot states the appropriate ATIS broadcast code.

4. Pertinent information on known airport conditions if they are considered necessary to the safe operation of the aircraft concerned.

5. Lost communication procedures as specified in paragraph 5−10−4, Lost Communications.

b. Before starting final approach:

NOTE−
1. *ASR approach procedures may be prescribed for specific runways, for an airport/heliport, and for helicopters only to a "point-in-space," i.e., a MAP from which a helicopter must be able to proceed to the landing area by visual reference to a prescribed surface route.*

2. *Occasionally, helicopter PAR approaches are available to runways where conventional PAR approaches have been established. In those instances where the two PAR approaches serve the same runway, the helicopter approach will have a steeper glide slope and a lower decision height. By the controllers designating the approach to be flown, the helicopter pilot understands which of the two approaches he/she has been vectored for and which set of minima apply.*

1. Inform the aircraft of the type of approach, runway, airport, heliport, or other point, as appropriate, to which the approach will be made. Specify the airport name when the approach is to a secondary airport.

PHRASEOLOGY–
THIS WILL BE A P–A–R/SURVEILLANCE APPROACH TO:

RUNWAY (runway number),

or

(airport name) AIRPORT, RUNWAY (runway number),

or

(airport name) AIRPORT/HELIPORT.

THIS WILL BE A COPTER P–A–R APPROACH TO:

RUNWAY (runway number),

or

(airport name) AIRPORT, RUNWAY (runway number),

or

(airport name) AIRPORT/HELIPORT.

2. For surveillance approaches, specify the location of the MAP in relation to the runway/airport/heliport.

PHRASEOLOGY–
MISSED APPROACH POINT IS (distance) MILE(S) FROM RUNWAY/AIRPORT/HELIPORT,

or for a point-in-space approach,

A MISSED APPROACH POINT (distance) MILE(S) (direction from landing area) OF (airport name) AIRPORT/HELIPORT.

EXAMPLE–
Helicopter point-in-space approach:

"Army copter Zulu Two, this will be a surveillance approach to a missed approach point, three point five miles south of Creedon Heliport."

REFERENCE–
FAA Order JO 7110.65, Para 5–12–10, Elevation Failure.

c. Inform an aircraft making an approach to an airport not served by a tower that no traffic or landing runway information is available for that airport.

PHRASEOLOGY–
NO TRAFFIC OR LANDING RUNWAY INFORMATION AVAILABLE FOR THE AIRPORT.

REFERENCE–
FAA Order JO 7110.65, Para 2–7–2, Altimeter Setting Issuance Below Lowest Usable FL.
FAA Order JO 7110.65, Para 5–9–2, Final Approach Course Interception.

5–10–3. NO-GYRO APPROACH

When an aircraft will make a no-gyro surveillance or a PAR approach:

a. Before issuing a vector, inform the aircraft of the type of approach.

PHRASEOLOGY–
THIS WILL BE A NO-GYRO SURVEILLANCE/P–A–R APPROACH.

b. Instruct the aircraft when to start and stop turn.

PHRASEOLOGY–
TURN LEFT/RIGHT. STOP TURN.

c. After turn on to final approach has been made and prior to the aircraft reaching the approach gate, instruct the aircraft to make half-standard rate turns.

PHRASEOLOGY–
MAKE HALF-STANDARD RATE TURNS.

REFERENCE–
FAA Order JO 7110.65, Para 5–9–2, Final Approach Course Interception.
FAA Order JO 7110.65, Para 5–12–10, Elevation Failure.

5–10–4. LOST COMMUNICATIONS

When weather reports indicate that an aircraft will likely encounter IFR weather conditions during the approach, take the following action as soon as possible after establishing radar identification and radio communications (may be omitted after the first approach when successive approaches are made and the instructions remain the same):

NOTE–
Air traffic control facilities at U.S. Army and U.S. Air Force installations are not required to transmit lost communications instructions to military aircraft. All military facilities will issue specific lost communications instructions to civil aircraft when required.

a. If lost communications instructions will require the aircraft to fly on an unpublished route, issue an appropriate altitude to the pilot. If the lost communications instructions are the same for both pattern and final, the pattern/vector controller must issue both. Advise the pilot that if radio communications are lost for a specified time interval (not more than 1 minute) on vector to final approach, 15 seconds on a surveillance final approach, or 5 seconds on a PAR final approach to:

1. Attempt contact on a secondary or a tower frequency.

2. Proceed in accordance with visual flight rules if possible.

3. Proceed with an approved nonradar approach, or execute the specific lost communications procedure for the radar approach being used.

NOTE–
The approved procedures are those published on the FAA Forms 8260 or applicable military document.

PHRASEOLOGY–
IF NO TRANSMISSIONS ARE RECEIVED FOR (time interval) IN THE PATTERN OR FIVE/FIFTEEN SECONDS ON FINAL APPROACH, ATTEMPT CONTACT ON (frequency), AND

if the possibility exists,

PROCEED VFR. IF UNABLE:

if approved,

PROCEED WITH (nonradar approach), MAINTAIN (altitude) UNTIL ESTABLISHED ON/OVER FIX/NAVAID/ APPROACH PROCEDURE,

or

(alternative instructions).

PHRASEOLOGY–
USN. *For ACLS operations using Mode I, IA, and II,*

IF NO TRANSMISSIONS ARE RECEIVED FOR FIVE SECONDS AFTER LOSS OF DATA LINK, ATTEMPT CONTACT ON (frequency), AND

if the possibility exists,

PROCEED VFR. IF UNABLE:

if approved,

PROCEED WITH (nonradar approach), MAINTAIN (altitude) UNTIL ESTABLISHED ON/OVER FIX/NAVAID/ APPROACH PROCEDURE,

or

(alternative instructions).

b. If the final approach lost communications instructions are changed, differ from those for the pattern, or are not issued by the pattern controller, they must be issued by the final controller.

c. If the pilot states that he/she cannot accept a lost communications procedure due to weather conditions or other reasons, request the pilot's intention.

NOTE–
The pilot is responsible for determining the adequacy of lost communications procedures with respect to aircraft performance, equipment capability, or reported weather.

REFERENCE–
FAA Order JO 7110.65, Para 5–9–2, Final Approach Course Interception.
FAA Order JO 7110.65, Para 5–10–2, Approach Information.
FAA Order JO 7110.65, Para 5–12–10, Elevation Failure.

5–10–5. RADAR CONTACT LOST

If radar contact is lost during an approach and the aircraft has not started final approach, clear the aircraft to an appropriate NAVAID/fix for an instrument approach.

REFERENCE–
FAA Order JO 7110.65, Para 5–9–2, Final Approach Course Interception.
FAA Order JO 7110.65, Para 5–10–14, Final Approach Abnormalities.
FAA Order JO 7110.65, Para 5–12–10, Elevation Failure.

5–10–6. LANDING CHECK

USA/USN. Advise the pilot to perform landing check while the aircraft is on downwind leg and in time to complete it before turning base leg. If an incomplete pattern is used, issue this before handoff to the final controller for a PAR approach, or before starting descent on final approach for surveillance approach.

PHRASEOLOGY–
PERFORM LANDING CHECK.

REFERENCE–
FAA Order JO 7110.65, Para 5–9–2, Final Approach Course Interception.
FAA Order JO 7110.65, Para 5–12–10, Elevation Failure.

5–10–7. POSITION INFORMATION

Inform the aircraft of its position at least once before starting final approach.

PHRASEOLOGY–
(Number) MILES (direction) OF (airport name) AIRPORT,

or

(number) MILES (direction) OF (airport name) AIRPORT ON DOWNWIND/BASE LEG.

REFERENCE–
FAA Order JO 7110.65, Para 5–9–2, Final Approach Course Interception.
FAA Order JO 7110.65, Para 5–12–10, Elevation Failure.

5–10–8. FINAL CONTROLLER CHANGEOVER

When instructing the aircraft to change frequency for final approach guidance, include the name of the facility.

PHRASEOLOGY–
CONTACT (name of facility) FINAL CONTROLLER ON (frequency).

REFERENCE–
FAA Order JO 7110.65, Para 2–1–17, Radio Communications.
FAA Order JO 7110.65, Para 5–9–2, Final Approach Course Interception.
FAA Order JO 7110.65, Para 5–9–4, Arrival Instructions.
FAA Order JO 7110.65, Para 5–12–10, Elevation Failure.

5–10–9. COMMUNICATIONS CHECK

On initial contact with the final controller, ask the aircraft for a communication check.

PHRASEOLOGY–
(Aircraft call sign), (name of facility) FINAL CONTROLLER. HOW DO YOU HEAR ME?

REFERENCE–
FAA Order JO 7110.65, Para 5–9–2, Final Approach Course Interception.
FAA Order JO 7110.65, Para 5–12–10, Elevation Failure.

5–10–10. TRANSMISSION ACKNOWLEDGMENT

After contact has been established with the final controller and while on the final approach course, instruct the aircraft not to acknowledge further transmissions.

PHRASEOLOGY–
DO NOT ACKNOWLEDGE FURTHER TRANSMISSIONS.

REFERENCE–
FAA Order JO 7110.65, Para 5–9–2, Final Approach Course Interception.
FAA Order JO 7110.65, Para 5–12–10, Elevation Failure.

5–10–11. MISSED APPROACH

Before an aircraft starts final descent for a full stop landing and weather reports indicate that any portion of the final approach will be conducted in IFR conditions, issue a specific missed approach procedure approved for the radar approach being conducted.

PHRASEOLOGY–
YOUR MISSED APPROACH PROCEDURE IS (missed approach procedure).

NOTE–
1. *The specific missed approach procedure is published on FAA Form 8260–4 or applicable military document.*

2. *USAF. At locations where missed approach instructions are published in base flying regulations, controllers need not issue missed approach instructions to locally assigned/attached aircraft.*

REFERENCE–
FAA Order JO 7110.65, Para 5–9–2, Final Approach Course Interception.
FAA Order JO 7110.65, Para 5–12–10, Elevation Failure.

5–10–12. LOW APPROACH AND TOUCH-AND-GO

Before an aircraft which plans to execute a low approach or touch-and-go begins final descent, issue appropriate departure instructions to be followed upon completion of the approach. Climb-out instructions must include a specific heading and altitude except when the aircraft will maintain VFR and contact the tower.

PHRASEOLOGY–
AFTER COMPLETING LOW APPROACH/TOUCH AND GO:

CLIMB AND MAINTAIN (altitude).

TURN (right or left) HEADING (degrees)/FLY RUNWAY HEADING,

or

MAINTAIN VFR, CONTACT TOWER,

or

(other instructions as appropriate).

NOTE–
This may be omitted after the first approach if instructions remain the same.

REFERENCE–
FAA Order JO 7110.65, Para 5–9–2, Final Approach Course Interception.
FAA Order JO 7110.65, Para 5–12–10, Elevation Failure.

5–10–13. TOWER CLEARANCE

a. When an aircraft is on final approach to an airport served by a tower, obtain a clearance to land, touch-and-go, or make low approach. Issue the clearance and the surface wind to the aircraft.

b. If the clearance is not obtained or is canceled, inform the aircraft and issue alternative instructions.

PHRASEOLOGY–
TOWER CLEARANCE CANCELED/NOT RECEIVED (alternative instructions).

REFERENCE–
FAA Order JO 7110.65, Para 5–9–2, Final Approach Course Interception.
FAA Order JO 7110.65, Para 5–12–10, Elevation Failure.

5–10–14. FINAL APPROACH ABNORMALITIES

Instruct the aircraft if runway environment not in sight, execute a missed approach if previously given; or climb to or maintain a specified altitude and fly a specified course whenever the completion of a safe approach is questionable because one or more of the following conditions exists. The conditions in subparagraphs a, b, and c do not apply after the aircraft passes decision height on a PAR approach.

EXAMPLE–
Typical reasons for issuing missed approach instructions:
"Radar contact lost."
"Too high/low for safe approach."
"Too far right/left for safe approach."

REFERENCE–
FAA Order JO 7110.65, Para 5–12–7, Position Advisories.

a. Safety limits are exceeded or radical target deviations are observed.

b. Position or identification of the aircraft is in doubt.

c. Radar contact is lost or a malfunctioning radar is suspected.

PHRASEOLOGY–
(Reason) IF RUNWAY/APPROACH LIGHTS/RUNWAY LIGHTS NOT IN SIGHT, EXECUTE MISSED APPROACH/(alternative instructions).

NOTE–
If the pilot requests, approval may be granted to proceed with the approach via ILS or another navigational aid/approach aid.

REFERENCE–
FAA Order JO 7110.65, Para 5–10–5, Radar Contact Lost.

d. Airport conditions or traffic preclude approach completion.

PHRASEOLOGY–
EXECUTE MISSED APPROACH/(alternative instructions), (reason).

REFERENCE–
FAA Order JO 7110.65, Para 5–9–2, Final Approach Course Interception.
FAA Order JO 7110.65, Para 5–12–10, Elevation Failure.

5–10–15. MILITARY SINGLE FREQUENCY APPROACHES

a. Utilize single frequency approach procedures as contained in a letter of agreement.

b. Do not require a frequency change from aircraft on a single frequency approach after the approach has begun unless:

1. Landing or low approach has been completed.

2. The aircraft is in visual flight rules (VFR) conditions during daylight hours.

3. The pilot requests the frequency change.

4. An emergency situation exists.

5. The aircraft is cleared for a visual approach.

6. The pilot cancels instrument flight rules (IFR).

c. Accomplish the following steps to complete communications transfer on single frequency approaches after completion of a handoff:

1. Transferring controller: Position transmitter selectors to preclude further transmissions on the special use frequencies.

2. Receiving controller: Position transmitter and receiver selectors to enable communications on the special use frequencies.

3. Do not require or expect the flight to check on frequency unless an actual frequency change is transmitted to the pilot.

Section 11. Surveillance Approaches– Terminal

5–11–1. ALTITUDE INFORMATION

Provide recommended altitudes on final approach if the pilot requests. If recommended altitudes are requested, inform the pilot that recommended altitudes which are at or above the published MDA will be given for each mile on final.

REFERENCE–
FAA Order JO 7210.3, Para 10–5–7, Recommended Altitudes for Surveillance Approaches.
FAA Order JO 7110.65, Para 5–11–5, Final Approach Guidance.

PHRASEOLOGY–
RECOMMENDED ALTITUDES WILL BE PROVIDED FOR EACH MILE ON FINAL TO MINIMUM DESCENT ALTITUDE/CIRCLING MINIMUM DESCENT ALTITUDE.

5–11–2. VISUAL REFERENCE REPORT

Aircraft may be requested to report the runway, approach/runway lights, or airport in sight. Helicopters making a "point-in-space" approach may be requested to report when able to proceed to the landing area by visual reference to a prescribed surface route.

PHRASEOLOGY–
REPORT (runway, approach/runway lights or airport) IN SIGHT.

REPORT WHEN ABLE TO PROCEED VISUALLY TO AIRPORT/HELIPORT.

5–11–3. DESCENT NOTIFICATION

a. Issue advance notice of where descent will begin and issue the straight-in MDA prior to issuing final descent for the approaches.

NOTE–
The point at which descent to the minimum descent altitude is authorized is the final approach fix unless an altitude limiting stepdown-fix is prescribed.

b. When it is determined that the surveillance approach will terminate in a circle to land maneuver, request the aircraft approach category from the pilot. After receiving the aircraft approach category, provide him/her with the applicable circling MDA prior to issuing final descent for the approach.

NOTE–
Pilots are normally expected to furnish the aircraft approach category to the controller when it is determined that the surveillance approach will terminate in a circle to land maneuver. If this information is not voluntarily given, solicit the aircraft approach category from the pilot, and then issue him/her the applicable circling MDA.

PHRASEOLOGY–
PREPARE TO DESCEND IN (number) MILE(S).

for straight-in approaches,

MINIMUM DESCENT ALTITUDE (altitude).

for circling approaches,

REQUEST YOUR AIRCRAFT APPROACH CATEGORY. (Upon receipt of aircraft approach category), PUBLISHED CIRCLING MINIMUM DESCENT ALTITUDE (altitude).

5–11–4. DESCENT INSTRUCTIONS

When an aircraft reaches the descent point, issue one of the following as appropriate:

REFERENCE–
FAA Order JO 7110.65, Para 5–12–10, Elevation Failure.

a. Unless a descent restriction exists, advise the aircraft to descend to the MDA.

PHRASEOLOGY–
(Number) MILES FROM RUNWAY/AIRPORT/HELIPORT. DESCEND TO YOUR MINIMUM DESCENT ALTITUDE.

b. When a descent restriction exists, specify the prescribed restriction altitude. When the aircraft has passed the altitude limiting point, advise to continue descent to MDA.

PHRASEOLOGY–
(Number) MILES FROM RUNWAY/AIRPORT/HELIPORT. DESCEND AND MAINTAIN (restriction altitude).

DESCEND TO YOUR MINIMUM DESCENT ALTITUDE.

5–11–5. FINAL APPROACH GUIDANCE

a. Issue course guidance, inform the aircraft when it is on course, and frequently inform the aircraft of any deviation from course. Transmissions with aircraft on surveillance final approach should occur approximately every 15 seconds.

PHRASEOLOGY–
HEADING (heading),

ON COURSE,

or

SLIGHTLY/WELL LEFT/RIGHT OF COURSE.

NOTE–
Controllers should not key the radio transmitter continuously during radar approaches to preclude a lengthy communications block. The decision on how often transmitters are unkeyed is the controller's prerogative.

b. Issue trend information, as required, to indicate target position with respect to the extended runway centerline and to describe the target movement as appropriate corrections are issued. Trend information may be modified by the terms "RAPIDLY" and "SLOWLY" as appropriate.

EXAMPLE–
"Going left/right of course."
"Left/right of course and holding/correcting."

c. Inform the aircraft of its distance from the runway, airport/heliport, or MAP, as appropriate, each mile on final.

PHRASEOLOGY–
(Number) MILE(S) FROM RUNWAY/AIRPORT/HELIPORT OR MISSED APPROACH POINT.

d. Recommended altitudes must be furnished, if requested, in accordance with paragraph 5–11–1, Altitude Information.

PHRASEOLOGY–
If requested,

ALTITUDE SHOULD BE (altitude).

5–11–6. APPROACH GUIDANCE TERMINATION

a. Discontinue surveillance approach guidance when:

1. Requested by the pilot.

2. In your opinion, continuation of a safe approach to the MAP is questionable.

3. The aircraft is over the MAP.

b. Surveillance approach guidance may be discontinued when the pilot reports the runway or approach/runway lights in sight or if a "point-in-space" approach, he/she reports able to proceed to the landing area by visual reference to a prescribed surface route.

c. When approach guidance is discontinued in accordance with subparagraph a and the aircraft has reported the runway or approach/runway lights in sight, advise the aircraft of its position and to proceed visually.

PHRASEOLOGY–
(Distance) MILE(S) FROM RUNWAY/AIRPORT/HELIPORT,

or

OVER MISSED APPROACH POINT.

PROCEED VISUALLY (additional instructions/clearance as required.)

d. When approach guidance is discontinued in accordance with subparagraph a above and the aircraft has not reported the runway or approach/runway lights in sight, advise the aircraft of its position and to execute a missed approach unless the runway or approach/runway lights are in sight or, if a "point-in-space" approach, unless able to proceed visually.

PHRASEOLOGY–
(Distance) MILE(S) FROM RUNWAY,

or

OVER MISSED APPROACH POINT.
IF RUNWAY,

or

APPROACH/RUNWAY LIGHTS NOT IN SIGHT, EXECUTE MISSED APPROACH/(missed approach instructions). (Additional instructions/clearance, as required.)

(Distance and direction) FROM AIRPORT/HELIPORT/MISSED APPROACH POINT.

IF UNABLE TO PROCEED VISUALLY, EXECUTE MISSED APPROACH. (Additional instructions/clearance, if required.)

NOTE–
Terminal instrument approach procedures and flight inspection criteria require establishment of a MAP for each procedure including the point to which satisfactory radar guidance can be provided.

Section 12. PAR Approaches- Terminal

5-12-1. GLIDEPATH NOTIFICATION

Inform the aircraft when it is approaching glidepath (approximately 10 to 30 seconds before final descent).

PHRASEOLOGY-
APPROACHING GLIDEPATH.

5-12-2. DECISION HEIGHT (DH) NOTIFICATION

Provide the DH to any pilot who requests it.

PHRASEOLOGY-
DECISION HEIGHT (number of feet).

5-12-3. DESCENT INSTRUCTION

When an aircraft reaches the point where final descent is to start, instruct it to begin descent.

PHRASEOLOGY-
BEGIN DESCENT.

5-12-4. GLIDEPATH AND COURSE INFORMATION

a. Issue course guidance and inform the aircraft when it is on glidepath and on course, and frequently inform the aircraft of any deviation from glidepath or course. Transmissions with aircraft on precision final approach should occur approximately every 5 seconds.

PHRASEOLOGY-
HEADING (heading).

ON GLIDEPATH.

ON COURSE,

or

SLIGHTLY/WELL ABOVE/BELOW GLIDEPATH.

SLIGHTLY/WELL LEFT/RIGHT OF COURSE.

NOTE-
Controllers should not key the radio transmitter continuously during radar approaches to preclude a lengthy communications block. The decision on how often transmitters are unkeyed is the controller's prerogative.

b. Issue trend information as required, to indicate target position with respect to the azimuth and elevation cursors and to describe target movement as appropriate corrections are issued. Trend information may be modified by the terms "RAPIDLY" or "SLOWLY," as appropriate.

EXAMPLE-
"Going above/below glidepath."
"Going right/left of course."
"Above/below glidepath and coming down/up."
"Above/below glidepath and holding."
"Left/right of course and holding/correcting."

REFERENCE-
FAA Order JO 7110.65, Para 5-12-7, Position Advisories.

5-12-5. DISTANCE FROM TOUCHDOWN

Inform the aircraft of its distance from touchdown at least once each mile on final approach.

PHRASEOLOGY-
(Number of miles) MILES FROM TOUCHDOWN.

5-12-6. DECISION HEIGHT

Inform the aircraft when it reaches the published decision height.

PHRASEOLOGY-
AT DECISION HEIGHT.

5-12-7. POSITION ADVISORIES

a. Continue to provide glidepath and course information prescribed in paragraph 5-12-4, Glidepath and Course Information, subparagraphs a and b, until the aircraft passes over threshold.

NOTE-
Glidepath and course information provided below decision height is advisory only. 14 CFR Section 91.175 outlines pilot responsibilities for descent below decision height.

b. Inform the aircraft when it is passing over the approach lights.

PHRASEOLOGY-
OVER APPROACH LIGHTS.

c. Inform the aircraft when it is passing over the landing threshold and inform it of its position with respect to the final approach course.

PHRASEOLOGY-
OVER LANDING THRESHOLD, (position with respect to course).

REFERENCE-
FAA Order JO 7110.65, Para 5-10-14, Final Approach Abnormalities.

5-12-8. APPROACH GUIDANCE TERMINATION

a. Discontinue precision approach guidance when:

1. Requested by the pilot.

2. In your opinion, continuation of a safe approach to the landing threshold is questionable.

3. The aircraft passes over landing threshold.

4. The pilot reports the runway/approach lights in sight and requests to or advises that he/she will proceed visually.

NOTE-
A pilot's report of "runway in sight" or "visual" is not a request to proceed visually.

b. When precision approach guidance is discontinued in accordance with subparagraph a, advise the aircraft of its position and to proceed visually.

PHRASEOLOGY-
(Distance) MILE(S) FROM TOUCHDOWN, PROCEED VISUALLY (additional instructions/clearance as required).

c. After a pilot has reported the runway/approach lights in sight and requested to or advised that he/she will proceed visually, and has been instructed to proceed visually, all PAR approach procedures must be discontinued.

d. Continue to monitor final approach and frequency. Pilots must remain on final controller's frequency until touchdown or otherwise instructed.

REFERENCE-
FAA Order JO 7110.65, Para 5-10-14, Final Approach Abnormalities.

5-12-9. COMMUNICATION TRANSFER

Issue communications transfer instructions.

PHRASEOLOGY-
CONTACT (terminal control function) (frequency, if required) AFTER LANDING.

NOTE-
Communications transfer instructions should be delayed slightly until the aircraft is on the landing roll-out to preclude diversion of the pilot's attention during transition and touchdown.

REFERENCE-
FAA Order JO 7110.65, Para 2-1-17, Radio Communications.

5-12-10. ELEVATION FAILURE

a. If the elevation portion of PAR equipment fails during a precision approach:

1. Discontinue PAR instructions and tell the aircraft to take over visually or if unable, to execute a missed approach. If the aircraft executes a missed approach, apply subparagraph 2 below.

PHRASEOLOGY-
NO GLIDEPATH INFORMATION AVAILABLE. IF RUNWAY, APPROACH/RUNWAY LIGHTS, NOT IN SIGHT, EXECUTE MISSED APPROACH/(alternative instructions).

2. If a surveillance approach, ASR or PAR without glide slope, is established for the same runway, inform the aircraft that a surveillance approach can be given. Use ASR or the azimuth portion of the PAR to conduct the approach and apply Chapter 5, Radar, Section 11, Surveillance Approaches- Terminal. When the PAR azimuth is used, inform the pilot that mileage information will be from touchdown, and at those runways where specific minima have been established for PAR without glideslope, inform the pilot that the PAR azimuth will be used for the approach.

EXAMPLE-
1. *Approach information when PAR azimuth used:*
"This will be a surveillance approach to runway three six. Mileages will be from touchdown."
or
"This will be a surveillance approach to runway three six using P-A-R azimuth. Mileages will be from touchdown."

2. *Descent Instructions:*
"Five miles from touchdown, descend to your minimum descent altitude/minimum altitude."

REFERENCE-
FAA Order JO 7110.65, Para 5-10-2, Approach Information.
FAA Order JO 7110.65, Para 5-11-4, Descent Instructions.

b. If the elevation portion of the PAR equipment is inoperative before starting a precision approach, apply subparagraph a2.

5-12-11. SURVEILLANCE UNUSABLE

PAR approaches may be conducted when the ASR is unusable provided a nonradar instrument approach will position the aircraft over a navigational aid or DME fix within the precision radar coverage, or an adjacent radar facility can provide a direct radar handoff to the PAR controller.

NOTE-
The display of the NAVAID or DME fix in accordance with paragraph 5-3-2, Primary Radar Identification Methods, is not required provided the NAVAID or DME fix can be correlated on a PAR scope.

Section 13. Automation– En Route

5–13–1. CONFLICT ALERT (CA) AND MODE C INTRUDER (MCI) ALERT

a. When a CA or MCI alert is displayed, evaluate the reason for the alert without delay and take appropriate action.

REFERENCE–
FAA Order JO 7110.65, Para 2–1–6, Safety Alert.

b. If another controller is involved in the alert, initiate coordination to ensure an effective course of action. Coordination is not required when immediate action is dictated.

c. Suppressing/Inhibiting CA/MCI alert.

1. The controller may suppress the display of a CA/MCI alert from a control position with the application of one of the following suppress/inhibit computer functions:

(a) The Conflict Suppress (CO) function may be used to suppress the CA/MCI display between specific aircraft for a specific alert.

NOTE–
See NAS–MD–678 for the EARTS conflict suppress message.

(b) The Group Suppression (SG) function must be applied exclusively to inhibit the displaying of alerts among military aircraft engaged in special military operations where standard en route separation criteria does not apply.

NOTE–
Special military operations where the SG function would typically apply involve those activities where military aircraft routinely operate in proximities to each other that are less than standard en route separation criteria; i.e., air refueling operations, ADC practice intercept operations, etc.

2. The computer entry of a message suppressing a CA/MCI alert constitutes acknowledgment for the alert and signifies that appropriate action has or will be taken.

3. The CA/MCI alert may not be suppressed or inhibited at or for another control position without being coordinated.

5–13–2. EN ROUTE MINIMUM SAFE ALTITUDE WARNING (E-MSAW)

a. When an E-MSAW alert is displayed, immediately analyze the situation and take the appropriate action to resolve the alert.

NOTE–
Caution should be exercised when issuing a clearance to an aircraft in reaction to an E-MSAW alert to ensure that adjacent MIA areas are not a factor.

REFERENCE–
FAA Order JO 7110.65, Para 2–1–6, Safety Alert.

b. The controller may suppress the display of an E-MSAW alert from his/her control position with the application of one of the following suppress/inhibit computer functions:

1. The specific alert suppression message may be used to inhibit the E-MSAW alerting display on a single flight for a specific alert.

2. The indefinite alert suppression message must be used exclusively to inhibit the display of E-MSAW alerts on aircraft known to be flying at an altitude that will activate the alert feature of one or more MIA areas within an ARTCC.

NOTE–
1. *The indefinite alert suppression message will remain in effect for the duration of the referenced flight's active status within the ARTCC unless modified by controller action.*

2. *The indefinite alert suppression message would typically apply to military flights with clearance to fly low-level type routes that routinely require altitudes below established minimum IFR altitudes.*

c. The computer entry of a message suppressing or inhibiting E-MSAW alerts constitutes acknowledgment for the alert and indicates that appropriate action has or will be taken to resolve the situation.

5-13-3. COMPUTER ENTRY OF FLIGHT PLAN INFORMATION

a. Altitude

1. The altitude field(s) of the data block must always reflect the current status of the aircraft unless otherwise specified in an appropriate facility directive.

2. Unless otherwise specified in a facility directive or letter of agreement, do not modify assigned or interim altitude information prior to establishing communication with an aircraft that is outside your area of jurisdiction unless verbal coordination identifying who will modify the data block has been accomplished.

NOTE–
1. *A local interim altitude (LIA) can be used as a means of recording interfacility coordination.*
2. *Conflict probe in EDST does not probe for the LIA.*

3. Whenever an aircraft is cleared to maintain an altitude different from that in the flight plan database, enter into the computer one of the following:

(a) The new assigned altitude if the aircraft will (climb or descend to and) maintain the new altitude, or

(b) An interim altitude if the aircraft will (climb or descend to and) maintain the new altitude for a short period of time and subsequently be recleared to the altitude in the flight plan database or a new altitude or a new interim altitude, or

ERAM

(c) A procedure altitude if the aircraft is cleared to vertically navigate (VNAV) on a SID/STAR with published restrictions, or

(d) Where appropriate for interfacility handoffs, an LIA when the assigned altitude differs from the coordinated altitude unless verbally coordinated or specified in a letter of agreement or facility directive.

NOTE–
A facility directive may be published, in accordance with JO 7210.3, paragraph 8-2-7, Waiver to Interim Altitude Requirements, deleting the interim altitude computer entry requirements of subparagraph 3.

b. Flight Plan Route Data

This information must not be modified outside of the controller's area of jurisdiction unless verbally coordinated or specified in a Letter of Agreement or Facility Directive.

5-13-4. ENTRY OF REPORTED ALTITUDE

Whenever Mode C altitude information is either not available or is unreliable, enter reported altitudes into the computer as follows:

NOTE–
Altitude updates are required to assure maximum accuracy in applying slant range correction formulas.

a. When an aircraft reaches the assigned altitude.

b. When an aircraft at an assigned altitude is issued a clearance to climb or descend.

c. A minimum of each 10,000 feet during climb to or descent from FL 180 and above.

5-13-5. SELECTED ALTITUDE LIMITS

The display of Mode C targets and limited data blocks is necessary for application of Merging Target Procedures. Sectors must ensure the display of Mode C targets and data blocks by entering appropriate altitude limits and display filters to include, as a minimum, the altitude stratum of the sector plus:

a. 1,200 feet above the highest and below the lowest altitude or flight level of the sector where 1,000 feet vertical separation is applicable; and

b. 2,200 feet above the highest and below the lowest flight level of the sector where 2,000 feet vertical separation is applicable.

NOTE–
1. *The data block, for purposes of this paragraph, must contain the Mode C altitude and call sign or beacon code_at a minimum.*

2. *Exception to these requirements may be authorized for specific altitudes in certain ARTCC sectors if defined in appropriate facility directives and approved by the respective service area operations directorate.*

5–13–6. SECTOR ELIGIBILITY

The use of the OK function is allowed to override sector eligibility only when one of the following conditions is met:

a. Prior coordination is effected.

b. The flight is within the control jurisdiction of the sector.

5–13–7. COAST TRACKS

Do not use coast tracks in the application of either radar or nonradar separation criteria.

5–13–8. CONTROLLER INITIATED COAST TRACKS

a. Initiate coast tracks only in Flight Plan Aided Tracking (FLAT) mode, except "free" coast tracking may be used as a reminder that aircraft without corresponding computer-stored flight plan information are under your control.

NOTE–
To ensure tracks are started in FLAT mode, perform a start track function at the aircraft's most current reported position, then immediately "force" the track into coast tracking by performing another start function with "CT" option in field 64. Making amendments to the stored route with trackball entry when the aircraft is rerouted, and repositioning the data block to coincide with the aircraft's position reports are methods of maintaining a coast track in FLAT mode.

b. Prior to initiating a coast track, ensure that a departure message or progress report corresponding with the aircraft's current position is entered into the computer.

c. As soon as practicable after the aircraft is in radar surveillance, initiate action to cause radar tracking to begin on the aircraft.

5–13–9. ERAM COMPUTER ENTRY OF HOLD INFORMATION

a. When an aircraft is issued holding instructions, the delay is ATC initiated, and the EFC is other than "no delay expected:"

1. Enter a hold message.

2. Maintain a paired track.

3. Enter an EFC time via a hold message, the Hold Data Menu, or the Hold View.

4. Enter non-published holding instructions via a hold message or the Hold Data Menu.

NOTE–
The ERAM hold message allows automatic calculation and reporting of aggregate delays.

b. Unless otherwise specified in a facility directive, verbally coordinate non-published holding instructions when handing off an aircraft in hold status to another ERAM sector.

c. An EFC time entered into the Hold Data Menu, Hold View, or the hold message constitutes coordination of the EFC between ERAM sectors.

REFERENCE–
FAA Order JO 7210.3, Para 8–2–9, ERAM Hold Information Facility Directive Requirements.

5–13–10. ERAM VISUAL INDICATOR OF SPECIAL ACTIVITY AIRSPACE (SAA) STATUS

Sector controllers shall ensure the situation display accurately reflects the status of all SAAs that impact their area of control responsibility. When "SAA DOWN" is displayed in the Outage View, manually create visual indicators on the situation display to reflect changes to airspace status.

NOTE–
The "SAA DOWN" message in the Outage View means that SAA status is no longer being updated. The status of each SAA at the time of the failure, whether "on" or "off", will continue to be displayed. Status changes will not be automatically updated on the display until the outage is resolved.

Section 14. Standard Terminal Automation Replacement System (STARS)–Terminal

5–14–1. APPLICATION

STARS may be used for identifying aircraft assigned a discrete beacon code, maintaining identity of targets, and performing handoffs of these targets between controllers. All procedures for the terminal domain related to air traffic control services using STARS apply to the FUSION target.

5–14–2. RESPONSIBILITY

This equipment does not relieve the controller of the responsibility to ensure proper identification, maintenance of identity, handoff of the correct target associated with the alphanumeric data, and separation of aircraft.

5–14–3. FUNCTIONAL USE

In addition to other uses specified herein, terminal automation may be used for the following functions:

a. Tracking.

b. Tagging.

c. Handoff.

d. Altitude information.

REFERENCE–
FAA Order JO 7110.65, Para 5–2–21, Altitude Filters.

e. Coordination.

f. Ground speed.

g. Identification.

5–14–4. SYSTEM REQUIREMENTS

Use terminal automation systems as follows:

NOTE–
Locally developed procedures, operating instructions, and training material are required because of differences in equipment capability. Such locally developed procedures must be supplemental to those contained in this section and must be designed to make maximum use of the STARS equipment.

a. Inform all appropriate positions before terminating or reinstating use of the terminal automation system at a control position. When terminating the use of terminal automation systems, all pertinent flight data of that position must be transferred or terminated.

b. Inform other interfaced facilities of scheduled and unscheduled shutdowns.

c. Initiate a track/tag on all aircraft to the maximum extent possible. As a minimum, aircraft identification should be entered, and automated handoff functions should be used.

d. Assigned altitude, if displayed, must be kept current at all times. Climb and descent arrows, where available, must be used to indicate other than level flight.

e. When operating in FUSION mode, the assigned or pilot reported altitude must be displayed and kept current when the aircraft is in level flight.

f. The automatic altitude readout of an aircraft under another controller's jurisdiction may be used for vertical separation purposes without verbal coordination provided:

1. Operation is conducted using single-site radar coverage or when operating in FUSION mode.

2. Prearranged coordination procedures are contained in a facility directive in accordance with paragraph 5-4-9, Prearranged Coordination, and FAA Order JO 7210.3, paragraph 3-6-7, Prearranged Coordination.

3. Do not use Mode C to effect vertical separation within a Mosaic radar configuration.

5-14-5. INFORMATION DISPLAYED

a. Two-letter ICAO designators or three-letter designators, as appropriate, must be used unless program limitations dictate the use of a single letter alpha prefix.

b. Use of the inhibit/select functions to remove displayed information no longer required must be in accordance with local directives, which should ensure maximum required use of the equipment.

c. Information displayed must be in accordance with national orders and specified in local directives.

5-14-6. CA/MCI

a. When a CA or MCI alert is displayed, evaluate the reason for the alert without delay and take appropriate action.

REFERENCE-
FAA Order JO 7110.65, Para 2-1-6, Safety Alert.

b. If another controller is involved in the alert, initiate coordination to ensure an effective course of action. Coordination is not required when immediate action is dictated.

c. Suppressing/Inhibiting CA/MCI alert.

1. The suppress function may be used to suppress the display of a specific CA/MCI alert.

2. The inhibit function must only be used to inhibit the display of CA for aircraft routinely engaged in operations where approved separation criteria do not apply.

NOTE-
Examples of operations where approved separation criteria do not apply are ADC practice intercept operations and air shows.

3. Computer entry of a message suppressing a CA/MCI alert constitutes acknowledgment for the alert and signifies that appropriate action has or will be taken.

4. CA/MCI alert may not be suppressed or inhibited at or for another control position without being coordinated.

5-14-7. INHIBITING MINIMUM SAFE ALTITUDE WARNING (MSAW)

a. Inhibit MSAW processing of VFR aircraft and aircraft that cancel instrument flight rules (IFR) flight plans unless the pilot specifically requests otherwise.

REFERENCE-
FAA Order JO 7110.65, Para 10-2-7, VFR Aircraft in Weather Difficulty.
FAA Order JO 7110.65, Para 10-2-8, Radar Assistance to VFR Aircraft in Weather Difficulty.

b. A low altitude alert may be suppressed from the control position. Computer entry of the suppress message constitutes an acknowledgment for the alert and indicates that appropriate action has or will be taken.

5-14-8. TRACK SUSPEND FUNCTION

Use the track suspend function only when data block overlap in holding patterns or in proximity of the final approach create an unworkable situation. If necessary to suspend tracks, those which are not displaying automatic altitude readouts must be suspended. If the condition still exists, those displaying automatic altitude readouts may then be suspended.

Chapter 6. Nonradar

Section 1. General

6–1–1. DISTANCE

Use mileage-based (DME and/or ATD) procedures and minima only when direct pilot/controller VHF or UHF voice communications are maintained.

6–1–2. NONRECEIPT OF POSITION REPORT

When a position report affecting separation is not received, take action to obtain the report no later than 5 minutes after the aircraft was estimated over the fix.

REFERENCE–
FAA Order JO 7110.65, Para 9–2–6, IFR Military Training Routes.

6–1–3. DUPLICATE POSITION REPORTS

Do not require an aircraft to make the same position report to more than one facility.

6–1–4. ADJACENT AIRPORT OPERATION

TERMINAL

WAKE TURBULENCE APPLICATION

The ATC facility having control jurisdiction at adjacent airports must separate arriving or departing IFR aircraft on a course that will cross the flight path of an aircraft requiring wake turbulence separation in accordance with the following:

a. Heavy, large, or small behind super – *3 minutes.*

b. Heavy, large, or small behind heavy – *2 minutes.*

c. Small behind B757 - *2 minutes.*

FIG 6–1–1
Adjacent Airport Operation -- Arrival

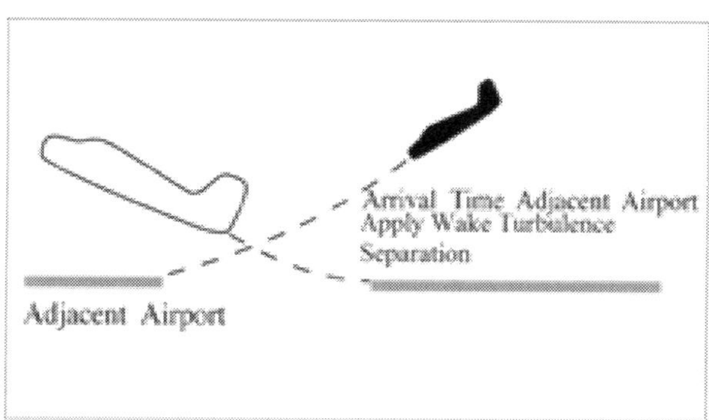

FIG 6-1-2
Adjacent Airport Operation -- Departure

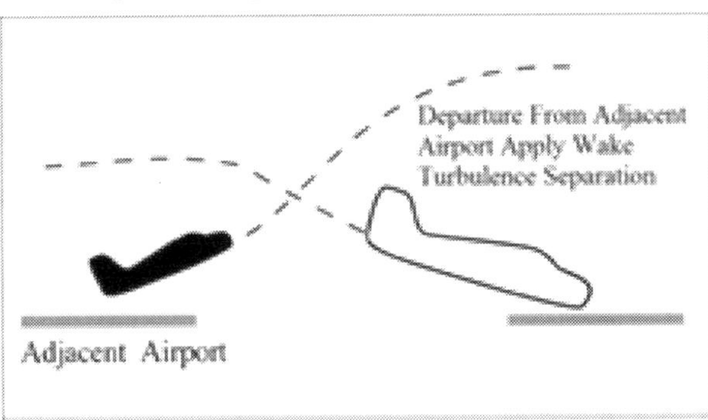

6-1-5. ARRIVAL MINIMA

TERMINAL

WAKE TURBULENCE APPLICATION

a. Separate IFR aircraft landing behind an arriving aircraft to the same runway:

1. Behind super:

(a) Heavy or large – *3 minutes.*

(b) Small – *4 minutes.*

2. Behind heavy:

(a) Heavy or large – *2 minutes.*

(b) Small – *3 minutes.*

3. Small behind B757 – *3 minutes.*

b. Separate IFR aircraft landing behind an arriving aircraft to a parallel runway separated by less than 2,500 feet, or a crossing runway if projected flight paths will cross:

1. Heavy, large, or small behind super – *3 minutes.*

2. Heavy, large, or small behind heavy – *2 minutes.*

3. Small behind B757 – *2 minutes.*

FIG 6-1-3
Arrival Minima Landing Behind an Arriving Aircraft Requiring Wake Turbulence Separation

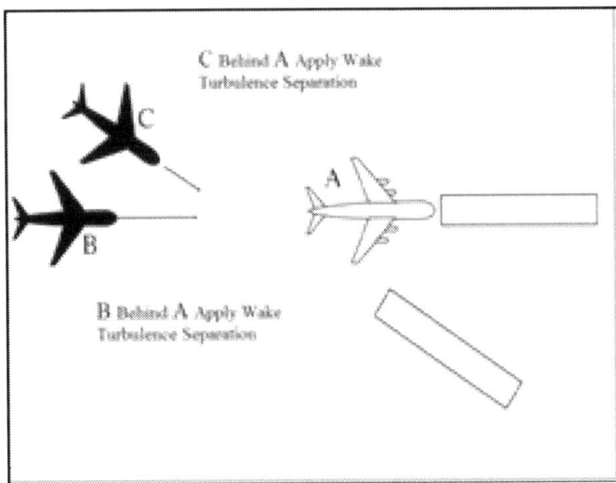

Section 2. Initial Separation of Successive Departing Aircraft

6–2–1. MINIMA ON DIVERGING COURSES

Separate aircraft that will fly courses diverging by 45 degrees or more after departing the same or adjacent airports by use of one of the following minima:

NOTE–

1. *Consider known aircraft performance characteristics when applying initial separation to successive departing aircraft.*

2. *When one or both of the departure surfaces is a helipad, use the takeoff course of the helicopter as a reference, comparable to the centerline of a runway and the helipad center as the threshold.*

a. When aircraft will fly diverging courses:

1. Immediately after takeoff – *1 minute* until courses diverge. (See FIG 6–2–1.)

FIG 6–2–1
Minima on Diverging Courses

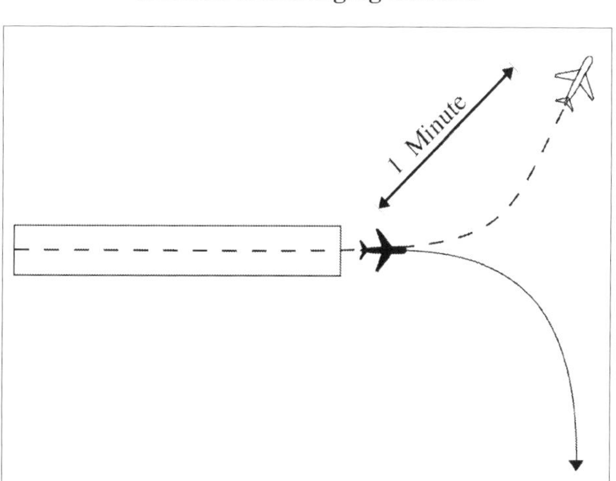

2. Within 5 minutes after takeoff– *2 minutes* until courses diverge. (See FIG 6–2–2.)

FIG 6–2–2
Minima on Diverging Courses

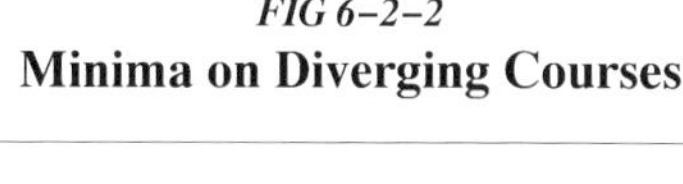

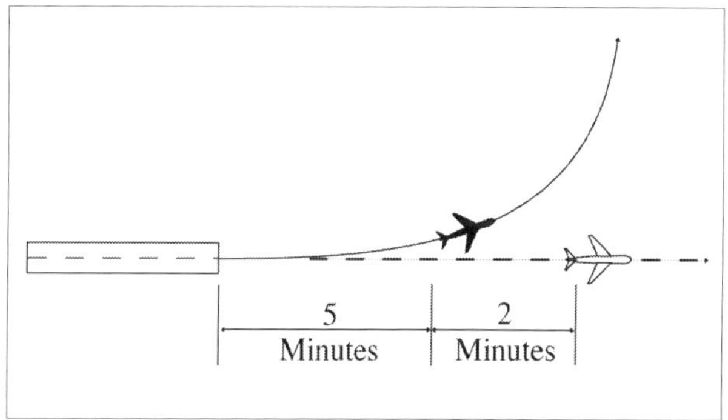

3. Within 13 miles DME/ATD after takeoff – *3 miles* until courses diverge. (See FIG 6–2–3.)

FIG 6-2-3
Minima on Diverging Courses

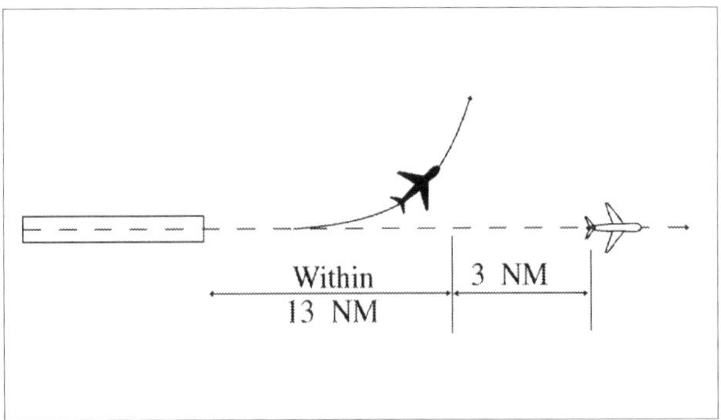

b. *TERMINAL.* Between aircraft departing in the same direction from different runways whose centerlines are parallel and separated by at least 3,500 feet, authorize simultaneous takeoffs when the aircraft will fly diverging courses immediately after takeoff. (See FIG 6-2-4.)

FIG 6-2-4
Minima on Diverging Courses

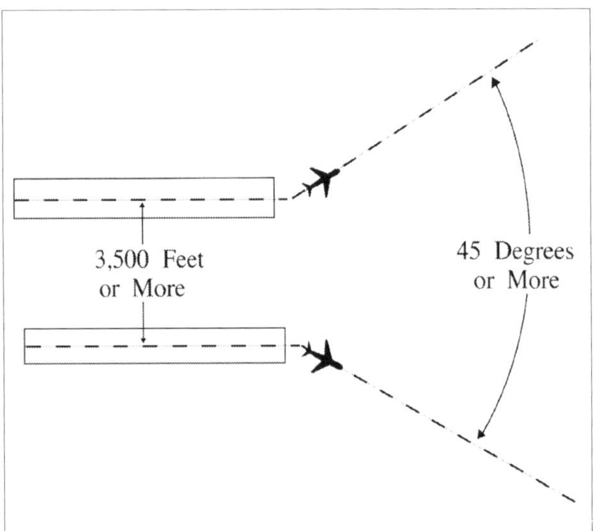

c. *TERMINAL.* Between aircraft that will fly diverging courses immediately after takeoff from diverging runways: (See FIG 6-2-5.)

1. Nonintersecting runways. Authorize simultaneous takeoffs when either of the following conditions exist:

(a) The runways diverge by 30 degrees or more.

(b) The distance between runway centerlines at and beyond the points where takeoffs begin is at least:

(1) 2,000 feet and the runways diverge by 15 to 29 degrees inclusive.

(2) 3,500 feet and the runways diverge by less than 15 degrees.

FIG 6–2–5
Minima on Diverging Courses

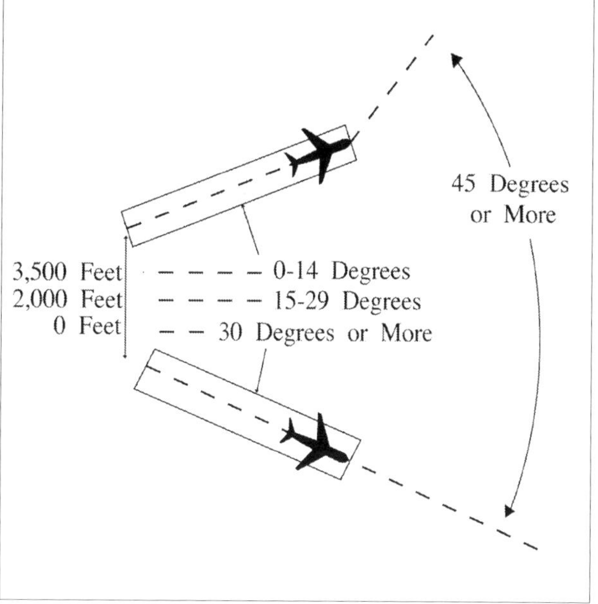

2. Intersecting runways. Authorize takeoff of a succeeding aircraft when the preceding aircraft has passed the point of runway intersection, and

(a) The runways diverge by 30 degrees or more. (See FIG 6–2–6.)

FIG 6–2–6
Minima on Diverging Courses

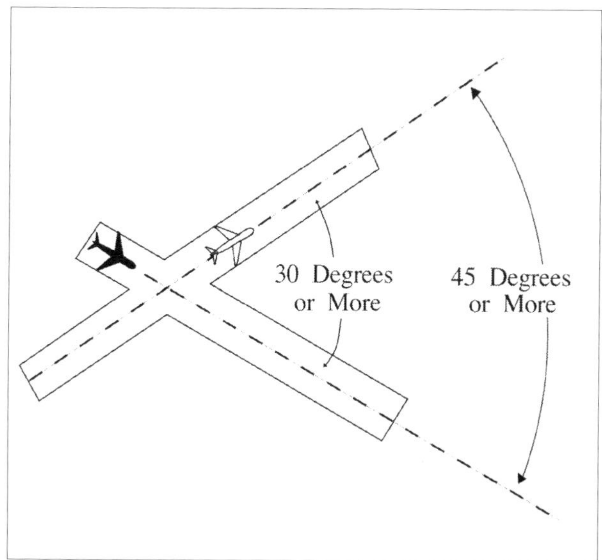

(b) The runways diverge by 15 to 29 degrees inclusive and the preceding aircraft has commenced a turn. (See FIG 6–2–7.)

FIG 6–2–7
Minima on Diverging Courses

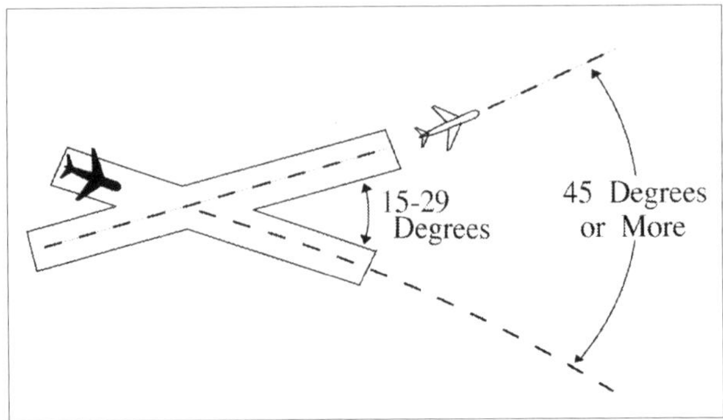

6–2–2. MINIMA ON SAME COURSE

Separate aircraft that will fly the same course when the following aircraft will climb through the altitude assigned to the leading aircraft by using a minimum of *3 minutes* until the following aircraft passes through the assigned altitude of the leading aircraft; or *5 miles* between DME equipped aircraft; RNAV equipped aircraft using ATD; and between DME and ATD aircraft provided the DME aircraft is either 10,000 feet or below or outside of 10 miles from the DME NAVAID. (See FIG 6–2–8 and FIG 6–2–9.)

FIG 6–2–8
Minima on Same Course

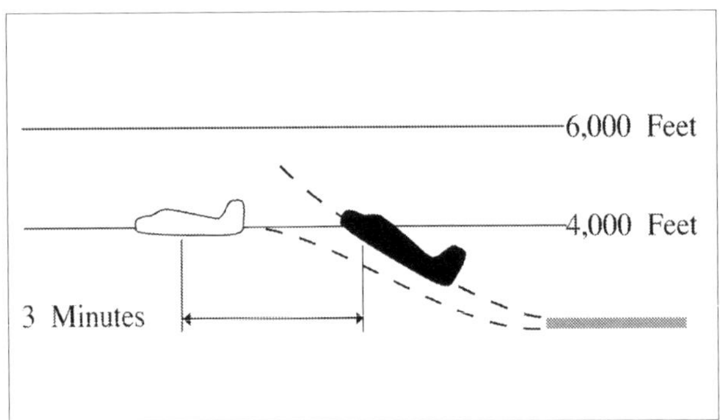

FIG 6–2–9
Minima on Same Course

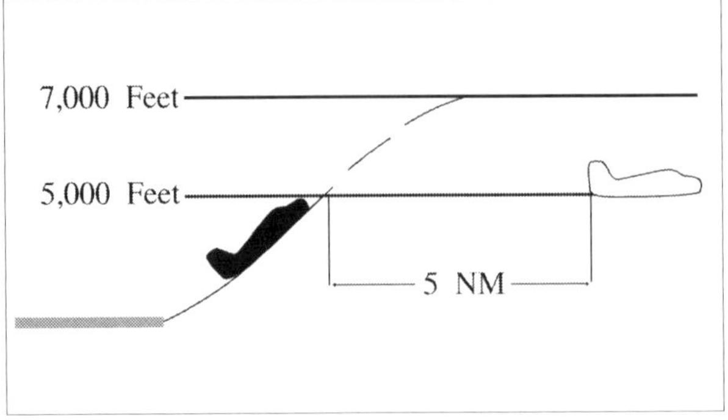

Section 3. Initial Separation of Departing and Arriving Aircraft

6–3–1. SEPARATION MINIMA

Separate a departing aircraft from an arriving aircraft making an instrument approach to the same airport by using one of the following minima until vertical or lateral separation is achieved:

a. *TERMINAL.* When takeoff direction differs by at least 45 degrees from the reciprocal of the final approach course, the departing aircraft takes off before the arriving aircraft leaves a fix inbound not less than *4 miles* from the airport.

b. *TERMINAL.* When takeoff direction is other than in subparagraph a, the departing aircraft takes off so that it is established on a course diverging by at least 45 degrees from the reciprocal of the final approach course before the arriving aircraft leaves a fix inbound not less than *4 miles* from the airport.

c. *TERMINAL.* When the absence of an appropriate fix precludes the application of subparagraphs a or b and at airports where approach control service is not provided, the separation in subparagraphs d or e must be applied.

d. When takeoff direction differs by at least 45 degrees from the reciprocal of the final approach course, the departing aircraft takes off *3 minutes* before the arriving aircraft is estimated at the airport. (See FIG 6–3–1.)

FIG 6–3–1
Separation Minima

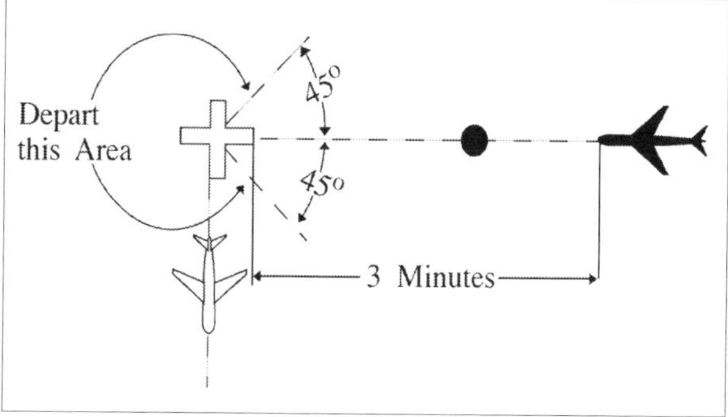

e. When takeoff direction is other than in subparagraph d, the departing aircraft takes off so that it is established on a course diverging by at least 45 degrees from the reciprocal of the final approach course *5 minutes* before the arriving aircraft is estimated at the airport or before it starts procedure turn. (See FIG 6–3–2 and FIG 6–3–3.)

FIG 6–3–2
Separation Minima

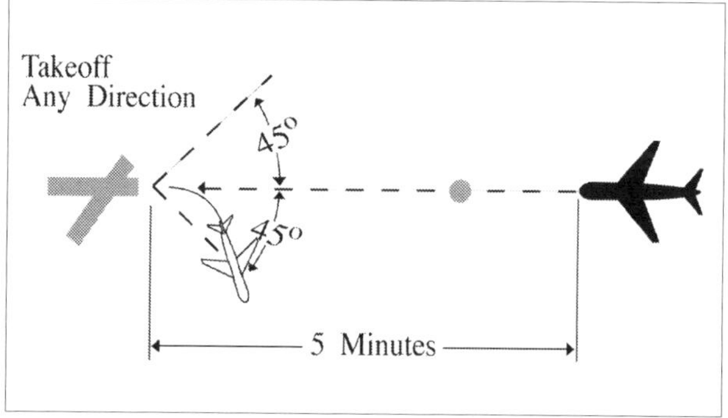

FIG 6-3-3
Separation Minima

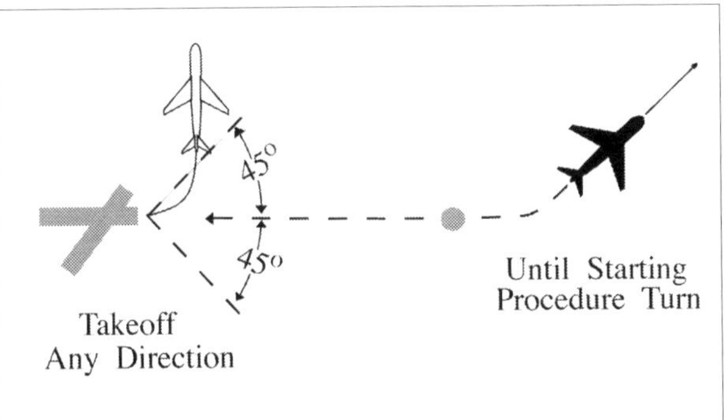

Section 4. Longitudinal Separation

6–4–1. APPLICATION

Separate aircraft longitudinally by requiring them to do one of the following, as appropriate:

a. Depart at a specified time.

b. Arrive at a fix at a specified time.

PHRASEOLOGY–
CROSS (fix) AT OR BEFORE (time).

CROSS (fix) AT OR AFTER (time).

c. Hold at a fix until a specified time.

d. Change altitude at a specified time or fix.

REFERENCE–
FAA Order JO 7110.65, Para 4–5–7, Altitude Information.

6–4–2. MINIMA ON SAME, CONVERGING, OR CROSSING COURSES

Separate aircraft on the same, converging, or crossing courses by an interval expressed in time or distance, using the following minima:

a. When the leading aircraft maintains a speed at least 44 knots faster than the following aircraft – *5 miles* between DME equipped aircraft; RNAV equipped aircraft using ATD; and between DME and ATD aircraft provided the DME aircraft is either 10,000 feet or below or outside of 10 miles from the DME NAVAID, or *3 minutes* between other aircraft if, in either case, one of the following conditions is met:

1. A departing aircraft follows a preceding aircraft which has taken off from the same or adjacent airport. (See FIG 6–4–1.)

FIG 6–4–1
Minima on Same Course
44 Knots or More Separation

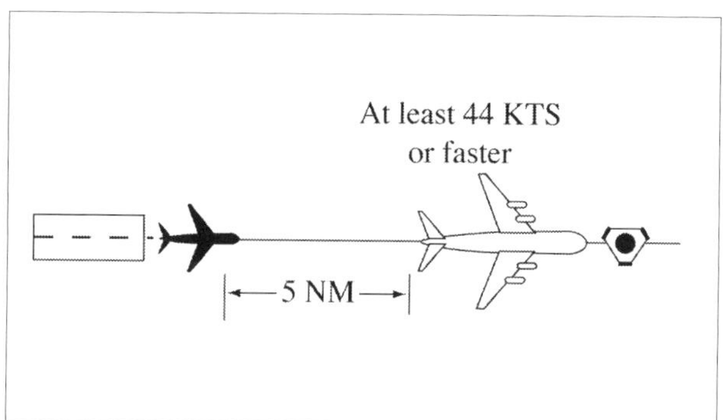

2. A departing aircraft follows a preceding en route aircraft which has reported over a fix serving the departure airport. (See FIG 6–4–2.)

FIG 6-4-2
Minima on Converging Courses
44 Knots or More Separation

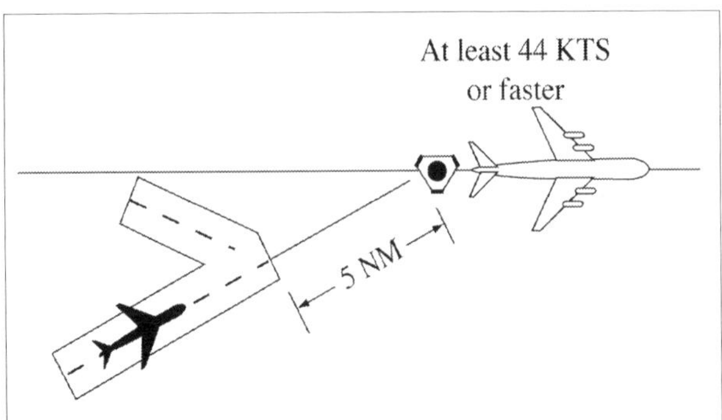

3. An en route aircraft follows a preceding en route aircraft which has reported over the same fix. (See FIG 6-4-3.)

FIG 6-4-3
Minima on Crossing Courses
44 Knots or More Separation

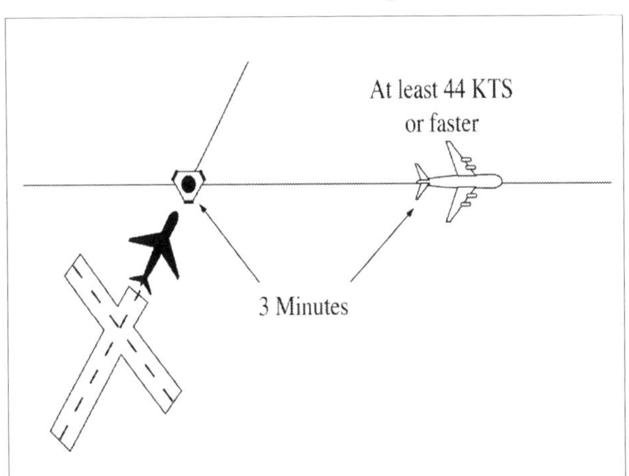

b. When the leading aircraft maintains a speed at least 22 knots faster than the following aircraft – *10 miles* between DME equipped aircraft; RNAV equipped aircraft using ATD; and between DME and ATD aircraft provided the DME aircraft is either 10,000 feet or below or outside of 10 miles from the DME NAVAID; or *5 minutes* between other aircraft if, in either case, one of the following conditions exists:

1. A departing aircraft follows a preceding aircraft which has taken off from the same or an adjacent airport. (See FIG 6-4-4.)

FIG 6−4−4
Minima on Same Course
22 Knots or More Separation

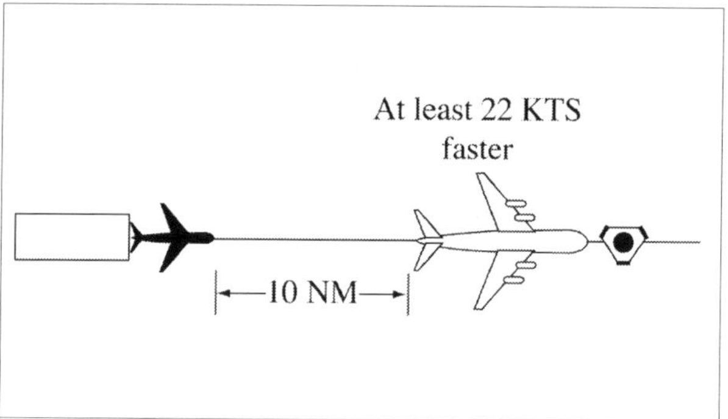

2. A departing aircraft follows a preceding en route aircraft which has reported over a fix serving the departure airport. (See FIG 6−4−5.)

FIG 6−4−5
Minima on Converging Courses
22 Knots or More Separation

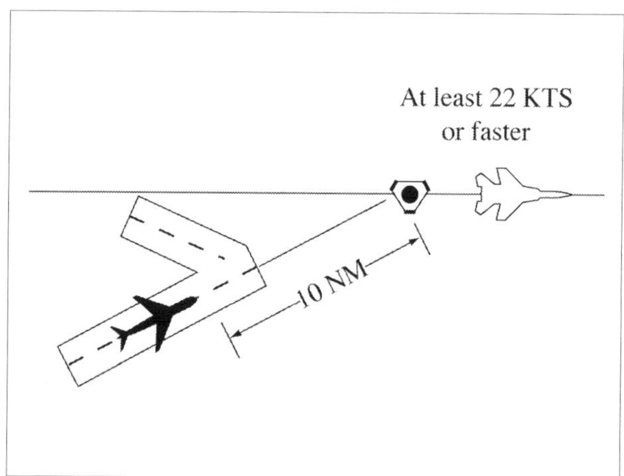

3. An en route aircraft follows a preceding en route aircraft which has reported over the same fix. (See FIG 6−4−6.)

FIG 6−4−6
Minima on Crossing Courses
22 Knots or More Separation

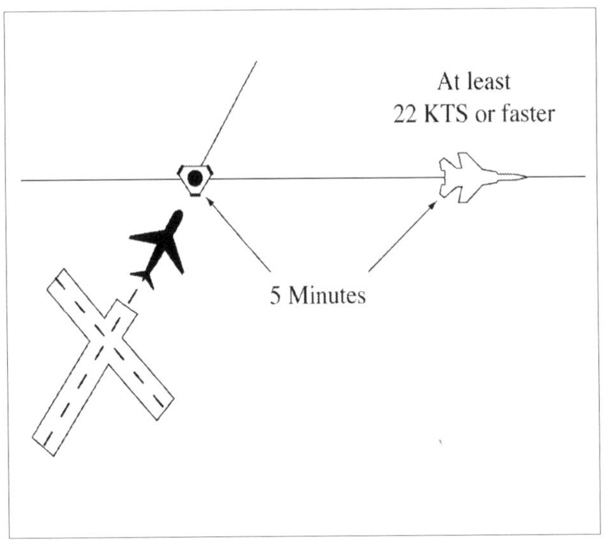

c. When an aircraft is climbing or descending through the altitude of another aircraft:

1. Between DME equipped aircraft; RNAV equipped aircraft using ATD; and between DME and ATD aircraft provided the DME aircraft is either 10,000 feet or below or outside of 10 miles from the DME NAVAID− *10 miles,* if the descending aircraft is leading or the climbing aircraft is following. (See FIG 6−4−7 and FIG 6−4−8.)

FIG 6−4−7
Descending Through Another Aircraft's Altitude DME Separation

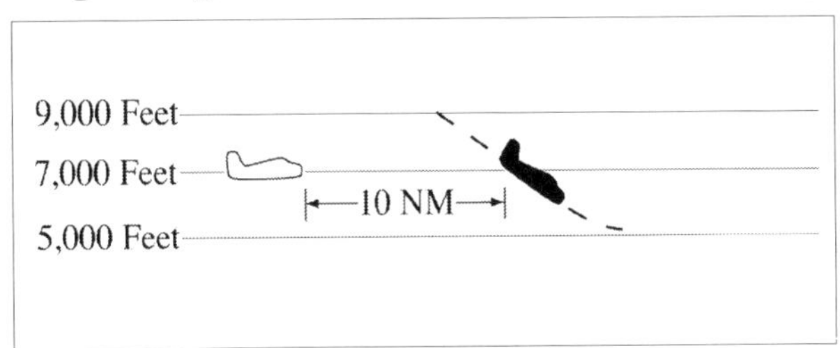

FIG 6−4−8
Climbing Through Another Aircraft's Altitude DME Separation

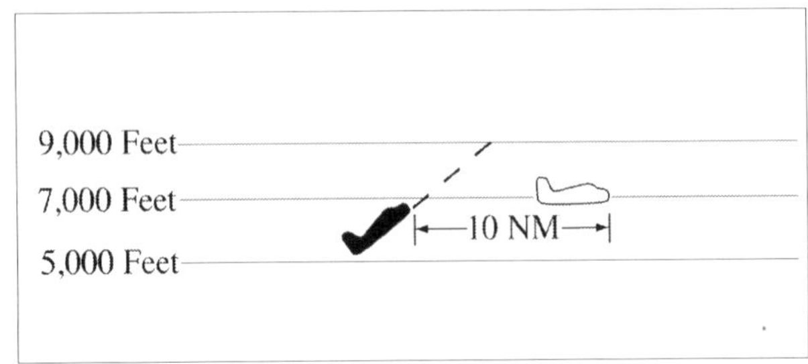

2. Between other aircraft− *5 minutes*, if all of the following conditions are met: (See FIG 6−4−9 and FIG 6−4−10.)

(a) The descending aircraft is leading or climbing aircraft is following.

(b) The aircraft are separated by not more than 4,000 feet when the altitude change started.

(c) The change is started within 10 minutes after a following aircraft reports over a fix reported over by the leading aircraft or has acknowledged a clearance specifying the time to cross the same fix.

3. Between RNAV aircraft that are operating along an RNAV route that is eight miles or less in width– *10 miles* provided the following conditions are met:

(a) The descending aircraft is leading or the climbing aircraft is following.

(b) The aircraft were separated by not more than 4,000 feet when the altitude change started.

FIG 6–4–9
Descending Through Another Aircraft's Altitude Timed Separation

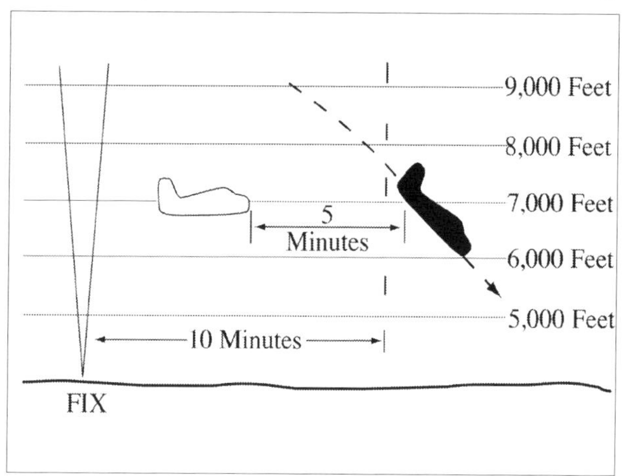

FIG 6–4–10
Climbing Through Another Aircraft's Altitude Timed Separation

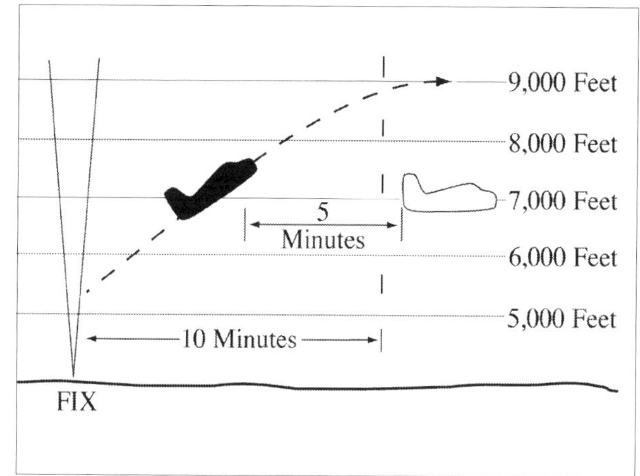

d. When the conditions of subparagraphs a, b, or c cannot be met– *20 miles* between DME equipped aircraft; RNAV equipped aircraft using ATD; and between DME and ATD aircraft provided the DME aircraft is either 10,000 feet or below or outside of 10 miles from the DME NAVAID; or *10 minutes* between other aircraft. (See FIG 6–4–11, FIG 6–4–12, FIG 6–4–13, FIG 6–4–14, FIG 6–4–15, and FIG 6–4–16.)

FIG 6-4-11
Minima for Same Course Separation

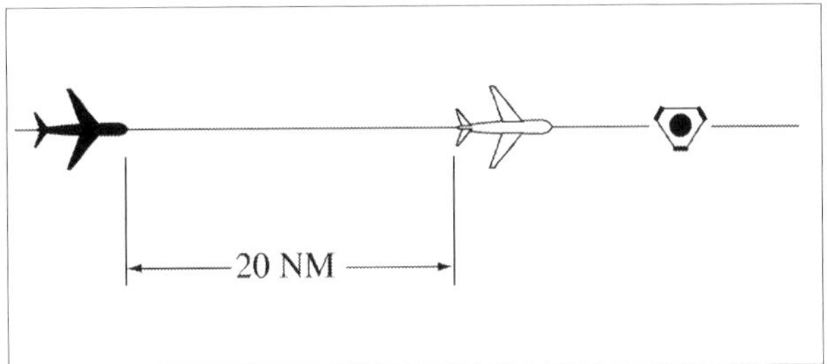

FIG 6-4-12
Minima for Crossing Courses Separation

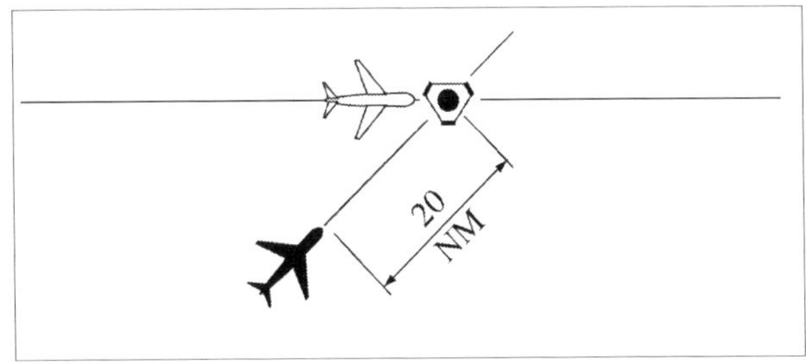

FIG 6-4-13
Minima for Same Course Separation

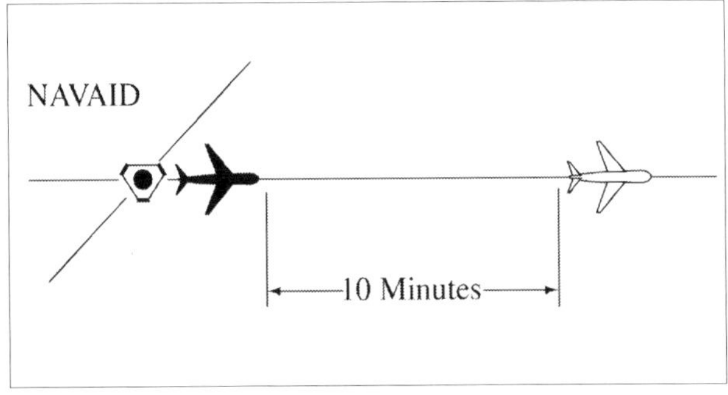

FIG 6-4-14
Minima for Crossing Courses Separation

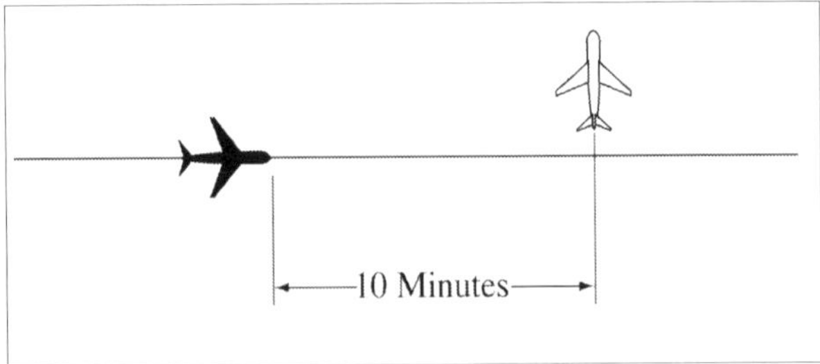

FIG 6-4-15
Climbing Through Another Aircraft's Altitude Separation

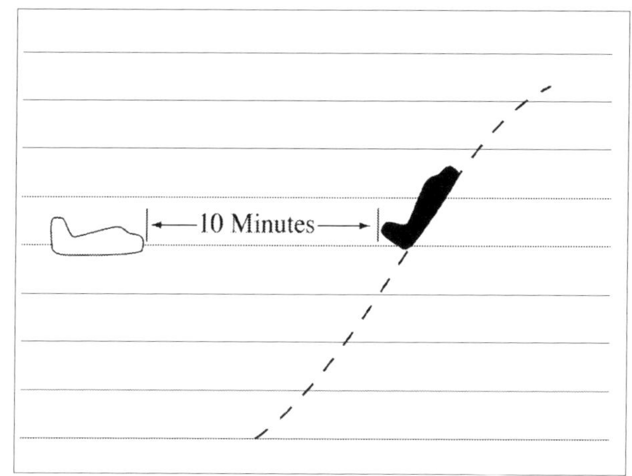

FIG 6-4-16
Descending Through Another Aircraft's Altitude Separation

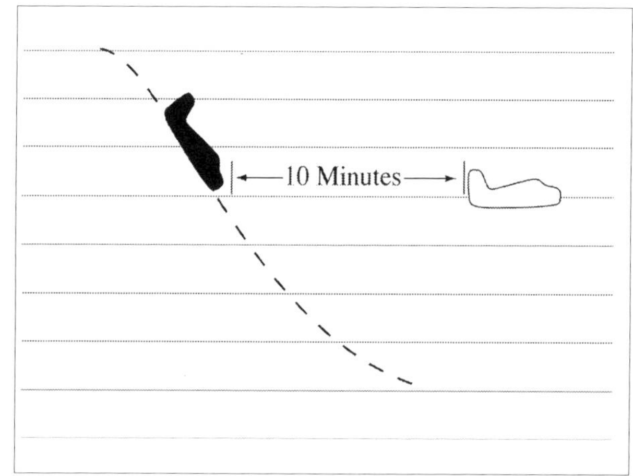

e. Between aircraft, when one aircraft is using DME/ATD and the other is not− *30 miles* if both the following conditions are met: (See FIG 6−4−17 and FIG 6−4−18.)

FIG 6-4-17
Minima for Same Course Separation

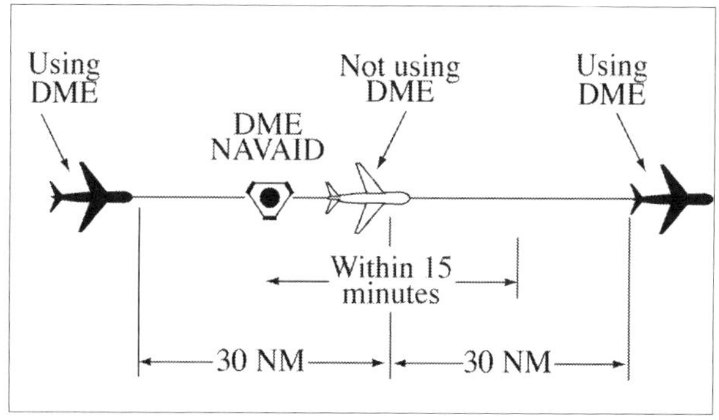

FIG 6–4–18
Minima for Crossing Courses Separation

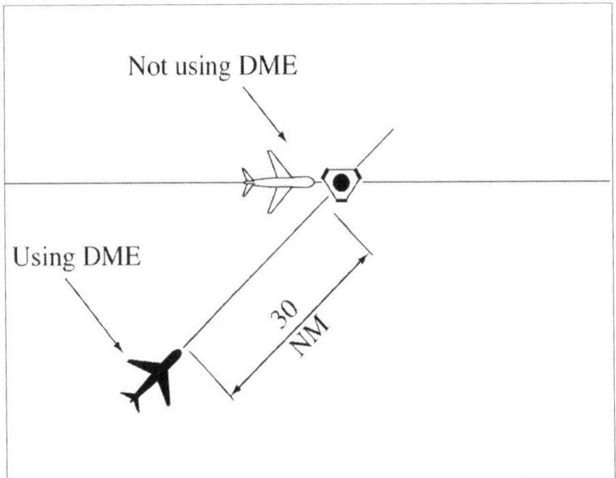

1. The aircraft using DME/ATD derives distance information by reference to the same NAVAID or waypoint over which the aircraft not using DME/ATD has reported.

2. The aircraft not using DME/ATD is within 15 minutes of the NAVAID.

6–4–3. MINIMA ON OPPOSITE COURSES

Separate aircraft traveling opposite courses by assigning different altitudes consistent with the approved vertical separation from *10 minutes* before, until *10 minutes* after they are estimated to pass. Vertical separation may be discontinued after one of the following conditions is met: (See FIG 6–4–19.)

FIG 6–4–19
Minima for Opposite Courses Separation

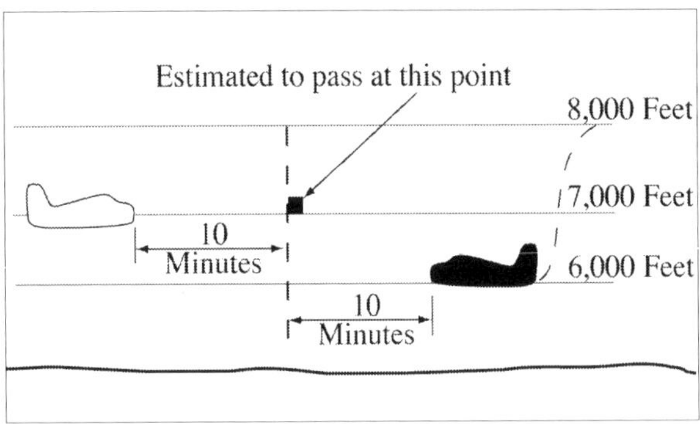

NOTE–
RNAV route segments that have been expanded in the proximity to reference facilities for slant-range effect are not to be considered "expanded" for purposes of applying separation criteria in this paragraph.

a. Both aircraft have reported passing NAVAIDs, DME fixes, or waypoints indicating they have passed each other. (See FIG 6–4–20.)

FIG 6−4−20
Minima for Opposite Courses Separation

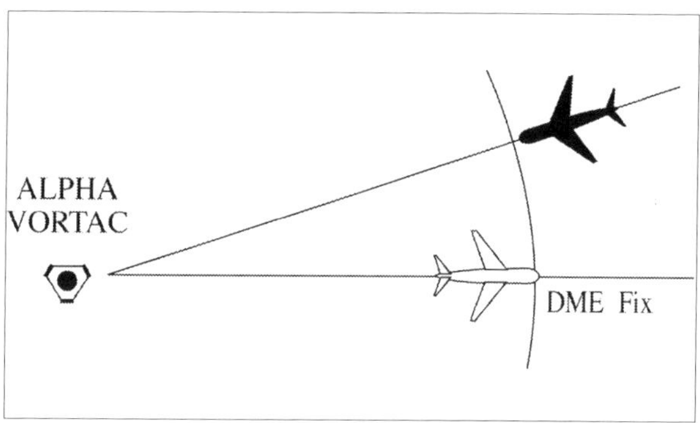

NOTE−
It is not intended to limit application of this procedure only to aircraft operating in opposite directions along the same airway or radial. This procedure may also be applied to aircraft established on diverging airways or radials of the same NAVAID.

b. Both aircraft have reported passing the same intersection/waypoint and they are at least *3 minutes* apart.

c. Two RNAV aircraft have reported passing the same position and are at least *8 miles* apart if operating along a route that is 8 miles or less in width; or *18 miles* apart if operating along any route segment that is greater than 8 miles in width; except that *30 miles* must be applied if operating along that portion of any route segment defined by a navigation station requiring extended usable distance limitations beyond 130 miles.

d. An aircraft utilizing RNAV and an aircraft utilizing VOR have reported passing the same position and the RNAV aircraft is at least 4 miles beyond the reported position when operating along a route that is 8 miles or less in width; 9 miles beyond the point when operating along any route segment that is greater than 8 miles in width; except that 15 miles must be applied if operating along that portion of any route segment defined by a navigation station requiring extended usable distance limitation beyond 130 miles; or 3 minutes apart whichever is greater.

NOTE−
Except for GNSS-equipped aircraft /G, /L, /S, and /V, not on a random impromptu route, paragraph 5−5−1, Application, requires radar separation be provided to RNAV aircraft operating at and below FL450 on Q routes or random RNAV routes, excluding oceanic airspace.

6−4−4. SEPARATION BY PILOTS

When pilots of aircraft on the same course in direct radio communication with each other concur, you may authorize the following aircraft to maintain longitudinal separation of *10 minutes;* or *20 miles* between DME equipped aircraft; RNAV equipped aircraft using ATD; and between DME and ATD aircraft provided the DME aircraft is either 10,000 feet or below or outside of 10 miles from the DME NAVAID.

PHRASEOLOGY−
MAINTAIN AT LEAST ONE ZERO MINUTES/TWO ZERO MILES SEPARATION FROM (ident).

6−4−5. RNAV AIRCRAFT ALONG VOR AIRWAYS/ROUTES

Advise the pilot to use DME distances when applying DME separation to an RNAV aircraft operating along VOR airways/routes.

PHRASEOLOGY−
USE DME DISTANCES.

NOTE−
ATD derived from area navigation devices having slant-range correction will not coincide with the direct DME readout.

Section 5. Lateral Separation

6-5-1. SEPARATION METHODS

Separate aircraft by one of the following methods:

a. Clear aircraft on different airways or routes whose widths or protected airspace do not overlap.

b. Clear aircraft below 18,000 to proceed to and report over or hold at different geographical locations determined visually or by reference to NAVAIDs.

c. Clear aircraft to hold over different fixes whose holding pattern airspace areas do not overlap each other or other airspace to be protected.

d. Clear departing aircraft to fly specified headings which diverge by at least 45 degrees.

6-5-2. MINIMA ON DIVERGING RADIALS

a. Consider separation to exist between aircraft:

1. Established on radials of the same NAVAID that diverge by at least 15 degrees when either aircraft is clear of the airspace to be protected for the other aircraft.

2. With non-VOR/DME based navigational equipment established on tracks of the same waypoint that diverge by at least 15 degrees when either aircraft is clear of the airspace to be protected for the other aircraft.

FIG 6-5-1
Minima on Diverging Radials

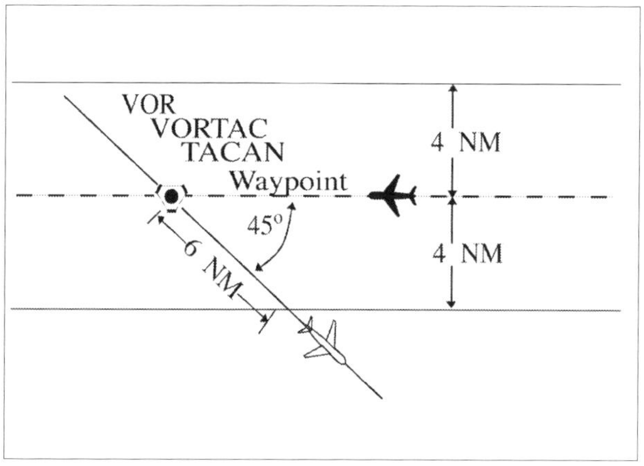

NOTE-
The procedure may be applied to converging as well as diverging aircraft. (See FIG 6-5-1.) The aircraft depicted 6 miles from the NAVAID/waypoint would require vertical separation until reaching the 6-mile point. Reversing direction, the same aircraft would require vertical separation before passing the 6-mile point. Due to the nature of GPS equipment, issue crossing restrictions in reference to the next waypoint, since the pilot receives tracking "to" data rather than tracking "from" the last waypoint.

b. Use TBL 6-5-1 and TBL 6-5-2 to determine the distance required for various divergence angles to clear the airspace to be protected. For divergence that falls between two values, use the lesser divergence value to obtain the distance.

TBL 6–5–1
Non–DME Divergence Distance Minima

Divergence (Degrees)	Distance (NM)
15	16
20	12
25	10
30	8
35	7
45	6
55	5
90	4
NOTE: *This table is for non–DME application only.*	

TBL 6–5–2
Divergence Distance Minima

Divergence (Degrees)	Distance (NM)	
	Below FL 180	FL 180 through FL 450
15	17	18
20	13	15
25	11	13
30	9	11
35	8	11
45	7	11
55	6	11
90	5	11
NOTE: *This table is for DME application and compensates for DME slant-range error.*		

NOTE–
For altitudes of 3,000 feet or less above the elevation of the NAVAID, DME slant-range error is negligible and the values in TBL 6–5–1 may be used.

6–5–3. DME ARC MINIMA

Apply lateral DME separation by requiring aircraft using DME to fly an arc about a NAVAID at a specified distance using the following minima: (See FIG 6–5–2.)

FIG 6–5–2
DME Arc Minima

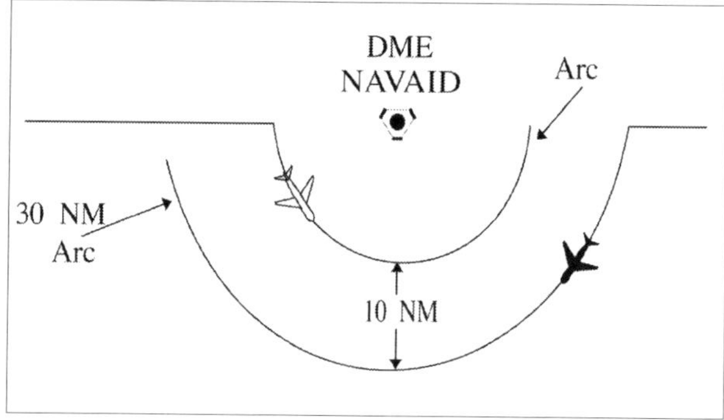

REFERENCE–
FAA Order JO 7110.65, Para 2–5–2, NAVAID Terms.

a. Between different arcs about a NAVAID regardless of direction of flight:

1. At 35 miles or less from the NAVAID– *10 miles.*

2. More than 35 miles from the NAVAID– *20 miles.*

b. Between an arc about a NAVAID and other airspace to be protected: (See FIG 6–5–3.)

FIG 6–5–3
DME Arc Minima

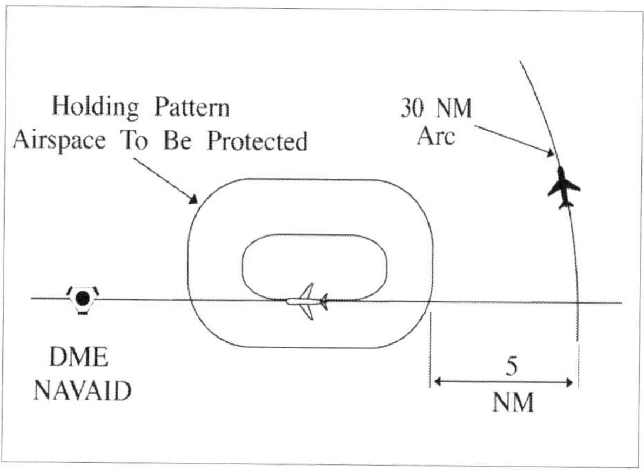

NOTE–
The other airspace to be protected may be a MOA, a holding pattern, airway or route, ATCAA, Warning Area, Restricted Area, Prohibited Area, etc.

1. At 35 miles or less from the NAVAID– *5 miles.*

2. More than 35 miles from the NAVAID– *10 miles.*

PHRASEOLOGY–
VIA (number of miles) MILE ARC (direction) OF (name of DME NAVAID).

6–5–4. MINIMA ALONG OTHER THAN ESTABLISHED AIRWAYS OR ROUTES

Protect airspace along other than established airways or routes as follows: (See FIG 6–5–4.)

FIG 6-5-4
Minima Along Other Than Established Airways or Routes

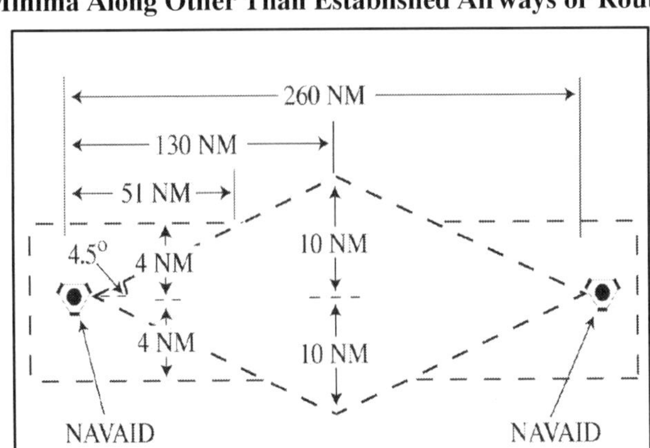

REFERENCE–
P/CG Term – Airway.
P/CG Term – Route.

a. Direct courses and course changes of 15 degrees or less:

1. Via NAVAIDs or radials FL 600 and below– *4 miles* on each side of the route to a point 51 miles from the NAVAID, then increasing in width on a 4 $^1/_2$ degree angle to a width of *10 miles* on each side of the route at a distance of 130 miles from the NAVAID.

2. Via degree-distance fixes for aircraft authorized under paragraph 4–4–3, Degree–Distance Route Definition for Military Operations.

(a) Below FL 180– *4 miles* on each side of the route.

(b) FL 180 to FL 600 inclusive– *10 miles* on each side of the route.

3. Via degree-distance fixes for RNAV flights above FL 450– *10 miles* on each side of the route.

NOTE–
Except for GNSS-equipped aircraft /G, /L, /S, and /V, not on a random impromptu route, paragraph 5–5–1, Application, requires radar separation be provided to RNAV aircraft operating at and below FL450 on Q routes or random RNAV routes, excluding oceanic airspace.

REFERENCE–
FAA Order JO 7110.65, Para 4–4–2, Route Structure Transitions.
FAA Order JO 7110.65, Para 5–5–1, Application.
P/CG Term – Global Navigation Satellite System (GNSS)[ICAO].

4. GNSS-equipped RNAV aircraft provided nonradar separation on random RNAV routes must be cleared via or reported to be established on point-to-point route segments.

(a) The points must be published NAVAIDs, waypoints, fixes, or airports recallable from the aircraft's navigation database. The points must be displayed on controller video maps or depicted on the controller chart displayed at the control position. The maximum distance between points must not exceed 500 miles.

(b) Protect 4 miles either side of the route centerline.

(c) Assigned altitudes must be at or above the highest MIA along the projected route segment being flown, including the protected airspace of that route segment.

EXAMPLE–
A pilot has filed a point–to–point route from XYZ to ABC at 13,000 feet. Departure procedures from the originating airport place the aircraft a significant distance from XYZ; however, the aircraft can establish itself along the route segment from XYZ to ABC. Ascertain when the pilot is established on the point–to–point route segment and at an altitude that meets or exceeds the highest MVA/MIA projected along the route of flight, then issue a clearance. "Verify when you are established on the XYZ to ABC route segment at or above 6,000 feet."

(d) When the GNSS aircraft is being provided radar service and is transitioning to nonradar airspace, provide clearance direct to the named point in nonradar airspace in accordance with subparagraphs a4(a) through (c).

5. If transitioning between two random point–to–point routes, GNSS–equipped aircraft being provided nonradar separation may be cleared via an impromptu route when the following conditions are met:

(a) The impromptu route segment must not exceed the distance to the nearest available recallable fix/waypoint consistent with the direction of flight; and

(b) Assigned altitudes must be at or above the highest MIA along the projected route segment being flown; and

(c) Aircraft conducting the impromptu route must be separated vertically from other aircraft until established on the new point-to-point route.

REFERENCE–
FAA Order JO 7110.65, Para 4–4–1, Route Use.
FAA Order JO 7110.65, Para 4–4–2, Route Structure Transitions.
FAA Order JO 7110.65, Para 5–5–1, Application.

b. When course change is 16 degrees through 90 degrees, protect the airspace on the overflown side beginning at the point where the course changes as follows: (See FIG 6–5–5.)

FIG 6–5–5
Overflown Side Minima
16 to 90 Degrees

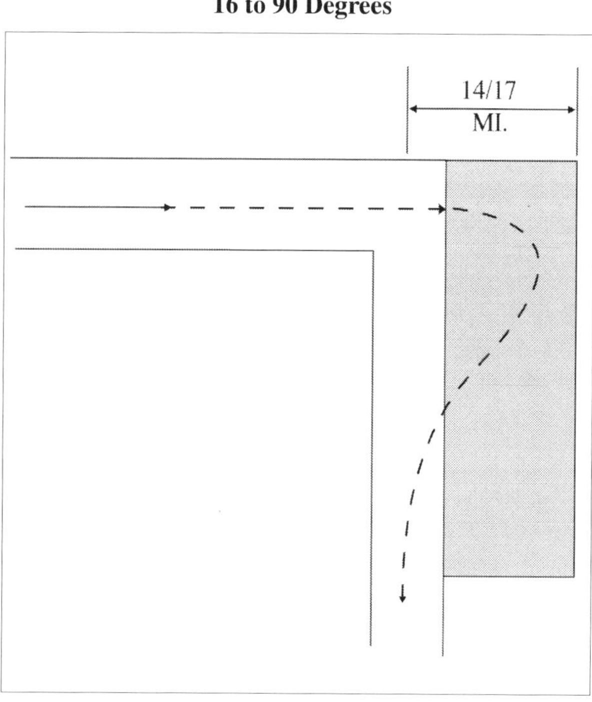

1. Below FL 180– same as subparagraphs a1 or 2.

2. FL 180 to FL 230 inclusive– *14 miles.*

3. Above FL 230 to FL 600 inclusive– *17 miles.*

c. When course change is 91 degrees through 180 degrees, protect the airspace on the overflown side beginning at the point where the course changes as follows: (See FIG 6–5–6.)

1. Below FL 180– same as subparagraphs a1 or 2.

2. FL 180 to FL 230 inclusive– *28 miles.*

3. Above FL 230 to FL 600 inclusive– *34 miles.*

FIG 6–5–6
Overflown Side Minima
91 to 180 Degrees

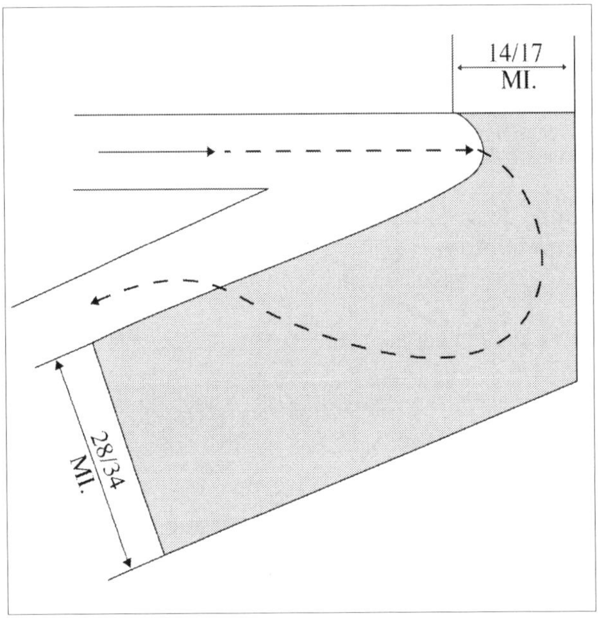

d. After the course changes specified in subparagraphs b or c have been completed and the aircraft is back on course, the appropriate minima in subparagraph a may be used.

6–5–5. RNAV MINIMA– DIVERGING/CROSSING COURSES

Consider lateral separation to exist when an RNAV aircraft is beyond the point where the lateral protected airspace of that aircraft has ceased to overlap the lateral protected airspace of another by at least:
(See FIG 6–5–7 and FIG 6–5–8.)

FIG 6–5–7
RNAV Minima

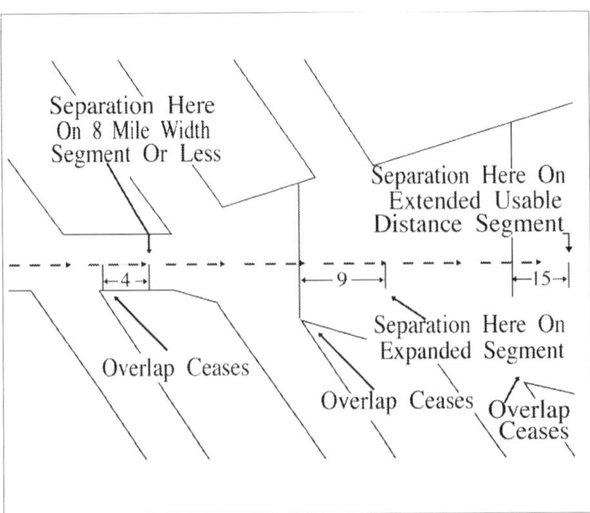

a. When operating along a route that is 8 miles or less in width– *4 miles.*

b. When operating along any route segment that is greater than 8 miles in width – *9 miles,* except that *15 miles* must be applied along that portion of any route segment requiring extended usable distance limitation beyond 130 miles of the reference facility.

NOTE–
Except for GNSS-equipped aircraft /G, /L, /S, and /V, not on a random impromptu route, paragraph 5–5–1, Application, requires radar separation be provided to RNAV aircraft operating at and below FL450 on Q routes or random RNAV routes, excluding oceanic airspace.

FIG 6–5–8
RNAV Minima

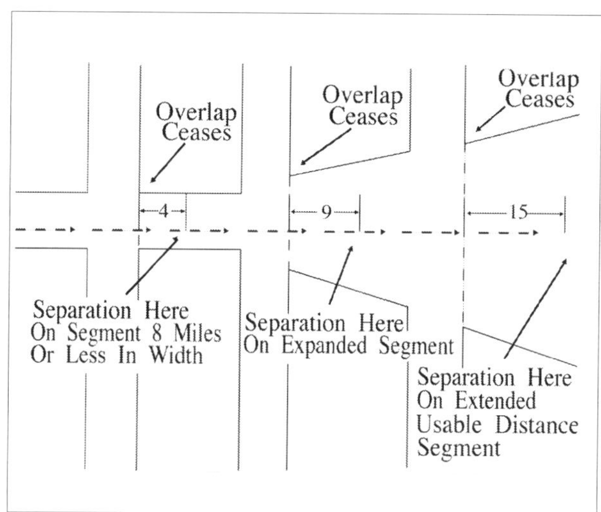

Section 6. Vertical Separation

6–6–1. APPLICATION

Assign an altitude to an aircraft after the aircraft previously at that altitude has reported leaving the altitude.

PHRASEOLOGY–
REPORT LEAVING/REACHING (altitude/flight level).

REPORT LEAVING ODD/EVEN ALTITUDES/FLIGHT LEVELS.

(If aircraft is known to be operating below the lowest useable flight level),

SAY ALTITUDE.

or

(If aircraft is known to be operating at or above the lowest useable flight level),

SAY FLIGHT LEVEL.

or

If aircraft's position relative to the lowest useable flight level is unknown),

SAY ALTITUDE OR FLIGHT LEVEL.

NOTE–
Consider known aircraft performance characteristics, pilot furnished and/or Mode C detected information which indicate that climb/descent will not be consistent with the rates recommended in the AIM.

REFERENCE–
FAA Order JO 7110.65, Para 2–1–3, Procedural Preference.
FAA Order JO 7110.65, Para 4–5–1, Vertical Separation Minima.
FAA Order JO 7110.65, Para 7–7–3, Separation.
FAA Order JO 7110.65, Para 7–8–3, Separation.
FAA Order JO 7110.65, Para 7–9–4, Separation.

6–6–2. EXCEPTIONS

Assign an altitude to an aircraft only after the aircraft previously at that altitude has reported at or passing through another altitude separated from the first by the appropriate minimum when:

a. Severe turbulence is reported.

b. Aircraft are conducting military aerial refueling.

REFERENCE–
FAA Order JO 7110.65, Para 9–2–13, Military Aerial Refueling.

c. The aircraft previously at the altitude has been:

1. Issued a clearance permitting climb/descent at pilot's discretion.

2. Cleared to CRUISE (altitude). However, do not use Mode C to effect separation with an aircraft on a cruise clearance.

NOTE–
An aircraft assigned a cruise clearance is assigned a block of airspace from the minimum IFR altitude up to and including the assigned cruising altitude, and climb/descent within the block is at pilot's discretion. When the pilot verbally reports leaving an altitude in descent, he/she may not return to that altitude.

REFERENCE–
P/CG Term – Cruise.

6–6–3. SEPARATION BY PILOTS

When pilots of aircraft in direct radio communication with each other during climb and descent concur, you may authorize the lower aircraft, if climbing, or the upper aircraft, if descending, to maintain vertical separation.

Section 7. Timed Approaches

6–7–1. APPLICATION

Timed approaches using either nonradar procedures or radar vectors to the final approach course may be used at airports served by a tower if the following conditions are met:

NOTE–
These procedures require NAVAIDs and standard/special instrument approach procedures or adequate radar coverage which permit an aircraft to:

1. *Hold at a fix located on the approach course or to be radar vectored to the final approach course for a straight-in approach in accordance with the minima specified in paragraph 6–7–5, Interval Minima.*

2. *Proceed in the direction of the airport along the approach course crossing the holding/approach fix at a specified altitude if required.*

3. *Continue descent for an approach to destination airport.*

a. Direct communication is maintained with the aircraft until the pilot is instructed to contact the tower.

b. If more than one missed approach procedure is available, none require course reversal.

c. If only one missed approach procedure is available, the following conditions are met:

1. Course reversal is not required.

2. Reported ceiling and visibility are equal to or greater than the highest prescribed circling minimums for the instrument approach procedure in use.

NOTE–
Determination of whether or not an existing ceiling meets minima is accomplished by comparing MDA (MSL) with ceiling (AGL) plus the airport elevation.

REFERENCE–
FAA Order JO 7110.65, Para 6–7–2, Approach Sequence.

6–7–2. APPROACH SEQUENCE

When an aircraft passes the final approach fix inbound (nonprecision approach) or the outer marker or the fix used in lieu of the outer marker inbound (precision approach), issue clearances for a succeeding timed approach in accordance with the following:

REFERENCE–
FAA Order JO 7110.65, Para 5–9–5, Approach Separation Responsibility.
FAA Order JO 7110.65, Para 6–7–4, Level Flight Restriction.
FAA Order JO 7110.65, Para 6–7–7, Missed Approaches.

a. Clear the succeeding aircraft for approach, to descend to the altitude vacated by the preceding aircraft, and to leave the final approach fix inbound (nonprecision approach) or the outer marker or the fix used in lieu of the outer marker inbound (precision approach) at a specified time; or when using radar to sequence and position aircraft on the final approach course, vector aircraft to cross the final approach fix/outer marker or the fix used in lieu of the outer marker in compliance with paragraph 6–7–5, Interval Minima.

FIG 6-7-1
Timed Approach Procedures
Using ILS and Longitudinal Separation Only

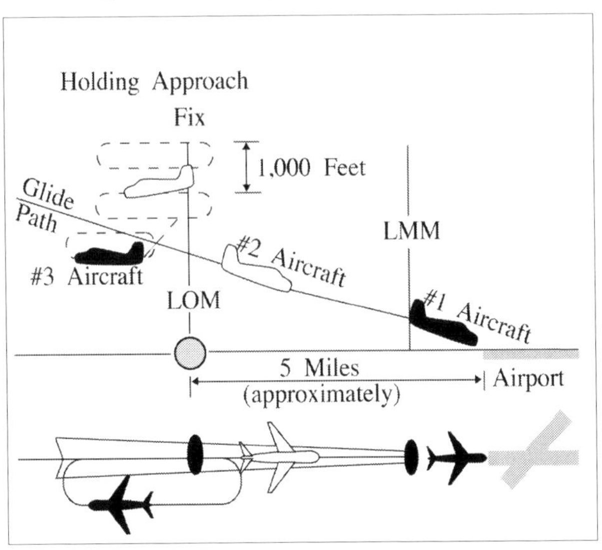

NOTE–
FIG 6-7-1 depicts the application of timed approach procedures using an ILS and applying longitudinal separation only. Using an interval of 2 minutes between successive approaches, the #1 and #2 aircraft have already passed the outer locator (LOM) on final approach, and the #3 aircraft has been cleared for approach and to depart the LOM 2 minutes after the #2 aircraft reported leaving the LOM inbound on final approach. After aircraft in the approach sequence depart the holding/approach fix (LOM) inbound, vertical separation is no longer provided and longitudinal separation is utilized.

REFERENCE–
FAA Order JO 7110.65, Para 5-9-2, Final Approach Course Interception.

b. If an alternative missed approach procedure is not available and weather conditions are less than required by paragraph 6-7-1, Application, subparagraph c, clear the succeeding aircraft for an approach when the preceding aircraft has landed or canceled its IFR flight plan.

FIG 6-7-2
Timed Approach Procedures Using a Bearing on an NDB and Longitudinal and Vertical Separation

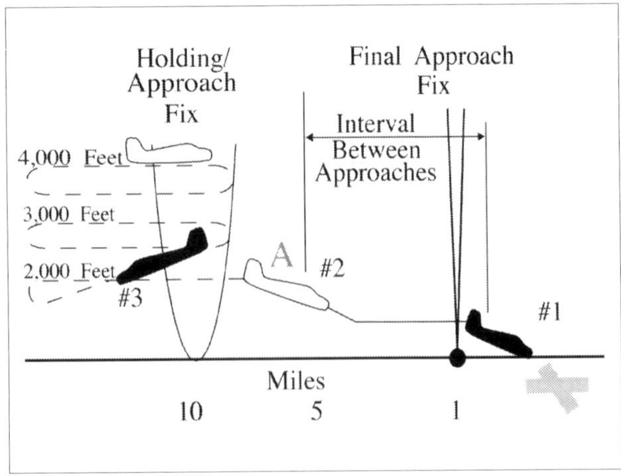

NOTE–
FIG 6-7-2 depicts the application of timed approach procedures using a holding/approach fix on a bearing of an NDB and applying a combination of longitudinal and vertical separation. The #3 aircraft has been instructed to descend to 2,000 after the #2 aircraft has reported departing the holding/approach fix inbound and leaving 2,000 at point A. The #2 aircraft has

departed the holding/approach fix inbound at the designated time, maintaining 2,000 until cleared for approach at point A. The #1 aircraft has been sighted, enabling the controller to issue approach clearance to the #2 aircraft at point A.

INTERPRETATION–

7110.65, 5–9–5b, Approach Separation Responsibility and Chapter 6, Section 7, Timed Approaches (6–19–2015)

c. Release the aircraft to the tower before it reaches the final approach fix.

6–7–3. SEQUENCE INTERRUPTION

Interrupt the established timed approach sequence if necessary to allow an aircraft to execute a different type of approach.

6–7–4. LEVEL FLIGHT RESTRICTION

If the weather report indicates an aircraft will be in IFR conditions over the final approach fix (nonprecision approach) or the outer marker or the fix used in lieu of the outer marker (precision approach) when paragraph 6–7–2, Approach Sequence, subparagraph b is applied, clear the second aircraft for an approach early enough to allow at least 1 minute of level flight before crossing the final approach fix/outer marker or the fix used in lieu of the outer marker.

6–7–5. INTERVAL MINIMA

a. Except as provided in subparagraph b, use a *2–minute* or a *5–mile* radar interval as the minimum between successive approaches.

REFERENCE–

FAA Order JO 7110.65, Para 5–9–5, Approach Separation Responsibility.
FAA Order JO 7110.65, Para 6–7–1, Application.
FAA Order JO 7110.65, Para 6–7–2, Approach Sequence.

WAKE TURBULENCE APPLICATION

b. Use the following time or radar interval as the minimum interval:

1. Behind super:

(a) Heavy – *3 minutes* or *6 miles.*

(b) Large – *3 minutes* or *7 miles.*

(c) Small – *4 minutes* or *8 miles.*

2. Small behind heavy – *3 minutes* or *6 miles.*

c. Increase the interval, as necessary, taking into account the:

1. Relative speeds of the aircraft concerned.

2. Existing weather conditions.

3. Distance between the approach fix and the airport.

4. Type of approach being made.

6–7–6. TIME CHECK

Issue a time check to an aircraft before specifying a time to leave the approach fix inbound unless the aircraft is vectored to the final approach course.

6–7–7. MISSED APPROACHES

a. If weather conditions are such that an aircraft will likely miss an approach, issue an alternative missed approach procedure to the next aircraft.

b. If an aircraft misses an approach, allow the next aircraft to continue the approach if it has been assigned an alternative missed approach procedure. Retain radar control or hold any remaining aircraft at assigned altitudes until traffic conditions permit the issuance of approach clearances.

c. When paragraph 6−7−2, Approach Sequence, subparagraph b is applied and the first aircraft misses an approach, retain radar control or clear the second aircraft to maintain the last assigned altitude (minimum holding altitude) and return to the holding/approach fix to hold until traffic conditions permit the issuance of approach clearances.

Chapter 7. Visual

Section 1. General

7-1-1. CLASS A AIRSPACE RESTRICTIONS

Do not apply visual separation or issue VFR or "VFR-on-top" clearances in Class A airspace.

7-1-2. VFR CONDITIONS

a. You may clear aircraft to maintain "VFR conditions" if one of the following conditions exists:

1. The pilot of an aircraft on an IFR flight plan requests a VFR climb/descent.

2. *TERMINAL.* The clearance will result in noise abatement benefits where part of the IFR departure route does not conform to an FAA- approved noise abatement route or altitude.

PHRASEOLOGY-
MAINTAIN VFR CONDITIONS.

MAINTAIN VFR CONDITIONS UNTIL (time or fix).

MAINTAIN VFR CONDITIONS ABOVE/BELOW (altitude).

CLIMB/DESCEND VFR,

and if required,

BETWEEN (altitude) AND (altitude)

or

ABOVE/BELOW (altitude).

b. When, in your judgment, there is reason to believe that flight in VFR conditions may become impractical, issue an alternative clearance which will ensure separation from all other aircraft for which you have separation responsibility.

PHRASEOLOGY-
IF UNABLE, (alternative procedure), AND ADVISE.

7-1-3. APPROACH CONTROL SERVICE FOR VFR ARRIVING AIRCRAFT

Issue the following where procedures have been established for arriving VFR aircraft to contact approach control for landing information:

a. Wind, runway, and altimeter setting at the airport of intended landing. This information may be omitted if contained in the ATIS broadcast and the pilot states the appropriate ATIS code or if the pilot uses the phrase, "have numbers."

NOTE-
Pilot use of "have numbers" does not indicate receipt of the ATIS broadcast.

b. Traffic information on a workload permitting basis.

c. Time or place at which the aircraft is to contact the tower on local control frequency for further landing information.

d. An aircraft may be instructed to contact approach control for landing and traffic information upon initial contact with the tower.

REFERENCE–
FAA Order JO 7110.65, Para 7–6–1, Application.
FAA Order JO 7110.65, Para 7–6–2, Service Availability.

7–1–4. VISUAL HOLDING OF VFR AIRCRAFT

TERMINAL

When it becomes necessary to hold VFR aircraft at visual holding fixes, take the following actions:

a. Clear aircraft to hold at selected, prominent geographical fixes which can be easily recognized from the air, preferably those depicted on sectional charts.

NOTE–
At some locations, VFR checkpoints are depicted on Sectional Aeronautical and Terminal Area Charts. In selecting geographical fixes, depicted VFR checkpoints are preferred unless the pilot exhibits a familiarity with the local area.

REFERENCE–
FAA Order JO 7110.65, Para 4–6–5, Visual Holding Points.

b. Issue traffic information to aircraft cleared to hold at the same fix.

PHRASEOLOGY–
HOLD AT (location) UNTIL (time or other condition),

TRAFFIC (description) HOLDING AT (fix, altitude if known),

or

PROCEEDING TO (fix) FROM (direction or fix).

REFERENCE–
FAA Order JO 7110.65, Para 7–6–5, Holding.

Section 2. Visual Separation

7–2–1. VISUAL SEPARATION

Visual separation may be applied when other approved separation is assured before and after the application of visual separation. To ensure that other separation will exist, consider aircraft performance, wake turbulence, closure rate, routes of flight, known weather conditions, and aircraft position. Weather conditions must allow the aircraft to remain within sight until other separation exists. Visual separation is not authorized when the lead aircraft is a super.

REFERENCE–
FAA Order JO 7110.65, Para 2–1–20, Wake Turbulence Cautionary Advisories.
FAA Order JO 7110.65, Para 2–1–21, Traffic Advisories.
FAA Order JO 7110.65, Para 3–1–9, Use of Tower Radar Displays.
FAA Order JO 7110.65, Para 5–9–5, Approach Separation Responsibility.
FAA Order JO 7110.65, Para 7–4–1, Visual Approach.
FAA Order JO 7110.65, Para 7–4–2, Vectors for Visual Approach.
FAA Order JO 7110.65, Para 7–4–4, Approaches to Multiple Runways.
FAA Order JO 7210.3, Para 4–3–2, Appropriate Subjects.
FAA Order JO 7210.3, Para 10–3–9, Visual Separation.
P/CG Term – Visual Approach.
P/CG Term – Visual Separation.

a. TERMINAL. Visual separation may be applied between aircraft up to but not including FL180 under the following conditions:

1. Tower-applied visual separation.

(a) Maintain communication with at least one of the aircraft involved or ensure there is an ability to communicate immediately with applicable military aircraft as prescribed in paragraph 3–9–3, Departure Control Instructions, subparagraph a2.

(b) The tower visually observes the aircraft, issues timely traffic advisories, and provides visual separation between the aircraft.

(c) Issue control instructions as necessary to ensure continued separation between the applicable aircraft.

(d) Do not apply visual separation between successive departures when departure routes and/or aircraft performance preclude maintaining separation.

(e) The use of tower-applied visual separation is not authorized when wake turbulence separation is required.

(f) ATCTs at adjacent airports may be authorized to apply visual separation between their traffic and the other facility's traffic. All provisions of FAA Order JO 7110.65, paragraph 7–2–1a1, still apply.

NOTE–
Additional requirements are listed in FAA Order JO 7210.3, paragraph 10–3–9, Visual Separation.

2. Pilot-applied visual separation.

(a) Maintain communication with at least one of the aircraft involved and ensure there is an ability to communicate with the other aircraft.

(b) The pilot sees another aircraft and is instructed to maintain visual separation from the aircraft as follows:

(1) Tell the pilot about the other aircraft. Include position, direction, type, and, unless it is obvious, the other aircraft's intention.

(2) Obtain acknowledgment from the pilot that the other aircraft is in sight.

(3) Instruct the pilot to maintain visual separation from that aircraft.

PHRASEOLOGY–
(ACID), TRAFFIC, (clock position and distance), (direction) BOUND, (type of aircraft), (intentions and other relevant information).

If required,
(ACID), REPORT TRAFFIC IN SIGHT or DO YOU HAVE IT IN SIGHT?

If the pilot reports traffic in sight, or the answer is in the affirmative,

(ACID), MAINTAIN VISUAL SEPARATION

NOTE–
Towers must use the procedures contained in paragraph 3–1–6, Traffic Information, subparagraph b or c, as appropriate.

(c) If the pilot reports the traffic in sight and will maintain visual separation from it (the pilot must state both), the controller may "approve" the operation instead of restating the instructions.

PHRASEOLOGY–
(ACID), APPROVED.

NOTE–
Pilot-applied visual separation between aircraft is achieved when the controller has instructed the pilot to maintain visual separation and the pilot acknowledges with their call sign or when the controller has approved pilot-initiated visual separation.

REFERENCE–
FAA Order JO 7110.65, Para 5–4–5, Transferring Controller Handoff.

(d) If aircraft are on converging courses, inform the other aircraft of the traffic and that visual separation is being applied.

PHRASEOLOGY–
(ACID), TRAFFIC, (clock position and distance), (direction) BOUND, (type of aircraft), HAS YOU IN SIGHT AND WILL MAINTAIN VISUAL SEPARATION.

(e) Advise the pilots if the targets appear likely to merge.

NOTE–
Issue this advisory in conjunction with the instruction to maintain visual separation, the advisory to the other aircraft of the converging course, or thereafter if the controller subsequently becomes aware that the targets are merging.

EXAMPLE–
"Targets appear likely to merge."

(f) Control of aircraft maintaining visual separation may be transferred to an adjacent position/sector/facility. Coordination procedures must be specified in an LOA or facility directive.

REFERENCE–
FAA Order JO 7210.3, Para 4-3-1, Letters of Agreement.

b. *EN ROUTE.* Visual separation may be used up to but not including FL 180 when the following conditions are met:

1. Direct communication is maintained with one of the aircraft involved and there is an ability to communicate with the other.

2. A pilot sees another aircraft and is instructed to maintain visual separation from it as follows:

(a) Tell the pilot about the other aircraft including position, direction, and type. If it is not obvious, include the other aircraft's intentions.

REFERENCE–
FAA Order JO 7110.65, Para 2–1–21, Traffic Advisories.

(b) Obtain acknowledgment from the pilot that the other aircraft is in sight.

(c) Instruct the pilot to maintain visual separation from that aircraft.

PHRASEOLOGY–
(ACID), TRAFFIC, (clock position and distance), (direction) BOUND, (type of aircraft), (intentions and other relevant information). If required, (ACID), REPORT TRAFFIC IN SIGHT or DO YOU HAVE IT IN SIGHT? If the pilot reports traffic in sight, or the answer is in the affirmative, (ACID), MAINTAIN VISUAL SEPARATION

(d) If the pilot reports the traffic in sight and will maintain visual separation (the pilot must state both), the controller may "approve" the operation instead of restating the instructions.

PHRASEOLOGY–
(ACID), APPROVED.

NOTE–
Pilot-applied visual separation between aircraft is achieved when the controller has instructed the pilot to maintain visual separation and the pilot acknowledges with their call sign or when the controller has approved pilot-initiated visual separation.

(e) If the aircraft are on converging courses, inform the other aircraft of the traffic and that visual separation is being applied.

(f) Advise the pilots if the radar targets appear likely to merge.

NOTE–
Issue this advisory in conjunction with the instruction to maintain visual separation, the advisory to the other aircraft of the converging course, or thereafter if the controller subsequently becomes aware that the targets are merging.

EXAMPLE–
"Radar targets appear likely to merge."

PHRASEOLOGY–
(ACID) TRAFFIC, (clock position and distance), (direction)–BOUND, (type of aircraft), ON CONVERGING COURSE, HAS YOU IN SIGHT AND WILL MAINTAIN VISUAL SEPARATION.

REFERENCE–
FAA Order JO 7110.65, Para 7–4–1, Visual Approach.
FAA Order JO 7110.65, Para 7–4–2, Vectors for Visual Approach.

(g) Advise the pilots if either aircraft is a heavy.

(h) Issue wake turbulence cautionary advisories in accordance with paragraph 2–1–20.

INTERPRETATION–
7110.65, 7–2–1b, Visual Separation (5–24–2017)
7110.65, 7–2–1c, Visual Separation (7–17–2015)

c. Nonapproach control towers may be authorized to provide visual separation between aircraft within surface areas or designated areas when approved separation is provided before and after the application of visual separation. The nonapproach control tower must apply the procedures contained in subparagraph a1 or a2, when applying visual separation.

PHRASEOLOGY–
VISUAL SEPARATION APPROVED BETWEEN (ACID) AND (ACID),

and for departing aircraft,

(departing/succeeding aircraft) (ACID), RELEASED.

d. If the nonapproach control tower controller states to the radar controller that they will provide visual separation between arrivals, departures/arrivals and/or successive departures, and states the call signs of all aircraft involved, the radar controller can approve the application of visual separation as requested.

PHRASEOLOGY–
VISUAL SEPARATION APPROVED and for departing/succeeding aircraft, (ACIDs) RELEASED

NOTE–
A nonapproach control tower by accepting authorization for visual separation becomes responsible for ensuring that separation. Separation of IFR aircraft before and after application of visual separation is an IFR control function that must

be applied by the Approach/Departure/En Route facility. Separation requirements also apply to VFR aircraft when IFR, Class B, Class C or TRSA separation services are required.

REFERENCE−
FAA Order JO 7110.65, Para 4−8−11, Practice Approaches.
FAA Order JO 7110.65, Para 5−6−1, Application.
FAA Order JO 7110.65, Para 7−4−2, Vectors for Visual Approach.
FAA Order JO 7110.65, Para 7−6−1, Application.
FAA Order JO 7110.65, Para 7−7−1, Application.
FAA Order JO 7110.65, Para 7−7−2, Issuance of EFC.
FAA Order JO 7110.65, Para 7−7−3, Separation.
FAA Order JO 7110.65, Para 7−7−4, Helicopter Traffic.
FAA Order JO 7110.65, Para 7−7−5, Altitude Assignments.
FAA Order JO 7110.65, Para 7−7−6, Approach Interval.
FAA Order JO 7110.65, Para 7−7−7, TRSA Departure Information.
FAA Order JO 7110.65, Para 7−8−2, Class C Services.
FAA Order JO 7110.65, Para 7−8−3, Separation.
FAA Order JO 7110.65, Para 7−8−4, Establishing Two−Way Communications.
FAA Order JO 7110.65, Para 7−8−5, Altitude Assignments.
FAA Order JO 7110.65, Para 7−8−6, Exceptions.
FAA Order JO 7110.65, Para 7−9−1, Application.
FAA Order JO 7110.65, Para 7−9−3, Methods.
FAA Order JO 7110.65, Para 7−9−4, Separation.
FAA Order JO 7110.65, Para 7−9−6, Helicopter Traffic.
FAA Order JO 7110.65, Para 7−9−7, Altitude Assignments.

Section 3. VFR-On-Top

7–3–1. VFR-ON-TOP

a. You may clear an aircraft to maintain "VFR-on-top" if the pilot of an aircraft on an IFR flight plan requests the clearance.

PHRASEOLOGY–
MAINTAIN VFR-ON-TOP.

NOTE–
1. *When an aircraft has been cleared to maintain "VFR-on-top," the pilot is responsible to fly at an appropriate VFR altitude, comply with VFR visibility and distance from cloud criteria, and to be vigilant so as to see and avoid other aircraft. The pilot is also responsible to comply with instrument flight rules applicable to the flight (e.g., adherence to ATC clearances).*

2. *Although IFR separation is not applied, controllers must continue to provide traffic advisories and safety alerts, and apply merging target procedures to aircraft operating VFR-on-top.*

REFERENCE–
FAA Order JO 7110.65, Para 2–1–6, Safety Alert.
FAA Order JO 7110.65, Para 2–1–21, Traffic Advisories.
FAA Order JO 7110.65, Para 5–1–4, Merging Target Procedures.
FAA Order JO 7110.65, Para 7–1–1, Class A Airspace Restrictions.
AIM, Para 5–5–13, VFR–on–top.
14 CFR Section 91.157, Special VFR Weather Minimums.
14 CFR Section 91.159, VFR Cruising Altitude or Flight Level.

b. You may clear an aircraft to climb through clouds, smoke, haze, or other meteorological formations and then to maintain "VFR-on-top" if the following conditions are met:

1. The pilot requests the clearance.

2. You inform the pilot of the reported height of the tops of the meteorological formation, or

3. You inform the pilot that no top report is available.

4. When necessary, you ensure separation from all other traffic for which you have separation responsibility by issuing an alternative clearance.

5. When an aircraft is climbing to and reports reaching "VFR-on-top," reclear the aircraft to maintain "VFR-on-top."

PHRASEOLOGY–
CLIMB TO AND REPORT REACHING VFR-ON-TOP,

and

TOPS REPORTED (altitude),

or

NO TOPS REPORTS.

IF NOT ON TOP AT (altitude), MAINTAIN (altitude), AND ADVISE.

MAINTAIN VFR-ON-TOP.

c. Do not clear an aircraft to maintain "VFR-on-top" between sunset and sunrise to separate holding aircraft from each other or from en route aircraft unless restrictions are applied to ensure the appropriate IFR vertical separation.

PHRASEOLOGY–
MAINTAIN VFR-ON-TOP AT OR ABOVE/BELOW/BETWEEN (altitudes).

EXAMPLE–
"Maintain VFR-on-top at or above one three thousand five hundred."

"Maintain VFR-on-top at or below one two thousand five hundred."

"Maintain VFR-on-top at or between six thousand and one zero thousand."

d. When, in your judgment, there is reason to believe that flight in VFR conditions may become impractical, issue an alternative clearance which will ensure separation from all other aircraft for which you have separation responsibility.

PHRASEOLOGY–
IF UNABLE, (alternative procedure), AND ADVISE.

REFERENCE–
FAA Order JO 7110.65, Para 9–3–3, VFR-On-Top.

7–3–2. ALTITUDE FOR DIRECTION OF FLIGHT

Inform an aircraft maintaining "VFR-on-top" when a report indicates the pilot is not complying with 14 CFR Section 91.159(a).

NOTE–
As required by 14 CFR Section 91.159(a), the appropriate VFR altitudes for aircraft (not in a holding pattern of 2 minutes or less, or turning) operating more than 3,000 feet above the surface to and including 18,000 feet MSL:

Magnetic courses 0–179– odd cardinal altitudes plus 500 feet; e.g., 3,500, 5,500.

Magnetic courses 180–359– even cardinal altitudes plus 500 feet; e.g., 4,500, 8,500.

PHRASEOLOGY–
VFR-ON-TOP CRUISING LEVELS FOR YOUR DIRECTION OF FLIGHT ARE:

more than 3,000 feet above the surface to FL 180:

ODD/EVEN ALTITUDES/FLIGHT LEVELS PLUS FIVE HUNDRED FEET.

Section 4. Approaches

7–4–1. VISUAL APPROACH

A visual approach is an ATC authorization for an aircraft on an IFR flight plan to proceed visually and clear of clouds to the airport of intended landing. A visual approach is not a standard instrument approach procedure and has no missed approach segment. An aircraft unable to complete a landing from a visual approach must be handled as any go–around and appropriate IFR separation must be provided until the aircraft lands or the pilot cancels their IFR flight plan.

a. At airports with an operating control tower, aircraft executing a go–around may be directed to:

1. Enter the traffic pattern for landing. An altitude assignment is not required. The pilot is expected to climb to pattern altitude and is responsible to maintain terrain and obstruction avoidance. ATC must provide approved separation or visual separation from other IFR aircraft, or

2. Proceed as otherwise instructed by ATC. The pilot is expected to comply with assigned instructions, and responsible to maintain terrain and obstruction avoidance until reaching an ATC assigned altitude. ATC is responsible to provide instructions to the pilot to facilitate a climb to the minimum altitude for instrument operations. ATC must provide approved separation or visual separation from other IFR aircraft.

NOTE–
The pilot is responsible for their own terrain and obstruction avoidance during a go–around after conducting a visual approach. The facility can assign headings towards the lowest terrain and obstructions.

b. At airports without an operating control tower, aircraft executing a go–around are expected to complete a landing as soon as possible or contact ATC for further clearance. ATC must maintain approved separation from other IFR aircraft.

REFERENCE–
FAA Order JO 7110.65, Para 2–1–4, Operational Priority.
FAA Order JO 7110.65, Para 2–1–20, Wake Turbulence Cautionary Advisories.
FAA Order JO 7110.65, Para 3–10–2, Forwarding Approach Information by Nonapproach Control Facilities.
FAA Order JO 7110.65, Para 7–2–1, Visual Separation.
FAA Order JO 7110.65, Para 7–4–4, Approaches to Multiple Runways.
FAA Order JO 7210.3, Para 10–3–15, Go–around/Missed Approach.
P/CG Term – Go–around.
AIM, Para 5–4–23, Visual Approach.

7–4–2. VECTORS FOR VISUAL APPROACH

A vector for a visual approach may be initiated if the reported ceiling at the airport of intended landing is at least 500 feet above the MVA/MIA and the visibility is 3 miles or greater. At airports without weather reporting service there must be reasonable assurance (e.g. area weather reports, PIREPs, etc.) that descent and flight to the airport can be made visually, and the pilot must be informed that weather information is not available.

PHRASEOLOGY–
(Ident) FLY HEADING

or
TURN RIGHT/LEFT HEADING (degrees) VECTOR FOR VISUAL APPROACH TO (airport name).

(If appropriate)

WEATHER NOT AVAILABLE.

NOTE–
At airports where weather information is not available, a pilot request for a visual approach indicates that descent and flight to the airport can be made visually and clear of clouds.

REFERENCE–
FAA Order JO 7110.65, Para 5–9–1, Vectors to Final Approach Course.
FAA Order JO 7110.65, Para 7–2–1, Visual Separation.
FAA Order JO 7110.65, Para 7–4–3, Clearance for Visual Approach.
FAA Order JO 7110.65, Para 7–4–4, Approaches to Multiple Runways.
FAA Order JO 7110.65, Para 7–6–7, Sequencing.
FAA Order JO 7110.65, Para 7–7–3, Separation.

7–4–3. CLEARANCE FOR VISUAL APPROACH

ARTCCs and approach controls may clear aircraft for visual approaches using the following procedures:

NOTE–
Towers may exercise this authority when authorized by a LOA with the facility that provides the IFR service, or by a facility directive at collocated facilities.

a. Controllers may initiate, or pilots may request, a visual approach even when an aircraft is being vectored for an instrument approach and the pilot subsequently reports:

1. The airport or the runway in sight at airports with operating control towers.

2. The airport in sight at airports without a control tower.

b. Resolve potential conflicts with all other aircraft, advise an overtaking aircraft of the distance to the preceding aircraft and speed difference, and ensure that weather conditions at the airport are VFR or that the pilot has been informed that weather is not available for the destination airport. Upon pilot request, advise the pilot of the frequency to receive weather information where AWOS/ASOS is available.

REFERENCE–
FAA Order JO 7110.65, Para 7–2–1, Visual Separation.

INTERPRETATION–
7110.65 7–4–3b, Clearance for Visual Approach and 4–7–10b(2), Approach Information (12–1–2014)

c. Clear an aircraft for a visual approach when:

1. The aircraft is number one in the approach sequence, or

2. At locations with an operating control tower, the aircraft is to follow a preceding aircraft and the pilot reports the preceding aircraft in sight and is instructed to follow it to the same runway, or

NOTE–
The pilot need not report the airport/runway in sight.

3. At locations with an operating control tower, the pilot reports the airport or runway in sight but not the preceding aircraft. Radar separation must be maintained until visual separation is provided.

4. At locations without an operating control tower or where part–time towers are closed, do not specify a runway when issuing a visual approach clearance, issue a visual approach clearance to the airport only.

PHRASEOLOGY–
(at locations with an operating control tower)

(Call sign) (control instructions as required) CLEARED VISUAL APPROACH RUNWAY number);

or

(at locations without an operating control tower)

(Call sign) (control instructions as required) CLEARED VISUAL APPROACH TO (airport name)

(and if appropriate)

WEATHER NOT AVAILABLE

or

VERIFY THAT YOU HAVE THE (airport) WEATHER.

REFERENCE−
FAA Order JO 7110.65, Para 7−2−1, Visual Separation.

d. All aircraft following a heavy, or a small aircraft following a B757, must be informed of the airplane manufacturer and/or model.

EXAMPLE−
"Cessna Three Four Juliett, following a Boeing 757, 12 o'clock, six miles."

or

"Cessna Three Four Juliett, following a Seven fifty seven, 12 o'clock, six miles."

REFERENCE−
FAA Order JO 7110.65, Para 2−4−21, Description of Aircraft Types.

NOTE−
Visual separation is not authorized when the lead aircraft is a super.

REFERENCE−
FAA Order JO 7110.65, Para 7−2−1, Visual Separation.

e. Inform the tower of the aircraft's position prior to communications transfer at controlled airports. STARS functions may be used provided a facility directive or LOA specifies control and communication transfer points.

f. In addition to the requirements of paragraph 7−4−2, Vectors for Visual Approach, and subparagraphs a, b, c, d, and e, ensure that the location of the destination airport is provided when the pilot is asked to report the destination airport in sight.

g. In those instances where airports are located in close proximity, also provide the location of the airport that may cause the confusion.

EXAMPLE−
"Cessna Five Six November, Cleveland Burke Lakefront Airport is at 12 o'clock, 5 miles. Cleveland Hopkins Airport is at 1 o'clock 12 miles. Report Cleveland Hopkins in sight."

REFERENCE−
FAA Order JO 7110.65, Para 7−4−4, Approaches to Multiple Runways.

7−4−4. APPROACHES TO MULTIPLE RUNWAYS

a. All aircraft must be informed that approaches are being conducted to parallel, intersecting, or converging runways. This may be accomplished through use of the ATIS.

b. When conducting visual approaches to multiple runways ensure the following:

1. Do not permit the respective aircrafts' primary radar targets/fusion target symbols to touch unless visual separation is being applied.

2. When the aircraft flight paths intersect, ensure approved separation is maintained until visual separation is applied.

c. The following conditions apply to visual approaches being conducted simultaneously to parallel, intersecting, and converging runways, as appropriate:

1. Parallel runways separated by less than 2,500 feet. Unless approved separation is provided, an aircraft must report sighting a preceding aircraft making an approach (instrument or visual) to the adjacent parallel runway. When an aircraft reports another aircraft in sight on the adjacent extended runway centerline and visual separation is applied, controllers must advise the succeeding aircraft to maintain visual separation. Do not permit an aircraft to overtake another aircraft when wake turbulence separation is required.

2. Parallel runways separated by 2,500 feet but less than 4,300 feet.

(a) When aircraft are approaching from opposite base legs, or one aircraft is turning to final and another aircraft is established on the extended centerline for the adjacent runway, approved separation is provided until the aircraft are:

(1) Established on a heading or established on a direct course to a fix or cleared on an RNAV/ instrument approach procedure which will intercept the extended centerline of the runway at an angle not greater than 30 degrees, and,

INTERPRETATION–
7110.65 7–4–4, Approaches to Multiple Runways (8–14–2015)

(2) One pilot has acknowledged receipt of a visual approach clearance and the other pilot has acknowledged receipt of a visual or instrument approach clearance.

(b) When aircraft are approaching from the same side of the airport and the lead aircraft is assigned the nearer runway, approved separation is maintained or pilot–applied visual separation is provided by the succeeding aircraft until intercepting the farther adjacent extended runway centerline.

(c) Provided that aircraft flight paths do not intersect, when the provisions of subparagraphs (a), (b), or (d) are met, it is not necessary to apply any other type of separation with aircraft on the adjacent extended runway centerline.

(d) When aircraft are approaching from the same side of the airport and the lead aircraft is assigned the farther runway, the succeeding aircraft must be assigned a heading that will intercept the extended centerline of the nearer runway at an angle not greater than 30 degrees. Approved separation must be maintained or pilot–applied visual separation must be provided by the succeeding aircraft until it is established on the extended centerline of the nearer runway.

NOTE–

1. *The intent of the 30 degree intercept angle is to reduce the potential for overshoots of the extended centerline of the runway and preclude side-by-side operations with one or both aircraft in a "belly-up" configuration during the turn. Aircraft performance, speed, and the number of degrees of the turn are factors to be considered when vectoring aircraft to parallel runways.*

2. *The 30-degree intercept angle is not necessary when approved separation is maintained until the aircraft are established on the extended centerline of the assigned runway.*

3. *Variances between heading assigned to intercept the extended centerline of the runway and aircraft ground track are expected due to the effect of wind and course corrections after completion of the turn and pilot acknowledgment of a visual approach clearance.*

4. *Procedures using Radius-to-Fix legs that intercept final may be used in lieu of the 30-degree intercept provisions contained in this paragraph.*

3. Parallel runways separated by 4,300 feet or more.

(a) When aircraft are approaching from opposite base legs, or one aircraft is turning to final and another aircraft is established on the extended centerline for the adjacent runway, approved separation is provided until the aircraft are:

(1) Assigned a heading or established on a direct course to a fix or cleared on an RNAV/instrument approach procedure which will intercept the extended centerline of the runway at an angle not greater than 30 degrees, and,

(2) One of the aircraft has been issued and the pilot has acknowledged receipt of the visual approach clearance.

(b) When aircraft are approaching from the same side of the airport and the lead aircraft is assigned the nearer runway, approved separation is maintained or pilot–applied visual separation is provided by the succeeding aircraft until intercepting the farther adjacent extended runway centerline.

(c) Provided that aircraft flight paths do not intersect, when the provisions of subparagraphs (a), (b), or (d) are met, it is not necessary to apply any other type of separation with aircraft on the adjacent extended runway centerline.

(d) When aircraft are approaching from the same side of the airport and the lead aircraft is assigned the farther runway, the succeeding aircraft must be assigned a heading that will intercept the extended centerline of the nearer runway at an angle not greater than 30 degrees. Approved separation must be maintained or pilot–applied visual separation must be provided by the succeeding aircraft until it is established on the extended centerline of the nearer runway.

NOTE–

1. *The intent of the 30 degree intercept angle is to reduce the potential for overshoots of the extended centerline of the runway and preclude side-by-side operations with one or both aircraft in a "belly-up" configuration during the turn. Aircraft performance, speed, and the number of degrees of the turn are factors to be considered when vectoring aircraft to parallel runways.*

2. *The 30–degree intercept angle is not necessary when approved separation is maintained until the aircraft are established on the extended centerline of the assigned runway.*

3. *Variances between heading assigned to intercept the extended centerline of the runway and aircraft ground track are expected due to the effect of wind and course corrections after completion of the turn and pilot acknowledgment of a visual approach clearance.*

4. *Procedures using Radius-to-Fix legs that intercept final may be used in lieu of 30-degree intercept provisions contained in this paragraph.*

(e) Visual approaches may be conducted to one runway while visual or instrument approaches are conducted simultaneously to other runways, provided the conditions of subparagraph (a), (b), or (d) are met.

4. Intersecting and converging runways. Visual approaches may be conducted simultaneously with visual or instrument approaches to other runways, provided:

(a) Approved separation is maintained until the aircraft conducting the visual approach has been issued, and the pilot has acknowledged receipt of, the visual approach clearance.

(b) When aircraft flight paths intersect, approved separation must be maintained until visual separation is provided.

NOTE–

Although simultaneous approaches may be conducted to intersecting runways, staggered approaches may be necessary to meet the airport separation requirements specified in paragraph 3–10–4, Intersecting Runway/Intersecting Flight Path Separation.

REFERENCE–
FAA Order JO 7110.65, Para 7–7–3, Separation.
FAA Order JO 7110.65, Para 7–8–3, Separation.
FAA Order JO 7110.65, Para 7–9–4, Separation.

7–4–5. CHARTED VISUAL FLIGHT PROCEDURES (CVFP). USA/USN NOT APPLICABLE

Clear an aircraft for a CVFP only when the following conditions are met:

a. There is an operating control tower.

b. The published name of the CVFP and the landing runway are specified in the approach clearance, the reported ceiling at the airport of intended landing is at least 500 feet above the MVA/MIA, and the visibility is 3 miles or more, unless higher minimums are published for the particular CVFP.

c. When using parallel or intersecting/converging runways, the criteria specified in paragraph 7–4–4, Approaches to Multiple Runways, are applied.

d. An aircraft not following another aircraft on the approach reports sighting a charted visual landmark, or reports sighting a preceding aircraft landing on the same runway and has been instructed to follow that aircraft.

PHRASEOLOGY–

(Ident) CLEARED (name of CVFP) APPROACH.

7–4–6. RNAV VISUAL FLIGHT PROCEDURES (RVFP)

RNAV Visual Flight Procedures (RVFPs) are special procedures flown in VMC and clear of clouds and used by authorized operators only. Clear an aircraft for an RVFP when:

a. Requested by the pilot, or if necessary, as addressed in a Letter of Agreement (LOA).

b. The pilot reports the airport in sight or, at locations with an operating control tower, the preceding aircraft in sight.

c. An altitude is assigned at or above the MVA/MIA, before issuing an approach clearance when conducting an RVFP. The pilot should join the RVFP at the beginning of the charted procedure, or if necessary, may join at another waypoint along the path of the charted procedure, except for waypoints beginning or within an RF leg.

d. The official weather at the airport of intended landing indicates VFR and should meet or exceed the ceiling and visibility specified on the RVFP.

e. The published name of the RVFP and the landing runway are specified in the approach clearance.

PHRASEOLOGY–
(Ident) CLEARED RNAV VISUAL RUNWAY (number) APPROACH

NOTE–
Refer to the facility RVFP LOAs, if applicable, to determine the authorized operators.

REFERENCE–
FAA Order 8260.60, Special Procedures.

7–4–7. CONTACT APPROACH

Clear an aircraft for a contact approach only if the following conditions are met:

a. The pilot has requested it.

NOTE–
When executing a contact approach, the pilot is responsible for maintaining the required flight visibility, cloud clearance, and terrain/obstruction clearance. Unless otherwise restricted, the pilot may find it necessary to descend, climb, and/or fly a circuitous route to the airport to maintain cloud clearance and/or terrain/obstruction clearance. It is not in any way intended that controllers will initiate or suggest a contact approach to a pilot.

b. The reported ground visibility is at least 1 statute mile.

c. A standard or special instrument approach procedure has been published and is functioning for the airport of intended landing.

d. Approved separation is applied between aircraft so cleared and other IFR or SVFR aircraft. When applying vertical separation, do not assign a fixed altitude but clear the aircraft at or below an altitude which is at least 1,000 feet below any IFR traffic but not below the minimum safe altitude prescribed in 14 CFR Section 91.119.

NOTE–
14 CFR Section 91.119 specifies the minimum safe altitude to be flown:
(a) Anywhere.
(b) Over congested areas.
(c) Other than congested areas. To provide for an emergency landing in the event of power failure and without undue hazard to persons or property on the surface.
(d) Helicopters. May be operated at less than the minimums prescribed in (b) and (c) above if the operation is conducted without hazard to persons or property on the surface.

e. An alternative clearance is issued when weather conditions are such that a contact approach may be impracticable.

PHRASEOLOGY–
CLEARED CONTACT APPROACH,

And if required,
AT OR BELOW (altitude) (routing).

IF NOT POSSIBLE, (alternative procedures), AND ADVISE.

Section 5. Special VFR (SVFR)

7-5-1. AUTHORIZATION

a. SVFR operations in weather conditions less than basic VFR minima are authorized:

REFERENCE–
FAA Order JO 7110.65, Para 2-1-4, Operational Priority.

1. At any location not prohibited by 14 CFR Part 91, Appendix D or when an exemption to 14 CFR Part 91 has been granted and an associated LOA established. 14 CFR Part 91 does not prohibit SVFR helicopter operations.

2. Only within the lateral boundaries of Class B, Class C, Class D, or Class E surface areas, below 10,000 feet MSL.

3. Only when requested by the pilot.

4. On the basis of weather conditions reported at the airport of intended landing/departure.

REFERENCE–
FAA Order JO 7110.65, Para 7-5-6, Climb to VFR.
FAA Order JO 7110.65, Para 7-5-7, Ground Visibility Below One Mile.

5. When weather conditions are not reported at the airport of intended landing/departure and the pilot advises that VFR cannot be maintained and requests SVFR.

PHRASEOLOGY–
CLEARED TO ENTER/OUT OF/THROUGH, (name) SURFACE AREA

and if required,

(direction) OF (name) AIRPORT (specified routing),
and

MAINTAIN SPECIAL V-F-R CONDITIONS,

and if required,

AT OR BELOW (altitude below 10,000 feet MSL)

or as applicable under an exemption from 14 CFR Part 91,

CLEARED FOR (coded arrival or departure procedure) ARRIVAL/DEPARTURE, (additional instructions as required).

REFERENCE–
FAA Order JO 7110.65, Para 2-4-22, Airspace Classes.

b. SVFR operations may be authorized for aircraft operating in or transiting a Class B, Class C, Class D, or Class E surface area when the primary airport is reporting VFR but the pilot advises that basic VFR cannot be maintained.

NOTE–
The basic requirements for issuance of a SVFR clearance in subparagraph a apply with the obvious exception that weather conditions at the controlling airport are not required to be less than basic VFR minima.

7-5-2. PRIORITY

a. SVFR flights may be approved only if arriving and departing IFR aircraft are not delayed.

EXAMPLE–
1. *A SVFR aircraft has been cleared to enter a Class B, Class C, Class D, or Class E surface area and subsequently an IFR*

aircraft is ready to depart or is in position to begin an approach. Less overall delay might accrue to the IFR aircraft if the SVFR aircraft is allowed to proceed to the airport and land, rather than leave, a Class B, Class C, Class D, or Class E surface area or be repositioned to provide IFR priority.

2. *A SVFR aircraft is number one for takeoff and located in such a position that the number two aircraft, an IFR flight, cannot taxi past to gain access to the runway. Less overall delay might accrue to the IFR aircraft by releasing the SVFR departure rather than by having the aircraft taxi down the runway to a turnoff point so the IFR aircraft could be released first.*

NOTE−
The priority afforded IFR aircraft over SVFR aircraft is not intended to be so rigidly applied that inefficient use of airspace results. The controller has the prerogative of permitting completion of a SVFR operation already in progress when an IFR aircraft becomes a factor if better overall efficiency will result.

b. Inform an aircraft of the anticipated delay when a SVFR clearance cannot be granted because of IFR traffic. Do not issue an EFC or expected departure time.

PHRASEOLOGY−
EXPECT (number) MINUTES DELAY, (additional instructions as necessary).

REFERENCE−
FAA Order JO 7110.65, Para 2−1−4, Operational Priority.
FAA Order JO 7110.65, Para 5−6−1, Application.

7−5−3. SEPARATION

a. Apply nonradar or visual separation between:

1. SVFR fixed−wing aircraft.

2. SVFR fixed−wing aircraft and SVFR Helicopters.

3. SVFR fixed−wing aircraft and IFR aircraft.

NOTE−
1. *Vertical separation is authorized between SVFR fixed-wing aircraft and IFR aircraft as prescribed in FAA Order JO 7110.65, paragraph 7−5−4, Altitude Assignments*

2. *Due to the requirements for SVFR fixed−wing aircraft to maintain 1-mile flight visibility and to remain clear of clouds, radar separation is not authorized during SVFR fixed−wing operations. Radar vectors are authorized, as prescribed in paragraph 5−6−1, Application, subparagraph f, to expedite the entrance, exit, and transition of SVFR fixed-wing aircraft through the appropriate surface area.*

REFERENCE−
FAA Order JO 7110.65, Chapter 6, Nonradar.
FAA Order JO 7110.65, Para 7−2−1, Visual Separation.
FAA Order JO 7110.65, Para 7−5−4, Altitude Assignment.

b. Apply nonradar, visual, or IFR radar separation between:

1. SVFR Helicopters.

2. SVFR Helicopters and IFR aircraft.

NOTE−
1. *Vertical separation is authorized between SVFR helicopters and IFR aircraft as prescribed in FAA Order JO 7110.65, paragraph 7−5−4, Altitude Assignments.*

2. *Radar separation as prescribed in Chapter 5 may be applied provided that the facility conducting the operation is authorized to provide radar separation services in accordance with FAA Order JO 7210.3, paragraph 10-5-3, Functional Use of Certified Tower Radar Displays (CTRD), subparagraph b5, and subparagraph d. Facilities that are not delegated airspace or separation responsibility must use CTRDs in accordance with FAA Order JO 7110.65, paragraph 3−1−9, Use of Tower Radar Displays, subparagraph b.*

c. Alternate SVFR helicopter separation minima may be established when warranted by the volume and/or complexity of local helicopter operations. Alternate SVFR helicopter separation minima must be established with an LOA with the helicopter operator which must specify, as a minimum, that SVFR helicopters are to maintain visual reference to the surface and adhere to the following aircraft separation minima:

1. Between a SVFR helicopter and an arriving or departing IFR aircraft:

(a) $^{1}/_{2}$ mile. If the IFR aircraft is less than 1 mile from the landing airport.

(b) 1 mile. If the IFR aircraft is 1 mile or more from the airport.

2. 1 mile between SVFR helicopters. This separation may be reduced to 200 feet if:

(a) Both helicopters are departing simultaneously on courses that diverge by at least 30 degrees and:

(1) The tower can determine this separation by reference to surface markings; or

(2) One of the departing helicopters is instructed to remain at least 200 feet from the other.

NOTE–

1. *Vertical separation is authorized between SVFR helicopters and IFR aircraft as prescribed in FAA Order JO 7110.65, paragraph 7–5–4, Altitude Assignments.*

2. *Radar separation as prescribed in Chapter 5 may be applied provided that the facility conducting the operation is authorized to provide radar separation services in accordance with FAA Order JO 7210.3, paragraph 10-5-3, Functional Use of Certified Tower Radar Displays (CTRD), subparagraph b5, and subparagraph d. Facilities that are not delegated airspace or separation responsibility must use CTRDs in accordance with FAA Order JO 7110.65, paragraph 3–1–9, Use of Tower Radar Displays, subparagraph b.*

REFERENCE–
FAA Order JO 7110.65, Para 2–1–4, Operational Priority.
FAA Order JO 7110.65, Para 7–2–1, Visual Separation.
FAA Order JO 7110.65, Para 7–5–4, Altitude Assignment.
FAA Order JO 7110.65, Chapter 6, Nonradar.
FAA Order JO 7210.3, Para 10-5-3, Functional Use of Certified Tower Radar Displays.

7–5–4. ALTITUDE ASSIGNMENT

Do not assign a fixed altitude when applying vertical separation, but clear the SVFR aircraft at or below an altitude which is at least 500 feet below any conflicting IFR traffic but not below the MSA prescribed in 14 CFR Section 91.119.

PHRASEOLOGY–
MAINTAIN SPECIAL V–F–R CONDITIONS AT OR BELOW (altitude).

NOTE–

1. *SVFR aircraft are not assigned fixed altitudes to maintain because of the clearance from clouds requirement.*

2. *The MSAs are:*

(a) Over congested areas, an altitude at least 1,000 feet above the highest obstacle, and

(b) Over other than congested areas, an altitude at least 500 feet above the surface.

(c) Helicopters may be operated at less than the minimum altitudes prescribed in (a) and (b) above.

REFERENCE–
FAA Order JO 7110.65, Para 2–1–4, Operational Priority.
FAA Order JO 7110.65, Para 5–6–1, Application.
14 CFR Section 91.119, Minimum Safe Altitudes: General.

7–5–5. LOCAL OPERATIONS

a. Authorize local SVFR operations for a specified period (series of landings and takeoffs, etc.) upon request if the aircraft can be recalled when traffic or weather conditions require. Where warranted, LOAs may be consummated.

PHRASEOLOGY–
LOCAL SPECIAL V–F–R OPERATIONS IN THE IMMEDIATE VICINITY OF (name) AIRPORT ARE AUTHORIZED UNTIL (time). MAINTAIN SPECIAL V–F–R CONDITIONS.

REFERENCE–
FAA Order JO 7210.3, Para 4–3–2, Appropriate Subjects.

b. Control facilities may also authorize an FSS to transmit SVFR clearances so that only one aircraft at a time operates in the Class B, Class C, Class D, or Class E surface areas unless pilots agree that they will maintain visual separation with other aircraft operating in the Class B, Class C, Class D, or Class E surface areas. Such authorization concerning visual separation by pilots must be contained in a LOA between the control facility and the FSS.

REFERENCE–
FAA Order JO 7210.3, Para 4–3–3, Developing LOA.
FAA Order JO 7110.65, Para 2–1–4, Operational Priority.

7–5–6. CLIMB TO VFR

Authorize an aircraft to climb to VFR upon request if the only weather limitation is restricted visibility.

PHRASEOLOGY–
CLIMB TO V–F–R WITHIN (name) SURFACE AREA/WITHIN (a specified distance) MILES FROM (airport name) AIRPORT, MAINTAIN SPECIAL V–F–R CONDITIONS UNTIL REACHING V–F–R.

REFERENCE–
FAA Order JO 7110.65, Para 2–1–4, Operational Priority.
FAA Order JO 7110.65, Para 2–4–22, Airspace Classes.
FAA Order JO 7110.65, Para 7–5–1, Authorization.

7–5–7. GROUND VISIBILITY BELOW 1 MILE

14 CFR Part 91 does not prohibit helicopter SVFR flight when the visibility is less than 1 mile. Treat requests for SVFR fixed–wing operations as follows when the ground visibility is officially reported at an airport as less than 1 mile:

a. Inform departing aircraft that ground visibility is less than 1 mile and that a clearance cannot be issued.

b. Inform arriving aircraft, operating outside of a Class B, Class C, Class D, or Class E surface area, that ground visibility is less than 1 mile and that, unless an emergency exists, a clearance cannot be issued.

c. Inform arriving aircraft, operating VFR/SVFR within a Class B, Class C, Class D, or Class E surface area, that ground visibility is less than 1 mile and request the pilot to advise intentions.

PHRASEOLOGY–
(Name of airport) VISIBILITY LESS THAN 1 MILE. ADVISE INTENTIONS.

NOTE–
Clear an aircraft to land at an airport with an operating control tower, traffic permitting, if the pilot reports the airport in sight. The pilot is responsible to continue to the airport or exit the surface area. 14 CFR Section 91.157 prohibits VFR aircraft (other than helicopters) from landing at any airport within a surface area when ground visibility is less than 1 mile. A pilot could inadvertently encounter conditions that are below SVFR minimums after entering a surface area due to rapidly changing weather. The pilot is best suited to determine the action to be taken since pilots operating under SVFR between sunrise and sunset are not required to be instrument rated, and the possibility exists that flight visibility may not be the same as ground visibility. 14 CFR Section 91.3 authorizes a pilot encountering an inflight emergency requiring immediate action to deviate from any rule of 14 CFR Part 91 to the extent required to meet that emergency. Flight into adverse weather conditions may require the pilot to execute the emergency authority granted in 14 CFR Section 91.3 and continue inbound to land.

d. Authorize scheduled air carrier aircraft in the U.S. to conduct operations if ground visibility is not less than $^1/_2$ statute mile.

NOTE–
14 CFR Part 121 permits landing or takeoff by domestic scheduled air carriers where a local surface restriction to visibility is not less than 1/2 statute mile, provided all turns after takeoff or before landing and all flights beyond 1 statute mile from the airport boundary can be accomplished above or outside the area so restricted. The pilot is solely responsible for determining if the nature of the visibility restriction will permit compliance with the provisions of 14 CFR Part 121.

e. Clear an aircraft to fly through the Class B, Class C, Class D, or Class E surface area if the aircraft reports flight visibility is at least 1 statute mile.

REFERENCE–
FAA Order JO 7110.65, Para 2–1–4, Operational Priority.
FAA Order JO 7110.65, Para 7–5–1, Authorization.

7-5-8. FLIGHT VISIBILITY BELOW 1 MILE

Treat requests for SVFR fixed-wing operations as follows when weather conditions are not reported at an airport and the pilot advises the flight visibility is less than 1 mile:

NOTE–
14 CFR Part 91 prescribes the visibility for basic VFR and SVFR operations as the official reported ground visibility at airports where provided and landing or takeoff "flight visibility" where there is no official reported ground visibility.

a. Inform departing aircraft that a clearance cannot be issued.

b. Inform arriving aircraft operating outside of a Class B, Class C, Class D or Class E surface area that a clearance cannot be issued unless an emergency exists.

c. Request the intentions of an arriving aircraft operating within a Class B, Class C, Class D, or Class E surface area.

NOTE–
Clear an aircraft to land at an airport with an operating control tower, traffic permitting, if the pilot reports the airport in sight. The pilot is responsible to continue to the airport or exit the surface area. 14 CFR Section 91.157 prohibits VFR aircraft (other than helicopters) from landing at any airport within a surface area when flight visibility is less than 1 mile. A pilot could inadvertently encounter conditions that are below SVFR minimums after entering a surface area due to rapidly changing weather. The pilot is best suited to determine the action to be taken since pilots operating under SVFR between sunrise and sunset are not required to be instrument rated, and the possibility exists that flight visibility may not be the same as ground visibility. 14 CFR Section 91.3 authorizes a pilot encountering an inflight emergency requiring immediate action to deviate from any rule of 14 CFR Part 91 to the extent required to meet that emergency. Flight into adverse weather conditions may require the pilot to execute the emergency authority granted in 14 CFR Section 91.3 and continue inbound to land.

REFERENCE–
FAA Order JO 7110.65, Para 2-1-4, Operational Priority.

Section 6. Basic Radar Service to VFR Aircraft– Terminal

7–6–1. APPLICATION

a. Basic radar services for VFR aircraft must include:

1. Safety alerts.

2. Traffic advisories.

3. Limited radar vectoring when requested by the pilot.

4. Sequencing at locations where procedures have been established for this purpose and/or when covered by a LOA.

b. Apply the procedures contained in paragraph 7–1–3, Approach Control Service for VFR Arriving Aircraft, when arriving VFR aircraft are handled by approach control and provide vectoring service in accordance with Chapter 5, Radar, Section 7, Speed Adjustment, in addition to the radar services prescribed in paragraph 5–6–1, Application, and paragraph 5–6–2, Methods.

REFERENCE–
FAA Order JO 7110.65, Para 2–1–16, Surface Areas.
FAA Order JO 7110.65, Para 7–6–1, Application.
FAA Order JO 7210.3, Chapter 12, Section 1, Terminal VFR Radar Services.
AIM, Para 4–1–18, Terminal Radar Services for VFR Aircraft.

7–6–2. SERVICE AVAILABILITY

a. Inform aircraft on initial contact whenever this service cannot be provided because of radar outage and apply paragraph 7–1–3, Approach Control Service for VFR Arriving Aircraft.

b. Provide the service, to the extent possible using an available frequency, if an aircraft desires the service but cannot communicate on the appropriate frequencies. Aircraft which do not desire radar service may be fitted into the landing sequence by the tower. Coordination of these aircraft must be accomplished with the approach control unless a facility directive/LOA prescribes otherwise. Nonparticipating aircraft must, to the extent possible, be given the same landing sequence they would have received had they been sequenced by radar vectors.

c. Radar sequencing to the primary airport, when local procedures have been developed, must be provided unless the pilot states that the service is not requested. Arriving aircraft are assumed to want radar service unless the pilot states "Negative radar service," or makes a similar comment.

7–6–3. INITIAL CONTACT

An aircraft sighted by the local controller at the time of first radio contact may be positioned in the landing sequence after coordination with approach control.

7–6–4. IDENTIFICATION

Identify the aircraft before taking action to position it in the approach sequence.

7–6–5. HOLDING

Hold VFR aircraft over the initial reporting fix or a fix near the airport when holding is required to establish an approach sequence.

REFERENCE–
FAA Order JO 7110.65, Para 7–1–4, Visual Holding of VFR Aircraft.

7–6–6. APPROACH SEQUENCE

Do not assign landing sequence numbers, when establishing aircraft in the approach sequence, unless this responsibility has been delegated in a LOA or facility directive.

NOTE–
The landing sequence is ordinarily established by the tower.

7–6–7. SEQUENCING

a. Establish radar contact before instructing a VFR aircraft to enter the traffic pattern at a specified point or vectoring the aircraft to a position in the approach sequence. Inform the pilot of the aircraft to follow when the integrity of the approach sequence is dependent on following a preceding aircraft. Ensure visual contact is established with the aircraft to follow and provide instruction to follow that aircraft.

PHRASEOLOGY–
FOLLOW (description) (position, if necessary).

b. Direct a VFR aircraft to a point near the airport to hold when a position is not available in the approach sequence for the runway in use. The aircraft may be vectored to another runway after coordination with the tower.

c. Apply the following procedures to a VFR aircraft being radar sequenced:

1. The provisions of paragraph 5–5–4, Minima, subparagraphs f and g.

2. When parallel runways are less than 2,500 feet apart, do not permit a super or heavy aircraft to overtake any aircraft, nor a B757 or other large aircraft to overtake a small aircraft established on final within the facility's area of responsibility.

7–6–8. CONTROL TRANSFER

a. Inform the tower of the aircraft's position and then instruct the pilot to contact the tower.

b. The aircraft may be instructed to contact the tower prior to the tower being advised of the aircraft's position provided:

1. The tower advises the aircraft is in sight, and

2. Space is available in the landing sequence.

c. Instruct the pilot to contact the tower at the appropriate point when the approach control STARS track data is being displayed on the tower's TDW display, the aircraft is tagged by STARS, and a facility directive specifies change of communications and control jurisdiction points.

NOTE–
The point at which an aircraft is instructed to contact the tower is determined by prior coordination between the tower and approach control and will vary, depending on the runway in use, weather, etc. The transfer of communications ordinarily occurs at least 5 miles from the runway. The point for the transfer of communications should be a sufficient distance from the airport to permit the tower to properly sequence the aircraft, but not at a distance that could derogate the provision of radar traffic information service.

7–6–9. ABANDONED APPROACH

Instruct the aircraft to change to approach control for sequencing when an aircraft, under tower control, abandons the approach and coordination with approach control reveals no immediate space in the approach sequence.

7–6–10. VFR DEPARTURE INFORMATION

Inform departing VFR aircraft who request radar traffic advisories when to contact departure control and the frequency to use. Provide traffic advisories in accordance with paragraph 2–1–21, Traffic Advisories, after the departure is radar identified.

NOTE–
Departing aircraft desiring traffic information are expected to request the service and to state their proposed direction of flight upon initial contact with ground control.

7–6–11. TERMINATION OF SERVICE

Basic radar services should be provided to the extent possible, workload permitting. Terminate radar service to aircraft landing at airports other than those where sequencing service is provided at a sufficient distance from the airport to permit the pilot to change to the appropriate frequency for traffic and airport information.

PHRASEOLOGY–
RADAR SERVICE TERMINATED, SQUAWK ONE TWO ZERO ZERO,

or

SQUAWK VFR,

then

CHANGE TO ADVISORY FREQUENCY APPROVED,

or

CONTACT (frequency identification),

or

FREQUENCY CHANGE APPROVED.

7–6–12. SERVICE PROVIDED WHEN TOWER IS INOPERATIVE

a. Provide the following services during hours when the tower is not in operation:

1. Wind direction and velocity.

NOTE–
Issue information provided from the FSS or WSO. Otherwise, inform the pilot that wind information is not available.

2. Traffic information.

3. Inform aircraft when radar service is terminated.

REFERENCE–
FAA Order JO 7110.65, Para 5–1–9, Radar Service Termination.

b. Do not assign landing sequence.

Section 7. Terminal Radar Service Area (TRSA)– Terminal

7–7–1. APPLICATION

Apply TRSA procedures within the designated TRSA in addition to the basic services described in Chapter 7, Visual, Section 6, Basic Radar Service to VFR Aircraft– Terminal.

REFERENCE–
FAA Order JO 7110.65, Para 7–2–1, Visual Separation.

7–7–2. ISSUANCE OF EFC

Inform the pilot when to expect further clearance when VFR aircraft are held either inside or outside the TRSA.

REFERENCE–
FAA Order JO 7110.65, Para 7–2–1, Visual Separation.

7–7–3. SEPARATION

Separate participating VFR aircraft from IFR aircraft and other participating VFR aircraft by any one of the following:

a. Visual separation, as specified in paragraph 7–2–1, Visual Separation, paragraph 7–4–2, Vectors for Visual Approach, and paragraph 7–6–7, Sequencing.

NOTE–
Issue wake turbulence cautionary advisories in accordance with paragraph 2–1–20, Wake Turbulence Cautionary Advisories.

b. 500 feet vertical separation.

c. Target resolution, except when ISR is being displayed.

NOTE–
Apply the provisions of paragraph 5–5–4, Minima, subparagraphs g and h, when wake turbulence separation is required.

REFERENCE–
FAA Order JO 7110.65, Para 7–2–1, Visual Separation.

7–7–4. HELICOPTER TRAFFIC

Helicopters need not be separated from other helicopters. Traffic information must be exchanged, as necessary.

REFERENCE–
FAA Order JO 7110.65, Para 7–2–1, Visual Separation.

7–7–5. ALTITUDE ASSIGNMENTS

a. Altitude information contained in a clearance, instruction, or advisory to VFR aircraft must meet MVA, MSA, or minimum IFR altitude criteria.

REFERENCE–
FAA Order JO 7110.65, Para 4–5–2, Flight Direction.
FAA Order JO 7110.65, Para 4–5–3, Exceptions.
FAA Order JO 7110.65, Para 4–5–6, Minimum En Route Altitudes.

b. If required, issue altitude assignments, consistent with the provisions of 14 CFR Section 91.119.

NOTE–
The MSAs are:

1. *Over congested areas, an altitude at least 1,000 feet above the highest obstacle; and*

2. *Over other than congested areas, an altitude at least 500 feet above the surface.*

c. When necessary to assign an altitude for separation purposes to VFR aircraft contrary to 14 CFR Section 91.159, advise the aircraft to resume altitudes appropriate for the direction of flight when the altitude assignment is no longer needed for separation or when leaving the TRSA.

PHRASEOLOGY–
RESUME APPROPRIATE VFR ALTITUDES.

REFERENCE–
FAA Order JO 7110.65, Para 4–8–11, Practice Approaches.
FAA Order JO 7110.65, Para 5–6–1, Application.
FAA Order JO 7110.65, Para 7–2–1, Visual Separation.

7–7–6. APPROACH INTERVAL

The tower must specify the approach interval.

REFERENCE–
FAA Order JO 7110.65, Para 7–2–1, Visual Separation.

7–7–7. TRSA DEPARTURE INFORMATION

a. At controlled airports within the TRSA, inform a departing aircraft proposing to operate within the TRSA when to contact departure control and the frequency to use. If the aircraft is properly equipped, ground control or clearance delivery must issue the appropriate beacon code.

NOTE–
Departing aircraft are assumed to want TRSA service unless the pilot states, "negative TRSA service," or makes a similar comment. Pilots are expected to inform the controller of intended destination and/or route of flight and altitude.

b. Provide separation until the aircraft leaves the TRSA.

c. Inform participating VFR aircraft when leaving the TRSA.

PHRASEOLOGY–
LEAVING THE (name) TRSA,

and as appropriate,

RESUME OWN NAVIGATION, REMAIN THIS FREQUENCY FOR TRAFFIC ADVISORIES, RADAR SERVICE TERMINATED, SQUAWK ONE TWO ZERO ZERO.

d. Aircraft departing satellite controlled airports that will penetrate the TRSA should be provided the same service as those aircraft departing the primary airport. Procedures for handling this situation must be covered in a letter of agreement or facility directives, as appropriate.

e. Procedures for handling aircraft departing uncontrolled satellite airports must be advertised in a facility bulletin and service provided accordingly.

REFERENCE–
FAA Order JO 7110.65, Para 7–2–1, Visual Separation.

Section 8. Class C Service– Terminal

7–8–1. APPLICATION

Apply Class C service procedures within the designated Class C airspace and the associated outer area. Class C services are designed to keep ATC informed of all aircraft within Class C airspace, not to exclude operations. Two-way radio communications and operational transponder are normally required for operations within Class C airspace, but operations without radio communications or transponder can be conducted by LOA, facility directive, or special arrangement with Class C airspace controlling facility.

REFERENCE–
FAA Order JO 7110.65, Para 7–2–1, Visual Separation.
14 CFR Section 91.215, ATC Transponder and Altitude Reporting Equipment and Use.

7–8–2. CLASS C SERVICES

a. Class C services include the following:

1. Sequencing of all aircraft to the primary airport.

2. Standard IFR services to IFR aircraft.

3. Separation, traffic advisories, and safety alerts between IFR and VFR aircraft.

4. Mandatory traffic advisories and safety alerts between VFR aircraft.

b. Provide Class C services to all aircraft operating within Class C airspace.

c. Provide Class C services to all participating aircraft in the outer area.

d. Aircraft should not normally be held. However, if holding is necessary, inform the pilot of the expected length of delay.

e. When an outage occurs, affecting the preferred radar sensor, advise aircraft that Class C services are not available and, if appropriate, when to contact the tower, except when other radar resources are available and to the extent that coverage is sufficient, continue to provide radar services.

NOTE–
Limited radar coverage in one portion of a Class C area does not justify denial of Class C radar service in the entire area.

REFERENCE–
FAA Order JO 7110.65, Para 7–2–1, Visual Separation.

7–8–3. SEPARATION

Separate VFR aircraft from IFR aircraft by any one of the following:

a. Visual separation as specified in paragraph 7–2–1, Visual Separation, paragraph 7–4–2, Vectors for Visual Approach, and paragraph 7–6–7, Sequencing.

NOTE–
Issue wake turbulence cautionary advisories in accordance with paragraph 2–1–20, Wake Turbulence Cautionary Advisories.

b. 500 feet vertical separation.

c. Target resolution, except when ISR is being displayed.

NOTE–
Apply the provisions of paragraph 5–5–4, Minima, subparagraphs g and h, when wake turbulence separation is required.

REFERENCE–
FAA Order JO 7110.65, Para 7–2–1, Visual Separation.

7–8–4. ESTABLISHING TWO-WAY COMMUNICATIONS

Class C service requires pilots to establish two-way radio communications before entering Class C airspace. If the controller responds to a radio call with, "(a/c call sign) standby," radio communications have been established and the pilot can enter Class C airspace. If workload or traffic conditions prevent immediate provision of Class C services, inform the pilot to remain outside Class C airspace until conditions permit the services to be provided.

PHRASEOLOGY–
(A/c call sign) REMAIN OUTSIDE CHARLIE AIRSPACE AND STANDBY.

REFERENCE–
FAA Order JO 7110.65, Para 7–2–1, Visual Separation.

7–8–5. ALTITUDE ASSIGNMENTS

a. When necessary to assign altitudes to VFR aircraft, assign altitudes that meet the MVA, MSA, or minimum IFR altitude criteria.

b. Aircraft assigned altitudes which are contrary to 14 CFR Section 91.159 must be advised to resume altitudes appropriate for the direction of flight when the altitude is no longer needed for separation, when leaving the outer area, or when terminating Class C service.

PHRASEOLOGY–
RESUME APPROPRIATE VFR ALTITUDES.

REFERENCE–
FAA Order JO 7110.65, Para 7–2–1, Visual Separation.

7–8–6. EXCEPTIONS

a. VFR helicopters need not be separated from IFR helicopters. Traffic information and safety alerts must be issued as appropriate.

b. Hot air balloons need not be separated from IFR aircraft. Traffic information and safety alerts must be issued as appropriate.

7–8–7. ADJACENT AIRPORT OPERATIONS

a. Aircraft that will penetrate Class C airspace after departing controlled airports within or adjacent to Class C airspace must be provided the same services as those aircraft departing the primary airport. Procedures for handling this situation must be covered in a LOA or a facility directive, as appropriate.

b. Aircraft departing uncontrolled airports within Class C airspace must be handled using procedures advertised in a Letter to Airmen.

7–8–8. TERMINATION OF SERVICE

Unless aircraft are landing at secondary airports or have requested termination of service while in the outer area, provide services until the aircraft departs the associated outer area. Terminate Class C service to aircraft landing at other than the primary airport at a sufficient distance from the airport to allow the pilot to change to the appropriate frequency for traffic and airport information.

PHRASEOLOGY–
CHANGE TO ADVISORY FREQUENCY APPROVED,

or

CONTACT (facility identification).

Section 9. Class B Service Area– Terminal

7–9–1. APPLICATION

a. Apply Class B services and procedures within the designated Class B airspace.

b. No person may operate an aircraft within Class B airspace unless:

1. The aircraft has an operable two-way radio capable of communications with ATC on appropriate frequencies for that Class B airspace.

2. The aircraft is equipped with the applicable operating transponder and automatic altitude reporting equipment specified in paragraph (a) of 14 CFR Section 91.215, except as provided in paragraph (d) of that section.

7–9–2. VFR AIRCRAFT IN CLASS B AIRSPACE

a. VFR aircraft must obtain an ATC clearance to operate in Class B airspace.

REFERENCE–
FAA Order JO 7110.65, Para 2–1–18, Operational Requests.
FAA Order JO 7110.65, Para 2–4–22, Airspace Classes.

PHRASEOLOGY–
CLEARED THROUGH/TO ENTER/OUT OF BRAVO AIRSPACE,

and as appropriate,

VIA (route). MAINTAIN (altitude) WHILE IN BRAVO AIRSPACE.

or

CLEARED AS REQUESTED.

(Additional instructions, as necessary.)

REMAIN OUTSIDE BRAVO AIRSPACE. (When necessary, reason and/or additional instructions.)

NOTE–
1. *Assignment of radar headings, routes, or altitudes is based on the provision that a pilot operating in accordance with VFR is expected to advise ATC if compliance will cause violation of any part of the CFR.*

2. *Separation and sequencing for VFR aircraft is dependent upon radar. Efforts should be made to segregate VFR traffic from IFR traffic flows when a radar outage occurs.*

b. Approve/deny requests from VFR aircraft to operate in Class B airspace based on workload, operational limitations and traffic conditions.

c. Inform the pilot when to expect further clearance when VFR aircraft are held either inside or outside Class B airspace.

d. Inform VFR aircraft when leaving Class B airspace.

PHRASEOLOGY–
LEAVING (name) BRAVO AIRSPACE,

and as appropriate,

RESUME OWN NAVIGATION, REMAIN THIS FREQUENCY FOR TRAFFIC ADVISORIES, RADAR SERVICE TERMINATED, SQUAWK ONE TWO ZERO ZERO.

7–9–3. METHODS

a. To the extent practical, clear large turbine engine-powered airplanes to/from the primary airport using altitudes and routes that avoid VFR corridors and airspace below the Class B airspace floor where VFR aircraft are operating.

NOTE–
Pilots operating in accordance with VFR are expected to advise ATC if compliance with assigned altitudes, headings, or routes will cause violation of any part of the CFR.

b. Vector aircraft to remain in Class B airspace after entry. Inform the aircraft when leaving and reentering Class B airspace if it becomes necessary to extend the flight path outside Class B airspace for spacing.

NOTE–
14 CFR Section 91.131 states that "Unless otherwise authorized by ATC, each person operating a large turbine engine-powered airplane to or from a primary airport for which a Class B airspace area is designated must operate at or above the designated floors of the Class B airspace area while within the lateral limits of that area." Such authorization should be the exception rather than the rule.

REFERENCE–
FAA Order JO 7110.65, Para 5–1–6, Deviation Advisories.

c. Aircraft departing controlled airports within Class B airspace will be provided the same services as those aircraft departing the primary airport.

REFERENCE–
FAA Order JO 7110.65, Para 2–1–18, Operational Requests.

7–9–4. SEPARATION

a. Standard IFR services to IFR aircraft.

b. VFR aircraft must be separated from VFR/IFR aircraft/ helicopter/rotorcraft that weigh more than 19,000 pounds and turbojets by no less than:

1. 1 ½ miles separation, or

NOTE–
When ISR is being displayed, discontinue 1 ½ –NM separation.

2. 500 feet vertical separation, or

NOTE–
Apply the provisions of paragraph 5–5–4, Minima, when wake turbulence separation is required.

3. Visual separation, as specified in paragraph 7–2–1, Visual Separation, paragraph 7–4–2, Vectors for Visual Approach, and paragraph 7–6–7, Sequencing.

NOTE–
Issue wake turbulence cautionary advisories in accordance with paragraph 2–1–20, Wake Turbulence Cautionary Advisories.

c. For the application of Class Bravo airspace separation requirements, the V-22 Osprey must be treated as a helicopter/rotorcraft.

d. VFR aircraft must be separated from all VFR/IFR aircraft which weigh 19,000 pounds or less by a minimum of:

1. Target resolution, except when ISR is being displayed, or

2. 500 feet vertical separation, or

NOTE–
1. *Apply the provisions of paragraph 5–5–4, Minima, when wake turbulence separation is required.*

2. *Aircraft weighing 19,000 pounds or less are listed in FAA Order JO 7360.1, Aircraft Type Designators.*

REFERENCE–
FAA Order JO 7360.1, Para 2–2, How Designators are Formulated.

3. Visual separation, as specified in paragraph 7–2–1, Visual Separation, paragraph 7–4–2, Vectors for Visual Approach, and paragraph 7–6–7, Sequencing.

NOTE–
Issue wake turbulence cautionary advisories in accordance with paragraph 2–1–20, Wake Turbulence Cautionary Advisories.

REFERENCE–
P/CG Term – Lateral Separation.
P/CG Term – Radar Separation.
P/CG Term – Target Resolution.
P/CG Term – Visual Separation.

7–9–5. TRAFFIC ADVISORIES

a. Provide mandatory traffic advisories and safety alerts, between all aircraft.

b. Apply merging target procedures in accordance with paragraph 5–1–4, Merging Target Procedures.

7–9–6. HELICOPTER TRAFFIC

VFR helicopters need not be separated from VFR or IFR helicopters. Traffic advisories and safety alerts must be issued as appropriate.

7–9–7. ALTITUDE ASSIGNMENTS

a. Altitude information contained in a clearance, instruction, or advisory to VFR aircraft must meet MVA, MSA, or minimum IFR altitude criteria.

b. Issue altitude assignments, if required, consistent with the provisions of 14 CFR Section 91.119.

NOTE–
The MSAs are:
1. *Over congested areas, an altitude at least 1,000 feet above the highest obstacle,*
2. *Over other than congested areas, an altitude at least 500 feet above the surface.*

REFERENCE–
FAA Order JO 7110.65, Para 4–5–2, Flight Direction.
FAA Order JO 7110.65, Para 4–5–3, Exceptions.
FAA Order JO 7110.65, Para 4–5–6, Minimum En Route Altitudes.

c. Aircraft assigned altitudes which are contrary to 14 CFR Section 91.159 must be advised to resume altitudes appropriate for the direction of flight when the altitude assignment is no longer required or when leaving Class B airspace.

PHRASEOLOGY–
RESUME APPROPRIATE VFR ALTITUDES.

7–9–8. APPROACH INTERVAL

The tower must specify the approach interval.

Chapter 8. Offshore/Oceanic Procedures

Section 1. General

8-1-1. ATC SERVICE

Provide air traffic control service in oceanic controlled airspace in accordance with the procedures in this chapter except when other procedures/minima are prescribed in a directive or a letter of agreement.

REFERENCE–
FAA Order JO 7110.65, Para 1-1-10, Procedural Letters of Agreement (LOA).

8-1-2. OPERATIONS IN OFFSHORE AIRSPACE AREAS

Provide air traffic control service in offshore airspace areas in accordance with procedures and minima in this chapter. For those situations not covered by this chapter, the provisions in this Order must apply.

8-1-3. VFR FLIGHT PLANS

VFR flights in Oceanic FIRs may be conducted in meteorological conditions equal to or greater than those specified in 14 CFR Section 91.155, Basic VFR weather minimums. Operations on a VFR flight plan are permitted only between sunrise and sunset and only within:

a. Miami, Houston, and San Juan Oceanic Control Areas (CTAs) below FL 180.

b. Within the Oakland FIR when operating less than 100 NM seaward from the shoreline within controlled airspace.

c. All Oceanic FIR airspace below the Oceanic CTAs.

8-1-4. TYPES OF SEPARATION

Separation must consist of at least one of the following:

a. Vertical separation;

b. Horizontal separation, either;

1. Longitudinal; or

2. Lateral;

c. Radar separation, as specified in Chapter 5, Radar, where radar coverage is adequate.

8-1-5. ALTIMETER SETTING

Within oceanic control areas, unless directed and/or charted otherwise, altitude assignment must be based on flight levels and a standard altimeter setting of 29.92 inches Hg.

8-1-6. RECEIPT OF POSITION REPORTS

When a position report affecting separation is not received, take action to obtain the report no later than *10 minutes* after the control estimate, unless otherwise specified.

8-1-7. OCEANIC ERROR REPORT PROCEDURES

FAA Order JO 7210.632 establishes procedures for reporting Gross Navigation Errors (GNE), height errors, time (longitudinal) errors, intervention, and Special Area of Operations (SAO) verification in oceanic airspace. This data is needed for risk modeling activities to support separation standard reductions.

8-1-8. USE OF CONTROL ESTIMATES

Control estimates are the estimated position of aircraft, with reference to time as determined by the ATC automation system in use or calculated by the controller using known wind patterns, previous aircraft transit times, pilot progress reports, and pilot estimates. These estimates may be updated through the receipt of automated position reports and/or manually updated by the controller. Control estimates must be used when applying time-based separation minima.

8-1-9. RVSM OPERATIONS

Controller responsibilities for non-RVSM aircraft operating in RVSM airspace must include but not be limited to the following:

a. Ensure non-RVSM aircraft are not permitted in RVSM airspace unless they meet the criteria of excepted aircraft and are previously approved by the operations supervisor/CIC.

b. In addition to those aircraft listed in Chapter 2, Section 1, paragraph 2-1-29, RVSM Operations, in this order, the following aircraft operating within oceanic airspace or transiting to/from oceanic airspace are excepted:

1. Aircraft being initially delivered to the State of Registry or Operator;

2. Aircraft that was formerly RVSM approved but has experienced an equipment failure and is being flown to a maintenance facility for repair in order to meet RVSM requirements and/or obtain approval;

3. Aircraft being utilized for mercy or humanitarian purposes;

4. Within the Oakland, Anchorage, and Arctic FIR's, an aircraft transporting a spare engine mounted under the wing.

(a) These exceptions are accommodated on a workload or traffic-permitting basis.

(b) All other requirements contained in paragraph 2-1-29, RVSM Operations are applicable to this section.

REFERENCE-
FAA Order JO 7110.65, Para 2-1-29, RVSM Operations.

8-1-10. PROCEDURES FOR WEATHER DEVIATIONS AND OTHER CONTINGENCIES IN OCEANIC CONTROLLED AIRSPACE

Aircraft must request an ATC clearance to deviate. Since aircraft will not fly into adverse meteorological conditions, weather deviation requests should take priority over routine requests. If there is no traffic in the horizontal dimension, ATC must issue clearance to deviate from track; or if there is conflicting traffic in the horizontal dimension, ATC must separate aircraft by establishing vertical separation, then issue clearance to deviate from track. If there is conflicting traffic and ATC is unable to establish required separation, ATC must:

a. Advise the pilot unable to issue clearance for requested deviation;

b. Advise the pilot of conflicting traffic; and

c. Request pilot's intentions.

PHRASEOLOGY-
UNABLE (requested deviation), TRAFFIC IS (call sign, position, altitude, direction), SAY INTENTIONS.

NOTE-
1. *The pilot will advise ATC of intentions by the most expeditious means available.*

2. *In the event that pilot/controller communications cannot be established or a revised ATC clearance is not available, pilots will follow the procedures outlined in the Aeronautical Information Publication (AIP), Section ENR 7.3, Special Procedures for In-flight Contingencies in Oceanic Airspace; and AC 91-70, Oceanic and Remote Continental Airspace Operations.*

Section 2. Coordination

8-2-1. GENERAL

ARTCCs must:

a. Forward to appropriate ATS facilities, as a flight progresses, current flight plan and control information.

b. Coordinate flight plan and control information in sufficient time to permit the receiving facility to analyze the data and to effect any necessary additional coordination. This may be specified in a letter of agreement.

c. Coordinate with adjacent ATS facilities when airspace to be protected will overlap the common boundary.

d. Forward revisions of estimates of *3 minutes* or more to the appropriate ATS facility.

e. Coordinate with adjacent facilities on IFR and VFR flights to ensure the continuation of appropriate air traffic services.

8-2-2. TRANSFER OF CONTROL AND COMMUNICATIONS

a. Only one air traffic control unit must control an aircraft at any given time.

b. The control of an aircraft must be transferred from one control unit to another at the time the aircraft is estimated to cross the control boundary or at such other point or time agreed upon by the two units.

c. The transferring unit must forward to the accepting unit any changed flight plan or control data which are pertinent to the transfer.

d. The accepting unit must notify the transferring unit if it is unable to accept control under the terms specified, or it must specify the changes or conditions required so that the aircraft can be accepted.

e. The accepting unit must not alter the clearance of an aircraft that has not yet reached the transfer of control point without the prior approval of the transferring unit.

f. Where nonradar separation minima are being applied, the transfer of air-ground communications with an aircraft must be made *5 minutes* before the time at which the aircraft is estimated to reach the boundary unless otherwise agreed to by the control and/or communication units concerned.

8-2-3. AIR TRAFFIC SERVICES INTERFACILITY DATA COMMUNICATIONS (AIDC)

Where interfacility data communications capability has been implemented, its use for ATC coordination should be accomplished in accordance with regional Interface Control Documents, and supported by letters of agreement between the facilities concerned.

Section 3. Longitudinal Separation

8-3-1. APPLICATION

a. Longitudinal separation must be applied so that the spacing between the estimated positions of the aircraft being separated is never less than a prescribed minimum.

NOTE-
Consider separation to exist when the estimated positions of the aircraft being separated are never less than a prescribed minimum.

b. In situations where one aircraft requires a different time-based longitudinal standard than another, apply the larger of the two standards between the aircraft concerned.

c. Longitudinal separation expressed in distance may be applied as prescribed in Chapter 6, Nonradar.

d. In situations where an update to a control estimate indicates that the minimum being applied no longer exists, controllers must ensure that separation is reestablished. Issue traffic information as necessary.

8-3-2. SEPARATION METHODS

a. For the purpose of application of longitudinal separation, the terms *same track* must be considered identical to *same course*, *reciprocal tracks* must be considered identical to *reciprocal courses*, and *crossing tracks*, must be considered identical to *crossing courses*.

NOTE-
Refer to paragraph 1-2-2, Course Definitions.

b. Separate aircraft longitudinally in accordance with the following:

1. Same track. Ensure that the estimated spacing between aircraft is not less than the applicable minimum required. (See FIG 8-3-1.)

FIG 8-3-1
Same Courses

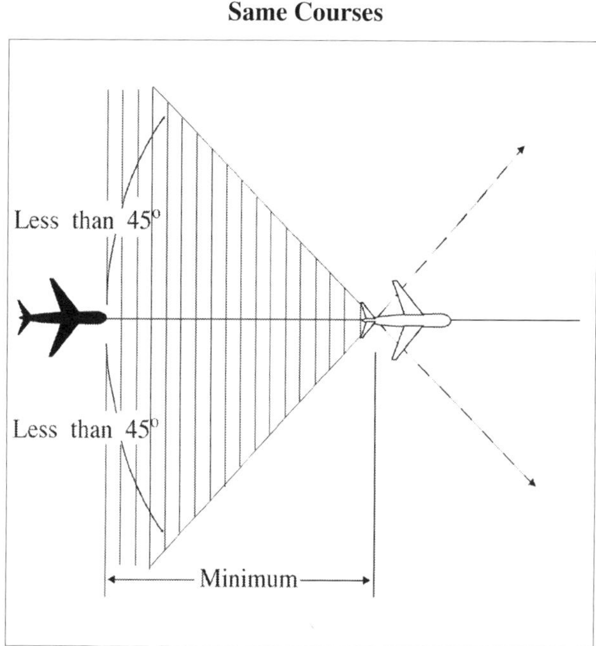

2. Crossing tracks. Ensure that the estimated spacing at the point of intersection is not less than the applicable minimum required. (See FIG 8-3-2.)

FIG 8-3-2
Crossing Courses

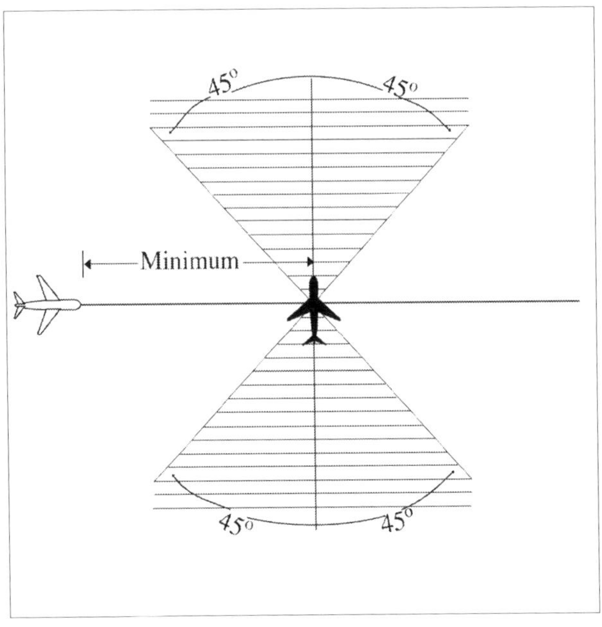

3. Reciprocal tracks:

(a) Ensure that aircraft are vertically separated for a time interval equal to the applicable minimum required before and after the aircraft are estimated to pass. (See FIG 8-3-3.)

FIG 8-3-3
Reciprocal Courses

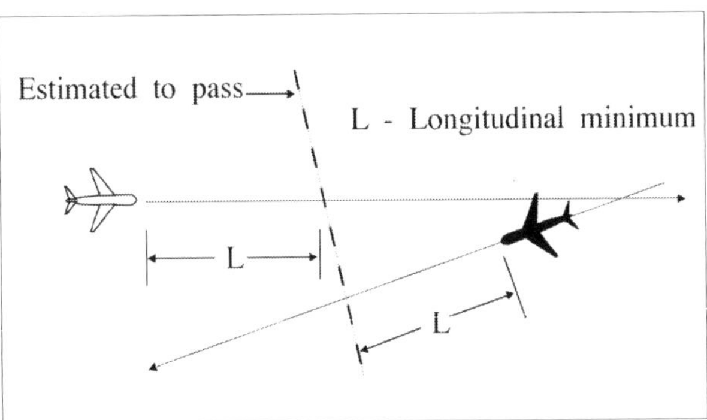

(b) Vertical separation may be discontinued after one of the following conditions is met:

(1) Both aircraft have reported passing a significant point and the aircraft are separated by at least the applicable minimum required for the same direction longitudinal spacing; (See FIG 8-3-4.) or

FIG 8-3-4
Vertical Separation

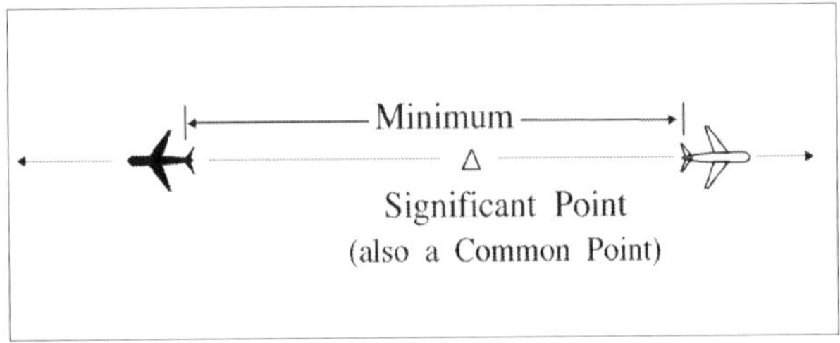

(2) Both aircraft have reported passing ground-based NAVAIDs or DME fixes indicating that they have passed each other.

8-3-3. MACH NUMBER TECHNIQUE

The use of Mach number technique allows for the application of reduced longitudinal separation minima. The following conditions must be met when the Mach number technique is being applied:

a. Aircraft Types: Turbojet aircraft only.

b. Routes:

1. The aircraft follow the same track or continuously diverging tracks, and

2. The aircraft concerned have reported over a common point; or

3. If the aircraft have *not* reported over a common point, the appropriate time interval being applied between aircraft exists and will exist at the common point; or,

4. If a common point does not exist, the appropriate time interval being applied between aircraft exists and will exist at significant points along each track.

c. Altitudes: The aircraft concerned are in level, climbing or descending flight.

d. Mach Number Assignment:

1. A Mach number (or, when appropriate, a range of Mach numbers) must be issued to each aircraft unless otherwise prescribed on the basis of ICAO regional agreement.

NOTE–

1. *The application of Mach number technique requires pilots to strictly adhere to the last assigned Mach number (or range of Mach numbers), even during climbs and descents, unless revised by ATC. Turbojet aircraft must request ATC approval before making any changes. If it is essential to make an immediate temporary change in the Mach number (e.g., due to turbulence), ATC must be notified as soon as possible that such a change has been made.*

2. *When it is necessary to issue crossing restrictions to ensure the appropriate time interval, it may be impossible for an aircraft to comply with both the clearance to meet the crossing restrictions and the clearance to maintain a single, specific Mach number.*

REFERENCE–
ICAO DOC 9426–AN/924, Part II, Section 2, Para 2.3.4, Para 2.4.7, and Para 2.5.3.

EXAMPLE–
"Maintain Mach point eight four or greater."
"Maintain Mach point eight three or less."
"Maintain Mach point eight two or greater; do not exceed Mach point eight four."

e. Longitudinal Minima:

When the Mach number technique is applied, minimum longitudinal separation must be:

1. *10 minutes*, provided that:

(a) The preceding aircraft maintains a Mach number equal to, or greater than that maintained by the following aircraft; or

(b) When the following aircraft is faster than the preceding aircraft, at least *10 minutes* exists until another form of separation is achieved; or

2. Between *9 and 5 minutes* inclusive, provided that the preceding aircraft is maintaining a Mach number greater than the following aircraft in accordance with the following:

(a) *9 minutes*, if the preceding aircraft is Mach 0.02 faster than the following aircraft;

(b) *8 minutes*, if the preceding aircraft is Mach 0.03 faster than the following aircraft;

(c) *7 minutes*, if the preceding aircraft is Mach 0.04 faster than the following aircraft;

(d) *6 minutes*, if the preceding aircraft is Mach 0.05 faster than the following aircraft;

(e) *5 minutes*, if the preceding aircraft is Mach 0.06 faster than the following aircraft.

NOTE–
A "rule–of–thumb" may be applied to assist in providing the required estimated spacing over the oceanic exit point when either conflict probe is not in use or when requested by another facility. This rule–of–thumb can be stated as follows: For each 600 NM in distance between the entry and exit points of the area where the Mach Number Technique is used, add 1 minute for each 0.01 difference in Mach number for the two aircraft concerned to compensate for the fact that the second aircraft is overtaking the first aircraft. (See TBL 8–3–1.)

TBL 8–3–1

Application of the Mach Number Technique When the Following Aircraft is Faster

Difference in Mach	Distance to Fly and Separation (in Minutes) Required at Entry Point				
	001–600 NM	601–1200 NM	1201–1800 NM	1801–2400 NM	2401–3000 NM
0.01	11	12	13	14	15
0.02	12	14	16	18	20
0.03	13	16	19	22	25
0.04	14	18	22	26	30
0.05	15	20	25	30	35
0.06	16	22	28	34	40
0.07	17	24	31	38	45
0.08	18	26	34	42	50
0.09	19	28	37	46	55
0.10	20	30	40	50	60

Section 4. Lateral Separation

8–4–1. APPLICATION

Separate aircraft by assigning different flight paths whose widths or protected airspace do not overlap.

Within that portion of the Gulf of Mexico Low Offshore airspace, use 12 NM between aircraft whose flight paths are defined by published Grid System waypoints.

NOTE–

1. *The Grid System is defined as those waypoints contained within the Gulf of Mexico Low Offshore airspace and published on the IFR Vertical Flight Reference Chart.*

2. *Lateral separation minima is contained in:*

Section 7, North Atlantic ICAO Region.
Section 8, Caribbean ICAO Region.
Section 9, Pacific ICAO Region.
Section 10, North American ICAO Region– Arctic CTA.

8–4–2. SEPARATION METHODS

Lateral separation exists for:

a. Nonintersecting flight paths:

1. When the required distance is maintained between the flight paths; or (See FIG 8–4–1.)

FIG 8–4–1
Separation Methods

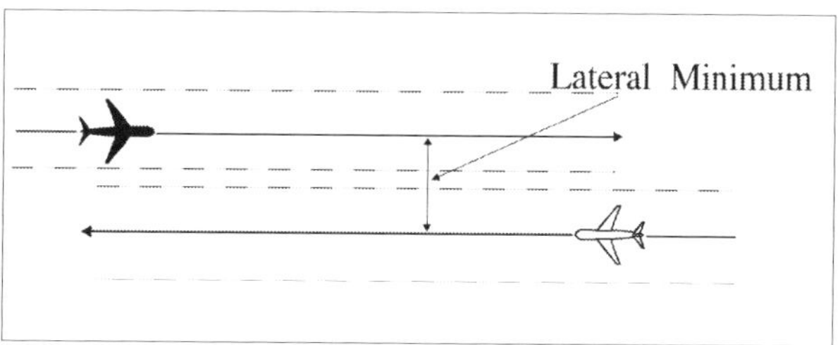

2. When reduced route protected airspace is applicable, and the protected airspace of the flight paths do not overlap; or (See FIG 8–4–2.)

FIG 8–4–2
Separation Methods

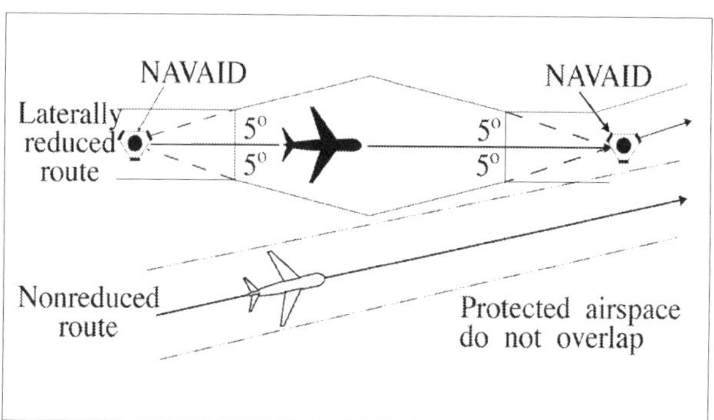

3. When aircraft are crossing an oceanic boundary and are entering an airspace with a larger lateral minimum than the airspace being exited; and

(a) The smaller separation exists at the boundary; and

(b) Flight paths diverge by 15° or more until the larger minimum is established. (See FIG 8–4–3.)

FIG 8–4–3
Separation Methods

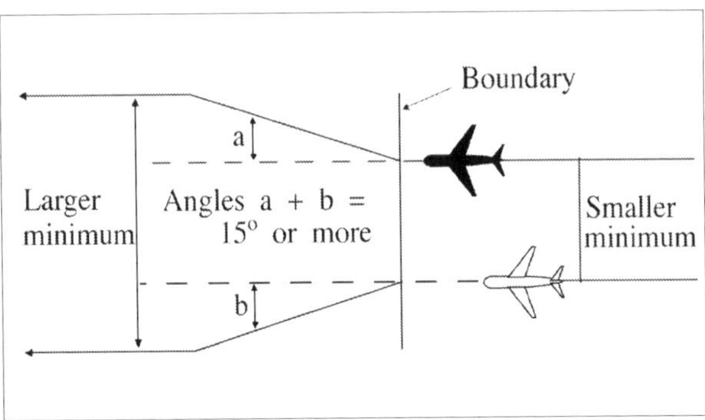

b. Intersecting flight paths with constant and same width protected airspace when either aircraft is at or beyond a distance equal to the applicable lateral separation minimum measured perpendicular to the flight path of the other aircraft. (See FIG 8–4–4.)

FIG 8–4–4
Separation Methods

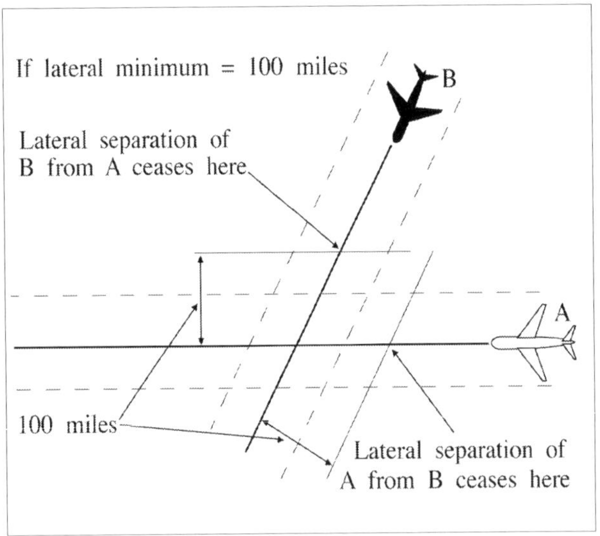

c. Intersecting flight paths with constant but different width protected airspace when either aircraft is at or beyond a distance equal to the sum of the protected airspace of both flight paths measured perpendicular to the flight path of the other aircraft. (See FIG 8–4–5.)

FIG 8–4–5

Separation Methods

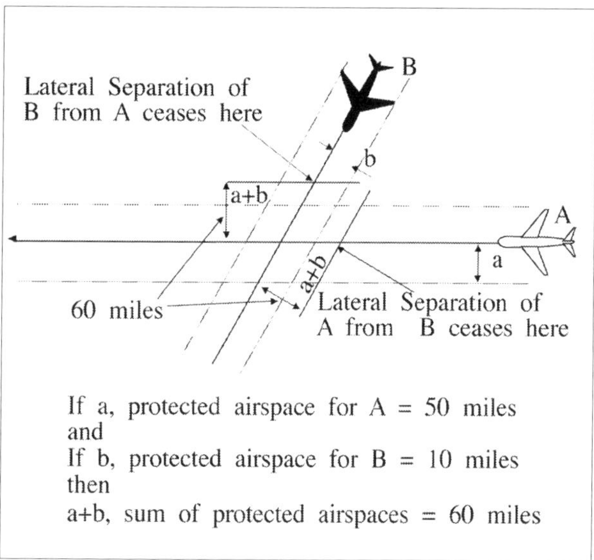

d. Intersecting flight paths with variable width protected airspace when either aircraft is at or beyond a distance equal to the sum of the protected airspace of both flight paths measured perpendicular to the flight path of the other aircraft. Measure protected airspace for each aircraft perpendicular to its flight path at the first point or the last point, as applicable, of protected airspace overlap.

NOTE–

In FIG 8–4–5, the protected airspace for westbound flight A is distance "a" (50 miles), and for southwestbound flight B, distance "b" (10 miles). Therefore, the sum of distances "a" and "b"; i.e., the protected airspace of Aircrafts A and B, establishes the lateral separation minimum (60 miles) applicable for either flight relevant to the other.

FIG 8-4-6
Separation Methods

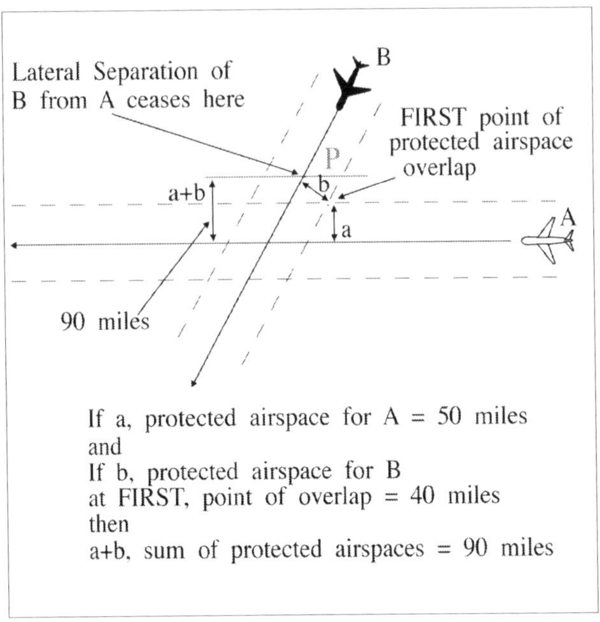

NOTE-
(See FIG 8-4-6.) At the first point of protected airspace overlap, the protected airspace for westbound flight A is distance "a" (50 miles), and for southbound flight B, distance "b" (40 miles). The sum of distances "a" and "b" (90 miles) establishes the lateral separation minimum applicable in this example for either flight as it approaches the intersection. For example, Aircraft B should be vertically separated from Aircraft A by the time it reaches point "p."

FIG 8-4-7
Separation Methods

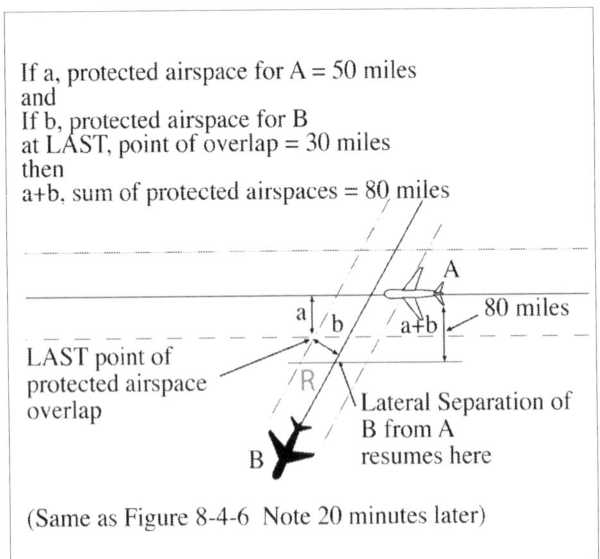

NOTE-
(See FIG 8-4-7.) Distance "a" (50 miles) and "b" (30 miles) are determined at the last point of protected airspace overlap. The sum of the distances "a" and "b" (80 miles) establishes the lateral separation minima applicable for either flight after it passes beyond the intersection. For example, Aircraft B could be cleared to, or through, Aircraft A's altitude after passing point "r."

8-4-3. REDUCTION OF ROUTE PROTECTED AIRSPACE

When routes have been satisfactorily flight checked and notice has been given to users, reduction in route protected airspace may be made as follows:

a. Below FL 240, reduce the width of the protected airspace to 5 miles on each side of the route centerline to a distance of 57.14 miles from the NAVAID, then increasing in width on a 5° angle from the route centerline, measured at the NAVAID, to the maximum width allowable within the lateral minima; for example, 50 miles of protected airspace on each side of centerline; i.e., a lateral minimum of 100 miles. (See FIG 8-4-8.)

FIG 8-4-8

Reduction of Route Protected Airspace

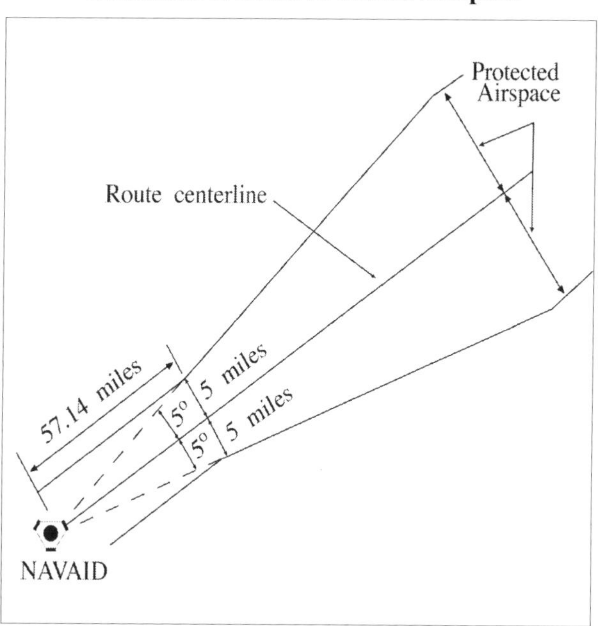

b. At and above FL 240, reduce the width of the protected airspace to 10 miles on each side of the route centerline to a distance of 114.29 miles from the NAVAID, then increasing in width on a 5° angle from the route centerline, as measured at the NAVAID, to the maximum width allowable within the lateral minima; for example, 60 miles of protected airspace on each side of the centerline; i.e., a lateral separation minimum of 120 miles. (See FIG 8-4-9.)

FIG 8-4-9
Reduction of Route Protected Airspace

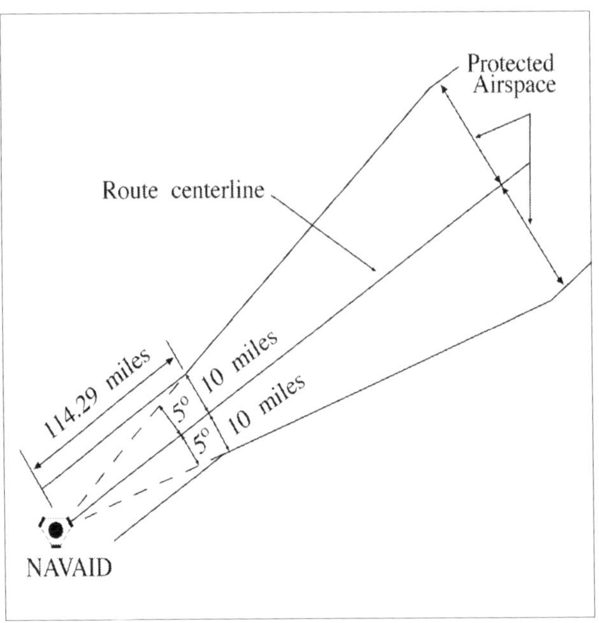

8-4-4. TRACK SEPARATION

Apply track separation between aircraft by requiring aircraft to fly specified tracks or radials and with specified spacings as follows:

a. ***Same NAVAID:***

1. VOR/VORTAC/TACAN. Consider separation to exist between aircraft established on radials of the same NAVAID that diverge by at least 15 degrees when either aircraft is clear of the airspace to be protected for the other aircraft. Use TBL 8-4-1 to determine the flight distance required for various divergence angles and altitudes to clear the airspace to be protected. (See FIG 8-4-10.)

TBL 8-4-1
Divergence-Distance Minima
VOR/VORTAC/TACAN

Divergence (degrees)	Distance (mile)	
	FL 230 and below	FL 240 through FL 450
15-25	17	18
26-35	11	13
36-90	8	11
Note: *This table compensates for DME slant range error.*		

FIG 8−4−10
Track Separation VOR

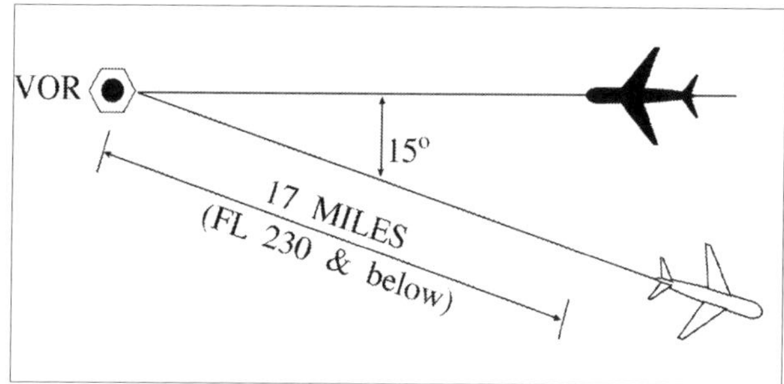

2. ***NDB:***

(a) Consider separation to exist between aircraft established on tracks of the same NAVAID that diverge by at least 30 degrees and one aircraft is at least 15 miles from the NAVAID. This separation must not be used when one or both aircraft are inbound to the aid unless the distance of the aircraft from the facility can be readily determined by reference to the NAVAID. Use TBL 8−4−2 to determine the flight distance required for various divergence angles to clear the airspace to be protected. For divergence that falls between two values, use the lesser value to obtain the distance. (See FIG 8−4−11.)

TBL 8−4−2
Divergence-Distance Minima (NDB)

Divergence (degrees)	Distance (mile)	
	FL 230 and below	FL 240 through FL 450
30	15	17
45	13	14
60	9	10
75	7	8
90	6	7

Note: *This table compensates for DME slant range error.*

FIG 8−4−11
Track Separation NDB

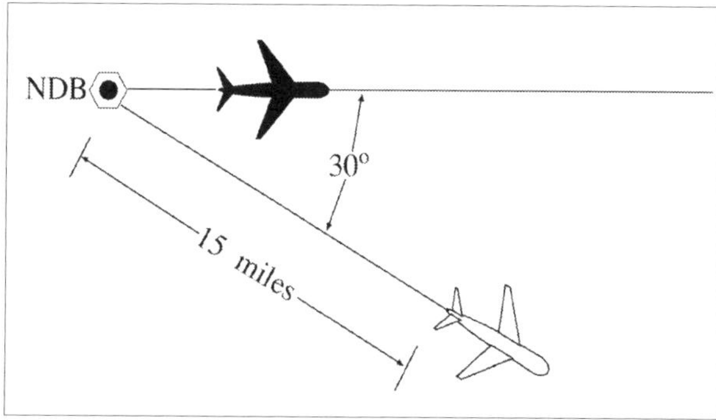

(b) Clear aircraft navigating on NDB facilities in accordance with paragraph 2−5−2, NAVAID Terms.

b. Different NAVAIDs: Separate aircraft using different navigation aids by assigning tracks so that their protected airspace does not overlap. (See FIG 8−4−12.)

FIG 8-4-12
Track Separation
Different NAVAIDs

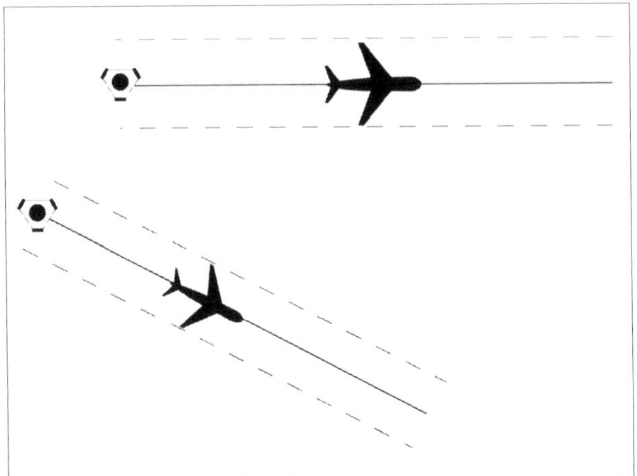

c. Dead Reckoning (DR):

1. Consider separation to exist between aircraft established on tracks that diverge by at least 45 degrees when one aircraft is at least 15 miles from the point of intersection of the tracks. This point may be determined either visually or by reference to a ground-based navigation aid. (See FIG 8-4-13.)

FIG 8-4-13
Track Separation
Dead Reckoning

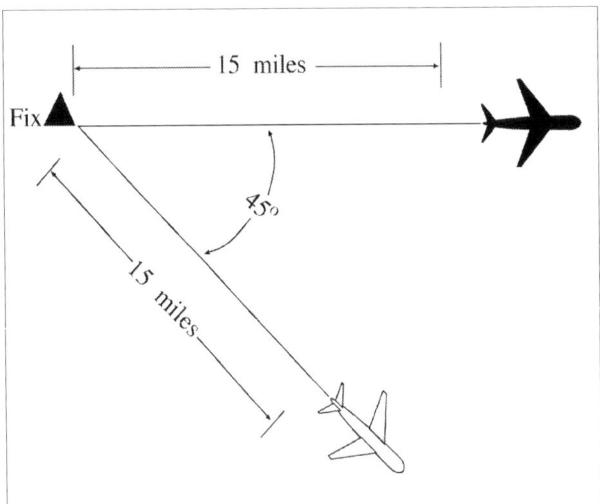

Section 5. Offshore/Oceanic Transition Procedures

8–5–1. ALTITUDE/FLIGHT LEVEL TRANSITION

When vertical separation is applied between aircraft crossing the offshore/oceanic airspace boundary below FL 180, control action must be taken to ensure that differences between the standard altimeter setting (QNE) and local altimeter setting (QNH) do not compromise separation. (See FIG 8–5–1.)

FIG 8–5–1
Standard and Local Altimeter Setting Differences

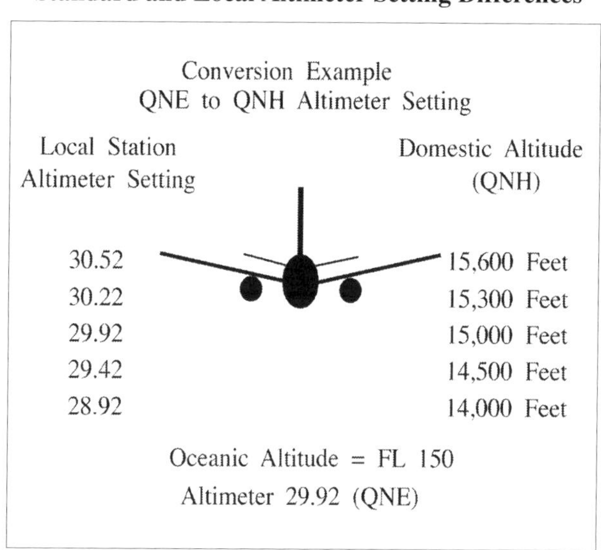

8–5–2. COURSE DIVERGENCE

When aircraft are entering oceanic airspace, separation will exist in oceanic airspace when:

a. Aircraft are established on courses that diverge by at least 15 degrees until oceanic lateral separation is established, and

b. The aircraft are horizontally radar separated and separation is increasing at the edge of known radar coverage.

8–5–3. OPPOSITE DIRECTION

When transitioning from an offshore airspace area to oceanic airspace, an aircraft may climb through opposite direction oceanic traffic provided vertical separation above that traffic is established:

a. Before the outbound crosses the offshore/oceanic boundary; and

b. 15 minutes before the aircraft are estimated to pass. (See FIG 8–5–2.)

FIG 8–5–2
Transitioning From Offshore to Oceanic Airspace Opposite Direction

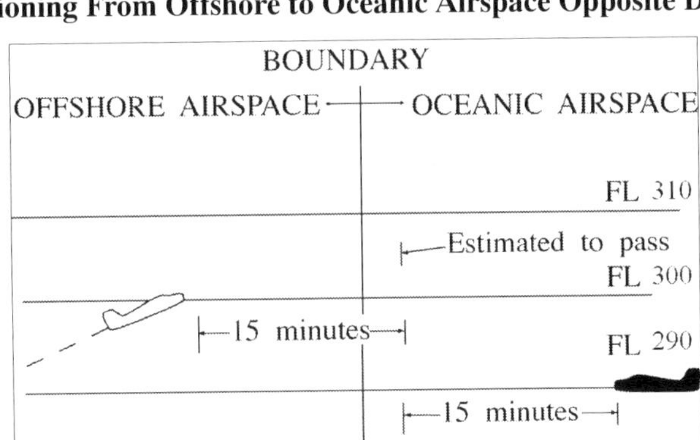

8–5–4. SAME DIRECTION

When transitioning from an offshore airspace area to oceanic airspace or while within oceanic airspace, apply 5 minutes minimum separation when a following aircraft on the same course is climbing through the altitude of the preceding aircraft if the following conditions are met:

a. The preceding aircraft is level at the assigned altitude and is maintaining a speed equal to or greater than the following aircraft; and

b. The minimum of *5 minutes* is maintained between the preceding and following aircraft; and

c. The following aircraft is separated by not more than 4,000 feet from the preceding aircraft when the climb clearance is issued; and

d. The following aircraft commences climb within *10 minutes* after passing:

1. An exact reporting point (DME fix or intersection formed from NAVAIDs) which the preceding aircraft has reported; or

2. A radar observed position over which the preceding aircraft has been observed; and

e. The following aircraft is in direct communication with air traffic control until vertical separation is established. (See FIG 8–5–3.)

FIG 8-5-3
Transitioning From Offshore to Oceanic Airspace Same Direction

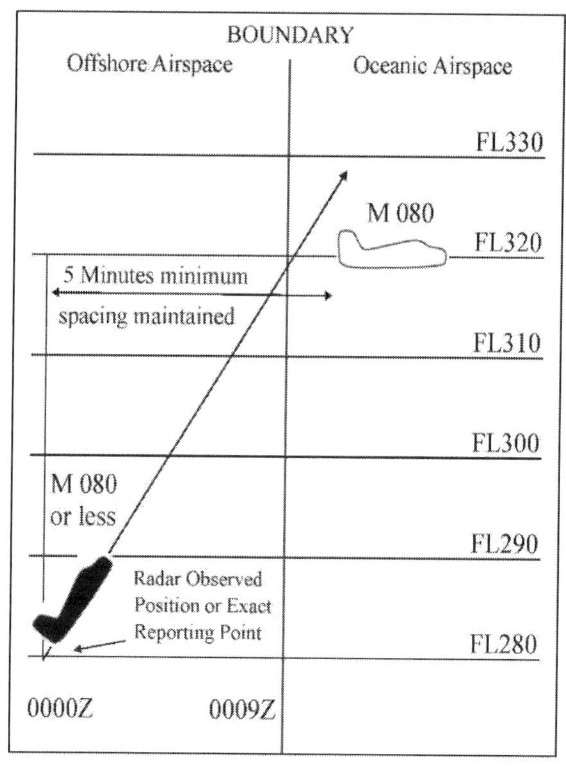

8-5-5. RADAR IDENTIFICATION APPLICATION

Radar separation standards may be applied between radar identified aircraft and another aircraft not yet identified that is in transit from oceanic airspace or nonradar offshore airspace into an area of known radar coverage where radar separation is applied provided:

a. Direct radio communications is maintained with one of the aircraft involved and there is an ability to communicate with the other;

b. The transiting aircraft is RNAV equipped;

c. The performance of the radar/system is adequate;

REFERENCE-
FAA Order JO 7110.65, Para 5-1-1, Presentation and Equipment Performance.

d. Flight data on the aircraft that has not been radar identified indicate that it is equipped with a standard transponder and there is no known information that the transponder is not operating;

e. Radar separation standards are maintained between the radar identified aircraft and any other observed targets until the transitioning aircraft is radar identified or nonradar separation is established;

f. The facility has identified areas of known radar coverage, incorporated those areas into facility standard operating procedures (SOP), and provided training to the controllers.

g. This procedure is also applicable to aircraft in transit from oceanic airspace into Guam Control Area (CTA), San Juan CTA and Honolulu CTA radar coverage areas.

h. EXCEPTION: This procedure is not authorized if there is insufficient time for the controller to establish other approved separation in the event of a delay or inability to establish radar identification of the transiting aircraft taking into consideration factors such as aircraft performance characteristics, type, and speed; weather, traffic conditions; workload; frequency congestion; etc.

REFERENCE–
FAA Order JO 7110.65, Para 2–2–6, IFR Flight Progress Data, Subpara b.
FAA Order JO 7110.65, Para 8–1–8, Use of Control Estimates.

Section 6. Separation from Airspace Reservations

8–6–1. TEMPORARY STATIONARY AIRSPACE RESERVATIONS

Separate aircraft from a temporary stationary reservation by one of two methods:

a. Laterally: Clear aircraft so that the protected airspace along the route of flight does not overlap the geographical area of the stationary reservation. (See FIG 8–6–1.)

FIG 8–6–1
Temporary Stationary Airspace Reservations
Lateral Separation

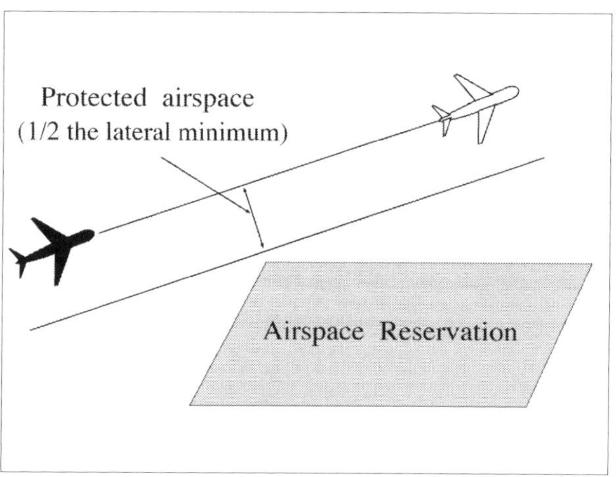

b. Vertically: Clear aircraft so that vertical separation exists while the aircraft is within a geographical area defined as the stationary reservation plus a buffer around the perimeter equivalent to one-half the lateral separation minimum. (See FIG 8–6–2.)

FIG 8–6–2
Temporary Stationary Airspace Reservations
Vertical Separation

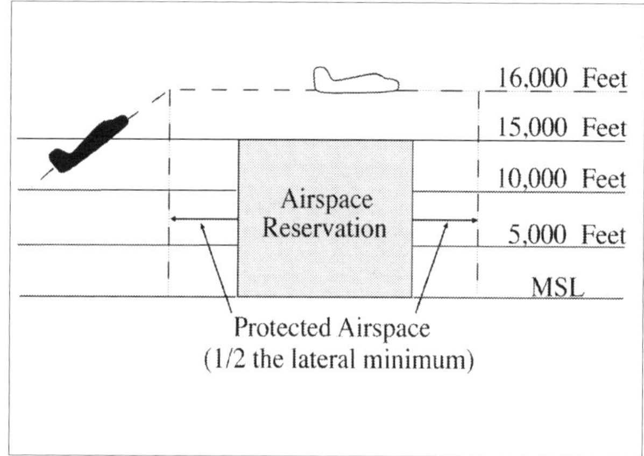

8–6–2. REFUSAL OF AVOIDANCE CLEARANCE

If a pilot refuses to accept a clearance to avoid a reservation, inform him/her of the potential hazard, advise him/her that services will not be provided while the flight is within the reservation and, if possible, inform the appropriate using agency.

8-6-3. TEMPORARY MOVING AIRSPACE RESERVATIONS

Separate aircraft from a temporary moving airspace reservation by one of the following methods:

a. Laterally: Clear aircraft so that the protected airspace along the route of flight does not overlap the (time-dependent) geographical area of the moving airspace reservation.

b. Longitudinally: Clear aircraft so that the appropriate longitudinal minimum exists ahead of the first or behind the last aircraft operating within the reservation.

c. Vertically: Clear aircraft so that vertical separation exists while the aircraft is within a (time-dependent) geographical area defined as the moving airspace reservation plus a buffer around the perimeter equivalent to one-half the lateral separation minimum.

Section 7. North Atlantic ICAO Region

8-7-1. APPLICATION

Provide air traffic control services in the North Atlantic ICAO Region with the procedures and minima contained in this section except when noted otherwise.

8-7-2. VERTICAL SEPARATION

Provide vertical separation in accordance with Chapter 4, IFR, Section 5, Altitude Assignment and Verification.

8-7-3. LONGITUDINAL SEPARATION

In accordance with Chapter 8, Offshore/Oceanic Procedures, Section 3, Longitudinal Separation, apply the following:

a. Supersonic flight:

1. *10 minutes* provided that:

(a) both aircraft are in level flight at the same Mach number or the aircraft are of the same type and are both operating in cruise climb, and one of the following;

(1) The aircraft concerned have reported over a common point; or,

(2) If the aircraft have not reported over a common point, the appropriate time interval being applied between aircraft exists and will exist at the common point; or,

(3) If a common point does not exist, the appropriate time interval being applied between aircraft exists and will exist at significant points along each track.

2. *15 minutes* between aircraft in supersonic flight not covered in subparagraph a1 above.

b. Turbojet operations *(subsonic flight)*:

1. Apply the prescribed minima in accordance with paragraph 8-3-3, Mach Number Technique; or

2. Where tracks diverge from the common point and the following aircraft is maintaining a greater Mach Number than the preceding aircraft:

(a) At least *10 minutes* longitudinal separation exists at the point where the tracks diverge; and

(b) At least *5 minutes* longitudinal separation will exist where minimum lateral separation is achieved *(whichever is estimated to occur first)*;

(1) At or before the next significant point (normally within ten degrees of longitude along track(s)), or

(2) Within 90 minutes of the time the following aircraft passes the common point, or

(3) Within 600 NM of the common point.

3. Apply *15 minutes* between all other turbojet aircraft.

c. Nonturbojet operations:

1. Apply *20 minutes* between aircraft operating in the West Atlantic (WAT), or

2. Apply *30 minutes* between aircraft operating outside of the WAT.

NOTE−
The WAT area is defined as beginning at a point 27°00'N/77°00'W direct to 20°00'N/67°00'W direct to 18°00'N/62°00'W

direct to 18°00'N/60°00'W direct to 38°30'N/60°00'W direct to 38°30'N/69°15'W, thence counterclockwise along the New York Oceanic CTA/FIR boundary to the Miami Oceanic CTA/FIR boundary, thence southbound along the Miami Oceanic CTA/FIR boundary to the point of beginning.

d. Clear an aircraft for an ADS-B In Trail Procedure (ITP) climb or descent provided the following conditions are satisfied:

1. The ITP climb or descent has been requested by the pilot;

2. The aircraft identification of each reference aircraft in the ITP request exactly matches the Item 7 - aircraft identification of the corresponding aircraft's filed flight plan;

3. The reported ITP distance between the ITP aircraft and any reference aircraft is 15 NM or more;

4. Both the ITP aircraft and reference aircraft are either on:

(a) same identical tracks and any turn at a waypoint shall be limited to less than 45 degrees; or

(b) same tracks with no turns permitted that reduce required separation during the ITP.

NOTE–
Same identical tracks are where the angular difference is zero degrees.

5. No speed or route change clearance shall be issued to the ITP aircraft until the ITP climb or descent is completed;

6. The altitude difference between the ITP aircraft and any reference aircraft shall be 2000 ft or less;

7. No instruction to amend speed, altitude or route shall be issued to any reference aircraft until the ITP climb or descent is completed;

8. The maximum closing speed between the ITP aircraft and each reference aircraft shall be Mach 0.06; and

9. The ITP aircraft shall not be a reference aircraft in another ITP clearance.

NOTE–
ATOP is designed to check for the above criteria prior to allowing the minima to be provided.

e. Minima based on distance using Automatic Dependent Surveillance – Contract (ADS-C):

1. Apply the minima as specified in TBL 8–7–1 between aircraft on the same track within airspace designated for Required Navigation Performance (RNP), provided:

(a) Direct controller/pilot communication via voice or Controller Pilot Data Link Communications (CPDLC) is established, and

(b) The required ADS-C periodic reports are maintained and monitored by an automated flight data processor (for example, ATOP).

TBL 8–7–1
ADS–C Criteria

Minima				
Standard	**RNP**	**RCP See Note 1**	**RSP See Note 2**	**Maximum ADS-C Periodic Reporting Interval**
50 NM	10	240	180	27 minutes
50 NM	4	240	180	32 minutes
30 NM	4	240	180	10 minutes

NOTE–
1. *Required Communication Performance (RCP).*
2. *Required Surveillance Performance (RSP).*

2. Aircraft on reciprocal tracks may be cleared to climb or descend to or through the altitude(s) occupied by another aircraft provided:

(a) An ADS-C position report on at least one of the aircraft has been received beyond the passing point, and

(b) The aircraft have passed each other by the applicable separation minimum.

NOTE–
ATOP has been designed to check for the above criteria prior to allowing the minima to be provided.

3. When an ADS-C periodic or waypoint change event report is overdue by *3 minutes*, the controller must take action to obtain an ADS-C report.

4. If no report is received within *6 minutes* of the time the original report was due, the controller must take action to apply another form of separation.

5. Aircraft on the same track may be cleared to climb or descend through the level of another aircraft provided:

(a) The longitudinal distance between the aircraft is determined from near simultaneous ADS–C demand reports and the ATOP software is used to ensure the following conditions are met;

(b) The longitudinal distance between the aircraft, as determined in a) above, is not less than:

(1) 15 NM when the preceding aircraft is at the same speed or faster than the following aircraft; or

(2) 25 NM when the following aircraft is not more than Mach 0.02 faster than the preceding aircraft

(c) The altitude difference between aircraft is not more than 2000 ft;

(d) The clearance is for a climb or descent of 4000 ft or less;

(e) Both aircraft are filed as single flights not flying in formation with other aircraft;

(f) Both aircraft are in level flight at a single altitude;

(g) Both aircraft are same direction;

(h) Neither aircraft are on a weather deviation;

(i) Neither aircraft have an open CPDLC request for a weather deviation;

(j) Neither aircraft are on an offset with a rejoin clearance; and

(k) The clearance is issued with a restriction that ensures vertical separation is re–established within 15 minutes from the first demand report request.

8–7–4. LATERAL SEPARATION

In accordance with Chapter 8, Offshore/Oceanic Procedures, Section 4, Lateral Separation, apply the following:

a. *23 NM* to approved aircraft (at a minimum, RNP 4, RCP 240, and RSP 180) operating within airspace designated for *23 NM* lateral separation when direct controller/pilot communications via voice or Controller Pilot Data Link Communications (CPDLC), and the required ADS–C contracts are maintained and monitored by an automated flight data processor (e.g., ATOP).

b. *50 NM* between Required Navigation Performance (RNP 4 or RNP 10) approved aircraft that operate in the New York Oceanic CTA/FIR or the San Juan Oceanic CTA/FIR or the Atlantic portion of the Miami Oceanic CTA/FIR.

NOTE–
This reduced lateral separation must not be used if track–keeping capability of the aircraft has been reduced for any reason.

c. *60 NM or 1 degree latitude* between:

1. Supersonic aircraft operating above FL 275.

2. Aircraft which have MNPS or NAT HLA authorization and which:

(a) Operate within NAT HLA; or

(b) Are in transit to or from NAT HLA; or

(c) Operate for part of their flight within, above, or below NAT HLA.

NOTE–
This reduced lateral separation must not be used if track–keeping capability of the aircraft has been reduced for any reason.

d. *90 NM or 1 and 1/2 degrees latitude* between aircraft not approved for RNP 4 or RNP 10 and which:

1. Operate on routes or in areas within WAT, the San Juan CTA/FIR or the Atlantic portion of the Miami CTA/FIR;

2. Operate between points in the U.S. or Canada, and Bermuda;

3. Operate west of 55° West between the U.S., Canada, or Bermuda and points in the Caribbean ICAO Region.

e. *120 NM or 2 degrees latitude* between aircraft not covered by subparagraphs a, c or d above.

NOTE–
Tracks may be spaced with reference to their difference in latitude, provided that in any interval of 10 degrees of longitude the change in latitude of at least one of the tracks does not exceed 3 degrees when operating south of 58° North.

Section 8. Caribbean ICAO Region

8-8-1. APPLICATION

Provide air traffic control services in the Caribbean ICAO Region with the procedures and minima contained in this section except when noted otherwise.

8-8-2. VERTICAL SEPARATION

Provide vertical separation in accordance with Chapter 4, IFR, Section 5, Altitude Assignment and Verification.

8-8-3. LONGITUDINAL SEPARATION

Provide longitudinal separation between aircraft as follows:

a. Supersonic flight:

1. *10 minutes* provided both aircraft are in level flight at the same Mach number or the aircraft are of the same type and are both operating in cruise climb, and one of the following;

(a) Both aircraft have reported over a common point; or,

(b) If both aircraft have not reported over a common point, the appropriate time interval being applied between aircraft exists and will exist at the common point; or,

(c) If a common point does not exist, the appropriate time interval being applied between aircraft exists and will exist at significant points along each track.

2. *15 minutes* between all other aircraft.

b. Turbojet operations at or above FL 200 in the Miami Oceanic, Houston Oceanic and San Juan CTAs/FIRs and all altitudes in the West Atlantic Route System (WATRS) and New York Oceanic CTA/FIR *(subsonic flight)*:

1. Apply the prescribed minima in accordance with paragraph 8-3-3, Mach Number Technique; or

2. In the New York CTA/FIR, where tracks diverge from the common point and the following aircraft is maintaining a greater Mach number than the preceding aircraft:

(a) At least *10 minutes* longitudinal separation exists at the point where the tracks diverge; and

(b) At least *5 minutes* longitudinal separation will exist where minimum lateral separation is achieved *(whichever is estimated to occur first)*;

(1) At or before the next significant point (normally within ten degrees of longitude along track(s)), or

(2) Within *90 minutes* of the time the following aircraft passes the common point, or

(3) Within *600 NM* of the common point; or

3. Apply *15 minutes* between all other turbojet aircraft.

c. Turbojet operations below FL 200 *(subsonic flight)*:

Apply *20 minutes* between turbojet aircraft operating below FL 200 in the San Juan Oceanic *(outside the WATRS area)*, Miami Oceanic and Houston Oceanic CTAs/FIRs.

d. Nonturbojet operations.

1. Apply *20 minutes* between aircraft operating in the WATRS; or

2. Apply *20 minutes* between aircraft operating below FL 200 in the Miami Oceanic, Houston Oceanic and San Juan CTAs/FIRs; or

3. Apply *30 minutes* between aircraft operating outside of the WATRS in the New York CTA/FIR.

NOTE–
The WATRS area is defined as beginning at a point 27°00'N/77°00'W direct to 20°00'N/67°00'W direct to 18°00'N/62°00'W direct to 18°00'N/60°00'W direct to 38°30'N/60°00'W direct to 38°30'N/69°15'W, thence counterclockwise along the New York Oceanic CTA/FIR boundary to the Miami Oceanic CTA/FIR boundary, thence southbound along the Miami Oceanic CTA/FIR boundary to the point of beginning.

e. Clear an aircraft for an ADS-B In Trail Procedure (ITP) climb or descent provided the following conditions are satisfied:

1. The ITP climb or descent has been requested by the pilot;

2. The aircraft identification of each reference aircraft in the ITP request exactly matches the Item 7_-aircraft identification of the corresponding aircraft's filed flight plan;

3. The reported ITP distance between the ITP aircraft and any reference aircraft is 15 NM or more;

4. Both the ITP aircraft and reference aircraft are either on:

(a) same identical tracks and any turn at a waypoint shall be limited to less than 45 degrees; or

(b) same tracks with no turns permitted that reduce required separation during the ITP.

NOTE–
Same identical tracks are where the angular difference is zero degrees.

5. No speed or route change clearance shall be issued to the ITP aircraft until the ITP climb or descent is completed;

6. The altitude difference between the ITP aircraft and any reference aircraft shall be 2000 ft or less;

7. No instruction to amend speed, altitude or route shall be issued to any reference aircraft until the ITP climb or descent is completed;

8. The maximum closing speed between the ITP aircraft and each reference aircraft shall be Mach 0.06; and

9. The ITP aircraft shall not be a reference aircraft in another ITP clearance.

NOTE–
ATOP is designed to check for the above criteria prior to allowing the minima to be provided.

f. Minima based on distance using Automatic Dependent Surveillance – Contract (ADS-C):

1. Apply the minima as specified in TBL 8–8–1 between aircraft on the same track within airspace designated for Required Navigation Performance (RNP), provided:

(a) Direct controller/pilot communication via voice or Controller Pilot Data Link Communications (CPDLC) is established, and

(b) The required ADS-C periodic reports are maintained and monitored by an automated flight data processor (for example, ATOP).

TBL 8–8–1
ADS–C Criteria

Minima				
Standard	**RNP**	**RCP**	**RSP**	**Maximum ADS-C Periodic Reporting Interval**
50 NM	10	240	180	27 minutes
50 NM	4	240	180	32 minutes
30 NM	4	240	180	10 minutes

2. Aircraft on reciprocal tracks may be cleared to climb or descend to or through the altitude(s) occupied by another aircraft provided:

(a) An ADS-C position report on at least one of the aircraft has been received beyond the passing point, and

(b) The aircraft have passed each other by the applicable separation minimum.

NOTE–
ATOP has been designed to check for the above criteria prior to allowing the minima to be provided.

3. When an ADS-C periodic or waypoint change event report is overdue by *3 minutes*, the controller must take action to obtain an ADS-C report.

4. If no report is received within *6 minutes* of the time the original report was due, the controller must take action to apply another form of separation.

5. Aircraft on the same track may be cleared to climb or descend through the level of another aircraft provided:

(a) The longitudinal distance between the aircraft is determined from near simultaneous ADS–C demand reports and the ATOP software is used to ensure the following conditions are met;

(b) The longitudinal distance between the aircraft, as determined in a) above, is not less than:

(1) 15 NM when the preceding aircraft is at the same speed or faster than the following aircraft; or

(2) 25 NM when the following aircraft is not more than Mach 0.02 faster than the preceding aircraft

(c) The altitude difference between aircraft is not more than 2000 ft;

(d) The clearance is for a climb or descent of 4000 ft or less;

(e) Both aircraft are filed as single flights not flying in formation with other aircraft;

(f) Both aircraft are in level flight at a single altitude;

(g) Both aircraft are same direction;

(h) Neither aircraft are on a weather deviation;

(i) Neither aircraft have an open CPDLC request for a weather deviation;

(j) Neither aircraft are on an offset with a rejoin clearance; and

(k) The clearance is issued with a restriction that ensures vertical separation is re–established within 15 minutes from the first demand report request.

8–8–4. LATERAL SEPARATION

In accordance with Chapter 8, Offshore/Oceanic Procedures, Section 4, Lateral Separation, apply the following:

a. *23 NM* to approved aircraft (at a minimum, RNP 4, RCP 240, and RSP 180) operating within airspace designated for *23 NM* lateral separation when direct controller/pilot communications via voice or Controller Pilot Data Link Communications (CPDLC), and the required ADS–C contracts are maintained and monitored by an automated flight data processor (e.g., ATOP).

b. *50 NM* between Required Navigation Performance (RNP 4 or RNP 10) approved aircraft that:

1. Operate in the New York Oceanic CTA/FIR; or

2. Operate in the San Juan Oceanic CTA/FIR; or

3. Operate in the Houston Oceanic CTA/FIR; or

4. Operate in the Atlantic or Gulf of Mexico portion of the Miami CTA/FIR.

NOTE–
This reduced lateral separation must not be used if track–keeping capability of the aircraft has been reduced for any reason.

c. *60 NM* between:

1. Supersonic aircraft operating above FL 275 within the New York oceanic CTA/FIR.

2. Supersonic aircraft operating at or above FL 450 not covered in subparagraph 1 above.

3. Aircraft which have MNPS or NAT HLA authorization and which:

(a) Operate within NTA HLA; or

(b) Are in transit to or from NAT HLA; or

(c) Operate for part of their flight within, above, or below NAT HLA.

NOTE–
This reduced lateral separation must not be used if track–keeping capability of the aircraft has been reduced for any reason.

d. *90 NM* between aircraft not approved for RNP 4 or RNP 10 and which:

1. Operate within *WAT*; or

2. Operate west of 55° West between the U.S., Canada, or Bermuda and points in the Caribbean ICAO Region.

e. *100 NM* between aircraft operating west of 55°West not covered by subparagraphs a, c, or d above.

f. *120 NM* between aircraft operating east of 55°West.

8–8–5. VFR CLIMB AND DESCENT

a. In the Houston, Miami, and San Juan CTAs, IFR flights may be cleared to climb and descend in VFR conditions only:

1. When requested by the pilot; and

2. Between sunrise and sunset.

b. Apply the following when the flight is cleared:

1. If there is a possibility that VFR conditions may become impractical, issue alternative instructions.

2. Issue traffic information to aircraft that are not separated in accordance with the minima in this section.

Section 9. Pacific ICAO Region

8-9-1. APPLICATION

Provide air traffic control services in the Pacific ICAO Region with the procedures and minima contained in this section except when noted otherwise.

8-9-2. VERTICAL SEPARATION

Provide vertical separation in accordance with Chapter 4, IFR, Section 5, Altitude Assignment and Verification.

8-9-3. LONGITUDINAL SEPARATION

In accordance with Chapter 8, Offshore/Oceanic Procedures, Section 3, Longitudinal Separation, apply the following:

a. Minima based on time:

1. *15 minutes* between aircraft; or

2. *10 minutes* between turbojet aircraft whether in level, climbing or descending flight, provided that the aircraft concerned follow the same track or continuously diverging tracks until some other form of separation is provided; or

3. The prescribed minima in accordance with paragraph 8-3-3, Mach Number Technique.

4. Reciprocal track aircraft – Where lateral separation is not provided, vertical separation must be provided at least *10 minutes* before and after the time the aircraft are estimated to pass or are estimated to have passed.

b. Clear an aircraft for an ADS-B In Trail Procedure (ITP) climb or descent provided the following conditions are satisfied:

1. The ITP climb or descent has been requested by the pilot;

2. The aircraft identification of each reference aircraft in the ITP request exactly matches the Item 7 - aircraft identification of the corresponding aircraft's filed flight plan;

3. The reported ITP distance between the ITP aircraft and any reference aircraft is 15 NM or more;

4. Both the ITP aircraft and reference aircraft are either on:

(a) Same identical tracks and any turn at a waypoint shall be limited to less than 45 degrees; or

(b) same tracks with no turns permitted that reduce required separation during the ITP.

NOTE–
Same identical tracks are where the angular difference is zero degrees.

5. No speed or route change clearance shall be issued to the ITP aircraft until the ITP climb or descent is completed;

6. The altitude difference between the ITP aircraft and any reference aircraft shall be 2000 ft or less;

7. No instruction to amend speed, altitude or route shall be issued to any reference aircraft until the ITP climb or descent is completed;

8. The maximum closing speed between the ITP aircraft and each reference aircraft shall be Mach 0.06; and

9. The ITP aircraft shall not be a reference aircraft in another ITP clearance.

NOTE–
ATOP is designed to check for the above criteria prior to allowing the minima to be provided.

c. Minima based on distance using Automatic Dependent Surveillance – Contract (ADS–C):

1. Apply the minima as specified in TBL 8–9–1, ADS–C Criteria, between aircraft on the same track within airspace designated for Required Navigation Performance (RNP), provided:

(a) Direct controller/pilot communication via voice or Controller Pilot Data Link Communications (CPDLC) is established, and

(b) The required ADS–C periodic reports are maintained and monitored by an automated flight data processor (e.g., ATOP);

TBL 8–9–1
ADS–C Criteria

Minima				
Standard	**RNP**	**RCP**	**RSP**	**Maximum ADS-C Periodic Reporting Interval**
50 NM	10	240	180	27 minutes
50 NM	4	240	180	32 minutes
30 NM	4	240	180	10 minutes

2. Aircraft on reciprocal tracks may be cleared to climb or descend to or through the altitude(s) occupied by another aircraft provided that:

(a) An ADS–C position report on at least one of the aircraft has been received beyond the passing point, and

(b) The aircraft have passed each other by the applicable separation minimum.

NOTE–
ATOP has been designed to check for the above criteria prior to allowing the minima to be provided.

3. When an ADS–C periodic or waypoint change event report is overdue by *3 minutes*, the controller must take action to obtain an ADS–C report.

4. If no report is received within *6 minutes* of the time the original report was due, the controller must take action to apply another form of separation.

5. Aircraft on the same track may be cleared to climb or descend through the level of another aircraft provided:

(a) The longitudinal distance between the aircraft is determined from near simultaneous ADS–C demand reports and the ATOP software is used to ensure the following conditions are met;

(b) The longitudinal distance between the aircraft, as determined in a) above, is not less than:

(1) 15 NM when the preceding aircraft is at the same speed or faster than the following aircraft; or

(2) 25 NM when the following aircraft is not more than Mach 0.02 faster than the preceding aircraft

(c) The altitude difference between aircraft is not more than 2000 ft;

(d) The clearance is for a climb or descent of 4000 ft or less;

(e) Both aircraft are filed as single flights not flying in formation with other aircraft;

(f) Both aircraft are in level flight at a single altitude;

(g) Both aircraft are same direction;

(h) Neither aircraft are on a weather deviation;

(i) Neither aircraft have an open CPDLC request for a weather deviation;

(j) Neither aircraft are on an offset with a rejoin clearance; and

(k) The clearance is issued with a restriction that ensures vertical separation is re−established within 15 minutes from the first demand report request.

d. Minima based on distance *without* ADS−C:

1. Apply *50 NM* between aircraft cruising, climbing or descending on the same track or reciprocal track that meet the requirements for and are operating within airspace designated for RNP−10 operations provided:

(a) Direct controller/pilot communication via voice or CPDLC is maintained; and

(b) Separation is established by ensuring that at least *50 NM* longitudinal separation minima exists between aircraft positions as reported by reference to the same waypoint.

(1) *Same track aircraft* – whenever possible ahead of both; or

(2) *Reciprocal track aircraft* – provided that it has been positively established that the aircraft have passed each other.

2. Distance verification must be obtained from each aircraft at least every *24 minutes* to verify that separation is maintained.

3. If an aircraft fails to report its position within *3 minutes* after the expected time, the controller must take action to establish communication. If communication is not established within *8 minutes* after the time the report should have been received, the controller must take action to apply another form of separation.

NOTE−
When same track aircraft are at, or are expected to reduce to, the minima, speed control techniques should be applied in order to maintain the required separation.

8−9−4. LATERAL SEPARATION

In accordance with Chapter 8, Offshore/Oceanic Procedures, Section 4, Lateral Separation, apply the following:

a. Within areas where Required Navigation Performance separation and procedures are authorized, apply *50 NM* to RNP 4 or RNP 10 approved aircraft.

b. Apply *23 NM* to approved aircraft (at a minimum, RNP 4, RCP 240, and RSP 180) operating within airspace designated for *23 NM* lateral separation when direct controller/pilot communications via voice or Controller Pilot Data Link Communications (CPDLC), and the required ADS−C contracts are maintained and monitored by an automated flight data processor (e.g., ATOP).

c. Apply *100 NM* to aircraft not covered by subparagraphs a and b.

Section 10. North American ICAO Region

8-10-1. APPLICATION

Provide air traffic control services in the North American ICAO Region with the procedures and minima contained in this section.

8-10-2. VERTICAL SEPARATION

Provide vertical separation in accordance with:

a. Chapter 4, IFR, Section 5, Altitude Assignment and Verification; and

b. Facility directives depicting the transition between flight levels and metric altitudes.

8-10-3. LONGITUDINAL SEPARATION

In accordance with Chapter 8, Offshore/Oceanic Procedures, Section 3, Longitudinal Separation, apply the following:

a. Minima based on time:

1. *15 minutes* between turbojet aircraft.

2. The prescribed minima in accordance with paragraph 8-3-3, Mach Number Technique.

3. *20 minutes* between other aircraft.

b. Clear an aircraft for an ADS-B In Trail Procedure (ITP) climb or descent provided the following conditions are satisfied:

1. The ITP climb or descent has been requested by the pilot;

2. The aircraft identification of each reference aircraft in the ITP request exactly matches the Item 7 - aircraft identification of the corresponding aircraft's filed flight plan;

3. The reported ITP distance between the ITP aircraft and any reference aircraft is 15 NM or more;

4. Both the ITP aircraft and reference aircraft are either on:

(a) same identical tracks and any turn at a waypoint shall be limited to less than 45 degrees; or

(b) same tracks with no turns permitted that reduce required separation during the ITP.

NOTE-
Same identical tracks are where the angular difference is zero degrees.

5. No speed or route change clearance shall be issued to the ITP aircraft until the ITP climb or descent is completed;

6. The altitude difference between the ITP aircraft and any reference aircraft shall be 2000 ft or less;

7. No instruction to amend speed, altitude or route shall be issued to any reference aircraft until the ITP climb or descent is completed;

8. The maximum closing speed between the ITP aircraft and each reference aircraft shall be Mach 0.06; and

9. The ITP aircraft shall not be a reference aircraft in another ITP clearance.

NOTE-
ATOP is designed to check for the above criteria prior to allowing the minima to be provided.

c. Minima based on distance using Automatic Dependent Surveillance – Contract (ADS-C) in the Anchorage Oceanic and Anchorage Continental CTAs only:

NOTE–
The minima described in this paragraph are not applicable within airspace in the Anchorage Arctic CTA.

1. Apply the minima as specified in TBL 8–10–1 between aircraft on the same track within airspace in the Anchorage Oceanic and Anchorage Continental CTAs designated for Required Navigation Performance (RNP), provided:

(a) Direct controller/pilot communication via voice or Controller Pilot Data Link Communications (CPDLC) is established, and

(b) The required ADS-C periodic reports are maintained and monitored by an automated flight data processor (for example, ATOP).

TBL 8-10-1
ADS-C Criteria

Minima				
Standard	**RNP**	**RCP**	**RSP**	**Maximum ADS-C Periodic Reporting Interval**
50 NM	10	240	180	27 minutes
50 NM	4	240	180	32 minutes
30 NM	4	240	180	10 minutes

2. Aircraft on reciprocal tracks in the Anchorage Oceanic and Anchorage Continental CTAs may be cleared to climb or descend to or through the altitude(s) occupied by another aircraft provided:

(a) An ADS-C position report on at least one of the aircraft has been received beyond the passing point, and

(b) The aircraft have passed each other by the applicable separation minimum.

NOTE–
ATOP has been designed to check for the above criteria prior to allowing the minima to be provided.

3. When an ADS-C periodic or waypoint change event report is overdue by *3 minutes*, the controller must take action to obtain an ADS-C report.

4. If no report is received within *6 minutes* of the time the original report was due, the controller must take action to apply another form of separation.

5. Aircraft on the same track may be cleared to climb or descend through the level of another aircraft provided:

(a) The longitudinal distance between the aircraft is determined from near simultaneous ADS–C demand reports and the ATOP software is used to ensure the following conditions are met;

(b) The longitudinal distance between the aircraft, as determined in a) above, is not less than:

(1) 15 NM when the preceding aircraft is at the same speed or faster than the following aircraft; or

(2) 25 NM when the following aircraft is not more than Mach 0.02 faster than the preceding aircraft.

(c) The altitude difference between aircraft is not more than 2000 ft;

(d) The clearance is for a climb or descent of 4000 ft or less;

(e) Both aircraft are filed as single flights not flying in formation with other aircraft;

(f) Both aircraft are in level flight at a single altitude;

(g) Both aircraft are same direction;

(h) Neither aircraft are on a weather deviation;

(i) Neither aircraft have an open CPDLC request for a weather deviation;

(j) Neither aircraft are on an offset with a rejoin clearance; and

(k) The clearance is issued with a restriction that ensures vertical separation is re–established within 15 minutes from the first demand report request.

d. Minima based on DME/RNAV:

Apply the following DME/RNAV minima in Control 1234H, Control 1487H, and the Norton Sound High Control areas to turbojet aircraft established on or transitioning to the North Pacific (NOPAC) Route System.

1. *30 NM* between aircraft when DME reports or radar observations are used to establish the distance, otherwise at least *40 NM* based on RNAV must be applied; and

2. Unless both aircraft are radar identified, both aircraft must provide DME/RNAV distance reports via direct voice that indicates the appropriate separation exists; and

3. Application of DME/RNAV separation without direct voice communications may not continue for more than *90 minutes;* and

4. The preceding aircraft is assigned the same or greater Mach number than the following aircraft; and

5. Both aircraft must be advised of the other aircraft involved, including the distance relative to the flights.

EXAMPLE–
"Maintain Mach point eight four, same direction traffic, twelve o'clock, three five miles."

REFERENCE–
FAA Order JO 7110.65, Para 2–1–21, Traffic Advisories.

8–10–4. LATERAL SEPARATION

In accordance with Chapter 8, Offshore/Oceanic Procedures, Section 4, Lateral Separation, apply the following:

a. Within areas where Required Navigation Performance separation and procedures are authorized, apply *50 NM* to RNP 4 or RNP 10 approved aircraft.

b. Apply *23 NM* to approved aircraft (at a minimum, RNP 4, RCP 240, and RSP 180) operating within the Anchorage Oceanic CTA and Anchorage Continental CTA when direct controller/pilot communications via voice or Controller Pilot Data Link Communications (CPDLC) and the required ADS–C contracts are maintained and monitored by an automated flight data processor (e.g., ATOP).

NOTE–
The minimum described in subparagraph b is not applicable within airspace in the Anchorage Arctic CTA.

c. *90 NM* to aircraft not covered by subparagraphs a or b.

Chapter 9. Special Flights

Section 1. General

9–1–1. GENERAL

Provide aircraft engaged in the flight inspection of NAVAIDs with maximum assistance. Unless otherwise agreed to, maintain direct contact with the pilot and exchange information regarding known traffic in the area and his/her intentions.

NOTE–

1. *Many flight inspections are accomplished using automatic recording equipment, and an uninterrupted flight is necessary for successful completion of the mission. The workload for the limited number of aircraft engaged in these activities requires strict adherence to a schedule.*

2. *Flight inspection operations which require special participation of ground personnel, specific communications, or radar operation capabilities are considered to require special handling. These flights are coordinated with appropriate facilities before departure.*

REFERENCE–
FAA Order 8200.1, United States Standard Flight Inspection Manual.
FAA Order 8240.41, Flight Inspection/Air Traffic On–Site Coordination Requirements.

9–1–2. SPECIAL HANDLING

a. Clear the aircraft according to pilot request as soon as practicable. Do not ask the pilot to deviate from his/her planned action except to preclude an emergency situation.

REFERENCE–
FAA Order 8240.41, Flight Inspection/Air Traffic On–Site Coordination Requirements, Appendix 1, describes certain flight inspection maneuvers in detail.

b. Issue radar advisories to the flight inspection aircraft where adequate coverage exists and to the extent permitted by workload.

c. Suggest flight path adjustments, as required, for any aircraft which will enter or penetrate an area in which a flight inspection function is being performed.

d. Provide special handling, as required, to FAA aircraft conducting flight inspections using the call sign "Flight Check." The call sign "Flight Check (Nr) recorded" indicates automated flight inspections are in progress in terminal areas.

NOTE–

1. *FAA flight inspection aircraft will file flight plans using the call sign "FLIGHT CHECK" during flight inspections or when inbound to conduct flight inspections. Flight plan remarks may indicate type NAVAID inspection to be accomplished; e.g., "FC OKC P."*

2. *Authorized non-FAA Service Providers conducting Flight Validation activities use the call sign "FLIGHT VAL." Although these activities are similar to Flight Inspection activities, no additional priority is granted with this call sign.*

9–1–3. FLIGHT CHECK AIRCRAFT

a. Provide special handling, as required, to expedite flight inspection of NAVAIDs and RADAR by flight check aircraft.

NOTE–
Certain flight inspection maneuvers require operations in close proximity to the surface. These maneuvers can only be performed during daylight visual meteorological conditions. Preplanned automatic flight places the following limitations on the capability of the pilot to adhere to normal ATC clearances:

1. *Route of flight – orbital from 6 nautical miles to a maximum of 40 nautical miles from the facility depending on the type of inspection. During commissioning flight checks all SIDs, STARs, airways, DME fixes, and approaches must be flown.*

2. *Altitude assignment – from 1,000 feet above the antenna site up to the minimum en route altitude (MEA).*

REFERENCE–
FAA Order JO 7110.65, Para 2–1–4, Operational Priority.
FAA Order 8240.41, Flight Inspection/Air Traffic On–Site Coordination Requirements, Appendix 1, describes certain flight inspection maneuvers in detail.

b. Avoid changes in the route or altitude from that filed by the pilot in the initial flight plan.

c. Do not impose air traffic control delays in the flight except to preclude emergency situations.

d. Do not change the previously assigned discrete beacon code of special radar accuracy flight check aircraft.

REFERENCE–
FAA Order JO 7210.3, Para 7–1–2, Special Radar Accuracy Checks.
FAA Order JO 7210.3, Para 10–5–4, ASR Performance Checks.

Section 2. Special Operations

9-2-1. AIRCRAFT CARRYING DANGEROUS MATERIALS

a. Provide the following special handling to military aircraft or military contracted aircraft carrying dangerous materials when:

1. The words "dangerous cargo," or "inert devices," or both are contained in the remarks section of the filed flight plan, or

NOTE-
1. *Certain types of military flights carrying dangerous materials require strict adherence to military regulations and flight planning along carefully selected routes. These flights must avoid heavily populated areas.*

2. *"Inert devices" are devices containing no dangerous materials but closely resembling nuclear or explosive items that are classified as dangerous and could be easily mistaken for their dangerous counterparts.*

2. The pilot uses these words in radio communication.

b. If it becomes necessary to issue a clearance to amend the route/altitude, advise the pilot:

1. Of the proposed change, and

2. The amount of delay to expect if it is necessary to maintain the present route/altitude.

c. When it becomes necessary for the pilot to refuse a clearance amending his/her route/altitude, he/she will advise if the traffic delay is acceptable or if an alternate route/altitude is desired. In such cases, offer all possible assistance.

d. When the aircraft is provided an en route descent, do not vector the aircraft from the planned route unless the pilot concurs.

e. Use special patterns and routings in areas where they have been developed for these flights. If special patterns and routings have not been developed, employ normal procedures.

9-2-2. CELESTIAL NAVIGATION TRAINING

EN ROUTE

a. Approve flight plans specifying celestial navigation only when it is requested for USAF or USN aircraft.

NOTE-
An ATC clearance must be obtained by the pilot before discontinuing conventional navigation to begin celestial navigation training. The pilot will advise when discontinuing celestial navigation and resuming conventional navigation. Celestial navigation training will be conducted within 30 NM of the route centerline specified in the en route clearance unless otherwise authorized by ATC. During celestial navigation training, the pilot will advise ATC before initiating any heading changes which exceed 20 degrees.

b. Within conterminous U.S. airspace, limit celestial navigation training to transponder-equipped aircraft within areas of ARTCC radar coverage.

c. Prior to control transfer, ensure that the receiving controller is informed of the nature of the celestial navigation training leg.

REFERENCE-
FAA Order JO 7110.65, Para 2-2-6, IFR Flight Progress Data.

9-2-3. EXPERIMENTAL AIRCRAFT OPERATIONS

a. When notified that an experimental aircraft requires special handling:

NOTE–
14 CFR Section 91.319(d)(3) requires that each person operating an aircraft with an experimental certificate must notify the control tower of the experimental nature of the aircraft when operating into or out of airports with operating control towers.

1. Clear the aircraft according to pilot requests as traffic permits and if not contrary to ATC procedures.

2. Once approved, do not ask the pilot to deviate from a planned action except to preclude an emergency situation.

b. At locations where volume or complexity of experimental aircraft operations warrant, a letter of agreement may be consummated between the facility and operator.

9–2–4. FAA RESEARCH AND DEVELOPMENT FLIGHTS

When coordinated in advance and traffic permits, approve requests for special flight procedures from aircraft participating in FAA research and development test activities. These special procedures must be applied to participating aircraft/vehicles.

NOTE–
Special flight procedures for FAA research and development test activities must be approved by the facility air traffic manager prior to their use.

9–2–5. FLYNET

ATC personnel at the first facility establishing contact with an aircraft using the code word FLYNET must:

a. Provide expeditious handling.

b. Report it to the operations supervisor (OS)/controller-in-charge (CIC), for reporting to the National Tactical Security Operations (NTSO) Air Traffic Security Coordinator (ATSC) through the Domestic Events Network (DEN).

c. Add to the remarks section of the flight plan that DEN notification has been accomplished.

NOTE–
The code word FLYNET indicates that an aircraft is transporting a nuclear emergency support team or other disaster response teams to a potential or actual nuclear/radiological incident, or to a potential or actual incident involving dangerous chemical agents or other hazardous materials. It is in the public interest that they reach their destination as rapidly as possible.

EXAMPLE–
"Miami Center, Energy One Two FLYNET, request clearance direct Dulles."

REFERENCE–
FAA Order JO 7110.65, Para 2–1–4, Operational Priority.
FAA Order JO 7610.4, Para 9–4–1, FLYNET Flights, Nuclear Emergency Support Teams.

9–2–6. IFR MILITARY TRAINING ROUTES

a. Except for aircraft operating in the same altitude reservation, clear aircraft into an MTR provided separation will be applied between successive aircraft unless otherwise covered in a letter of agreement between the military scheduling activity and the concerned ATC facility.

PHRASEOLOGY–
CLEARED INTO IR (designator).
MAINTAIN (altitude),

or

MAINTAIN IR (designator) ALTITUDE(S),

or

MAINTAIN AT OR BELOW (altitude),

or

CRUISE (altitude),

and if required,

CROSS (fix) AT OR LATER THAN (time).

b. Unless otherwise covered in a letter of agreement between the military scheduling activity and the concerned FAA facility, clear aircraft to exit an MTR.

PHRASEOLOGY−
CLEARED TO (destination/clearance limit) FROM IR (designator/exit fix) VIA (route).
MAINTAIN (altitude).

c. If the provisions of subparagraph a above cannot be accomplished, MTRs may be designated for MARSA operations. To preclude an inadvertent compromise of MARSA standards by ATC, appropriate MARSA application for such routes must be covered in a letter of agreement with the military scheduling activity. Establish separation between aircraft as soon as practicable after operation on the designated MARSA route is ended.

NOTE−
For designated MARSA routes, the military assumes responsibility for separation for MTR aircraft that have passed the primary/alternate entry fix until separation is established by ATC after operations on the MARSA route are completed.

d. The lateral airspace to be protected along an MTR is the designated width of the route.

e. Prior to an aircraft entering an MTR, request the pilot's estimate for the route's exit/alternate exit fix, the pilot's requested altitude after exiting and, if applicable, the number of reentries on a Strategic Training Range.

PHRASEOLOGY−
(Call sign) VERIFY YOUR EXIT FIX ESTIMATE AND REQUESTED ALTITUDE AFTER EXIT,

and if applicable,

THE NUMBER OF REENTRIES.

f. Forward estimates for exit/alternate exit fixes, requested altitude after exit, and, if applicable, the number of reentries on the Strategic Training Range.

g. Apply the procedures of paragraph 6−1−2, Nonreceipt of Position Report, based upon the pilot's estimate for the route exit fix.

h. Clearance may be issued to amend or restrict operations on a route for ATC considerations. Where a route has been designated MARSA in accordance with subparagraph c, ATC must not amend or restrict operations in such a manner as to compromise MARSA provisions.

NOTE−
When MARSA is provided through route scheduling and circumstances prevent the pilot from entering the route within established time limits, it must be the responsibility of the pilot to inform the ATC facility and advise his/her intentions.

i. If an aircraft on an IR experiences a two-way radio communications failure and you are unable to determine if the aircraft is proceeding VFR in accordance with 14 CFR Section 91.185(b) or the aircraft has not been positively radar identified:

1. Provide separation to the destination airport based on the aircraft complying with the following:

(a) Maintain to the exit/alternate exit fix the higher of the following altitudes:

(1) The minimum IFR altitude for each of the remaining route segment(s) remaining on the route.

(2) The highest altitude assigned in the last ATC clearance.

(b) Depart the exit/alternate exit fix at the appropriate altitude specified in subparagraph (a) above, then climb/descend to the altitude filed in the flight plan for the remainder of the flight, or

NOTE–
In the event of a two-way communications failure, ATC will be based on the following anticipated pilot action at the exit fix. Unless otherwise covered in a letter of agreement, and if the pilot is unable to comply with the VFR provisions of 14 CFR Section 91.185/FLIP IFR Supplement, the pilot will exercise his/her emergency authority, squawk transponder ***Code 7700****, depart the exit/alternate exit fix and climb/descend (continuing to squawk 7700) to the altitude filed in the flight plan. Subsequent transponder operations will be in accordance with paragraph 10–4–4, Communications Failure. Air traffic controller action from the exit fix is as prescribed in paragraph 10–1–1, Emergency Determinations.*

(c) Proceed in accordance with the lost communication procedure contained in letters of agreement.

2. Continue to monitor the last ATC assigned discrete code.

NOTE–
Pilots who experience a two-way radio failure will adjust their transponder to ***Code 7700*** *during climb/descent to altitude filed for the next leg of the flight plan; then change to* ***Code 7600*** *for a period of 15 minutes. At the end of each 15–minute period, he/she will squawk 7700 for a period of 1 minute; all other times he/she will squawk 7600.*

j. Impose delays, if needed, to eliminate conflict with nonparticipating IFR aircraft when necessary to preclude denial of IR usage. Advise the pilot of the expected length and reason for delay.

9–2–7. INTERCEPTOR OPERATIONS

Provide maximum assistance to expedite the movement of interceptor aircraft on active air defense (scrambles) missions until the unknown aircraft is identified in accordance with the policies and procedures published in FAA Order JO 7610.4, Sensitive Procedures and Requirements for Special Operations.

NOTE–
The FAA and the military have mutually agreed to the implementation of policies and procedures for control of air defense interceptor operations. Effective coordination and cooperation between FAA and the military at all levels are essential if policy objectives are to be met.

a. The ADCF initiating the SCRAMBLE must identify the mission as an active air defense mission.

b. ATC services must be used for active air defense missions insofar as the circumstances and situation permits.

c. Upon request, the ATC facility must expedite transfer of the control jurisdiction of the interceptors to the requesting ADCF.

9–2–8. SPECIAL INTEREST SITES

a. Immediately relay any reports or information regarding unusual aircraft activities in the vicinity of special interest sites such as nuclear power plants, power plants, dams, refineries, etc., to supervisory/CIC personnel.

NOTE–
Air traffic controllers have no responsibilities to monitor or observe aircraft in the vicinity of special interest sites unless directed by supervisory/CIC personnel.

9–2–9. SPECIAL AIR TRAFFIC RULES (SATR) AND SPECIAL FLIGHT RULES AREA (SFRA)

The Code of Federal Regulations prescribes special air traffic rules for aircraft operating within the boundaries of certain designated airspace. These areas are listed in 14 CFR Part 93 and can be found throughout the NAS. Procedures, nature of operations, configuration, size, and density of traffic vary among the identified areas.

a. Special Flight Rules Areas are areas of airspace wherein the flight of aircraft is subject to special air traffic rules set forth in 14 CFR Part 93, unless otherwise authorized by air traffic control. Not all areas listed in 14 CFR Part 93 are Special Flight Rules Areas, but special air traffic rules apply to all areas designated as SFRA.

REFERENCE–
14 CFR Part 93, Special Air Traffic Rules.
P/CG, SPECIAL AIR TRAFFIC RULES (SATR)
P/CG, SPECIAL FLIGHT RULES AREA (SFRA)

b. Each person operating an aircraft to, from, or within airspace designated as a SATR area or SFRA must adhere to the special air traffic rules set forth in 14 CFR Part 93, as applicable, unless otherwise authorized or required by ATC.

9–2–10. ATC SECURITY SERVICES FOR THE WASHINGTON, DC, SPECIAL FLIGHT RULES AREA (DC SFRA)

Provide ATC security services at locations where procedures are required for tracking aircraft in security services airspace. ATC security services are designed to support the national security mission of the FAA and other agencies. Two–way radio communications, flight planning, and an operational transponder on an assigned code are required for operations in the designated area.

a. When the assigned code is observed, advise the aircraft to proceed on course/as requested but to remain outside of Class B, C, and/or D airspace as appropriate.

PHRASEOLOGY–
(ACID) TRANSPONDER OBSERVED PROCEED ON COURSE/AS REQUESTED; REMAIN OUTSIDE (class) AIRSPACE.

1. Maintain continuous security tracking of VFR aircraft operating in the designated area to assist security forces in situational awareness. Immediately report all instances of loss of radio communication or the inability to conduct security tracking of an aircraft to the operations supervisor (OS)/CIC and wait for instructions.

2. Basic separation services to aircraft, for example, IFR, SVFR, Class B, Class C, TRSA, do not apply to ATC security tracking.

INTERPRETATION–
7110.65, 9–2–10, Washington, DC, Special Flight Rules Area (DC SFRA)/ATC Security Services (9–27–2016)

3. Aircraft with operating transponders, but without operating Mode C (altitude), require specific authorization from ATC to operate in the SFRA. ATC must coordinate with the Domestic Events Network (DEN) before approval.

4. Aircraft flying too low for radar coverage must be instructed to report landing or exiting the SFRA. Keep flight progress strips on these aircraft until pilot reports landing or exiting the SFRA. If a flight progress strip does not exist for the aircraft, record the call sign, transponder code, entry point (for example, north, northeast, east), and time of entry into the SFRA.

PHRASEOLOGY–
(Call sign), REPORT LANDING OR LEAVING THE SFRA.

5. United States military, law enforcement, and aeromedical flights are exempt from filing flight plans.

b. Establishing two–way Communications.

1. Pilots must establish two–way radio communications with ATC prior to entering the security service area. Responding to a radio call with, "(a/c call sign) standby," establishes radio communications and the pilot may enter the area, provided all other security requirements have been satisfied.

2. Aircraft requesting security services should not normally be held. However, if holding is necessary or workload/traffic conditions prevent immediate provision of ATC security services, inform the pilot to remain outside the designated area until conditions permit the provision of ATC security services. Inform the pilot of the expected length of delay.

PHRASEOLOGY–
(A/C call sign) REMAIN OUTSIDE OF THE (location) AND STANDBY. EXPECT (time) MINUTES DELAY.

c. Termination of Service.

1. If the aircraft is not landing within the designated area, provide security services until the aircraft exits the area and then advise the aircraft to squawk VFR and that frequency change is approved.

PHRASEOLOGY–
SQUAWK VFR, FREQUENCY CHANGE APPROVED.

or

CONTACT (facility identification).

2. When an aircraft is landing at an airport inside the area, instruct the pilot to remain on the assigned transponder code until after landing.

PHRASEOLOGY–
(ACID) REMAIN ON YOUR ASSIGNED TRANSPONDER CODE UNTIL YOU LAND, FREQUENCY CHANGE APPROVED.

3. Using approved handoff functionality, transfer the data blocks of all security tracked aircraft that will enter another sector/position for coordination of aircraft information/location. Upon acceptance of the transferred information, instruct the pilot to contact the next sector/positions' frequency.

9–2–11. SECURITY NOTICE (SECNOT)

Upon receiving notification of a SECNOT, the controller must forward all information on the subject aircraft to the OS/CIC. If information is not known, broadcast call sign on all frequencies and advise the OS/CIC of the response.

REFERENCE–
P/CG Term – Security Notice.
FAA Order JO 7210.3, Chapter 20, Section 9, Security Notice (SECNOT).

9–2–12. LAW ENFORCEMENT AND SENSITIVE GOVERNMENT MISSIONS

a. Provide the maximum assistance possible to law enforcement aircraft when requested.

1. If requested by the pilot/flight crew, communicate with law enforcement aircraft on a separate and unique communications frequency whenever possible.

2. Ensure assistance to law enforcement aircraft does not compromise approved separation minima or place the aircraft in unsafe proximity to terrain, obstructions or other aircraft.

3. When requested, assist law enforcement in locating suspect aircraft.

4. Forward any information received pertaining to stolen aircraft to the OS/CIC for reporting on the Domestic Events Network (DEN).

REFERENCE–
FAA Order JO 7210.3, Para 2–7–7, Cooperation With Law Enforcement Agencies.

b. Sensitive government missions.

1. Sensitive government missions include inflight identification, surveillance, interdiction and pursuit activities conducted by government aircraft for national defense, homeland security, and intelligence or law enforcement purposes.

2. Provide support to national security and homeland defense activities as specified in paragraph 2–1–2, Duty Priority.

3. To facilitate accomplishment of sensitive government missions, exemptions from specified parts of Title 14 of the Code of Federal Regulations have been granted to designated departments and agencies. Each organization's exemption identifies its responsibilities for notifying ATC of its intent to operate under an exemption before commencing operations.

REFERENCE–
FAA Order JO 7210.3, Para 19–3–1, Authorizations and Exemptions from Title 14, Code of Federal Regulations (14 CFR).

4. Departments and agencies that conduct sensitive government missions are assigned U.S. special call signs. Additionally, some have pre–assigned beacon codes to permit them to apprise ATC of ongoing mission activities and solicit air traffic assistance. To support these sensitive government missions, ATC must:

(a) Not change the sensitive beacon codes requested or displayed by these operators.

(b) To the maximum extent possible, ensure the full call sign designator of aircraft conducting sensitive government operations is entered into FAA automation systems.

(c) Not alter or abbreviate the U.S. special call signs used by aircraft for sensitive government operations.

REFERENCE–
FAA Order JO 7110.67, Air Traffic Management Security Procedures and Requirements for Special Operations.

9–2–13. MILITARY AERIAL REFUELING

Authorize aircraft to conduct aerial refueling along published or special tracks at their flight plan altitudes, unless otherwise requested.

PHRASEOLOGY–
CLEARED TO CONDUCT REFUELING ALONG (number) TRACK,

or

FROM (fix) TO (fix),

and

MAINTAIN BLOCK (altitude) THROUGH (altitude),

or

COMMENCING AT (altitude), DESCENDING TO (altitude).

NOTE–
1. *During aerial refueling, tanker aircraft are responsible for receiver aircraft communication with ATC and for their navigation along the track.*

2. *Aerial refueling airspace is not sterilized airspace and other aircraft may transit this airspace provided vertical or lateral separation is provided from refueling aircraft.*

3. *MARSA begins between the tanker and receiver when the tanker and receiver(s) have entered the air refueling airspace and the tanker advises ATC that he/she is accepting MARSA.*

4. *MARSA ends between the tanker and receiver when the tanker advises ATC that the tanker and receiver aircraft are vertically positioned within the air refueling airspace and ATC advises MARSA is terminated.*

REFERENCE–
FAA Order JO 7110.65, Para 2–1–11, Use of MARSA.
FAA Order JO 7110.65, Para 5–5–8, Additional Separation for Formation Flights.
FAA Order JO 7610.14, Chapter 5, Aerial Refueling.

a. Provide radar assistance to the rendezvous for participating aircraft:

1. When requested, and

2. By providing vertical separation prior to MARSA declaration.

b. Do not request receiver aircraft that have been cleared to conduct air refueling and have departed the ARIP to:

1. Make code changes when less than 5 miles from the tanker.

2. Squawk standby when less than 1 mile or more than 3 miles from the tanker.

NOTE–
Requests for receiver aircraft to make code changes during air refueling diverts the receiver pilot's attention during a critical phase of flight.

c. When issuing an initial air refueling clearance, you may request a receiver to squawk standby when the receiver reaches a point 3 miles from the tanker.

NOTE–
1. *Receiver aircraft will squawk normal when separation from the tanker is greater than 3 miles.*

2. *Once rendezvous is completed, heading and altitude assignments may be made with the tanker concurrence with MARSA remaining in effect.*

3. *Upon rendezvous completion, the tanker must keep receiver aircraft within 3 miles of the tanker until MARSA is terminated.*

d. After MARSA has been declared, you should avoid issuing course or altitude changes prior to rendezvous.

NOTE–
Altitude or course changes issued will automatically void MARSA.

e. Do not use the altitude vacated during the refueling operation until the refueling aircraft has reported reaching the next IFR altitude.

REFERENCE–
FAA Order JO 7110.65, Para 6–6–2, Exceptions.

f. Approve requests by the tanker pilot for vectors or alternative routes or altitudes as follows:

1. Furnish vectors or alternative altitudes at any time.

2. Furnish nonradar routes only after the refueling aircraft have passed the ARCP.

NOTE–
1. *To meet a training requirement that aerial refueling be accomplished in a nonradar environment, the military has requested that vectors be furnished only upon request.*

2. *The tanker commander is responsible for coordinating all inflight requests with other aircraft in the refueling mission before submission of such requests to the center.*

3. *Normally, aircraft conducting aerial refueling operations will utilize at least three consecutive altitudes.*

g. Unless a vector or alternative route has been furnished, clear the aircraft to depart the refueling track at a navigational reference point or egress fix.

h. Request an aircraft to report the ARIP, ARCP, or egress fix as necessary.

PHRASEOLOGY–
REPORT:

A–R–I–P,

or

A–R–C–P,

or

EGRESS FIX.

i. Expect the following procedures in addition to those required by the appropriate parts of Title 14 of the Code of Federal Regulations in the event of two-way communications failure:

1. The tanker will depart the track from the highest altitude in the block.

2. The receiver will depart the track from the lowest altitude in the block.

3. Aircraft will squawk 7600 for at least 2 minutes prior to departing the track.

REFERENCE–
FAA Order JO 7110.65, Para 9–2–14, Military Operations Above FL 600.

9–2–14. MILITARY OPERATIONS ABOVE FL 600

Control aircraft operating above FL 600 using the following procedures:

a. Flight plans involving supersonic flight are required 16 hours in advance of proposed departure times for processing and approval by the ARTCCs concerned. The originating ARTCC, where the flight plan is first filed, may waive the 16–hour advance filing requirement.

b. The route of flight must be defined by at least one high altitude fix within each ARTCC area without regard to the distance between fixes. Additionally, the entry and exit points of turns of 90 degrees or more will be designated.

c. Elapsed times from takeoff to the first fix in each ARTCC area must be included in the route of flight.

d. The ARTCC which originates the flight plan must forward departure times to all ARTCCs responsible for processing the flight plan.

e. Approval of the flight plan indicates approval of both route and flight levels (if stated) including operations below FL 600 (aerial refueling).

PHRASEOLOGY–
CLEARED AS FILED VIA ROUTE AND FLIGHT LEVELS.

REFERENCE–
FAA Order JO 7110.65, Para 9–2–13, Military Aerial Refueling.

f. Separation. Use the following as minima in lieu of the corresponding type of separation prescribed in:

NOTE–
The primary method described to provide separation between two supersonic aircraft is to descend the aircraft at the lower FL and provide vertical separation since the aircraft at the higher FL may not be able to climb rapidly enough to establish the required separation. Another aspect which should be considered is that supersonic aircraft during turns, either programmed or as the result of vectors, will lose a few thousand feet. Vectoring supersonic aircraft seriously affects the range and mission objectives. Radar separation is the preferred method of separating a subsonic aircraft both from another subsonic aircraft or from a supersonic aircraft.

1. Paragraph 4–5–1, Vertical Separation Minima: *5,000 feet.*

NOTE–
1. *The security requirements of the military services preclude the transmission of actual altitude information on the air/ground or landline circuits. Altitude information for the day should be readily available to the controllers at their positions of operation. The classification requirements of the altitude information remains unchanged.*

2. *Pilots will report their altitude, using the coded plan, and intended flight profile on initial contact with each ARTCC.*

2. Paragraph 6–5–4, Minima Along Other Than Established Airways or Routes: Protect the airspace 25 miles either side of the route centerline. For turns by supersonic aircraft, protect the airspace 75 miles on the overflown side and 25 miles on the other side. For turns by subsonic aircraft, protect the airspace 34 miles on the overflown side and 25 miles on the other side.

REFERENCE–
FAA Order JO 7110.65, Para 4–3–3, Abbreviated Departure Clearance.

9–2–15. MILITARY SPECIAL USE FREQUENCIES

a. Assign special use frequency to:

NOTE–
Special use frequencies are assigned to ARTCCs in such a manner that adjacent ARTCCs will not have the same frequency. They are to be used within the ARTCC area jurisdiction from the established FL base of the high altitude sectors and above. Each high altitude sector should have the capability to use the special use frequency on a shared basis.

1. USAF, U.S. Navy, and Air National Guard (ANG) single-pilot jet aircraft formations operating at night or in instrument weather conditions. Formations of five or more USAF aircraft deploying either to a continental U.S. staging base or nonstop to an overseas location are authorized to use special use frequencies at any time. Normally these deployments will be conducted within an altitude reservation.

2. U–2 and B–57 (pressure suit flights) aircraft at all altitudes/FLs except where terminal operations require the assignment of other frequencies.

NOTE–
Aerial refueling operations may require that aircraft leave the special use frequency for communications with the tanker. This will occur when the receiver is approximately 200 miles from the ARCP. The tanker aircraft will remain on the ARTCC assigned frequency and will relay clearances to the receiver as required. An alternate means of communications between the tanker and receiver is HF radio.

3. All aircraft during supersonic flight.

NOTE–
Pilots are expected to request assignment of the special use frequency in the remarks section of the flight plan or before entering supersonic flight. B–57 aircraft engaged in pressure suit operations will use the static call sign KITE and flights will normally be conducted from Dover, Eielson, Ellington, Hickman, Howard, Kirtland, and McClellan Air Force Bases.

4. E–3A AWACS mission crews when operations are being conducted as an MRU in accordance with appropriate letters of agreement.

b. The special use frequency may be assigned as "backup" for the high-altitude sector when direct communications are essential because of a potential emergency control situation.

c. Do not assign the special use frequency to the aircraft in subparagraph a1 above, when they will operate in airspace assigned for special military operations.

9–2–16. AVOIDANCE OF AREAS OF NUCLEAR RADIATION

a. Advise pilots whenever their proposed flight path will traverse a reported or forecasted area of hazardous radiation and reroute the aircraft when requested by the pilot.

REFERENCE–
FAA Order JO 7610.4, Para 4–4–4, Avoidance of Hazardous Radiation Areas.

b. Inform pilots when an airfield of intended landing lies within a reported or forecasted area of hazardous radiation and request the pilot to advise his/her intentions.

9–2–17. SAMP FLIGHTS

Provide special handling to USAF or other government aircraft using the "SAMP" call sign and engaged in aerial sampling/surveying missions for nuclear, chemical, or hazardous material contamination. Approve inflight clearance requests for altitude and route changes to the maximum extent possible. Other IFR aircraft may be recleared so that requests by SAMP aircraft are approved.

REFERENCE–
FAA Order JO 7110.65, Para 2–1–4, Operational Priority.
FAA Order JO 7110.65, Para 2–4–20, Aircraft Identification.
FAA Order JO 7610.4, Para 4–4–4, Avoidance of Hazardous Radiation Areas.
FAA Order JO 7210.3, Para 5–3–2, Aerial Sampling/Surveying for Airborne Contamination.

9–2–18. AWACS/NORAD SPECIAL FLIGHTS

Do not delay E–3 AWACS aircraft identified as "AWACS/NORAD Special" flights. The following control actions are acceptable while expediting these aircraft to the destination orbit.

a. En route altitude changes +/– 2,000 feet from the requested flight level.

b. Radar vectors or minor route changes that do not impede progress towards the destination orbit.

NOTE–
NORAD has a requirement to position E–3 AWACS aircraft at selected locations on a time-critical basis. To the extent possible these flights will utilize routes to the destination orbit that have been precoordinated with the impacted ATC facilities. To identify these flights, the words "AWACS/NORAD SPECIAL" will be included as the first item in the remarks section of the flight plan.

9–2–19. WEATHER RECONNAISSANCE FLIGHTS

TEAL and NOAA mission aircraft fly reconnaissance flights to gather meteorological data on winter storms, (NWSOP missions), hurricanes and tropical cyclones (NHOP missions). The routes and timing of these flights are determined by movement of the storm areas and not by traffic flows.

a. When a dropsonde release time is received from a TEAL or NOAA mission aircraft, workload and priorities permitting, controllers must advise the mission aircraft of any traffic estimated to pass through the area of the drop at altitudes below that of the mission aircraft. This traffic advisory must include:

1. Altitude.

2. Direction of flight.

3. ETA at the point closest to drop area (or at the fix/intersection where drop will occur).

NOTE–
A dropsonde is a 14–inch long cardboard cylinder about 2.75 inches in diameter, that weighs approximately 14 ounces (400 grams), and has a parachute attached. When released from the aircraft it will fall at a rate of approximately 2,500 feet per minute. Controllers should recognize that a dropsonde released at FL 310 will be a factor for traffic at FL 210 four minutes later. It is the aircraft commanders responsibility to delay release of dropsondes if traffic is a factor. Aircraft commanders will delay release of dropsondes based solely upon traffic as issued by ATC.

b. When advised that an airborne TEAL or NOAA aircraft is requesting a clearance via CARCAH, issue the clearance in accordance with Chapter 4, IFR, Section 2, Clearances.

REFERENCE–
FAA Order JO 7110.65, Para 4–2–1, Clearance Items.
FAA Order JO 7110.65, Para 4–2–2, Clearance Prefix.
FAA Order JO 7110.65, Para 4–2–3, Delivery Instructions.

c. If a TEAL or NOAA mission aircraft must be contacted but is out of VHF, UHF, and HF radio range, advise the supervisory traffic management coordinator–in–charge.

REFERENCE–
FAA Order JO 7210.3, Para 5–3–4, Weather Reconnaissance Flights.
FAA Order JO 7110.65, Para 2–1–4, Operational Priority.

d. Aircraft operations associated with a Weather Reconnaissance Area (WRA) must be conducted in accordance with the Memorandum of Agreement between the National Oceanic and Atmospheric Administration Aircraft Operations Center, U.S. Air Force Reserve Command 53rd Weather Reconnaissance Squadron, and the Federal Aviation Administration Air Traffic Organization in Support of the National Hurricane Operations Plan (FAA Order JO 7610.14, Appendix 3, Document 1), and the associated letters of agreement.

9–2–20. EVASIVE ACTION MANEUVER

Approve a pilot request to conduct an evasive action maneuver only on the basis of a permissible traffic situation. Specify the following items, as necessary, when issuing approval:

NOTE–
The "evasive action" maneuver is performed by a bomber/fighter bomber aircraft at or above FL 250 along a 60 NM long segment of the flight plan route overlying a RBS or other site and includes:
1. *Flying a zigzag pattern on both the left and right side of the flight plan route centerline. Altitude deviations are made in conjunction with the lateral maneuvering.*
2. *Lateral deviations from the route centerline will not normally exceed 12 miles. Altitude variations must not exceed plus or minus 1,000 feet of the assigned flight level; i.e., confined within a 2,000 foot block.*

a. Specific route segment on which the maneuver will take place.

b. Distance of maximum route deviation from the centerline in miles.

c. Altitude.

PHRASEOLOGY−
CLEARED TO CONDUCT EVASIVE ACTION MANEUVER FROM (fix) TO (fix),

and

(number of miles) EITHER SIDE OF CENTERLINE,

and

MAINTAIN (altitude) THROUGH (altitude),

and

COMPLETE MANEUVER AT (fix) AT (altitude).

9−2−21. NONSTANDARD FORMATION/CELL OPERATIONS

Occasionally the military is required to operate in a nonstandard cell formation and controllers should be knowledgeable of the various tactics employed and the procedures used.

REFERENCE−
FAA Order JO 7610.14, Chapter 7, Section 3, Military Formation Flight.

a. Formation leaders are responsible for obtaining ATC approval to conduct nonstandard formation/cell operations.

b. When nonstandard formation/cell operations have been approved, controllers must assign sufficient altitudes to allow intra-cell vertical spacing of 500 feet between each aircraft in the formation.

c. Control nonstandard formation/cell operations on the basis that MARSA is applicable between the participating aircraft until they establish approved separation which is acknowledged by ATC.

d. Apply approved separation criteria between the approved nonstandard formation/cell envelope and nonparticipating aircraft.

e. Clear aircraft operating in a nonstandard formation/cell to the breakup fix as the clearance limit. Forward data pertaining to route or altitude beyond the breakup point to the center concerned as a part of the routine flight plan information.

f. *EN ROUTE.* If the breakup occurs in your area, issue appropriate clearances to authorize transition from formation to individual routes or altitudes. If a breakup cannot be approved, issue an appropriate clearance for the flight to continue as a formation.

Section 3. Special Use, ATC–Assigned Airspace, and Stationary ALTRVs

9–3–1. APPLICATION

Apply the procedures in this section to aircraft operating in proximity to special use, ATC-assigned airspace (ATCAA), and stationary ALTRVs unless the airspace is designated an alert area/controlled firing area or one of the following conditions exist:

NOTE–
These procedures are not applicable to Alert Areas or Controlled Firing Areas.

REFERENCE–
P/CG Term – Special Use Airspace.

a. The pilot informs you that permission has been obtained from the using agency to operate in the airspace.

b. The using agency informs you they have given permission for the aircraft to operate in the airspace.

NOTE–
Using agency permission may be relayed to the pilot.

c. The restricted/warning area, MOA, ATCAA, or stationary ALTRV has been released to the controlling agency.

d. The aircraft is on an approved ALTRV, unless the airspace area in question is an ATCAA.

NOTE–
Mission project officers are responsible for obtaining approval for ALTRV operations within prohibited/ restricted/warning areas, MOAs, and stationary ALTRVs.

REFERENCE–
FAA Order JO 7110.65, Para 9–3–4, Transiting Active SUA/ATCAA.

e. Operations in special use airspace and stationary ALTRVs located in offshore/oceanic airspace will be conducted in accordance with the procedures in Chapter 8, Offshore/Oceanic Procedures.

9–3–2. SEPARATION MINIMA

Unless clearance of nonparticipating aircraft in/through/adjacent to a prohibited/restricted/warning area/MOA/ATCAA/stationary ALTRV is provided for in a letter of agreement (LOA) or letter of procedure (LOP), separate nonparticipating aircraft from active special use airspace, ATCAAs, and stationary ALTRVs by the following minima:

NOTE–
Nonparticipating aircraft refers to those aircraft for which you have separation responsibility and which have not been authorized by the using agency to operate in/through the special use airspace, ATCAA, or stationary ALTRV. VFR traffic is not prohibited from transiting stationary ALTRVs or transitional hazard areas (THA).

a. Assign an altitude consistent with paragraph 4–5–2, Flight Direction, and 4–5–3, Exceptions, which is at least 500 feet (above FL 290-1000 feet) above/below the upper/lower limit of the prohibited/ restricted/warning area/MOA/ATCAA/stationary ALTRV.

REFERENCE–
FAA Order JO 7210.3, Para 2-1-18, Prohibited/Restricted Areas and Stationary ALTRVs.

b. Provide radar separation of 3 miles (FL 600 and above – 6 miles) from the special use airspace, ATCAA, or stationary ALTRV peripheral boundary. EXCEPTIONS:

1. Some prohibited/restricted/warning areas are established for security reasons or to contain hazardous activities and do not require radar separation of 3 miles (FL 600 and above – 6 miles) from the special use airspace. Where facility management has identified these areas as outlined in FAA Order JO 7210.3, Facility Operation and Administration, vector aircraft to remain clear of the peripheral boundary.

2. For stationary ALTRVs issued for the purpose of space launch or reentry operations, ensure aircraft remain clear of the peripheral boundary.

c. Clear aircraft on airways or routes whose widths or protected airspace do not overlap the peripheral boundary.

d. For stationary ALTRVs and temporary flight restrictions (TFR) issued for the purpose of space launch or reentry operations to protect aircraft hazard areas (AHA):

1. Do not allow nonparticipating aircraft to operate in an AHA unless real−time notifications of the actual start of activity and end of activity of the AHA is provided to affected facilities via ATO Space Operations coordination.

2. Do not provide ATC services to aircraft at airports that lie within an AHA unless real−time notifications of the actual start of activity and end of activity of the AHA is provided to affected facilities via ATO Space Operations coordination.

REFERENCE−
FAA Order JO 7210.3, Para 20−6−4, Airports within Aircraft Hazard Areas and Transitional Hazard Areas.

e. For NOTAMs issued for the purpose of space launch or reentry operations to protect THAs:

1. Aircraft may enter provided they are not holding, loitering, or hovering, and are cleared on:

(a) Routing approved by ATO Space Operations that has an angular difference of 30 through 150 degrees from the launch/reentry course, or

(b) Crossing courses that have an angular difference of 45 through 135 degrees from the launch/reentry course.

NOTE−
The intent is to provide a crossing angle that accounts for the effects of wind.

REFERENCE−
FAA Order JO 7110.65, Para 1−2−2, Course Definitions.

2. Do not provide ATC services to aircraft at airports that lie within a THA unless real−time notifications of the actual start of activity and end of activity of the THA is provided to affected facilities via ATO Space Operations coordination.

REFERENCE−
FAA Order JO 7210.3, Para 20−6−4, Airports within Aircraft Hazard Areas and Transitional Hazard Areas.

9−3−3. VFR-ON-TOP

If the aircraft's route, track, or altitude may cause it to enter an active Prohibited/Restricted/Warning Area, MOA, or ATCAA:

a. Inform the pilot to conduct flight "VFR−on−top" at least 500 feet above the upper limit or below the lower limit of the airspace (subject to paragraph 7−3−1, VFR−on−top); or

PHRASEOLOGY−
MAINTAIN VFR-ON-TOP AT LEAST 500 FEET ABOVE/BELOW (upper/lower limit of airspace) ACROSS (name or number of airspace) BETWEEN (fix) AND (fix);

and if the airspace is an ATCAA,

(name of ATCAA) IS ATC ASSIGNED AIRSPACE.

REFERENCE−
FAA Order JO 7110.65, Para 7−1−1, Class A Airspace Restrictions.

b. Clear the aircraft via a routing which provides approved separation from the airspace.

c. *Exception:* Some Prohibited/Restricted Areas are established for security reasons or to contain hazardous activities not involving aircraft operations. The addition of 500 (or 1,000) feet to the upper/lower limit of these Prohibited/Restricted Areas is not required if the areas have been identified by facility management.

REFERENCE–
FAA Order JO 7210.3, Para 2–1–18, Prohibited/Restricted Areas.

9–3–4. TRANSITING ACTIVE SUA/ATCAA

If a LOA/LOP has been coordinated with the Using Agency and permission has been granted to transit the area:

a. Comply with the instruction/clearances issued by the Using Agency and provide the applicable separation minima between aircraft when two or more aircraft are transiting the area; or

NOTE–
Some Using Agencies are also air traffic control facilities.

b. If unable to comply with instructions/clearances, clear the aircraft in accordance with paragraph 9–3–2, Separation Minima.

NOTE–
The FAA has no jurisdictional authority over the use of nonjoint use prohibited/restricted/warning area airspace; therefore, clearance cannot be issued for flight therein without the appropriate approval.

Section 4. Fuel Dumping

9–4–1. INFORMATION REQUIREMENTS

When information is received that an aircraft plans to dump fuel, determine the route and altitude it will fly and the weather conditions in which the operation will be conducted.

9–4–2. ROUTING

Except when it is dumping fuel for emergency reasons, an aircraft in either VFR or IFR conditions may be requested to fly a different route.

9–4–3. ALTITUDE ASSIGNMENT

If an aircraft is dumping fuel in IFR conditions, assign an altitude at least 2,000 feet above the highest obstacle within 5 miles of the route or pattern being flown.

9–4–4. SEPARATION MINIMA

Separate known aircraft from the aircraft dumping fuel as follows:

a. IFR aircraft by one of the following:

1. *1,000 feet* above it; or in accordance with paragraph 4–5–1, Vertical Separation Minima, whichever is greater.

2. *2,000 feet* below it.

3. *5 miles* radar.

4. *5 miles* laterally.

b. VFR radar-identified aircraft by *5 miles* and in accordance with paragraph 5–6–1, Application.

9–4–5. INFORMATION DISSEMINATION

a. If you are in contact with an aircraft when it starts dumping fuel, inform other controllers and facilities which might be concerned. Facilities concerned must broadcast an advisory on appropriate radio frequencies at 3–minute intervals until the dumping stops.

PHRASEOLOGY–
ATTENTION ALL AIRCRAFT.
FUEL DUMPING IN PROGRESS OVER (location) AT (altitude) BY (type aircraft) (flight direction).

b. Broadcast a terminating advisory when the fuel dumping operation is completed.

PHRASEOLOGY–
ATTENTION ALL AIRCRAFT.
FUEL DUMPING OVER (location) TERMINATED.

Section 5. Jettisoning of External Stores

9–5–1. JETTISONING OF EXTERNAL STORES

At locations where a drop area has been established for radar assistance in jettisoning of external stores, provide vectoring service upon request to:

NOTE–
1. *Where required, a mutually satisfactory drop area for the jettisoning of external stores will be determined by radar-equipped towers and centers in cooperation with the local USAF units, Air Division, or civil operators and civil aircraft companies concerned.*

2. *FAA and Headquarters, USAF, have agreed to allow FAA facilities to vector USAF, Air Force Reserve, and Air National Guard aircraft for jettisoning of all external stores; i.e., tip tanks, JATO racks, special weapons, etc. Any similar vectoring service given to civil operators and civil aircraft companies operating Air Force type aircraft requires written agreement between the FAA and the user to relieve the FAA of possible liability. The regional counsel's office acts for FAA in executing this agreement.*

a. USAF, ANG, and Air Force Reserve aircraft at any time.

b. Civil operators and civil aircraft when a written agreement is in effect for your location.

Section 6. Unmanned Free Balloons

9–6–1. APPLICATION

FIG 9–6–1
Shapes of 11 Million Cubic Feet Balloon at Various Altitudes

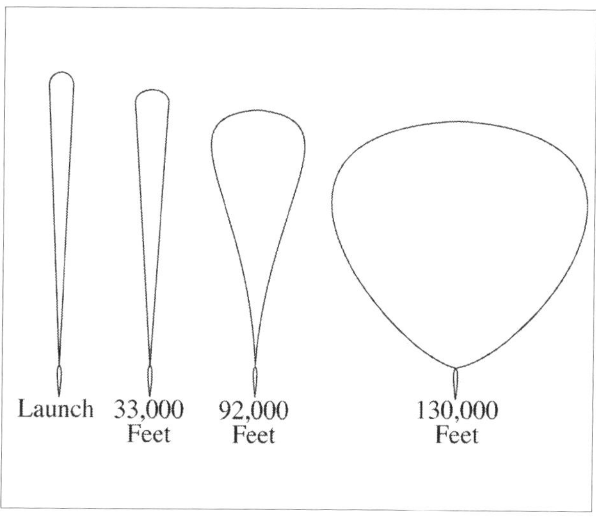

Apply the following procedures, as appropriate, when unmanned free balloons are within airspace for which you have control jurisdiction:

NOTE–
These procedures apply to unmanned free balloons that carry payloads as described in 14 CFR Section 101.1(a)(4). Payloads may weigh several hundred pounds and the physical shape of the balloons change at various altitudes/flight levels. (See FIG 9–6–1.) Balloon and payload ascend at an average rate of 400 feet a minute. Over the descent area, the payload is normally released from the balloon and descends by parachute at a minimum rate of 1,000 feet a minute. The balloon is normally deflated automatically when the payload is released. The operator is required to advise ATC 1 hour in advance of descent in accordance with 14 CFR Section 101.39.

a. Post the balloon flight on flight progress strips along the planned trajectory and revise routing as tracking/position reports require.

NOTE–
The prelaunch notice information should be posted on flight progress strips for planning and operational purposes.

b. Radar flight follow balloons to the extent that equipment capabilities permit. If radar flight following is not possible, tracking should be attempted by communication with the "chase plane," telephone contact with the operator, pilot, or ground observation reports.

NOTE–
Some operators have equipped their balloons with transponder beacons in addition to a radar reflection device or material required by 14 CFR Section 101.35, but at cruise altitude, the balloon's communications equipment and transponder, if so equipped, are operated intermittently to conserve battery energy.

c. With pilot concurrence, provide separation between aircraft and balloons when you are satisfied that the balloon information is sufficiently reliable to provide the service. Do not attempt to separate aircraft from the balloon by using vertical separation unless you have accurate balloon altitude information.

d. Provide traffic advisories to all affected aircraft during initial contact specifying the balloon's known or estimated position, direction of movement, and altitude as "unknown" or "reported," as appropriate.

NOTE–
Unless ATC requires otherwise, operators of unmanned free balloons are required to monitor the course of the balloon and record its position at least every two hours. As required in 14 CFR Section 101.39a, balloon position reports are not forwarded by the operator unless requested by ATC.

PHRASEOLOGY–
UNMANNED FREE BALLOON OVER (name of location),

or

ESTIMATED OVER (name of location), MOVING (direction of movement).

LAST REPORTED ALTITUDE AT (altitude as reported by the operator or determined from pilot report),

or

ALTITUDE UNKNOWN.

e. To transfer flight following responsibility of balloons between facilities or between controllers, forward the following information when available:

REFERENCE–
14 CFR Section 101.37, Notice Requirements.
14 CFR Section 101.39, Balloon Position Reports.

1. Identification and type; e.g., Flight 804 Balloon.

2. Last known position and altitude.

3. General direction of movement and speed.

4. ETA over facility boundary, sector boundary, or other point if believed to be reasonably accurate.

5. Other pertinent information.

6. If in radar contact, physically point out the target to the receiving controller.

7. The name and the telephone number of the location where tracking is being accomplished.

REFERENCE–
FAA Order JO 7110.65, Para 9–6–2, Derelict Balloons.

9–6–2. DERELICT BALLOONS

Balloons become derelict when a moored balloon slips its mooring and becomes a hazard to air navigation or when an unmanned free balloon flight cannot be terminated as planned. When this occurs:

a. In the case of a moored balloon which has slipped its moorings, issue traffic advisories.

b. In the case of an unmanned free balloon, flight follow the balloon and, to the extent possible, provide aircraft under your control separation from the balloon.

c. Forward balloon position information received from pilot reports or derived from radar returns to your supervisor for further dissemination.

d. If radar contact with the balloon is lost, broadcast an advisory to all aircraft operating in the airspace affected by the derelict balloon at 10–minute intervals continuing until the derelict balloon is no longer a factor.

PHRASEOLOGY–
ADVISORY TO ALL AIRCRAFT.

DERELICT BALLOON REPORTED IN THE VICINITY OF (location),

or

ESTIMATED IN VICINITY OF (location),

or

REPORTED OVER (location),

or

RADAR REPORTED OVER (location).

LAST REPORTED ALTITUDE/FLIGHT LEVEL AT (altitude/flight level as reported by operator or pilot report),

or

ALTITUDE/FLIGHT LEVEL UNKNOWN.

e. Transfer flight following responsibility as outlined in paragraph 9–6–1, Application, subparagraph e.

REFERENCE–
FAA Order JO 7210.3, Para 19–5–2, Derelict Balloons/Objects.

Section 7. Parachute Operations

9–7–1. COORDINATION

Coordinate any pertinent information prior to and at the end of each parachute jump or series of jumps which begins or ends in your area of jurisdiction with other affected ATC facilities/sectors.

NOTE–
14 CFR Section 105.15 prescribes the information required from each person requesting authorization or submitting notification for nonemergency parachute jumping activity.

REFERENCE–
FAA Order JO 7210.3, Para 19–4–1, Nonemergency Parachute Jump Operations.
14 CFR Part 105, Parachute Operations.

9–7–2. CLASS A, CLASS B, AND CLASS C AIRSPACE

a. Authorize parachute operations only within airspace designated for the jumping activity.

b. Separate aircraft, other than those participating in the jump operation, from the airspace authorized for the jumping activity.

c. Impose, as necessary, any conditions and restrictions which in your judgment would promote the safety of the operation.

REFERENCE–
14 CFR Section 105.25, Parachute Operations in Designated Airspace.

9–7–3. CLASS D AIRSPACE

TERMINAL

Handle requests to conduct jump operations in or into Class D airspace in which there is a functioning control tower as follows:

a. Authorize parachute jumping with respect to known or observed traffic.

b. Issue advisory information to the jump aircraft and to nonparticipating aircraft as necessary for the safe conduct of the jump operation.

9–7–4. OTHER CONTROL AIRSPACE

Handle notifications to conduct jump operations in other Class E airspace as follows:

a. Issue a traffic advisory to the jump aircraft before the jump. Include aircraft type, altitude, and direction of flight of all known traffic which will transit the airspace within which the jump will be conducted.

NOTE–
14 CFR Section 105.13, Radio Equipment and Use Requirements, prescribes that, except when otherwise authorized by ATC, parachute jumping is not allowed in or into Class E airspace unless radio communications have been established between the aircraft and the FAA ATC facility having jurisdiction over the affected airspace of the first intended exit altitude at least 5 minutes before the jumping activity is to begin for the purpose of receiving information in the aircraft about known air traffic in the vicinity of the jump aircraft.

b. Issue advisories to all known aircraft which will transit the airspace within which the jump operations will be conducted. Advisories must consist of the location, time, duration, and altitude from which the jump will be made.

c. When time or numbers of aircraft make individual transmissions impractical, advisories to nonparticipating aircraft may be broadcast on appropriate control frequencies, or when available, the ATIS broadcast.

d. When requested by the pilot and to the extent possible, assist nonparticipating aircraft to avoid the airspace within which the jump will be conducted.

Section 8. Unidentified Flying Object (UFO) Reports

9-8-1. GENERAL

a. Persons wanting to report UFO/unexplained phenomena activity should contact a UFO/unexplained phenomena reporting data collection center, such as the National UFO Reporting Center, etc.

b. If concern is expressed that life or property might be endangered, report the activity to the local law enforcement department.

Chapter 10. Emergencies

Section 1. General

10–1–1. EMERGENCY DETERMINATIONS

a. An emergency can be either a *Distress* or an *Urgency* condition as defined in the "Pilot/Controller Glossary."

b. A pilot who encounters a *Distress* condition should declare an emergency by beginning the initial communication with the word "Mayday," preferably repeated three times. For an *Urgency* condition, the word "Pan-Pan" should be used in the same manner.

c. If the words "Mayday" or "Pan–Pan" are not used but you believe an emergency or an urgent situation exists, handle it as though it were an emergency.

d. Because of the infinite variety of possible emergency situations, specific procedures cannot be prescribed. However, when you believe an emergency exists or is imminent, select and pursue a course of action which appears to be most appropriate under the circumstances and which most nearly conforms to the instructions in this manual.

REFERENCE–
FAA Order JO 7110.65, Para 9–2–6, IFR Military Training Routes.

10–1–2. OBTAINING INFORMATION

a. Use the information provided or solicit more information as necessary to assist the distressed aircraft. Provide assistance that is consistent with the requests of the pilot. If you believe an alternative course of action may prove more beneficial, transmit your recommendation(s) to the pilot.

REFERENCE–
14 CFR § 91.3 Responsibilities and authority of pilot in command.

b. If an emergency was declared by an Emergency Autoland system, the aircraft may transmit the following:

1. Callsign.

2. That Emergency Autoland has been activated.

3. Position (mileage and direction) relative to a nearby airport.

4. The intended emergency landing airport and the planned landing runway.

5. An ETE to the emergency landing airport.

EXAMPLE–
"Aircraft, N123B, pilot incapacitation, 12 miles southwest of KOJC, landing KIXD airport. Emergency Autoland in 13 minutes on runway 36."

NOTE–
1. *System configurations may vary between manufacturers. All systems should be configured to transmit enough information for the controller to respond effectively to the emergency.*

2. *In the event of frequency congestion, an Emergency Autoland system may transmit on 121.5 or CTAF instead of the last assigned ATC frequency.*

10–1–3. PROVIDING ASSISTANCE

Provide maximum assistance to aircraft in distress. Enlist the services of available radar facilities operated by the FAA, the military services, and the Federal Communications Commission, as well as their emergency services and facilities, when the pilot requests or when you deem necessary.

REFERENCE–
FAA Order JO 7110.65, Para 2–1–4, Operational Priority.

10–1–4. RESPONSIBILITY

a. If you are in communication with an aircraft in distress, handle the emergency and coordinate and direct the activities of assisting facilities. Transfer this responsibility to another facility only when you feel better handling of the emergency will result.

b. When you receive information about an aircraft in distress, forward detailed data to the center in whose area the emergency exists.

NOTE–
1. *Centers serve as the central points for collecting information, for coordinating with SAR, and for conducting a communications search by distributing any necessary ALNOTs concerning:*

a. *Overdue or missing IFR aircraft.*

b. *Aircraft in an emergency situation occurring in their respective area.*

c. *Aircraft on a combination VFR/IFR or an airfiled IFR flight plan and 30 minutes have passed since the pilot requested IFR clearance and neither communication nor radar contact can be established with it. For SAR purposes, these aircraft are treated the same as IFR aircraft.*

d. *Overdue or missing aircraft which have been authorized to operate in accordance with special VFR clearances.*

2. *Notifying the center about a VFR aircraft emergency allows provision of IFR separation if considered necessary.*

REFERENCE–
FAA Order JO 7110.65, Para 10–2–5, Emergency Situations.
FAA Order JO 7110.65, Para 10–3–2, Information to be Forwarded to ARTCC.
FAA Order JO 7110.65, Para 10–3–3, Information to be Forwarded to RCC.

c. If the aircraft involved is operated by a foreign air carrier, notify the center serving the departure or destination point, when either point is within the U.S., for relay to the operator of the aircraft.

d. The ARTCC must be responsible for receiving and relaying all pertinent ELT signal information to the appropriate authorities.

REFERENCE–
FAA Order JO 7110.65, Para 10–2–10, Emergency Locator Transmitter (ELT) Signals.

e. When consideration is given to the need to escort an aircraft in distress, evaluate the close formation required by both aircraft. Special consideration should be given if the maneuver takes the aircraft through the clouds.

f. Before a determination is made to have an aircraft in distress be escorted by another aircraft, ask the pilots if they are familiar with and capable of formation flight.

1. Do not allow aircraft to join up in formation during emergency conditions, unless:

(a) The pilots involved are familiar with and capable of formation flight.

(b) They can communicate with one another, and have visual contact with each other.

2. If there is a need for aircraft that are not designated as search and rescue aircraft to get closer to one another than radar separation standards allow, the maneuver must be accomplished, visually, by the aircraft involved.

10–1–5. COORDINATION

Coordinate efforts to the extent possible to assist any aircraft believed overdue, lost, or in emergency status.

10–1–6. AIRPORT GROUND EMERGENCY

TERMINAL

a. When an emergency occurs on the airport proper, control other air and ground traffic to avoid conflicts in the area where the emergency is being handled. This also applies when routes within the airport proper are required for movement of local emergency equipment going to or from an emergency which occurs outside the airport proper.

NOTE–
Aircraft operated in proximity to accident or other emergency or disaster locations may cause hindrances to airborne and surface rescue or relief operations. Congestion, distraction or other effects, such as wake turbulence from nearby airplanes and helicopters, could prevent or delay proper execution of these operations.

REFERENCE–
FAA Order JO 7210.3, Chapter 20, Temporary Flight Restrictions.
14 CFR Section 91.137, Temporary Flight Restrictions.

b. Workload permitting, monitor the progress of emergency vehicles responding to a situation. If necessary, provide available information to assist responders in finding the accident/incident scene.

10–1–7. INFLIGHT EMERGENCIES INVOLVING MILITARY FIGHTER-TYPE AIRCRAFT

a. The design and complexity of military fighter-type aircraft places an extremely high workload on the pilot during an inflight emergency. The pilot's full attention is required to maintain control of the aircraft. Therefore, radio frequency and transponder code changes should be avoided and radio transmissions held to a minimum, especially when the aircraft experiencing the emergency is at low altitude.

b. Pilots of military fighter–type aircraft, normally single engine, experiencing or anticipating loss of engine power or control may execute a flameout pattern in an emergency situation. Circumstances may dictate that the pilot, depending on the position and nature of the emergency, modify the pattern based on actual emergency recovery requirements.

c. Military airfields with an assigned flying mission may conduct practice emergency approaches. Participating units maintain specific procedures for conducting these operations.

REFERENCE–
FAA Order JO 7110.65, Para 3–10–13, Simulated Flameout (SFO) Approaches/Emergency Landing Pattern (ELP) Operations/Practice Precautionary Approaches.

Section 2. Emergency Assistance

10–2–1. INFORMATION REQUIREMENTS

a. Start assistance as soon as enough information has been obtained upon which to act. Information requirements will vary, depending on the existing situation. Minimum required information for inflight emergencies is:

NOTE–
In the event of an ELT signal see paragraph 10–2–10, Emergency Locator Transmitter (ELT) Signals.

1. Aircraft identification and type.

2. Nature of the emergency.

3. Pilot's desires.

b. After initiating action, obtain the following items or any other pertinent information from the pilot or aircraft operator, as necessary:

NOTE–
1. *Emergency Autoland systems may not provide all of the required information for emergencies. Use the information provided to develop an appropriate course of action to assist the aircraft.*

2. *If an emergency has been declared by an Emergency Autoland system, transmissions to the aircraft may go unanswered.*

3. *Normally, do not request this information from military fighter–type aircraft that are at low altitudes (for example, on approach, immediately after departure, on a low level route). However, request the position of an aircraft that is not visually sighted or displayed on radar if the location is not given by the pilot.*

1. Aircraft altitude.

2. Fuel remaining in time.

3. Pilot reported weather.

4. Pilot capability for IFR flight.

5. Time and place of last known position.

6. Heading since last known position.

7. Airspeed.

8. Navigation equipment capability.

9. NAVAID signals received.

10. Visible landmarks.

11. Aircraft color.

12. Number of people on board.

13. Point of departure and destination.

14. Emergency equipment on board.

10–2–2. FREQUENCY CHANGES

Although 121.5 MHz and 243.0 MHz are emergency frequencies, it might be best to keep the aircraft on the initial contact frequency. Change frequencies only when there is a valid reason.

10–2–3. AIRCRAFT ORIENTATION

Orientate an aircraft by the means most appropriate to the circumstances. Recognized methods include:

a. Radar.

b. NAVAIDs.

c. Pilotage.

d. Sighting by other aircraft.

10–2–4. ALTITUDE CHANGE FOR IMPROVED RECEPTION

When you consider it necessary and if weather and circumstances permit, recommend that the aircraft maintain or increase altitude to improve communications or radar.

NOTE–
Aircraft with high-bypass turbofan engines (such as B747) encountering volcanic ash clouds have experienced total loss of power to all engines. Damage to engines due to volcanic ash ingestion increases as engine power is increased, therefore, climb while in the ash cloud is to be avoided where terrain permits.

REFERENCE–
AIM, Para 7–5–9, Flight Operations in Volcanic Ash.

10–2–5. EMERGENCY SITUATIONS

Consider that an aircraft emergency exists and inform the RCC or ARTCC if:

NOTE–
USAF facilities are only required to notify the ARTCC.

a. An emergency is declared by any of the following:

1. The pilot.

2. Facility personnel.

3. Officials responsible for the operation of the aircraft.

4. A system–generated transmission from an aircraft.

b. There is unexpected loss of radar contact and radio communications with any IFR or VFR aircraft.

c. Reports indicate it has made a forced landing, is about to do so, or its operating efficiency is so impaired that a forced landing will be necessary.

d. Reports indicate the crew has abandoned the aircraft or is about to do so.

e. An emergency transponder code is displayed or reported.

NOTE–
EN ROUTE. ERAM: Code 7700 causes an emergency indicator to blink in the data block.

f. Intercept or escort aircraft services are required.

g. The need for ground rescue appears likely.

h. An Emergency Locator Transmitter (ELT) signal is heard or reported.

REFERENCE–
FAA Order JO 7110.65, Para 10–1–3, Providing Assistance.
FAA Order JO 7110.65, Para 10–2–10, Emergency Locator Transmitter (ELT) Signals.

10–2–6. HIJACKED AIRCRAFT

Hijack attempts or actual events are a matter of national security and require special handling. FAA Order JO 7610.4, Sensitive Procedures and Requirements for Special Operations, describes additional procedures and reporting requirements that must be followed.

REFERENCE–
FAA Order JO 7610.4, Chapter 7, Procedures for Handling Suspicious Flight Situations and Hijacked Aircraft.
FAA Order JO 7110.65, Para 5–2–11, Code Monitor.

a. When a pilot notifies ATC verbally of a hijacking situation, assign code 7500 to the subject aircraft.

PHRASEOLOGY–
(Identification) SQUAWK SEVEN FIVE ZERO ZERO.

1. Should the pilot acknowledge assignment of code 7500 without further communication, or fail to acknowledge or communicate further, assume that the flight is being subject to hijack.

2. No reference to the hijacking must be made in subsequent communications unless initiated by the pilot, or unless directed by the Domestic Events Network (DEN) Air Traffic Security Coordinator.

3. Immediately inform the operations manager, supervisor or CIC.

NOTE–
When an aircraft squawks code 7500, ERAM will display "HIJK," and STARS/MEARTS will display "HJ" in the data block.

b. When a pilot notifies ATC of a hijacking situation by squawking code 7500, use the following phraseology to verify that the aircrew intentionally selected code 7500.

PHRASEOLOGY–
(Identification)(name of facility) VERIFY SQUAWKING SEVEN FIVE ZERO ZERO.

1. Should the pilot fail to acknowledge or communicate further, assume that the flight is being subject to hijack.

2. No reference to the hijacking must be made in subsequent communications unless initiated by the pilot, or unless directed by the DEN Air Traffic Security Coordinator.

3. Immediately inform the operations manager, supervisor or CIC.

10–2–7. VFR AIRCRAFT IN WEATHER DIFFICULTY

a. If VFR aircraft requests assistance when it encounters or is about to encounter IFR weather conditions, determine the facility best able to provide service. If a frequency change is necessary, advise the pilot of the reason for the change, and request the aircraft contact the appropriate control facility. Inform that facility of the situation. If the aircraft is unable to communicate with the control facility, relay information and clearances.

b. The following must be accomplished on a Mode C equipped VFR aircraft which is in emergency but no longer requires the assignment of **Code 7700**:

1. *TERMINAL.* Assign a beacon code that will permit terminal minimum safe altitude warning (MSAW) alarm processing.

2. *EN ROUTE.* An appropriate keyboard entry must be made to ensure en route MSAW (EMSAW) alarm processing.

10–2–8. RADAR ASSISTANCE TO VFR AIRCRAFT IN WEATHER DIFFICULTY

a. If a VFR aircraft requests radar assistance when it encounters or is about to encounter IFR weather conditions, ask the pilot if he/she is qualified for and capable of conducting IFR flight.

b. If the pilot states he/she is qualified for and capable of IFR flight, request him/her to file an IFR flight plan and then issue clearance to destination airport, as appropriate.

c. If the pilot states he/she is not qualified for or not capable of conducting IFR flight, or if he/she refuses to file an IFR flight plan, take whichever of the following actions is appropriate:

1. Inform the pilot of airports where VFR conditions are reported, provide other available pertinent weather information, and ask if he/she will elect to conduct VFR flight to such an airport.

2. If the action in subparagraph 1 above is not feasible or the pilot declines to conduct VFR flight to another airport, provide radar assistance if the pilot:

(a) Declares an emergency.

(b) Refuses to declare an emergency and you have determined the exact nature of the radar services the pilot desires.

3. If the aircraft has already encountered IFR conditions, inform the pilot of the appropriate terrain/obstacle clearance minimum altitude. If the aircraft is below appropriate terrain/obstacle clearance minimum altitude and sufficiently accurate position information has been received or radar identification is established, furnish a heading or radial on which to climb to reach appropriate terrain/obstacle clearance minimum altitude.

d. The following must be accomplished on a Mode C equipped VFR aircraft which is in emergency but no longer requires the assignment of **Code 7700**:

1. *TERMINAL.* Assign a beacon code that will permit terminal minimum safe altitude warning (MSAW) alarm processing.

2. *EN ROUTE.* An appropriate keyboard entry must be made to ensure en route MSAW (EMSAW) alarm processing.

10–2–9. RADAR ASSISTANCE TECHNIQUES

Use the following techniques to the extent possible when you provide radar assistance to a pilot not qualified to operate in IFR conditions:

a. Avoid radio frequency changes except when necessary to provide a clear communications channel.

b. Make turns while the aircraft is in VFR conditions so it will be in a position to fly a straight course while in IFR conditions.

c. Have pilot lower gear and slow aircraft to approach speed while in VFR conditions.

d. Avoid requiring a climb or descent while in a turn if in IFR conditions.

e. Avoid abrupt maneuvers.

f. Vector aircraft to VFR conditions.

g. The following must be accomplished on a Mode C equipped VFR aircraft which is in emergency but no longer requires the assignment of **Code 7700**:

1. *TERMINAL.* Assign a beacon code that will permit terminal minimum safe altitude warning (MSAW) alarm processing.

2. *EN ROUTE.* An appropriate keyboard entry must be made to ensure en route MSAW (EMSAW) alarm processing.

10–2–10. EMERGENCY LOCATOR TRANSMITTER (ELT) SIGNALS

When an ELT signal is heard or reported:

a. *EN ROUTE.* Notify the Rescue Coordination Center (RCC).

NOTE–
FAA Form 7210–8, ELT INCIDENT, contains standardized format for coordination with the RCC.

REFERENCE–
FAA Order JO 7210.3, Para 9–3–1, FAA Form 7210–8, ELT Incident.

b. *TERMINAL.* Notify the ARTCC which will coordinate with the RCC.

NOTE–
1. *Operational ground testing of emergency locator transmitters (ELTs) has been authorized during the first 5 minutes of each hour. To avoid confusing the tests with an actual alarm, the testing is restricted to no more than three audio sweeps.*

2. *Controllers can expect pilots to report aircraft position and time the signal was first heard, aircraft position and time the signal was last heard, aircraft position at maximum signal strength, flight altitude, and frequency of the emergency signal (121.5/243.0). (See AIM, paragraph 6–2–4, Emergency Locator Transmitter (ELT).)*

c. *TERMINAL.* Attempt to obtain fixes or bearings on the signal.

d. Solicit the assistance of other aircraft known to be operating in the signal area.

e. *TERMINAL.* Forward fixes or bearings and any other pertinent information to the ARTCC.

NOTE–
Fix information in relation to a VOR or VORTAC (radial- distance) facilitates accurate ELT plotting by RCC and should be provided when possible.

f. *EN ROUTE.* When the ELT signal strength indicates the signal may be emanating from somewhere on an airport or vicinity thereof, notify the on-site technical operations personnel and the Regional Operations Center (ROC) for their actions. This action is in addition to the above.

g. *TERMINAL.* When the ELT signal strength indicates the signal may be emanating from somewhere on the airport or vicinity thereof, notify the on-site technical operations personnel and the ARTCC for their action. This action is in addition to the above.

h. Air traffic personnel must not leave their required duty stations to locate an ELT signal source.

NOTE–
Portable handcarried receivers assigned to air traffic facilities (where no technical operations personnel are available) may be loaned to responsible airport personnel or local authorities to assist in locating the ELT signal source.

i. *EN ROUTE.* Notify the RCC and the ROC if signal source is located/terminated.

j. *TERMINAL.* Notify the ARTCC if signal source is located/terminated.

REFERENCE–
FAA Order JO 7110.65, Para 10–1–4, Responsibility.
FAA Order JO 7110.65, Para 10–2–1, Information Requirements.

10–2–11. AIRCRAFT BOMB THREATS

a. When information is received from any source that a bomb has been placed on, in, or near an aircraft for the purpose of damaging or destroying such aircraft, notify your supervisor or the facility air traffic manager. If the threat is general in nature, handle it as a "Suspicious Activity." When the threat is targeted against a specific aircraft and you are in contact with the suspect aircraft, take the following actions as appropriate:

REFERENCE–
FAA Order JO 7610.4, Chapter 7, Procedures for Handling Suspicious Flight Situations and Hijacked Aircraft.

1. Advise the pilot of the threat.

2. Inform the pilot that technical assistance can be obtained from an FAA aviation explosives expert.

NOTE–
An FAA aviation explosive expert is on call at all times and may be contacted by calling the FAA Operations Center, Washington, DC, Area Code 202–267–3333, ETN 521–0111, or DSN 851–3750. Technical advice can be relayed to assist civil or military air crews in their search for a bomb and in determining what precautionary action to take if one is found.

3. Ask the pilot if he/she desires to climb or descend to an altitude that would equalize or reduce the outside air pressure/existing cabin air pressure differential. Issue or relay an appropriate clearance considering MEA, MOCA, MRA, and weather.

NOTE–
Equalizing existing cabin air pressure with outside air pressure is a key step which the pilot may wish to take to minimize the damage potential of a bomb.

4. Handle the aircraft as an emergency and/or provide the most expeditious handling possible with respect to the safety of other aircraft, ground facilities, and personnel.

NOTE–
Emergency handling is discretionary and should be based on the situation. With certain types of threats, plans may call for a low-key action or response.

5. Issue or relay clearances to a new destination if requested.

6. When a pilot requests technical assistance or if it is apparent that a pilot may need such assistance, do NOT suggest what actions the pilot should take concerning a bomb, but obtain the following information and notify your supervisor who will contact the FAA aviation explosives expert:

NOTE–
This information is needed by the FAA aviation explosives expert so that he/she can assess the situation and make immediate recommendations to the pilot. The aviation explosives expert may not be familiar with all military aircraft configurations but he/she can offer technical assistance which would be beneficial to the pilot.

(a) Type, series, and model of the aircraft.

(b) Precise location/description of the bomb device if known.

(c) Other details which may be pertinent.

NOTE–
The following details may be of significance if known, but it is not intended that the pilot should disturb a suspected bomb/bomb container to ascertain the information: The altitude or time set for the bomb to explode, type of detonating action (barometric, time, anti-handling, remote radio transmitter), power source (battery, electrical, mechanical), type of initiator (blasting cap, flash bulb, chemical), and the type of explosive/incendiary charge (dynamite, black powder, chemical).

b. When a bomb threat involves an aircraft on the ground and you are in contact with the suspect aircraft, take the following actions in addition to those discussed in the preceding paragraphs which may be appropriate:

1. If the aircraft is at an airport where tower control or FSS advisory service is not available, or if the pilot ignores the threat at any airport, recommend that takeoff be delayed until the pilot or aircraft operator establishes that a bomb is not aboard in accordance with 14 CFR Part 121. If the pilot insists on taking off and in your opinion the operation will not adversely affect other traffic, issue or relay an ATC clearance.

REFERENCE–
14 CFR Section 121.538, Airplane Security.

2. Advise the aircraft to remain as far away from other aircraft and facilities as possible, to clear the runway, if appropriate, and to taxi to an isolated or designated search area. When it is impractical or if the pilot takes an alternative action; e.g., parking and off-loading immediately, advise other aircraft to remain clear of the suspect aircraft by at least 100 yards if able.

NOTE–
Passenger deplaning may be of paramount importance and must be considered before the aircraft is parked or moved away from service areas. The decision to use ramp facilities rests with the pilot, aircraft operator/airport manager.

c. If you are unable to inform the suspect aircraft of a bomb threat or if you lose contact with the aircraft, advise your supervisor and relay pertinent details to other sectors or facilities as deemed necessary.

d. When a pilot reports the discovery of a bomb or suspected bomb on an aircraft which is airborne or on the ground, determine the pilot's intentions and comply with his/her requests in so far as possible. Take all of the actions discussed in the preceding paragraphs which may be appropriate under the existing circumstances.

e. The handling of aircraft when a hijacker has or is suspected of having a bomb requires special considerations. Be responsive to the pilot's requests and notify supervisory personnel. Apply hijacking procedures and offer assistance to the pilot according to the preceding paragraphs, if needed.

10–2–12. EXPLOSIVE DETECTION K–9 TEAMS

Take the following actions should you receive an aircraft request for the location of the nearest explosive detection K–9 team.

REFERENCE–
FAA Order JO 7210.3, Para 2–1–12, Explosives Detection K–9 Teams.

a. Obtain the aircraft identification and position and advise your supervisor of the pilot request.

b. When you receive the nearest location of the explosive detection K−9 team, relay the information to the pilot.

c. If the aircraft wishes to divert to the airport location provided, obtain an estimated arrival time from the pilot and advise your supervisor.

10−2−13. MANPADS ALERT

When a threat or attack from Man−Portable Air Defense Systems (MANPADS) is determined to be real, notify and advise aircraft as follows:

a. Do not withhold landing clearance. To the extent possible, issue information on MANPADS threats, confirmed attacks, or post−event activities in time for it to be useful to the pilot. The pilot or parent company will determine the pilot's actions.

b. MANPADS information will be disseminated via the ATIS and/or controller−to−pilot transmissions.

c. Disseminate via controller−to−pilot transmission until the appropriate MANPADS information is broadcast via the ATIS and pilots indicate they have received the appropriate ATIS code. MANPADS information will include nature and location of threat or incident, whether reported or observed and by whom, time (if known), and when transmitting to an individual aircraft, a request for pilot's intentions.

PHRASEOLOGY−
ATTENTION (aircraft identification), MANPADS ALERT. EXERCISE EXTREME CAUTION. MANPADS THREAT/ ATTACK/POST−EVENT ACTIVITY OBSERVED/ REPORTED BY (reporting agency) (location) AT (time, if known). (When transmitting to an individual aircraft) SAY INTENTIONS.

EXAMPLE−
"Attention Eastern Four Seventeen, MANPADS alert. Exercise extreme caution. MANPADS threat reported by TSA, LaGuardia vicinity. Say intentions."

"Attention all aircraft, MANPADS alert. Exercise extreme caution. MANPADS post−event activity observed by tower south of airport at two−one−zero−zero Zulu."

d. Report MANPADS threat/attack/post−event activity via the ATIS and/or controller−to−pilot transmissions until notified otherwise by the Domestic Events Network (DEN) Air Traffic Security Coordinator (ATSC).

REFERENCE−
FAA Order JO 7110.65, Para 2−9−3, Content.
FAA Order JO 7210.3, Para 2−1−10, Handling MANPADS Incidents.
FAA Order JO 7610.4, Para 3−1−3, Responsibilities.

10−2−14. UNAUTHORIZED LASER ILLUMINATION OF AIRCRAFT

a. When a laser event is reported to an air traffic facility, broadcast on all appropriate frequencies a general caution warning every five minutes for 20 minutes following the last report.

PHRASEOLOGY−
UNAUTHORIZED LASER ILLUMINATION EVENT, (location), (altitude).

b. Terminal facilities must include reported unauthorized laser illumination events on the ATIS broadcast for one hour following the last report. Include the time, location, altitude, color, and direction of the laser as reported by the pilot.

NOTE−
All personnel can expect aircrews to regard lasers as an inflight emergency and may take evasive action to avoid laser illumination. Additionally, other aircraft may request clearance to avoid the area.

REFERENCE−
FAA Order JO 7110.65, Para 2−9−3, Content.
FAA Order JO 7210.3, Para 2−1−30, Reporting Unauthorized Laser Illumination of Aircraft.

10−2−15. EMERGENCY AIRPORT RECOMMENDATION

a. Consider the following factors when recommending an emergency airport:

1. Remaining fuel in relation to airport distances.

2. Weather conditions.

NOTE–
Depending on the nature of the emergency, certain weather phenomena may deserve weighted consideration when recommending an airport; e.g., a pilot may elect to fly farther to land at an airport with VFR instead of IFR conditions.

3. Airport conditions.

4. NAVAID status.

5. Aircraft type.

6. Pilot's qualifications.

7. Vectoring or homing capability to the emergency airport.

NOTE–
In the event of an Emergency Autoland system activation, the system will select a suitable airport and advise ATC. The Emergency Autoland system does not consider closed runways, equipment on the runway, construction, or other possible airport hazards when selecting a suitable airport.

b. Consideration to the provisions of subparagraph a and paragraph 10–2–16, Guidance to Emergency Airport, must be used in conjunction with the information derived from any automated emergency airport information source.

10–2–16. GUIDANCE TO EMERGENCY AIRPORT

a. When necessary, use any of the following for guidance to the airport:

1. Radar.

2. Following another aircraft.

3. NAVAIDs.

4. Pilotage by landmarks.

5. Compass headings.

b. Consideration to the provisions of paragraph 10–2–15, Emergency Airport Recommendation, must be used in conjunction with the information derived from any automated emergency airport information source.

10–2–17. EMERGENCY OBSTRUCTION VIDEO MAP (EOVM)

a. The EOVM is intended to facilitate advisory service to an aircraft in an emergency situation wherein an appropriate terrain/obstacle clearance minimum altitude cannot be maintained. It must only be used and the service provided under the following conditions:

1. The pilot has declared an emergency, or

2. The controller has determined that an emergency condition exists or is imminent because of the pilot's inability to maintain an appropriate terrain/obstacle clearance minimum altitude.

NOTE–
Appropriate terrain/obstacle clearance minimum altitudes may be defined as Minimum IFR Altitude (MIA), Minimum En Route Altitude (MEA), Minimum Obstruction Clearance Altitude (MOCA), or Minimum Vectoring Altitude (MVA).

b. When providing emergency vectoring service, the controller must advise the pilot that any headings issued are emergency advisories intended only to direct the aircraft toward and over an area of lower terrain/obstacle elevation.

NOTE–
Altitudes and obstructions depicted on the EOVM are the actual altitudes and locations of the obstacle/terrain and contain no lateral or vertical buffers for obstruction clearance.

REFERENCE–
FAA Order JO 7210.3, Para 3–8–4, Emergency Obstruction Video Map (EOVM).

10–2–18. VOLCANIC ASH

a. If a volcanic ash cloud is known or forecast to be present:

1. Relay all information available to pilots to ensure that they are aware of the ash cloud's position and altitude(s).

2. Suggest appropriate reroutes to avoid the area of known or forecast ash clouds.

NOTE–
Volcanic ash clouds are not normally detected by airborne or air traffic radar systems.

b. If advised by an aircraft that it has entered a volcanic ash cloud and indicates that a distress situation exists:

1. Consider the aircraft to be in an emergency situation.

2. Do not initiate any climb clearances to turbine–powered aircraft until the aircraft has exited the ash cloud.

3. Do not attempt to provide escape vectors without pilot concurrence.

NOTE–
1. *The recommended escape maneuver is to reverse course and begin a descent (if terrain permits). However, it is the pilot's responsibility to determine the safest escape route from the ash cloud.*

2. *Controllers should be aware of the possibility of complete loss of power to any turbine–powered aircraft that encounters an ash cloud.*

REFERENCE–
FAA Order JO 7110.65, Para 10–2–4, Altitude Change for Improved Reception.
AIM, Para 7–5–9, Flight Operations in Volcanic Ash.

10–2–19. REPORTING DEATH, ILLNESS, OR OTHER PUBLIC HEALTH RISK ON BOARD AIRCRAFT

a. If an air traffic controller receives a report of the death of person, an illness, and/or other public health risk obtain the following information and notify the operations manager in charge (OMIC)/operations supervisor (OS)/controller-in-charge (CIC) as soon as possible.

1. Call sign.

2. Number of suspected cases of illness on board.

3. Nature of the illnesses or other public health risk, if known.

4. Number of persons on board.

5. Number of deaths, if applicable.

6. Pilot's intent (for example, continue to destination or divert).

7. Any request for assistance (for example, needing emergency medical services to meet the aircraft at arrival).

b. The OMIC/OS/CIC must relay the information to the DEN as soon as possible.

NOTE–
1. *If the ATC facility is not actively monitoring the DEN or does not have a dedicated line to the DEN, they must call into the DEN directly via 844–432–2962 (toll free).*

2. *Except in extraordinary circumstances, such as a situation requiring ATC intervention, follow-on coordination regarding the incident will not involve ATC frequencies.*

3. *The initial report to a U.S. ATC facility may be passed from a prior ATC facility along the route of flight.*

REFERENCE–
FAA Order JO 7210.3, Para 2–1–37, Reporting Death, Illness, or Other Public Health Risk On Board Aircraft.

Section 3. Overdue Aircraft

10-3-1. OVERDUE AIRCRAFT/OTHER SITUATIONS

a. Consider an aircraft to be overdue and initiate the procedures stated in this section to issue an ALNOT when neither communications nor radar contact can be established and 30 minutes have passed since:

NOTE-
The procedures in this section also apply to an aircraft referred to as "missing" or "unreported."

1. Its ETA over a specified or compulsory reporting point or at a clearance limit in your area.

2. Its clearance void time.

3. A VFR or IFR aircraft arriving at an airport not served by an air traffic control tower or flight service station fails to cancel a flight plan after receiving instructions on how to cancel.

NOTE-
If you have reason to believe that an aircraft is overdue prior to 30 minutes, take the appropriate action immediately.

b. Consider an aircraft to be in an emergency status and initiate ALNOT procedures in this section immediately when there is an abnormal simultaneous loss of radar and communications with an IFR aircraft or VFR/SVFR aircraft receiving flight following services. This situation may be applicable to an aircraft operating in a nonradar environment and an unexpected/abnormal loss of communications occurs.

c. The ARTCC in whose area the aircraft is reported as overdue, missing or lost will make these determinations and takes any subsequent action required.

d. If you have reason to believe that an aircraft is overdue prior to 30 minutes, take the appropriate action immediately.

e. The center in whose area the aircraft is first unreported or overdue will make these determinations and takes any subsequent action required.

REFERENCE-
FAA Order JO 7110.65, Para 4-3-4, Departure Release, Hold for Release, Release Times, Departure Restrictions, and Clearance Void Times.

10-3-2. INFORMATION TO BE FORWARDED TO ARTCC

TERMINAL

When an aircraft is considered to be in emergency status that may require SAR procedures, or an IFR aircraft is overdue, the terminal facility must alert the appropriate ARTCC and forward the following information, as available:

a. Flight plan, including color of aircraft, if known.

b. Time of last transmission received, by whom, and frequency used.

c. Last position report and how determined.

d. Aircraft beacon code.

e. Number of persons on board.

f. Fuel status.

g. Facility working aircraft and frequency.

h. Last known position, how determined, time,_estimated present position, and maximum range of flight of the aircraft based on remaining fuel and airspeed.

i. Position of other aircraft near aircraft's route of flight, when requested.

j. Whether or not an ELT signal has been heard or reported in the vicinity of the last known position.

k. Other pertinent information.

REFERENCE–
FAA Order JO 7110.65, Para 10–1–4, Responsibility.
FAA Order JO 7110.65, Para 10–2–5, Emergency Situations.

NOTE–
FSSs serve as the central points for collecting and disseminating information on an overdue or missing aircraft which is not on an IFR flight plan. Non–FSS ATC facilities that receive telephone calls or other inquiries regarding these flights must refer these calls and inquiries to the appropriate FSS.

10–3–3. INFORMATION TO BE FORWARDED TO RCC

EN ROUTE

When an aircraft is considered to be in emergency status or an IFR aircraft is overdue, the ARTCC must alert the RCC and forward the following information, as available:

a. Facility and person calling.

b. Flight plan, including color of aircraft, if known.

c. Time of last transmission received, by whom, and frequency used.

d. Last position report and how determined.

e. Aircraft beacon code.

f. Action taken by reporting facility and proposed action.

g. Number of persons on board.

h. Fuel status.

i. Facility working aircraft and frequency.

j. Last known position, how determined, time, estimated present position, and maximum range of flight of the aircraft based on remaining fuel and airspeed.

k. Position of other aircraft near aircraft's route of flight, when requested.

l. Whether or not an ELT signal has been heard or reported in the vicinity of the last known position.

m. Other pertinent information.

REFERENCE–
FAA Order JO 7110.65, Para 10–1–4, Responsibility.
FAA Order JO 7110.65, Para 10–2–5, Emergency Situations.

NOTE–
FSSs serve as the central points for collecting and disseminating information on an overdue or missing aircraft which is not on an IFR flight plan. Non–FSS ATC facilities that receive telephone calls or other inquiries regarding these flights must refer these calls and inquiries to the appropriate FSS.

10–3–4. ALNOT

EN ROUTE

a. In addition to routing to the regional office operations center for the area in which the facility is located, issue an ALNOT to all centers and Area B circuits, generally 50 miles on either side of the route of flight from the last reported position to destination. Include the original or amended flight plan, as appropriate, and the last known position of the aircraft. At the recommendation of the RCC or at your discretion, the ALNOT may be issued to cover the maximum range of the aircraft.

NOTE–
1. *An ALNOT must be issued before the RCC can begin search and rescue procedures.*

2. Flight plan information on military aircraft is available at the FSS serving as a tie-in station for the departure or destination airport. FAA tie-in stations for airports in the continental U.S. are listed in FAA Order JO 7350.8, Location Identifiers. In the West Flight Services Area Office, tie–in stations are listed in service area publications entitled, "Flight Plan Routing and Airport Search Directory." For flights with overseas departure points, the information is available through the destination FSS or the appropriate IFSS.

b. Upon receipt of an INREQ or ALNOT, check the position records to determine whether the aircraft has contacted your facility. Notify the originator of the results or status of this check within one hour of the time the alert was received. Retain the alert in an active status, and immediately notify the originator of subsequent contact, until cancellation is received.

c. Include pertinent information in the ALNOT that will aid the RCC and SAR Teams in conducting the SAR mission. When known, include:

1. Last known position.

2. Time.

3. Aircraft beacon code.

d. When information is obtained not previously contained in the ALNOT, issue an amended ALNOT to update information that will assist the SAR providers.

10–3–5. RESPONSIBILITY TRANSFER TO RCC

EN ROUTE

Transfer responsibility for further search to the RCC when one of the following occurs:

a. Thirty minutes have elapsed after the estimated aircraft fuel exhaustion time.

b. The aircraft has not been located within one hour after ALNOT issuance.

c. The ALNOT search has been completed with negative results.

10–3–6. LAST KNOWN POSITION DETERMINATION

a. To assist the RCC and SAR Teams in the conduct of the SAR mission, provide the most accurate latitude and longitude available to the FAA using en route and terminal radar sensor data near the aircraft's last known position.

b. If necessary to prevent an undue delay, utilize any available method to determine the initial latitude and longitude. Follow-up as soon as possible with a formal latitude and longitude using the appropriate terminal or en route facility data extraction tools.

c. If available, solicit the assistance of other_aircraft known to be operating near the aircraft in distress.

d. Forward this information to the RCC or the ARTCC as appropriate.

10–3–7. ALNOT CANCELLATION

EN ROUTE

a. When directed by the RCC, cancel the ALNOT when the aircraft is located or the search is abandoned.

b. Include pertinent information in the cancellation that will aid the RCC, SAR Teams, and FAA SAR management to include the location where the aircraft or wreckage was found.

Section 4. Control Actions

10-4-1. TRAFFIC RESTRICTIONS

IFR traffic which could be affected by an overdue or unreported aircraft must be restricted or suspended unless radar separation is used. The facility responsible must restrict or suspend IFR traffic for a period of 30 minutes following the applicable time listed in subparagraphs a through e:

a. The time at which approach clearance was delivered to the pilot.

b. The EFC time delivered to the pilot.

c. The arrival time over the NAVAID serving the destination airport.

d. The current estimate, either the control facility's or the pilot's, whichever is later, at:

1. The appropriate en route NAVAID or fix, and

2. The NAVAID serving the destination airport.

e. The release time and, if issued, the clearance void time.

REFERENCE–
FAA Order JO 7110.65, Para 4-3-4, Departure Release, Hold for Release, Release Times, Departure Restrictions, and Clearance Void Times.

10-4-2. LIGHTING REQUIREMENTS

a. *EN ROUTE.* At nontower or non-FSS locations, request the airport management to light all runway lights, approach lights, and all other required airport lighting systems for at least 30 minutes before the ETA of the unreported aircraft until the aircraft has been located or for 30 minutes after its fuel supply is estimated to be exhausted.

b. *TERMINAL.* Operate runway lights, approach lights, and all other required airport lighting systems for at least 30 minutes before the ETA of the unreported aircraft until the aircraft has been located or for 30 minutes after its fuel supply is estimated to be exhausted.

REFERENCE–
FAA Order JO 7110.65, Para 3-4-1, Emergency Lighting.

10-4-3. TRAFFIC RESUMPTION

After the 30-minute traffic suspension period has expired, resume normal air traffic control if the operators or pilots of other aircraft concur. This concurrence must be maintained for a period of 30 minutes after the suspension period has expired.

REFERENCE–
FAA Order JO 7110.65, Para 4-3-4, Departure Release, Hold for Release, Release Times, Departure Restrictions, and Clearance Void Times.

10-4-4. COMMUNICATIONS FAILURE

Take the following actions, as appropriate, if two-way radio communications are lost with an aircraft:

NOTE–
1. *When an IFR aircraft experiences two-way radio communications failure, air traffic control is based on anticipated pilot actions. Pilot procedures and recommended practices are set forth in the AIM, CFRs, and pertinent military regulations.*

2. *Should the pilot of an aircraft equipped with a coded radar beacon transponder experience a loss of two-way radio capability, the pilot can be expected to adjust the transponder to reply on Mode 3/A* ***Code 7600.***

a. In the event of lost communications with an aircraft under your control jurisdiction use all appropriate means available to reestablish communications with the aircraft. These may include, but are not limited to, emergency frequencies, NAVAIDs that are equipped with voice capability, FSS, New York Radio, San Francisco Radio, etc.

NOTE–
1. *New York Radio and San Francisco Radio are operated by Collins Aerospace (formerly ARINC, Incorporated) under contract with the FAA for communications services. These Radio facilities have the capability of relaying information to/from ATC facilities throughout the country.*

2. *Aircraft communications addressing and reporting system (ACARS) or selective calling (SELCAL) may be utilized to reestablish radio communications with suitably equipped aircraft. ACARS can be utilized by contacting San Francisco Radio at (800)–621–0140 or New York Radio at (800) 645–1095. Provide the aircraft call sign, approximate location, and contact instructions. In order to utilize the SELCAL system, the SELCAL code for the subject aircraft must be known. If the SELCAL code is not contained in the remarks section of the flight plan, contact the pertinent air carrier dispatch office to determine the code. Then contact San Francisco Radio (for aircraft over the Pacific, U.S. or Mexico) or New York Radio (for aircraft over the Atlantic, Gulf of Mexico, or Caribbean) and provide the aircraft call sign, SELCAL code, approximate location, and contact instructions.*

b. Broadcast clearances through any available means of communications including the voice feature of NAVAIDs.

NOTE–
1. *Some UHF equipped aircraft have VHF navigation equipment and can receive 121.5 MHz.*

2. *"Any available means" includes the use of FSS and New York Radio or San Francisco Radio.*

REFERENCE–
FAA Order JO 7110.65, Para 4–2–2, Clearance Prefix.

c. Attempt to re-establish communication by having the aircraft use its transponder or make turns to acknowledge clearances and answer questions. Request any of the following in using the transponder:

1. Request the aircraft to reply Mode 3/A "IDENT."

2. Request the aircraft to reply on Code 7600.

3. Request the aircraft to change to "stand-by" for sufficient time for you to be sure that the lack of a target is the result of the requested action.

PHRASEOLOGY–
REPLY NOT RECEIVED, (appropriate instructions).

(Action) OBSERVED, (additional instructions/information if necessary).

d. Broadcast a clearance for the aircraft to proceed to its filed alternate airport at the MEA if the aircraft operator concurs.

REFERENCE–
FAA Order JO 7110.65, Para 5–2–4, Radio Failure.
FAA Order JO 7110.65, Para 9–2–6, IFR Military Training Routes.

e. If radio communications have not been (re) established with the aircraft after 5 minutes, consider the aircraft's or pilot's activity to be suspicious and report it to the OS/CIC per FAA Order JO 7610.4, Chapter 7, Procedures for Handling Suspicious Flight Situations and Hijacked Aircraft, and paragraph 2–1–26f, Supervisory Notification, of this order.

Section 5. Miscellaneous Operations

10-5-1. EXPLOSIVE CARGO

TERMINAL

When you receive information that an emergency landing will be made with explosive cargo aboard, inform the pilot of the safest or least congested airport areas. Relay the explosive cargo information to:

a. The emergency equipment crew.

b. The airport management.

c. The appropriate military agencies, when requested by the pilot.

10-5-2. DEBRIS-GENERATING SPACE LAUNCH OR REENTRY VEHICLE MISHAPS

A debris-generating space launch or reentry vehicle mishap is an emergency situation in the NAS.

a. In the event of a debris-generating space launch or reentry vehicle mishap, issue an alert broadcast to all affected aircraft informing them of the mishap, and, if known, the approximate location of the debris fall area. If a debris response area (DRA) has been activated, issue the approximate location of the response area instead.

EXAMPLE-
"Attention all aircraft, due to a space vehicle mishap, possible debris falling in the NAS from approximately Brownsville, Texas, extending east for approximately five hundred miles. Stand by for individual instructions."

"Attention all aircraft, due to a space vehicle mishap, a debris response area has been activated beginning at approximately Cape Canaveral, extending northeast for approximately three hundred miles. Stand by for individual instructions."

1. When workload permits, reissue the alert broadcast approximately every 15 minutes.

2. When advised that falling debris is no longer a factor, or the DRA has been deactivated, issue a broadcast to advise all aircraft of this information.

EXAMPLE-
"Attention all aircraft, falling debris no longer a factor."

"Attention all aircraft, the debris response area is no longer active."

b. In the event of a debris response area activation:

1. Issue instructions and/or clearances to prevent aircraft from entering the debris response area, unless a higher priority duty already exists.

REFERENCE-
FAA Order JO 7110.65, Para 2-1-2a, Duty Priority.

2. For airborne aircraft already within an activated DRA:

(a) Assist aircraft to exit the DRA expeditiously;

(b) Do not withhold landing or approach clearances.

3. For airports that underlie an active DRA:

(a) Do not issue departure releases or takeoff clearances;

(b) To the extent possible do not clear aircraft onto the movement area.

Section 6. Oceanic Emergency Procedures

10–6–1. APPLICATION

The procedures in this section are to be used solely in oceanic airspace.

10–6–2. PHASES OF EMERGENCY

Emergency phases are described as follows:

a. Uncertainty phase (INCERFA). When there is concern about the safety of an aircraft or its occupants, an INCERFA exists:

1. When communication from an aircraft has not been received within 30 minutes after the time a communication should have been received or after the time an unsuccessful attempt to establish communication with such aircraft was first made, whichever is earlier; or

2. When an aircraft fails to arrive within 30 minutes after the time of arrival last estimated by the pilot or by the ATC units, whichever is later.

b. Alert phase (ALERFA). When there is apprehension about the safety of an aircraft and its occupants, an ALERFA exists:

1. Following the uncertainty phase when subsequent attempts to establish communications with the aircraft, or inquiries to other relevant sources have failed to reveal any information about the aircraft; or

2. When information has been received which indicates that the operating efficiency of the aircraft has been impaired but not to the extent that a forced landing is likely; or

3. When communication from an aircraft has not been received within 60 minutes after the time a communication should have been received or after the time an unsuccessful attempt to establish communication with such aircraft was first made, whichever is earlier.

c. Distress phase (DETRESFA). When there is reasonable certainty that the aircraft and its occupants are threatened by grave and imminent danger, a DETRESFA exists:

1. Following the alert phase when further attempts to establish communications with the aircraft and more widespread inquiries are unsuccessful; or

2. When the fuel on board is considered to be exhausted or to be insufficient for the aircraft to reach safety; or

3. When information is received which indicates that the operating efficiency of the aircraft has been impaired to the extent that a forced landing is likely; or

4. When information is received or it is reasonably certain that the aircraft is about to make or has made a forced landing.

10–6–3. ALERTING SERVICE AND SPECIAL ASSISTANCE

a. Provide alerting service to:

1. All aircraft receiving ATC service;

2. All other aircraft which have filed a flight plan or which are otherwise known to the ATC unit; and

3. Any aircraft known or believed to be the subject of unlawful interference.

b. When alerting service is required, the responsibility for coordinating such service must, unless otherwise established by letter of agreement, rest with the facility serving the FIR or CTA:

1. Within which the aircraft was flying at the time of last air-ground radio contact; or

2. Which the aircraft was about to enter if the last air-ground contact was established at or close to the boundary; or

3. Within which the point of destination is located if the aircraft:

(a) Was not equipped with suitable two-way radio communications equipment; or

(b) Was not under obligation to transmit position reports.

REFERENCE–
FAA Order JO 7110.65, Chapter 8, Section 2, Coordination.

c. The responsible Area Control Center (ACC) must serve as the control point for:

1. Collecting all information relevant to a state of emergency of an aircraft;

2. Forwarding that information to the appropriate RCC; and

3. Coordinating with other facilities concerned.

d. The responsibility of the ACC to provide alerting service for military aircraft may be waived upon a written or recorded request from a military agency. In this case, the military request must state that the military agency assumes full responsibility for their aircraft while the aircraft are operating in the oceanic airspace.

e. Responsibility to provide alerting service for flight operations conducted under the "due regard" or "operational" prerogative of military aircraft is assumed by the military. When "due regard" operations are scheduled to end with aircraft filed under ICAO procedures, the ACC may, if specified in a letter of agreement, assume responsibility for alerting service at proposed time filed.

f. In the event of INCERFA, ALERFA, or DETRESFA, notify the following:

1. When practicable, the aircraft operator.

2. The appropriate RCC.

3. Aeronautical stations having en route communications guard responsibilities at the point of departure, along or adjacent to the route of flight, and at the destination.

4. ACCs having jurisdiction over the proposed route of flight from the last reported position to the destination airport.

g. INCERFA, ALERFA, and DETRESFA messages must include the following information, if available, in the order listed:

1. INCERFA, ALERFA, or DETRESFA according to the phase of the emergency.

2. Agency and person originating the message.

3. Nature of the emergency.

4. Significant flight plan information.

5. The air traffic unit which made the last radio contact, the time, and the frequency used.

6. The aircraft's last position report, how it was received, and what facility received it.

7. Color and distinctive marks of aircraft.

8. Any action taken by reporting office.

9. Other pertinent remarks.

h. An INCERFA phase ends with the receipt of any information or position report on the aircraft. Cancel the INCERFA by a message addressed to the same stations as the INCERFA message.

1. An ALERFA ends when:

(a) Evidence exists that would ease apprehension about the safety of the aircraft and its occupants; or

(b) The concerned aircraft lands. Cancel the ALERFA message by a message addressed to the same stations as the ALERFA message.

2. A DETRESFA ends when the:

(a) Aircraft successfully lands; or

(b) RCC advises of a successful rescue; or

(c) RCC advises of termination of SAR activities. Cancel the DETRESFA by a message addressed to the same stations as the DETRESFA message.

i. A separate chronological record should be kept on each ALERFA and DETRESFA together with a chart which displays the projected route of the aircraft, position reports received, route of interceptor aircraft, and other pertinent information.

10–6–4. INFLIGHT CONTINGENCIES

a. If an aircraft over water requests weather, sea conditions, ditching information, and/or assistance from surface vessels, or if the controller feels that this information may be necessary for aircraft safety, it should be requested from the RCC. Also, an appropriate AMVER SURPIC should be asked for if requested by the aircraft or deemed beneficial by control personnel.

NOTE–
The AMVER Center can deliver, in a matter of minutes, a SURPIC of vessels in the area of a SAR incident, including their predicted positions and their characteristics.

b. In all cases of aircraft ditching, the airspace required for SAR operations must be determined by the RCC. The ACC must block that airspace until the RCC advises the airspace is no longer required. An International Notice to Air Missions (NOTAM) must be issued describing the airspace affected.

c. The following actions will be taken in the event an aircraft must make an emergency descent:

1. In the event an aircraft requests an emergency descent:

(a) Issue a clearance to the requested altitude if approved separation can be provided.

(b) Advise the aircraft of the traffic, and request its intentions if traffic prevents an unrestricted descent.

PHRASEOLOGY–
ATC ADVISES (aircraft identification) UNABLE TO APPROVE UNRESTRICTED DESCENT.
TRAFFIC (traffic information).
REQUEST INTENTIONS.

2. In the event an aircraft is making or will make an emergency descent without a clearance:

(a) Advise other aircraft of the emergency descent.

PHRASEOLOGY–
ATC ADVISES (aircraft identification/all aircraft) BE ALERT FOR EMERGENCY DESCENT IN THE VICINITY OF (latitude/longitude) FROM (altitude/FL) TO (altitude/FL).

(b) Advise other aircraft when the emergency descent is complete.

PHRASEOLOGY–
(Aircraft identification/all aircraft) EMERGENCY DESCENT AT (location) COMPLETED.

3. Upon notification that an aircraft is making an emergency descent through other traffic, take action immediately to safeguard all aircraft concerned.

4. When appropriate, broadcast by ATC communications, by radio navigation aids, and/or through aeronautical communication stations/services an emergency message to all aircraft in the vicinity of the descending aircraft. Include the following information:

(a) Location of emergency descent.

(b) Direction of flight.

(c) Type aircraft.

(d) Route if appropriate.

(e) Altitude vacated.

(f) Other information.

EXAMPLE–
"Attention all aircraft in the vicinity of Trout, a northbound D-C Ten on A-T-S Route Alfa Seven Hundred is making an emergency descent from flight level three three zero." (Repeat as you deem appropriate.)

5. If traffic conditions permit, provide traffic information to the affected aircraft.

6. Immediately after an emergency broadcast or traffic information has been made, issue appropriate clearances or instructions, as necessary, to all aircraft involved.

10–6–5. SERVICES TO RESCUE AIRCRAFT

a. Provide IFR separation between the SAR and the aircraft in distress, except when visual or radar contact has been established by the search and rescue aircraft and the pilots of both aircraft concur, IFR separation may be discontinued.

b. Clear the SAR aircraft to a fixed clearance limit rather than to the aircraft in distress, which is a moving fix. Issue route clearances that are consistent with that of the distressed aircraft.

c. Advise the rescue aircraft, as soon as practicable, of any factors that could adversely affect its mission; e.g., unfavorable weather conditions, anticipated problems, the possibility of not being able to approve an IFR descent through en route traffic, etc.

d. Advise the appropriate rescue agency of all pertinent information as it develops.

e. Forward immediately any information about the action being taken by the RCC, other organizations, or aircraft to the aircraft concerned.

f. Advise the aircraft operator of the current status of the SAR operation as soon as practicable.

g. Since prompt, correct, and complete information is the key to successful rescue operations, ensure that this information is swiftly and smoothly supplied to those organizations actively engaged in rescue operations.

Section 7. Ground Missile Emergencies

10−7−1. INFORMATION RELAY

When you receive information concerning a ground missile emergency, notify other concerned facilities and take action to have alerting advisories issued by:

a. *EN ROUTE.* Air carrier company radio stations for each VFR company aircraft which is or will be operating in the vicinity of the emergency.

b. *EN ROUTE.* FSSs adjacent to the emergency location.

c. *TERMINAL.* Relay all information concerning a ground missile emergency to the ARTCC within whose area the emergency exists and disseminate as a NOTAM.

REFERENCE−
P/CG Term − Notice to Air Missions.

10−7−2. IFR AND SVFR MINIMA

Reroute IFR and SVFR aircraft as necessary to avoid the emergency location by one of the following minima, or by greater minima when suggested by the notifying official:

a. Lateral separation− *1 mile* between the emergency location and either of the following:

1. An aircraft under radar control and the emergency location which can be accurately determined by reference to the radar scope.

2. The airspace to be protected for the route being flown.

b. Vertical separation− *6,000 feet* above the surface over the emergency location.

10−7−3. VFR MINIMA

Advise all known VFR aircraft which are, or will be, operating in the vicinity of a ground missile emergency, to avoid the emergency location by 1 mile laterally or 6,000 feet vertically, or by a greater distance or altitude, when suggested by the notifying official.

10−7−4. SMOKE COLUMN AVOIDANCE

Advise all aircraft to avoid any observed smoke columns in the vicinity of a ground missile emergency.

10−7−5. EXTENDED NOTIFICATION

EN ROUTE

When reports indicate that an emergency will exist for an extended period of time, a Notice to Air Missions may be issued.

Chapter 11. Traffic Management Procedures

Section 1. General

11–1–1. DUTY RESPONSIBILITY

a. The mission of the traffic management system is to balance air traffic demand with system capacity to ensure the maximum efficient utilization of the NAS.

b. TBFM must be used to the maximum extent feasible in preference to miles-in-trail initiatives.

c. It is recognized that the ATCS is integral in the execution of the traffic management mission.

NOTE–
Complete details of TBM, traffic management initiatives and programs can be found in FAA Order JO 7210.3, Facility Operation and Administration.

11–1–2. DUTIES AND RESPONSIBILITIES

a. Supervisory Traffic Management Coordinator–in–Charge (STMCIC) must:

1. Ensure an operational briefing is conducted at least once during the day and evening shifts. Participants must include, at a minimum, the STMCIC, Operations Supervisor–in–Charge (OSMIC)/Controller–in–Charge (CIC) and other interested personnel as designated by facility management. Discussions at the meeting should include meteorological conditions (present and forecasted), staffing, equipment status, runways in use, Airport Arrival Rate (AAR), TBM use, and Traffic Management Initiatives (TMIs) (present and anticipated).

2. Assume responsibility for TMC duties when not staffed.

3. Ensure that TBM operations and TMIs are carried out by personnel providing traffic management services.

4. Where authorized, perform EDST data entries to keep the activation status of designated EDST Airspace Configuration Elements current.

5. Perform assigned actions in the event of an EDST outage or degradation, in accordance with the requirements of FAA Order JO 7210.3, Facility Operation and Administration, and as designated by facility directive.

6. Ensure changes to TBM operations and TMIs are implemented in a timely manner.

b. OS/CIC must:

1. Keep the TMU and affected sectors apprised of situations or circumstances that may cause congestion or delays.

2. Coordinate with the TMU and personnel providing air traffic services to develop appropriate TBM operations or TMIs for sectors and airports in their area of responsibility.

3. Continuously review TBM operations and TMIs affecting their area of responsibility and coordinate with TMU for extensions, revisions, or cancellations.

4. Ensure that TBM operations and TMIs are carried out by personnel providing air traffic services.

5. Where authorized, perform data entries to keep the activation status of designated EDST Airspace Configuration Elements current.

6. Perform assigned actions in the event of an EDST outage or degradation, in accordance with the requirements of FAA Order JO 7210.3, Facility Operation and Administration, and as designated by facility directive.

7. Ensure changes to TBM operations and TMIs are implemented in a timely manner.

c. Personnel providing air traffic services must:

1. Ensure that TBM operations and TMIs are enforced within their area of responsibility. TBM operations and TMIs do not have priority over maintaining:

(a) Separation of aircraft.

(b) Procedural integrity of the sector.

2. Keep the OS/CIC and TMU apprised of situations or circumstances that may cause congestion or delays.

3. Continuously review TBM operations and TMIs affecting their area of responsibility and coordinate with OS/CIC and TMU for extensions, revisions, or cancellations.

4. Where authorized, perform data entries to keep the activation status of designated EDST Airspace Configuration Elements current.

5. Perform assigned actions in the event of an EDST outage or degradation, in accordance with the requirements of FAA Order JO 7210.3, Facility Operation and Administration, and as designated by facility directive.

d. ARTCCs, unless otherwise coordinated, must:

1. Support TBFM operations and monitor TBFM equipment to improve situational awareness for a system approach to TBM operations.

2. Monitor arrival flow for potential metering actions/changes and, if necessary, initiate coordination with all facilities to discuss the change to the metering plan.

e. TRACONs, unless otherwise coordinated, must:

1. Support TBFM operations and monitor TBFM equipment to improve situational awareness for a system approach to TBM operations.

2. Monitor arrival flow for potential metering actions/changes and, if necessary, initiate coordination with all facilities to discuss the change to the metering plan.

3. Schedule internal departures in accordance with specific written procedures and agreements developed with overlying ARTCCs and adjacent facilities.

f. ATCTs, unless otherwise coordinated, must:

1. Monitor TBFM equipment to improve situational awareness for a system approach to TBM operations.

2. When equipped, and departure scheduling is in effect, use automation to obtain a departure release time from the TBM system.

3. When departure scheduling or Call for Release is in effect, release aircraft so they are airborne within a window that extends from 2 minutes prior and ends 1 minute after the assigned time, unless otherwise coordinated.

NOTE–
Coordination may be verbal, electronic, or written.

11–1–3. TIME BASED FLOW MANAGEMENT (TBFM)

During periods of metering, personnel providing air traffic services must:

a. Display TBFM schedule information on the situation display.

b. Comply with TBFM-generated metering times within +/- 1 minute.

1. If TBFM–generated metering time accuracy within +/– 1 minute cannot be used for specific aircraft due to significant jumps in the delay countdown timer (DCT), then TMIs may be used between those aircraft such as miles–in–trail (MIT) or minutes–in–trail (MINIT) to assist in delay absorption until stability resumes.

2. An exception to the requirement to comply within +/- 1 minute may be authorized for certain ARTCC sectors if explicitly defined in an appropriate facility directive.

c. When compliance is not possible, coordinate with OS/CIC, personnel providing traffic management services, and adjacent facilities/sectors as appropriate.

NOTE–
TBFM accuracy of generated metering times is predicated on several factors, including vectoring outside of TBFM route conformance boundaries (route recovery logic), certain trajectory ground speed calculations, and when TMU resequences a specific flight or flight list. Caution should be used in these situations to minimize impact on surrounding sector traffic and complexity levels, flight efficiencies, and user preferences.

Chapter 12. Canadian Airspace Procedures

Section 1. General Control

12−1−1. APPLICATION

Where control responsibility within Canadian airspace has been formally delegated to the FAA by the Transport Canada Aviation Group, apply basic FAA procedures except for the Canadian procedures contained in this chapter.

NOTE−
In 1985, the U.S. and Canada established an agreement recognizing the inherent safety of the ATC procedures exercised by the other country. This agreement permits the use of ATC procedures of one country when that country is exercising ATC in the airspace over the territory of the other country insofar as they are not inconsistent with, or repugnant to, the laws and regulations or unique operational requirements of the country over whose territory such airspace is located. Accordingly, this chapter was revised to include only those Canadian procedures that must be used because of a Canadian regulatory or unique operational requirement.

12−1−2. AIRSPACE CLASSIFICATION

a. Class A airspace. Controlled airspace within which only IFR flights are permitted. Airspace designated from the base of all controlled high level airspace up to and including FL 600.

b. Class B airspace. Controlled airspace within which only IFR and Controlled VFR (CVFR) flights are permitted. Includes all controlled low level airspace above 12,500 feet ASL or at and above the minimum en route IFR altitude, (whichever is higher) up to but not including 18,000 feet ASL. ATC procedures pertinent to IFR flights must be applied to CVFR aircraft.

NOTE−
The CVFR pilot is responsible to maintain VFR flight and visual reference to the ground at all times.

c. Class C airspace. Controlled airspace within which both IFR and VFR flights are permitted, but VFR flights require a clearance from ATC to enter.

d. Class D airspace. Controlled airspace within which both IFR and VFR flights are permitted, but VFR flights do not require a clearance from ATC to enter, however, they must establish two−way communications with the appropriate ATC agency prior to entering the airspace.

e. Class E airspace. Airspace within which both IFR and VFR flights are permitted, but for VFR flight there are no special requirements.

f. Class F airspace. Airspace of defined dimensions within which activities must be confined because of their nature, or within which limitations are imposed upon aircraft operations that are not a part of those activities, or both. Special use airspace may be classified as Class F advisory or Class F restricted.

g. Class G airspace. Uncontrolled airspace within which ATC has neither the authority nor responsibility for exercising control over air traffic.

12−1−3. ONE THOUSAND−ON−TOP

Clear an aircraft to maintain "at least 1,000 feet-on-top" in lieu of "VFR−on−top," provided:

a. The pilot requests it.

NOTE−
It is the pilot's responsibility to ensure that the requested operation can be conducted at least 1,000 feet above all cloud, haze, smoke, or other formation, with a flight visibility of 3 miles or more. A pilot's request can be considered as confirmation that conditions are adequate.

b. The pilot will not operate within Class A or Class B airspace.

12-1-4. SEPARATION

Apply a lateral, longitudinal, or vertical separation minimum between aircraft operating in accordance with an IFR or CVFR clearance, regardless of the weather conditions.

12-1-5. DEPARTURE CLEARANCE/COMMUNICATION FAILURE

Base controller action regarding radio failures in Canadian airspace on the requirement for pilots to comply with Canadian Airspace Regulations, which are similar to 14 CFR Section 91.185; however, the following major difference must be considered when planning control actions. Except when issued alternate radio failure instructions by ATC, pilots will adhere to the following: If flying a turbine-powered (turboprop or turbojet) aircraft and cleared on departure to a point other than the destination, proceed to the destination airport in accordance with the flight plan, maintaining the last assigned altitude or flight level or the minimum en route IFR altitude, whichever is higher, until 10 minutes beyond the point specified in the clearance (clearance limit), and then proceed at altitude(s) or flight level(s) filed in the flight plan. When the aircraft will enter U.S. airspace within 10 minutes after passing the clearance limit, the climb to the flight planned border crossing altitude is to be commenced at the estimated time of crossing the Canada/U.S. boundary.

12-1-6. PARACHUTE JUMPING

Do not authorize parachute jumping without prior permission from the appropriate Canadian authority.

NOTE–
Canadian regulations require written authority from the Ministry of Transport.

12-1-7. SPECIAL VFR (SVFR)

NOTE–
Pilots do not have to be IFR qualified to fly SVFR at night, nor does the aircraft have to be equipped for IFR flight.

a. Within a control zone where there is an airport controller on duty, approve or refuse a pilot's request for SVFR on the basis of current or anticipated IFR traffic only. If approved, specify the period of time during which SVFR flight is permitted.

b. Within a control zone where there is no airport controller on duty, authorize or refuse an aircraft's request for SVFR on the basis of:

1. Current or anticipated IFR traffic, and

2. Official ceiling and visibility reports.

c. Canadian SVFR weather minimums for:

1. Aircraft other than helicopters. Flight visibility (ground visibility when reported) 1 mile.

2. Helicopters. Flight visibility (ground visibility when available) 1/2 mile.

Chapter 13. Decision Support Tools

Section 1. ERAM – En Route

13–1–1. DESCRIPTION

En Route Decision Support Tool (EDST) is an integrated function of ERAM that is used by the sector team in performing its strategic planning responsibilities. EDST uses current plan data, forecast winds, aircraft performance characteristics, and track data to derive expected aircraft trajectories, and to predict conflicts between aircraft and between aircraft and special use or designated airspace. It also provides trial planning and enhanced flight data management capabilities.

NOTE–
For use by the EDST, the current plan is what the En Route Automation System (EAS) predicts an aircraft will fly. This may include clearances that have not yet been issued to the aircraft. Current plans are used to model a flight trajectory and, when applicable, for detecting conflicts.

13–1–2. CONFLICT DETECTION AND RESOLUTION

a. Actively scan EDST information for predicted aircraft-to-aircraft and aircraft-to-airspace alerts.

b. When a conflict probe alert is displayed, evaluate the alert and take appropriate action as early as practical, in accordance with duty priorities.

c. Prioritize the evaluation and resolution of conflict probe alerts to ensure the safe, expeditious, and efficient flow of air traffic.

NOTE–
Conflict probe alerts are based on approved radar separation. Conflict probe does not account for instances in which greater separation may be needed (e.g., non–standard formations, A380) or where reduced separation is permitted (e.g., 3 mile airspace).

d. When a conflict probe alert is displayed and when sector priorities permit, give consideration to the following in determining a solution:

1. Solutions that involve direct routing, altitude changes, removal of a flight direction constraint (i.e., inappropriate altitude for direction of flight), and/or removal of a static restriction for one or more pertinent aircraft.

2. Impact on surrounding sector traffic and complexity levels, flight efficiencies, and user preferences.

e. When the Stop Probe feature is activated for an aircraft, conflict probe for that aircraft shall be restarted before transfer of control, unless otherwise coordinated.

NOTE–
The requirement in subparagraph 13–1–2e does not apply to aircraft entering a non EDST facility.

13–1–3. TRIAL PLANNING

When EDST is operational at the sector and when sector priorities permit, use the trial plan capability to evaluate:

a. Solutions to predicted conflicts.

b. The feasibility of granting user requests.

c. The feasibility of removing a flight direction constraint (i.e., inappropriate altitude for direction of flight) for an aircraft.

d. The feasibility of removing a static restriction for an aircraft.

13-1-4. CONFLICT PROBE-BASED CLEARANCES

When the results of a trial plan based upon a user request indicate the absence of alerts, every effort should be made to grant the user request, unless the change is likely to adversely affect operations at another sector.

13-1-5. THE AIRCRAFT LIST (ACL), DEPARTURE LIST (DL) AND FLIGHT DATA MANAGEMENT

a. The ACL must be used as the sector team's primary source of flight data.

b. Actively scan EDST to identify automated notifications that require sector team action.

c. When an ACL or DL entry has a Remarks indication, the Remarks field of the flight plan must be reviewed. Changes to the Remarks field must also be reviewed.

d. Highlighting an entry on the ACL or DL must be used to indicate the flight requires an action or special attention.

e. The Special Posting Area (SPA) should be used to group aircraft that have special significance (e.g., aircraft to be sequenced, air refueling missions, formations).

f. Sector teams shall post flight progress strips for any nonradar flights.

g. A flight progress strip shall be posted for any flight plan not contained in the EAS.

h. Sector teams shall post any flight progress strip(s) that are deemed necessary for safe or efficient operations. The sector team shall comply with all applicable facility directives to maintain posted flight progress strips.

i. The Drop Track Delete option shall be used in accordance with facility directives.

13-1-6. MANUAL COORDINATION AND THE COORDINATION MENU

a. Where automated coordination with a facility is not available (e.g., an international facility, a VFR tower), use the Coordination Menu or a flight progress strip to annotate manual coordination status, in accordance with facility directives.

b. When the Coordination Menu is used and the flight plan is subsequently changed, remove the yellow coding from the Coordination Indicator after any appropriate action has been taken.

13-1-7. HOLDING

For flights in hold, use the Hold View, Hold Data_Menu, hold message, a flight progress strip, or a facility approved worksheet, to annotate holding instructions, in accordance with facility directives.

13-1-8. RECORDING OF CONTROL DATA

a. All control information not otherwise recorded via automation recordings or voice recordings must be manually recorded using approved methods.

b. When a verbal point out has been approved, remove the yellow color coding on the ACL.

c. When the ACL or DL Free Text Area is used to enter control information, authorized abbreviations must be used. You may use:

1. The clearance abbreviations authorized in TBL 13-1-1.

TBL 13-1-1

Clearance Abbreviations

Abbreviation	Meaning
A	Cleared to airport (point of intended landing)
B	Center clearance delivered
C	ATC clears (when clearance relayed through non-ATC facility)
CAF	Cleared as filed
D	Cleared to depart from the fix
F	Cleared to the fix
H	Cleared to hold and instructions issued
N	Clearance not delivered
O	Cleared to the outer marker
PD	Cleared to climb/descend at pilot's discretion
Q	Cleared to fly specified sectors of a NAVAID defined in terms of courses, bearings, radials, or quadrants within a designated radius
T	Cleared through (for landing and takeoff through intermediate point)
V	Cleared over the fix
X	Cleared to cross (airway, route, radial) at (point)
Z	Tower jurisdiction

2. The miscellaneous abbreviations authorized in TBL 13-1-2.

3. The EDST equivalents for control information symbols authorized in TBL 13-1-3.

4. Plain language markings when it will aid in understanding information.

5. Locally approved abbreviations.

d. When the ACL or DL Free Text Area is used to enter control information, the Free Text Area must remain open and visible. When no longer relevant, the information entered into the Free Text Area must be updated or deleted.

e. Control information entered in the Free Text Area must be used for reference purposes only.

NOTE-
Information entered into the Free Text Area does not pass on handoff and, if necessary, must be coordinated.

TBL 13-1-2

Miscellaneous Abbreviations

Abbreviation	Meaning
BC	Back course approach
CT	Contact approach
FA	Final approach
FMS	Flight management system approach
GPS	GPS approach
I	Initial approach
ILS	ILS approach
MA	Missed approach
NDB	Nondirectional radio beacon approach
OTP	VFR conditions-on-top
PA	Precision approach
PT	Procedure turn
RA	Resolution advisory (Pilot-reported TCAS event)
RH	Runway heading
RNAV	Area navigation approach
RP	Report immediately upon passing (fix/altitude)
RX	Report crossing
SA	Surveillance approach
SI	Straight-in approach
TA	TACAN approach
TL	Turn left
TR	Turn right
VA	Visual approach
VR	VOR approach

TBL 13-1-3

EDST Equivalents for Control Information Symbols

Abbreviation	Meaning
T *dir*	Depart (direction if specified)
↑	Climb and maintain
↓	Descend and maintain
CR	Cruise
AT	At
X	Cross
M	Maintain
/*airway*	Join or intercept (airway, jet route, track, or course)
=	While in controlled airspace
WICA	While in control area
dir ECA	Enter control area
dir OOCA	Out of control area
dir ESA	Cleared to enter surface area. Indicated direction of flight by appropriate compass letter(s)
TSA *alt*	Through surface area and altitude indicated direction of flight by appropriate compass letter(s). Maintain special VFR conditions (altitude if appropriate) while in surface area
250 K	Aircraft requested to adjust speed to 250 knots
–20 K	Aircraft requested to reduce speed 20 knots
+30 K	Aircraft requested to increase speed 30 knots
SVFR	Local Special VFR operations in the vicinity of (name) airport are authorized until (time). Maintain special VFR conditions (altitude if appropriate)
B4	Before
AF	After or Past
/	Until
instructions	Alternate instructions
REST	Restriction
AOB	At or Below
AOA	At or Above

Abbreviation	Meaning
–	From–to (route, time, etc.)
(Alt)B(Alt)	Indicates a block altitude assignment. Altitudes are inclusive, and the first altitude must be lower than the second (Example 310B370)
V *time*	Clearance void if aircraft not off ground by *time*
CL	Pilot canceled flight plan
+*info*+	Information or revised information forwarded
alt	Other than assigned altitude reported Example: **50**
ARC *mi. dir.*	DME arc of VORTAC or TACAN
C *freq.*	Contact (facility) or (freq.), (time, fix, or altitude if appropriate). Insert frequency only when it is other than standard
R	Radar contact
R *alt*	Requested altitude
R/	Radar service terminated
RX	Radar Contact Lost
RV	Radar vector
RVX	Pilot resumed own navigation
HO	Handoff completed
E	Emergency
W	Warning
P	Point out initiated. Indicate the appropriate facility, sector, or position.
FUEL	Minimum fuel
EFC *time*	Expect further clearance at (time)
–*fix*	Direct to fix
FRC	Full route clearance
IAF	Initial approach fix
NORDO	No Radio
PT	Procedure turn
RLS	Release
REQ	Request
SI	Straight in

13-1-9. ACKNOWLEDGEMENT OF AUTOMATED NOTIFICATION

a. The EDST Inappropriate Altitude for Direction of Flight (IAFDOF) feature must be used in the automatic mode (i.e., IAFDOF Manual must remain deselected) unless otherwise authorized in a facility directive.

b. Completion of any required coordination for IAFDOF must be acknowledged on the ACL by removing the IAFDOF coding.

c. Completion of appropriate coordination for an Unsuccessful Transmission Message (UTM) must be acknowledged on the ACL by removing the UTM coding.

d. Issuance of the Expect Departure Clearance Time (EDCT) to the pilot or other control facility must be acknowledged on the DL by removing the EDCT coding.

e. IAFDOF, UTM, or EDCT coding must be acknowledged only after the appropriate action has been completed.

f. The first sector which displays Embedded Route Text (ERT) coding must issue and send/acknowledge the route prior to initiating a hand-off unless verbally coordinated or as specified in appropriate facility directives. Do not send/acknowledge ERT coding unless the sector has track control for the flight or it has been otherwise coordinated.

g. Route Action Notifications (RAN) such as ATC preferred routes or route processing errors must be amended at the first control position that displays the RAN unless verbally coordinated or as specified in appropriate facility directives. Do not remove RAN coding unless the sector has track control or it has been otherwise coordinated.

13-1-10. CURRENCY OF TRAJECTORY INFORMATION

a. The sector team shall perform automation entries in a timely manner.

NOTE–

1. *Conflict probe accuracy requires timely updates of data used to model each flight's trajectory. If this data is not current, the aircraft entries and notification of probe results for surrounding sectors and facilities, as well as the subject sector, may be misleading.*

2. *Data used to model an individual aircraft's trajectory includes route of flight, assigned and interim altitudes, application/removal of an adapted restriction for that flight, and aircraft type.*

b. An exception to the requirement to enter or update interim altitudes may be authorized for certain ARTCC sectors if explicitly defined in an appropriate facility directive.

NOTE–

Conflict probe accuracy in assigning alert notification is dependent upon entry/update of a flight's interim altitude.

13-1-11. DELAY REPORTING

a. Adhere to all applicable delay reporting directives.

b. Delay information must be recorded. Delay information may be automatically recorded via use of the ERAM Hold Data Menu, ERAM Hold View, a hold message, or manually on flight progress strips or facility-approved worksheets, in accordance with the facility-defined standard.

NOTE–

When using the ERAM Hold Data Menu or Hold View, delays are automatically recorded when the aircraft is cleared out of hold.

13-1-12. OVERDUE AIRCRAFT

Upon receipt of the overdue aircraft notification take appropriate actions set forth in Chapter 10, Section 3, Overdue aircraft.

NOTE–
ESDT overdue aircraft notification is based on radar track data. Updating an aircraft's route of fight will remove the overdue aircraft notification.

13–1–13. USE OF GRAPHICS PLAN DISPLAY (GPD)

a. Graphic depictions of flight trajectories may be used only to aid in situational awareness and strategic planning.

b. Do not use trajectory–based positions as a substitute for radar track position.

c. Do not use trajectory–based altitude in lieu of Mode C for altitude confirmation.

d. Do not use the GPD for radar identification, position information, transfer of radar identification, radar separation, correlation, or point outs.

13–1–14. FORECAST WINDS

In the event that current forecast wind data are not available, continue use of conflict probe and trial planning with appropriate recognition that alert and trajectory data may be affected.

13–1–15. INTERFACILITY CONNECTIVITY

In the event of a loss of connectivity to an adjacent ERAM facility, continue use of EDST with appropriate recognition that alert data may be affected.

13–1–16. SURVEILLANCE AND FLIGHT DATA OUTAGES

In the event of a surveillance or flight data outage, electronic flight data may be used to support situational awareness while the facility transitions to alternate automation capabilities or non radar procedures.

13–1–17. AIRSPACE CONFIGURATION ELEMENTS

a. Airspace Configuration Elements are:

1. Special Activity Airspace (SAA).

2. Airport Stream Filters (ASF).

3. Adapted restrictions.

b. Where assigned as a sector responsibility by facility directive, the sector team shall update Airspace Configuration Elements to reflect current status.

NOTE–
Unless otherwise covered in an LOA or facility directive, activating or scheduling the SAA in the Airspace Status View does NOT constitute coordination for activation of airspace.

c. For Airspace Configuration Elements designated as a sector responsibility, notify the operations supervisor when the status of an Airspace Configuration Element has been modified.

Section 2. ATOP - Oceanic

The following procedures are applicable to the operation of the ATOP Oceanic Air Traffic Control (ATC) System.

13-2-1. DESCRIPTION

a. The ATOP ATC System is utilized in designated en route/oceanic airspace. ATOP includes both surveillance and flight data processing, which provides the controllers with automated decision support tools to establish, monitor and maintain separation between aircraft, and aircraft to airspace and terrain.

b. ATOP capabilities include:

1. MEARTS based radar surveillance processing.

2. Conflict Prediction and Reporting.

3. Automatic Dependent Surveillance- Broadcast (ADS-B).

4. Automatic Dependent Surveillance- Contract (ADS-C).

5. Controller Pilot Data Link Communications (CPDLC).

6. ATS Interfacility Data Communications (AIDC).

7. Additional Decision Support Tools used primarily for situational awareness.

8. Electronic Flight Data including Electronic Flight Strips.

13-2-2. CONFLICT DETECTION AND RESOLUTION

The controller must use the most accurate information available to initiate, monitor, and maintain separation.

a. Apply the following procedures in airspace where conflict probe is being utilized as a decision support tool:

1. Conflict Probe Results.

(a) Controllers must assume that the conflict probe separation calculations are accurate.

(b) Unless otherwise prescribed in subparagraph a3, controllers must utilize the results from conflict probe to initiate and maintain the prescribed separation minima.

2. Conflict Resolution.

(a) When a controller is alerted to a conflict, which will occur in his/her sector, take the appropriate action to resolve the conflict.

(b) The controller responsible for resolving a conflict must evaluate the alert and take appropriate action as early as practical, in accordance with duty priorities, alert priority, and operational considerations.

(c) Unless otherwise specified in facility directives, the controller must take immediate action to resolve any "red" conflicts.

3. Overriding Conflict Probe.

(a) Controllers must not override conflict probe except for the following situations:

(1) The application of a separation standard not recognized by conflict probe listed in subparagraph a8(a), or as identified by facility directive.

(2) When action has been taken to resolve the identified conflict and separation has been ensured, or

(3) Control responsibility has been delegated to another sector or facility, or

(4) Other situations as specified in facility directives.

(b) Controllers must continue to ensure that separation is maintained until the overridden conflict is resolved.

4. Use of Probe when Issuing Clearances. Utilize conflict probe results when issuing a clearance to ensure that any potential conflict has been given thorough consideration.

5. Use of Probe when Accepting Manual Transfers. Prior to manually accepting an aircraft transfer from an external facility ensure that the coordinated flight profile is accurately entered, conflict probe initiated and, if necessary, action is taken to resolve any potential conflicts.

6. Trial Probe. The controller can utilize trial probe to assess whether there are any potential conflicts with a proposed clearance or when performing manual coordination.

NOTE–
Once initiated, trial probe does not take into account any changes made to the proposed profile or to any other flight profile in the system. It is an assessment by conflict probe of the current situation at the time the controller enters the trial probe. A trial probe does not alleviate the controller from performing a conflict probe when issuing a clearance or accepting a transfer.

7. System Unable to Perform Conflict Probe for a Specific Aircraft.

(a) If a flight's profile becomes corrupted, conflict probe may not be able to correctly monitor separation for that flight. Take the necessary steps to correct an aircraft's flight plan when conflict probe could not be performed.

(b) In addition, after verifying flight plan data accuracy, utilize other decision support tools to establish and maintain the appropriate separation minima until such time that conflict probe can be utilized.

8. Conflict Probe Limitations.

(a) Conflict Probe does not support the following separation minima:

(1) Subparagraph 8–4–2a2 – Nonintersecting paths.

(2) Subparagraph 8–4–2d – Intersecting flight paths with variable width protected airspace.

(3) Subparagraph 8–4–3a – Reduction of Route Protected Airspace, below FL 240.

(4) Subparagraph 8–4–3b – Reduction of Route Protected Airspace, at and above FL 240.

(5) Subparagraph 8–4–4a1 – Same NAVAID: VOR/VORTAC/TACAN.

(6) Subparagraph 8–4–4a2 – Same NAVAID: NDB.

(7) Subparagraph 8–4–4c – Dead Reckoning.

(8) Paragraph 8–5–4 – Same Direction.

(9) Paragraph 8–8–5 – VFR Climb and Descent.

b. Additional Decision Support Tools: These support tools include: range/bearing, time of passing, intercept angle, the aircraft situation display (ASD) and electronic flight data.

1. The results provided by these additional decision support/controller tools can be used by the controller for maintaining situational awareness and monitoring flight profile information, and for establishing and maintaining separation standards not supported by probe, or when probe is unavailable.

2. Under no circumstances must the controller utilize any of the additional decision support tools to override probe results when the applicable separation standard is supported by probe and none of the other conditions for overriding probe apply.

13–2–3. INFORMATION MANAGEMENT

a. Currency of Information: The sector team is responsible for ensuring that manually entered data is accurate and timely. Ensure that nonconformant messages are handled in a timely manner and that the flight's profile is updated as necessary.

NOTE–
Conflict probe accuracy requires timely updates of data used to model each flight's trajectory. If this data is not current, the aircraft flight profile and probe results may be misleading.

b. Data Block Management.

1. Ensure that the data block reflects the most current flight information and controller applied indicators as specified in facility directives.

2. Ensure that appropriate and timely action is taken when a special condition code is indicated in the data block.

c. Electronic Flight Strip Management.

1. Electronic flight strips must be maintained in accordance with facility directives and the following:

(a) Annotations. Ensure that annotations are kept up to date.

(b) Reduced Separation Flags. Ensure the flags listed below are selected appropriately for each flight:

(1) M– Mach Number Technique (MNT).

(2) R– Reduced MNT.

(3) D– Distance–based longitudinal.

(4) W– Reduced Vertical Separation Minimum (RVSM).

(c) Degraded RNP. Select when an aircraft has notified ATC of a reduction in navigation capability that affects the applicable separation minima.

(d) Restrictions. Ensure restrictions accurately reflect the cleared profile.

d. Queue Management.

1. Manage all sector and coordination queues in accordance with the appropriate message priority and the controller's priority of duties.

2. In accordance with facility directives, ensure that the messages directed to the error queue are processed in a timely manner.

e. Window/List Management.

1. Ensure that the situation display window title bar is not obscured by other windows and/or lists.

NOTE–
The title bar changes color to denote when priority information on the ASD is being obscured or is out of view.

2. In accordance with facility directives, ensure that designated windows and/or lists are displayed at all times.

13–2–4. CONTROLLER PILOT DATA LINK COMMUNICATIONS (CPDLC)

a. Means of communication.

1. When CPDLC is available and CPDLC connected aircraft are operating outside of VHF coverage, CPDLC must be used as the primary means of communication.

2. Voice communications may be utilized for CPDLC aircraft when it will provide an operational advantage and/or when workload or equipment capabilities demand.

3. When CPDLC is being utilized, a voice backup must exist (e.g., HF, SATCOM, Third party).

4. When a pilot communicates via CPDLC, the response should be via CPDLC.

5. To the extent possible, the CPDLC message set should be used in lieu of free text messages.

NOTE–
The use of the CPDLC message set ensures the proper "closure" of CPDLC exchanges.

b. Transfer of Communications to the Next Facility.

1. When the receiving facility is capable of CPDLC communications, the data link transfer is automatic and is accomplished within facility adapted parameters.

2. When a receiving facility is not CPDLC capable, the transfer of communications must be made in accordance with local directives and Letters of Agreement (LOAs).

c. Abnormal conditions.

1. If any portion of the automated transfer fails, the controller should attempt to initiate the transfer manually. If unable to complete the data link transfer, the controller should advise the pilot to log on to the next facility and send an End Service (EOS) message.

2. If CPDLC fails, voice communications must be utilized until CPDLC connections can be reestablished.

3. If the CPDLC connection is lost on a specific aircraft, the controller should send a connection request message (CR1) or advise the pilot via backup communications to log on again.

4. If CPDLC service is to be canceled, the controller must advise the pilot as early as possible to facilitate a smooth transition to voice communications. Workload permitting, the controller should also advise the pilot of the reason for the termination of data link.

5. When there is uncertainty that a clearance was delivered to an aircraft via CPDLC, the controller must continue to protect the airspace associated with the clearance until an appropriate operational response is received from the flight crew. If an expected operational response to a clearance is not received, the controller will initiate appropriate action to ensure that the clearance was received by the flight crew. On initial voice contact with aircraft preface the message with the following:

PHRASEOLOGY–
(Call Sign) CPDLC Failure, (message).

13–2–5. COORDINATION

In addition to the requirements set forth in Chapter 8, Offshore/Oceanic Procedures, Section 2, Coordination, automated coordination must constitute complete coordination between ATOP sectors, both internally and between sectors across adjacent ATOP facilities, except:

a. When the aircraft is in conflict with another in the receiving sector, or

b. When otherwise specified in facility directives or LOA.

13–2–6. TEAM RESPONSIBILITIES – MULTIPLE PERSON OPERATION

a. When operating in a multiple controller operation at a workstation, ensure all ATC tasks are completed according to their priority of duties.

b. Multiple controller operation must be accomplished according to facility directives.

Appendix A. Standard Operating Practice (SOP) for the Transfer of Position Responsibility

1. PURPOSE

This appendix prescribes the method and step−by−step process for conducting a position relief briefing and transferring position responsibility from one specialist to another.

2. DISCUSSION

a. In all operational facilities, the increase in traffic density and the need for the expeditious movement of traffic without compromising safety have emphasized the importance of the position relief process.

b. The contents, methods, and practices used for position relief and briefings vary among personnel, and pertinent information is often forgotten or incompletely covered. Major problems occur whenever there is a heavy reliance upon memory, unsupported by routines or systematic reminders. This SOP addresses the complete task of transferring position responsibility and the associated relief briefing.

c. Position relief unavoidably provides workload for specialists at the time of relief. The intent of this SOP is to make the transfer of position responsibility take place smoothly and to ensure a complete transfer of information with a minimum amount of workload. The method takes advantage of a self−briefing concept in which the relieving specialist obtains needed status information by reading from the Status Information Area/s to begin the relief process. Up to the moment information related to the control of aircraft or vehicular movements requires verbal exchanges between specialists during the relief process. The method also specifies the moment when the transfer of position responsibility occurs.

d. In the final part of the relief process, the specialist being relieved monitors and reviews the position to ensure that nothing has been overlooked or incorrectly displayed and that the transfer of position responsibility occurred with a complete briefing.

3. TERMS

The following terms are important for a complete understanding of this SOP:

a. Status Information Area (SIA). Manual or automatic displays of the current status of position related equipment and operational conditions or procedures.

b. Written Notes. Manually recorded items of information kept at designated locations on the position of operation. They may be an element of the Status Information Area/s.

c. Checklist. An ordered listing of items to be covered during a position relief.

4. PRECAUTIONS

a. Specialists involved in the position relief process should not rush or be influenced to rush.

b. During position operation, each item of status information which is or may be an operational factor for the relieving specialist should be recorded as soon as it is operationally feasible so that it will not be forgotten or incorrectly recorded.

c. Extra care should be taken when more than one specialist relieves or is being relieved from a position at the same time; e.g., combining or decombining positions. Such simultaneous reliefs should be approached with caution.

5. RESPONSIBILITIES

a. The specialist being relieved must be responsible for ensuring that any pertinent status information of which he/she is aware is relayed to the relieving specialist and is either:

1. Accurately displayed in the Status Information Area/s for which he/she has responsibility, or

2. Relayed to the position having responsibility for accurately displaying the status information.

b. The relieving specialist must be responsible for ensuring that, prior to accepting responsibility for the position, any unresolved questions pertaining to the operation of the position are resolved.

c. The relieving specialist and the specialist being relieved must share equal responsibility for the completeness and accuracy of the position relief briefing.

d. The specialists engaged in a position relief must conduct the relief process at the position being relieved unless other procedures have been established and authorized by the facility air traffic manager.

NOTE–
The "sharing" of this responsibility means that the specialist being relieved is obligated to provide a complete, accurate briefing and the relieving specialist is obligated to ensure that a briefing takes place and is to his/her total satisfaction.

6. STEP–BY–STEP PROCESS

a. PREVIEW THE POSITION

Relieving Specialist	Specialist Being Relieved
1. Follow checklist and review the Status Information Area(s).	
NOTE– *This sub-step may be replaced by an authorized pre–position briefing provided an equivalent review of checklist items is accomplished.*	
2. Observe position equipment, operational situation, and the work environment. **3.** Listen to voice communications and observe other operational actions. **4.** Observe current and pending aircraft and vehicular traffic and correlate with flight and other movement information. **5.** Indicate to the specialist being relieved that the position has been previewed and that the verbal briefing may begin.	
NOTE– *Substeps 6a2, 3, and 4 may be conducted concurrently or in any order.*	

b. VERBAL BRIEFING

Relieving Specialist	Specialist Being Relieved
	1. Brief the relieving specialist on the abnormal status of items not listed on the Status Information Area(s) as well as on any items of special interest calling for verbal explanation or additional discussion. **2.** Brief on reported weather and other weather related information. **3.** Brief on traffic if applicable. **4.** Brief communication status of all known aircraft except for ERAM facilities using Voice Communication Indicator (VCI).
5. Ask questions necessary to ensure a complete understanding of the operational situation.	
	6. Completely answer any questions asked.

c. ASSUMPTION OF POSITION RESPONSIBILITY

Relieving Specialist	Specialist Being Relieved
1. Make a statement or otherwise indicate to the specialist being relieved that position responsibility has been assumed.	
	2. Release the position to the relieving specialist and mentally note the time.

d. REVIEW THE POSITION

Relieving Specialist	Specialist Being Relieved
1. Check, verify, and update the information obtained in steps 6a and b.	
2. Check position equipment in accordance with existing directives.	
	3. Review checklist, Status Information Area/s, written notes, and other prescribed sources of information and advise the relieving specialist of known omissions, updates, or inaccuracies.
	4. Observe overall position operation to determine if assistance is needed.
	5. If assistance is needed, provide or summon it as appropriate.
	6. Advise the appropriate position regarding known Status Information Area(s) omissions, updates, or inaccuracies.
	7. Sign-on the relieving specialist with the time as noted in step 6c2.
	8. Sign off the position in accordance with existing directives or otherwise indicate that the relief process is complete.

Appendix B. Standard Operating Practice (SOP) for Aircraft Deviating for Weather Near Active Special Activity Airspace (SAA)

The procedures listed below must be applied and contained in a facility SOP when aircraft deviate into and/or near an active or scheduled SAA:

1. PURPOSE

This appendix prescribes the method and step–by–step process for handling aircraft deviations for weather near active Special Activity Airspace (SAA). The procedures are intended to work in parallel to the preventive procedures outlined in FAA Order JO 7210.3, Facility Operation and Administration, subparagraph 18–2–4a9, which must be applied when weather is scheduled to impact an active or scheduled SAA.

2. DISCUSSION

a. In all operational facilities, the increase in traffic density and the need for the expeditious movement of traffic without compromising safety have emphasized the importance of handling aircraft deviations for weather in the vicinity of active SAA.

b. The methods, and practices used for handling aircraft requesting or initiating deviations off of their filed route due to weather require time critical responses to the request or in response to observed course deviations. Major issues can occur whenever there is a heavy reliance upon reactive control actions when not performed according to this handbook and the procedures outlined in FAA Order JO 7210.3.

c. Course deviations in areas near active SAA's increase the workload for specialists at the time of their request or observation. The intent of this SOP is to make the handling of the requested deviation or to correct the observed course deviation take place smoothly and to ensure a safe operation with a minimum amount of workload.

3. TERMS

The following terms are important for a complete understanding of this SOP:

a. Status Information Area (SIA). Manual or automatic displays of the current status of position related equipment and operational conditions or procedures.

b. Special Activity Airspace (SAA). Airspace of defined dimensions as an Alert Area, Controlled Firing Area, Military Operations Area (MOA), Prohibited Area, Restricted Area or Warning Area.

c. Deviations. A departure from a current clearance, such as an off course maneuvers to avoid weather or turbulence.

d. Using Agency. The using agency is the military unit or other organization whose activity established the requirement for the SAA. The using agency is responsible for ensuring that:

1. The airspace is used only for its designated purpose.

2. Proper scheduling procedures are established and utilized.

3. The controlling agency is kept informed of changes in scheduled activity, to include the completion of activities for the day.

4. A point of contact is made available to enable the controlling agency to verify schedules, and coordinate access for emergencies, weather diversions, etc.

5. An ATC facility may be designated as the using agency for joint–use areas when that facility has been granted priority for use of the airspace in a joint–use letter of procedure or letter of agreement.

4. PRECAUTIONS

a. Unless clearance of nonparticipating aircraft in/through/adjacent to an active SAA is provided for in a Letter of Agreement or Letter of Procedure, any clearance issued to a nonparticipating aircraft must ensure separation from that SAA by the appropriate minima specified in paragraph 9–3–2.

b. The specialist receiving a request for a route deviation in the vicinity of an active SAA cannot issue a clearance into the active SAA airspace, unless the provisions of paragraph 9–3–4 of this handbook are applied. The FAA has no jurisdictional authority over the use of non–joint use prohibited/restricted/warning area airspace; therefore, clearance cannot be issued for flight therein without appropriate approval.

c. If the specialist is able to coordinate approval for entry into the SAA from the using agency, a clearance to the aircraft complying with the provisions coordinated with the using agency can be issued; the specialist must notify the OS/CIC of this situation and of subsequent requests or deviations from other aircraft in the same area.

d. Use of Code 7700 for aircraft deviations into active SAA is not encouraged, particularly in situations involving multiple aircraft. Positive identification of aircraft may be lost if an aircraft deviates from flight plan track, particularly in the event of a momentary loss of radar or other interruption in tracking.

5. RESPONSIBILITY:

If a deviation occurs that causes an aircraft to enter SAA the air traffic team must follow the procedures outlined below:

a. Attempt the following:

1. Handoff the aircraft to the Using Agency and transfer communications; or

2. Point Out the aircraft to the Using Agency. The controller must:

(a) Continue to provide safety alerts and traffic advisories, as appropriate, to the affected aircraft.

(b) Continue to coordinate with the Using Agency until the situation is resolved.

(c) Assist the aircraft in exiting the SAA.

3. If the handoff or point out is unsuccessful, the controller must:

(a) If able, advise the Using Agency of the pilot's actions.

(b) Provide safety alerts and traffic advisories, as appropriate.

(c) Assist the aircraft in exiting the SAA as quickly as the weather allows.

(d) Continue to coordinate with the Using Agency until the situation is resolved.

4. If no approval to enter the SAA is given by the using agency:

(a) The specialist must advise the aircraft requesting the course deviation, or deviating toward the SAA, the status of the SAA, and that no clearance can be issued permitting entry into the airspace or;

(b) If an alternative course, which remains clear of the active SAA, is available, offer it to the pilot of the aircraft in question.

5. If the pilot of the nonparticipating aircraft exercises their discretion to deviate from that clearance which ensures separation from an active SAA, and the track of the aircraft will not maintain the required minima from an active SAA, controllers must ascertain if the pilot is exercising emergency authority:

(a) If so, provide assistance and obtain information as provided in Chapter 10, Emergencies.

(b) If not, provide appropriate pilot deviation notification as specified in paragraph 2–1–26, Pilot Deviation Notification.

PILOT/CONTROLLER GLOSSARY

PURPOSE

a. This Glossary was compiled to promote a common understanding of the terms used in the Air Traffic Control system. It includes those terms which are intended for pilot/controller communications. Those terms most frequently used in pilot/controller communications are printed in ***bold italics***. The definitions are primarily defined in an operational sense applicable to both users and operators of the National Airspace System. Use of the Glossary will preclude any misunderstandings concerning the system's design, function, and purpose.

b. Because of the international nature of flying, terms used in the Lexicon, published by the International Civil Aviation Organization (ICAO), are included when they differ from FAA definitions. These terms are followed by "[ICAO]." For the reader's convenience, there are also cross references to related terms in other parts of the Glossary and to other documents, such as the Code of Federal Regulations (CFR) and the Aeronautical Information Manual (AIM).

c. Terms used in this glossary that apply to flight service station (FSS) roles are included when they differ from air traffic control functions. These terms are followed by "[FSS]."

d. This Glossary will be revised, as necessary, to maintain a common understanding of the system.

EXPLANATION OF CHANGES

e. Terms Added:
CHART SUPPLEMENT
CHART SUPPLEMENT ALASKA
CHART SUPPLEMENT PACIFIC

f. Terms Modified:
AERONAUTICAL INFORMATION PUBLICATION (AIP)
AIR TRAFFIC CONTROL SYSTEM COMMAND CENTER (ATCSCC)
ALPHANUMERIC DISPLAY
ALTITUDE READOUT
AUTOMATED UNICOM
CHART SUPPLEMENT U.S.
NAVAID CLASSES
PRECIPITATION RADAR WEATHER DESCRIPTIONS
ROUTE ACTION NOTIFICATION
SAFETY LOGIC SYSTEM ALERTS
TERMINAL VFR RADAR SERVICE
TIE–IN FACILITY
UNICOM
VOT

g. Editorial/format changes were made where necessary. Revision bars were not used due to the insignificant nature of the changes.

A

AAM–
(See ADVANCED AIR MOBILITY.)

AAR–
(See AIRPORT ARRIVAL RATE.)
(See ADAPTED ROUTES.)

ABBREVIATED IFR FLIGHT PLANS– An authorization by ATC requiring pilots to submit only that information needed for the purpose of ATC. It includes only a small portion of the usual IFR flight plan information. In certain instances, this may be only aircraft identification, location, and pilot request. Other information may be requested if needed by ATC for separation/control purposes. It is frequently used by aircraft which are airborne and desire an instrument approach or by aircraft which are on the ground and desire a climb to VFR-on-top.
(See VFR-ON-TOP.)
(Refer to AIM.)

ABEAM– An aircraft is "abeam" a fix, point, or object when that fix, point, or object is approximately 90 degrees to the right or left of the aircraft track. Abeam indicates a general position rather than a precise point.

ABORT– To terminate a preplanned aircraft maneuver; e.g., an aborted takeoff.

ABRR–
(See AIRBORNE REROUTE)

AC–
(See ADVISORY CIRCULAR.)

ACC [ICAO]–
(See ICAO term AREA CONTROL CENTER.)

ACCELERATE-STOP DISTANCE AVAILABLE– The runway plus stopway length declared available and suitable for the acceleration and deceleration of an airplane aborting a takeoff.

ACCELERATE-STOP DISTANCE AVAILABLE [ICAO]– The length of the take-off run available plus the length of the stopway if provided.

ACDO–
(See AIR CARRIER DISTRICT OFFICE.)

ACKNOWLEDGE– Let me know that you have received and understood this message.

ACL–
(See AIRCRAFT LIST.)

ACLS–
(See AUTOMATIC CARRIER LANDING SYSTEM.)

ACROBATIC FLIGHT– An intentional maneuver involving an abrupt change in an aircraft's attitude, an abnormal attitude, or abnormal acceleration not necessary for normal flight.
(See ICAO term ACROBATIC FLIGHT.)
(Refer to 14 CFR Part 91.)

ACROBATIC FLIGHT [ICAO]– Maneuvers intentionally performed by an aircraft involving an abrupt change in its attitude, an abnormal attitude, or an abnormal variation in speed.

ACTIVE RUNWAY–
(See RUNWAY IN USE/ACTIVE RUNWAY/DUTY RUNWAY.)

ACTUAL NAVIGATION PERFORMANCE (ANP)−
(See REQUIRED NAVIGATION PERFORMANCE.)

ADAPTED ROUTES− Departure and/or arrival routes that are adapted in ARTCC ERAM computers to accomplish inter/intrafacility controller coordination and to ensure that flight data is posted at the proper control positions. Adapted routes are automatically applied to flight plans where appropriate. When the workload or traffic situation permits, controllers may provide radar vectors or assign requested routes to minimize circuitous routing. Adapted routes are usually confined to one ARTCC's area and are referred to by the following names or abbreviations:

a. Adapted Arrival Route (AAR). A specific arrival route from an appropriate en route point to an airport or terminal area. It may be included in a Standard Terminal Arrival (STAR) or a Preferred IFR Route.

b. Adapted Departure Route (ADR). A specific departure route from an airport or terminal area to an en route point where there is no further need for flow control. It may be included in an Instrument Departure Procedure (DP) or a Preferred IFR Route.

c. Adapted Departure and Arrival Route (ADAR). A route between two terminals which are within or immediately adjacent to one ARTCC's area. ADARs are similar to Preferred IFR Routes and may share components, but they are not synonymous.
(See PREFFERED IFR ROUTES.)

ADAR−
(See ADAPTED ROUTES.)

ADDITIONAL SERVICES− Advisory information provided by ATC which includes but is not limited to the following:

a. Traffic advisories.

b. Vectors, when requested by the pilot, to assist aircraft receiving traffic advisories to avoid observed traffic.

c. Altitude deviation information of 300 feet or more from an assigned altitude as observed on a verified (reading correctly) automatic altitude readout (Mode C).

d. Advisories that traffic is no longer a factor.

e. Weather and chaff information.

f. Weather assistance.

g. Bird activity information.

h. Holding pattern surveillance. Additional services are provided to the extent possible contingent only upon the controller's capability to fit them into the performance of higher priority duties and on the basis of limitations of the radar, volume of traffic, frequency congestion, and controller workload. The controller has complete discretion for determining if he/she is able to provide or continue to provide a service in a particular case. The controller's reason not to provide or continue to provide a service in a particular case is not subject to question by the pilot and need not be made known to him/her.
(See TRAFFIC ADVISORIES.)
(Refer to AIM.)

ADF−
(See AUTOMATIC DIRECTION FINDER.)

ADIZ−
(See AIR DEFENSE IDENTIFICATION ZONE.)

ADLY−
(See ARRIVAL DELAY.)

ADMINISTRATOR− The Federal Aviation Administrator or any person to whom he/she has delegated his/her authority in the matter concerned.

ADR−
(See ADAPTED ROUTES.)
(See AIRPORT DEPARTURE RATE.)

ADS [ICAO]–
(See ICAO term AUTOMATIC DEPENDENT SURVEILLANCE.)

ADS–B–
(See AUTOMATIC DEPENDENT SURVEILLANCE–BROADCAST.)

ADS–C–
(See AUTOMATIC DEPENDENT SURVEILLANCE–CONTRACT.)

ADVANCED AIR MOBILITY (AAM)–A transportation system that transports people and property by air between two points in the NAS using aircraft with advanced technologies, including electric aircraft or electric vertical takeoff and landing aircraft, in both controlled and uncontrolled airspace.

ADVISE INTENTIONS– Tell me what you plan to do.

ADVISORY– Advice and information provided to assist pilots in the safe conduct of flight and aircraft movement.
(See ADVISORY SERVICE.)

ADVISORY CIRCULAR (AC)– An FAA publication, advisory and descriptive in nature, which is not regulatory.

ADVISORY FREQUENCY– The appropriate frequency to be used for Airport Advisory Service.
(See LOCAL AIRPORT ADVISORY.)
(See UNICOM.)
(Refer to ADVISORY CIRCULAR NO. 90-66.)
(Refer to AIM.)

ADVISORY SERVICE– Advice and information provided by a facility to assist pilots in the safe conduct of flight and aircraft movement.
(See ADDITIONAL SERVICES.)
(See LOCAL AIRPORT ADVISORY.)
(See RADAR ADVISORY.)
(See SAFETY ALERT.)
(See TRAFFIC ADVISORIES.)
(Refer to AIM.)

ADW–
(See ARRIVAL DEPARTURE WINDOW)

AERIAL REFUELING– A procedure used by the military to transfer fuel from one aircraft to another during flight.
(Refer to VFR/IFR Wall Planning Charts.)

AERODROME– A defined area on land or water (including any buildings, installations and equipment) intended to be used either wholly or in part for the arrival, departure, and movement of aircraft.

AERODROME BEACON [ICAO]– Aeronautical beacon used to indicate the location of an aerodrome from the air.

AERODROME CONTROL SERVICE [ICAO]– Air traffic control service for aerodrome traffic.

AERODROME CONTROL TOWER [ICAO]– A unit established to provide air traffic control service to aerodrome traffic.

AERODROME ELEVATION [ICAO]– The elevation of the highest point of the landing area.

AERODROME TRAFFIC CIRCUIT [ICAO]– The specified path to be flown by aircraft operating in the vicinity of an aerodrome.

AERONAUTICAL BEACON− A visual NAVAID displaying flashes of white and/or colored light to indicate the location of an airport, a heliport, a landmark, a certain point of a Federal airway in mountainous terrain, or an obstruction.

(See AIRPORT ROTATING BEACON.)
(Refer to AIM.)

AERONAUTICAL CHART− A map used in air navigation containing all or part of the following: topographic features, hazards and obstructions, navigation aids, navigation routes, designated airspace, and airports. Commonly used aeronautical charts are:

a. Sectional Aeronautical Charts (1:500,000)− Designed for visual navigation of slow or medium speed aircraft. Topographic information on these charts features the portrayal of relief and a judicious selection of visual check points for VFR flight. Aeronautical information includes visual and radio aids to navigation, airports, controlled airspace, permanent special use airspace (SUA), obstructions, and related data.

b. VFR Terminal Area Charts (1:250,000)− Depict Class B airspace which provides for the control or segregation of all the aircraft within Class B airspace. The chart depicts topographic information and aeronautical information which includes visual and radio aids to navigation, airports, controlled airspace, permanent SUA, obstructions, and related data.

c. En Route Low Altitude Charts− Provide aeronautical information for en route instrument navigation (IFR) in the low altitude stratum. Information includes the portrayal of airways, limits of controlled airspace, position identification and frequencies of radio aids, selected airports, minimum en route and minimum obstruction clearance altitudes, airway distances, reporting points, permanent SUA, and related data. Area charts, which are a part of this series, furnish terminal data at a larger scale in congested areas.

d. En Route High Altitude Charts− Provide aeronautical information for en route instrument navigation (IFR) in the high altitude stratum. Information includes the portrayal of jet routes, identification and frequencies of radio aids, selected airports, distances, time zones, special use airspace, and related information.

e. Instrument Approach Procedure (IAP) Charts− Portray the aeronautical data which is required to execute an instrument approach to an airport. These charts depict the procedures, including all related data, and the airport diagram. Each procedure is designated for use with a specific type of electronic navigation system including NDB, TACAN, VOR, ILS RNAV and GLS. These charts are identified by the type of navigational aid(s)/equipment required to provide final approach guidance.

f. Instrument Departure Procedure (DP) Charts− Designed to expedite clearance delivery and to facilitate transition between takeoff and en route operations. Each DP is presented as a separate chart and may serve a single airport or more than one airport in a given geographical location.

g. Standard Terminal Arrival (STAR) Charts− Designed to expedite air traffic control arrival procedures and to facilitate transition between en route and instrument approach operations. Each STAR procedure is presented as a separate chart and may serve a single airport or more than one airport in a given geographical location.

h. Airport Taxi Charts− Designed to expedite the efficient and safe flow of ground traffic at an airport. These charts are identified by the official airport name; e.g., Ronald Reagan Washington National Airport.

(See ICAO term AERONAUTICAL CHART.)

AERONAUTICAL CHART [ICAO]− A representation of a portion of the earth, its culture and relief, specifically designated to meet the requirements of air navigation.

AERONAUTICAL INFORMATION MANUAL (AIM)− A primary FAA publication whose purpose is to instruct airmen about operating in the National Airspace System of the U.S. It provides basic flight information, ATC Procedures and general instructional information concerning health, medical facts, factors affecting flight safety, accident and hazard reporting, and types of aeronautical charts and their use.

AERONAUTICAL INFORMATION PUBLICATION (AIP) [ICAO]− A publication issued by or with the authority of a State and containing aeronautical information of a lasting character essential to air navigation.

(See CHART SUPPLEMENT.)

AERONAUTICAL INFORMATION SERVICES (AIS)− A facility in Silver Spring, MD, established by FAA to operate a central aeronautical information service for the collection, validation, and dissemination of aeronautical data in support of the activities of government, industry, and the aviation community. The information is published in the National Flight Data Digest.

(See NATIONAL FLIGHT DATA DIGEST.)

AFFIRMATIVE– Yes.

AFIS–

(See AUTOMATIC FLIGHT INFORMATION SERVICE – ALASKA FSSs ONLY.)

AFP–

(See AIRSPACE FLOW PROGRAM.)

AHA–

(See AIRCRAFT HAZARD AREA.)

AIM–

(See AERONAUTICAL INFORMATION MANUAL.)

AIP [ICAO]–

(See ICAO term AERONAUTICAL INFORMATION PUBLICATION.)

AIR CARRIER DISTRICT OFFICE– An FAA field office serving an assigned geographical area, staffed with Flight Standards personnel serving the aviation industry and the general public on matters related to the certification and operation of scheduled air carriers and other large aircraft operations.

AIR DEFENSE EMERGENCY– A military emergency condition declared by a designated authority. This condition exists when an attack upon the continental U.S., Alaska, Canada, or U.S. installations in Greenland by hostile aircraft or missiles is considered probable, is imminent, or is taking place.

(Refer to AIM.)

AIR DEFENSE IDENTIFICATION ZONE (ADIZ)– An area of airspace over land or water in which the ready identification, location, and control of all aircraft (except for Department of Defense and law enforcement aircraft) is required in the interest of national security.

Note: ADIZ locations and operating and flight plan requirements for civil aircraft operations are specified in 14 CFR Part 99.

(Refer to AIM.)

AIR NAVIGATION FACILITY– Any facility used in, available for use in, or designed for use in, aid of air navigation, including landing areas, lights, any apparatus or equipment for disseminating weather information, for signaling, for radio-directional finding, or for radio or other electrical communication, and any other structure or mechanism having a similar purpose for guiding or controlling flight in the air or the landing and takeoff of aircraft.

(See NAVIGATIONAL AID.)

AIR ROUTE SURVEILLANCE RADAR– Air route traffic control center (ARTCC) radar used primarily to detect and display an aircraft's position while en route between terminal areas. The ARSR enables controllers to provide radar air traffic control service when aircraft are within the ARSR coverage. In some instances, ARSR may enable an ARTCC to provide terminal radar services similar to but usually more limited than those provided by a radar approach control.

AIR ROUTE TRAFFIC CONTROL CENTER (ARTCC)– A facility established to provide air traffic control service to aircraft operating on IFR flight plans within controlled airspace and principally during the en route phase of flight. When equipment capabilities and controller workload permit, certain advisory/assistance services may be provided to VFR aircraft.

(See EN ROUTE AIR TRAFFIC CONTROL SERVICES.)

(Refer to AIM.)

AIR TAXI– Used to describe a helicopter/VTOL aircraft movement conducted above the surface but normally not above 100 feet AGL. The aircraft may proceed either via hover taxi or flight at speeds more than 20 knots. The pilot is solely responsible for selecting a safe airspeed/altitude for the operation being conducted.

(See HOVER TAXI.)
(Refer to AIM.)

AIR TRAFFIC– Aircraft operating in the air or on an airport surface, exclusive of loading ramps and parking areas.

(See ICAO term AIR TRAFFIC.)

AIR TRAFFIC [ICAO]– All aircraft in flight or operating on the maneuvering area of an aerodrome.

AIR TRAFFIC CLEARANCE– An authorization by air traffic control for the purpose of preventing collision between known aircraft, for an aircraft to proceed under specified traffic conditions within controlled airspace. The pilot-in-command of an aircraft may not deviate from the provisions of a visual flight rules (VFR) or instrument flight rules (IFR) air traffic clearance except in an emergency or unless an amended clearance has been obtained. Additionally, the pilot may request a different clearance from that which has been issued by air traffic control (ATC) if information available to the pilot makes another course of action more practicable or if aircraft equipment limitations or company procedures forbid compliance with the clearance issued. Pilots may also request clarification or amendment, as appropriate, any time a clearance is not fully understood, or considered unacceptable because of safety of flight. Controllers should, in such instances and to the extent of operational practicality and safety, honor the pilot's request. 14 CFR Part 91.3(a) states: "The pilot in command of an aircraft is directly responsible for, and is the final authority as to, the operation of that aircraft." THE PILOT IS RESPONSIBLE TO REQUEST AN AMENDED CLEARANCE if ATC issues a clearance that would cause a pilot to deviate from a rule or regulation, or in the pilot's opinion, would place the aircraft in jeopardy.

(See ATC INSTRUCTIONS.)
(See ICAO term AIR TRAFFIC CONTROL CLEARANCE.)

AIR TRAFFIC CONTROL– A service operated by appropriate authority to promote the safe, orderly and expeditious flow of air traffic.

(See ICAO term AIR TRAFFIC CONTROL SERVICE.)

AIR TRAFFIC CONTROL CLEARANCE [ICAO]– Authorization for an aircraft to proceed under conditions specified by an air traffic control unit.

Note 1: For convenience, the term air traffic control clearance is frequently abbreviated to clearance when used in appropriate contexts.

Note 2: The abbreviated term clearance may be prefixed by the words taxi, takeoff, departure, en route, approach or landing to indicate the particular portion of flight to which the air traffic control clearance relates.

AIR TRAFFIC CONTROL SERVICE–

(See AIR TRAFFIC CONTROL.)

AIR TRAFFIC CONTROL SERVICE [ICAO]– A service provided for the purpose of:

a. Preventing collisions:

1. Between aircraft; and

2. On the maneuvering area between aircraft and obstructions.

b. Expediting and maintaining an orderly flow of air traffic.

AIR TRAFFIC CONTROL SPECIALIST– A person authorized to provide air traffic control service.

(See AIR TRAFFIC CONTROL.)
(See FLIGHT SERVICE STATION.)
(See ICAO term CONTROLLER.)

AIR TRAFFIC CONTROL SYSTEM COMMAND CENTER (ATCSCC)– An Air Traffic Tactical Operations facility responsible for monitoring and managing the flow of air traffic throughout the NAS, producing a safe, orderly, and expeditious flow of traffic while minimizing delays. The following functions are located at the ATCSCC:

a. Central Altitude Reservation Function (CARF). Responsible for coordinating, planning, and approving special user requirements under the Altitude Reservation (ALTRV) concept.
(See ALTITUDE RESERVATION.)

b. Airport Reservation Office (ARO). Monitors the operation and allocation of reservations for unscheduled operations at airports designated by the Administrator as High Density Airports. These airports are generally known as slot controlled airports. The ARO allocates reservations on a first come, first served basis determined by the time the request is received at the ARO.
(Refer to 14 CFR Part 93.)
(See CHART SUPPLEMENT.)

c. U.S. Notice to Air Missions (NOTAM) Office. Responsible for collecting, maintaining, and distributing NOTAMs for the U.S. civilian and military, as well as international aviation communities.
(See NOTICE TO AIR MISSIONS.)

d. Weather Unit. Monitor all aspects of weather for the U.S. that might affect aviation including cloud cover, visibility, winds, precipitation, thunderstorms, icing, turbulence, and more. Provide forecasts based on observations and on discussions with meteorologists from various National Weather Service offices, FAA facilities, airlines, and private weather services.

e. Air Traffic Organization (ATO) Space Operations and Unmanned Aircraft System (UAS); the Office of Primary Responsibility (OPR) for all space and upper class E tactical operations in the National Airspace System (NAS).

AIR TRAFFIC SERVICE– A generic term meaning:

a. Flight Information Service.

b. Alerting Service.

c. Air Traffic Advisory Service.

d. Air Traffic Control Service:

1. Area Control Service,

2. Approach Control Service, or

3. Airport Control Service.

AIR TRAFFIC ORGANIZATION (ATO) – The FAA line of business responsible for providing safe and efficient air navigation services in the national airspace system.

AIR TRAFFIC SERVICE (ATS) ROUTES – The term "ATS Route" is a generic term that includes "VOR Federal airways," "colored Federal airways," "jet routes," and "RNAV routes." The term "ATS route" does not replace these more familiar route names, but serves only as an overall title when listing the types of routes that comprise the United States route structure.

AIRBORNE– An aircraft is considered airborne when all parts of the aircraft are off the ground.

AIRBORNE DELAY– Amount of delay to be encountered in airborne holding.

AIRBORNE REROUTE (ABRR)– A capability within the Traffic Flow Management System used for the timely development and implementation of tactical reroutes for airborne aircraft. This capability defines a set of aircraft–specific reroutes that address a certain traffic flow problem and then electronically transmits them to En Route Automation Modernization (ERAM) for execution by the appropriate sector controllers.

AIRCRAFT– Device(s) that are used or intended to be used for flight in the air, and when used in air traffic control terminology, may include the flight crew.
(See ICAO term AIRCRAFT.)

AIRCRAFT [ICAO]– Any machine that can derive support in the atmosphere from the reactions of the air other than the reactions of the air against the earth's surface.

AIRCRAFT APPROACH CATEGORY− A grouping of aircraft based on a speed of 1.3 times the stall speed in the landing configuration at maximum gross landing weight. An aircraft must fit in only one category. If it is necessary to maneuver at speeds in excess of the upper limit of a speed range for a category, the minimums for the category for that speed must be used. For example, an aircraft which falls in Category A, but is circling to land at a speed in excess of 91 knots, must use the approach Category B minimums when circling to land. The categories are as follows:

a. Category A− Speed less than 91 knots.

b. Category B− Speed 91 knots or more but less than 121 knots.

c. Category C− Speed 121 knots or more but less than 141 knots.

d. Category D− Speed 141 knots or more but less than 166 knots.

e. Category E− Speed 166 knots or more.

(Refer to 14 CFR Part 97.)

AIRCRAFT CLASSES− For the purposes of Wake Turbulence Separation Minima, ATC classifies aircraft as Super, Heavy, Large, and Small as follows:

a. Super. The Airbus A-380-800 (A388) and the Antonov An-225 (A225) are classified as super.

b. Heavy− Aircraft capable of takeoff weights of 300,000 pounds or more whether or not they are operating at this weight during a particular phase of flight.

c. Large− Aircraft of more than 41,000 pounds, maximum certificated takeoff weight, up to but not including 300,000 pounds.

d. Small− Aircraft of 41,000 pounds or less maximum certificated takeoff weight.

(Refer to AIM.)

AIRCRAFT CONFLICT− Predicted conflict, within EDST of two aircraft, or between aircraft and airspace. A Red alert is used for conflicts when the predicted minimum separation is 5 nautical miles or less. A Yellow alert is used when the predicted minimum separation is between 5 and approximately 12 nautical miles. A Blue alert is used for conflicts between an aircraft and predefined airspace.

(See EN ROUTE DECISION SUPPORT TOOL.)

AIRCRAFT LIST (ACL)− A view available with EDST that lists aircraft currently in or predicted to be in a particular sector's airspace. The view contains textual flight data information in line format and may be sorted into various orders based on the specific needs of the sector team.

(See EN ROUTE DECISION SUPPORT TOOL.)

AIRCRAFT SURGE LAUNCH AND RECOVERY− Procedures used at USAF bases to provide increased launch and recovery rates in instrument flight rules conditions. ASLAR is based on:

a. Reduced separation between aircraft which is based on time or distance. Standard arrival separation applies between participants including multiple flights until the DRAG point. The DRAG point is a published location on an ASLAR approach where aircraft landing second in a formation slows to a predetermined airspeed. The DRAG point is the reference point at which MARSA applies as expanding elements effect separation within a flight or between subsequent participating flights.

b. ASLAR procedures shall be covered in a Letter of Agreement between the responsible USAF military ATC facility and the concerned Federal Aviation Administration facility. Initial Approach Fix spacing requirements are normally addressed as a minimum.

AIRCRAFT HAZARD AREA (AHA)− Used by ATC to segregate air traffic from a launch vehicle, reentry vehicle, amateur rocket, jettisoned stages, hardware, or falling debris generated by failures associated with any of these activities. An AHA is designated via NOTAM as either a TFR or stationary ALTRV. Unless otherwise specified, the vertical limits of an AHA are from the surface to unlimited.

(See CONTINGENCY HAZARD AREA.)
(See REFINED HAZARD AREA.)
(See TRANSITIONAL HAZARD AREA.)

AIRCRAFT WAKE TURBULENCE CATEGORIES– For the purpose of Wake Turbulence Recategorization (RECAT) Separation Minima, ATC groups aircraft into categories ranging from Category A through Category I, dependent upon the version of RECAT that is applied. Specific category assignments vary and are listed in the RECAT Orders.

AIRMEN'S METEOROLOGICAL INFORMATION (AIRMET)– A concise description of an occurrence or expected occurrence of specified en route weather phenomena that may affect the safety of aircraft operations, but at intensities lower than those that require the issuance of a SIGMET. An AIRMET may be issued when any of the following weather phenomena are occurring or expected to occur:

a. Moderate turbulence

b. Low–level windshear

c. Strong surface winds greater than 30 knots

d. Moderate icing

e. Freezing level

f. Mountain obscuration

g. IFR

(See CONVECTIVE SIGMET.)
(See CWA.)
(See GRAPHICAL AIRMEN'S METEOROLOGICAL INFORMATION.)
(See SAW.)
(See SIGMET.)
(Refer to AIM.)

AIRPORT– An area on land or water that is used or intended to be used for the landing and takeoff of aircraft and includes its buildings and facilities, if any.

AIRPORT ADVISORY AREA– The area within ten miles of an airport without a control tower or where the tower is not in operation, and on which a Flight Service Station is located.
(See LOCAL AIRPORT ADVISORY.)
(Refer to AIM.)

AIRPORT ARRIVAL RATE (AAR)– A dynamic input parameter specifying the number of arriving aircraft which an airport or airspace can accept from the ARTCC per hour. The AAR is used to calculate the desired interval between successive arrival aircraft.

AIRPORT DEPARTURE RATE (ADR)– A dynamic parameter specifying the number of aircraft which can depart an airport and the airspace can accept per hour.

AIRPORT ELEVATION– The highest point of an airport's usable runways measured in feet from mean sea level.
(See TOUCHDOWN ZONE ELEVATION.)
(See ICAO term AERODROME ELEVATION.)

AIRPORT LIGHTING– Various lighting aids that may be installed on an airport. Types of airport lighting include:

a. Approach Light System (ALS)– An airport lighting facility which provides visual guidance to landing aircraft by radiating light beams in a directional pattern by which the pilot aligns the aircraft with the extended centerline of the runway on his/her final approach for landing. Condenser-Discharge Sequential Flashing Lights/Sequenced Flashing Lights may be installed in conjunction with the ALS at some airports. Types of Approach Light Systems are:

1. ALSF-1– Approach Light System with Sequenced Flashing Lights in ILS Cat-I configuration.

2. ALSF-2– Approach Light System with Sequenced Flashing Lights in ILS Cat-II configuration. The ALSF-2 may operate as an SSALR when weather conditions permit.

3. SSALF– Simplified Short Approach Light System with Sequenced Flashing Lights.

4. SSALR– Simplified Short Approach Light System with Runway Alignment Indicator Lights.

5. MALSF– Medium Intensity Approach Light System with Sequenced Flashing Lights.

6. MALSR– Medium Intensity Approach Light System with Runway Alignment Indicator Lights.

7. RLLS– Runway Lead-in Light System Consists of one or more series of flashing lights installed at or near ground level that provides positive visual guidance along an approach path, either curving or straight, where special problems exist with hazardous terrain, obstructions, or noise abatement procedures.

8. RAIL– Runway Alignment Indicator Lights– Sequenced Flashing Lights which are installed only in combination with other light systems.

9. ODALS– Omnidirectional Approach Lighting System consists of seven omnidirectional flashing lights located in the approach area of a nonprecision runway. Five lights are located on the runway centerline extended with the first light located 300 feet from the threshold and extending at equal intervals up to 1,500 feet from the threshold. The other two lights are located, one on each side of the runway threshold, at a lateral distance of 40 feet from the runway edge, or 75 feet from the runway edge when installed on a runway equipped with a VASI.

(Refer to FAA Order JO 6850.2, Visual Guidance Lighting Systems.)

b. Runway Lights/Runway Edge Lights– Lights having a prescribed angle of emission used to define the lateral limits of a runway. Runway lights are uniformly spaced at intervals of approximately 200 feet, and the intensity may be controlled or preset.

c. Touchdown Zone Lighting– Two rows of transverse light bars located symmetrically about the runway centerline normally at 100 foot intervals. The basic system extends 3,000 feet along the runway.

d. Runway Centerline Lighting– Flush centerline lights spaced at 50-foot intervals beginning 75 feet from the landing threshold and extending to within 75 feet of the opposite end of the runway.

e. Threshold Lights– Fixed green lights arranged symmetrically left and right of the runway centerline, identifying the runway threshold.

f. Runway End Identifier Lights (REIL)– Two synchronized flashing lights, one on each side of the runway threshold, which provide rapid and positive identification of the approach end of a particular runway.

g. Visual Approach Slope Indicator (VASI)– An airport lighting facility providing vertical visual approach slope guidance to aircraft during approach to landing by radiating a directional pattern of high intensity red and white focused light beams which indicate to the pilot that he/she is "on path" if he/she sees red/white, "above path" if white/white, and "below path" if red/red. Some airports serving large aircraft have three-bar VASIs which provide two visual glide paths to the same runway.

h. Precision Approach Path Indicator (PAPI)– An airport lighting facility, similar to VASI, providing vertical approach slope guidance to aircraft during approach to landing. PAPIs consist of a single row of either two or four lights, normally installed on the left side of the runway, and have an effective visual range of about 5 miles during the day and up to 20 miles at night. PAPIs radiate a directional pattern of high intensity red and white focused light beams which indicate that the pilot is "on path" if the pilot sees an equal number of white lights and red lights, with white to the left of the red; "above path" if the pilot sees more white than red lights; and "below path" if the pilot sees more red than white lights.

i. Boundary Lights– Lights defining the perimeter of an airport or landing area.

(Refer to AIM.)

AIRPORT MARKING AIDS– Markings used on runway and taxiway surfaces to identify a specific runway, a runway threshold, a centerline, a hold line, etc. A runway should be marked in accordance with its present usage such as:

a. Visual.

b. Nonprecision instrument.

c. Precision instrument.

(Refer to AIM.)

AIRPORT REFERENCE POINT (ARP)– The approximate geometric center of all usable runway surfaces.

AIRPORT RESERVATION OFFICE– Office responsible for monitoring the operation of slot controlled airports. It receives and processes requests for unscheduled operations at slot controlled airports.

AIRPORT ROTATING BEACON– A visual NAVAID operated at many airports. At civil airports, alternating white and green flashes indicate the location of the airport. At military airports, the beacons flash alternately white and green, but are differentiated from civil beacons by dualpeaked (two quick) white flashes between the green flashes.

(See INSTRUMENT FLIGHT RULES.)
(See SPECIAL VFR OPERATIONS.)
(See ICAO term AERODROME BEACON.)
(Refer to AIM.)

AIRPORT SURFACE DETECTION EQUIPMENT (ASDE)– Surveillance equipment specifically designed to detect aircraft, vehicular traffic, and other objects, on the surface of an airport, and to present the image on a tower display. Used to augment visual observation by tower personnel of aircraft and/or vehicular movements on runways and taxiways. There are three ASDE systems deployed in the NAS:

a. ASDE–3– a Surface Movement Radar.

b. ASDE–X– a system that uses an X–band Surface Movement Radar, multilateration, and ADS–B.

c. Airport Surface Surveillance Capability (ASSC)– A system that uses Surface Movement Radar, multilateration, and ADS–B.

AIRPORT SURVEILLANCE RADAR– Approach control radar used to detect and display an aircraft's position in the terminal area. ASR provides range and azimuth information but does not provide elevation data. Coverage of the ASR can extend up to 60 miles.

AIRPORT TAXI CHARTS–
(See AERONAUTICAL CHART.)

AIRPORT TRAFFIC CONTROL SERVICE– A service provided by a control tower for aircraft operating on the movement area and in the vicinity of an airport.

(See MOVEMENT AREA.)
(See TOWER.)
(See ICAO term AERODROME CONTROL SERVICE.)

AIRPORT TRAFFIC CONTROL TOWER–
(See TOWER.)

AIRSPACE CONFLICT– Predicted conflict of an aircraft and active Special Activity Airspace (SAA).

AIRSPACE FLOW PROGRAM (AFP)– AFP is a Traffic Management (TM) process administered by the Air Traffic Control System Command Center (ATCSCC) where aircraft are assigned an Expect Departure Clearance Time (EDCT) in order to manage capacity and demand for a specific area of the National Airspace System (NAS). The purpose of the program is to mitigate the effects of en route constraints. It is a flexible program and may be implemented in various forms depending upon the needs of the air traffic system.

AIRSPACE HIERARCHY– Within the airspace classes, there is a hierarchy and, in the event of an overlap of airspace: Class A preempts Class B, Class B preempts Class C, Class C preempts Class D, Class D preempts Class E, and Class E preempts Class G.

AIRSPEED– The speed of an aircraft relative to its surrounding air mass. The unqualified term "airspeed" means one of the following:

a. Indicated Airspeed– The speed shown on the aircraft airspeed indicator. This is the speed used in pilot/controller communications under the general term "airspeed."

(Refer to 14 CFR Part 1.)

b. True Airspeed– The airspeed of an aircraft relative to undisturbed air. Used primarily in flight planning and en route portion of flight. When used in pilot/controller communications, it is referred to as "true airspeed" and not shortened to "airspeed."

AIRSPACE RESERVATION– The term used in oceanic ATC for airspace utilization under prescribed conditions normally employed for the mass movement of aircraft or other special user requirements which cannot otherwise be accomplished. Airspace reservations must be classified as either "moving" or "stationary."

(See MOVING AIRSPACE RESERVATION)
(See STATIONARY AIRSPACE RESERVATION.)
(See ALTITUDE RESERVATION.)

AIRSTART– The starting of an aircraft engine while the aircraft is airborne, preceded by engine shutdown during training flights or by actual engine failure.

AIRWAY– A Class E airspace area established in the form of a corridor, the centerline of which is defined by radio navigational aids.

(See FEDERAL AIRWAYS.)
(See ICAO term AIRWAY.)
(Refer to 14 CFR Part 71.)
(Refer to AIM.)

AIRWAY [ICAO]– A control area or portion thereof established in the form of corridor equipped with radio navigational aids.

AIRWAY BEACON– Used to mark airway segments in remote mountain areas. The light flashes Morse Code to identify the beacon site.

(Refer to AIM.)

AIS–

(See AERONAUTICAL INFORMATION SERVICES.)

AIT–

(See AUTOMATED INFORMATION TRANSFER.)

ALERFA (Alert Phase) [ICAO]– A situation wherein apprehension exists as to the safety of an aircraft and its occupants.

ALERT– A notification to a position that there is an aircraft-to-aircraft or aircraft-to-airspace conflict, as detected by Automated Problem Detection (APD).

ALERT AREA–

(See SPECIAL USE AIRSPACE.)

ALERT NOTICE (ALNOT)– A request originated by a flight service station (FSS) or an air route traffic control center (ARTCC) for an extensive communication search for overdue, unreported, or missing aircraft.

ALERTING SERVICE– A service provided to notify appropriate organizations regarding aircraft in need of search and rescue aid and assist such organizations as required.

ALNOT–

(See ALERT NOTICE.)

ALONG-TRACK DISTANCE (ATD)– The horizontal distance between the aircraft's current position and a fix measured by an area navigation system that is not subject to slant range errors.

ALPHANUMERIC DISPLAY– Letters and numerals used to show identification, altitude, beacon code, and other information concerning a target on a radar display.

ALTERNATE AERODROME [ICAO]– An aerodrome to which an aircraft may proceed when it becomes either impossible or inadvisable to proceed to or to land at the aerodrome of intended landing.

Note: The aerodrome from which a flight departs may also be an en-route or a destination alternate aerodrome for the flight.

ALTERNATE AIRPORT– An airport at which an aircraft may land if a landing at the intended airport becomes inadvisable.

(See ICAO term ALTERNATE AERODROME.)

ALTIMETER SETTING− The barometric pressure reading used to adjust a pressure altimeter for variations in existing atmospheric pressure or to the standard altimeter setting (29.92).
(Refer to 14 CFR Part 91.)
(Refer to AIM.)

ALTITUDE− The height of a level, point, or object measured in feet Above Ground Level (AGL) or from Mean Sea Level (MSL).
(See FLIGHT LEVEL.)

a. MSL Altitude− Altitude expressed in feet measured from mean sea level.

b. AGL Altitude− Altitude expressed in feet measured above ground level.

c. Indicated Altitude− The altitude as shown by an altimeter. On a pressure or barometric altimeter it is altitude as shown uncorrected for instrument error and uncompensated for variation from standard atmospheric conditions.
(See ICAO term ALTITUDE.)

ALTITUDE [ICAO]− The vertical distance of a level, a point or an object considered as a point, measured from mean sea level (MSL).

ALTITUDE READOUT− An aircraft's altitude, transmitted via the Mode C transponder feature, that is visually displayed in 100-foot increments on a radar scope having readout capability.
(See ALPHANUMERIC DISPLAY.)
(Refer to AIM.)

ALTITUDE RESERVATION (ALTRV)− Airspace utilization under prescribed conditions normally employed for the mass movement of aircraft or other special user requirements which cannot otherwise be accomplished. ALTRVs are approved by the appropriate FAA facility. ALTRVs must be classified as either "moving" or "stationary."
(See MOVING ALTITUDE RESERVATION.)
(See STATIONARY ALTITUDE RESERVATION.)
(See AIR TRAFFIC CONTROL SYSTEM COMMAND CENTER.)

ALTITUDE RESTRICTION− An altitude or altitudes, stated in the order flown, which are to be maintained until reaching a specific point or time. Altitude restrictions may be issued by ATC due to traffic, terrain, or other airspace considerations.

ALTITUDE RESTRICTIONS ARE CANCELED− Adherence to previously imposed altitude restrictions is no longer required during a climb or descent.

ALTRV−
(See ALTITUDE RESERVATION.)

AMVER−
(See AUTOMATED MUTUAL-ASSISTANCE VESSEL RESCUE SYSTEM.)

APB−
(See AUTOMATED PROBLEM DETECTION BOUNDARY.)

APD−
(See AUTOMATED PROBLEM DETECTION.)

APDIA−
(See AUTOMATED PROBLEM DETECTION INHIBITED AREA.)

APPROACH CLEARANCE− Authorization by ATC for a pilot to conduct an instrument approach. The type of instrument approach for which a clearance and other pertinent information is provided in the approach clearance when required.
(See CLEARED APPROACH.)
(See INSTRUMENT APPROACH PROCEDURE.)
(Refer to AIM.)
(Refer to 14 CFR Part 91.)

APPROACH CONTROL FACILITY– A terminal ATC facility that provides approach control service in a terminal area.

(See APPROACH CONTROL SERVICE.)
(See RADAR APPROACH CONTROL FACILITY.)

APPROACH CONTROL SERVICE– Air traffic control service provided by an approach control facility for arriving and departing VFR/IFR aircraft and, on occasion, en route aircraft. At some airports not served by an approach control facility, the ARTCC provides limited approach control service.

(See ICAO term APPROACH CONTROL SERVICE.)
(Refer to AIM.)

APPROACH CONTROL SERVICE [ICAO]– Air traffic control service for arriving or departing controlled flights.

APPROACH GATE– An imaginary point used within ATC as a basis for vectoring aircraft to the final approach course. The gate will be established along the final approach course 1 mile from the final approach fix on the side away from the airport and will be no closer than 5 miles from the landing threshold.

APPROACH/DEPARTURE HOLD AREA– The locations on taxiways in the approach or departure areas of a runway designated to protect landing or departing aircraft. These locations are identified by signs and markings.

APPROACH LIGHT SYSTEM–

(See AIRPORT LIGHTING.)

APPROACH SEQUENCE– The order in which aircraft are positioned while on approach or awaiting approach clearance.

(See LANDING SEQUENCE.)
(See ICAO term APPROACH SEQUENCE.)

APPROACH SEQUENCE [ICAO]– The order in which two or more aircraft are cleared to approach to land at the aerodrome.

APPROACH SPEED– The recommended speed contained in aircraft manuals used by pilots when making an approach to landing. This speed will vary for different segments of an approach as well as for aircraft weight and configuration.

APPROACH WITH VERTICAL GUIDANCE (APV)– A term used to describe RNAV approach procedures that provide lateral and vertical guidance but do not meet the requirements to be considered a precision approach.

APPROPRIATE ATS AUTHORITY [ICAO]– The relevant authority designated by the State responsible for providing air traffic services in the airspace concerned. In the United States, the "appropriate ATS authority" is the Program Director for Air Traffic Planning and Procedures, ATP-1.

APPROPRIATE AUTHORITY–

a. Regarding flight over the high seas: the relevant authority is the State of Registry.

b. Regarding flight over other than the high seas: the relevant authority is the State having sovereignty over the territory being overflown.

APPROPRIATE OBSTACLE CLEARANCE MINIMUM ALTITUDE– Any of the following:

(See MINIMUM EN ROUTE IFR ALTITUDE.)
(See MINIMUM IFR ALTITUDE.)
(See MINIMUM OBSTRUCTION CLEARANCE ALTITUDE.)
(See MINIMUM VECTORING ALTITUDE.)

APPROPRIATE TERRAIN CLEARANCE MINIMUM ALTITUDE– Any of the following:

(See MINIMUM EN ROUTE IFR ALTITUDE.)
(See MINIMUM IFR ALTITUDE.)
(See MINIMUM OBSTRUCTION CLEARANCE ALTITUDE.)
(See MINIMUM VECTORING ALTITUDE.)

APRON– A defined area on an airport or heliport intended to accommodate aircraft for purposes of loading or unloading passengers or cargo, refueling, parking, or maintenance. With regard to seaplanes, a ramp is used for access to the apron from the water.

(See ICAO term APRON.)

APRON [ICAO]– A defined area, on a land aerodrome, intended to accommodate aircraft for purposes of loading or unloading passengers, mail or cargo, refueling, parking or maintenance.

ARC– The track over the ground of an aircraft flying at a constant distance from a navigational aid by reference to distance measuring equipment (DME).

AREA CONTROL CENTER [ICAO]– An air traffic control facility primarily responsible for ATC services being provided IFR aircraft during the en route phase of flight. The U.S. equivalent facility is an air route traffic control center (ARTCC).

AREA NAVIGATION (RNAV)– A method of navigation which permits aircraft operation on any desired flight path within the coverage of ground– or space–based navigation aids or within the limits of the capability of self-contained aids, or a combination of these.

Note: Area navigation includes performance–based navigation as well as other operations that do not meet the definition of performance–based navigation.

AREA NAVIGATION (RNAV) APPROACH CONFIGURATION:

a. STANDARD T– An RNAV approach whose design allows direct flight to any one of three initial approach fixes (IAF) and eliminates the need for procedure turns. The standard design is to align the procedure on the extended centerline with the missed approach point (MAP) at the runway threshold, the final approach fix (FAF), and the initial approach/intermediate fix (IAF/IF). The other two IAFs will be established perpendicular to the IF.

b. MODIFIED T– An RNAV approach design for single or multiple runways where terrain or operational constraints do not allow for the standard T. The “T” may be modified by increasing or decreasing the angle from the corner IAF(s) to the IF or by eliminating one or both corner IAFs.

c. STANDARD I– An RNAV approach design for a single runway with both corner IAFs eliminated. Course reversal or radar vectoring may be required at busy terminals with multiple runways.

d. TERMINAL ARRIVAL AREA (TAA)– The TAA is controlled airspace established in conjunction with the Standard or Modified T and I RNAV approach configurations. In the standard TAA, there are three areas: straight-in, left base, and right base. The arc boundaries of the three areas of the TAA are published portions of the approach and allow aircraft to transition from the en route structure direct to the nearest IAF. TAAs will also eliminate or reduce feeder routes, departure extensions, and procedure turns or course reversal.

1. STRAIGHT-IN AREA– A 30 NM arc centered on the IF bounded by a straight line extending through the IF perpendicular to the intermediate course.

2. LEFT BASE AREA– A 30 NM arc centered on the right corner IAF. The area shares a boundary with the straight-in area except that it extends out for 30 NM from the IAF and is bounded on the other side by a line extending from the IF through the FAF to the arc.

3. RIGHT BASE AREA– A 30 NM arc centered on the left corner IAF. The area shares a boundary with the straight-in area except that it extends out for 30 NM from the IAF and is bounded on the other side by a line extending from the IF through the FAF to the arc.

AREA NAVIGATION (RNAV) GLOBAL POSITIONING SYSTEM (GPS) PRECISION RUNWAY MONITORING (PRM) APPROACH–
A GPS approach, which requires vertical guidance, used in lieu of another type of PRM approach to conduct approaches to parallel runways whose extended centerlines are separated by less than 4,300 feet and at least 3,000 feet, where simultaneous close parallel approaches are permitted. Also used in lieu of an ILS PRM and/or LDA PRM approach to conduct Simultaneous Offset Instrument Approach (SOIA) operations.

ARMY AVIATION FLIGHT INFORMATION BULLETIN– A bulletin that provides air operation data covering Army, National Guard, and Army Reserve aviation activities.

ARO–
(See AIRPORT RESERVATION OFFICE.)

ARRESTING SYSTEM– A safety device consisting of two major components, namely, engaging or catching devices and energy absorption devices for the purpose of arresting both tailhook and/or nontailhook-equipped aircraft. It is used to prevent aircraft from overrunning runways when the aircraft cannot be stopped after landing or during aborted takeoff. Arresting systems have various names; e.g., arresting gear, hook device, wire barrier cable.
(See ABORT.)
(Refer to AIM.)

ARRIVAL CENTER– The ARTCC having jurisdiction for the impacted airport.

ARRIVAL DELAY– A parameter which specifies a period of time in which no aircraft will be metered for arrival at the specified airport.

ARRIVAL/DEPARTURE WINDOW (ADW)– A depiction presented on an air traffic control display, used by the controller to prevent possible conflicts between arrivals to, and departures from, a runway. The ADW identifies that point on the final approach course by which a departing aircraft must have begun takeoff.

ARRIVAL SECTOR (En Route)– An operational control sector containing one or more meter fixes on or near the TRACON boundary.

ARRIVAL TIME– The time an aircraft touches down on arrival.

ARSR–
(See AIR ROUTE SURVEILLANCE RADAR.)

ARTCC–
(See AIR ROUTE TRAFFIC CONTROL CENTER.)

ASDA–
(See ACCELERATE-STOP DISTANCE AVAILABLE.)

ASDA [ICAO]–
(See ICAO Term ACCELERATE-STOP DISTANCE AVAILABLE.)

ASDE–
(See AIRPORT SURFACE DETECTION EQUIPMENT.)

ASLAR–
(See AIRCRAFT SURGE LAUNCH AND RECOVERY.)

ASR–
(See AIRPORT SURVEILLANCE RADAR.)

ASR APPROACH–
(See SURVEILLANCE APPROACH.)

ASSOCIATED– A radar target displaying a data block with flight identification and altitude information.
(See UNASSOCIATED.)

ATC–
(See AIR TRAFFIC CONTROL.)

ATC ADVISES– Used to prefix a message of noncontrol information when it is relayed to an aircraft by other than an air traffic controller.
(See ADVISORY.)

ATC ASSIGNED AIRSPACE– Airspace of defined vertical/lateral limits, assigned by ATC, for the purpose of providing air traffic segregation between the specified activities being conducted within the assigned airspace and other IFR air traffic.
(See SPECIAL USE AIRSPACE.)

ATC CLEARANCE–
(See AIR TRAFFIC CLEARANCE.)

ATC CLEARS– Used to prefix an ATC clearance when it is relayed to an aircraft by other than an air traffic controller.

ATC INSTRUCTIONS– Directives issued by air traffic control for the purpose of requiring a pilot to take specific actions; e.g., "Turn left heading two five zero," "Go around," "Clear the runway."
(Refer to 14 CFR Part 91.)

ATC PREFERRED ROUTE NOTIFICATION– EDST notification to the appropriate controller of the need to determine if an ATC preferred route needs to be applied, based on destination airport.
(See ROUTE ACTION NOTIFICATION.)
(See EN ROUTE DECISION SUPPORT TOOL.)

ATC PREFERRED ROUTES– Preferred routes that are not automatically applied by Host.

ATC REQUESTS– Used to prefix an ATC request when it is relayed to an aircraft by other than an air traffic controller.

ATC SECURITY SERVICES– Communications and security tracking provided by an ATC facility in support of the DHS, the DoD, or other Federal security elements in the interest of national security. Such security services are only applicable within designated areas. ATC security services do not include ATC basic radar services or flight following.

ATC SECURITY SERVICES POSITION– The position responsible for providing ATC security services as defined. This position does not provide ATC, IFR separation, or VFR flight following services, but is responsible for providing security services in an area comprising airspace assigned to one or more ATC operating sectors. This position may be combined with control positions.

ATC SECURITY TRACKING– The continuous tracking of aircraft movement by an ATC facility in support of the DHS, the DoD, or other security elements for national security using radar (i.e., radar tracking) or other means (e.g., manual tracking) without providing basic radar services (including traffic advisories) or other ATC services not defined in this section.

ATS SURVEILLANCE SERVICE [ICAO]– A term used to indicate a service provided directly by means of an ATS surveillance system.

ATC SURVEILLANCE SOURCE– Used by ATC for establishing identification, control and separation using a target depicted on an air traffic control facility's video display that has met the relevant safety standards for operational use and received from one, or a combination, of the following surveillance sources:

a. Radar (See RADAR.)

b. ADS-B (See AUTOMATIC DEPENDENT SURVEILLANCE–BROADCAST.)

c. WAM (See WIDE AREA MULTILATERATION.)

(See INTERROGATOR.)
(See TRANSPONDER.)
(See ICAO term RADAR.)
(Refer to AIM.)

ATS SURVEILLANCE SYSTEM [ICAO]– A generic term meaning variously, ADS–B, PSR, SSR or any comparable ground–based system that enables the identification of aircraft.

Note: A comparable ground–based system is one that has been demonstrated, by comparative assessment or other methodology, to have a level of safety and performance equal to or better than monopulse SSR.

ATCAA–
(See ATC ASSIGNED AIRSPACE.)

ATCRBS–
(See RADAR.)

ATCSCC–
(See AIR TRAFFIC CONTROL SYSTEM COMMAND CENTER.)

ATCT–
(See TOWER.)

ATD–
(See ALONG–TRACK DISTANCE.)

ATIS–
(See AUTOMATIC TERMINAL INFORMATION SERVICE.)

ATIS [ICAO]–
(See ICAO Term AUTOMATIC TERMINAL INFORMATION SERVICE.)

ATO–
(See AIR TRAFFIC ORGANIZATION.)

ATPA–
(See AUTOMATED TERMINAL PROXIMITY ALERT.)

ATS ROUTE [ICAO]– A specified route designed for channeling the flow of traffic as necessary for the provision of air traffic services.

Note: The term "ATS Route" is used to mean variously, airway, advisory route, controlled or uncontrolled route, arrival or departure, etc.

ATTENTION ALL USERS PAGE (AAUP)- The AAUP provides the pilot with additional information relative to conducting a specific operation, for example, PRM approaches and RNAV departures.

AUTOLAND APPROACH–An autoland system aids by providing control of aircraft systems during a precision instrument approach to at least decision altitude and possibly all the way to touchdown, as well as in some cases, through the landing rollout. The autoland system is a sub-system of the autopilot system from which control surface management occurs. The aircraft autopilot sends instructions to the autoland system and monitors the autoland system performance and integrity during its execution.

AUTOMATED EMERGENCY DESCENT–
(See EMERGENCY DESCENT MODE.)

AUTOMATED INFORMATION TRANSFER (AIT)– A precoordinated process, specifically defined in facility directives, during which a transfer of altitude control and/or radar identification is accomplished without verbal coordination between controllers using information communicated in a full data block.

AUTOMATED MUTUAL-ASSISTANCE VESSEL RESCUE SYSTEM– A facility which can deliver, in a matter of minutes, a surface picture (SURPIC) of vessels in the area of a potential or actual search and rescue incident, including their predicted positions and their characteristics.
(See FAA Order JO 7110.65, Para 10–6–4, INFLIGHT CONTINGENCIES.)

AUTOMATED PROBLEM DETECTION (APD)– An Automation Processing capability that compares trajectories in order to predict conflicts.

AUTOMATED PROBLEM DETECTION BOUNDARY (APB)– The adapted distance beyond a facilities boundary defining the airspace within which EDST performs conflict detection.
(See EN ROUTE DECISION SUPPORT TOOL.)

AUTOMATED PROBLEM DETECTION INHIBITED AREA (APDIA)– Airspace surrounding a terminal area within which APD is inhibited for all flights within that airspace.

AUTOMATED SERVICES–Services delivered via an automated system (that is, without human interaction). For example, flight plans, Notices to Air Missions (NOTAM), interactive maps, computer–generated text–to–speech messages, short message service, or email.

AUTOMATED TERMINAL PROXIMITY ALERT (ATPA)− Monitors the separation of aircraft on the Final Approach Course (FAC), displaying a graphical notification (cone and/or mileage) when a potential loss of separation is detected. The warning cone (Yellow) will display at 45 seconds and the alert cone (Red) will display at 24 seconds prior to predicted loss of separation. Current distance between two aircraft on final will be displayed in line 3 of the full data block of the trailing aircraft in corresponding colors.

AUTOMATED WEATHER SYSTEM− Any of the automated weather sensor platforms that collect weather data at airports and disseminate the weather information via radio and/or landline. The systems currently consist of the Automated Surface Observing System (ASOS) and Automated Weather Observation System (AWOS).

AUTOMATED UNICOM− Provides completely automated weather, radio check capability and airport advisory information on an Automated UNICOM system. These systems offer a variety of features, typically selectable by microphone clicks, on the UNICOM frequency. Availability will be published in the Chart Supplement and approach charts.

AUTOMATIC ALTITUDE REPORT−
(See ALTITUDE READOUT.)

AUTOMATIC ALTITUDE REPORTING− That function of a transponder which responds to Mode C interrogations by transmitting the aircraft's altitude in 100-foot increments.

AUTOMATIC CARRIER LANDING SYSTEM− U.S. Navy final approach equipment consisting of precision tracking radar coupled to a computer data link to provide continuous information to the aircraft, monitoring capability to the pilot, and a backup approach system.

AUTOMATIC DEPENDENT SURVEILLANCE (ADS) [ICAO]− A surveillance technique in which aircraft automatically provide, via a data link, data derived from on−board navigation and position fixing systems, including aircraft identification, four dimensional position and additional data as appropriate.

AUTOMATIC DEPENDENT SURVEILLANCE−BROADCAST (ADS-B)− A surveillance system in which an aircraft or vehicle to be detected is fitted with cooperative equipment in the form of a data link transmitter. The aircraft or vehicle periodically broadcasts its GNSS−derived position and other required information such as identity and velocity, which is then received by a ground−based or space−based receiver for processing and display at an air traffic control facility, as well as by suitably equipped aircraft.
(See AUTOMATIC DEPENDENT SURVEILLANCE−BROADCAST IN.)
(See AUTOMATIC DEPENDENT SURVEILLANCE−BROADCAST OUT.)
(See COOPERATIVE SURVEILLANCE.)
(See GLOBAL POSITIONING SYSTEM.)
(See SPACE−BASED ADS−B.)

AUTOMATIC DEPENDENT SURVEILLANCE−BROADCAST IN (ADS−B In)− Aircraft avionics capable of receiving ADS−B Out transmissions directly from other aircraft, as well as traffic or weather information transmitted from ground stations.
(See AUTOMATIC DEPENDENT SURVEILLANCE−BROADCAST OUT.)
(See AUTOMATIC DEPENDENT SURVEILLANCE−REBROADCAST.)
(See FLIGHT INFORMATION SERVICE−BROADCAST.)
(See TRAFFIC INFORMATION SERVICE−BROADCAST.)

AUTOMATIC DEPENDENT SURVEILLANCE−BROADCAST OUT (ADS−B Out)− The transmitter onboard an aircraft or ground vehicle that periodically broadcasts its GNSS−derived position along with other required information, such as identity, altitude, and velocity.
(See AUTOMATIC DEPENDENT SURVEILLANCE−BROADCAST.)
(See AUTOMATIC DEPENDENT SURVEILLANCE−BROADCAST IN.)

AUTOMATIC DEPENDENT SURVEILLANCE−CONTRACT (ADS−C)− A data link position reporting system, controlled by a ground station, that establishes contracts with an aircraft's avionics that occur automatically whenever specific events occur, or specific time intervals are reached.

AUTOMATIC DEPENDENT SURVEILLANCE- REBROADCAST (ADS-R)– A datalink translation function of the ADS–B ground system required to accommodate the two separate operating frequencies (978 MHz and 1090 MHz). The ADS–B system receives the ADS–B messages transmitted on one frequency and ADS–R translates and reformats the information for rebroadcast and use on the other frequency. This allows ADS–B In equipped aircraft to see nearby ADS–B Out traffic regardless of the operating link of the other aircraft. Aircraft operating on the same ADS–B frequency exchange information directly and do not require the ADS–R translation function.

AUTOMATIC DIRECTION FINDER– An aircraft radio navigation system which senses and indicates the direction to a L/MF nondirectional radio beacon (NDB) ground transmitter. Direction is indicated to the pilot as a magnetic bearing or as a relative bearing to the longitudinal axis of the aircraft depending on the type of indicator installed in the aircraft. In certain applications, such as military, ADF operations may be based on airborne and ground transmitters in the VHF/UHF frequency spectrum.

(See BEARING.)
(See NONDIRECTIONAL BEACON.)

AUTOMATIC FLIGHT INFORMATION SERVICE (AFIS) – ALASKA FSSs ONLY– The continuous broadcast of recorded non–control information at airports in Alaska where a FSS provides local airport advisory service. The AFIS broadcast automates the repetitive transmission of essential but routine information such as weather, wind, altimeter, favored runway, braking action, airport NOTAMs, and other applicable information. The information is continuously broadcast over a discrete VHF radio frequency (usually the ASOS/AWOS frequency).

AUTOMATIC TERMINAL INFORMATION SERVICE– The continuous broadcast of recorded noncontrol information in selected terminal areas. Its purpose is to improve controller effectiveness and to relieve frequency congestion by automating the repetitive transmission of essential but routine information; e.g., "Los Angeles information Alfa. One three zero zero Coordinated Universal Time. Weather, measured ceiling two thousand overcast, visibility three, haze, smoke, temperature seven one, dew point five seven, wind two five zero at five, altimeter two niner niner six. I-L-S Runway Two Five Left approach in use, Runway Two Five Right closed, advise you have Alfa."

(See ICAO term AUTOMATIC TERMINAL INFORMATION SERVICE.)
(Refer to AIM.)

AUTOMATIC TERMINAL INFORMATION SERVICE [ICAO]– The provision of current, routine information to arriving and departing aircraft by means of continuous and repetitive broadcasts throughout the day or a specified portion of the day.

AUTOROTATION– A rotorcraft flight condition in which the lifting rotor is driven entirely by action of the air when the rotorcraft is in motion.

a. Autorotative Landing/Touchdown Autorotation. Used by a pilot to indicate that the landing will be made without applying power to the rotor.

b. Low Level Autorotation. Commences at an altitude well below the traffic pattern, usually below 100 feet AGL and is used primarily for tactical military training.

c. 180 degrees Autorotation. Initiated from a downwind heading and is commenced well inside the normal traffic pattern. "Go around" may not be possible during the latter part of this maneuver.

AVAILABLE LANDING DISTANCE (ALD)– The portion of a runway available for landing and roll-out for aircraft cleared for LAHSO. This distance is measured from the landing threshold to the hold-short point.

AVIATION WATCH NOTIFICATION MESSAGE– The Storm Prediction Center (SPC) issues Aviation Watch Notification Messages (SAW) to provide an area threat alert for the aviation meteorology community to forecast organized severe thunderstorms that may produce tornadoes, large hail, and/or convective damaging winds as indicated in Public Watch Notification Messages within the Continental U.S. A SAW message provides a description of the type of watch issued by SPC, a valid time, an approximation of the area in a watch, and primary hazard(s).

AVIATION WEATHER SERVICE− A service provided by the National Weather Service (NWS) and FAA which collects and disseminates pertinent weather information for pilots, aircraft operators, and ATC. Available aviation weather reports and forecasts are displayed at each NWS office and FAA FSS.

(See TRANSCRIBED WEATHER BROADCAST.)

(See WEATHER ADVISORY.)

(Refer to AIM.)

B

B4UFLY– A free downloadable application, which allows operators to check airspace and local advisories before flying.

BACK-TAXI– A term used by air traffic controllers to taxi an aircraft on the runway opposite to the traffic flow. The aircraft may be instructed to back-taxi to the beginning of the runway or at some point before reaching the runway end for the purpose of departure or to exit the runway.

BASE LEG–
(See TRAFFIC PATTERN.)

BEACON–
(See AERONAUTICAL BEACON.)
(See AIRPORT ROTATING BEACON.)
(See AIRWAY BEACON.)
(See MARKER BEACON.)
(See NONDIRECTIONAL BEACON.)
(See RADAR.)

BEARING– The horizontal direction to or from any point, usually measured clockwise from true north, magnetic north, or some other reference point through 360 degrees.
(See NONDIRECTIONAL BEACON.)

BELOW MINIMUMS– Weather conditions below the minimums prescribed by regulation for the particular action involved; e.g., landing minimums, takeoff minimums.

BEYOND VISUAL LINE OF SIGHT (BVLOS)– The operation of a UAS beyond the visual capability of the flight crew members (i.e., remote pilot in command [RPIC], the person manipulating the controls, and visual observer [VO]), if used to see the aircraft with vision unaided by any device other than corrective lenses, spectacles, and contact lenses.

BLAST FENCE– A barrier that is used to divert or dissipate jet or propeller blast.

BLAST PAD– A surface adjacent to the ends of a runway provided to reduce the erosive effect of jet blast and propeller wash.

BLIND SPEED– The rate of departure or closing of a target relative to the radar antenna at which cancellation of the primary radar target by moving target indicator (MTI) circuits in the radar equipment causes a reduction or complete loss of signal.
(See ICAO term BLIND VELOCITY.)

BLIND SPOT– An area from which radio transmissions and/or radar echoes cannot be received. The term is also used to describe portions of the airport not visible from the control tower.

BLIND TRANSMISSION–
(See TRANSMITTING IN THE BLIND.)

BLIND VELOCITY [ICAO]– The radial velocity of a moving target such that the target is not seen on primary radars fitted with certain forms of fixed echo suppression.

BLIND ZONE–
(See BLIND SPOT.)

BLOCKED– Phraseology used to indicate that a radio transmission has been distorted or interrupted due to multiple simultaneous radio transmissions.

BOTTOM ALTITUDE– In reference to published altitude restrictions on a STAR or STAR runway transition, the lowest altitude authorized.

BOUNDARY LIGHTS–
(See AIRPORT LIGHTING.)

BRAKING ACTION (GOOD, GOOD TO MEDIUM, MEDIUM, MEDIUM TO POOR, POOR, OR NIL)– A report of conditions on the airport movement area providing a pilot with a degree/quality of braking to expect. Braking action is reported in terms of good, good to medium, medium, medium to poor, poor, or nil.
(See RUNWAY CONDITION READING.)
(See RUNWAY CONDITION REPORT.)
(See RUNWAY CONDITION CODES.)

BRAKING ACTION ADVISORIES– When tower controllers receive runway braking action reports which include the terms "medium," "poor," or "nil," or whenever weather conditions are conducive to deteriorating or rapidly changing runway braking conditions, the tower will include on the ATIS broadcast the statement, "Braking Action Advisories are in Effect." During the time braking action advisories are in effect, ATC will issue the most current braking action report for the runway in use to each arriving and departing aircraft. Pilots should be prepared for deteriorating braking conditions and should request current runway condition information if not issued by controllers. Pilots should also be prepared to provide a descriptive runway condition report to controllers after landing.

BREAKOUT– A technique to direct aircraft out of the approach stream. In the context of simultaneous (independent) parallel operations, a breakout is used to direct threatened aircraft away from a deviating aircraft.

BROADCAST– Transmission of information for which an acknowledgement is not expected.
(See ICAO term BROADCAST.)

BROADCAST [ICAO]– A transmission of information relating to air navigation that is not addressed to a specific station or stations.

BUFFER AREA– As applied to an MVA or MIA chart, a depicted 3 NM or 5 NM radius MVA/MIA sector isolating a displayed obstacle for which the sector is established. A portion of a buffer area can also be inclusive of a MVA/MIA sector polygon boundary.

BVLOS–
(See BEYOND VISUAL LINE OF SIGHT.)

C

CALCULATED LANDING TIME– A term that may be used in place of tentative or actual calculated landing time, whichever applies.

CALIBRATED AIRSPEED (CAS) – The indicated airspeed of an aircraft, corrected for position and instrument error. Calibrated airspeed is equal to true airspeed in standard atmosphere at sea level.

CALL FOR RELEASE– Wherein the overlying ARTCC requires a terminal facility to initiate verbal coordination to secure ARTCC approval for release of a departure into the en route environment.

CALL UP– Initial voice contact between a facility and an aircraft, using the identification of the unit being called and the unit initiating the call.
(Refer to AIM.)

CANADIAN MINIMUM NAVIGATION PERFORMANCE SPECIFICATION AIRSPACE– That portion of Canadian domestic airspace within which MNPS separation may be applied.

CARDINAL ALTITUDES– "Odd" or "Even" thousand-foot altitudes or flight levels; e.g., 5,000, 6,000, 7,000, FL 250, FL 260, FL 270.
(See ALTITUDE.)
(See FLIGHT LEVEL.)

CARDINAL FLIGHT LEVELS–
(See CARDINAL ALTITUDES.)

CAT–
(See CLEAR-AIR TURBULENCE.)

CATCH POINT– A fix/waypoint that serves as a transition point from the high altitude waypoint navigation structure to an arrival procedure (STAR) or the low altitude ground–based navigation structure.

CBO–
(See COMMUNITY–BASED ORGANIZATION.)

CEILING– The heights above the earth's surface of the lowest layer of clouds or obscuring phenomena that is reported as "broken," "overcast," or "obscuration," and not classified as "thin" or "partial."
(See ICAO term CEILING.)

CEILING [ICAO]– The height above the ground or water of the base of the lowest layer of cloud below 6,000 meters (20,000 feet) covering more than half the sky.

CENTER–
(See AIR ROUTE TRAFFIC CONTROL CENTER.)

CENTER'S AREA– The specified airspace within which an air route traffic control center (ARTCC) provides air traffic control and advisory service.
(See AIR ROUTE TRAFFIC CONTROL CENTER.)
(Refer to AIM.)

CENTER WEATHER ADVISORY– An unscheduled weather advisory issued by Center Weather Service Unit meteorologists for ATC use to alert pilots of existing or anticipated adverse weather conditions within the next 2 hours. A CWA may modify or redefine a SIGMET.
(See AIRMET.)
(See CONVECTIVE SIGMET.)
(See GRAPHICAL AIRMEN'S METEOROLOGICAL INFORMATION.)
(See SAW.)
(See SIGMET.)
(Refer to AIM.)

CENTRAL EAST PACIFIC– An organized route system between the U.S. West Coast and Hawaii.

CEP–
(See CENTRAL EAST PACIFIC.)

CERAP–
(See COMBINED CENTER-RAPCON.)

CERTIFICATE OF WAIVER OR AUTHORIZATION (COA)– An FAA grant of approval for a specific flight operation or airspace authorization or waiver.

CERTIFIED TOWER RADAR DISPLAY (CTRD)– An FAA radar display certified for use in the NAS.

CFR–
(See CALL FOR RELEASE.)

CHA
(See CONTINGENCY HAZARD AREA)

CHAFF– Thin, narrow metallic reflectors of various lengths and frequency responses, used to reflect radar energy. These reflectors, when dropped from aircraft and allowed to drift downward, result in large targets on the radar display.

CHART SUPPLEMENT– A series of civil/military flight information publications issued by FAA every 56 days consisting of the Chart Supplement U.S., Chart Supplement Alaska, and Chart Supplement Pacific.

CHART SUPPLEMENT ALASKA– A flight information publication designed for use with appropriate IFR or VFR charts which contains data on all airports, seaplane bases, and heliports open to the public including communications data, navigational facilities, airport diagrams, certain special notices, and non–regulatory procedures. Also included in this publication are selected entries needed to support the unique geographical operational conditions of Alaska. This publication is issued in one volume for the state of Alaska.

CHART SUPPLEMENT PACIFIC– A flight information publication designed for use with appropriate IFR or VFR charts which contains data on all airports, seaplane bases, and heliports open to the public including communications data, navigational facilities, airport diagrams, certain special notices, and non–regulatory procedures. Also included in this publication are Instrument Approach Procedures (IAP), Departure Procedures (DP), and Standard Terminal Arrival (STAR) charts, along with selected entries needed to support the unique geographical operational conditions of the Pacific Oceanic region. This publication is issued in one volume for the Hawaiian Islands and other selected Pacific Islands.

CHART SUPPLEMENT U.S.– A flight information publication designed for use with appropriate IFR or VFR charts which contains data on all airports, seaplane bases, and heliports open to the public including communications data, navigational facilities, airport diagrams, certain special notices, and non–regulatory procedures. This publication is issued for the conterminous U.S., Puerto Rico, and the Virgin Islands in seven volumes according to geographical area.

CHARTED VFR FLYWAYS– Charted VFR Flyways are flight paths recommended for use to bypass areas heavily traversed by large turbine-powered aircraft. Pilot compliance with recommended flyways and associated altitudes is strictly voluntary. VFR Flyway Planning charts are published on the back of existing VFR Terminal Area charts.

CHARTED VISUAL FLIGHT PROCEDURE APPROACH– An approach conducted while operating on an instrument flight rules (IFR) flight plan which authorizes the pilot of an aircraft to proceed visually and clear of clouds to the airport via visual landmarks and other information depicted on a charted visual flight procedure. This approach must be authorized and under the control of the appropriate air traffic control facility. Weather minimums required are depicted on the chart.

CHASE– An aircraft flown in proximity to another aircraft normally to observe its performance during training or testing.

CHASE AIRCRAFT–
(See CHASE.)

CHOP– A form of turbulence.

a. Light Chop– Turbulence that causes slight, rapid and somewhat rhythmic bumpiness without appreciable changes in altitude or attitude.

b. Moderate Chop– Turbulence similar to Light Chop but of greater intensity. It causes rapid bumps or jolts without appreciable changes in aircraft altitude or attitude.
(See TURBULENCE.)

CIRCLE-TO-LAND MANEUVER– A maneuver initiated by the pilot to align the aircraft with a runway for landing when a straight-in landing from an instrument approach is not possible or is not desirable. At tower controlled airports, this maneuver is made only after ATC authorization has been obtained and the pilot has established required visual reference to the airport.
(See CIRCLE TO RUNWAY.)
(See LANDING MINIMUMS.)
(Refer to AIM.)

CIRCLE TO RUNWAY (RUNWAY NUMBER)– Used by ATC to inform the pilot that he/she must circle to land because the runway in use is other than the runway aligned with the instrument approach procedure. When the direction of the circling maneuver in relation to the airport/runway is required, the controller will state the direction (eight cardinal compass points) and specify a left or right downwind or base leg as appropriate; e.g., "Cleared VOR Runway Three Six Approach circle to Runway Two Two," or "Circle northwest of the airport for a right downwind to Runway Two Two."
(See CIRCLE-TO-LAND MANEUVER.)
(See LANDING MINIMUMS.)
(Refer to AIM.)

CIRCLING APPROACH–
(See CIRCLE-TO-LAND MANEUVER.)

CIRCLING MANEUVER–
(See CIRCLE-TO-LAND MANEUVER.)

CIRCLING MINIMA–
(See CONTROLLED AIRSPACE.)

CIVIL AIRCRAFT OPERATION (CAO)– Aircraft operations other than public use.

CLASS A AIRSPACE–
(See CONTROLLED AIRSPACE.)

CLASS B AIRSPACE–
(See CONTROLLED AIRSPACE.)

CLASS C AIRSPACE–
(See CONTROLLED AIRSPACE.)

CLASS D AIRSPACE–
(See CONTROLLED AIRSPACE.)

CLASS E AIRSPACE–
(See CONTROLLED AIRSPACE.)

CLASS G AIRSPACE– Airspace that is not designated in 14 CFR Part 71 as Class A, Class B, Class C, Class D, or Class E controlled airspace is Class G (uncontrolled) airspace.
(See UNCONTROLLED AIRSPACE.)

CLEAR AIR TURBULENCE (CAT)– Turbulence encountered in air where no clouds are present. This term is commonly applied to high-level turbulence associated with wind shear. CAT is often encountered in the vicinity of the jet stream.

(See WIND SHEAR.)
(See JET STREAM.)

CLEAR OF THE RUNWAY–

a. Taxiing aircraft, which is approaching a runway, is clear of the runway when all parts of the aircraft are held short of the applicable runway holding position marking.

b. A pilot or controller may consider an aircraft, which is exiting or crossing a runway, to be clear of the runway when all parts of the aircraft are beyond the runway edge and there are no restrictions to its continued movement beyond the applicable runway holding position marking.

c. Pilots and controllers shall exercise good judgment to ensure that adequate separation exists between all aircraft on runways and taxiways at airports with inadequate runway edge lines or holding position markings.

CLEARANCE–

(See AIR TRAFFIC CLEARANCE.)

CLEARANCE LIMIT– The fix, point, or location to which an aircraft is cleared when issued an air traffic clearance.

(See ICAO term CLEARANCE LIMIT.)

CLEARANCE LIMIT [ICAO]– The point to which an aircraft is granted an air traffic control clearance.

CLEARANCE VOID IF NOT OFF BY (TIME)– Used by ATC to advise an aircraft that the departure release is automatically canceled if takeoff is not made prior to a specified time. The expiration of a clearance void time does not cancel the departure clearance or IFR flight plan. It withdraws the pilot's authority to depart IFR until a new departure release/release time has been issued by ATC. Pilots who choose to depart VFR after their clearance void time has expired should not depart using the previously assigned IFR transponder code.

(See ICAO term CLEARANCE VOID TIME.)

CLEARANCE VOID TIME [ICAO]– A time specified by an air traffic control unit at which a clearance ceases to be valid unless the aircraft concerned has already taken action to comply therewith.

CLEARED APPROACH– ATC authorization for an aircraft to execute any standard or special instrument approach procedure for that airport. Normally, an aircraft will be cleared for a specific instrument approach procedure.

(See CLEARED (Type of) APPROACH.)
(See INSTRUMENT APPROACH PROCEDURE.)
(Refer to 14 CFR Part 91.)
(Refer to AIM.)

CLEARED (Type of) APPROACH– ATC authorization for an aircraft to execute a specific instrument approach procedure to an airport; e.g., "Cleared ILS Runway Three Six Approach."

(See APPROACH CLEARANCE.)
(See INSTRUMENT APPROACH PROCEDURE.)
(Refer to 14 CFR Part 91.)
(Refer to AIM.)

CLEARED AS FILED– Means the aircraft is cleared to proceed in accordance with the route of flight filed in the flight plan. This clearance does not include the altitude, DP, or DP Transition.

(See REQUEST FULL ROUTE CLEARANCE.)
(Refer to AIM.)

CLEARED FOR TAKEOFF– ATC authorization for an aircraft to depart. It is predicated on known traffic and known physical airport conditions.

CLEARED FOR THE OPTION– ATC authorization for an aircraft to make a touch-and-go, low approach, missed approach, stop and go, or full stop landing at the discretion of the pilot. It is normally used in training so that an instructor can evaluate a student's performance under changing situations. Pilots should advise ATC if they decide to remain on the runway, of any delay in their stop and go, delay clearing the runway, or are unable to comply with the instruction(s).

(See OPTION APPROACH.)
(Refer to AIM.)

CLEARED THROUGH– ATC authorization for an aircraft to make intermediate stops at specified airports without refiling a flight plan while en route to the clearance limit.

CLEARED TO LAND– ATC authorization for an aircraft to land. It is predicated on known traffic and known physical airport conditions.

CLEARWAY– An area beyond the takeoff runway under the control of airport authorities within which terrain or fixed obstacles may not extend above specified limits. These areas may be required for certain turbine-powered operations and the size and upward slope of the clearway will differ depending on when the aircraft was certificated.

(Refer to 14 CFR Part 1.)

CLIMB TO VFR– ATC authorization for an aircraft to climb to VFR conditions within Class B, C, D, and E surface areas when the only weather limitation is restricted visibility. The aircraft must remain clear of clouds while climbing to VFR.

(See SPECIAL VFR CONDITIONS.)
(Refer to AIM.)

CLIMBOUT– That portion of flight operation between takeoff and the initial cruising altitude.

CLIMB VIA– An abbreviated ATC clearance that requires compliance with the procedure lateral path, associated speed restrictions, and altitude restrictions along the cleared route or procedure.

CLOSE PARALLEL RUNWAYS– Two parallel runways whose extended centerlines are separated by less than 4,300 feet and at least 3000 feet (750 feet for SOIA operations) for which ATC is authorized to conduct simultaneous independent approach operations. PRM and simultaneous close parallel appear in approach title. Dual communications, special pilot training, an Attention All Users Page (AAUP), NTZ monitoring by displays that have aural and visual alerting algorithms are required. A high update rate surveillance sensor is required for certain runway or approach course spacing.

CLOSED LOOP CLEARANCE– A vector or reroute clearance that includes a return to route point and updates ERAM to accurately reflect the anticipated route (e.g., a QU route pick that anticipates length of vector and includes the next fix that ties into the route of flight.)

CLOSED RUNWAY– A runway that is unusable for aircraft operations. Only the airport management/military operations office can close a runway.

CLOSED TRAFFIC– Successive operations involving takeoffs and landings or low approaches where the aircraft does not exit the traffic pattern.

CLOUD– A cloud is a visible accumulation of minute water droplets and/or ice particles in the atmosphere above the Earth's surface. Cloud differs from ground fog, fog, or ice fog only in that the latter are, by definition, in contact with the Earth's surface.

CLT–

(See CALCULATED LANDING TIME.)

CLUTTER– In radar operations, clutter refers to the reception and visual display of radar returns caused by precipitation, chaff, terrain, numerous aircraft targets, or other phenomena. Such returns may limit or preclude ATC from providing services based on radar.
(See CHAFF.)
(See GROUND CLUTTER.)
(See PRECIPITATION.)
(See TARGET.)
(See ICAO term RADAR CLUTTER.)

CMNPS–
(See CANADIAN MINIMUM NAVIGATION PERFORMANCE SPECIFICATION AIRSPACE.)

COA–
(See CERTIFICATE OF WAIVER OR AUTHORIZATION.)

COASTAL FIX– A navigation aid or intersection where an aircraft transitions between the domestic route structure and the oceanic route structure.

CODES– The number assigned to a particular multiple pulse reply signal transmitted by a transponder.
(See DISCRETE CODE.)

COLD TEMPERATURE CORRECTION– A correction in feet, based on height above airport and temperature, that is added to the aircraft's indicated altitude to offset the effect of cold temperature on true altitude.

COLLABORATIVE TRAJECTORY OPTIONS PROGRAM (CTOP)– CTOP is a traffic management program administered by the Air Traffic Control System Command Center (ATCSCC) that manages demand through constrained airspace, while considering operator preference with regard to both route and delay as defined in a Trajectory Options Set (TOS).

COMBINED CENTER-RAPCON– An air traffic facility which combines the functions of an ARTCC and a radar approach control facility.
(See AIR ROUTE TRAFFIC CONTROL CENTER.)
(See RADAR APPROACH CONTROL FACILITY.)

COMMON POINT– A significant point over which two or more aircraft will report passing or have reported passing before proceeding on the same or diverging tracks. To establish/maintain longitudinal separation, a controller may determine a common point not originally in the aircraft's flight plan and then clear the aircraft to fly over the point.
(See SIGNIFICANT POINT.)

COMMON PORTION–
(See COMMON ROUTE.)

COMMON ROUTE– That segment of a North American Route between the inland navigation facility and the coastal fix.

OR

COMMON ROUTE–
(See SEGMENTS OF A SID/STAR)

COMMON TRAFFIC ADVISORY FREQUENCY (CTAF)– A frequency designed for the purpose of carrying out airport advisory practices while operating to or from an airport without an operating control tower. The CTAF may be a UNICOM, Multicom, FSS, or tower frequency and is identified in appropriate aeronautical publications.
(See DESIGNATED COMMON TRAFFIC ADVISORY FREQUENCY (CTAF) AREA.)
(Refer to AC 90-66, Non-Towered Airport Flight Operations.)

COMMUNITY-BASED ORGANIZATION (CBO)– A membership-based entity, described under Section 501(a,c), whose mission is the furtherance of model aviation. (see also, 49 United States Code (USC) §44809 (h) and Advisory Circular (AC) 91-57).

COMPASS LOCATOR– A low power, low or medium frequency (L/MF) radio beacon installed at the site of the outer or middle marker of an instrument landing system (ILS). It can be used for navigation at distances of approximately 15 miles or as authorized in the approach procedure.

a. Outer Compass Locator (LOM)– A compass locator installed at the site of the outer marker of an instrument landing system.

(See OUTER MARKER.)

b. Middle Compass Locator (LMM)– A compass locator installed at the site of the middle marker of an instrument landing system.

(See MIDDLE MARKER.)
(See ICAO term LOCATOR.)

COMPASS ROSE– A circle, graduated in degrees, printed on some charts or marked on the ground at an airport. It is used as a reference to either true or magnetic direction.

COMPLY WITH RESTRICTIONS– An ATC instruction that requires an aircraft being vectored back onto an arrival or departure procedure to comply with all altitude and/or speed restrictions depicted on the procedure. This term may be used in lieu of repeating each remaining restriction that appears on the procedure.

COMPOSITE FLIGHT PLAN– A flight plan which specifies VFR operation for one portion of flight and IFR for another portion. It is used primarily in military operations.

(Refer to AIM.)

COMPULSORY REPORTING POINTS– Reporting points which must be reported to ATC. They are designated on aeronautical charts by solid triangles or filed in a flight plan as fixes selected to define direct routes. These points are geographical locations which are defined by navigation aids/fixes. Pilots should discontinue position reporting over compulsory reporting points when informed by ATC that their aircraft is in "radar contact."

COMPUTER NAVIGATION FIX (CNF)– A Computer Navigation Fix is a point defined by a latitude/longitude coordinate and is required to support Performance-Based Navigation (PBN) operations. A five-letter identifier denoting a CNF can be found next to an "x" on en route charts and on some approach charts. Eventually, all CNFs will be labeled and begin with the letters "CF" followed by three consonants (e.g., 'CFWBG'). CNFs are not recognized by ATC, are not contained in ATC fix or automation databases, and are not used for ATC purposes. Pilots should not use CNFs for point-to-point navigation (e.g., proceed direct), filing a flight plan, or in aircraft/ATC communications. Use of CNFs has not been adopted or recognized by the International Civil Aviation Organization (ICAO).

(REFER to AIM 1-1-17b5(i)(2), Global Positioning System (GPS).

CONDITIONS NOT MONITORED– When an airport operator cannot monitor the condition of the movement area or airfield surface area, this information is issued as a NOTAM. Usually necessitated due to staffing, operating hours or other mitigating factors associated with airport operations.

CONFIDENCE MANEUVER– A confidence maneuver consists of one or more turns, a climb or descent, or other maneuver to determine if the pilot in command (PIC) is able to receive and comply with ATC instructions.

CONFLICT ALERT– A function of certain air traffic control automated systems designed to alert radar controllers to existing or pending situations between tracked targets (known IFR or VFR aircraft) that require his/her immediate attention/action.

(See MODE C INTRUDER ALERT.)

CONFLICT RESOLUTION– The resolution of potential conflictions between aircraft that are radar identified and in communication with ATC by ensuring that radar targets do not touch. Pertinent traffic advisories shall be issued when this procedure is applied.

Note: This procedure shall not be provided utilizing mosaic radar systems.

CONFORMANCE– The condition established when an aircraft's actual position is within the conformance region constructed around that aircraft at its position, according to the trajectory associated with the aircraft's Current Plan.

CONFORMANCE REGION– A volume, bounded laterally, vertically, and longitudinally, within which an aircraft must be at a given time in order to be in conformance with the Current Plan Trajectory for that aircraft. At a given time, the conformance region is determined by the simultaneous application of the lateral, vertical, and longitudinal conformance bounds for the aircraft at the position defined by time and aircraft's trajectory.

CONSOLAN– A low frequency, long-distance NAVAID used principally for transoceanic navigations.

CONSOLIDATED WAKE TURBULENCE (CWT)– A version of RECAT that has nine categories, A through I, that refines the grouping of aircraft while optimizing wake turbulence separation.

CONSTRAINT SATISFACTION POINT (CSP)– Meter Reference Elements (MREs) that are actively scheduled by TBFM. Constraint satisfaction occurs when the Scheduled Time of Arrival generated for each metered flight conforms to all the scheduling constraints specified at all the applicable CSPs.

CONTACT–

a. Establish communication with (followed by the name of the facility and, if appropriate, the frequency to be used).

b. A flight condition wherein the pilot ascertains the attitude of his/her aircraft and navigates by visual reference to the surface.

(See CONTACT APPROACH.)
(See RADAR CONTACT.)

CONTACT APPROACH– An approach wherein an aircraft on an IFR flight plan, having an air traffic control authorization, operating clear of clouds with at least 1 mile flight visibility and a reasonable expectation of continuing to the destination airport in those conditions, may deviate from the instrument approach procedure and proceed to the destination airport by visual reference to the surface. This approach will only be authorized when requested by the pilot and the reported ground visibility at the destination airport is at least 1 statute mile.

(Refer to AIM.)

CONTAMINATED RUNWAY– A runway is considered contaminated whenever standing water, ice, snow, slush, frost in any form, heavy rubber, or other substances are present. A runway is contaminated with respect to rubber deposits or other friction-degrading substances when the average friction value for any 500-foot segment of the runway within the ALD fails below the recommended minimum friction level and the average friction value in the adjacent 500-foot segments falls below the maintenance planning friction level.

CONTERMINOUS U.S.– The 48 adjoining States and the District of Columbia.

CONTINENTAL UNITED STATES– The 49 States located on the continent of North America and the District of Columbia.

CONTINGENCY HAZARD AREA (CHA)– Used by ATC. Areas of airspace that are defined and distributed in advance of a launch or reentry operation and are activated in response to a failure.

(See AIRCRAFT HAZARD AREA.)
(See REFINED HAZARD AREA.)
(See TRANSITIONAL HAZARD AREA.)

CONTINUE– When used as a control instruction should be followed by another word or words clarifying what is expected of the pilot. Example: "continue taxi," "continue descent," "continue inbound," etc.

CONTROL AREA [ICAO]– A controlled airspace extending upwards from a specified limit above the earth.

CONTROL SECTOR– An airspace area of defined horizontal and vertical dimensions for which a controller or group of controllers has air traffic control responsibility, normally within an air route traffic control center or an approach control facility. Sectors are established based on predominant traffic flows, altitude strata, and

controller workload. Pilot communications during operations within a sector are normally maintained on discrete frequencies assigned to the sector.
(See DISCRETE FREQUENCY.)

CONTROL SLASH− A radar beacon slash representing the actual position of the associated aircraft. Normally, the control slash is the one closest to the interrogating radar beacon site. When ARTCC radar is operating in narrowband (digitized) mode, the control slash is converted to a target symbol.

CONTROLLED AIRSPACE− An airspace of defined dimensions within which air traffic control service is provided to IFR flights and to VFR flights in accordance with the airspace classification.

a. Controlled airspace is a generic term that covers Class A, Class B, Class C, Class D, and Class E airspace.

b. Controlled airspace is also that airspace within which all aircraft operators are subject to certain pilot qualifications, operating rules, and equipment requirements in 14 CFR Part 91 (for specific operating requirements, please refer to 14 CFR Part 91). For IFR operations in any class of controlled airspace, a pilot must file an IFR flight plan and receive an appropriate ATC clearance. Each Class B, Class C, and Class D airspace area designated for an airport contains at least one primary airport around which the airspace is designated (for specific designations and descriptions of the airspace classes, please refer to 14 CFR Part 71).

c. Controlled airspace in the United States is designated as follows:

1. CLASS A− Generally, that airspace from 18,000 feet MSL up to and including FL 600, including the airspace overlying the waters within 12 nautical miles of the coast of the 48 contiguous States and Alaska. Unless otherwise authorized, all persons must operate their aircraft under IFR.

2. CLASS B− Generally, that airspace from the surface to 10,000 feet MSL surrounding the nation's busiest airports in terms of airport operations or passenger enplanements. The configuration of each Class B airspace area is individually tailored and consists of a surface area and two or more layers (some Class B airspace areas resemble upside-down wedding cakes), and is designed to contain all published instrument procedures once an aircraft enters the airspace. An ATC clearance is required for all aircraft to operate in the area, and all aircraft that are so cleared receive separation services within the airspace. The cloud clearance requirement for VFR operations is "clear of clouds."

3. CLASS C− Generally, that airspace from the surface to 4,000 feet above the airport elevation (charted in MSL) surrounding those airports that have an operational control tower, are serviced by a radar approach control, and that have a certain number of IFR operations or passenger enplanements. Although the configuration of each Class C area is individually tailored, the airspace usually consists of a surface area with a 5 NM radius, a circle with a 10 NM radius that extends no lower than 1,200 feet up to 4,000 feet above the airport elevation, and an outer area that is not charted. Each person must establish two-way radio communications with the ATC facility providing air traffic services prior to entering the airspace and thereafter maintain those communications while within the airspace. VFR aircraft are only separated from IFR aircraft within the airspace.
(See OUTER AREA.)

4. CLASS D− Generally, that airspace from the surface to 2,500 feet above the airport elevation (charted in MSL) surrounding those airports that have an operational control tower. The configuration of each Class D airspace area is individually tailored and when instrument procedures are published, the airspace will normally be designed to contain the procedures. Arrival extensions for instrument approach procedures may be Class D or Class E airspace. Unless otherwise authorized, each person must establish two-way radio communications with the ATC facility providing air traffic services prior to entering the airspace and thereafter maintain those communications while in the airspace. No separation services are provided to VFR aircraft.

5. CLASS E− Generally, if the airspace is not Class A, Class B, Class C, or Class D, and it is controlled airspace, it is Class E airspace. Class E airspace extends upward from either the surface or a designated altitude to the overlying or adjacent controlled airspace. When designated as a surface area, the airspace will be configured to contain all instrument procedures. Also in this class are Federal airways, airspace beginning at either 700 or 1,200 feet AGL used to transition to/from the terminal or en route environment, en route domestic, and offshore airspace areas designated below 18,000 feet MSL. Unless designated at a lower altitude, Class E airspace begins at 14,500 MSL over the United States, including that airspace overlying the waters within 12 nautical miles of the coast of the 48 contiguous States and Alaska, up to, but not including 18,000 feet MSL, and the airspace above FL 600.

CONTROLLED AIRSPACE [ICAO]– An airspace of defined dimensions within which air traffic control service is provided to IFR flights and to VFR flights in accordance with the airspace classification.

Note: Controlled airspace is a generic term which covers ATS airspace Classes A, B, C, D, and E.

CONTROLLED TIME OF ARRIVAL– Arrival time assigned during a Traffic Management Program. This time may be modified due to adjustments or user options.

CONTROLLER–
(See AIR TRAFFIC CONTROL SPECIALIST.)

CONTROLLER [ICAO]– A person authorized to provide air traffic control services.

CONTROLLER PILOT DATA LINK COMMUNICATIONS (CPDLC)– A two–way digital communications system that conveys textual air traffic control messages between controllers and pilots using ground or satellite-based radio relay stations.

CONVECTIVE SIGMET– A weather advisory concerning convective weather significant to the safety of all aircraft. Convective SIGMETs are issued for tornadoes, lines of thunderstorms, embedded thunderstorms of any intensity level, areas of thunderstorms greater than or equal to VIP level 4 with an area coverage of $^{4}/_{10}$ (40%) or more, and hail $^{3}/_{4}$ inch or greater.
(See AIRMET.)
(See CWA.)
(See GRAPHICAL AIRMEN'S METEOROLOGICAL INFORMATION.)
(See SAW.)
(See SIGMET.)
(Refer to AIM.)

CONVECTIVE SIGNIFICANT METEOROLOGICAL INFORMATION–
(See CONVECTIVE SIGMET.)

COOPERATIVE SURVEILLANCE– Any surveillance system, such as secondary surveillance radar (SSR), wide–area multilateration (WAM), or ADS–B, that is dependent upon the presence of certain equipment onboard the aircraft or vehicle to be detected.
(See AUTOMATIC DEPENDENT SURVEILLANCE–BROADCAST.)
(See NON–COOPERATIVE SURVEILLANCE.)
(See RADAR.)
(See WIDE AREA MULTILATERATION.)

COORDINATES– The intersection of lines of reference, usually expressed in degrees/minutes/seconds of latitude and longitude, used to determine position or location.

COORDINATION FIX– The fix in relation to which facilities will handoff, transfer control of an aircraft, or coordinate flight progress data. For terminal facilities, it may also serve as a clearance for arriving aircraft.

COPTER–
(See HELICOPTER.)

CORRECTION– An error has been made in the transmission and the correct version follows.

COUPLED APPROACH– An instrument approach performed by the aircraft autopilot, and/or visually depicted on the flight director, which is receiving position information and/or steering commands from onboard navigational equipment. In general, coupled non-precision approaches must be flown manually (autopilot disengaged) at altitudes lower than 50 feet AGL below the minimum descent altitude, and coupled precision approaches must be flown manually (autopilot disengaged) below 50 feet AGL unless authorized to conduct autoland operations. Coupled instrument approaches are commonly flown to the allowable IFR weather minima established by the operator or PIC, or flown VFR for training and safety.

COUPLED SCHEDULING (CS)/ EXTENDED METERING (XM)– Adds additional Constraint Satisfaction Points for metered aircraft along their route. This provides the ability to merge flows upstream from the meter fix and results in a more optimal distribution of delays over a greater distance from the airport, increased meter list accuracy, and more accurate delivery to the meter fix.

COURSE–

a. The intended direction of flight in the horizontal plane measured in degrees from north.

b. The ILS localizer signal pattern usually specified as the front course or the back course.

(See BEARING.)
(See INSTRUMENT LANDING SYSTEM.)
(See RADIAL.)

CPDLC–

(See CONTROLLER PILOT DATA LINK COMMUNICATIONS.)

CPL [ICAO]–

(See ICAO term CURRENT FLIGHT PLAN.)

CREWMEMBER (UAS)– A person assigned to perform an operational duty. A UAS crewmember includes the remote pilot in command, the person manipulating the controls, and visual observers but may also include other persons as appropriate or required to ensure the safe operation of the UAS (e.g., sensor operator, ground control station operator).

CRITICAL ENGINE– The engine which, upon failure, would most adversely affect the performance or handling qualities of an aircraft.

CROSS (FIX) AT (ALTITUDE)– Used by ATC when a specific altitude restriction at a specified fix is required.

CROSS (FIX) AT OR ABOVE (ALTITUDE)– Used by ATC when an altitude restriction at a specified fix is required. It does not prohibit the aircraft from crossing the fix at a higher altitude than specified; however, the higher altitude may not be one that will violate a succeeding altitude restriction or altitude assignment.

(See ALTITUDE RESTRICTION.)
(Refer to AIM.)

CROSS (FIX) AT OR BELOW (ALTITUDE)– Used by ATC when a maximum crossing altitude at a specific fix is required. It does not prohibit the aircraft from crossing the fix at a lower altitude; however, it must be at or above the minimum IFR altitude.

(See ALTITUDE RESTRICTION.)
(See MINIMUM IFR ALTITUDES.)
(Refer to 14 CFR Part 91.)

CROSSWIND–

a. When used concerning the traffic pattern, the word means "crosswind leg."

(See TRAFFIC PATTERN.)

b. When used concerning wind conditions, the word means a wind not parallel to the runway or the path of an aircraft.

(See CROSSWIND COMPONENT.)

CROSSWIND COMPONENT– The wind component measured in knots at 90 degrees to the longitudinal axis of the runway.

CRUISE– Used in an ATC clearance to authorize a pilot to conduct flight at any altitude from the minimum IFR altitude up to and including the altitude specified in the clearance. The pilot may level off at any intermediate altitude within this block of airspace. Climb/descent within the block is to be made at the discretion of the pilot. However, once the pilot starts descent and verbally reports leaving an altitude in the block, he/she may not return to that altitude without additional ATC clearance. Further, it is approval for the pilot to proceed to and make an approach at destination airport and can be used in conjunction with:

a. An airport clearance limit at locations with a standard/special instrument approach procedure. The CFRs require that if an instrument letdown to an airport is necessary, the pilot shall make the letdown in accordance with a standard/special instrument approach procedure for that airport, or

b. An airport clearance limit at locations that are within/below/outside controlled airspace and without a standard/special instrument approach procedure. Such a clearance is NOT AUTHORIZATION for the pilot to descend under IFR conditions below the applicable minimum IFR altitude nor does it imply that ATC is exercising control over aircraft in Class G airspace; however, it provides a means for the aircraft to proceed to destination airport, descend, and land in accordance with applicable CFRs governing VFR flight operations. Also, this provides search and rescue protection until such time as the IFR flight plan is closed.
(See INSTRUMENT APPROACH PROCEDURE.)

CRUISE CLIMB– A climb technique employed by aircraft, usually at a constant power setting, resulting in an increase of altitude as the aircraft weight decreases.

CRUISING ALTITUDE– An altitude or flight level maintained during en route level flight. This is a constant altitude and should not be confused with a cruise clearance.
(See ALTITUDE.)
(See ICAO term CRUISING LEVEL.)

CRUISING LEVEL–
(See CRUISING ALTITUDE.)

CRUISING LEVEL [ICAO]– A level maintained during a significant portion of a flight.

CSP–
(See CONSTRAINT SATISFACTION POINT)

CT MESSAGE– An EDCT time generated by the ATCSCC to regulate traffic at arrival airports. Normally, a CT message is automatically transferred from the traffic management system computer to the NAS en route computer and appears as an EDCT. In the event of a communication failure between the traffic management system computer and the NAS, the CT message can be manually entered by the TMC at the en route facility.

CTA–
(See CONTROLLED TIME OF ARRIVAL.)
(See ICAO term CONTROL AREA.)

CTAF–
(See COMMON TRAFFIC ADVISORY FREQUENCY.)

CTOP–
(See COLLABORATIVE TRAJECTORY OPTIONS PROGRAM)

CTRD–
(See CERTIFIED TOWER RADAR DISPLAY.)

CURRENT FLIGHT PLAN [ICAO]– The flight plan, including changes, if any, brought about by subsequent clearances.

CVFP APPROACH–
(See CHARTED VISUAL FLIGHT PROCEDURE APPROACH.)

CWA–
(See CENTER WEATHER ADVISORY and WEATHER ADVISORY.)

CWT–
(See CONSOLIDATED WAKE TURBULENCE.)

D

D–ATIS–
(See DIGITAL-AUTOMATIC TERMINAL INFORMATION SERVICE.)

D–ATIS [ICAO]–
(See ICAO Term DATA LINK AUTOMATIC TERMINAL INFORMATION SERVICE.)

DA [ICAO]–
(See ICAO Term DECISION ALTITUDE/DECISION HEIGHT.)

DAIR–
(See DIRECT ALTITUDE AND IDENTITY READOUT.)

DANGER AREA [ICAO]– An airspace of defined dimensions within which activities dangerous to the flight of aircraft may exist at specified times.

Note: The term "Danger Area" is not used in reference to areas within the United States or any of its possessions or territories.

DAS–
(See DELAY ASSIGNMENT.)

DATA BLOCK–
(See ALPHANUMERIC DISPLAY.)

DATA LINK AUTOMATIC TERMINAL INFORMATION SERVICE (D–ATIS) [ICAO]– The provision of ATIS via data link.

DCT–
(See DELAY COUNTDOWN TIMER.)

DEAD RECKONING– Dead reckoning, as applied to flying, is the navigation of an airplane solely by means of computations based on airspeed, course, heading, wind direction, and speed, groundspeed, and elapsed time.

DEBRIS RESPONSE AREA (DRA)– Used by ATC. Areas of airspace that may be activated in response to unplanned falling debris in the NAS.

DECISION ALTITUDE/DECISION HEIGHT [ICAO Annex 6]- A specified altitude or height (A/H) in the precision approach at which a missed approach must be initiated if the required visual reference to continue the approach has not been established.
1. Decision altitude (DA) is referenced to mean sea level and decision height (DH) is referenced to the threshold elevation.
2. Category II and III minima are expressed as a DH and not a DA. Minima is assessed by reference to a radio altimeter and not a barometric altimeter, which makes the minima a DH.
3. The required visual reference means that section of the visual aids or of the approach area which should have been in view for sufficient time for the pilot to have made an assessment of the aircraft position and rate of change of position, in relation to the desired flight path.

DECISION ALTITUDE (DA)– A specified altitude (mean sea level (MSL)) on an instrument approach procedure (ILS, GLS, vertically guided RNAV) at which the pilot must decide whether to continue the approach or initiate an immediate missed approach if the pilot does not see the required visual references.

DECISION HEIGHT (DH)– With respect to the operation of aircraft, means the height at which a decision must be made during an ILS or PAR instrument approach to either continue the approach or to execute a missed approach.
(See ICAO term DECISION ALTITUDE/DECISION HEIGHT.)

DECODER– The device used to decipher signals received from ATCRBS transponders to effect their display as select codes.
(See CODES.)
(See RADAR.)

DEFENSE AREA– Any airspace of the contiguous United States that is not an ADIZ in which the control of aircraft is required for reasons of national security.

DEFENSE VISUAL FLIGHT RULES– Rules applicable to flights within an ADIZ conducted under the visual flight rules in 14 CFR Part 91.
(See AIR DEFENSE IDENTIFICATION ZONE.)
(Refer to 14 CFR Part 91.)
(Refer to 14 CFR Part 99.)

DELAY ASSIGNMENT (DAS)– Delays are distributed to aircraft based on the traffic management program parameters. The delay assignment is calculated in 15–minute increments and appears as a table in Traffic Flow Management System (TFMS).

DELAY COUNTDOWN TIMER (DCT)– The display of the delay that must be absorbed by a flight prior to crossing a Meter Reference Element (MRE) to meet the TBFM Scheduled Time of Arrival (STA). It is calculated by taking the difference between the frozen STA and the Estimated Time of Arrival (ETA).

DELAY INDEFINITE (REASON IF KNOWN) EXPECT FURTHER CLEARANCE (TIME)– Used by ATC to inform a pilot when an accurate estimate of the delay time and the reason for the delay cannot immediately be determined; e.g., a disabled aircraft on the runway, terminal or center area saturation, weather below landing minimums, etc.
(See EXPECT FURTHER CLEARANCE (TIME).)

DEPARTURE CENTER– The ARTCC having jurisdiction for the airspace that generates a flight to the impacted airport.

DEPARTURE CONTROL– A function of an approach control facility providing air traffic control service for departing IFR and, under certain conditions, VFR aircraft.
(See APPROACH CONTROL FACILITY.)
(Refer to AIM.)

DEPARTURE SEQUENCING PROGRAM– A program designed to assist in achieving a specified interval over a common point for departures.

DEPARTURE TIME– The time an aircraft becomes airborne.

DEPARTURE VIEWER– A capability within the Traffic Flow Management System (TFMS) that provides combined displays for monitoring departure by fixes and departure airports. Traffic management personnel can customize the displays by selecting the departure airports and fixes of interest. The information displayed is the demand for the resource (fix or departure airport) in time bins with the flight list and a flight history for one flight at a time. From the display, flights can be selected for route amendment, one or more at a time, and the Route Amendment Dialogue (RAD) screen automatically opens for easy route selection and execution. Reroute options are based on Coded Departure Route (CDR) database and Trajectory Options Set (TOS) (when available).

DESCEND VIA– An abbreviated ATC clearance that requires compliance with a published procedure lateral path and associated speed restrictions and provides a pilot-discretion descent to comply with published altitude restrictions.

DESCENT SPEED ADJUSTMENTS– Speed deceleration calculations made to determine an accurate VTA. These calculations start at the transition point and use arrival speed segments to the vertex.

DESIGNATED COMMON TRAFFIC ADVISORY FREQUENCY (CTAF) AREA– In Alaska, in addition to being designated for the purpose of carrying out airport advisory practices while operating to or from an airport without an operating airport traffic control tower, a CTAF may also be designated for the purpose of carrying out advisory practices for operations in and through areas with a high volume of VFR traffic.

DESIRED COURSE–

a. True– A predetermined desired course direction to be followed (measured in degrees from true north).

b. Magnetic– A predetermined desired course direction to be followed (measured in degrees from local magnetic north).

DESIRED TRACK– The planned or intended track between two waypoints. It is measured in degrees from either magnetic or true north. The instantaneous angle may change from point to point along the great circle track between waypoints.

DETRESFA (DISTRESS PHASE) [ICAO]– The code word used to designate an emergency phase wherein there is reasonable certainty that an aircraft and its occupants are threatened by grave and imminent danger or require immediate assistance.

DEVIATIONS–

a. A departure from a current clearance, such as an off course maneuver to avoid weather or turbulence.

b. Where specifically authorized in the CFRs and requested by the pilot, ATC may permit pilots to deviate from certain regulations.

DH–
(See DECISION HEIGHT.)

DH [ICAO]–
(See ICAO Term DECISION ALTITUDE/ DECISION HEIGHT.)

DIGITAL-AUTOMATIC TERMINAL INFORMATION SERVICE (D-ATIS)– The service provides text messages to aircraft, airlines, and other users outside the standard reception range of conventional ATIS via landline and data link communications to the cockpit. Also, the service provides a computer–synthesized voice message that can be transmitted to all aircraft within range of existing transmitters. The Terminal Data Link System (TDLS) D-ATIS application uses weather inputs from local automated weather sources or manually entered meteorological data together with preprogrammed menus to provide standard information to users. Airports with D-ATIS capability are listed in the Chart Supplement U.S.

DIGITAL TARGET– A computer–generated symbol representing an aircraft's position, based on a primary return or radar beacon reply, shown on a digital display.

DIGITAL TERMINAL AUTOMATION SYSTEM (DTAS)– A system where digital radar and beacon data is presented on digital displays and the operational program monitors the system performance on a real–time basis.

DIGITIZED TARGET– A computer–generated indication shown on an analog radar display resulting from a primary radar return or a radar beacon reply.

DIRECT– Straight line flight between two navigational aids, fixes, points, or any combination thereof. When used by pilots in describing off-airway routes, points defining direct route segments become compulsory reporting points unless the aircraft is under radar contact.

DIRECTLY BEHIND– An aircraft is considered to be operating directly behind when it is following the actual flight path of the lead aircraft over the surface of the earth except when applying wake turbulence separation criteria.

DISCRETE BEACON CODE–
(See DISCRETE CODE.)

DISCRETE CODE– As used in the Air Traffic Control Radar Beacon System (ATCRBS), any one of the 4096 selectable Mode 3/A aircraft transponder codes except those ending in zero zero; e.g., discrete codes: 0010, 1201, 2317, 7777; nondiscrete codes: 0100, 1200, 7700. Nondiscrete codes are normally reserved for radar facilities that are not equipped with discrete decoding capability and for other purposes such as emergencies (7700), VFR aircraft (1200), etc.

(See RADAR.)
(Refer to AIM.)

DISCRETE FREQUENCY− A separate radio frequency for use in direct pilot-controller communications in air traffic control which reduces frequency congestion by controlling the number of aircraft operating on a particular frequency at one time. Discrete frequencies are normally designated for each control sector in en route/terminal ATC facilities. Discrete frequencies are listed in the Chart Supplement U.S. and the DoD FLIP IFR En Route Supplement.

(See CONTROL SECTOR.)

DISPLACED THRESHOLD− A threshold that is located at a point on the runway other than the designated beginning of the runway.

(See THRESHOLD.)
(Refer to AIM.)

DISTANCE MEASURING EQUIPMENT (DME)− Equipment (airborne and ground) used to measure, in nautical miles, the slant range distance of an aircraft from the DME navigational aid.

(See TACAN.)
(See VORTAC.)

DISTRESS− A condition of being threatened by serious and/or imminent danger and of requiring immediate assistance.

DIVE BRAKES−

(See SPEED BRAKES.)

DIVERSE VECTOR AREA− In a radar environment, that area in which a prescribed departure route is not required as the only suitable route to avoid obstacles. The area in which random radar vectors below the MVA/MIA, established in accordance with the TERPS criteria for diverse departures, obstacles and terrain avoidance, may be issued to departing aircraft.

DIVERSION (DVRSN)− Flights that are required to land at other than their original destination for reasons beyond the control of the pilot/company, e.g. periods of significant weather.

DME−

(See DISTANCE MEASURING EQUIPMENT.)

DME FIX− A geographical position determined by reference to a navigational aid which provides distance and azimuth information. It is defined by a specific distance in nautical miles and a radial, azimuth, or course (i.e., localizer) in degrees magnetic from that aid.

(See DISTANCE MEASURING EQUIPMENT.)
(See FIX.)

DME SEPARATION− Spacing of aircraft in terms of distances (nautical miles) determined by reference to distance measuring equipment (DME).

(See DISTANCE MEASURING EQUIPMENT.)

DoD FLIP− Department of Defense Flight Information Publications used for flight planning, en route, and terminal operations. FLIP is produced by the National Geospatial−Intelligence Agency (NGA) for world-wide use. United States Government Flight Information Publications (en route charts and instrument approach procedure charts) are incorporated in DoD FLIP for use in the National Airspace System (NAS).

DOMESTIC AIRSPACE− Airspace which overlies the continental land mass of the United States plus Hawaii and U.S. possessions. Domestic airspace extends to 12 miles offshore.

DOMESTIC NOTICE− A special notice or notice containing graphics or plain language text pertaining to almost every aspect of aviation, such as military training areas, large scale sporting events, air show information, Special

Traffic Management Programs (STMPs), and airport−specific information. These notices are applicable to operations within the United States and can be found on the Domestic Notices website.

DOWNBURST− A strong downdraft which induces an outburst of damaging winds on or near the ground. Damaging winds, either straight or curved, are highly divergent. The sizes of downbursts vary from 1/2 mile or less to more than 10 miles. An intense downburst often causes widespread damage. Damaging winds, lasting 5 to 30 minutes, could reach speeds as high as 120 knots.

DOWNWIND LEG−
(See TRAFFIC PATTERN.)

DP−
(See INSTRUMENT DEPARTURE PROCEDURE.)

DRA−
(See DEBRIS RESPONSE AREA.)

DRAG CHUTE− A parachute device installed on certain aircraft which is deployed on landing roll to assist in deceleration of the aircraft.

DROP ZONE− Any pre-determined area upon which parachutists or objects land after making an intentional parachute jump or drop.
(Refer to 14 CFR §105.3, Definitions)

DSP−
(See DEPARTURE SEQUENCING PROGRAM.)

DTAS−
(See DIGITAL TERMINAL AUTOMATION SYSTEM.)

DUE REGARD− A phase of flight wherein an aircraft commander of a State-operated aircraft assumes responsibility to separate his/her aircraft from all other aircraft.
(See also FAA Order JO 7110.65, Para 1−2−1, WORD MEANINGS.)

DUTY RUNWAY−
(See RUNWAY IN USE/ACTIVE RUNWAY/DUTY RUNWAY.)

DVA−
(See DIVERSE VECTOR AREA.)

DVFR−
(See DEFENSE VISUAL FLIGHT RULES.)

DVFR FLIGHT PLAN− A flight plan filed for a VFR aircraft which intends to operate in airspace within which the ready identification, location, and control of aircraft are required in the interest of national security.

DVRSN−
(See DIVERSION.)

DYNAMIC− Continuous review, evaluation, and change to meet demands.

DYNAMIC RESTRICTIONS− Those restrictions imposed by the local facility on an "as needed" basis to manage unpredictable fluctuations in traffic demands.

E

EAS–
(See EN ROUTE AUTOMATION SYSTEM.)

EDCT–
(See EXPECT DEPARTURE CLEARANCE TIME.)

EDST–
(See EN ROUTE DECISION SUPPORT TOOL)

EFC–
(See EXPECT FURTHER CLEARANCE (TIME).)

ELT–
(See EMERGENCY LOCATOR TRANSMITTER.)

EMBEDDED ROUTE TEXT– An EDST notification that an ADR/ADAR/AAR has been applied to the flight plan. Within the route field, sub–fields consisting of an adapted route or an embedded change in the route are color–coded in cyan with cyan brackets around the sub–field.
(See EN ROUTE DECISION SUPPORT TOOL.)

EMERGENCY– A distress or an urgency condition.

EMERGENCY AUTOLAND SYSTEM– This system, if activated, will determine an optimal airport, plot a course, broadcast the aircraft's intentions, fly to the airport, land, and (depending on the model) shut down the engines. Though the system will broadcast the aircraft's intentions, the controller should assume that transmissions to the aircraft will not be acknowledged.

EMERGENCY DESCENT MODE– This automated system senses conditions conducive to hypoxia (cabin depressurization). If an aircraft is equipped and the system is activated, it is designed to turn the aircraft up to 90 degrees, then descend to a lower altitude and level off, giving the pilot(s) time to recover.

EMERGENCY LOCATOR TRANSMITTER (ELT)– A radio transmitter attached to the aircraft structure which operates from its own power source on 121.5 MHz and 243.0 MHz. It aids in locating downed aircraft by radiating a downward sweeping audio tone, 2-4 times per second. It is designed to function without human action after an accident.
(Refer to 14 CFR Part 91.)
(Refer to AIM.)

E-MSAW–
(See EN ROUTE MINIMUM SAFE ALTITUDE WARNING.)

ENHANCED FLIGHT VISION SYSTEM (EFVS)– An EFVS is an installed aircraft system which uses an electronic means to provide a display of the forward external scene topography (the natural or man–made features of a place or region especially in a way to show their relative positions and elevation) through the use of imaging sensors, including but not limited to forward–looking infrared, millimeter wave radiometry, millimeter wave radar, or low–light level image intensification. An EFVS includes the display element, sensors, computers and power supplies, indications, and controls. An operator's authorization to conduct an EFVS operation may have provisions which allow pilots to conduct IAPs when the reported weather is below minimums prescribed on the IAP to be flown.

ENHANCED SPECIAL REPORTING SERVICE (eSRS)– An automated service used to enhance search and rescue operations that provides flight service specialists in Alaska direct information from the aircraft's registered tracking device.

EN ROUTE AIR TRAFFIC CONTROL SERVICES– Air traffic control service provided aircraft on IFR flight plans, generally by centers, when these aircraft are operating between departure and destination terminal areas.

When equipment, capabilities, and controller workload permit, certain advisory/assistance services may be provided to VFR aircraft.
(See AIR ROUTE TRAFFIC CONTROL CENTER.)
(Refer to AIM.)

EN ROUTE AUTOMATION SYSTEM (EAS)– The complex integrated environment consisting of situation display systems, surveillance systems and flight data processing, remote devices, decision support tools, and the related communications equipment that form the heart of the automated IFR air traffic control system. It interfaces with automated terminal systems and is used in the control of en route IFR aircraft.
(Refer to AIM.)

EN ROUTE CHARTS–
(See AERONAUTICAL CHART.)

EN ROUTE DECISION SUPPORT TOOL (EDST)– An automated tool provided at each Radar Associate position in selected En Route facilities. This tool utilizes flight and radar data to determine present and future trajectories for all active and proposal aircraft and provides enhanced automated flight data management.

EN ROUTE DESCENT– Descent from the en route cruising altitude which takes place along the route of flight.

EN ROUTE HIGH ALTITUDE CHARTS–
(See AERONAUTICAL CHART.)

EN ROUTE LOW ALTITUDE CHARTS–
(See AERONAUTICAL CHART.)

EN ROUTE MINIMUM SAFE ALTITUDE WARNING (E–MSAW)– A function of the EAS that aids the controller by providing an alert when a tracked aircraft is below or predicted by the computer to go below a predetermined minimum IFR altitude (MIA).

EN ROUTE TRANSITION–
(See SEGMENTS OF A SID/STAR.)

EN ROUTE TRANSITION WAYPOINT
(See SEGMENTS OF A SID/STAR.)

eSRS–
(See ENHANCED SPECIAL REPORTING SERVICE.)

EST–
(See ESTIMATED.)

ESTABLISHED– To be stable or fixed at an altitude or on a course, route, route segment, heading, instrument approach or departure procedure, etc.

ESTABLISHED ON RNP (EoR) CONCEPT– A system of authorized instrument approaches, ATC procedures, surveillance, and communication requirements that allow aircraft operations to be safely conducted with approved reduced separation criteria once aircraft are established on a PBN segment of a published instrument flight procedure.

ESTIMATED (EST)–When used in NOTAMs "EST" is a contraction that is used by the issuing authority only when the condition is expected to return to service prior to the expiration time. Using "EST" lets the user know that this NOTAM has the possibility of returning to service earlier than the expiration time. Any NOTAM which includes an "EST" will be auto–expired at the designated expiration time.

ESTIMATED ELAPSED TIME [ICAO]– The estimated time required to proceed from one significant point to another.
(See ICAO Term TOTAL ESTIMATED ELAPSED TIME.)

ESTIMATED OFF-BLOCK TIME [ICAO]– The estimated time at which the aircraft will commence movement associated with departure.

ESTIMATED POSITION ERROR (EPE)–
(See Required Navigation Performance)

ESTIMATED TIME OF ARRIVAL– The time the flight is estimated to arrive at the gate (scheduled operators) or the actual runway on times for nonscheduled operators.

ESTIMATED TIME EN ROUTE– The estimated flying time from departure point to destination (lift-off to touchdown).

ETA–
(See ESTIMATED TIME OF ARRIVAL.)

ETE–
(See ESTIMATED TIME EN ROUTE.)

EXECUTE MISSED APPROACH– Instructions issued to a pilot making an instrument approach which means continue inbound to the missed approach point and execute the missed approach procedure as described on the Instrument Approach Procedure Chart or as previously assigned by ATC. The pilot may climb immediately to the altitude specified in the missed approach procedure upon making a missed approach. No turns should be initiated prior to reaching the missed approach point. When conducting an ASR or PAR approach, execute the assigned missed approach procedure immediately upon receiving instructions to "execute missed approach."
(Refer to AIM.)

EXPECT (ALTITUDE) AT (TIME) or (FIX)– Used under certain conditions to provide a pilot with an altitude to be used in the event of two-way communications failure. It also provides altitude information to assist the pilot in planning.
(Refer to AIM.)

EXPECT DEPARTURE CLEARANCE TIME (EDCT)– The runway release time assigned to an aircraft in a traffic management program and shown on the flight progress strip as an EDCT.
(See GROUND DELAY PROGRAM.)

EXPECT FURTHER CLEARANCE (TIME)– The time a pilot can expect to receive clearance beyond a clearance limit.

EXPECT FURTHER CLEARANCE VIA (AIRWAYS, ROUTES OR FIXES)– Used to inform a pilot of the routing he/she can expect if any part of the route beyond a short range clearance limit differs from that filed.

EXPEDITE– Used by ATC when prompt compliance is required to avoid the development of an imminent situation. Expedite climb/descent normally indicates to a pilot that the approximate best rate of climb/descent should be used without requiring an exceptional change in aircraft handling characteristics.

F

FAA−RECOGNIZED IDENTIFICATION AREA (FRIA)− A defined geographic area where persons can operate UAS without remote identification, provided they maintain visual line of sight.

FAF−
(See FINAL APPROACH FIX.)

FALLEN HERO− Remains of fallen members of the United States military are often returned home by aircraft. These flights may be identified with the phrase "FALLEN HERO" added to the remarks section of the flight plan, or they may be transmitted via air/ground communications. If able, these flights will receive priority handling.

FAST FILE− An FSS system whereby a pilot files a flight plan via telephone that is recorded and later transcribed for transmission to the appropriate air traffic facility. (Alaska only.)

FAWP− Final Approach Waypoint

FEATHERED PROPELLER− A propeller whose blades have been rotated so that the leading and trailing edges are nearly parallel with the aircraft flight path to stop or minimize drag and engine rotation. Normally used to indicate shutdown of a reciprocating or turboprop engine due to malfunction.

FEDERAL AIRWAYS−
(See LOW ALTITUDE AIRWAY STRUCTURE.)

FEEDER FIX− The fix depicted on Instrument Approach Procedure Charts which establishes the starting point of the feeder route.

FEEDER ROUTE− A route depicted on instrument approach procedure charts to designate routes for aircraft to proceed from the en route structure to the initial approach fix (IAF).
(See INSTRUMENT APPROACH PROCEDURE.)

FERRY FLIGHT− A flight for the purpose of:

a. Returning an aircraft to base.

b. Delivering an aircraft from one location to another.

c. Moving an aircraft to and from a maintenance base. Ferry flights, under certain conditions, may be conducted under terms of a special flight permit.

FIELD ELEVATION−
(See AIRPORT ELEVATION.)

FILED− Normally used in conjunction with flight plans, meaning a flight plan has been submitted to ATC.

FILED EN ROUTE DELAY− Any of the following preplanned delays at points/areas along the route of flight which require special flight plan filing and handling techniques.

a. Terminal Area Delay. A delay within a terminal area for touch-and-go, low approach, or other terminal area activity.

b. Special Use Airspace Delay. A delay within a Military Operations Area, Restricted Area, Warning Area, or ATC Assigned Airspace.

c. Aerial Refueling Delay. A delay within an Aerial Refueling Track or Anchor.

FILED FLIGHT PLAN− The flight plan as filed with an ATS unit by the pilot or his/her designated representative without any subsequent changes or clearances.

FINAL− Commonly used to mean that an aircraft is on the final approach course or is aligned with a landing area.
(See FINAL APPROACH COURSE.)
(See FINAL APPROACH-IFR.)
(See SEGMENTS OF AN INSTRUMENT APPROACH PROCEDURE.)

FINAL APPROACH [ICAO]– That part of an instrument approach procedure which commences at the specified final approach fix or point, or where such a fix or point is not specified.

a. At the end of the last procedure turn, base turn or inbound turn of a racetrack procedure, if specified; or

b. At the point of interception of the last track specified in the approach procedure; and ends at a point in the vicinity of an aerodrome from which:

1. A landing can be made; or

2. A missed approach procedure is initiated.

FINAL APPROACH COURSE– A bearing/radial/track of an instrument approach leading to a runway or an extended runway centerline all without regard to distance.

FINAL APPROACH FIX– The fix from which the final approach (IFR) to an airport is executed and which identifies the beginning of the final approach segment. It is designated on Government charts by the Maltese Cross symbol for nonprecision approaches and the lightning bolt symbol, designating the PFAF, for precision approaches; or when ATC directs a lower-than-published glideslope/path or vertical path intercept altitude, it is the resultant actual point of the glideslope/path or vertical path intercept.

(See FINAL APPROACH POINT.)
(See GLIDESLOPE INTERCEPT ALTITUDE.)
(See SEGMENTS OF AN INSTRUMENT APPROACH PROCEDURE.)

FINAL APPROACH-IFR– The flight path of an aircraft which is inbound to an airport on a final instrument approach course, beginning at the final approach fix or point and extending to the airport or the point where a circle-to-land maneuver or a missed approach is executed.

(See FINAL APPROACH COURSE.)
(See FINAL APPROACH FIX.)
(See FINAL APPROACH POINT.)
(See SEGMENTS OF AN INSTRUMENT APPROACH PROCEDURE.)
(See ICAO term FINAL APPROACH.)

FINAL APPROACH POINT– The point, applicable only to a nonprecision approach with no depicted FAF (such as an on airport VOR), where the aircraft is established inbound on the final approach course from the procedure turn and where the final approach descent may be commenced. The FAP serves as the FAF and identifies the beginning of the final approach segment.

(See FINAL APPROACH FIX.)
(See SEGMENTS OF AN INSTRUMENT APPROACH PROCEDURE.)

FINAL APPROACH SEGMENT–

(See SEGMENTS OF AN INSTRUMENT APPROACH PROCEDURE.)

FINAL APPROACH SEGMENT [ICAO]– That segment of an instrument approach procedure in which alignment and descent for landing are accomplished.

FINAL CONTROLLER– The controller providing information and final approach guidance during PAR and ASR approaches utilizing radar equipment.

(See RADAR APPROACH.)

FINAL GUARD SERVICE– A value added service provided in conjunction with LAA/RAA only during periods of significant and fast changing weather conditions that may affect landing and takeoff operations.

FINAL MONITOR AID– A high resolution color display that is equipped with the controller alert system hardware/software used to monitor the no transgression zone (NTZ) during simultaneous parallel approach operations. The display includes alert algorithms providing the target predictors, a color change alert when a target penetrates or is predicted to penetrate the no transgression zone (NTZ), synthesized voice alerts, and digital mapping.

(See RADAR APPROACH.)

FINAL MONITOR CONTROLLER– Air Traffic Control Specialist assigned to radar monitor the flight path of aircraft during simultaneous parallel (approach courses spaced less than 9000 feet/9200 feet above 5000 feet) and simultaneous close parallel approach operations. Each runway is assigned a final monitor controller during simultaneous parallel and simultaneous close parallel ILS approaches.

FIR–
(See FLIGHT INFORMATION REGION.)

FIRST PERSON VIEW– UAS operation in which imagery is transmitted to the UAS pilot by an onboard UA camera.

FIRST TIER CENTER– An ARTCC immediately adjacent to the impacted center.

FIS–B–
(See FLIGHT INFORMATION SERVICE–BROADCAST.)

FIX– A geographical position determined by visual reference to the surface, by reference to one or more radio NAVAIDs, by celestial plotting, or by another navigational device.

FIX BALANCING– A process whereby aircraft are evenly distributed over several available arrival fixes reducing delays and controller workload.

FLAG– A warning device incorporated in certain airborne navigation and flight instruments indicating that:

a. Instruments are inoperative or otherwise not operating satisfactorily, or

b. Signal strength or quality of the received signal falls below acceptable values.

FLAG ALARM–
(See FLAG.)

FLAMEOUT– An emergency condition caused by a loss of engine power.

FLAMEOUT PATTERN– An approach normally conducted by a single-engine military aircraft experiencing loss or anticipating loss of engine power or control. The standard overhead approach starts at a relatively high altitude over a runway (“high key”) followed by a continuous 180 degree turn to a high, wide position (“low key”) followed by a continuous 180 degree turn final. The standard straight-in pattern starts at a point that results in a straight-in approach with a high rate of descent to the runway. Flameout approaches terminate in the type approach requested by the pilot (normally fullstop).

FLIGHT CHECK– A call sign prefix used by FAA aircraft engaged in flight inspection/certification of navigational aids and flight procedures. The word “recorded” may be added as a suffix; e.g., “Flight Check 320 recorded” to indicate that an automated flight inspection is in progress in terminal areas.
(See FLIGHT INSPECTION.)
(Refer to AIM.)

FLIGHT DATA [FSS]– The primary task of the FSS flight data position is information management. Flight data services include the development, translation, processing, and coordination of aeronautical, meteorological, and aviation information.

FLIGHT FOLLOWING–
(See TRAFFIC ADVISORIES.)

FLIGHT INFORMATION REGION– An airspace of defined dimensions within which Flight Information Service and Alerting Service are provided.

a. Flight Information Service. A service provided for the purpose of giving advice and information useful for the safe and efficient conduct of flights.

b. Alerting Service. A service provided to notify appropriate organizations regarding aircraft in need of search and rescue aid and to assist such organizations as required.

FLIGHT INFORMATION SERVICE– A service provided for the purpose of giving advice and information useful for the safe and efficient conduct of flights.

FLIGHT INFORMATION SERVICE–BROADCAST (FIS–B)– A ground broadcast service provided through the ADS–B Broadcast Services network over the UAT data link that operates on 978 MHz. The FIS–B system provides pilots and flight crews of properly equipped aircraft with a cockpit display of certain aviation weather and aeronautical information.

FLIGHT INSPECTION– Inflight investigation and evaluation of a navigational aid to determine whether it meets established tolerances.

(See FLIGHT CHECK.)
(See NAVIGATIONAL AID.)

FLIGHT LEVEL– A level of constant atmospheric pressure related to a reference datum of 29.92 inches of mercury. Each is stated in three digits that represent hundreds of feet. For example, flight level (FL) 250 represents a barometric altimeter indication of 25,000 feet; FL 255, an indication of 25,500 feet.

(See ICAO term FLIGHT LEVEL.)

FLIGHT LEVEL [ICAO]– A surface of constant atmospheric pressure which is related to a specific pressure datum, 1013.2 hPa (1013.2 mb), and is separated from other such surfaces by specific pressure intervals.

Note 1: A pressure type altimeter calibrated in accordance with the standard atmosphere:

a. When set to a QNH altimeter setting, will indicate altitude;
b. When set to a QFE altimeter setting, will indicate height above the QFE reference datum; and
c. When set to a pressure of 1013.2 hPa
(1013.2 mb), may be used to indicate flight levels.

Note 2: The terms 'height' and 'altitude,' used in Note 1 above, indicate altimetric rather than geometric heights and altitudes.

FLIGHT LINE– A term used to describe the precise movement of a civil photogrammetric aircraft along a predetermined course(s) at a predetermined altitude during the actual photographic run.

FLIGHT MANAGEMENT SYSTEMS– A computer system that uses a large data base to allow routes to be preprogrammed and fed into the system by means of a data loader. The system is constantly updated with respect to position accuracy by reference to conventional navigation aids. The sophisticated program and its associated data base ensures that the most appropriate aids are automatically selected during the information update cycle.

FLIGHT PATH– A line, course, or track along which an aircraft is flying or intended to be flown.

(See COURSE.)
(See TRACK.)

FLIGHT PLAN– Specified information relating to the intended flight of an aircraft that is filed electronically, orally, or in writing with an FSS, third–party vendor, or an ATC facility.

(See FAST FILE.)
(See FILED.)
(Refer to AIM.)

FLIGHT PLAN AREA (FPA)– The geographical area assigned to a flight service station (FSS) for the purpose of establishing primary responsibility for services that may include search and rescue for VFR aircraft, issuance of NOTAMs, pilot briefings, inflight services, broadcast services, emergency services, flight data processing, international operations, and aviation weather services. Large consolidated FSS facilities may combine FPAs into larger areas of responsibility (AOR).

(See FLIGHT SERVICE STATION.)
(See TIE-IN FACILITY.)

FLIGHT RECORDER– A general term applied to any instrument or device that records information about the performance of an aircraft in flight or about conditions encountered in flight. Flight recorders may make records of airspeed, outside air temperature, vertical acceleration, engine RPM, manifold pressure, and other pertinent variables for a given flight.

(See ICAO term FLIGHT RECORDER.)

FLIGHT RECORDER [ICAO]− Any type of recorder installed in the aircraft for the purpose of complementing accident/incident investigation.

Note: See Annex 6 Part I, for specifications relating to flight recorders.

FLIGHT SERVICE STATION (FSS)− An air traffic facility which provides pilot briefings, flight plan processing, en route flight advisories, search and rescue services, and assistance to lost aircraft and aircraft in emergency situations. FSS also relay ATC clearances, process Notices to Air Missions, and broadcast aviation weather and aeronautical information. In Alaska, FSS provide Airport Advisory Services.
(See FLIGHT PLAN AREA.)
(See TIE-IN FACILITY.)

FLIGHT STANDARDS DISTRICT OFFICE− An FAA field office serving an assigned geographical area and staffed with Flight Standards personnel who serve the aviation industry and the general public on matters relating to the certification and operation of air carrier and general aviation aircraft. Activities include general surveillance of operational safety, certification of airmen and aircraft, accident prevention, investigation, enforcement, etc.

FLIGHT TERMINATION− The intentional and deliberate process of terminating the flight of a UA in the event of an unrecoverable lost link, loss of_control, or other failure that compromises the safety of flight.

FLIGHT TEST− A flight for the purpose of:

a. Investigating the operation/flight characteristics of an aircraft or aircraft component.

b. Evaluating an applicant for a pilot certificate or rating.

FLIGHT VISIBILITY−
(See VISIBILITY.)

FLIP−
(See DoD FLIP.)

FLY-BY WAYPOINT− A fly-by waypoint requires the use of turn anticipation to avoid overshoot of the next flight segment.

FLY HEADING (DEGREES)− Informs the pilot of the heading he/she should fly. The pilot may have to turn to, or continue on, a specific compass direction in order to comply with the instructions. The pilot is expected to turn in the shorter direction to the heading unless otherwise instructed by ATC.

FLY-OVER WAYPOINT− A fly-over waypoint precludes any turn until the waypoint is overflown and is followed by an intercept maneuver of the next flight segment.

FLY VISUAL TO AIRPORT−
(See PUBLISHED INSTRUMENT APPROACH PROCEDURE VISUAL SEGMENT.)

FLYAWAY− When the pilot is unable to effect control of the aircraft and, as a result, the UA is not operating in a predictable or planned manner.

FMA−
(See FINAL MONITOR AID.)

FMS−
(See FLIGHT MANAGEMENT SYSTEM.)

FORMATION FLIGHT− More than one aircraft which, by prior arrangement between the pilots, operate as a single aircraft with regard to navigation and position reporting. Separation between aircraft within the formation is the responsibility of the flight leader and the pilots of the other aircraft in the flight. This includes transition periods when aircraft within the formation are maneuvering to attain separation from each other to effect individual control and during join-up and breakaway.

a. A standard formation is one in which a proximity of no more than 1 mile laterally or longitudinally and within 100 feet vertically from the flight leader is maintained by each wingman.

b. Nonstandard formations are those operating under any of the following conditions:

1. When the flight leader has requested and ATC has approved other than standard formation dimensions.

2. When operating within an authorized altitude reservation (ALTRV) or under the provisions of a letter of agreement.

3. When the operations are conducted in airspace specifically designed for a special activity.

(See ALTITUDE RESERVATION.)
(Refer to 14 CFR Part 91.)

FRC–
(See REQUEST FULL ROUTE CLEARANCE.)

FREEZE/FROZEN– Terms used in referring to arrivals which have been assigned ACLTs and to the lists in which they are displayed.

FREEZE HORIZON– The time or point at which an aircraft's STA becomes fixed and no longer fluctuates with each radar update. This setting ensures a constant time for each aircraft, necessary for the metering controller to plan his/her delay technique. This setting can be either in distance from the meter fix or a prescribed flying time to the meter fix.

FREEZE SPEED PARAMETER– A speed adapted for each aircraft to determine fast and slow aircraft. Fast aircraft freeze on parameter FCLT and slow aircraft freeze on parameter MLDI.

FRIA–
(See FAA–RECOGNIZED IDENTIFICATION AREA.)

FRICTION MEASUREMENT– A measurement of the friction characteristics of the runway pavement surface using continuous self-watering friction measurement equipment in accordance with the specifications, procedures and schedules contained in AC 150/5320–12, Measurement, Construction, and Maintenance of Skid Resistant Airport Pavement Surfaces.

FSDO–
(See FLIGHT STANDARDS DISTRICT OFFICE.)

FSPD–
(See FREEZE SPEED PARAMETER.)

FSS–
(See FLIGHT SERVICE STATION.)

FUEL DUMPING– Airborne release of usable fuel. This does not include the dropping of fuel tanks.
(See JETTISONING OF EXTERNAL STORES.)

FUEL REMAINING– A phrase used by either pilots or controllers when relating to the fuel remaining on board until actual fuel exhaustion. When transmitting such information in response to either a controller question or pilot initiated cautionary advisory to air traffic control, pilots will state the APPROXIMATE NUMBER OF MINUTES the flight can continue with the fuel remaining. All reserve fuel SHOULD BE INCLUDED in the time stated, as should an allowance for established fuel gauge system error.

FUEL SIPHONING– Unintentional release of fuel caused by overflow, puncture, loose cap, etc.

FUEL VENTING–
(See FUEL SIPHONING.)

FUSED TARGET-
(See DIGITAL TARGET)

FUSION [STARS]- the combination of all available surveillance sources (airport surveillance radar [ASR], air route surveillance radar [ARSR], ADS-B, etc.) into the display of a single tracked target for air traffic control separation services. FUSION is the equivalent of the current single-sensor radar display. FUSION performance is characteristic of a single-sensor radar display system. Terminal areas use mono-pulse secondary surveillance radar (ASR 9, Mode S or ASR 11, MSSR).

G

GATE HOLD PROCEDURES− Procedures at selected airports to hold aircraft at the gate or other ground location whenever departure delays exceed or are anticipated to exceed 15 minutes. The sequence for departure will be maintained in accordance with initial call−up unless modified by flow control restrictions. Pilots should monitor the ground control/clearance delivery frequency for engine start/taxi advisories or new proposed start/taxi time if the delay changes.

GCA−
(See GROUND CONTROLLED APPROACH.)

GDP−
(See GROUND DELAY PROGRAM.)

GENERAL AVIATION− That portion of civil aviation that does not include scheduled or unscheduled air carriers or commercial space operations.
(See ICAO term GENERAL AVIATION.)

GENERAL AVIATION [ICAO]− All civil aviation operations other than scheduled air services and nonscheduled air transport operations for remuneration or hire.

GEO MAP− The digitized map markings associated with the ASR-9 Radar System.

GLIDEPATH−
(See GLIDESLOPE.)

GLIDEPATH [ICAO]− A descent profile determined for vertical guidance during a final approach.

GLIDEPATH INTERCEPT ALTITUDE−
(See GLIDESLOPE INTERCEPT ALTITUDE.)

GLIDESLOPE− Provides vertical guidance for aircraft during approach and landing. The glideslope/glidepath is based on the following:

a. Electronic components emitting signals which provide vertical guidance by reference to airborne instruments during instrument approaches such as ILS; or,

b. Visual ground aids, such as VASI, which provide vertical guidance for a VFR approach or for the visual portion of an instrument approach and landing.

c. PAR. Used by ATC to inform an aircraft making a PAR approach of its vertical position (elevation) relative to the descent profile.
(See ICAO term GLIDEPATH.)

GLIDESLOPE INTERCEPT ALTITUDE− The published minimum altitude to intercept the glideslope in the intermediate segment of an instrument approach. Government charts use the lightning bolt symbol to identify this intercept point. This intersection is called the Precise Final Approach fix (PFAF). ATC directs a higher altitude, the resultant intercept becomes the PFAF.
(See FINAL APPROACH FIX.)
(See SEGMENTS OF AN INSTRUMENT APPROACH PROCEDURE.)

GLOBAL NAVIGATION SATELLITE SYSTEM (GNSS)− GNSS refers collectively to the worldwide positioning, navigation, and timing determination capability available from one or more satellite constellations. A GNSS constellation may be augmented by ground stations and/or geostationary satellites to improve integrity and position accuracy.
(See GROUND−BASED AUGMENTATION SYSTEM.)
(See SATELLITE−BASED AUGMENTATION SYSTEM.)

GLOBAL NAVIGATION SATELLITE SYSTEM MINIMUM EN ROUTE IFR ALTITUDE (GNSS MEA)– The minimum en route IFR altitude on a published ATS route or route segment which assures acceptable Global Navigation Satellite System reception and meets obstacle clearance requirements.

(Refer to 14 CFR Part 91.)
(Refer to 14 CFR Part 95.)

GLOBAL POSITIONING SYSTEM (GPS)– GPS refers to the worldwide positioning, navigation and timing determination capability available from the U.S. satellite constellation. The service provided by GPS for civil use is defined in the GPS Standard Positioning System Performance Standard. GPS is composed of space, control, and user elements.

GNSS [ICAO]–
(See GLOBAL NAVIGATION SATELLITE SYSTEM.)

GNSS MEA–
(See GLOBAL NAVIGATION SATELLITE SYSTEM MINIMUM EN ROUTE IFR ALTITUDE.)

GO AHEAD– Proceed with your message. Not to be used for any other purpose.

GO AROUND– Instructions for a pilot to abandon his/her approach to landing. Additional instructions may follow. Unless otherwise advised by ATC, a VFR aircraft or an aircraft conducting visual approach should overfly the runway while climbing to traffic pattern altitude and enter the traffic pattern via the crosswind leg. A pilot on an IFR flight plan making an instrument approach should execute the published missed approach procedure or proceed as instructed by ATC; e.g., "Go around" (additional instructions if required).

(See LOW APPROACH.)
(See MISSED APPROACH.)

GPD–
(See GRAPHIC PLAN DISPLAY.)

GPS–
(See GLOBAL POSITIONING SYSTEM.)

GRAPHICAL AIRMEN'S METEOROLOGICAL INFORMATION– A graphical depiction of weather that may be hazardous to aircraft, but are less severe than SIGMETs. G–AIRMETS are issued 3 hours apart for a period of up to 12 hours into the future for the lower 48 states and coastal waters. The weather hazards depicted can be:

a. Moderate turbulence

b. Low-level windshear

c. Strong surface winds greater than 30 knots

d. Moderate icing

e. Freezing level

f. Mountain obscuration

g. IFR

(See AIRMET.)
(See CONVECTIVE SIGMET.)
(See CWA.)
(See SAW.)
(See SIGMET.)
(Refer to AIM.)

GRAPHIC PLAN DISPLAY (GPD)– A view available with EDST that provides a graphic display of aircraft, traffic, and notification of predicted conflicts. Graphic routes for Current Plans and Trial Plans are displayed upon controller request.

(See EN ROUTE DECISION SUPPORT TOOL.)

GROSS NAVIGATION ERROR (GNE) – A lateral deviation of 10 NM or more from the aircraft's cleared route.

GROUND BASED AUGMENTATION SYSTEM (GBAS)– A ground based GNSS station which provides local differential corrections, integrity parameters and approach data via VHF data broadcast to GNSS users to meet real-time performance requirements for CAT I precision approaches. The aircraft applies the broadcast data to improve the accuracy and integrity of its GNSS signals and computes the deviations to the selected approach. A single ground station can serve multiple runway ends up to an approximate radius of 23 NM.

GROUND BASED AUGMENTATION SYSTEM (GBAS) LANDING SYSTEM (GLS)- A type of precision IAP based on local augmentation of GNSS data using a single GBAS station to transmit locally corrected GNSS data, integrity parameters and approach information. This improves the accuracy of aircraft GNSS receivers' signal in space, enabling the pilot to fly a precision approach with much greater flexibility, reliability and complexity. The GLS procedure is published on standard IAP charts, features the title GLS with the designated runway and minima as low as 200 feet DA. Future plans are expected to support Cat II and CAT III operations.

GROUND–BASED INTERVAL MANAGEMENT–SPACING (GIM–S), SPEED ADVISORY– A calculated speed that will allow aircraft to meet the TBFM schedule at en route and TRACON boundary meter fixes.

GROUND CLUTTER– A pattern produced on the radar scope by ground returns which may degrade other radar returns in the affected area. The effect of ground clutter is minimized by the use of moving target indicator (MTI) circuits in the radar equipment resulting in a radar presentation which displays only targets which are in motion.
(See CLUTTER.)

GROUND COMMUNICATION OUTLET (GCO)– An unstaffed, remotely controlled, ground/ground communications facility. Pilots at uncontrolled airports may contact ATC and FSS via VHF radio to a telephone connection. If the connection goes to ATC, the pilot can obtain an IFR clearance or close an IFR flight plan. If the connection goes to Flight Service, the pilot can open or close a VFR flight plan; obtain an updated weather briefing prior to takeoff; close an IFR flight plan; or, for Alaska or MEDEVAC only, obtain an IFR clearance. Pilots will use four "key clicks" on the VHF radio to contact the appropriate ATC facility or six "key clicks" to contact the FSS. The GCO system is intended to be used only on the ground.

GROUND CONTROLLED APPROACH– A radar approach system operated from the ground by air traffic control personnel transmitting instructions to the pilot by radio. The approach may be conducted with surveillance radar (ASR) only or with both surveillance and precision approach radar (PAR). Usage of the term "GCA" by pilots is discouraged except when referring to a GCA facility. Pilots should specifically request a "PAR" approach when a precision radar approach is desired or request an "ASR" or "surveillance" approach when a nonprecision radar approach is desired.
(See RADAR APPROACH.)

GROUND DELAY PROGRAM (GDP)– A traffic management process administered by the ATCSCC, when aircraft are held on the ground. The purpose of the program is to support the TM mission and limit airborne holding. It is a flexible program and may be implemented in various forms depending upon the needs of the AT system. Ground delay programs provide for equitable assignment of delays to all system users.

GROUND SPEED– The speed of an aircraft relative to the surface of the earth.

GROUND STOP (GS)– The GS is a process that requires aircraft that meet a specific criteria to remain on the ground. The criteria may be airport specific, airspace specific, or equipment specific; for example, all departures to San Francisco, or all departures entering Yorktown sector, or all Category I and II aircraft going to Charlotte. GSs normally occur with little or no warning.

GROUND VISIBILITY–
(See VISIBILITY.)

GS–
(See GROUND STOP.)

H

HAA–
(See HEIGHT ABOVE AIRPORT.)

HAL–
(See HEIGHT ABOVE LANDING.)

HANDOFF– An action taken to transfer the radar identification of an aircraft from one controller to another if the aircraft will enter the receiving controller's airspace and radio communications with the aircraft will be transferred.

HAT–
(See HEIGHT ABOVE TOUCHDOWN.)

HAVE NUMBERS– Used by pilots to inform ATC that they have received runway, wind, and altimeter information only.

HAZARDOUS MATERIALS (HAZMAT)– Hazardous materials as defined by 49 Code of Federal Regulations (CFR) §171.8.
(Refer to 49 CFR Part 171.8)
(Refer to AIM)

HAZARDOUS WEATHER INFORMATION–Summary of significant meteorological information (SIGMET/WS), convective significant meteorological information (convective SIGMET/WST), urgent pilot weather reports (urgent PIREP/UUA), center weather advisories (CWA), airmen's meteorological information (AIRMET/WA), graphical airmen's meteorological information (G–AIRMET) and any other weather such as isolated thunderstorms that are rapidly developing and increasing in intensity, or low ceilings and visibilities that are becoming widespread which is considered significant and are not included in a current hazardous weather advisory.

HAZMAT–
(See HAZARDOUS MATERIALS.)

HEAVY (AIRCRAFT)–
(See AIRCRAFT CLASSES.)

HEIGHT ABOVE AIRPORT (HAA)– The height of the Minimum Descent Altitude above the published airport elevation. This is published in conjunction with circling minimums.
(See MINIMUM DESCENT ALTITUDE.)

HEIGHT ABOVE LANDING (HAL)– The height above a designated helicopter landing area used for helicopter instrument approach procedures.
(Refer to 14 CFR Part 97.)

HEIGHT ABOVE TOUCHDOWN (HAT)– The height of the Decision Height or Minimum Descent Altitude above the highest runway elevation in the touchdown zone (first 3,000 feet of the runway). HAT is published on instrument approach charts in conjunction with all straight-in minimums.
(See DECISION HEIGHT.)
(See MINIMUM DESCENT ALTITUDE.)

HELICOPTER– A heavier-than-air aircraft supported in flight chiefly by the reactions of the air on one or more power-driven rotors on substantially vertical axes.

HELIPAD– A small, designated area, usually with a prepared surface, on a heliport, airport, landing/takeoff area, apron/ramp, or movement area used for takeoff, landing, or parking of helicopters.

HELIPORT– An area of land, water, or structure used or intended to be used for the landing and takeoff of helicopters and includes its buildings and facilities if any.

HELIPORT REFERENCE POINT (HRP)– The geographic center of a heliport.

HERTZ– The standard radio equivalent of frequency in cycles per second of an electromagnetic wave. Kilohertz (kHz) is a frequency of one thousand cycles per second. Megahertz (MHz) is a frequency of one million cycles per second.

HF–
(See HIGH FREQUENCY.)

HF COMMUNICATIONS–
(See HIGH FREQUENCY COMMUNICATIONS.)

HIGH FREQUENCY– The frequency band between 3 and 30 MHz.
(See HIGH FREQUENCY COMMUNICATIONS.)

HIGH FREQUENCY COMMUNICATIONS– High radio frequencies (HF) between 3 and 30 MHz used for air-to-ground voice communication in overseas operations.

HIGH SPEED EXIT–
(See HIGH SPEED TAXIWAY.)

HIGH SPEED TAXIWAY– A long radius taxiway designed and provided with lighting or marking to define the path of aircraft, traveling at high speed (up to 60 knots), from the runway center to a point on the center of a taxiway. Also referred to as long radius exit or turn-off taxiway. The high speed taxiway is designed to expedite aircraft turning off the runway after landing, thus reducing runway occupancy time.

HIGH SPEED TURNOFF–
(See HIGH SPEED TAXIWAY.)

HIGH UPDATE RATE SURVEILLANCE– A surveillance system that provides a sensor update rate of less than 4.8 seconds.

HOLD FOR RELEASE– Used by ATC to delay an aircraft for traffic management reasons; i.e., weather, traffic volume, etc. Hold for release instructions (including departure delay information) are used to inform a pilot or a controller (either directly or through an authorized relay) that an IFR departure clearance is not valid until a release time or additional instructions have been received.
(See ICAO term HOLDING POINT.)

HOLD–IN–LIEU OF PROCEDURE TURN– A hold–in–lieu of procedure turn shall be established over a final or intermediate fix when an approach can be made from a properly aligned holding pattern. The hold–in–lieu of procedure turn permits the pilot to align with the final or intermediate segment of the approach and/or descend in the holding pattern to an altitude that will permit a normal descent to the final approach fix altitude. The hold–in–lieu of procedure turn is a required maneuver (the same as a procedure turn) unless the aircraft is being radar vectored to the final approach course, when "NoPT" is shown on the approach chart, or when the pilot requests or the controller advises the pilot to make a "straight–in" approach.

HOLD PROCEDURE– A predetermined maneuver which keeps aircraft within a specified airspace while awaiting further clearance from air traffic control. Also used during ground operations to keep aircraft within a specified area or at a specified point while awaiting further clearance from air traffic control.
(See HOLDING FIX.)
(Refer to AIM.)

HOLDING FIX– A specified fix identifiable to a pilot by NAVAIDs or visual reference to the ground used as a reference point in establishing and maintaining the position of an aircraft while holding.
(See FIX.)
(See VISUAL HOLDING.)
(Refer to AIM.)

HOLDING POINT [ICAO]– A specified location, identified by visual or other means, in the vicinity of which the position of an aircraft in flight is maintained in accordance with air traffic control clearances.

HOLDING PROCEDURE–
(See HOLD PROCEDURE.)

HOLD-SHORT POINT– A point on the runway beyond which a landing aircraft with a LAHSO clearance is not authorized to proceed. This point may be located prior to an intersecting runway, taxiway, predetermined point, or approach/departure flight path.

HOLD-SHORT POSITION LIGHTS– Flashing in-pavement white lights located at specified hold-short points.

HOLD-SHORT POSITION MARKING– The painted runway marking located at the hold-short point on all LAHSO runways.

HOLD-SHORT POSITION SIGNS– Red and white holding position signs located alongside the hold-short point.

HOMING– Flight toward a NAVAID, without correcting for wind, by adjusting the aircraft heading to maintain a relative bearing of zero degrees.
(See BEARING.)
(See ICAO term HOMING.)

HOMING [ICAO]– The procedure of using the direction-finding equipment of one radio station with the emission of another radio station, where at least one of the stations is mobile, and whereby the mobile station proceeds continuously towards the other station.

HOT SPOT– A location on an airport movement area with a history of potential risk of collision or runway incursion, and where heightened attention by pilots/drivers is necessary.

HOVER CHECK– Used to describe when a helicopter/VTOL aircraft requires a stabilized hover to conduct a performance/power check prior to hover taxi, air taxi, or takeoff. Altitude of the hover will vary based on the purpose of the check.

HOVER TAXI– Used to describe a helicopter/VTOL aircraft movement conducted above the surface and in ground effect at airspeeds less than approximately 20 knots. The actual height may vary, and some helicopters may require hover taxi above 25 feet AGL to reduce ground effect turbulence or provide clearance for cargo slingloads.
(See AIR TAXI.)
(See HOVER CHECK.)
(Refer to AIM.)

HOW DO YOU HEAR ME?– A question relating to the quality of the transmission or to determine how well the transmission is being received.

HZ–
(See HERTZ.)

I

***I SAY AGAIN*–** The message will be repeated.

IAF–

(See INITIAL APPROACH FIX.)

IAP–

(See INSTRUMENT APPROACH PROCEDURE.)

IAWP– Initial Approach Waypoint

ICAO–

(See ICAO Term INTERNATIONAL CIVIL AVIATION ORGANIZATION.)

ICAO 3LD–

(See ICAO Term ICAO Three–Letter Designator)

ICAO Three–Letter Designator (3LD)– An ICAO 3LD is an exclusive designator that, when used together with a flight number, becomes the aircraft call sign and provides distinct aircraft identification to air traffic control (ATC). ICAO approves 3LDs to enhance the safety and security of the air traffic system. An ICAO 3LD may be assigned to a company, agency, or organization and is used instead of the aircraft registration number for ATC operational and security purposes. An ICAO 3LD is also used for aircraft identification in the flight plan and associated messages and can be used for domestic and international flights. A telephony associated with an ICAO 3LD is used for radio communication.

ICING– The accumulation of airframe ice.

Types of icing are:

a. Rime Ice– Rough, milky, opaque ice formed by the instantaneous freezing of small supercooled water droplets.

b. Clear Ice– A glossy, clear, or translucent ice formed by the relatively slow freezing of large supercooled water droplets.

c. Mixed– A mixture of clear ice and rime ice.

Intensity of icing:

a. Trace– Ice becomes noticeable. The rate of accumulation is slightly greater than the rate of sublimation. A representative accretion rate for reference purposes is less than ¼ inch (6 mm) per hour on the outer wing. The pilot should consider exiting the icing conditions before they become worse.

b. Light– The rate of ice accumulation requires occasional cycling of manual deicing systems to minimize ice accretions on the airframe. A representative accretion rate for reference purposes is ¼ inch to 1 inch (0.6 to 2.5 cm) per hour on the unprotected part of the outer wing. The pilot should consider exiting the icing condition.

c. Moderate– The rate of ice accumulation requires frequent cycling of manual deicing systems to minimize ice accretions on the airframe. A representative accretion rate for reference purposes is 1 to 3 inches (2.5 to 7.5 cm) per hour on the unprotected part of the outer wing. The pilot should consider exiting the icing condition as soon as possible.

d. Severe– The rate of ice accumulation is such that ice protection systems fail to remove the accumulation of ice and ice accumulates in locations not normally prone to icing, such as areas aft of protected surfaces and any other areas identified by the manufacturer. A representative accretion rate for reference purposes is more than 3 inches (7.5 cm) per hour on the unprotected part of the outer wing. By regulation, immediate exit is required.

Note:

Severe icing is aircraft dependent, as are the other categories of icing intensity. Severe icing may occur at any ice accumulation rate when the icing rate or ice accumulations exceed the tolerance of the aircraft.

IDAC–
(See INTEGRATED DEPARTURE/ARRIVAL CAPABILITY.)

IDENT– A request for a pilot to activate the aircraft transponder identification feature. This will help the controller to confirm an aircraft identity or to identify an aircraft.
(Refer to AIM.)

IDENT FEATURE– The special feature in the Air Traffic Control Radar Beacon System (ATCRBS) equipment. It is used to immediately distinguish one displayed beacon target from other beacon targets.
(See IDENT.)

IDENTIFICATION [ICAO]– The situation which exists when the position indication of a particular aircraft is seen on a situation display and positively identified.

IF–
(See INTERMEDIATE FIX.)

IF NO TRANSMISSION RECEIVED FOR (TIME)– Used by ATC in radar approaches to prefix procedures which should be followed by the pilot in event of lost communications.
(See LOST COMMUNICATIONS.)

IFR–
(See INSTRUMENT FLIGHT RULES.)

IFR AIRCRAFT– An aircraft conducting flight in accordance with instrument flight rules.

IFR CONDITIONS– Weather conditions below the minimum for flight under visual flight rules.
(See INSTRUMENT METEOROLOGICAL CONDITIONS.)

IFR DEPARTURE PROCEDURE–
(See IFR TAKEOFF MINIMUMS AND DEPARTURE PROCEDURES.)
(Refer to AIM.)

IFR FLIGHT–
(See IFR AIRCRAFT.)

IFR LANDING MINIMUMS–
(See LANDING MINIMUMS.)

IFR MILITARY TRAINING ROUTES (IR)– Routes used by the Department of Defense and associated Reserve and Air Guard units for the purpose of conducting low-altitude navigation and tactical training in both IFR and VFR weather conditions below 10,000 feet MSL at airspeeds in excess of 250 knots IAS.

IFR TAKEOFF MINIMUMS AND DEPARTURE PROCEDURES– Title 14 Code of Federal Regulations Part 91, prescribes standard takeoff rules for certain civil users. At some airports, obstructions or other factors require the establishment of nonstandard takeoff minimums, departure procedures, or both to assist pilots in avoiding obstacles during climb to the minimum en route altitude. Those airports are listed in FAA/DoD Instrument Approach Procedures (IAPs) Charts under a section entitled "IFR Takeoff Minimums and Departure Procedures." The FAA/DoD IAP chart legend illustrates the symbol used to alert the pilot to nonstandard takeoff minimums and departure procedures. When departing IFR from such airports or from any airports where there are no departure procedures, DPs, or ATC facilities available, pilots should advise ATC of any departure limitations. Controllers may query a pilot to determine acceptable departure directions, turns, or headings after takeoff. Pilots should be familiar with the departure procedures and must assure that their aircraft can meet or exceed any specified climb gradients.

IF/IAWP– Intermediate Fix/Initial Approach Waypoint. The waypoint where the final approach course of a T approach meets the crossbar of the T. When designated (in conjunction with a TAA) this waypoint will be used as an IAWP when approaching the airport from certain directions, and as an IFWP when beginning the approach from another IAWP.

IFWP– Intermediate Fix Waypoint

ILS–
(See INSTRUMENT LANDING SYSTEM.)

ILS CATEGORIES– 1. Category I. An ILS approach procedure which provides for approach to a height above touchdown of not less than 200 feet and with runway visual range of not less than 1,800 feet.– 2. Special Authorization Category I. An ILS approach procedure which provides for approach to a height above touchdown of not less than 150 feet and with runway visual range of not less than 1,400 feet, HUD to DH. 3. Category II. An ILS approach procedure which provides for approach to a height above touchdown of not less than 100 feet and with runway visual range of not less than 1,200 feet (with autoland or HUD to touchdown and noted on authorization, RVR 1,000 feet).– 4. Special Authorization Category II with Reduced Lighting. An ILS approach procedure which provides for approach to a height above touchdown of not less than 100 feet and with runway visual range of not less than 1,200 feet with autoland or HUD to touchdown and noted on authorization (no touchdown zone and centerline lighting are required).– 5. Category III:

a. IIIA.–An ILS approach procedure which provides for approach without a decision height minimum and with runway visual range of not less than 700 feet.

b. IIIB.–An ILS approach procedure which provides for approach without a decision height minimum and with runway visual range of not less than 150 feet.

c. IIIC.–An ILS approach procedure which provides for approach without a decision height minimum and without runway visual range minimum.

IM–
(See INNER MARKER.)

IMC–
(See INSTRUMENT METEOROLOGICAL CONDITIONS.)

IMMEDIATELY– Used by ATC or pilots when such action compliance is required to avoid an imminent situation.

INCERFA (Uncertainty Phase) [ICAO]– A situation wherein uncertainty exists as to the safety of an aircraft and its occupants.

INCREASED SEPARATION REQUIRED (ISR)– Indicates the confidence level of the track requires 5 NM separation. 3 NM separation, 1 ½ NM separation, and target resolution cannot be used.

INCREASE SPEED TO (SPEED)–
(See SPEED ADJUSTMENT.)

INERTIAL NAVIGATION SYSTEM (INS)– An RNAV system which is a form of self-contained navigation.
(See Area Navigation/RNAV.)

INFLIGHT REFUELING–
(See AERIAL REFUELING.)

INFLIGHT SERVICES [FSS]– Services provided to or affecting aircraft inflight or otherwise operating on the airport surface. This includes services to airborne aircraft, such as the delivery of ATC clearances, advisories or requests, issuance of military flight advisory messages, NOTAM delivery, search and rescue communications searches, flight plan handling, transcribed or live broadcasts, weather observations, PIREPs, and pilot briefings.

INFLIGHT WEATHER ADVISORY–
(See WEATHER ADVISORY.)

INFORMATION REQUEST (INREQ)– A request originated by an FSS for information concerning an overdue VFR aircraft.

INITIAL APPROACH FIX (IAF)– The fixes depicted on instrument approach procedure charts that identify the beginning of the initial approach segment(s).
(See FIX.)
(See SEGMENTS OF AN INSTRUMENT APPROACH PROCEDURE.)

INITIAL APPROACH SEGMENT–
(See SEGMENTS OF AN INSTRUMENT APPROACH PROCEDURE.)

INITIAL APPROACH SEGMENT [ICAO]– That segment of an instrument approach procedure between the initial approach fix and the intermediate approach fix or, where applicable, the final approach fix or point.

INLAND NAVIGATION FACILITY– A navigation aid on a North American Route at which the common route and/or the noncommon route begins or ends.

INNER MARKER– A marker beacon used with an ILS (CAT II) precision approach located between the middle marker and the end of the ILS runway, transmitting a radiation pattern keyed at six dots per second and indicating to the pilot, both aurally and visually, that he/she is at the designated decision height (DH), normally 100 feet above the touchdown zone elevation, on the ILS CAT II approach. It also marks progress during a CAT III approach.
(See INSTRUMENT LANDING SYSTEM.)
(Refer to AIM.)

INNER MARKER BEACON–
(See INNER MARKER.)

INREQ–
(See INFORMATION REQUEST.)

INS–
(See INERTIAL NAVIGATION SYSTEM.)

INSTRUMENT APPROACH–
(See INSTRUMENT APPROACH PROCEDURE.)

INSTRUMENT APPROACH OPERATIONS [ICAO]– An approach and landing using instruments for navigation guidance based on an instrument approach procedure. There are two methods for executing instrument approach operations:

a. A two–dimensional (2D) instrument approach operation, using lateral navigation guidance only; and

b. A three–dimensional (3D) instrument approach operation, using both lateral and vertical navigation guidance.

Note: Lateral and vertical navigation guidance refers to the guidance provided either by:
a) a ground–based radio navigation aid; or
b) computer–generated navigation data from ground–based, space–based, self–contained navigation aids or a combination of these.

(See ICAO term INSTRUMENT APPROACH PROCEDURE.)

INSTRUMENT APPROACH PROCEDURE– A series of predetermined maneuvers for the orderly transfer of an aircraft under instrument flight conditions from the beginning of the initial approach to a landing or to a point from which a landing may be made visually. It is prescribed and approved for a specific airport by competent authority.
(See SEGMENTS OF AN INSTRUMENT APPROACH PROCEDURE.)
(Refer to 14 CFR Part 91.)
(Refer to AIM.)

a. U.S. civil standard instrument approach procedures are approved by the FAA as prescribed under 14 CFR Part 97 and are available for public use.

b. U.S. military standard instrument approach procedures are approved and published by the Department of Defense.

c. Special instrument approach procedures are approved by the FAA for individual operators but are not published in 14 CFR Part 97 for public use.
(See ICAO term INSTRUMENT APPROACH PROCEDURE.)

INSTRUMENT APPROACH PROCEDURE [ICAO]− A series of predetermined maneuvers by reference to flight instruments with specified protection from obstacles from the initial approach fix, or where applicable, from the beginning of a defined arrival route to a point from which a landing can be completed and thereafter, if a landing is not completed, to a position at which holding or en route obstacle clearance criteria apply.

(See ICAO term INSTRUMENT APPROACH OPERATIONS)

INSTRUMENT APPROACH PROCEDURE CHARTS−

(See AERONAUTICAL CHART.)

INSTRUMENT DEPARTURE PROCEDURE (DP)− A preplanned instrument flight rule (IFR) departure procedure published for pilot use, in graphic or textual format, that provides obstruction clearance from the terminal area to the appropriate en route structure. There are two types of DP, Obstacle Departure Procedure (ODP), printed either textually or graphically, and, Standard Instrument Departure (SID), which is always printed graphically.

(See IFR TAKEOFF MINIMUMS AND DEPARTURE PROCEDURES.)
(See OBSTACLE DEPARTURE PROCEDURES.)
(See STANDARD INSTRUMENT DEPARTURES.)
(Refer to AIM.)

INSTRUMENT DEPARTURE PROCEDURE (DP) CHARTS−

(See AERONAUTICAL CHART.)

INSTRUMENT FLIGHT RULES (IFR)− Rules governing the procedures for conducting instrument flight. Also a term used by pilots and controllers to indicate type of flight plan.

(See INSTRUMENT METEOROLOGICAL CONDITIONS.)
(See VISUAL FLIGHT RULES.)
(See VISUAL METEOROLOGICAL CONDITIONS.)
(See ICAO term INSTRUMENT FLIGHT RULES.)
(Refer to AIM.)

INSTRUMENT FLIGHT RULES [ICAO]− A set of rules governing the conduct of flight under instrument meteorological conditions.

INSTRUMENT LANDING SYSTEM (ILS)− A precision instrument approach system which normally consists of the following electronic components and visual aids:

a. Localizer.
(See LOCALIZER.)

b. Glideslope.
(See GLIDESLOPE.)

c. Outer Marker.
(See OUTER MARKER.)

d. Middle Marker.
(See MIDDLE MARKER.)

e. Approach Lights.
(See AIRPORT LIGHTING.)
(Refer to 14 CFR Part 91.)
(Refer to AIM.)

INSTRUMENT METEOROLOGICAL CONDITIONS (IMC)− Meteorological conditions expressed in terms of visibility, distance from cloud, and ceiling less than the minima specified for visual meteorological conditions.

(See INSTRUMENT FLIGHT RULES.)
(See VISUAL FLIGHT RULES.)
(See VISUAL METEOROLOGICAL CONDITIONS.)

INSTRUMENT RUNWAY− A runway equipped with electronic and visual navigation aids for which a precision or nonprecision approach procedure having straight-in landing minimums has been approved.

(See ICAO term INSTRUMENT RUNWAY.)

INSTRUMENT RUNWAY [ICAO]– One of the following types of runways intended for the operation of aircraft using instrument approach procedures:

a. Nonprecision Approach Runway– An instrument runway served by visual aids and a nonvisual aid providing at least directional guidance adequate for a straight-in approach.

b. Precision Approach Runway, Category I– An instrument runway served by ILS and visual aids intended for operations down to 60 m (200 feet) decision height and down to an RVR of the order of 800 m.

c. Precision Approach Runway, Category II– An instrument runway served by ILS and visual aids intended for operations down to 30 m (100 feet) decision height and down to an RVR of the order of 400 m.

d. Precision Approach Runway, Category III– An instrument runway served by ILS to and along the surface of the runway and:

1. Intended for operations down to an RVR of the order of 200 m (no decision height being applicable) using visual aids during the final phase of landing;

2. Intended for operations down to an RVR of the order of 50 m (no decision height being applicable) using visual aids for taxiing;

3. Intended for operations without reliance on visual reference for landing or taxiing.

Note 1: See Annex 10 Volume I, Part I, Chapter 3, for related ILS specifications.

Note 2: Visual aids need not necessarily be matched to the scale of nonvisual aids provided. The criterion for the selection of visual aids is the conditions in which operations are intended to be conducted.

INTEGRATED DEPARTURE/ARRIVAL CAPABILITY (IDAC)– A Tower/TRACON departure scheduling capability within TBFM that allows departures to be scheduled into either an arrival flow or an en route flow. IDAC provides a mechanism for electronic coordination of departure release times.

INTEGRITY– The ability of a system to provide timely warnings to users when the system should not be used for navigation.

INTERMEDIATE APPROACH SEGMENT–
(See SEGMENTS OF AN INSTRUMENT APPROACH PROCEDURE.)

INTERMEDIATE APPROACH SEGMENT [ICAO]– That segment of an instrument approach procedure between either the intermediate approach fix and the final approach fix or point, or between the end of a reversal, race track or dead reckoning track procedure and the final approach fix or point, as appropriate.

INTERMEDIATE FIX– The fix that identifies the beginning of the intermediate approach segment of an instrument approach procedure. The fix is not normally identified on the instrument approach chart as an intermediate fix (IF).
(See SEGMENTS OF AN INSTRUMENT APPROACH PROCEDURE.)

INTERMEDIATE LANDING– On the rare occasion that this option is requested, it should be approved. The departure center, however, must advise the ATCSCC so that the appropriate delay is carried over and assigned at the intermediate airport. An intermediate landing airport within the arrival center will not be accepted without coordination with and the approval of the ATCSCC.

INTERNATIONAL AIRPORT– Relating to international flight, it means:

a. An airport of entry which has been designated by the Secretary of Treasury or Commissioner of Customs as an international airport for customs service.

b. A landing rights airport at which specific permission to land must be obtained from customs authorities in advance of contemplated use.

c. Airports designated under the Convention on International Civil Aviation as an airport for use by international commercial air transport and/or international general aviation.
(See ICAO term INTERNATIONAL AIRPORT.)
(Refer to Chart Supplement U.S.)

INTERNATIONAL AIRPORT [ICAO]– Any airport designated by the Contracting State in whose territory it is situated as an airport of entry and departure for international air traffic, where the formalities incident to customs, immigration, public health, animal and plant quarantine and similar procedures are carried out.

INTERNATIONAL CIVIL AVIATION ORGANIZATION [ICAO]− A specialized agency of the United Nations whose objective is to develop the principles and techniques of international air navigation and to foster planning and development of international civil air transport.

INTERNATIONAL NOTICE− A notice containing flight prohibitions, potential hostile situations, or other international/foreign oceanic airspace matters. These notices can be found on the International Notices website.

INTERROGATOR− The ground-based surveillance radar beacon transmitter-receiver, which normally scans in synchronism with a primary radar, transmitting discrete radio signals which repetitiously request all transponders on the mode being used to reply. The replies received are mixed with the primary radar returns and displayed on the same plan position indicator (radar scope). Also, applied to the airborne element of the TACAN/DME system.

(See TRANSPONDER.)
(Refer to AIM.)

INTERSECTING RUNWAYS− Two or more runways which cross or meet within their lengths.

(See INTERSECTION.)

INTERSECTION−

a. A point defined by any combination of courses, radials, or bearings of two or more navigational aids.

b. Used to describe the point where two runways, a runway and a taxiway, or two taxiways cross or meet.

INTERSECTION DEPARTURE− A departure from any runway intersection except the end of the runway.

(See INTERSECTION.)

INTERSECTION TAKEOFF−

(See INTERSECTION DEPARTURE.)

IR−

(See IFR MILITARY TRAINING ROUTES.)

IRREGULAR SURFACE− A surface that is open for use but not per regulations.

ISR−

(See INCREASED SEPARATION REQUIRED.)

J

JAMMING− Denotes emissions that do not mimic Global Navigation Satellite System (GNSS) signals (e.g., GPS and WAAS), but rather interfere with the civil receiver's ability to acquire and track GNSS signals. Jamming can result in denial of GNSS navigation, positioning, timing and aircraft dependent functions.

JET BLAST− The rapid air movement produced by exhaust from jet engines.

JET ROUTE− A route designed to serve aircraft operations from 18,000 feet MSL up to and including flight level 450. The routes are referred to as "J" routes with numbering to identify the designated route; e.g., J105.
(See Class A AIRSPACE.)
(Refer to 14 CFR Part 71.)

JET STREAM− A migrating stream of high-speed winds present at high altitudes.

JETTISONING OF EXTERNAL STORES− Airborne release of external stores; e.g., tiptanks, ordnance.
(See FUEL DUMPING.)
(Refer to 14 CFR Part 91.)

JOINT USE RESTRICTED AREA−
(See RESTRICTED AREA.)

JUMP ZONE− The airspace directly associated with a Drop Zone. Vertical and horizontal limits may be locally defined.

K

KNOWN TRAFFIC− With respect to ATC clearances, means aircraft whose altitude, position, and intentions are known to ATC.

L

LAA–
(See LOCAL AIRPORT ADVISORY.)

LAANC–
(See LOW ALTITUDE AUTHORIZATION AND NOTIFICATION CAPABILITY.)

LAHSO– An acronym for "Land and Hold Short Operation." These operations include landing and holding short of an intersecting runway, a taxiway, a predetermined point, or an approach/departure flightpath.

LAHSO-DRY– Land and hold short operations on runways that are dry.

LAHSO-WET– Land and hold short operations on runways that are wet (but not contaminated).

LAND AND HOLD SHORT OPERATIONS– Operations which include simultaneous takeoffs and landings and/or simultaneous landings when a landing aircraft is able and is instructed by the controller to hold-short of the intersecting runway/taxiway or designated hold-short point. Pilots are expected to promptly inform the controller if the hold short clearance cannot be accepted.
(See PARALLEL RUNWAYS.)
(Refer to AIM.)

LAND–BASED AIR DEFENSE IDENTIFICATION ZONE (ADIZ)– An ADIZ over U.S. metropolitan areas, which is activated and deactivated as needed, with dimensions, activation dates, and other relevant information disseminated via NOTAM.
(See AIR DEFENSE IDENTIFICATION ZONE.)

LANDING AREA– Any locality either on land, water, or structures, including airports/heliports and intermediate landing fields, which is used, or intended to be used, for the landing and takeoff of aircraft whether or not facilities are provided for the shelter, servicing, or for receiving or discharging passengers or cargo.
(See ICAO term LANDING AREA.)

LANDING AREA [ICAO]– That part of a movement area intended for the landing or take-off of aircraft.

LANDING DIRECTION INDICATOR– A device which visually indicates the direction in which landings and takeoffs should be made.
(See TETRAHEDRON.)
(Refer to AIM.)

LANDING DISTANCE AVAILABLE (LDA)– The runway length declared available and suitable for a landing airplane.
(See ICAO term LANDING DISTANCE AVAILABLE.)

LANDING DISTANCE AVAILABLE [ICAO]– The length of runway which is declared available and suitable for the ground run of an aeroplane landing.

LANDING MINIMUMS– The minimum visibility prescribed for landing a civil aircraft while using an instrument approach procedure. The minimum applies with other limitations set forth in 14 CFR Part 91 with respect to the Minimum Descent Altitude (MDA) or Decision Height (DH) prescribed in the instrument approach procedures as follows:

a. Straight-in landing minimums. A statement of MDA and visibility, or DH and visibility, required for a straight-in landing on a specified runway, or

b. Circling minimums. A statement of MDA and visibility required for the circle-to-land maneuver.

Note: Descent below the MDA or DH must meet the conditions stated in 14 CFR Section 91.175.
(See CIRCLE-TO-LAND MANEUVER.)
(See DECISION HEIGHT.)
(See INSTRUMENT APPROACH PROCEDURE.)
(See MINIMUM DESCENT ALTITUDE.)
(See STRAIGHT-IN LANDING.)
(See VISIBILITY.)
(Refer to 14 CFR Part 91.)

LANDING ROLL– The distance from the point of touchdown to the point where the aircraft can be brought to a stop or exit the runway.

LANDING SEQUENCE– The order in which aircraft are positioned for landing.
(See APPROACH SEQUENCE.)

LAST ASSIGNED ALTITUDE– The last altitude/flight level assigned by ATC and acknowledged by the pilot.
(See MAINTAIN.)
(Refer to 14 CFR Part 91.)

LATERAL NAVIGATION (LNAV)– A function of area navigation (RNAV) equipment which calculates, displays, and provides lateral guidance to a profile or path.

LATERAL SEPARATION– The lateral spacing of aircraft at the same altitude by requiring operation on different routes or in different geographical locations.
(See SEPARATION.)

LDA–
(See LOCALIZER TYPE DIRECTIONAL AID.)
(See LANDING DISTANCE AVAILABLE.)
(See ICAO Term LANDING DISTANCE AVAILABLE.)

LF–
(See LOW FREQUENCY.)

LIGHTED AIRPORT– An airport where runway and obstruction lighting is available.
(See AIRPORT LIGHTING.)
(Refer to AIM.)

LIGHT GUN– A handheld directional light signaling device which emits a brilliant narrow beam of white, green, or red light as selected by the tower controller. The color and type of light transmitted can be used to approve or disapprove anticipated pilot actions where radio communication is not available. The light gun is used for controlling traffic operating in the vicinity of the airport and on the airport movement area.
(Refer to AIM.)

LIGHT-SPORT AIRCRAFT (LSA)– An FAA-registered aircraft, other than a helicopter or powered-lift, that meets certain weight and performance. Principally it is a single–engine aircraft with a maximum of two seats and weighing no more than 1,430 pounds if intended for operation on water, or 1,320 pounds if not. It must be of simple design (fixed landing gear (except if intended for operations on water or a glider), piston powered, nonpressurized, with a fixed or ground adjustable propeller). Performance is also limited to a maximum airspeed in level flight of not more than 120 knots calibrated airspeed (CAS), have a maximum never-exceed speed of not more than 120 knots CAS for a glider, and have a maximum stalling speed, without the use of lift-enhancing devices of not more than 45 knots CAS. It may be certificated as either Experimental LSA or as a Special LSA aircraft. A minimum of a sport pilot certificate is required to operate light-sport aircraft.
(Refer to 14 CFR Part 1, §1.1.)

LINE UP AND WAIT (LUAW)– Used by ATC to inform a pilot to taxi onto the departure runway to line up and wait. It is not authorization for takeoff. It is used when takeoff clearance cannot immediately be issued because of traffic or other reasons.
(See CLEARED FOR TAKEOFF.)

LOCAL AIRPORT ADVISORY (LAA)− A service available only in Alaska and provided by facilities that are located on the landing airport, have a discrete ground−to−air communication frequency or the tower frequency when the tower is closed, automated weather reporting with voice broadcasting, and a continuous ASOS/AWOS data display, other continuous direct reading instruments, or manual observations available to the specialist.
(See AIRPORT ADVISORY AREA.)

LOCAL TRAFFIC− Aircraft operating in the traffic pattern or within sight of the tower, or aircraft known to be departing or arriving from flight in local practice areas, or aircraft executing practice instrument approaches at the airport.
(See TRAFFIC PATTERN.)

LOCALIZER− The component of an ILS which provides course guidance to the runway.
(See INSTRUMENT LANDING SYSTEM.)
(See ICAO term LOCALIZER COURSE.)
(Refer to AIM.)

LOCALIZER COURSE [ICAO]− The locus of points, in any given horizontal plane, at which the DDM (difference in depth of modulation) is zero.

LOCALIZER OFFSET− An angular offset of the localizer aligned within 3° of the runway alignment.

LOCALIZER TYPE DIRECTIONAL AID (LDA)− A localizer with an angular offset that exceeds 3° of the runway alignment, used for nonprecision instrument approaches with utility and accuracy comparable to a localizer, but which are not part of a complete ILS.
(Refer to AIM.)

LOCALIZER TYPE DIRECTIONAL AID (LDA) PRECISION RUNWAY MONITOR (PRM) APPROACH− An approach, which includes a glideslope, used in conjunction with an ILS PRM, RNAV PRM or GLS PRM approach to an adjacent runway to conduct Simultaneous Offset Instrument Approaches (SOIA) to parallel runways whose centerlines are separated by less than 3,000 feet and at least 750 feet. NTZ monitoring is required to conduct these approaches.
(See SIMULTANEOUS OFFSET INSTRUMENT APPROACH (SOIA).)
(Refer to AIM)

LOCALIZER USABLE DISTANCE− The maximum distance from the localizer transmitter at a specified altitude, as verified by flight inspection, at which reliable course information is continuously received.
(Refer to AIM.)

LOCATOR [ICAO]− An LM/MF NDB used as an aid to final approach.
Note: A locator usually has an average radius of rated coverage of between 18.5 and 46.3 km (10 and 25 NM).

LONG RANGE NAVIGATION−
(See LORAN.)

LONGITUDINAL SEPARATION− The longitudinal spacing of aircraft at the same altitude by a minimum distance expressed in units of time or miles.
(See SEPARATION.)
(Refer to AIM.)

LORAN− An electronic navigational system by which hyperbolic lines of position are determined by measuring the difference in the time of reception of synchronized pulse signals from two fixed transmitters. Loran A operates in the 1750-1950 kHz frequency band. Loran C and D operate in the 100-110 kHz frequency band. In 2010, the U.S. Coast Guard terminated all U.S. LORAN-C transmissions.
(Refer to AIM.)

LOST COMMUNICATIONS− Loss of the ability to communicate by radio. Aircraft are sometimes referred to as NORDO (No Radio). Standard pilot procedures are specified in 14 CFR Part 91. Radar controllers issue procedures for pilots to follow in the event of lost communications during a radar approach when weather reports indicate that an aircraft will likely encounter IFR weather conditions during the approach.

(Refer to 14 CFR Part 91.)
(Refer to AIM.)

LOST LINK (LL)– An interruption or loss of the control link, or when the pilot is unable to effect control of the aircraft and, as a result, the UA will perform a predictable or planned maneuver. Loss of command and control link between the Control Station and the aircraft. There are two types of links:

a. An uplink which transmits command instructions to the aircraft, and

b. A downlink which transmits the status of the aircraft and provides situational awareness to the pilot.

LOST LINK PROCEDURE– Preprogrammed or predetermined mitigations to ensure the continued safe operation of the UA in the event of a lost link (LL). In the event positive link cannot be established, flight termination must be implemented.

LOW ALTITUDE AIRWAY STRUCTURE– The network of airways serving aircraft operations up to but not including 18,000 feet MSL.

(See AIRWAY.)
(Refer to AIM.)

LOW ALTITUDE ALERT, CHECK YOUR ALTITUDE IMMEDIATELY–

(See SAFETY ALERT.)

LOW ALTITUDE AUTHORIZATION AND NOTIFICATION CAPABILITY (LAANC)– FAA and industry collaboration which automates the process of obtaining a required authorization for operations in controlled airspace.

LOW APPROACH– An approach over an airport or runway following an instrument approach or a VFR approach including the go-around maneuver where the pilot intentionally does not make contact with the runway.

(Refer to AIM.)

LOW FREQUENCY (LF)– The frequency band between 30 and 300 kHz.

(Refer to AIM.)

LOCALIZER PERFORMANCE WITH VERTICAL GUIDANCE (LPV)– A type of approach with vertical guidance (APV) based on WAAS, published on RNAV (GPS) approach charts. This procedure takes advantage of the precise lateral guidance available from WAAS. The minima is published as a decision altitude (DA).

LUAW–

(See LINE UP AND WAIT.)

M

MAA−
(See MAXIMUM AUTHORIZED ALTITUDE.)

MACH NUMBER− The ratio of true airspeed to the speed of sound; e.g., MACH .82, MACH 1.6.
(See AIRSPEED.)

MACH TECHNIQUE [ICAO]− Describes a control technique used by air traffic control whereby turbojet aircraft operating successively along suitable routes are cleared to maintain appropriate MACH numbers for a relevant portion of the en route phase of flight. The principal objective is to achieve improved utilization of the airspace and to ensure that separation between successive aircraft does not decrease below the established minima.

MAHWP− Missed Approach Holding Waypoint

MAINTAIN−

a. Concerning altitude/flight level, the term means to remain at the altitude/flight level specified. The phrase "climb and" or "descend and" normally precedes "maintain" and the altitude assignment; e.g., "descend and maintain 5,000."

b. Concerning other ATC instructions, the term is used in its literal sense; e.g., maintain VFR.

MAINTENANCE PLANNING FRICTION LEVEL− The friction level specified in AC 150/5320-12, Measurement, Construction, and Maintenance of Skid Resistant Airport Pavement Surfaces, which represents the friction value below which the runway pavement surface remains acceptable for any category or class of aircraft operations but which is beginning to show signs of deterioration. This value will vary depending on the particular friction measurement equipment used.

MAKE SHORT APPROACH− Used by ATC to inform a pilot to alter his/her traffic pattern so as to make a short final approach.
(See TRAFFIC PATTERN.)

MAN PORTABLE AIR DEFENSE SYSTEMS (MANPADS)− MANPADS are lightweight, shoulder−launched, missile systems used to bring down aircraft and create mass casualties. The potential for MANPADS use against airborne aircraft is real and requires familiarity with the subject. Terrorists choose MANPADS because the weapons are low cost, highly mobile, require minimal set−up time, and are easy to use and maintain. Although the weapons have limited range, and their accuracy is affected by poor visibility and adverse weather, they can be fired from anywhere on land or from boats where there is unrestricted visibility to the target.

MANDATORY ALTITUDE− An altitude depicted on an instrument Approach Procedure Chart requiring the aircraft to maintain altitude at the depicted value.

MANPADS−
(See MAN PORTABLE AIR DEFENSE SYSTEMS.)

MAP−
(See MISSED APPROACH POINT.)

MARKER BEACON− An electronic navigation facility transmitting a 75 MHz vertical fan or boneshaped radiation pattern. Marker beacons are identified by their modulation frequency and keying code, and when received by compatible airborne equipment, indicate to the pilot, both aurally and visually, that he/she is passing over the facility.
(See INNER MARKER.)
(See MIDDLE MARKER.)
(See OUTER MARKER.)
(Refer to AIM.)

MARSA–
(See MILITARY AUTHORITY ASSUMES RESPONSIBILITY FOR SEPARATION OF AIRCRAFT.)

MAWP– Missed Approach Waypoint

MAXIMUM AUTHORIZED ALTITUDE– A published altitude representing the maximum usable altitude or flight level for an airspace structure or route segment. It is the highest altitude on a Federal airway, jet route, area navigation low or high route, or other direct route for which an MEA is designated in 14 CFR Part 95 at which adequate reception of navigation aid signals is assured.

MAXIMUM GROSS OPERATING WEIGHT (MGOW)– The maximum gross weight of an aircraft, including fuel and any external objects, at any point during the flight.

MAYDAY– The international radiotelephony distress signal. When repeated three times, it indicates imminent and grave danger and that immediate assistance is requested.
(See PAN-PAN.)
(Refer to AIM.)

MCA–
(See MINIMUM CROSSING ALTITUDE.)

MDA–
(See MINIMUM DESCENT ALTITUDE.)

MEA–
(See MINIMUM EN ROUTE IFR ALTITUDE.)

MEARTS–
(See MICRO-EN ROUTE AUTOMATED RADAR TRACKING SYSTEM.)

METEOROLOGICAL IMPACT STATEMENT– An unscheduled planning forecast describing conditions expected to begin within 4 to 12 hours which may impact the flow of air traffic in a specific center's (ARTCC) area.

METER FIX ARC– A semicircle, equidistant from a meter fix, usually in low altitude relatively close to the meter fix, used to help TBFM/ERAM calculate a meter time, and determine appropriate sector meter list assignments for aircraft not on an established arrival route or assigned a meter fix.

METER REFERENCE ELEMENT (MRE)– A constraint point through which traffic flows are managed. An MRE can be the runway threshold, a meter fix, or a meter arc.

METER REFERENCE POINT LIST (MRP)– A list of TBFM delay information conveyed to the controller on the situation display via the Meter Reference Point View, commonly known as the "Meter List."

METERING–A method of time–regulating traffic flows in the en route and terminal environments.

METERING AIRPORTS– Airports adapted for metering and for which optimum flight paths are defined. A maximum of 15 airports may be adapted.

METERING FIX– A fix along an established route from over which aircraft will be metered prior to entering terminal airspace. Normally, this fix should be established at a distance from the airport which will facilitate a profile descent 10,000 feet above airport elevation (AAE) or above.

MGOW–
(See MAXIMUM GROSS OPERATING WEIGHT.)

MHA–
(See MINIMUM HOLDING ALTITUDE.)

MIA–
(See MINIMUM IFR ALTITUDES.)

MICROBURST− A small downburst with outbursts of damaging winds extending 2.5 miles or less. In spite of its small horizontal scale, an intense microburst could induce wind speeds as high as 150 knots
(Refer to AIM.)

MICRO-EN ROUTE AUTOMATED RADAR TRACKING SYSTEM (MEARTS)− An automated radar and radar beacon tracking system capable of employing both short-range (ASR) and long-range (ARSR) radars. This microcomputer driven system provides improved tracking, continuous data recording, and use of full digital radar displays.

MID RVR−
(See VISIBILITY.)

MIDDLE COMPASS LOCATOR−
(See COMPASS LOCATOR.)

MIDDLE MARKER− A marker beacon that defines a point along the glideslope of an ILS normally located at or near the point of decision height (ILS Category I). It is keyed to transmit alternate dots and dashes, with the alternate dots and dashes keyed at the rate of 95 dot/dash combinations per minute on a 1300 Hz tone, which is received aurally and visually by compatible airborne equipment.
(See INSTRUMENT LANDING SYSTEM.)
(See MARKER BEACON.)
(Refer to AIM.)

MILES-IN-TRAIL− A specified distance between aircraft, normally, in the same stratum associated with the same destination or route of flight.

MILITARY AUTHORITY ASSUMES RESPONSIBILITY FOR SEPARATION OF AIRCRAFT (MARSA)− A condition whereby the military services involved assume responsibility for separation between participating military aircraft in the ATC system. It is used only for required IFR operations which are specified in letters of agreement or other appropriate FAA or military documents.

MILITARY LANDING ZONE− A landing strip used exclusively by the military for training. A military landing zone does not carry a runway designation.

MILITARY OPERATIONS AREA−
(See SPECIAL USE AIRSPACE.)

MILITARY TRAINING ROUTES− Airspace of defined vertical and lateral dimensions established for the conduct of military flight training at airspeeds in excess of 250 knots IAS.
(See IFR MILITARY TRAINING ROUTES.)
(See VFR MILITARY TRAINING ROUTES.)

MINIMA−
(See MINIMUMS.)

MINIMUM CROSSING ALTITUDE (MCA)− The lowest altitude at certain fixes at which an aircraft must cross when proceeding in the direction of a higher minimum en route IFR altitude (MEA).
(See MINIMUM EN ROUTE IFR ALTITUDE.)

MINIMUM DESCENT ALTITUDE (MDA)− The lowest altitude, expressed in feet above mean sea level, to which descent is authorized on final approach or during circle-to-land maneuvering in execution of a standard instrument approach procedure where no electronic glideslope is provided.
(See NONPRECISION APPROACH PROCEDURE.)

MINIMUM EN ROUTE IFR ALTITUDE (MEA)− The lowest published altitude between radio fixes which assures acceptable navigational signal coverage and meets obstacle clearance requirements between those fixes. The MEA prescribed for a Federal airway or segment thereof, area navigation low or high route, or other direct route applies to the entire width of the airway, segment, or route between the radio fixes defining the airway, segment, or route.

(Refer to 14 CFR Part 91.)
(Refer to 14 CFR Part 95.)
(Refer to AIM.)

MINIMUM FRICTION LEVEL– The friction level specified in AC 150/5320-12, Measurement, Construction, and Maintenance of Skid Resistant Airport Pavement Surfaces, that represents the minimum recommended wet pavement surface friction value for any turbojet aircraft engaged in LAHSO. This value will vary with the particular friction measurement equipment used.

MINIMUM FUEL– Indicates that an aircraft's fuel supply has reached a state where, upon reaching the destination, it can accept little or no delay. This is not an emergency situation but merely indicates an emergency situation is possible should any undue delay occur.

(Refer to AIM.)

MINIMUM HOLDING ALTITUDE– The lowest altitude prescribed for a holding pattern which assures navigational signal coverage, communications, and meets obstacle clearance requirements.

MINIMUM IFR ALTITUDES (MIA)– Minimum altitudes for IFR operations as prescribed in 14 CFR Part 91. These altitudes are published on aeronautical charts and prescribed in 14 CFR Part 95 for airways and routes, and in 14 CFR Part 97 for standard instrument approach procedures. If no applicable minimum altitude is prescribed in 14 CFR Part 95 or 14 CFR Part 97, the following minimum IFR altitude applies:

a. In designated mountainous areas, 2,000 feet above the highest obstacle within a horizontal distance of 4 nautical miles from the course to be flown; or

b. Other than mountainous areas, 1,000 feet above the highest obstacle within a horizontal distance of 4 nautical miles from the course to be flown; or

c. As otherwise authorized by the Administrator or assigned by ATC.

(See MINIMUM CROSSING ALTITUDE.)
(See MINIMUM EN ROUTE IFR ALTITUDE.)
(See MINIMUM OBSTRUCTION CLEARANCE ALTITUDE.)
(See MINIMUM SAFE ALTITUDE.)
(See MINIMUM VECTORING ALTITUDE.)
(Refer to 14 CFR Part 91.)

MINIMUM OBSTRUCTION CLEARANCE ALTITUDE (MOCA)– The lowest published altitude in effect between radio fixes on VOR airways, off-airway routes, or route segments which meets obstacle clearance requirements for the entire route segment and which assures acceptable navigational signal coverage only within 25 statute (22 nautical) miles of a VOR.

(Refer to 14 CFR Part 91.)
(Refer to 14 CFR Part 95.)

MINIMUM RECEPTION ALTITUDE (MRA)– The lowest altitude at which an intersection can be determined.

(Refer to 14 CFR Part 95.)

MINIMUM SAFE ALTITUDE (MSA)–

a. The Minimum Safe Altitude (MSA) specified in 14 CFR Part 91 for various aircraft operations.

b. Altitudes depicted on approach charts or departure procedure (DP) graphic charts which provide at least 1,000 feet of obstacle clearance for emergency use. These altitudes will be identified as Minimum Safe Altitudes or Emergency Safe Altitudes and are established as follows:

1. Minimum Safe Altitude (MSA). Altitudes depicted on approach charts or on a DP graphic chart which provide at least 1,000 feet of obstacle clearance within a 25–mile radius of the navigation facility, waypoint, or airport reference point upon which the MSA is predicated. MSAs are for emergency use only and do not necessarily assure acceptable navigational signal coverage.

(See ICAO term Minimum Sector Altitude.)

2. Emergency Safe Altitude (ESA). Altitudes depicted on approach charts which provide at least 1,000 feet of obstacle clearance in nonmountainous areas and 2,000 feet of obstacle clearance in designated mountainous areas within a 100-mile radius of the navigation facility or waypoint used as the ESA center. These altitudes are normally used only in military procedures and are identified on published procedures as "Emergency Safe Altitudes."

MINIMUM SAFE ALTITUDE WARNING (MSAW)− A function of the EAS and STARS computer that aids the controller by alerting him/her when a tracked Mode C equipped aircraft is below or is predicted by the computer to go below a predetermined minimum safe altitude.
(Refer to AIM.)

MINIMUM SECTOR ALTITUDE [ICAO]− The lowest altitude which may be used under emergency conditions which will provide a minimum clearance of 300 m (1,000 feet) above all obstacles located in an area contained within a sector of a circle of 46 km (25 NM) radius centered on a radio aid to navigation.

MINIMUMS− Weather condition requirements established for a particular operation or type of operation; e.g., IFR takeoff or landing, alternate airport for IFR flight plans, VFR flight, etc.
(See IFR CONDITIONS.)
(See IFR TAKEOFF MINIMUMS AND DEPARTURE PROCEDURES.)
(See LANDING MINIMUMS.)
(See VFR CONDITIONS.)
(Refer to 14 CFR Part 91.)
(Refer to AIM.)

MINIMUM VECTORING ALTITUDE (MVA)− The lowest MSL altitude at which an IFR aircraft will be vectored by a radar controller, except as otherwise authorized for radar approaches, departures, and missed approaches. The altitude meets IFR obstacle clearance criteria. It may be lower than the published MEA along an airway or J-route segment. It may be utilized for radar vectoring only upon the controller's determination that an adequate radar return is being received from the aircraft being controlled. Charts depicting minimum vectoring altitudes are normally available only to the controllers and not to pilots.
(Refer to AIM.)

MINUTES-IN-TRAIL− A specified interval between aircraft expressed in time. This method would more likely be utilized regardless of altitude.

MIS−
(See METEOROLOGICAL IMPACT STATEMENT.)

MISSED APPROACH−

a. A maneuver conducted by a pilot when an instrument approach cannot be completed to a landing. The route of flight and altitude are shown on instrument approach procedure charts. A pilot executing a missed approach prior to the Missed Approach Point (MAP) must continue along the final approach to the MAP.

b. A term used by the pilot to inform ATC that he/she is executing the missed approach.

c. At locations where ATC radar service is provided, the pilot should conform to radar vectors when provided by ATC in lieu of the published missed approach procedure.
(See MISSED APPROACH POINT.)
(Refer to AIM.)

MISSED APPROACH POINT (MAP)− A point prescribed in each instrument approach procedure at which a missed approach procedure shall be executed if the required visual reference does not exist.
(See MISSED APPROACH.)
(See SEGMENTS OF AN INSTRUMENT APPROACH PROCEDURE.)

MISSED APPROACH PROCEDURE [ICAO]− The procedure to be followed if the approach cannot be continued.

MISSED APPROACH SEGMENT–
(See SEGMENTS OF AN INSTRUMENT APPROACH PROCEDURE.)

MM–
(See MIDDLE MARKER.)

MOA–
(See MILITARY OPERATIONS AREA.)

MOCA–
(See MINIMUM OBSTRUCTION CLEARANCE ALTITUDE.)

MODE– The letter or number assigned to a specific pulse spacing of radio signals transmitted or received by ground interrogator or airborne transponder components of the Air Traffic Control Radar Beacon System (ATCRBS). Mode A (military Mode 3) and Mode C (altitude reporting) are used in air traffic control.
(See INTERROGATOR.)
(See RADAR.)
(See TRANSPONDER.)
(See ICAO term MODE.)
(Refer to AIM.)

MODE (SSR MODE) [ICAO]– The letter or number assigned to a specific pulse spacing of the interrogation signals transmitted by an interrogator. There are 4 modes, A, B, C and D specified in Annex 10, corresponding to four different interrogation pulse spacings.

MODE C INTRUDER ALERT– A function of certain air traffic control automated systems designed to alert radar controllers to existing or pending situations between a tracked target (known IFR or VFR aircraft) and an untracked target (unknown IFR or VFR aircraft) that requires immediate attention/action.
(See CONFLICT ALERT.)

MODEL AIRCRAFT– An unmanned aircraft that is: (1) capable of sustained flight in the atmosphere; (2) flown within visual line of sight of the person operating the aircraft; and (3) flown for hobby or recreational purposes.

MONITOR– (When used with communication transfer) listen on a specific frequency and stand by for instructions. Under normal circumstances do not establish communications.

MONITOR ALERT (MA)– A function of the TFMS that provides traffic management personnel with a tool for predicting potential capacity problems in individual operational sectors. The MA is an indication that traffic management personnel need to analyze a particular sector for actual activity and to determine the required action(s), if any, needed to control the demand.

MONITOR ALERT PARAMETER (MAP)– The number designated for use in monitor alert processing by the TFMS. The MAP is designated for each operational sector for increments of 15 minutes.

MOSAIC/MULTI–SENSOR MODE– Accepts positional data from multiple approved surveillance sources. Targets are displayed from a single source according to the hierarchy of the sources assigned in a given geographic area.

MOUNTAIN WAVE– Mountain waves occur when air is being blown over a mountain range or even the ridge of a sharp bluff area. As the air hits the upwind side of the range, it starts to climb, thus creating what is generally a smooth updraft which turns into a turbulent downdraft as the air passes the crest of the ridge. Mountain waves can cause significant fluctuations in airspeed and altitude with or without associated turbulence.
(Refer to AIM.)

MOVEMENT AREA– The runways, taxiways, and other areas of an airport/heliport which are utilized for taxiing/hover taxiing, air taxiing, takeoff, and landing of aircraft, exclusive of loading ramps and parking areas. At those airports/heliports with a tower, specific approval for entry onto the movement area must be obtained from ATC.
(See ICAO term MOVEMENT AREA.)

MOVEMENT AREA [ICAO]– That part of an aerodrome to be used for the takeoff, landing and taxiing of aircraft, consisting of the maneuvering area and the apron(s).

MOVING AIRSPACE RESERVATION– The term used in oceanic ATC for airspace that encompasses oceanic activities and advances with the mission progress; i.e., the reservation moves with the aircraft or flight.
(See MOVING ALTITUDE RESERVATION.)

MOVING ALTITUDE RESERVATION– An altitude reservation which encompasses en route activities and advances with the mission progress; i.e., the reservation moves with the aircraft or flight.

MOVING TARGET INDICATOR– An electronic device which will permit radar scope presentation only from targets which are in motion. A partial remedy for ground clutter.

MRA–
(See MINIMUM RECEPTION ALTITUDE.)

MRE–
(See METER REFERENCE ELEMENT.)

MRP
(See METER REFERENCE POINT LIST.)

MSA–
(See MINIMUM SAFE ALTITUDE.)

MSAW–
(See MINIMUM SAFE ALTITUDE WARNING.)

MTI–
(See MOVING TARGET INDICATOR.)

MTR–
(See MILITARY TRAINING ROUTES.)

MULTICOM– A mobile service not open to public correspondence used to provide communications essential to conduct the activities being performed by or directed from private aircraft.

MULTIPLE RUNWAYS– The utilization of a dedicated arrival runway(s) for departures and a dedicated departure runway(s) for arrivals when feasible to reduce delays and enhance capacity.

MVA–
(See MINIMUM VECTORING ALTITUDE.)

N

NAS–
(See NATIONAL AIRSPACE SYSTEM.)

NAT HLA–
(See NORTH ATLANTIC HIGH LEVEL AIRSPACE.)

NATIONAL AIRSPACE SYSTEM– The common network of U.S. airspace; air navigation facilities, equipment and services, airports or landing areas; aeronautical charts, information and services; rules, regulations and procedures, technical information, and manpower and material. Included are system components shared jointly with the military.

NATIONAL BEACON CODE ALLOCATION PLAN AIRSPACE (NBCAP)– Airspace over United States territory located within the North American continent between Canada and Mexico, including adjacent territorial waters outward to about boundaries of oceanic control areas (CTA)/Flight Information Regions (FIR).
(See FLIGHT INFORMATION REGION.)

NATIONAL FLIGHT DATA DIGEST (NFDD)– A daily (except weekends and Federal holidays) publication of flight information appropriate to aeronautical charts, aeronautical publications, Notices to Air Missions, or other media serving the purpose of providing operational flight data essential to safe and efficient aircraft operations.

NATIONAL SEARCH AND RESCUE PLAN– An interagency agreement which provides for the effective utilization of all available facilities in all types of search and rescue missions.

NATIONAL SECURITY AREA (NSA)–
(See SPECIAL USE AIRSPACE.)

NAVAID–
(See NAVIGATIONAL AID.)

NAVAID CLASSES– VOR, VORTAC, and TACAN aids are classed according to their operational use. The three classes of NAVAIDs are:

a. T– Terminal.

b. L– Low altitude.

c. H– High altitude.

Note: The normal service range for T, L, and H class aids is found in the AIM. Certain operational requirements make it necessary to use some of these aids at greater service ranges than specified. Extended range is made possible through flight inspection determinations. Some aids also have lesser service range due to location, terrain, frequency protection, etc. Restrictions to service range are listed in the Chart Supplement.

NAVIGABLE AIRSPACE– Airspace at and above the minimum flight altitudes prescribed in the CFRs including airspace needed for safe takeoff and landing.
(Refer to 14 CFR Part 91.)

NAVIGATION REFERENCE SYSTEM (NRS)– The NRS is a system of waypoints developed for use within the United States for flight planning and navigation without reference to ground based navigational aids. The NRS waypoints are located in a grid pattern along defined latitude and longitude lines. The initial use of the NRS will be in the high altitude environment. The NRS waypoints are intended for use by aircraft capable of point–to–point navigation.

NAVIGATION SPECIFICATION [ICAO]– A set of aircraft and flight crew requirements needed to support performance–based navigation operations within a defined airspace. There are two kinds of navigation specifications:

a. RNP specification. A navigation specification based on area navigation that includes the requirement for performance monitoring and alerting, designated by the prefix RNP; e.g., RNP 4, RNP APCH.

b. RNAV specification. A navigation specification based on area navigation that does not include the requirement for performance monitoring and alerting, designated by the prefix RNAV; e.g., RNAV 5, RNAV 1.

Note: The Performance-based Navigation Manual (Doc 9613), Volume II contains detailed guidance on navigation specifications.

NAVIGATIONAL AID– Any visual or electronic device airborne or on the surface which provides point-to-point guidance information or position data to aircraft in flight.
(See AIR NAVIGATION FACILITY.)

NAVSPEC-
(See NAVIGATION SPECIFICATION [ICAO].)

NBCAP AIRSPACE–
(See NATIONAL BEACON CODE ALLOCATION PLAN AIRSPACE.)

NDB–
(See NONDIRECTIONAL BEACON.)

NEGATIVE– "No," or "permission not granted," or "that is not correct."

NEGATIVE CONTACT– Used by pilots to inform ATC that:

a. Previously issued traffic is not in sight. It may be followed by the pilot's request for the controller to provide assistance in avoiding the traffic.

b. They were unable to contact ATC on a particular frequency.

NFDD–
(See NATIONAL FLIGHT DATA DIGEST.)

NIGHT– The time between the end of evening civil twilight and the beginning of morning civil twilight, as published in the Air Almanac, converted to local time.
(See ICAO term NIGHT.)

NIGHT [ICAO]– The hours between the end of evening civil twilight and the beginning of morning civil twilight or such other period between sunset and sunrise as may be specified by the appropriate authority.

Note: Civil twilight ends in the evening when the center of the sun's disk is 6 degrees below the horizon and begins in the morning when the center of the sun's disk is 6 degrees below the horizon.

NO GYRO APPROACH– A radar approach/vector provided in case of a malfunctioning gyro-compass or directional gyro. Instead of providing the pilot with headings to be flown, the controller observes the radar track and issues control instructions "turn right/left" or "stop turn" as appropriate.
(Refer to AIM.)

NO GYRO VECTOR–
(See NO GYRO APPROACH.)

NO TRANSGRESSION ZONE (NTZ)– The NTZ is a 2,000 foot wide zone, located equidistant between parallel runway or SOIA final approach courses, in which flight is normally not allowed.

NONAPPROACH CONTROL TOWER– Author-izes aircraft to land or takeoff at the airport controlled by the tower or to transit the Class D airspace. The primary function of a nonapproach control tower is the sequencing of aircraft in the traffic pattern and on the landing area. Nonapproach control towers also separate aircraft operating under instrument flight rules clearances from approach controls and centers. They provide ground control services to aircraft, vehicles, personnel, and equipment on the airport movement area.

NONCOMMON ROUTE/PORTION– That segment of a North American Route between the inland navigation facility and a designated North American terminal.

NON–COOPERATIVE SURVEILLANCE– Any surveillance system, such as primary radar, that is not dependent upon the presence of any equipment on the aircraft or vehicle to be tracked.

(See COOPERATIVE SURVEILLANCE.)
(See RADAR.)

NONDIRECTIONAL BEACON– An L/MF or UHF radio beacon transmitting nondirectional signals whereby the pilot of an aircraft equipped with direction finding equipment can determine his/her bearing to or from the radio beacon and "home" on or track to or from the station. When the radio beacon is installed in conjunction with the Instrument Landing System marker, it is normally called a Compass Locator.

(See AUTOMATIC DIRECTION FINDER.)
(See COMPASS LOCATOR.)

NONMOVEMENT AREAS– Taxiways and apron (ramp) areas not under the control of air traffic.

NONPRECISION APPROACH–

(See NONPRECISION APPROACH PROCEDURE.)

NONPRECISION APPROACH PROCEDURE– A standard instrument approach procedure in which no electronic glideslope is provided; e.g., VOR, TACAN, NDB, LOC, ASR, LDA, or SDF approaches.

NONRADAR– Precedes other terms and generally means without the use of radar, such as:

a. Nonradar Approach. Used to describe instrument approaches for which course guidance on final approach is not provided by ground-based precision or surveillance radar. Radar vectors to the final approach course may or may not be provided by ATC. Examples of nonradar approaches are VOR, NDB, TACAN, ILS, RNAV, and GLS approaches.

(See FINAL APPROACH COURSE.)
(See FINAL APPROACH-IFR.)
(See INSTRUMENT APPROACH PROCEDURE.)
(See RADAR APPROACH.)

b. Nonradar Approach Control. An ATC facility providing approach control service without the use of radar.

(See APPROACH CONTROL FACILITY.)
(See APPROACH CONTROL SERVICE.)

c. Nonradar Arrival. An aircraft arriving at an airport without radar service or at an airport served by a radar facility and radar contact has not been established or has been terminated due to a lack of radar service to the airport.

(See RADAR ARRIVAL.)
(See RADAR SERVICE.)

d. Nonradar Route. A flight path or route over which the pilot is performing his/her own navigation. The pilot may be receiving radar separation, radar monitoring, or other ATC services while on a nonradar route.

(See RADAR ROUTE.)

e. Nonradar Separation. The spacing of aircraft in accordance with established minima without the use of radar; e.g., vertical, lateral, or longitudinal separation.

(See RADAR SEPARATION.)

NON–RESTRICTIVE ROUTING (NRR)– Portions of a proposed route of flight where a user can flight plan the most advantageous flight path with no requirement to make reference to ground–based NAVAIDs.

NOPAC–

(See NORTH PACIFIC.)

NORDO (No Radio)– Aircraft that cannot or do not communicate by radio when radio communication is required are referred to as "NORDO."

(See LOST COMMUNICATIONS.)

NORMAL OPERATING ZONE (NOZ)– The NOZ is the operating zone within which aircraft flight remains during normal independent simultaneous parallel ILS approaches.

NORTH AMERICAN ROUTE– A numerically coded route preplanned over existing airway and route systems to and from specific coastal fixes serving the North Atlantic. North American Routes consist of the following:

a. Common Route/Portion. That segment of a North American Route between the inland navigation facility and the coastal fix.

b. Noncommon Route/Portion. That segment of a North American Route between the inland navigation facility and a designated North American terminal.

c. Inland Navigation Facility. A navigation aid on a North American Route at which the common route and/or the noncommon route begins or ends.

d. Coastal Fix. A navigation aid or intersection where an aircraft transitions between the domestic route structure and the oceanic route structure.

NORTH AMERICAN ROUTE PROGRAM (NRP)– The NRP is a set of rules and procedures which are designed to increase the flexibility of user flight planning within published guidelines.

NORTH ATLANTIC HIGH LEVEL AIRSPACE (NAT HLA)– That volume of airspace (as defined in ICAO Document 7030) between FL 285 and FL 420 within the Oceanic Control Areas of Bodo Oceanic, Gander Oceanic, New York Oceanic East, Reykjavik, Santa Maria, and Shanwick, excluding the Shannon and Brest Ocean Transition Areas. ICAO Doc 007 *North Atlantic Operations and Airspace Manual* provides detailed information on related aircraft and operational requirements.

NORTH PACIFIC– An organized route system between the Alaskan west coast and Japan.

NOT STANDARD– Varying from what is expected or published. For use in NOTAMs only.

NOT STD-
(See NOT STANDARD.)

NOTAM–
(See NOTICE TO AIR MISSIONS.)

NOTAM [ICAO]– A notice containing information concerning the establishment, condition or change in any aeronautical facility, service, procedure or hazard, the timely knowledge of which is essential to personnel concerned with flight operations.

a. I Distribution– Distribution by means of telecommunication.

b. II Distribution– Distribution by means other than telecommunications.

NOTICE TO AIR MISSIONS (NOTAM)– A notice containing information (not known sufficiently in advance to publicize by other means) concerning the establishment, condition, or change in any component (facility, service, or procedure of, or hazard in the National Airspace System) the timely knowledge of which is essential to personnel concerned with flight operations.

a. NOTAM (D)– A NOTAM given (in addition to local dissemination) distant dissemination beyond the area of responsibility of the Flight Service Station. These NOTAMs will be stored and available until canceled.

b. FDC NOTAM– A NOTAM regulatory in nature, transmitted by USNOF and given system wide dissemination.
(See ICAO term NOTAM.)

NRR–
(See NON–RESTRICTIVE ROUTING.)

NRS–
(See NAVIGATION REFERENCE SYSTEM.)

NUMEROUS TARGETS VICINITY (LOCATION)– A traffic advisory issued by ATC to advise pilots that targets on the radar scope are too numerous to issue individually.
(See TRAFFIC ADVISORIES.)

O

OBSTACLE− An existing object, object of natural growth, or terrain at a fixed geographical location or which may be expected at a fixed location within a prescribed area with reference to which vertical clearance is or must be provided during flight operation.

OBSTACLE DEPARTURE PROCEDURE (ODP)− A preplanned instrument flight rule (IFR) departure procedure printed for pilot use in textual or graphic form to provide obstruction clearance via the least onerous route from the terminal area to the appropriate en route structure. ODPs are recommended for obstruction clearance and may be flown without ATC clearance unless an alternate departure procedure (SID or radar vector) has been specifically assigned by ATC.

(See IFR TAKEOFF MINIMUMS AND DEPARTURE PROCEDURES.)
(See STANDARD INSTRUMENT DEPARTURES.)
(Refer to AIM.)

OBSTACLE FREE ZONE− The OFZ is a three−dimensional volume of airspace which protects the transition of aircraft to and from the runway. The OFZ clearing standard precludes taxiing and parked airplanes and object penetrations, except for frangible NAVAID locations that are fixed by function. Additionally, vehicles, equipment, and personnel may be authorized by air traffic control to enter the area using the provisions of FAA Order JO 7110.65, paragraph 3−1−5, Vehicles/Equipment/Personnel Near/On Runways. The runway OFZ and when applicable, the inner-approach OFZ, and the inner-transitional OFZ, comprise the OFZ.

a. Runway OFZ. The runway OFZ is a defined volume of airspace centered above the runway. The runway OFZ is the airspace above a surface whose elevation at any point is the same as the elevation of the nearest point on the runway centerline. The runway OFZ extends 200 feet beyond each end of the runway. The width is as follows:

1. For runways serving large airplanes, the greater of:

(a) 400 feet, or

(b) 180 feet, plus the wingspan of the most demanding airplane, plus 20 feet per 1,000 feet of airport elevation.

2. For runways serving only small airplanes:

(a) 300 feet for precision instrument runways.

(b) 250 feet for other runways serving small airplanes with approach speeds of 50 knots, or more.

(c) 120 feet for other runways serving small airplanes with approach speeds of less than 50 knots.

b. Inner-approach OFZ. The inner-approach OFZ is a defined volume of airspace centered on the approach area. The inner-approach OFZ applies only to runways with an approach lighting system. The inner-approach OFZ begins 200 feet from the runway threshold at the same elevation as the runway threshold and extends 200 feet beyond the last light unit in the approach lighting system. The width of the inner-approach OFZ is the same as the runway OFZ and rises at a slope of 50 (horizontal) to 1 (vertical) from the beginning.

c. Inner-transitional OFZ. The inner transitional surface OFZ is a defined volume of airspace along the sides of the runway and inner-approach OFZ and applies only to precision instrument runways. The inner-transitional surface OFZ slopes 3 (horizontal) to 1 (vertical) out from the edges of the runway OFZ and inner-approach OFZ to a height of 150 feet above the established airport elevation.

(Refer to AC 150/5300-13, Chapter 3.)
(Refer to FAA Order JO 7110.65, Para 3−1−5, Vehicles/Equipment/Personnel Near/On Runways.)

OBSTRUCTION− Any object/obstacle exceeding the obstruction standards specified by 14 CFR Part 77, Subpart C.

OBSTRUCTION LIGHT− A light or one of a group of lights, usually red or white, frequently mounted on a surface structure or natural terrain to warn pilots of the presence of an obstruction.

OCEANIC AIRSPACE− Airspace over the oceans of the world, considered international airspace, where oceanic separation and procedures per the International Civil Aviation Organization are applied. Responsibility for the provisions of air traffic control service in this airspace is delegated to various countries, based generally upon geographic proximity and the availability of the required resources.

OCEANIC ERROR REPORT− A report filed when ATC observes an Oceanic Error as defined by FAA Order JO 7210.632, Air Traffic Organization Occurrence Reporting.

OCEANIC PUBLISHED ROUTE− A route established in international airspace and charted or described in flight information publications, such as Route Charts, DoD En route Charts, Chart Supplements, NOTAMs, and Track Messages.

OCEANIC TRANSITION ROUTE− An ATS route established for the purpose of transitioning aircraft to/from an organized track system.

ODP−
(See OBSTACLE DEPARTURE PROCEDURE.)

OFF COURSE− A term used to describe a situation where an aircraft has reported a position fix or is observed on radar at a point not on the ATC-approved route of flight.

OFF−ROUTE OBSTRUCTION CLEARANCE ALTITUDE (OROCA)− A published altitude which provides terrain and obstruction clearance with a 1,000 foot buffer in non−mountainous areas and a 2,000 foot buffer in designated mountainous areas within the United States, and a 3,000 foot buffer outside the US ADIZ. These altitudes are not assessed for NAVAID signal coverage, air traffic control surveillance, or communications coverage, and are published for general situational awareness, flight planning, and in−flight contingency use.

OFF-ROUTE VECTOR− A vector by ATC which takes an aircraft off a previously assigned route. Altitudes assigned by ATC during such vectors provide required obstacle clearance.

OFFSET PARALLEL RUNWAYS− Staggered runways having centerlines which are parallel.

OFFSHORE/CONTROL AIRSPACE AREA− That portion of airspace between the U.S. 12 NM limit and the oceanic CTA/FIR boundary within which air traffic control is exercised. These areas are established to provide air traffic control services. Offshore/Control Airspace Areas may be classified as either Class A airspace or Class E airspace.

OFT−
(See OUTER FIX TIME.)

OM−
(See OUTER MARKER.)

ON COURSE−

a. Used to indicate that an aircraft is established on the route centerline.

b. Used by ATC to advise a pilot making a radar approach that his/her aircraft is lined up on the final approach course.
(See ON-COURSE INDICATION.)

ON-COURSE INDICATION− An indication on an instrument, which provides the pilot a visual means of determining that the aircraft is located on the centerline of a given navigational track, or an indication on a radar scope that an aircraft is on a given track.

ONE-MINUTE WEATHER− The most recent one minute updated weather broadcast received by a pilot from an uncontrolled airport ASOS/AWOS.

ONER−
(See OCEANIC NAVIGATIONAL ERROR REPORT.)

OOP−
(See OPERATIONS OVER PEOPLE.)

OPEN LOOP CLEARANCE– Provides a lateral vector solution that does not include a return to route point.

OPERATIONAL–
(See DUE REGARD.)

OPERATIONS OVER PEOPLE (OOP)– Operations of small unmanned aircraft over people.
(Refer to 14 CFR Part 107)

OPERATIONS SPECIFICATIONS [ICAO]– The authorizations, conditions and limitations associated with the air operator certificate and subject to the conditions in the operations manual.

OPERATOR (UAS)– The owner and/or remote pilot of a UAS.

OPPOSITE DIRECTION AIRCRAFT– Aircraft are operating in opposite directions when:

a. They are following the same track in reciprocal directions; or

b. Their tracks are parallel and the aircraft are flying in reciprocal directions; or

c. Their tracks intersect at an angle of more than 135°.

OPTION APPROACH– An approach requested and conducted by a pilot which will result in either a touch-and-go, missed approach, low approach, stop-and-go, or full stop landing. Pilots should advise ATC if they decide to remain on the runway, of any delay in their stop and go, delay clearing the runway, or are unable to comply with the instruction(s).
(See CLEARED FOR THE OPTION.)
(Refer to AIM.)

ORGANIZED TRACK SYSTEM– A series of ATS routes which are fixed and charted; i.e., CEP, NOPAC, or flexible and described by NOTAM; i.e., NAT TRACK MESSAGE.

OTR–
(See OCEANIC TRANSITION ROUTE.)

OTS–
(See ORGANIZED TRACK SYSTEM.)

OUT– The conversation is ended and no response is expected.

OUT OF SERVICE/UNSERVICEABLE (U/S)– When a piece of equipment, a NAVAID, a facility or a service is not operational, certified (if required) and immediately "available" for Air Traffic or public use.

OUTER AREA (associated with Class C airspace)– Non−regulatory airspace surrounding designated Class C airspace airports wherein ATC provides radar vectoring and sequencing on a full-time basis for all IFR and participating VFR aircraft. The service provided in the outer area is called Class C service which includes: IFR/IFR−IFR separation; IFR/VFR−traffic advisories and conflict resolution; and VFR/VFR−traffic advisories and, as appropriate, safety alerts. The normal radius will be 20 nautical miles with some variations based on site-specific requirements. The outer area extends outward from the primary Class C airspace airport and extends from the lower limits of radar/radio coverage up to the ceiling of the approach control's delegated airspace excluding the Class C charted area and other airspace as appropriate.
(See CONFLICT RESOLUTION.)
(See CONTROLLED AIRSPACE.)

OUTER COMPASS LOCATOR–
(See COMPASS LOCATOR.)

OUTER FIX– A general term used within ATC to describe fixes in the terminal area, other than the final approach fix. Aircraft are normally cleared to these fixes by an Air Route Traffic Control Center or an Approach Control Facility. Aircraft are normally cleared from these fixes to the final approach fix or final approach course.

OR

OUTER FIX– An adapted fix along the converted route of flight, prior to the meter fix, for which crossing times are calculated and displayed in the metering position list.

OUTER FIX ARC– A semicircle, usually about a 50–70 mile radius from a meter fix, usually in high altitude, which is used by CTAS/ERAM to calculate outer fix times and determine appropriate sector meter list assignments for aircraft on an established arrival route that will traverse the arc.

OUTER FIX TIME– A calculated time to depart the outer fix in order to cross the vertex at the ACLT. The time reflects descent speed adjustments and any applicable delay time that must be absorbed prior to crossing the meter fix.

OUTER MARKER– A marker beacon at or near the glideslope intercept altitude of an ILS approach. It is keyed to transmit two dashes per second on a 400 Hz tone, which is received aurally and visually by compatible airborne equipment. The OM is normally located four to seven miles from the runway threshold on the extended centerline of the runway.

(See INSTRUMENT LANDING SYSTEM.)
(See MARKER BEACON.)
(Refer to AIM.)

OVER– My transmission is ended; I expect a response.

OVERHEAD MANEUVER– A series of predetermined maneuvers prescribed for aircraft (often in formation) for entry into the visual flight rules (VFR) traffic pattern and to proceed to a landing. An overhead maneuver is not an instrument flight rules (IFR) approach procedure. An aircraft executing an overhead maneuver is considered VFR and the IFR flight plan is canceled when the aircraft reaches the "initial point" on the initial approach portion of the maneuver. The pattern usually specifies the following:

a. The radio contact required of the pilot.

b. The speed to be maintained.

c. An initial approach 3 to 5 miles in length.

d. An elliptical pattern consisting of two 180 degree turns.

e. A break point at which the first 180 degree turn is started.

f. The direction of turns.

g. Altitude (at least 500 feet above the conventional pattern).

h. A "Roll-out" on final approach not less than 1/4 mile from the landing threshold and not less than 300 feet above the ground.

OVERLYING CENTER– The ARTCC facility that is responsible for arrival/departure operations at a specific terminal.

P

P TIME–
(See PROPOSED DEPARTURE TIME.)

P-ACP–
(See PREARRANGED COORDINATION PROCEDURES.)

PAN-PAN– The international radio-telephony urgency signal. When repeated three times, indicates uncertainty or alert followed by the nature of the urgency.
(See MAYDAY.)
(Refer to AIM.)

PAO–
(See PUBLIC AIRCRAFT OPERATION.)

PAR–
(See PRECISION APPROACH RADAR.)

PAR [ICAO]–
(See ICAO Term PRECISION APPROACH RADAR.)

PARALLEL ILS APPROACHES– Approaches to parallel runways by IFR aircraft which, when established inbound toward the airport on the adjacent final approach courses, are radar-separated by at least 2 miles.
(See FINAL APPROACH COURSE.)
(See SIMULTANEOUS ILS APPROACHES.)

PARALLEL OFFSET ROUTE– A parallel track to the left or right of the designated or established airway/route. Normally associated with Area Navigation (RNAV) operations.
(See AREA NAVIGATION.)

PARALLEL RUNWAYS– Two or more runways at the same airport whose centerlines are parallel. In addition to runway number, parallel runways are designated as L (left) and R (right) or, if three parallel runways exist, L (left), C (center), and R (right).

PBCT–
(See PROPOSED BOUNDARY CROSSING TIME.)

PBN–
(See ICAO Term PERFORMANCE–BASED NAVIGATION.)

PDC–
(See PRE–DEPARTURE CLEARANCE.)

PDRR–
(See PRE–DEPARTURE REROUTE.)

PERFORMANCE–BASED NAVIGATION (PBN) [ICAO]– Area navigation based on performance requirements for aircraft operating along an ATS route, on an instrument approach procedure or in a designated airspace.

Note: Performance requirements are expressed in navigation specifications (RNAV specification, RNP specification) in terms of accuracy, integrity, continuity, availability, and functionality needed for the proposed operation in the context of a particular airspace concept.

PERMANENT ECHO– Radar signals reflected from fixed objects on the earth's surface; e.g., buildings, towers, terrain. Permanent echoes are distinguished from "ground clutter" by being definable locations rather than large areas. Under certain conditions they may be used to check radar alignment.

PERTI–
(See PLAN, EXECUTE, REVIEW, TRAIN, IMPROVE.)

PGUI–
(See PLANVIEW GRAPHICAL USER INTERFACE.)

PHOTO RECONNAISSANCE– Military activity that requires locating individual photo targets and navigating to the targets at a preplanned angle and altitude. The activity normally requires a lateral route width of 16 NM and altitude range of 1,500 feet to 10,000 feet AGL.

PILOT BRIEFING– The gathering, translation, interpretation, and summarization of weather and aeronautical information into a form usable by the pilot or flight supervisory personnel to assist in flight planning and decision–making for the safe and efficient operation of aircraft. These briefings may include, but are not limited to, weather observations, forecasts, and aeronautical information (for example, NOTAMs, military activities, flow control information, and temporary flight restrictions [TFR]).
(Refer to AIM.)

PILOT IN COMMAND– The pilot responsible for the operation and safety of an aircraft during flight time.
(Refer to 14 CFR Part 91.)

PILOT WEATHER REPORT– A report of meteorological phenomena encountered by aircraft in flight.
(Refer to AIM.)

PILOT'S DISCRETION– When used in conjunction with altitude assignments, means that ATC has offered the pilot the option of starting climb or descent whenever he/she wishes and conducting the climb or descent at any rate he/she wishes. He/she may temporarily level off at any intermediate altitude. However, once he/she has vacated an altitude, he/she may not return to that altitude.

PIREP–
(See PILOT WEATHER REPORT.)

PITCH POINT– A fix/waypoint that serves as a transition point from a departure procedure or the low altitude ground–based navigation structure into the high altitude waypoint system.

PLAN, EXECUTE, REVIEW, TRAIN, IMPROVE (PERTI)– A process that delivers a one–day detailed plan for NAS operations, and a two–day outlook, which sets NAS performance goals for high impact constraints. PLAN: Increase lead time for identifying aviation system constraint planning and goals while utilizing historical NAS performance data and constraints to derive successful and/or improved advance planning strategies. EXECUTE: Set goals and a strategy. The Air Traffic Control System Command Center (ATCSCC), FAA field facilities, and aviation stakeholders execute the strategy and work to achieve the desired/planned outcomes. REVIEW: Utilize post event analysis and lessons learned to define and implement future strategies and operational triggers based on past performance and outcomes, both positive and negative. TRAIN: Develop training that includes rapid and continuous feedback to operational personnel and provides increased data and weather knowledge and tools for analytical usage and planning. IMPROVE: Implement better information sharing processes, technologies, and procedures that improve the skills and technology needed to implement operational insights and improvements.

PLANS DISPLAY– A display available in EDST that provides detailed flight plan and predicted conflict information in textual format for requested Current Plans and all Trial Plans.
(See EN ROUTE DECISION SUPPORT TOOL)

PLANVIEW GRAPHICAL USER INTERFACE (PGUI)– A TBFM display that provides a spatial display of individual aircraft track information.

POFZ–
(See PRECISION OBSTACLE FREE ZONE.)

POINT OUT–
(See RADAR POINT OUT.)

POINT–TO–POINT (PTP)– A level of NRR service for aircraft that is based on traditional waypoints in their FMSs or RNAV equipage.

POLAR TRACK STRUCTURE– A system of organized routes between Iceland and Alaska which overlie Canadian MNPS Airspace.

POSITION REPORT– A report over a known location as transmitted by an aircraft to ATC.
(Refer to AIM.)

POSITION SYMBOL– A computer-generated indication shown on a radar display to indicate the mode of tracking.

POSITIVE CONTROL– The separation of all air traffic within designated airspace by air traffic control.

PRACTICE INSTRUMENT APPROACH– An instrument approach procedure conducted by a VFR or an IFR aircraft for the purpose of pilot training or proficiency demonstrations.

PRE–DEPARTURE CLEARANCE– An application with the Terminal Data Link System (TDLS) that provides clearance information to subscribers, through a service provider, in text to the cockpit or gate printer.

PRE–DEPARTURE REROUTE (PDRR)– A capability within the Traffic Flow Management System that enables ATC to quickly amend and execute revised departure clearances that mitigate en route constraints or balance en route traffic flows.

PREARRANGED COORDINATION– A standardized procedure which permits an air traffic controller to enter the airspace assigned to another air traffic controller without verbal coordination. The procedures are defined in a facility directive which ensures approved separation between aircraft.

PREARRANGED COORDINATION PROCEDURES– A facility's standardized procedure that describes the process by which one controller shall allow an aircraft to penetrate or transit another controller's airspace in a manner that assures approved separation without individual coordination for each aircraft.

PRECIPITATION– Any or all forms of water particles (rain, sleet, hail, or snow) that fall from the atmosphere and reach the surface.

PRECIPITATION RADAR WEATHER DESCRIPTIONS– Existing radar systems cannot detect turbulence. However, there is a direct correlation between the degree of turbulence and other weather features associated with thunderstorms and the weather radar precipitation intensity. Controllers will issue (where capable) precipitation intensity as observed by radar when using weather and radar processor (WARP) or NAS ground–based digital radars with weather capabilities. When precipitation intensity information is not available, the intensity will be described as UNKNOWN. When intensity levels can be determined, they shall be described as:

a. LIGHT (< 26 dBZ)

b. MODERATE (26 to 40 dBZ)

c. HEAVY (> 40 to 50 dBZ)

d. EXTREME (> 50 dBZ)

(Refer to the Aviation Weather Handbook, FAA–H–8083–28.)

PRECISION APPROACH–
(See PRECISION APPROACH PROCEDURE.)

PRECISION APPROACH PROCEDURE– A standard instrument approach procedure in which an electronic glideslope or other type of glidepath is provided; e.g., ILS, PAR, and GLS.
(See INSTRUMENT LANDING SYSTEM.)
(See PRECISION APPROACH RADAR.)

PRECISION APPROACH RADAR– Radar equipment in some ATC facilities operated by the FAA and/or the military services at joint-use civil/military locations and separate military installations to detect and display azimuth, elevation, and range of aircraft on the final approach course to a runway. This equipment may be used

to monitor certain nonradar approaches, but is primarily used to conduct a precision instrument approach (PAR) wherein the controller issues guidance instructions to the pilot based on the aircraft's position in relation to the final approach course (azimuth), the glidepath (elevation), and the distance (range) from the touchdown point on the runway as displayed on the radar scope.
(See GLIDEPATH.)
(See PAR.)
(See ICAO term PRECISION APPROACH RADAR.)
(Refer to AIM.)

PRECISION APPROACH RADAR [ICAO]– Primary radar equipment used to determine the position of an aircraft during final approach, in terms of lateral and vertical deviations relative to a nominal approach path, and in range relative to touchdown.

PRECISION OBSTACLE FREE ZONE (POFZ)– An 800 foot wide by 200 foot long area centered on the runway centerline adjacent to the threshold designed to protect aircraft flying precision approaches from ground vehicles and other aircraft when ceiling is less than 250 feet or visibility is less than 3/4 statute mile (or runway visual range below 4,000 feet.)

PRECISION RUNWAY MONITOR (PRM) SYSTEM– Provides air traffic controllers monitoring the NTZ during simultaneous close parallel PRM approaches with precision, high update rate secondary surveillance data. The high update rate surveillance sensor component of the PRM system is only required for specific runway or approach course separation. The high resolution color monitoring display, Final Monitor Aid (FMA) of the PRM system, or other FMA with the same capability, presents NTZ surveillance track data to controllers along with detailed maps depicting approaches and no transgression zone and is required for all simultaneous close parallel PRM NTZ monitoring operations.
(Refer to AIM.)

PREDICTIVE WIND SHEAR ALERT SYSTEM (PWS)– A self–contained system used on board some aircraft to alert the flight crew to the presence of a potential wind shear. PWS systems typically monitor 3 miles ahead and 25 degrees left and right of the aircraft's heading at or below 1200' AGL. Departing flights may receive a wind shear alert after they start the takeoff roll and may elect to abort the takeoff. Aircraft on approach receiving an alert may elect to go around or perform a wind shear escape maneuver.

PREFERRED IFR ROUTES– Routes established between busier airports to increase system efficiency and capacity. They normally extend through one or more ARTCC areas and are designed to achieve balanced traffic flows among high density terminals. IFR clearances are issued on the basis of these routes except when severe weather avoidance procedures or other factors dictate otherwise. Preferred IFR Routes are listed in the Chart Supplement U.S., and are also available at https://www.fly.faa.gov/rmt/nfdc_preferred_routes_database.jsp. If a flight is planned to or from an area having such routes but the departure or arrival point is not listed in the Chart Supplement U.S., pilots may use that part of a Preferred IFR Route which is appropriate for the departure or arrival point that is listed. Preferred IFR Routes may be defined by DPs, SIDs, or STARs; NAVAIDs, Waypoints, etc.; high or low altitude airways; or any combinations thereof. Because they often share elements with adapted routes, pilots' use of preferred IFR routes can minimize flight plan route amendments.
(See ADAPTED ROUTES.)
(See CENTER'S AREA.)
(See INSTRUMENT APPROACH PROCEDURE.)
(See INSTRUMENT DEPARTURE PROCEDURE.)
(See STANDARD TERMINAL ARRIVAL.)
(Refer to CHART SUPPLEMENT U.S.)

PRE-FLIGHT PILOT BRIEFING–
(See PILOT BRIEFING.)

PREVAILING VISIBILITY–
(See VISIBILITY.)

PRIMARY RADAR TARGET− An analog or digital target, exclusive of a secondary radar target, presented on a radar display.

PRM−
(See AREA NAVIGATION (RNAV) GLOBAL POSITIONING SYSTEM (GPS) PRECISION RUNWAY MONITORING (PRM) APPROACH.)
(See PRM APPROACH.)
(See PRECISION RUNWAY MONITOR SYSTEM.)

PRM APPROACH− An instrument approach procedure titled ILS PRM, RNAV PRM, LDA PRM, or GLS PRM conducted to parallel runways separated by less than 4,300 feet and at least 3,000 feet where independent closely spaced approaches are permitted. Use of an enhanced display with alerting, a No Transgression Zone (NTZ), secondary monitor frequency, pilot PRM training, and publication of an Attention All Users Page are required for all PRM approaches. Depending on the runway spacing, the approach courses may be parallel or one approach course must be offset. PRM procedures are also used to conduct Simultaneous Offset Instrument Approach (SOIA) operations. In SOIA, one straight−in ILS PRM, RNAV PRM, GLS PRM, and one offset LDA PRM, RNAV PRM or GLS PRM approach are utilized. PRM procedures are terminated and a visual segment begins at the offset approach missed approach point where the minimum distance between the approach courses is 3000 feet. Runway spacing can be as close as 750 feet.
(Refer to AIM.)

PROCEDURAL CONTROL [ICAO]− Term used to indicate that information derived from an ATS surveillance system is not required for the provision of air traffic control service.

PROCEDURAL SEPARATION [ICAO]− The separation used when providing procedural control.

PROCEDURE TURN− The maneuver prescribed when it is necessary to reverse direction to establish an aircraft on the intermediate approach segment or final approach course. The outbound course, direction of turn, distance within which the turn must be completed, and minimum altitude are specified in the procedure. However, unless otherwise restricted, the point at which the turn may be commenced and the type and rate of turn are left to the discretion of the pilot.
(See ICAO term PROCEDURE TURN.)

PROCEDURE TURN [ICAO]− A maneuver in which a turn is made away from a designated track followed by a turn in the opposite direction to permit the aircraft to intercept and proceed along the reciprocal of the designated track.

Note 1: Procedure turns are designated "left" or "right" according to the direction of the initial turn.

Note 2: Procedure turns may be designated as being made either in level flight or while descending, according to the circumstances of each individual approach procedure.

PROCEDURE TURN INBOUND− That point of a procedure turn maneuver where course reversal has been completed and an aircraft is established inbound on the intermediate approach segment or final approach course. A report of "procedure turn inbound" is normally used by ATC as a position report for separation purposes.
(See FINAL APPROACH COURSE.)
(See PROCEDURE TURN.)
(See SEGMENTS OF AN INSTRUMENT APPROACH PROCEDURE.)

PROFILE DESCENT− An uninterrupted descent (except where level flight is required for speed adjustment; e.g., 250 knots at 10,000 feet MSL) from cruising altitude/level to interception of a glideslope or to a minimum altitude specified for the initial or intermediate approach segment of a nonprecision instrument approach. The profile descent normally terminates at the approach gate or where the glideslope or other appropriate minimum altitude is intercepted.

PROGRESS REPORT−
(See POSITION REPORT.)

PROGRESSIVE TAXI− Precise taxi instructions given to a pilot unfamiliar with the airport or issued in stages as the aircraft proceeds along the taxi route.

PROHIBITED AREA–
(See SPECIAL USE AIRSPACE.)
(See ICAO term PROHIBITED AREA.)

PROHIBITED AREA [ICAO]– An airspace of defined dimensions, above the land areas or territorial waters of a State, within which the flight of aircraft is prohibited.

PROMINENT OBSTACLE– An obstacle that meets one or more of the following conditions:

a. An obstacle which stands out beyond the adjacent surface of surrounding terrain and immediately projects a noticeable hazard to aircraft in flight.

b. An obstacle, not characterized as low and close in, whose height is no less than 300 feet above the departure end of takeoff runway (DER) elevation, is within 10 NM from the DER, and that penetrates that airport/heliport's diverse departure obstacle clearance surface (OCS).

c. An obstacle beyond 10 NM from an airport/heliport that requires an obstacle departure procedure (ODP) to ensure obstacle avoidance.
(See OBSTACLE.)
(See OBSTRUCTION.)

PROPELLER (PROP) WASH (PROP BLAST)– The disturbed mass of air generated by the motion of a propeller.

PROPOSED BOUNDARY CROSSING TIME– Each center has a PBCT parameter for each internal airport. Proposed internal flight plans are transmitted to the adjacent center if the flight time along the proposed route from the departure airport to the center boundary is less than or equal to the value of PBCT or if airport adaptation specifies transmission regardless of PBCT.

PROPOSED DEPARTURE TIME– The time that the aircraft expects to become airborne.

PROTECTED AIRSPACE– The airspace on either side of an oceanic route/track that is equal to one-half the lateral separation minimum except where reduction of protected airspace has been authorized.

PROTECTED SEGMENT- The protected segment is a segment on the amended TFM route that is to be inhibited from automatic adapted route alteration by ERAM.

PT–
(See PROCEDURE TURN.)

PTP–
(See POINT–TO–POINT.)

PTS–
(See POLAR TRACK STRUCTURE.)

PUBLIC AIRCRAFT OPERATION (PAO)– A UAS operation meeting the qualifications and conditions required for the operation of a public aircraft.
(See AC–1.1)
(See AIM)

PUBLISHED INSTRUMENT APPROACH PROCEDURE VISUAL SEGMENT– A segment on an IAP chart annotated as "Fly Visual to Airport" or "Fly Visual." A dashed arrow will indicate the visual flight path on the profile and plan view with an associated note on the approximate heading and distance. The visual segment should be flown as a dead reckoning course while maintaining visual conditions.

PUBLISHED ROUTE– A route for which an IFR altitude has been established and published; e.g., Federal Airways, Jet Routes, Area Navigation Routes, Specified Direct Routes.

PWS–
(See PREDICTIVE WIND SHEAR ALERT SYSTEM.)

Q

Q ROUTE– 'Q' is the designator assigned to published RNAV routes used by the United States.

QFE– The atmospheric pressure at aerodrome elevation (or at runway threshold).

QNE– The barometric pressure used for the standard altimeter setting (29.92 inches Hg.).

QNH– The barometric pressure as reported by a particular station.

QUADRANT– A quarter part of a circle, centered on a NAVAID, oriented clockwise from magnetic north as follows: NE quadrant 000-089, SE quadrant 090-179, SW quadrant 180-269, NW quadrant 270-359.

QUEUING–
(See STAGING/QUEUING.)

QUICK LOOK– A feature of the EAS and STARS which provides the controller the capability to display full data blocks of tracked aircraft from other control positions.

R

RAD–
(See ROUTE AMENDMENT DIALOG.)

RADAR– A device that provides information on range, azimuth, and/or elevation of objects by measuring the time interval between transmission and reception of directional radio pulses and correlating the angular orientation of the radiated antenna beam or beams in azimuth and/or elevation.

a. Primary Radar– A radar system in which a minute portion of a radio pulse transmitted from a site is reflected by an object and then received back at that site for processing and display at an air traffic control facility.

b. Secondary Radar/Radar Beacon (ATCRBS)– A radar system in which the object to be detected is fitted with cooperative equipment in the form of a radio receiver/transmitter (transponder). Radar pulses transmitted from the searching transmitter/receiver (interrogator) site are received in the cooperative equipment and used to trigger a distinctive transmission from the transponder. This reply transmission, rather than a reflected signal, is then received back at the transmitter/receiver site for processing and display at an air traffic control facility.
(See COOPERATIVE SURVEILLANCE.)
(See INTERROGATOR.)
(See NON–COOPERATIVE SURVEILLANCE.)
(See TRANSPONDER.)
(See ICAO term RADAR.)
(Refer to AIM.)

RADAR [ICAO]– A radio detection device which provides information on range, azimuth and/or elevation of objects.

a. Primary Radar– Radar system which uses reflected radio signals.

b. Secondary Radar– Radar system wherein a radio signal transmitted from a radar station initiates the transmission of a radio signal from another station.

RADAR ADVISORY– The provision of advice and information based on radar observations.
(See ADVISORY SERVICE.)

RADAR ALTIMETER–
(See RADIO ALTIMETER.)

RADAR APPROACH– An instrument approach procedure which utilizes Precision Approach Radar (PAR) or Airport Surveillance Radar (ASR).
(See AIRPORT SURVEILLANCE RADAR.)
(See INSTRUMENT APPROACH PROCEDURE.)
(See PRECISION APPROACH RADAR.)
(See SURVEILLANCE APPROACH.)
(See ICAO term RADAR APPROACH.)
(Refer to AIM.)

RADAR APPROACH [ICAO]– An approach, executed by an aircraft, under the direction of a radar controller.

RADAR APPROACH CONTROL FACILITY– A terminal ATC facility that uses radar and nonradar capabilities to provide approach control services to aircraft arriving, departing, or transiting airspace controlled by the facility.
(See APPROACH CONTROL SERVICE.)

a. Provides radar ATC services to aircraft operating in the vicinity of one or more civil and/or military airports in a terminal area. The facility may provide services of a ground controlled approach (GCA); i.e., ASR and PAR approaches. A radar approach control facility may be operated by FAA, USAF, US Army, USN, USMC, or jointly by FAA and a military service. Specific facility nomenclatures are used for administrative purposes only and are related to the physical location of the facility and the operating service generally as follows:

1. Army Radar Approach Control (ARAC) (US Army).

2. Radar Air Traffic Control Facility (RATCF) (USN/FAA and USMC/FAA).

3. Radar Approach Control (RAPCON) (USAF/FAA, USN/FAA, and USMC/FAA).

4. Terminal Radar Approach Control (TRACON) (FAA).

5. Airport Traffic Control Tower (ATCT) (FAA). (Only those towers delegated approach control authority.)

RADAR ARRIVAL– An aircraft arriving at an airport served by a radar facility and in radar contact with the facility.
(See NONRADAR.)

RADAR BEACON–
(See RADAR.)

RADAR CLUTTER [ICAO]– The visual indication on a radar display of unwanted signals.

RADAR CONTACT–

a. Used by ATC to inform an aircraft that it is identified using an approved ATC surveillance source on an air traffic controller's display and that radar flight following will be provided until radar service is terminated. Radar service may also be provided within the limits of necessity and capability. When a pilot is informed of "radar contact," he/she automatically discontinues reporting over compulsory reporting points.
(See ATC SURVEILLANCE SOURCE.)
(See RADAR CONTACT LOST.)
(See RADAR FLIGHT FOLLOWING.)
(See RADAR SERVICE.)
(See RADAR SERVICE TERMINATED.)
(Refer to AIM.)

b. The term used to inform the controller that the aircraft is identified and approval is granted for the aircraft to enter the receiving controllers airspace.
(See ICAO term RADAR CONTACT.)

RADAR CONTACT [ICAO]– The situation which exists when the radar blip or radar position symbol of a particular aircraft is seen and identified on a radar display.

RADAR CONTACT LOST– Used by ATC to inform a pilot that the surveillance data used to determine the aircraft's position is no longer being received, or is no longer reliable and radar service is no longer being provided. The loss may be attributed to several factors including the aircraft merging with weather or ground clutter, the aircraft operating below radar line of sight coverage, the aircraft entering an area of poor radar return, failure of the aircraft's equipment, or failure of the surveillance equipment.
(See CLUTTER.)
(See RADAR CONTACT.)

RADAR ENVIRONMENT– An area in which radar service may be provided.
(See ADDITIONAL SERVICES.)
(See RADAR CONTACT.)
(See RADAR SERVICE.)
(See TRAFFIC ADVISORIES.)

RADAR FLIGHT FOLLOWING– The observation of the progress of radar–identified aircraft, whose primary navigation is being provided by the pilot, wherein the controller retains and correlates the aircraft identity with the appropriate target or target symbol displayed on the radar scope.
(See RADAR CONTACT.)
(See RADAR SERVICE.)
(Refer to AIM.)

RADAR IDENTIFICATION– The process of ascertaining that an observed radar target is the radar return from a particular aircraft.
(See RADAR CONTACT.)
(See RADAR SERVICE.)

RADAR IDENTIFIED AIRCRAFT– An aircraft, the position of which has been correlated with an observed target or symbol on the radar display.
(See RADAR CONTACT.)
(See RADAR CONTACT LOST.)

RADAR MONITORING–
(See RADAR SERVICE.)

RADAR NAVIGATIONAL GUIDANCE–
(See RADAR SERVICE.)

RADAR POINT OUT– An action taken by a controller to transfer the radar identification of an aircraft to another controller if the aircraft will or may enter the airspace or protected airspace of another controller and radio communications will not be transferred.

RADAR REQUIRED– A term displayed on charts and approach plates and included in FDC NOTAMs to alert pilots that segments of either an instrument approach procedure or a route are not navigable because of either the absence or unusability of a NAVAID. The pilot can expect to be provided radar navigational guidance while transiting segments labeled with this term.
(See RADAR ROUTE.)
(See RADAR SERVICE.)

RADAR ROUTE– A flight path or route over which an aircraft is vectored. Navigational guidance and altitude assignments are provided by ATC.
(See FLIGHT PATH.)
(See ROUTE.)

RADAR SEPARATION–
(See RADAR SERVICE.)

RADAR SERVICE– A term which encompasses one or more of the following services based on the use of radar which can be provided by a controller to a pilot of a radar identified aircraft.

a. Radar Monitoring– The radar flight-following of aircraft, whose primary navigation is being performed by the pilot, to observe and note deviations from its authorized flight path, airway, or route. When being applied specifically to radar monitoring of instrument approaches; i.e., with precision approach radar (PAR) or radar monitoring of simultaneous ILS,RNAV and GLS approaches, it includes advice and instructions whenever an aircraft nears or exceeds the prescribed PAR safety limit or simultaneous ILS RNAV and GLS no transgression zone.
(See ADDITIONAL SERVICES.)
(See TRAFFIC ADVISORIES.)

b. Radar Navigational Guidance– Vectoring aircraft to provide course guidance.

c. Radar Separation– Radar spacing of aircraft in accordance with established minima.
(See ICAO term RADAR SERVICE.)

RADAR SERVICE [ICAO]– Term used to indicate a service provided directly by means of radar.

a. Monitoring– The use of radar for the purpose of providing aircraft with information and advice relative to significant deviations from nominal flight path.

b. Separation– The separation used when aircraft position information is derived from radar sources.

RADAR SERVICE TERMINATED– Used by ATC to inform a pilot that he/she will no longer be provided any of the services that could be received while in radar contact. Radar service is automatically terminated, and the pilot is not advised in the following cases:

a. An aircraft cancels its IFR flight plan, except within Class B airspace, Class C airspace, a TRSA, or where Basic Radar service is provided.

b. An aircraft conducting an instrument, visual, or contact approach has landed or has been instructed to change to advisory frequency.

c. An arriving VFR aircraft, receiving radar service to a tower-controlled airport within Class B airspace, Class C airspace, a TRSA, or where sequencing service is provided, has landed; or to all other airports, is instructed to change to tower or advisory frequency.

d. An aircraft completes a radar approach.

RADAR SURVEILLANCE– The radar observation of a given geographical area for the purpose of performing some radar function.

RADAR TRAFFIC ADVISORIES– Advisories issued to alert pilots to known or observed radar traffic which may affect the intended route of flight of their aircraft.
(See TRAFFIC ADVISORIES.)

RADAR TRAFFIC INFORMATION SERVICE–
(See TRAFFIC ADVISORIES.)

RADAR VECTORING [ICAO]– Provision of navigational guidance to aircraft in the form of specific headings, based on the use of radar.

RADIAL– A magnetic bearing extending from a VOR/VORTAC/TACAN navigation facility.

RADIO–

a. A device used for communication.

b. Used to refer to a flight service station; e.g., "Seattle Radio" is used to call Seattle FSS.

RADIO ALTIMETER– Aircraft equipment which makes use of the reflection of radio waves from the ground to determine the height of the aircraft above the surface.

RADIO BEACON–
(See NONDIRECTIONAL BEACON.)

RADIO–CONTROLLED (RC)– The use of control signals transmitted radio to a remotely controlled device, as in radio–controlled model airplanes.

RADIO DETECTION AND RANGING–
(See RADAR.)

RADIO MAGNETIC INDICATOR– An aircraft navigational instrument coupled with a gyro compass or similar compass that indicates the direction of a selected NAVAID and indicates bearing with respect to the heading of the aircraft.

RAIS–
(See REMOTE AIRPORT INFORMATION SERVICE.)

RAMP–
(See APRON.)

RANDOM ALTITUDE– An altitude inappropriate for direction of flight and/or not in accordance with FAA Order JO 7110.65, paragraph 4–5–1, VERTICAL SEPARATION MINIMA.

RANDOM ROUTE– Any route not established or charted/published or not otherwise available to all users.

RC

(See RADIO–CONTROLLED.)

RC–

(See ROAD RECONNAISSANCE.)

RCAG–

(See REMOTE COMMUNICATIONS AIR/GROUND FACILITY.)

RCC–

(See RESCUE COORDINATION CENTER.)

RCO–

(See REMOTE COMMUNICATIONS OUTLET.)

RCR–

(See RUNWAY CONDITION READING.)

READ BACK– Repeat my message back to me.

RECEIVER AUTONOMOUS INTEGRITY MONITORING (RAIM)– A technique whereby a civil GNSS receiver/processor determines the integrity of the GNSS navigation signals without reference to sensors or non-DoD integrity systems other than the receiver itself. This determination is achieved by a consistency check among redundant pseudorange measurements.

RECEIVING CONTROLLER– A controller/facility receiving control of an aircraft from another controller/facility.

RECEIVING FACILITY–

(See RECEIVING CONTROLLER.)

RECONFORMANCE– The automated process of bringing an aircraft's Current Plan Trajectory into conformance with its track.

RECREATIONAL FLYER– Pilot of a UAS who is operating under 49 USC §44809, Exception for Limited Recreational Operations of Unmanned Aircraft.

REDUCE SPEED TO (SPEED)–

(See SPEED ADJUSTMENT.)

REDUCED VERTICAL SEPARATION MINIMUM (RVSM) AIRSPACE– RVSM airspace is defined as any airspace between FL 290 and FL 410 inclusive, where eligible aircraft are separated vertically by 1,000 feet. Authorization guidance for operations in this airspace is provided in Advisory Circular AC 91–85.

REFINED HAZARD AREA (RHA)– Used by ATC. Airspace that is defined and distributed after a failure of a launch or reentry operation to provide a more concise depiction of the hazard location than a Contingency Hazard Area.

(See AIRCRAFT HAZARD AREA.)
(See CONTINGENCY HAZARD AREA.)
(See TRANSITIONAL HAZARD AREA.)

REIL–

(See RUNWAY END IDENTIFIER LIGHTS.)

RELEASE TIME– A departure time restriction issued to a pilot by ATC (either directly or through an authorized relay) when necessary to separate a departing aircraft from other traffic.

(See ICAO term RELEASE TIME.)

RELEASE TIME [ICAO]– Time prior to which an aircraft should be given further clearance or prior to which it should not proceed in case of radio failure.

REMOTE AIRPORT INFORMATION SERVICE (RAIS)– A temporary service provided by facilities, which are not located on the landing airport, but have communication capability and automated weather reporting available to the pilot at the landing airport.

REMOTE COMMUNICATIONS AIR/GROUND FACILITY– An unmanned VHF/UHF transmitter/receiver facility which is used to expand ARTCC air/ground communications coverage and to facilitate direct contact between pilots and controllers. RCAG facilities are sometimes not equipped with emergency frequencies 121.5 MHz and 243.0 MHz.

(Refer to AIM.)

REMOTE COMMUNICATIONS OUTLET (RCO)– An unmanned communications facility remotely controlled by air traffic personnel. RCOs serve FSSs. Remote Transmitter/Receivers (RTR) serve terminal ATC facilities. An RCO or RTR may be UHF or VHF and will extend the communication range of the air traffic facility. There are several classes of RCOs and RTRs. The class is determined by the number of transmitters or receivers. Classes A through G are used primarily for air/ground purposes. RCO and RTR class O facilities are nonprotected outlets subject to undetected and prolonged outages. RCO (O's) and RTR (O's) were established for the express purpose of providing ground-to-ground communications between air traffic control specialists and pilots located at a satellite airport for delivering en route clearances, issuing departure authorizations, and acknowledging instrument flight rules cancellations or departure/landing times. As a secondary function, they may be used for advisory purposes whenever the aircraft is below the coverage of the primary air/ground frequency.

REMOTE IDENTIFICATION (RID)– A system for electronic identification and secure oversight of UAS.

(See 4 CFR Part 89)

(See AIM)

REMOTE PILOT– Pilot of a UAS who is not operating as a recreational flyer under 49 USC §44809, the Exception for Limited Recreational Operations of Unmanned Aircraft.

REMOTE PILOT IN COMMAND (RPIC)– The RPIC is directly responsible for and is the final authority as to the operation of the unmanned aircraft system.

REMOTE TRANSMITTER/RECEIVER (RTR)–

(See REMOTE COMMUNICATIONS OUTLET.)

REPORT– Used to instruct pilots to advise ATC of specified information; e.g., "Report passing Hamilton VOR."

REPORTING POINT– A geographical location in relation to which the position of an aircraft is reported.

(See COMPULSORY REPORTING POINTS.)

(See ICAO term REPORTING POINT.)

(Refer to AIM.)

REPORTING POINT [ICAO]– A specified geographical location in relation to which the position of an aircraft can be reported.

REQUEST FULL ROUTE CLEARANCE– Used by pilots to request that the entire route of flight be read verbatim in an ATC clearance. Such request should be made to preclude receiving an ATC clearance based on the original filed flight plan when a filed IFR flight plan has been revised by the pilot, company, or operations prior to departure.

REQUIRED NAVIGATION PERFORMANCE (RNP)– A statement of the navigational performance necessary for operation within a defined airspace. The following terms are commonly associated with RNP:

a. Required Navigation Performance Level or Type (RNP-X). A value, in nautical miles (NM), from the intended horizontal position within which an aircraft would be at least 95-percent of the total flying time.

b. Advanced – Required Navigation Performance (A–RNP). A navigation specification based on RNP that requires advanced functions such as scalable RNP, radius–to–fix (RF) legs, and tactical parallel offsets. This sophisticated Navigation Specification (NavSpec) is designated by the abbreviation "A–RNP".

c. Required Navigation Performance (RNP) Airspace. A generic term designating airspace, route(s), leg(s), operation(s), or procedure(s) where minimum required navigational performance (RNP) have been established.

d. Actual Navigation Performance (ANP). A measure of the current estimated navigational performance. Also referred to as Estimated Position Error (EPE).

e. Estimated Position Error (EPE). A measure of the current estimated navigational performance. Also referred to as Actual Navigation Performance (ANP).

f. Lateral Navigation (LNAV). A function of area navigation (RNAV) equipment which calculates, displays, and provides lateral guidance to a profile or path.

g. Vertical Navigation (VNAV). A function of area navigation (RNAV) equipment which calculates, displays, and provides vertical guidance to a profile or path.

REROUTE IMPACT ASSESSMENT (RRIA)– A capability within the Traffic Flow Management System that is used to define and evaluate a potential reroute prior to implementation, with or without miles–in–trail (MIT) restrictions. RRIA functions estimate the impact on demand (e.g., sector loads) and performance (e.g., flight delay). Using RRIA, traffic management personnel can determine whether the reroute will sufficiently reduce demand in the Flow Constraint Area and not create excessive "spill over" demand in the adjacent airspace on a specific route segment or point of interest (POI).

RESCUE COORDINATION CENTER (RCC)– A search and rescue (SAR) facility equipped and manned to coordinate and control SAR operations in an area designated by the SAR plan. The U.S. Coast Guard and the U.S. Air Force have responsibility for the operation of RCCs.

(See ICAO term RESCUE CO-ORDINATION CENTRE.)

RESCUE CO-ORDINATION CENTRE [ICAO]– A unit responsible for promoting efficient organization of search and rescue service and for coordinating the conduct of search and rescue operations within a search and rescue region.

RESOLUTION ADVISORY– A display indication given to the pilot by the Traffic alert and Collision Avoidance System (TCAS II) recommending a maneuver to increase vertical separation relative to an intruding aircraft. Positive, negative, and vertical speed limit (VSL) advisories constitute the resolution advisories. A resolution advisory is also classified as corrective or preventive.

RESTRICTED AREA–

(See SPECIAL USE AIRSPACE.)
(See ICAO term RESTRICTED AREA.)

RESTRICTED AREA [ICAO]– An airspace of defined dimensions, above the land areas or territorial waters of a State, within which the flight of aircraft is restricted in accordance with certain specified conditions.

RESUME NORMAL SPEED– Used by ATC to advise a pilot to resume an aircraft's normal operating speed. It is issued to terminate a speed adjustment where no published speed restrictions apply. It does not delete speed restrictions in published procedures of upcoming segments of flight. This does not relieve the pilot of those speed restrictions that are applicable to 14 CFR Section 91.117.

RESUME OWN NAVIGATION– Used by ATC to advise a pilot to resume his/her own navigational responsibility. It is issued after completion of a radar vector or when radar contact is lost while the aircraft is being radar vectored.

(See RADAR CONTACT LOST.)
(See RADAR SERVICE TERMINATED.)

RESUME PUBLISHED SPEED– Used by ATC to advise a pilot to resume published speed restrictions that are applicable to a SID, STAR, or other instrument procedure. It is issued to terminate a speed adjustment where speed restrictions are published on a charted procedure.

RHA–
(See REFINED HAZARD AREA.)

RID–
(See REMOTE IDENTIFICATION.)

RMI–
(See RADIO MAGNETIC INDICATOR.)

RNAV–
(See AREA NAVIGATION (RNAV).)

RNAV APPROACH– An instrument approach procedure which relies on aircraft area navigation equipment for navigational guidance.
(See AREA NAVIGATION (RNAV).)
(See INSTRUMENT APPROACH PROCEDURE.)

RNAV VISUAL FLIGHT PROCEDURE (RVFP)– An RVFP is a special visual flight procedure flown on an IFR flight plan. It is flown in visual conditions and clear of clouds must be maintained. An RVFP is flown using an approved RNAV system to maintain published lateral and vertical paths to runways without an instrument approach procedure. It requires an ATC clearance and may begin at other points along the path of the charted procedure when approved by ATC. An RVFP is not published in the Federal Register for public use and the operator is required to have a specific Operations Specification approval. Required ceiling and visibility minima are published on the procedure chart. An RVFP does not have a missed approach procedure and is not evaluated for obstacle protection.

ROAD RECONNAISSANCE (RC)– Military activity requiring navigation along roads, railroads, and rivers. Reconnaissance route/route segments are seldom along a straight line and normally require a lateral route width of 10 NM to 30 NM and an altitude range of 500 feet to 10,000 feet AGL.

ROGER– I have received all of your last transmission. It should not be used to answer a question requiring a yes or a no answer.
(See AFFIRMATIVE.)
(See NEGATIVE.)

ROLLOUT RVR–
(See VISIBILITY.)

ROTOR WASH– A phenomenon resulting from the vertical down wash of air generated by the main rotor(s) of a helicopter.

ROUND–ROBIN FLIGHT PLAN– A single flight plan filed from the departure airport to an intermediary destination(s) and then returning to the original departure airport.

ROUTE– A defined path, consisting of one or more courses in a horizontal plane, which aircraft traverse over the surface of the earth.
(See AIRWAY.)
(See JET ROUTE.)
(See PUBLISHED ROUTE.)
(See UNPUBLISHED ROUTE.)

ROUTE ACTION NOTIFICATION– EDST notification that an ADR/ADAR/AAR has been applied to the flight plan.
(See ATC PREFERRED ROUTE NOTIFICATION.)
(See EN ROUTE DECISION SUPPORT TOOL.)

ROUTE AMENDMENT DIALOG (RAD)– A capability within the Traffic Flow Management System that allows traffic management personnel to submit or edit a route amendment for one or more flights.

ROUTE SEGMENT– As used in Air Traffic Control, a part of a route that can be defined by two navigational fixes, two NAVAIDs, or a fix and a NAVAID.
(See FIX.)
(See ROUTE.)
(See ICAO term ROUTE SEGMENT.)

ROUTE SEGMENT [ICAO]– A portion of a route to be flown, as defined by two consecutive significant points specified in a flight plan.

RPIC–
(See REMOTE PILOT IN COMMAND.)

RRIA–
(See REROUTE IMPACT ASSESSMENT.)

RSA–
(See RUNWAY SAFETY AREA.)

RTR–
(See REMOTE TRANSMITTER/RECEIVER.)

RUNWAY– A defined rectangular area on a land airport prepared for the landing and takeoff run of aircraft along its length. Runways are normally numbered in relation to their magnetic direction rounded off to the nearest 10 degrees; e.g., Runway 1, Runway 25.
(See PARALLEL RUNWAYS.)
(See ICAO term RUNWAY.)

RUNWAY [ICAO]– A defined rectangular area on a land aerodrome prepared for the landing and takeoff of aircraft.

RUNWAY CENTERLINE LIGHTING–
(See AIRPORT LIGHTING.)

RUNWAY CONDITION CODES (RwyCC)– Numerical readings, provided by airport operators, that indicate runway surface contamination (for example, slush, ice, rain, etc.). These values range from "1" (poor) to "6" (dry) and must be included on the ATIS when the reportable condition is less than 6 in any one or more of the three runway zones (touchdown, midpoint, rollout).

RUNWAY CONDITION READING– Numerical decelerometer readings relayed by air traffic controllers at USAF and certain civil bases for use by the pilot in determining runway braking action. These readings are routinely relayed only to USAF and Air National Guard Aircraft.
(See BRAKING ACTION.)

RUNWAY CONDITION REPORT (RwyCR)– A data collection worksheet used by airport operators that correlates the runway percentage of coverage along with the depth and type of contaminant for the purpose of creating a FICON NOTAM.
(See RUNWAY CONDITION CODES.)

RUNWAY END IDENTIFIER LIGHTS (REIL)–
(See AIRPORT LIGHTING.)

RUNWAY ENTRANCE LIGHTS (REL)–An array of red lights which include the first light at the hold line followed by a series of evenly spaced lights to the runway edge aligned with the taxiway centerline, and one additional light at the runway centerline in line with the last two lights before the runway edge.

RUNWAY GRADIENT– The average slope, measured in percent, between two ends or points on a runway. Runway gradient is depicted on Government aerodrome sketches when total runway gradient exceeds 0.3%.

RUNWAY HEADING– The magnetic direction that corresponds with the runway centerline extended, not the painted runway number. When cleared to "fly or maintain runway heading," pilots are expected to fly or maintain the heading that corresponds with the extended centerline of the departure runway. Drift correction shall not be applied; e.g., Runway 4, actual magnetic heading of the runway centerline 044, fly 044.

RUNWAY IN USE/ACTIVE RUNWAY/DUTY RUNWAY– Any runway or runways currently being used for takeoff or landing. When multiple runways are used, they are all considered active runways. In the metering sense, a selectable adapted item which specifies the landing runway configuration or direction of traffic flow. The adapted optimum flight plan from each transition fix to the vertex is determined by the runway configuration for arrival metering processing purposes.

RUNWAY LIGHTS–
(See AIRPORT LIGHTING.)

RUNWAY MARKINGS–
(See AIRPORT MARKING AIDS.)

RUNWAY OVERRUN– In military aviation exclusively, a stabilized or paved area beyond the end of a runway, of the same width as the runway plus shoulders, centered on the extended runway centerline.

RUNWAY PROFILE DESCENT– An instrument flight rules (IFR) air traffic control arrival procedure to a runway published for pilot use in graphic and/or textual form and may be associated with a STAR. Runway Profile Descents provide routing and may depict crossing altitudes, speed restrictions, and headings to be flown from the en route structure to the point where the pilot will receive clearance for and execute an instrument approach procedure. A Runway Profile Descent may apply to more than one runway if so stated on the chart.
(Refer to AIM.)

RUNWAY SAFETY AREA– A defined surface surrounding the runway prepared, or suitable, for reducing the risk of damage to airplanes in the event of an undershoot, overshoot, or excursion from the runway. The dimensions of the RSA vary and can be determined by using the criteria contained within AC 150/5300-13, Airport Design, Chapter 3. Figure 3–1 in AC 150/5300-13 depicts the RSA. The design standards dictate that the RSA shall be:

a. Cleared, graded, and have no potentially hazardous ruts, humps, depressions, or other surface variations;

b. Drained by grading or storm sewers to prevent water accumulation;

c. Capable, under dry conditions, of supporting snow removal equipment, aircraft rescue and firefighting equipment, and the occasional passage of aircraft without causing structural damage to the aircraft; and,

d. Free of objects, except for objects that need to be located in the runway safety area because of their function. These objects shall be constructed on low impact resistant supports (frangible mounted structures) to the lowest practical height with the frangible point no higher than 3 inches above grade.
(Refer to AC 150/5300-13, Airport Design, Chapter 3.)

RUNWAY STATUS LIGHTS (RWSL) SYSTEM– The RWSL is a system of runway and taxiway lighting to provide pilots increased situational awareness by illuminating runway entry lights (REL) when the runway is unsafe for entry or crossing, and take-off hold lights (THL) when the runway is unsafe for departure.

RUNWAY TRANSITION–
(See SEGMENTS OF A SID/STAR)

RUNWAY TRANSITION WAYPOINT–
(See SEGMENTS OF A SID/STAR.)

RUNWAY USE PROGRAM– A noise abatement runway selection plan designed to enhance noise abatement efforts with regard to airport communities for arriving and departing aircraft. These plans are developed into runway use programs and apply to all turbojet aircraft 12,500 pounds or heavier; turbojet aircraft less than 12,500 pounds are included only if the airport proprietor determines that the aircraft creates a noise problem. Runway use programs are coordinated with FAA offices, and safety criteria used in these programs are developed by the

Office of Flight Operations. Runway use programs are administered by the Air Traffic Service as "Formal" or "Informal" programs.

a. Formal Runway Use Program– An approved noise abatement program which is defined and acknowledged in a Letter of Understanding between Flight Operations, Air Traffic Service, the airport proprietor, and the users. Once established, participation in the program is mandatory for aircraft operators and pilots as provided for in 14 CFR Section 91.129.

b. Informal Runway Use Program– An approved noise abatement program which does not require a Letter of Understanding, and participation in the program is voluntary for aircraft operators/pilots.

RUNWAY VISUAL RANGE (RVR)–
(See VISIBILITY.)

RVFP–
(See RNAV VISUAL FLIGHT PROCEDURE.)

RwyCC–
(See RUNWAY CONDITION CODES.)

RwyCR–
(See RUNWAY CONDITION REPORT.)

S

SAA–
(See SENSE AND AVOID.)
(See SPECIAL ACTIVITY AIRSPACE.)

SAFETY ALERT– A safety alert issued by ATC to aircraft under their control if ATC is aware the aircraft is at an altitude which, in the controller's judgment, places the aircraft in unsafe proximity to terrain, obstructions, or other aircraft. The controller may discontinue the issuance of further alerts if the pilot advises he/she is taking action to correct the situation or has the other aircraft in sight.

a. Terrain/Obstruction Alert– A safety alert issued by ATC to aircraft under their control if ATC is aware the aircraft is at an altitude which, in the controller's judgment, places the aircraft in unsafe proximity to terrain/obstructions; e.g., "Low Altitude Alert, check your altitude immediately."

b. Aircraft Conflict Alert– A safety alert issued by ATC to aircraft under their control if ATC is aware of an aircraft that is not under their control at an altitude which, in the controller's judgment, places both aircraft in unsafe proximity to each other. With the alert, ATC will offer the pilot an alternate course of action when feasible; e.g., "Traffic Alert, advise you turn right heading zero niner zero or climb to eight thousand immediately."

Note: The issuance of a safety alert is contingent upon the capability of the controller to have an awareness of an unsafe condition. The course of action provided will be predicated on other traffic under ATC control. Once the alert is issued, it is solely the pilot's prerogative to determine what course of action, if any, he/she will take.

SAFETY LOGIC SYSTEM– A software enhancement to ASDE–3, ASDE–X, and ASSC, that predicts the path of aircraft landing and/or departing, and/or vehicular movements on runways. Visual and aural alarms are activated when the safety logic projects a potential collision. The Airport Movement Area Safety System (AMASS) is a safety logic system enhancement to the ASDE–3. The Safety Logic System for ASDE–X and ASSC is an integral part of the software program.

SAFETY LOGIC SYSTEM ALERTS–

a. ALERT–

1. An actual situation involving two real Safety Logic tracks (aircraft/aircraft, aircraft/vehicle, or aircraft/other tangible object) that the Safety Logic System has predicted will result in an imminent collision, based upon the Safety Logic parameters.

2. An actual situation involving a single Safety Logic track arriving to, or departing from, a closed runway.

3. An actual situation involving a single Safety Logic track arriving to a taxiway.

b. FALSE ALERT–

1. Alerts generated by one or more false surface radar or cooperative surveillance targets, that the ASDE system has interpreted as real tracks and placed into Safety Logic.

2. Alerts in which the Safety Logic System did not perform correctly, based upon the design specifications and Safety Logic parameters.

3. Alerts generated by surface radar targets caused by moderate or greater precipitation.

c. NUISANCE ALERT– An alert in which one or more of the following is true:

1. The alert is generated by a known situation that is not considered an unsafe operation, such as LAHSO or other approved operations.

2. The alert is generated by inaccurate cooperative surveillance data received by the Safety Logic System.

3. One or more of the aircraft involved in the alert is not intending to use a runway/taxiway (helicopter, pipeline patrol, non–Mode C overflight, etc.).

d. VALID NON–ALERT– A situation in which the Safety Logic System correctly determines that an alert is not required, based upon the design specifications and Safety Logic parameters.

e. INVALID NON–ALERT– A situation in which the Safety Logic System did not issue an alert when an alert was required, based upon the design specifications and Safety Logic parameters.

SAIL BACK– A maneuver during high wind conditions (usually with power off) where float plane movement is controlled by water rudders/opening and closing cabin doors.

SAME DIRECTION AIRCRAFT– Aircraft are operating in the same direction when:

a. They are following the same track in the same direction; or

b. Their tracks are parallel and the aircraft are flying in the same direction; or

c. Their tracks intersect at an angle of less than 45 degrees.

SAR–
(See SEARCH AND RESCUE.)

SATELLITE–BASED AUGMENTATION SYSTEM (SBAS) – A wide coverage augmentation system in which the user receives augmentation information from a satellite–based transmitter.
(See WIDE–AREA AUGMENTATION SYSTEM (WAAS.)

SAW–
(See AVIATION WATCH NOTIFICATION MESSAGE.)

SAY AGAIN– Used to request a repeat of the last transmission. Usually specifies transmission or portion thereof not understood or received; e.g., "Say again all after ABRAM VOR."

SAY ALTITUDE– Used by ATC to ascertain an aircraft's specific altitude/flight level. When the aircraft is climbing or descending, the pilot should state the indicated altitude rounded to the nearest 100 feet.

SAY HEADING– Used by ATC to request an aircraft heading. The pilot should state the actual heading of the aircraft.

SCHEDULED TIME OF ARRIVAL (STA)– A STA is the desired time that an aircraft should cross a certain point (landing or metering fix). It takes other traffic and airspace configuration into account. A STA time shows the results of the TBFM scheduler that has calculated an arrival time according to parameters such as optimized spacing, aircraft performance, and weather.

SDF–
(See SIMPLIFIED DIRECTIONAL FACILITY.)

SE SAR–
(See SURVEILLANCE ENHANCED SEARCH AND RESCUE.)

SEA LANE– A designated portion of water outlined by visual surface markers for and intended to be used by aircraft designed to operate on water.

SEARCH AND RESCUE– A service which seeks missing aircraft and assists those found to be in need of assistance. It is a cooperative effort using the facilities and services of available Federal, state and local agencies. The U.S. Coast Guard is responsible for coordination of search and rescue for the Maritime Region, and the U.S. Air Force is responsible for search and rescue for the Inland Region. Information pertinent to search and rescue should be passed through any air traffic facility or be transmitted directly to the Rescue Coordination Center by telephone.
(See FLIGHT SERVICE STATION.)
(See RESCUE COORDINATION CENTER.)
(Refer to AIM.)

SEARCH AND RESCUE FACILITY– A facility responsible for maintaining and operating a search and rescue (SAR) service to render aid to persons and property in distress. It is any SAR unit, station, NET, or other operational activity which can be usefully employed during an SAR Mission; e.g., a Civil Air Patrol Wing, or a Coast Guard Station.
(See SEARCH AND RESCUE.)

SECNOT–
(See SECURITY NOTICE.)

SECONDARY RADAR TARGET– A target derived from a transponder return presented on a radar display.

SECTIONAL AERONAUTICAL CHARTS–
(See AERONAUTICAL CHART.)

SECTOR LIST DROP INTERVAL– A parameter number of minutes after the meter fix time when arrival aircraft will be deleted from the arrival sector list.

SECURITY NOTICE (SECNOT) – A SECNOT is a request originated by the Air Traffic Security Coordinator (ATSC) for an extensive communications search for aircraft involved, or suspected of being involved, in a security violation, or are considered a security risk. A SECNOT will include the aircraft identification, search area, and expiration time. The search area, as defined by the ATSC, could be a single airport, multiple airports, a radius of an airport or fix, or a route of flight. Once the expiration time has been reached, the SECNOT is considered to be canceled.

SECURITY SERVICES AIRSPACE – Areas established through the regulatory process or by NOTAM, issued by the Administrator under title 14, CFR, sections 99.7, 91.141, and 91.139, which specify that ATC security services are required; i.e., ADIZ or temporary flight rules areas.

SEE AND AVOID– When weather conditions permit, pilots operating IFR or VFR are required to observe and maneuver to avoid other aircraft. Right-of-way rules are contained in 14 CFR Part 91.

SEGMENTED CIRCLE– A system of visual indicators designed to provide traffic pattern information at airports without operating control towers.
(Refer to AIM.)

SEGMENTS OF A SID/STAR–

a. En Route Transition– The segment(s) of a SID/STAR that connect to/from en route flight. Not all SIDs/STARs will contain an en route transition.

b. En Route Transition Waypoint– The NAVAID/fix/waypoint that defines the beginning of the SID/STAR en route transition.

c. Common Route– The segment(s) of a SID/STAR procedure that provides a single route serving an airport/runway or multiple airports/runways. The common route may consist of a single point. Not all conventional SIDs will contain a common route.

d. Runway Transition– The segment(s) of a SID/STAR between the common route/point and the runway(s). Not all SIDs/STARs will contain a runway transition.

e. Runway Transition Waypoint (RTW)– On a STAR, the NAVAID/fix/waypoint that defines the end of the common route or en route transition and the beginning of a runway transition (In the arrival route description found on the STAR chart, the last fix of the common route and the first fix of the runway transition(s)).

SEGMENTS OF AN INSTRUMENT APPROACH PROCEDURE– An instrument approach procedure may have as many as four separate segments depending on how the approach procedure is structured.

a. Initial Approach– The segment between the initial approach fix and the intermediate fix or the point where the aircraft is established on the intermediate course or final approach course.
(See ICAO term INITIAL APPROACH SEGMENT.)

b. Intermediate Approach– The segment between the intermediate fix or point and the final approach fix.
(See ICAO term INTERMEDIATE APPROACH SEGMENT.)

c. Final Approach– The segment between the final approach fix or point and the runway, airport, or missed approach point.
(See ICAO term FINAL APPROACH SEGMENT.)

d. Missed Approach– The segment between the missed approach point or the point of arrival at decision height and the missed approach fix at the prescribed altitude.
(Refer to 14 CFR Part 97.)
(See ICAO term MISSED APPROACH PROCEDURE.)

SELF–BRIEFING– A self–briefing is a review, using automated tools, of all meteorological and aeronautical information that may influence the pilot in planning, altering, or canceling a proposed route of flight.

SENSE AND AVOID (SAA) – The capability of an unmanned aircraft to detect (sense) and avoid collisions with other aircraft and all obstacles, whether airborne or on the ground while operating in the NAS.

SEPARATION– In air traffic control, the spacing of aircraft to achieve their safe and orderly movement in flight and while landing and taking off.

(See SEPARATION MINIMA.)
(See ICAO term SEPARATION.)

SEPARATION [ICAO]– Spacing between aircraft, levels or tracks.

SEPARATION MINIMA– The minimum longitudinal, lateral, or vertical distances by which aircraft are spaced through the application of air traffic control procedures.

(See SEPARATION.)

SERVICE– A generic term that designates functions or assistance available from or rendered by air traffic control. For example, Class C service would denote the ATC services provided within a Class C airspace area.

SEVERE WEATHER AVOIDANCE PLAN (SWAP)– An approved plan to minimize the affect of severe weather on traffic flows in impacted terminal and/or ARTCC areas. A SWAP is normally implemented to provide the least disruption to the ATC system when flight through portions of airspace is difficult or impossible due to severe weather.

SEVERE WEATHER FORECAST ALERTS– Preliminary messages issued in order to alert users that a Severe Weather Watch Bulletin (WW) is being issued. These messages define areas of possible severe thunderstorms or tornado activity. The messages are unscheduled and issued as required by the Storm Prediction Center (SPC) at Norman, Oklahoma.

(See AIRMET.)
(See CONVECTIVE SIGMET.)
(See CWA.)
(See GRAPHICAL AIRMEN'S METEOROLOGICAL INFORMATION.)
(See SIGMET.)

SFA–
(See SINGLE FREQUENCY APPROACH.)

SFO–
(See SIMULATED FLAMEOUT.)

SGI
(See SPECIAL GOVERNMENT INTEREST.)

SHF–
(See SUPER HIGH FREQUENCY.)

SHORT RANGE CLEARANCE– A clearance issued to a departing IFR flight which authorizes IFR flight to a specific fix short of the destination while air traffic control facilities are coordinating and obtaining the complete clearance.

SHORT TAKEOFF AND LANDING AIRCRAFT (STOL)– An aircraft which, at some weight within its approved operating weight, is capable of operating from a runway in compliance with the applicable STOL characteristics, airworthiness, operations, noise, and pollution standards.

(See VERTICAL TAKEOFF AND LANDING AIRCRAFT.)

SIAP–
(See STANDARD INSTRUMENT APPROACH PROCEDURE.)

SID–
(See STANDARD INSTRUMENT DEPARTURE.)

SIDESTEP MANEUVER– A visual maneuver accomplished by a pilot at the completion of an instrument approach to permit a straight-in landing on a parallel runway not more than 1,200 feet to either side of the runway to which the instrument approach was conducted.

(Refer to AIM.)

SIGMET– A weather advisory issued concerning weather significant to the safety of all aircraft. SIGMET advisories cover severe and extreme turbulence, severe icing, and widespread dust or sandstorms that reduce visibility to less than 3 miles.

(See AIRMET.)
(See CONVECTIVE SIGMET.)
(See CWA.)
(See GRAPHICAL AIRMEN'S METEOROLOGICAL INFORMATION.)
(See ICAO term SIGMET INFORMATION.)
(See SAW.)
(Refer to AIM.)

SIGMET INFORMATION [ICAO]– Information issued by a meteorological watch office concerning the occurrence or expected occurrence of specified en-route weather phenomena which may affect the safety of aircraft operations.

SIGNIFICANT METEOROLOGICAL INFORMATION–

(See SIGMET.)

SIGNIFICANT POINT– A point, whether a named intersection, a NAVAID, a fix derived from a NAVAID(s), or geographical coordinate expressed in degrees of latitude and longitude, which is established for the purpose of providing separation, as a reporting point, or to delineate a route of flight.

SIMPLIFIED DIRECTIONAL FACILITY (SDF)– A NAVAID used for nonprecision instrument approaches. The final approach course is similar to that of an ILS localizer except that the SDF course may be offset from the runway, generally not more than 3 degrees, and the course may be wider than the localizer, resulting in a lower degree of accuracy.

(Refer to AIM.)

SIMULATED FLAMEOUT– A practice approach by a jet aircraft (normally military) at idle thrust to a runway. The approach may start at a runway (high key) and may continue on a relatively high and wide downwind leg with a continuous turn to final. It terminates in landing or low approach. The purpose of this approach is to simulate a flameout.

(See FLAMEOUT.)

SIMULTANEOUS CLOSE PARALLEL APPROACHES– A simultaneous, independent approach operation permitting ILS/RNAV/GLS approaches to airports having parallel runways separated by at least 3,000 feet and less than 4,300–feet between centerlines. Aircraft are permitted to pass each other during these simultaneous operations. Integral parts of a total system are radar, NTZ monitoring with enhanced FMA color displays that include aural and visual alerts and predictive aircraft position software, communications override, ATC procedures, an Attention All Users Page (AAUP), PRM in the approach name, and appropriate ground based and airborne equipment. High update rate surveillance sensor required for certain runway or approach course separations.

SIMULTANEOUS (CONVERGING) DEPENDENT APPROACHES- An approach operation permitting ILS/RNAV/GLS approaches to runways or missed approach courses that intersect where required minimum spacing between the aircraft on each final approach course is required.

SIMULTANEOUS (CONVERGING) INDEPENDENT APPROACHES- An approach operation permitting ILS/RNAV/GLS approaches to non-parallel runways where approach procedure design maintains the required aircraft spacing throughout the approach and missed approach and hence the operations may be conducted independently.

SIMULTANEOUS ILS APPROACHES– An approach system permitting simultaneous ILS approaches to airports having parallel runways separated by at least 4,300 feet between centerlines. Integral parts of a total system are ILS, radar, communications, ATC procedures, and appropriate airborne equipment.

(See PARALLEL RUNWAYS.)

(Refer to AIM.)

SIMULTANEOUS OFFSET INSTRUMENT APPROACH (SOIA)– An instrument landing system comprised of an ILS PRM, RNAV PRM or GLS PRM approach to one runway and an offset LDA PRM with glideslope or an RNAV PRM or GLS PRM approach utilizing vertical guidance to another where parallel runway spaced less than 3,000 feet and at least 750 feet apart. The approach courses converge by 2.5 to 3 degrees. Simultaneous close parallel PRM approach procedures apply up to the point where the approach course separation becomes 3,000 feet, at the offset MAP. From the offset MAP to the runway threshold, visual separation by the aircraft conducting the offset approach is utilized.

(Refer to AIM)

SIMULTANEOUS (PARALLEL) DEPENDENT APPROACHES- An approach operation permitting ILS/RNAV/GLS approaches to adjacent parallel runways where prescribed diagonal spacing must be maintained. Aircraft are not permitted to pass each other during simultaneous dependent operations. Integral parts of a total system ATC procedures, and appropriate airborne and ground based equipment.

SINGLE DIRECTION ROUTES– Preferred IFR Routes which are sometimes depicted on high altitude en route charts and which are normally flown in one direction only.

(See PREFERRED IFR ROUTES.)

(Refer to CHART SUPPLEMENT U.S.)

SINGLE FREQUENCY APPROACH– A service provided under a letter of agreement to military single-piloted turbojet aircraft which permits use of a single UHF frequency during approach for landing. Pilots will not normally be required to change frequency from the beginning of the approach to touchdown except that pilots conducting an en route descent are required to change frequency when control is transferred from the air route traffic control center to the terminal facility. The abbreviation “SFA” in the DoD FLIP IFR Supplement under “Communications” indicates this service is available at an aerodrome.

SINGLE-PILOTED AIRCRAFT– A military turbojet aircraft possessing one set of flight controls, tandem cockpits, or two sets of flight controls but operated by one pilot is considered single-piloted by ATC when determining the appropriate air traffic service to be applied.

(See SINGLE FREQUENCY APPROACH.)

SKYSPOTTER– A pilot who has received specialized training in observing and reporting inflight weather phenomena.

SLASH– A radar beacon reply displayed as an elongated target.

SLDI–

(See SECTOR LIST DROP INTERVAL.)

SLOW TAXI– To taxi a float plane at low power or low RPM.

SMALL UNMANNED AIRCRAFT SYSTEM (sUAS)– An unmanned aircraft weighing less than 55 pounds on takeoff, including everything that is on board or otherwise attached to the aircraft.

SN–

(See SYSTEM STRATEGIC NAVIGATION.)

SPACE–BASED ADS–B (SBA)– A constellation of satellites that receives ADS–B Out broadcasts and relays that information to the appropriate surveillance facility. The currently deployed SBA system is only capable of receiving broadcasts from 1090ES–equipped aircraft, and not from those equipped with only a universal access transceiver (UAT). Also, aircraft with a top–of–fuselage–mounted transponder antenna (required for TCAS II installations) will be better received by SBA, especially at latitudes below 45 degrees.

(See AUTOMATIC DEPENDENT SURVEILLANCE–BROADCAST.)

(See AUTOMATIC DEPENDENT SURVEILLANCE–BROADCAST OUT.)

SPACE LAUNCH AND REENTRY AREA– Locations where commercial space launch and/or reentry operations occur. For pilot awareness, a rocket–shaped symbol is used to depict space launch and reentry areas on sectional aeronautical charts.

SPEAK SLOWER– Used in verbal communications as a request to reduce speech rate.

SPECIAL GOVERNMENT INTEREST (SGI)– A near real–time airspace authorization for Part 91 or Part 107 UAS, which supports activities that answer significant and urgent governmental interests. These include: national defense, homeland security, law enforcement, and emergency operations objectives.

SPECIAL ACTIVITY AIRSPACE (SAA)– Airspace with defined dimensions within the National Airspace System wherein limitations may be imposed upon operations for national defense, homeland security, public interest, or public safety. Special activity airspace includes but is not limited to the following; Air Traffic Control Assigned Airspace (ATCAA), Altitude Reservations (ALTRV), Military Training Routes (MTR), Air Refueling Tracks and Anchors, Temporary Flight Restrictions (TFR), Special Security Instructions (SSI), etc. Special Use Airspace (SUA) is a subset of Special Activity Airspace.

(See SPECIAL USE AIRSPACE.)

SPECIAL AIR TRAFFIC RULES (SATR)– Rules that govern procedures for conducting flights in certain areas listed in 14 CFR Part 93. The term "SATR" is used in the United States to describe the rules for operations in specific areas designated in the Code of Federal Regulations.

(Refer to 14 CFR Part 93.)

SPECIAL EMERGENCY– A condition of air piracy or other hostile act by a person(s) aboard an aircraft which threatens the safety of the aircraft or its passengers.

SPECIAL FLIGHT RULES AREA (SFRA)– An area in the NAS, described in 14 CFR Part 93, wherein the flight of aircraft is subject to special traffic rules, unless otherwise authorized by air traffic control. Not all areas listed in 14 CFR Part 93 are designated SFRA, but special air traffic rules apply to all areas described in 14 CFR Part 93.

SPECIAL INSTRUMENT APPROACH PROCEDURE–

(See INSTRUMENT APPROACH PROCEDURE.)

SPECIAL USE AIRSPACE– Airspace of defined dimensions identified by an area on the surface of the earth wherein activities must be confined because of their nature and/or wherein limitations may be imposed upon aircraft operations that are not a part of those activities. Types of special use airspace are:

a. Alert Area– Airspace which may contain a high volume of pilot training activities or an unusual type of aerial activity, neither of which is hazardous to aircraft. Alert Areas are depicted on aeronautical charts for the information of nonparticipating pilots. All activities within an Alert Area are conducted in accordance with Federal Aviation Regulations, and pilots of participating aircraft as well as pilots transiting the area are equally responsible for collision avoidance.

b. Controlled Firing Area– Airspace wherein activities are conducted under conditions so controlled as to eliminate hazards to nonparticipating aircraft and to ensure the safety of persons and property on the ground.

c. Military Operations Area (MOA)– Permanent and temporary MOAs are airspace established outside of Class A airspace area to separate or segregate certain nonhazardous military activities from IFR traffic and to identify for VFR traffic where these activities are conducted. Permanent MOAs are depicted on Sectional Aeronautical, VFR Terminal Area, and applicable En Route Low Altitude Charts.

Note: Temporary MOAs are not charted.

(Refer to AIM.)

d. National Security Area (NSA)– Airspace of defined vertical and lateral dimensions established at locations where there is a requirement for increased security of ground facilities. Pilots are requested to voluntarily avoid flying through the depicted NSA. When a greater level of security is required, flight through an NSA may be temporarily prohibited by establishing a TFR under the provisions of 14 CFR Section 99.7. Such prohibitions will be issued by FAA Headquarters and disseminated via the U.S. NOTAM System.

(Refer to AIM)

e. Prohibited Area– Airspace designated under 14 CFR Part 73 within which no person may operate an aircraft without the permission of the using agency.

(Refer to AIM.)
(Refer to En Route Charts.)

f. Restricted Area– Permanent and temporary restricted areas are airspace designated under 14 CFR Part 73, within which the flight of aircraft, while not wholly prohibited, is subject to restriction. Most restricted areas are designated joint use and IFR/VFR operations in the area may be authorized by the controlling ATC facility when it is not being utilized by the using agency. Permanent restricted areas are depicted on Sectional Aeronautical, VFR Terminal Area, and applicable En Route charts. Where joint use is authorized, the name of the ATC controlling facility is also shown.

Note: Temporary restricted areas are not charted.

(Refer to 14 CFR Part 73.)
(Refer to AIM.)

g. Warning Area– A warning area is airspace of defined dimensions extending from 3 nautical miles outward from the coast of the United States, that contains activity that may be hazardous to nonparticipating aircraft. The purpose of such warning area is to warn nonparticipating pilots of the potential danger. A warning area may be located over domestic or international waters or both.

SPECIAL VFR CONDITIONS– Meteorological conditions that are less than those required for basic VFR flight in Class B, C, D, or E surface areas and in which some aircraft are permitted flight under visual flight rules.

(See SPECIAL VFR OPERATIONS.)
(Refer to 14 CFR Part 91.)

SPECIAL VFR FLIGHT [ICAO]– A VFR flight cleared by air traffic control to operate within Class B, C, D, and E surface areas in meteorological conditions below VMC.

SPECIAL VFR OPERATIONS– Aircraft operating in accordance with clearances within Class B, C, D, and E surface areas in weather conditions less than the basic VFR weather minima. Such operations must be requested by the pilot and approved by ATC.

(See SPECIAL VFR CONDITIONS.)
(See ICAO term SPECIAL VFR FLIGHT.)

SPECIALIST–PROVIDED SERVICES–
Services delivered directly by a flight service specialist via ground/ground communication, air/ground communication, in–person, or technology (for example, speech–to–text, email, or short message service).

SPEED–

(See AIRSPEED.)
(See GROUND SPEED.)

SPEED ADJUSTMENT– An ATC procedure used to request pilots to adjust aircraft speed to a specific value for the purpose of providing desired spacing. Pilots are expected to maintain a speed of plus or minus 10 knots or 0.02 Mach number of the specified speed. Examples of speed adjustments are:

a. "Increase/reduce speed to Mach point (number)."

b. "Increase/reduce speed to (speed in knots)" or "Increase/reduce speed (number of knots) knots."

SPEED ADVISORY– Speed advisories that are generated within Time–Based Flow Management to assist controllers to meet the Scheduled Time of Arrival (STA) at the meter fix/meter arc. See also Ground–Based Interval Management–Spacing (GIM–S) Speed Advisory.

SPEED BRAKES– Moveable aerodynamic devices on aircraft that reduce airspeed during descent and landing.

SPEED SEGMENTS– Portions of the arrival route between the transition point and the vertex along the optimum flight path for which speeds and altitudes are specified. There is one set of arrival speed segments adapted from each transition point to each vertex. Each set may contain up to six segments.

SPOOFING− Denotes emissions of GNSS−like signals that may be acquired and tracked in combination with or instead of the intended signals by civil receivers. The onset of spoofing effects can be instantaneous or delayed, and effects can persist after the spoofing has ended. Spoofing can result in false and potentially confusing, or hazardously misleading, position, navigation, and/or date/time information in addition to loss of GNSS use.

SQUAWK (Mode, Code, Function)− Used by ATC to instruct a pilot to activate the aircraft transponder and ADS−B Out with altitude reporting enabled, or (military) to activate only specific modes, codes, or functions. Examples: "Squawk five seven zero seven;" "Squawk three/alpha, two one zero five."

(See TRANSPONDER.)

STA−

(See SCHEDULED TIME OF ARRIVAL.)

STAGING/QUEUING− The placement, integration, and segregation of departure aircraft in designated movement areas of an airport by departure fix, EDCT, and/or restriction.

STAND BY− Means the controller or pilot must pause for a few seconds, usually to attend to other duties of a higher priority. Also means to wait as in "stand by for clearance." The caller should reestablish contact if a delay is lengthy. "Stand by" is not an approval or denial.

STANDARD INSTRUMENT APPROACH PROCEDURE (SIAP)−

(See INSTRUMENT APPROACH PROCEDURE.)

STANDARD INSTRUMENT DEPARTURE (SID)− A preplanned instrument flight rule (IFR) air traffic control (ATC) departure procedure printed for pilot/controller use in graphic form to provide obstacle clearance and a transition from the terminal area to the appropriate en route structure. SIDs are primarily designed for system enhancement to expedite traffic flow and to reduce pilot/controller workload. ATC clearance must always be received prior to flying a SID.

(See IFR TAKEOFF MINIMUMS AND DEPARTURE PROCEDURES.)
(See OBSTACLE DEPARTURE PROCEDURE.)
(Refer to AIM.)

STANDARD RATE TURN− A turn of three degrees per second.

STANDARD TERMINAL ARRIVAL (STAR)− A preplanned instrument flight rule (IFR) air traffic control arrival procedure published for pilot use in graphic and/or textual form. STARs provide transition from the en route structure to an outer fix or an instrument approach fix/arrival waypoint in the terminal area.

STANDARD TERMINAL ARRIVAL CHARTS−

(See AERONAUTICAL CHART.)

STANDARD TERMINAL AUTOMATION REPLACEMENT SYSTEM (STARS)−

(See DTAS.)

STAR−

(See STANDARD TERMINAL ARRIVAL.)

STATE AIRCRAFT− Aircraft used in military, customs and police service, in the exclusive service of any government or of any political subdivision thereof, including the government of any state, territory, or possession of the United States or the District of Columbia, but not including any government-owned aircraft engaged in carrying persons or property for commercial purposes.

STATIC RESTRICTIONS− Those restrictions that are usually not subject to change, fixed, in place, and/or published.

STATIONARY AIRSPACE RESERVATION− The term used in oceanic ATC for airspace that encompasses activities in a fixed volume of airspace to be occupied for a specified time period. Stationary Airspace Reservations may include activities such as special tests of weapons systems or equipment; certain U.S. Navy carrier, fleet, and anti−submarine operations; rocket, missile, and drone operations; and certain aerial refueling or similar operations.

(See STATIONARY ALTITUDE RESERVATION.)

STATIONARY ALTITUDE RESERVATION (STATIONARY ALTRV)− An altitude reservation which encompasses activities in a fixed volume of airspace to be occupied for a specified time period. Stationary ALTRVs may include activities such as special tests of weapons systems or equipment; certain U.S. Navy carrier, fleet, and anti−submarine operations; rocket, missile, and drone operations; and certain aerial refueling or similar operations.

STEP TAXI− To taxi a float plane at full power or high RPM.

STEP TURN− A maneuver used to put a float plane in a planing configuration prior to entering an active sea lane for takeoff. The STEP TURN maneuver should only be used upon pilot request.

STEPDOWN FIX− A fix permitting additional descent within a segment of an instrument approach procedure by identifying a point at which a controlling obstacle has been safely overflown.

STEREO ROUTE− A routinely used route of flight established by users and ARTCCs identified by a coded name; e.g., ALPHA 2. These routes minimize flight plan handling and communications.

STNR ALT RESERVATION− An abbreviation for Stationary Altitude Reservation commonly used in NOTAMs.
(See STATIONARY ALTITUDE RESERVATION.)

STOL AIRCRAFT−
(See SHORT TAKEOFF AND LANDING AIRCRAFT.)

STOP ALTITUDE SQUAWK− Used by ATC to instruct a pilot to turn off the automatic altitude reporting feature of the aircraft transponder and ADS−B Out. It is issued when a verbally reported altitude varies by 300 feet or more from the automatic altitude report.
(See ALTITUDE READOUT.)
(See TRANSPONDER.)

STOP AND GO− A procedure wherein an aircraft will land, make a complete stop on the runway, and then commence a takeoff from that point.
(See LOW APPROACH.)
(See OPTION APPROACH.)

STOP BURST−
(See STOP STREAM.)

STOP BUZZER−
(See STOP STREAM.)

STOP SQUAWK (Mode or Code)− Used by ATC to instruct a pilot to stop transponder and ADS−B transmissions, or to turn off only specified functions of the aircraft transponder (military).
(See STOP ALTITUDE SQUAWK.)
(See TRANSPONDER.)

STOP STREAM− Used by ATC to request a pilot to suspend electronic attack activity.
(See JAMMING.)

STOPOVER FLIGHT PLAN− A flight plan format which permits in a single submission the filing of a sequence of flight plans through interim full-stop destinations to a final destination.

STOPWAY− An area beyond the takeoff runway no less wide than the runway and centered upon the extended centerline of the runway, able to support the airplane during an aborted takeoff, without causing structural damage to the airplane, and designated by the airport authorities for use in decelerating the airplane during an aborted takeoff.

STRAIGHT-IN APPROACH IFR– An instrument approach wherein final approach is begun without first having executed a procedure turn, not necessarily completed with a straight-in landing or made to straight-in landing minimums.

(See LANDING MINIMUMS.)
(See STRAIGHT-IN APPROACH VFR.)
(See STRAIGHT-IN LANDING.)

STRAIGHT-IN APPROACH VFR– Entry into the traffic pattern by interception of the extended runway centerline (final approach course) without executing any other portion of the traffic pattern.

(See TRAFFIC PATTERN.)

STRAIGHT-IN LANDING– A landing made on a runway aligned within 30° of the final approach course following completion of an instrument approach.

(See STRAIGHT-IN APPROACH IFR.)

STRAIGHT-IN LANDING MINIMUMS–

(See LANDING MINIMUMS.)

STRAIGHT-IN MINIMUMS–

(See STRAIGHT-IN LANDING MINIMUMS.)

STRATEGIC PLANNING– Planning whereby solutions are sought to resolve potential conflicts.

sUAS–

(See SMALL UNMANNED AIRCRAFT SYSTEM.)

SUBSTITUTE ROUTE– A route assigned to pilots when any part of an airway or route is unusable because of NAVAID status. These routes consist of:

a. Substitute routes which are shown on U.S. Government charts.

b. Routes defined by ATC as specific NAVAID radials or courses.

c. Routes defined by ATC as direct to or between NAVAIDs.

SUNSET AND SUNRISE– The mean solar times of sunset and sunrise as published in the Nautical Almanac, converted to local standard time for the locality concerned. Within Alaska, the end of evening civil twilight and the beginning of morning civil twilight, as defined for each locality.

SUPPLEMENTAL WEATHER SERVICE LOCATION– Airport facilities staffed with contract personnel who take weather observations and provide current local weather to pilots via telephone or radio. (All other services are provided by the parent FSS.)

SUPPS– Refers to ICAO Document 7030 Regional Supplementary Procedures. SUPPS contain procedures for each ICAO Region which are unique to that Region and are not covered in the worldwide provisions identified in the ICAO Air Navigation Plan. Procedures contained in Chapter 8 are based in part on those published in SUPPS.

SURFACE AREA– The airspace contained by the lateral boundary of the Class B, C, D, or E airspace designated for an airport that begins at the surface and extends upward.

SURFACE METERING PROGRAM– A capability within Terminal Flight Data Manager that provides the user with the ability to tactically manage surface traffic flows through adjusting desired minimum and maximum departure queue lengths to balance surface demand with capacity. When a demand/capacity imbalance for a surface resource is predicted, a metering procedure is recommended.

SURFACE VIEWER– A capability within the Traffic Flow Management System that provides situational awareness for a user–selected airport. The Surface Viewer displays a top–down view of an airport depicting runways, taxiways, gate areas, ramps, and buildings. The display also includes icons representing aircraft and vehicles currently on the surface, with identifying information. In addition, the display includes current airport configuration information such as departure/arrival runways and airport departure/arrival rates.

SURPIC– A description of surface vessels in the area of a Search and Rescue incident including their predicted positions and their characteristics.

(Refer to FAA Order JO 7110.65, Para 10–6–4, INFLIGHT CONTINGENCIES.)

SURVEILLANCE APPROACH– An instrument approach wherein the air traffic controller issues instructions, for pilot compliance, based on aircraft position in relation to the final approach course (azimuth), and the distance (range) from the end of the runway as displayed on the controller's radar scope. The controller will provide recommended altitudes on final approach if requested by the pilot.

(Refer to AIM.)

SURVEILLANCE ENHANCED SEARCH AND RESCUE (SE SAR)– An automated service used to enhance search and rescue operations that provides federal contract flight service specialists direct information from the aircraft's registered tracking device.

SUSPICIOUS UAS– Suspicious UAS operations may include operating without authorization, loitering in the vicinity of sensitive locations, (e.g., national security, law enforcement facilities, and critical infrastructure), or disrupting normal air traffic operations resulting in runway changes, ground stops, pilot evasive action, etc. The report of a UAS operation alone does not constitute suspicious activity. Development of a comprehensive list of suspicious activities is not possible due to the vast number of situations that could be considered suspicious. ATC must exercise sound judgment when identifying situations that could constitute or indicate a suspicious activity.

SWAP–

(See SEVERE WEATHER AVOIDANCE PLAN.)

SWSL–

(See SUPPLEMENTAL WEATHER SERVICE LOCATION.)

SYSTEM STRATEGIC NAVIGATION– Military activity accomplished by navigating along a preplanned route using internal aircraft systems to maintain a desired track. This activity normally requires a lateral route width of 10 NM and altitude range of 1,000 feet to 6,000 feet AGL with some route segments that permit terrain following.

T

TACAN–
(See TACTICAL AIR NAVIGATION.)

TACAN-ONLY AIRCRAFT– An aircraft, normally military, possessing TACAN with DME but no VOR navigational system capability. Clearances must specify TACAN or VORTAC fixes and approaches.

TACTICAL AIR NAVIGATION (TACAN)– An ultra-high frequency electronic rho-theta air navigation aid which provides suitably equipped aircraft a continuous indication of bearing and distance to the TACAN station.
(See VORTAC.)
(Refer to AIM.)

TAILWIND– Any wind more than 90 degrees to the longitudinal axis of the runway. The magnetic direction of the runway shall be used as the basis for determining the longitudinal axis.

TAKEOFF AREA–
(See LANDING AREA.)

TAKEOFF DISTANCE AVAILABLE (TODA)– The takeoff run available plus the length of any remaining runway or clearway beyond the far end of the takeoff run available.
(See ICAO term TAKEOFF DISTANCE AVAILABLE.)

TAKEOFF DISTANCE AVAILABLE [ICAO]– The length of the takeoff run available plus the length of the clearway, if provided.

TAKEOFF HOLD LIGHTS (THL)– The THL system is composed of in-pavement lighting in a double, longitudinal row of lights aligned either side of the runway centerline. The lights are focused toward the arrival end of the runway at the "line up and wait" point, and they extend for 1,500 feet in front of the holding aircraft. Illuminated red lights indicate to an aircraft in position for takeoff or rolling that it is unsafe to takeoff because the runway is occupied or about to be occupied by an aircraft or vehicle.

TAKEOFF ROLL – The process whereby an aircraft is aligned with the runway centerline and the aircraft is moving with the intent to take off. For helicopters, this pertains to the act of becoming airborne after departing a takeoff area.

TAKEOFF RUN AVAILABLE (TORA) – The runway length declared available and suitable for the ground run of an airplane taking off.
(See ICAO term TAKEOFF RUN AVAILABLE.)

TAKEOFF RUN AVAILABLE [ICAO]– The length of runway declared available and suitable for the ground run of an aeroplane take-off.

TARGET– The indication shown on a display resulting from a primary radar return, a radar beacon reply, or an ADS–B report. The specific target symbol presented to ATC may vary based on the surveillance source and automation platform.
(See ASSOCIATED.)
(See DIGITAL TARGET.)
(See DIGITIZED RADAR TARGET.)
(See FUSED TARGET.)
(See PRIMARY RADAR TARGET.)
(See RADAR.)
(See SECONDARY RADAR TARGET.)
(See ICAO term TARGET.)
(See UNASSOCIATED.)

TARGET [ICAO]− In radar:

a. Generally, any discrete object which reflects or retransmits energy back to the radar equipment.

b. Specifically, an object of radar search or surveillance.

TARGET RESOLUTION− A process to ensure that correlated radar targets do not touch. Target resolution must be applied as follows:

a. Between the edges of two primary targets or the edges of the ASR-9/11 primary target symbol.

b. Between the end of the beacon control slash and the edge of a primary target.

c. Between the ends of two beacon control slashes.

Note 1: Mandatory traffic advisories and safety alerts must be issued when this procedure is used.

Note 2: This procedure must not be used when utilizing mosaic radar systems or multi−sensor mode.

TARGET SYMBOL−
(See TARGET.)
(See ICAO term TARGET.)

TARMAC DELAY− The holding of an aircraft on the ground either before departure or after landing with no opportunity for its passengers to deplane.

TARMAC DELAY AIRCRAFT− An aircraft whose pilot−in−command has requested to taxi to the ramp, gate, or alternate deplaning area to comply with the Three−hour Tarmac Rule.

TARMAC DELAY REQUEST− A request by the pilot−in−command to taxi to the ramp, gate, or alternate deplaning location to comply with the Three−hour Tarmac Rule.

TAS−
(See TERMINAL AUTOMATION SYSTEMS.)

TAWS−
(See TERRAIN AWARENESS WARNING SYSTEM.)

TAXI− The movement of an airplane under its own power on the surface of an airport (14 CFR Section 135.100 [Note]). Also, it describes the surface movement of helicopters equipped with wheels.
(See AIR TAXI.)
(See HOVER TAXI.)
(Refer to 14 CFR Section 135.100.)
(Refer to AIM.)

TAXI PATTERNS− Patterns established to illustrate the desired flow of ground traffic for the different runways or airport areas available for use.

TBM−
(See TIME−BASED MANAGEMENT.)

TBO−
(See TRAJECTORY−BASED OPERATIONS.)

TCAS−
(See TRAFFIC ALERT AND COLLISION AVOIDANCE SYSTEM.)

TCH−
(See THRESHOLD CROSSING HEIGHT.)

TDLS−
(See TERMINAL DATA LINK SYSTEM.)

TDZE−
(See TOUCHDOWN ZONE ELEVATION.)

TEMPORARY FLIGHT RESTRICTION (TFR)– A TFR is a regulatory action issued by the FAA via the U.S. NOTAM System, under the authority of United States Code, Title 49. TFRs are issued within the sovereign airspace of the United States and its territories to restrict certain aircraft from operating within a defined area on a temporary basis to protect persons or property in the air or on the ground. While not all inclusive, TFRs may be issued for disaster or hazard situations such as: toxic gas leaks or spills, fumes from flammable agents, aircraft accident/incident sites, aviation or ground resources engaged in wildfire suppression, or aircraft relief activities_following a disaster. TFRs may also be issued in support of VIP movements, for reasons of national security; or when determined necessary for the management of air traffic in the vicinity of aerial demonstrations or major sporting events. NAS users or other interested parties should contact a FSS for TFR information. Additionally, TFR information can be found in automated briefings, NOTAM publications, and on the internet at http://www.faa.gov. The FAA also distributes TFR information to aviation user groups for further dissemination.

TERMINAL AREA– A general term used to describe airspace in which approach control service or airport traffic control service is provided.

TERMINAL AREA FACILITY– A facility providing air traffic control service for arriving and departing IFR, VFR, Special VFR, and on occasion en route aircraft.

(See APPROACH CONTROL FACILITY.)

(See TOWER.)

TERMINAL AUTOMATION SYSTEMS (TAS)– TAS is used to identify the numerous automated tracking systems including STARS and MEARTS.

TERMINAL DATA LINK SYSTEM (TDLS)– A system that provides Digital Automatic Terminal Information Service (D–ATIS) both on a specified radio frequency and also, for subscribers, in a text message via data link to the cockpit or to a gate printer. TDLS also provides Pre–departure Clearances (PDC), at selected airports, to subscribers, through a service provider, in text to the cockpit or to a gate printer. In addition, TDLS will emulate the Flight Data Input/Output (FDIO) information within the control tower.

TERMINAL FLIGHT DATA MANAGER (TFDM)– An integrated tower flight data automation system to provide improved airport surface and terminal airspace management. TFDM enhances traffic flow management data integration with Time–Based Flow Management (TBFM) and Traffic Flow Management System (TFMS) to enable airlines, controllers, and airports to share and exchange real–time data. This improves surface traffic management and enhances capabilities of TFMS and TBFM. TFDM assists the Tower personnel with surface Traffic Flow Management (TFM) and Collaborative Decision Making (CDM) and enables a fundamental change in the Towers from a local airport–specific operation to a NAS–connected metering operation. The single platform consolidates multiple Tower automation systems, including: Departure Spacing Program (DSP), Airport Resource Management Tool (ARMT), Electronic Flight Strip Transfer System (EFSTS), and Surface Movement Advisor (SMA). TFDM data, integrated with other FAA systems such as TBFM and TFMS, allows airlines, controllers, and airports to manage the flow of aircraft more efficiently through all phases of flight from departure to arrival gate.

TERMINAL RADAR SERVICE AREA– Airspace surrounding designated airports wherein ATC provides radar vectoring, sequencing, and separation on a full-time basis for all IFR and participating VFR aircraft. The AIM contains an explanation of TRSA. TRSAs are depicted on VFR aeronautical charts. Pilot participation is urged but is not mandatory.

TERMINAL SEQUENCING AND SPACING (TSAS)– Extends scheduling and metering capabilities into the terminal area and provides metering automation tools to terminal controllers and terminal traffic management personnel. Those controllers and traffic management personnel become active participants in time–based metering operations as they work to deliver aircraft accurately to Constraint Satisfaction Points within terminal airspace to include the runway in accordance with scheduled times at those points. Terminal controllers are better able to utilize efficient flight paths, such as Standard Instrument Approach Procedures (SIAPs) that require a Navigational Specification (NavSpec) of RNP APCH with Radius–to–Fix (RF) legs, or Advanced RNP

(A–RNP), through tools that support the merging of mixed–equipage traffic flows. For example, merging aircraft flying RNP APCH AR with RF, A–RNP, and non–RNP approach procedures. Additional fields in the flight plan will identify those flights capable of flying the RNP APCH with RF or A–RNP procedures, and those flights will be scheduled for those types of procedures when available. TSAS will schedule these and the non–RNP aircraft to a common merge point. Terminal traffic management personnel have improved situation awareness using displays that allow for the monitoring of terminal metering operations, similar to the displays used today by center traffic management personnel to monitor en route metering operations.

TERMINAL VFR RADAR SERVICE– A national program instituted to extend the terminal radar services provided instrument flight rules (IFR) aircraft to visual flight rules (VFR) aircraft. The program is divided into four types service referred to as basic radar service, terminal radar service area (TRSA) service, Class B service and Class C service. The type of service provided at a particular location is contained in the Chart Supplement.

a. Basic Radar Service– These services are provided for VFR aircraft by all commissioned terminal radar facilities. Basic radar service includes safety alerts, traffic advisories, limited radar vectoring when requested by the pilot, and sequencing at locations where procedures have been established for this purpose and/or when covered by a letter of agreement. The purpose of this service is to adjust the flow of arriving IFR and VFR aircraft into the traffic pattern in a safe and orderly manner and to provide traffic advisories to departing VFR aircraft.

b. TRSA Service– This service provides, in addition to basic radar service, sequencing of all IFR and participating VFR aircraft to the primary airport and separation between all participating VFR aircraft. The purpose of this service is to provide separation between all participating VFR aircraft and all IFR aircraft operating within the area defined as a TRSA.

c. Class C Service– This service provides, in addition to basic radar service, approved separation between IFR and VFR aircraft, and sequencing of VFR aircraft, and sequencing of VFR arrivals to the primary airport.

d. Class B Service– This service provides, in addition to basic radar service, approved separation of aircraft based on IFR, VFR, and/or weight, and sequencing of VFR arrivals to the primary airport(s).

(See CONTROLLED AIRSPACE.)
(See TERMINAL RADAR SERVICE AREA.)
(Refer to AIM.)
(Refer to CHART SUPPLEMENT U.S.)

TERMINAL-VERY HIGH FREQUENCY OMNIDIRECTIONAL RANGE STATION (TVOR)– A very high frequency terminal omnirange station located on or near an airport and used as an approach aid.

(See NAVIGATIONAL AID.)
(See VOR.)

TERRAIN AWARENESS WARNING SYSTEM (TAWS)– An on–board, terrain proximity alerting system providing the aircrew ‘Low Altitude warnings’ to allow immediate pilot action.

TERRAIN FOLLOWING– The flight of a military aircraft maintaining a constant AGL altitude above the terrain or the highest obstruction. The altitude of the aircraft will constantly change with the varying terrain and/or obstruction.

TETRAHEDRON– A device normally located on uncontrolled airports and used as a landing direction indicator. The small end of a tetrahedron points in the direction of landing. At controlled airports, the tetrahedron, if installed, should be disregarded because tower instructions supersede the indicator.

(See SEGMENTED CIRCLE.)
(Refer to AIM.)

TF–

(See TERRAIN FOLLOWING.)

TFDM–

(See TERMINAL FLIGHT DATA MANAGER.)

TGUI–

(See TIMELINE GRAPHICAL USER INTERFACE.)

THAT IS CORRECT– The understanding you have is right.

THA–
(See TRANSITIONAL HAZARD AREA.)

THE RECREATIONAL UAS SAFETY TEST (TRUST)– The electronically administered free test required for all recreational UAS operators referred to as the aeronautical knowledge and safety test, under 49 USC §44809 (g).

THREE–HOUR TARMAC RULE– Rule that relates to Department of Transportation (DOT) requirements placed on airlines when tarmac delays are anticipated to reach 3 hours.

360 OVERHEAD–
(See OVERHEAD MANEUVER.)

THRESHOLD– The beginning of that portion of the runway usable for landing.
(See AIRPORT LIGHTING.)
(See DISPLACED THRESHOLD.)

THRESHOLD CROSSING HEIGHT– The theoretical height above the runway threshold at which the aircraft's glideslope antenna would be if the aircraft maintains the trajectory established by the mean ILS glideslope or the altitude at which the calculated glidepath of an RNAV or GPS approaches.
(See GLIDESLOPE.)
(See THRESHOLD.)

THRESHOLD LIGHTS–
(See AIRPORT LIGHTING.)

TIE-IN FACILITY– The FSS primarily responsible for providing FSS services, including telecommunications services for landing facilities or navigational aids located within the boundaries of a flight plan area (FPA). Three-letter identifiers are assigned to each FSS/FPA and are annotated as tie-in facilities in the Chart Supplement and FAA Order JO 7350.9, Location Identifiers. Large consolidated FSS facilities may have many tie-in facilities or FSS sectors within one facility.
(See FLIGHT PLAN AREA.)
(See FLIGHT SERVICE STATION.)

TIME–BASED FLOW MANAGEMENT (TBFM)– A foundational Decision Support Tool for time–based management in the en route and terminal environments. TBFM's core function is the ability to schedule aircraft within a stream of traffic to reach a defined constraint point (e.g., meter fix/meter arc) at specified times, creating a time–ordered sequence of traffic. The scheduled times allow for merging of traffic flows, efficiently utilizing airport and airspace capacity while minimizing coordination and reducing the need for vectoring/holding. The TBFM schedule is calculated using current aircraft estimated time of arrival at key defined constraint points based on wind forecasts, aircraft flight plan, the desired separation at the constraint point and other parameters. The schedule applies spacing only when needed to maintain the desired separation at one or more constraint points. This includes, but is not limited to, Single Center Metering (SCM), Adjacent Center Metering (ACM), En Route Departure Capability (EDC), Integrated Departure/Arrival Capability (IDAC), Ground–based Interval Management–Spacing (GIM–S), Departure Scheduling, and Extended/Coupled Metering.

TIME–BASED MANAGEMENT (TBM)– A methodology for managing the flow of air traffic through the assignment of time at specific points for an aircraft. TBM applies time to manage and condition air traffic flows to mitigate demand/capacity imbalances and enhance efficiency and predictability of the NAS. Where implemented, TBM tools will be used to manage traffic even during periods when demand does not exceed capacity. This will sustain operational predictability and assure the regional/national strategic plan is maintained. TBM uses capabilities within TFMS, TBFM, and TFDM. These programs are designed to achieve a specified interval between aircraft. Different types of programs accommodate different phases of flight.

TIME GROUP– Four digits representing the hour and minutes from the Coordinated Universal Time (UTC) clock. FAA uses UTC for all operations. The term "ZULU" may be used to denote UTC. The word "local" or the time zone equivalent shall be used to denote local when local time is given during radio and telephone communications. When written, a time zone designator is used to indicate local time; e.g., "0205M" (Mountain). The local time may be based on the 24-hour clock system. The day begins at 0000 and ends at 2359.

TIMELINE GRAPHICAL USER INTERFACE (TGUI)– A TBFM display that uses timelines to display the Estimated Time of Arrival and Scheduled Time of Arrival of each aircraft to specified constraint points. The TGUI can also display pre–departure and scheduled aircraft.

TIS–B–
(See TRAFFIC INFORMATION SERVICE–BROADCAST.)

TMI–
(See TRAFFIC MANAGEMENT INITIATIVE.)

TMPA–
(See TRAFFIC MANAGEMENT PROGRAM ALERT.)

TMU–
(See TRAFFIC MANAGEMENT UNIT.)

TOD–
(See TOP OF DESCENT.)

TODA–
(See TAKEOFF DISTANCE AVAILABLE.)
(See ICAO term TAKEOFF DISTANCE AVAILABLE.)

TOI–
(See TRACK OF INTEREST.)

TOP ALTITUDE– In reference to SID published altitude restrictions, the charted "maintain" altitude contained in the procedure description or assigned by ATC.

TOP OF DESCENT (TOD)– The point at which an aircraft begins the initial descent.

TORA–
(See TAKEOFF RUN AVAILABLE.)
(See ICAO term TAKEOFF RUN AVAILABLE.)

TORCHING– The burning of fuel at the end of an exhaust pipe or stack of a reciprocating aircraft engine, the result of an excessive richness in the fuel air mixture.

TOS–
(See TRAJECTORY OPTIONS SET)

TOTAL ESTIMATED ELAPSED TIME [ICAO]– For IFR flights, the estimated time required from takeoff to arrive over that designated point, defined by reference to navigation aids, from which it is intended that an instrument approach procedure will be commenced, or, if no navigation aid is associated with the destination aerodrome, to arrive over the destination aerodrome. For VFR flights, the estimated time required from takeoff to arrive over the destination aerodrome.
(See ICAO term ESTIMATED ELAPSED TIME.)

TOUCH-AND-GO– An operation by an aircraft that lands and departs on a runway without stopping or exiting the runway.

TOUCH-AND-GO LANDING–
(See TOUCH-AND-GO.)

TOUCHDOWN–

a. The point at which an aircraft first makes contact with the landing surface.

b. Concerning a precision radar approach (PAR), it is the point where the glide path intercepts the landing surface.

(See ICAO term TOUCHDOWN.)

TOUCHDOWN [ICAO]− The point where the nominal glide path intercepts the runway.

Note: Touchdown as defined above is only a datum and is not necessarily the actual point at which the aircraft will touch the runway.

TOUCHDOWN RVR−
(See VISIBILITY.)

TOUCHDOWN ZONE− The first 3,000 feet of the runway beginning at the threshold. The area is used for determination of Touchdown Zone Elevation in the development of straight-in landing minimums for instrument approaches.
(See ICAO term TOUCHDOWN ZONE.)

TOUCHDOWN ZONE [ICAO]− The portion of a runway, beyond the threshold, where it is intended landing aircraft first contact the runway.

TOUCHDOWN ZONE ELEVATION− The highest elevation in the first 3,000 feet of the landing surface. TDZE is indicated on the instrument approach procedure chart when straight-in landing minimums are authorized.
(See TOUCHDOWN ZONE.)

TOUCHDOWN ZONE LIGHTING−
(See AIRPORT LIGHTING.)

TOWER− A terminal facility that uses air/ground communications, visual signaling, and other devices to provide ATC services to aircraft operating in the vicinity of an airport or on the movement area. Authorizes aircraft to land or takeoff at the airport controlled by the tower or to transit the Class D airspace area regardless of flight plan or weather conditions (IFR or VFR). A tower may also provide approach control services (radar or nonradar).
(See AIRPORT TRAFFIC CONTROL SERVICE.)
(See APPROACH CONTROL FACILITY.)
(See APPROACH CONTROL SERVICE.)
(See MOVEMENT AREA.)
(See TOWER EN ROUTE CONTROL SERVICE.)
(See ICAO term AERODROME CONTROL TOWER.)
(Refer to AIM.)

TOWER EN ROUTE CONTROL SERVICE− The control of IFR en route traffic within delegated airspace between two or more adjacent approach control facilities. This service is designed to expedite traffic and reduce control and pilot communication requirements.

TOWER TO TOWER−
(See TOWER EN ROUTE CONTROL SERVICE.)

TRACEABLE PRESSURE STANDARD− The facility station pressure instrument, with certification/calibration traceable to the National Institute of Standards and Technology. Traceable pressure standards may be mercurial barometers, commissioned ASOS or dual transducer AWOS, or portable pressure standards or DASI.

TRACK− The actual flight path of an aircraft over the surface of the earth.
(See COURSE.)
(See FLIGHT PATH.)
(See ROUTE.)
(See ICAO term TRACK.)

TRACK [ICAO]− The projection on the earth's surface of the path of an aircraft, the direction of which path at any point is usually expressed in degrees from North (True, Magnetic, or Grid).

TRACK OF INTEREST (TOI)– Displayed data representing an airborne object that threatens or has the potential to threaten North America or National Security. Indicators may include, but are not limited to: noncompliance with air traffic control instructions or aviation regulations; extended loss of communications; unusual transmissions or unusual flight behavior; unauthorized intrusion into controlled airspace or an ADIZ; noncompliance with issued flight restrictions/security procedures; or unlawful interference with airborne flight crews, up to and including hijack. In certain circumstances, an object may become a TOI based on specific and credible intelligence pertaining to that particular aircraft/object, its passengers, or its cargo.

TRACK OF INTEREST RESOLUTION– A TOI will normally be considered resolved when: the aircraft/object is no longer airborne; the aircraft complies with air traffic control instructions, aviation regulations, and/or issued flight restrictions/security procedures; radio contact is re–established and authorized control of the aircraft is verified; the aircraft is intercepted and intent is verified to be nonthreatening/nonhostile; TOI was identified based on specific and credible intelligence that was later determined to be invalid or unreliable; or displayed data is identified and characterized as invalid.

TRAFFIC–

a. A term used by a controller to transfer radar identification of an aircraft to another controller for the purpose of coordinating separation action. Traffic is normally issued:

1. In response to a handoff or point out,

2. In anticipation of a handoff or point out, or

3. In conjunction with a request for control of an aircraft.

b. A term used by ATC to refer to one or more aircraft.

TRAFFIC ADVISORIES– Advisories issued to alert pilots to other known or observed air traffic which may be in such proximity to the position or intended route of flight of their aircraft to warrant their attention. Such advisories may be based on:

a. Visual observation.

b. Observation of radar identified and nonidentified aircraft targets on an ATC radar display, or

c. Verbal reports from pilots or other facilities.

Note 1: The word "traffic" followed by additional information, if known, is used to provide such advisories; e.g., "Traffic, 2 o'clock, one zero miles, southbound, eight thousand."

Note 2: Traffic advisory service will be provided to the extent possible depending on higher priority duties of the controller or other limitations; e.g., radar limitations, volume of traffic, frequency congestion, or controller workload. Radar/ nonradar traffic advisories do not relieve the pilot of his/her responsibility to see and avoid other aircraft. Pilots are cautioned that there are many times when the controller is not able to give traffic advisories concerning all traffic in the aircraft's proximity; in other words, when a pilot requests or is receiving traffic advisories, he/she should not assume that all traffic will be issued.

(Refer to AIM.)

TRAFFIC ALERT (aircraft call sign), TURN (left/right) IMMEDIATELY, (climb/descend) AND MAINTAIN (altitude).

(See SAFETY ALERT.)

TRAFFIC ALERT AND COLLISION AVOIDANCE SYSTEM (TCAS)– An airborne collision avoidance system based on radar beacon signals which operates independent of ground-based equipment. TCAS-I generates traffic advisories only. TCAS-II generates traffic advisories, and resolution (collision avoidance) advisories in the vertical plane.

TRAFFIC INFORMATION–

(See TRAFFIC ADVISORIES.)

TRAFFIC INFORMATION SERVICE–BROADCAST (TIS–B)– The broadcast of ATC derived traffic information to ADS–B equipped (1090ES or UAT) aircraft. The source of this traffic information is derived from ground–based air traffic surveillance sensors, typically from radar targets. TIS–B service will be available throughout the NAS where there are both adequate surveillance coverage (radar) and adequate broadcast coverage from ADS–B ground stations. Loss of TIS–B will occur when an aircraft enters an area not covered by the GBT network. If this occurs in an area with adequate surveillance coverage (radar), nearby aircraft that remain within the adequate broadcast coverage (ADS–B) area will view the first aircraft. TIS–B may continue when an aircraft enters an area with inadequate surveillance coverage (radar); nearby aircraft that remain within the adequate broadcast coverage (ADS–B) area will not view the first aircraft.

TRAFFIC IN SIGHT– Used by pilots to inform a controller that previously issued traffic is in sight.
(See NEGATIVE CONTACT.)
(See TRAFFIC ADVISORIES.)

TRAFFIC MANAGEMENT INITIATIVE (TMI)– Tools used to manage demand with capacity in the National Airspace System (NAS.) TMIs can be used to manage NAS resources (e.g., airports, sectors, airspace) or to increase the efficiency of the operation. TMIs can be either tactical (i.e., short term) or strategic (i.e., long term), depending on the type of TMI and the operational need.

TRAFFIC MANAGEMENT PROGRAM ALERT– A term used in a Notice to Air Missions (NOTAM) issued in conjunction with a special traffic management program to alert pilots to the existence of the program and to refer them to a special traffic management program advisory message for program details. The contraction TMPA is used in NOTAM text.

TRAFFIC MANAGEMENT UNIT– The entity in ARTCCs and designated terminals directly involved in the active management of facility traffic. Usually under the direct supervision of an assistant manager for traffic management.

TRAFFIC NO FACTOR– Indicates that the traffic described in a previously issued traffic advisory is no factor.

TRAFFIC NO LONGER OBSERVED– Indicates that the traffic described in a previously issued traffic advisory is no longer depicted on radar, but may still be a factor.

TRAFFIC PATTERN– The traffic flow that is prescribed for aircraft landing at, taxiing on, or taking off from an airport. The components of a typical traffic pattern are upwind leg, crosswind leg, downwind leg, base leg, and final approach.

a. Upwind Leg– A flight path parallel to the landing runway in the direction of landing.

b. Crosswind Leg– A flight path at right angles to the landing runway off its upwind end.

c. Downwind Leg– A flight path parallel to the landing runway in the direction opposite to landing. The downwind leg normally extends between the crosswind leg and the base leg.

d. Base Leg– A flight path at right angles to the landing runway off its approach end. The base leg normally extends from the downwind leg to the intersection of the extended runway centerline.

NOTE–
ATC may instruct a pilot to report a "2–mile left base" to Runway 22. This instruction means that the pilot is expected to maneuver their aircraft into a left base leg that will intercept a straight–in final 2 miles from the approach end of Runway 22 and advise ATC.

REFERENCE–
Pilot's Handbook of Aeronautical Knowledge, FAA–H–8083–25, Chapter 14, Airport Operations, Traffic Patterns.

e. Final Approach– A flight path in the direction of landing along the extended runway centerline. The final approach normally extends from the base leg to the runway. An aircraft making a straight-in approach VFR is also considered to be on final approach.

NOTE–
ATC may instruct a pilot to report "5–mile final" to Runway 22. This instruction means that the pilot should maneuver their aircraft onto a straight–in final and advise ATC when they are five miles from the approach end of Runway 22.

REFERENCE–
Pilot's Handbook of Aeronautical Knowledge, FAA–H–8083–25, Chapter 14, Airport Operations, Traffic Patterns.
(See STRAIGHT-IN APPROACH VFR.)
(See TAXI PATTERNS.)
(See ICAO term AERODROME TRAFFIC CIRCUIT.)
(Refer to 14 CFR Part 91.)
(Refer to AIM.)

TRAFFIC SITUATION DISPLAY (TSD)– TSD is a computer system that receives radar track data from all 20 CONUS ARTCCs, organizes this data into a mosaic display, and presents it on a computer screen. The display allows the traffic management coordinator multiple methods of selection and highlighting of individual aircraft or groups of aircraft. The user has the option of superimposing these aircraft positions over any number of background displays. These background options include ARTCC boundaries, any stratum of en route sector boundaries, fixes, airways, military and other special use airspace, airports, and geopolitical boundaries. By using the TSD, a coordinator can monitor any number of traffic situations or the entire systemwide traffic flows.

TRAJECTORY– A EDST representation of the path an aircraft is predicted to fly based upon a Current Plan or Trial Plan.
(See EN ROUTE DECISION SUPPORT TOOL.)

TRAJECTORY–BASED OPERATIONS (TBO)– An Air Traffic Management method for strategically planning and managing flights throughout the operation by using Time–Based Management (TBM), information exchange between air and ground systems, and the aircraft's ability to fly trajectories in time and space. Aircraft trajectory is defined in four dimensions – latitude, longitude, altitude, and time.

TRAJECTORY MODELING– The automated process of calculating a trajectory.

TRAJECTORY OPTIONS SET (TOS)– A TOS is an electronic message, submitted by the operator, that is used by the Collaborative Trajectory Options Program (CTOP) to manage the airspace captured in the traffic management program. The TOS will allow the operator to express the route and delay trade-off options that they are willing to accept.

TRANSFER OF CONTROL– That action whereby the responsibility for the separation of an aircraft is transferred from one controller to another.
(See ICAO term TRANSFER OF CONTROL.)

TRANSFER OF CONTROL [ICAO]– Transfer of responsibility for providing air traffic control service.

TRANSFERRING CONTROLLER– A controller/facility transferring control of an aircraft to another controller/facility.
(See ICAO term TRANSFERRING UNIT/CONTROLLER.)

TRANSFERRING FACILITY–
(See TRANSFERRING CONTROLLER.)

TRANSFERRING UNIT/CONTROLLER [ICAO]– Air traffic control unit/air traffic controller in the process of transferring the responsibility for providing air traffic control service to an aircraft to the next air traffic control unit/air traffic controller along the route of flight.
Note: See definition of accepting unit/controller.

TRANSITION– The general term that describes the change from one phase of flight or flight condition to another; e.g., transition from en route flight to the approach or transition from instrument flight to visual flight.

TRANSITION POINT– A point at an adapted number of miles from the vertex at which an arrival aircraft would normally commence descent from its en route altitude. This is the first fix adapted on the arrival speed segments.

TRANSITIONAL AIRSPACE– That portion of controlled airspace wherein aircraft change from one phase of flight or flight condition to another.

TRANSITIONAL HAZARD AREA (THA)– Used by ATC. Airspace normally associated with an Aircraft Hazard Area within which the flight of aircraft is subject to restrictions.
(See AIRCRAFT HAZARD AREA.)
(See CONTINGENCY HAZARD AREA.)
(See REFINED HAZARD AREA.)

TRANSMISSOMETER– An apparatus used to determine visibility by measuring the transmission of light through the atmosphere. It is the measurement source for determining runway visual range (RVR).
(See VISIBILITY.)

TRANSMITTING IN THE BLIND– A transmission from one station to other stations in circumstances where two-way communication cannot be established, but where it is believed that the called stations may be able to receive the transmission.

TRANSPONDER– The airborne radar beacon receiver/transmitter portion of the Air Traffic Control Radar Beacon System (ATCRBS) which automatically receives radio signals from interrogators on the ground, and selectively replies with a specific reply pulse or pulse group only to those interrogations being received on the mode to which it is set to respond.
(See INTERROGATOR.)
(See ICAO term TRANSPONDER.)
(Refer to AIM.)

TRANSPONDER [ICAO]– A receiver/transmitter which will generate a reply signal upon proper interrogation; the interrogation and reply being on different frequencies.

TRANSPONDER CODES–
(See CODES.)

TRANSPONDER OBSERVED – Phraseology used to inform a VFR pilot the aircraft's assigned beacon code and position have been observed. Specifically, this term conveys to a VFR pilot the transponder reply has been observed and its position correlated for transit through the designated area.

TRIAL PLAN– A proposed amendment which utilizes automation to analyze and display potential conflicts along the predicted trajectory of the selected aircraft.

TRSA–
(See TERMINAL RADAR SERVICE AREA.)

TRUST–
(See THE RECREATIONAL UAS SAFETY TEST.)

TSAS–
(See TERMINAL SEQUENCING AND SPACING.)

TSD–
(See TRAFFIC SITUATION DISPLAY.)

TURBOJET AIRCRAFT– An aircraft having a jet engine in which the energy of the jet operates a turbine which in turn operates the air compressor.

TURBOPROP AIRCRAFT– An aircraft having a jet engine in which the energy of the jet operates a turbine which drives the propeller.

TURBULENCE– An atmospheric phenomenon that causes changes in aircraft altitude, attitude, and or airspeed with aircraft reaction depending on intensity. Pilots report turbulence intensity according to aircraft's reaction as follows:

a. Light – Causes slight, erratic changes in altitude and or attitude (pitch, roll, or yaw).

b. Moderate– Similar to Light but of greater intensity. Changes in altitude and or attitude occur but the aircraft remains in positive control at all times. It usually causes variations in indicated airspeed.

c. Severe– Causes large, abrupt changes in altitude and or attitude. It usually causes large variations in indicated airspeed. Aircraft may be momentarily out of control.

d. Extreme– The aircraft is violently tossed about and is practically impossible to control. It may cause structural damage.

(See CHOP.)
(Refer to AIM.)

TURN ANTICIPATION– (maneuver anticipation).

TVOR–
(See TERMINAL-VERY HIGH FREQUENCY OMNIDIRECTIONAL RANGE STATION.)

TWO-WAY RADIO COMMUNICATIONS FAILURE–
(See LOST COMMUNICATIONS.)

U

UAM–
(See URBAN AIR MOBILITY.)

UAS FACILITY MAP (UASFM)– Defined grid squares showing maximum altitudes around airports where the FAA may authorize Part 107 sUAS operations without additional safety analysis. The maps should be consulted prior to conducting UAS operations (Part 91, Part 107 or Section 44809) in controlled airspace. The UASFM will aid in determining if the airspace authorization or waivers are necessary. UASFM(s) are charted on the UAS Data Delivery System (UDDS) at the following website address: https://faa.maps.arcgis.com/apps/webappviewer/index.html?id=9c2e4406710048e19806ebf6a06754ad.

UAS TEST SITE– Independently owned UAS test & research sites, recognized by the FAA.

UAS TRAFFIC MANAGEMENT (UTM)–The unmanned aircraft traffic management ecosystem that will allow multiple low altitude BVLOS operations and which is separate from, but complementary to, FAA's Air Traffic Control System.

UASFM–
(See UAS FACILITY MAP.)

UHF–
(See ULTRAHIGH FREQUENCY.)

ULTRAHIGH FREQUENCY (UHF)– The frequency band between 300 and 3,000 MHz. The bank of radio frequencies used for military air/ground voice communications. In some instances this may go as low as 225 MHz and still be referred to as UHF.

ULTRALIGHT VEHICLE– A single-occupant aeronautical vehicle operated for sport or recreational purposes which does not require FAA registration, an airworthiness certificate, or pilot certification. Operation of an ultralight vehicle in certain airspace requires authorization from ATC.
(Refer to 14 CFR Part 103.)

UNABLE– Indicates inability to comply with a specific instruction, request, or clearance.

UNASSOCIATED– A radar target that does not display a data block with flight identification and altitude information.
(See ASSOCIATED.)

UNCONTROLLED AIRSPACE– Airspace in which aircraft are not subject to controlled airspace (Class A, B, C, D, or E) separation criteria.

UNDER THE HOOD– Indicates that the pilot is using a hood to restrict visibility outside the cockpit while simulating instrument flight. An appropriately rated pilot is required in the other control seat while this operation is being conducted.
(Refer to 14 CFR Part 91.)

UNFROZEN– The Scheduled Time of Arrival (STA) tags, which are still being rescheduled by the time–based flow management (TBFM) calculations. The aircraft will remain unfrozen until the time the corresponding estimated time of arrival (ETA) tag passes the preset freeze horizon for that aircraft's stream class. At this point the automatic rescheduling will stop, and the STA becomes "frozen."

UNICOM– A nongovernment communication facility which may provide airport information at certain airports. Locations and frequencies of UNICOMs are shown on aeronautical charts and publications.
(See CHART SUPPLEMENT.)
(Refer to AIM.)

UNMANNED AIRCRAFT (UA)- A device used or intended to be used for flight that has no onboard pilot. This device can be any type of airplane, helicopter, airship, or powered-lift aircraft. Unmanned free balloons, moored balloons, tethered aircraft, gliders, and unmanned rockets are not considered to be a UA.

UNMANNED AIRCRAFT SYSTEM (UAS)- An unmanned aircraft and its associated elements related to safe operations, which may include control stations (ground, ship, or air based), control links, support equipment, payloads, flight termination systems, and launch/recovery equipment. It consists of three elements: unmanned aircraft, control station, and data link.

UNPUBLISHED ROUTE– A route for which no minimum altitude is published or charted for pilot use. It may include a direct route between NAVAIDs, a radial, a radar vector, or a final approach course beyond the segments of an instrument approach procedure.
(See PUBLISHED ROUTE.)
(See ROUTE.)

UNRELIABLE (GPS/WAAS)– An advisory to pilots indicating the expected level of service of the GPS and/or WAAS may not be available. Pilots must then determine the adequacy of the signal for desired use.

UNSERVICEABLE (U/S)
(See OUT OF SERVICE/UNSERVICEABLE.)

UPWIND LEG–
(See TRAFFIC PATTERN.)

URBAN AIR MOBILITY (UAM)– A subset of Advanced Air Mobility (AAM), referring to an air transportation system utilizing highly automated aircraft to transport passengers or cargo in urban/suburban areas.

URGENCY– A condition of being concerned about safety and of requiring timely but not immediate assistance; a potential distress condition.
(See ICAO term URGENCY.)

URGENCY [ICAO]– A condition concerning the safety of an aircraft or other vehicle, or of person on board or in sight, but which does not require immediate assistance.

USAFIB–
(See ARMY AVIATION FLIGHT INFORMATION BULLETIN.)

UTM–
(See UAS TRAFFIC MANAGEMENT.)

V

VASI–
(See VISUAL APPROACH SLOPE INDICATOR.)

VCOA–
(See VISUAL CLIMB OVER AIRPORT.)

VDP–
(See VISUAL DESCENT POINT.)

VECTOR– A heading issued to an aircraft to provide navigational guidance by radar.
(See ICAO term RADAR VECTORING.)

VERIFY– Request confirmation of information; e.g., "verify assigned altitude."

VERIFY SPECIFIC DIRECTION OF TAKEOFF (OR TURNS AFTER TAKEOFF)– Used by ATC to ascertain an aircraft's direction of takeoff and/or direction of turn after takeoff. It is normally used for IFR departures from an airport not having a control tower. When direct communication with the pilot is not possible, the request and information may be relayed through an FSS, dispatcher, or by other means.
(See IFR TAKEOFF MINIMUMS AND DEPARTURE PROCEDURES.)

VERTICAL NAVIGATION (VNAV)– A function of area navigation (RNAV) equipment which calculates, displays, and provides vertical guidance to a profile or path.

VERTICAL SEPARATION– Separation between aircraft expressed in units of vertical distance.
(See SEPARATION.)

VERTICAL TAKEOFF AND LANDING AIRCRAFT (VTOL)– Aircraft capable of vertical climbs and/or descents and of using very short runways or small areas for takeoff and landings. These aircraft include, but are not limited to, helicopters.
(See SHORT TAKEOFF AND LANDING AIRCRAFT.)

VERY HIGH FREQUENCY (VHF)– The frequency band between 30 and 300 MHz. Portions of this band, 108 to 118 MHz, are used for certain NAVAIDs; 118 to 136 MHz are used for civil air/ground voice communications. Other frequencies in this band are used for purposes not related to air traffic control.

VERY HIGH FREQUENCY OMNIDIRECTIONAL RANGE STATION–
(See VOR.)

VERY LOW FREQUENCY (VLF)– The frequency band between 3 and 30 kHz.

VFR–
(See VISUAL FLIGHT RULES.)

VFR AIRCRAFT– An aircraft conducting flight in accordance with visual flight rules.
(See VISUAL FLIGHT RULES.)

VFR CONDITIONS– Weather conditions equal to or better than the minimum for flight under visual flight rules. The term may be used as an ATC clearance/instruction only when:

a. An IFR aircraft requests a climb/descent in VFR conditions.

b. The clearance will result in noise abatement benefits where part of the IFR departure route does not conform to an FAA approved noise abatement route or altitude.

c. A pilot has requested a practice instrument approach and is not on an IFR flight plan.

Note: All pilots receiving this authorization must comply with the VFR visibility and distance from cloud criteria in 14 CFR Part 91. Use of the term does not relieve controllers of their responsibility to separate aircraft in

Class B and Class C airspace or TRSAs as required by FAA Order JO 7110.65. When used as an ATC clearance/instruction, the term may be abbreviated "VFR;" e.g., "MAINTAIN VFR," "CLIMB/DESCEND VFR," etc.

VFR FLIGHT–
(See VFR AIRCRAFT.)

VFR MILITARY TRAINING ROUTES (VR)– Routes used by the Department of Defense and associated Reserve and Air Guard units for the purpose of conducting low-altitude navigation and tactical training under VFR below 10,000 feet MSL at airspeeds in excess of 250 knots IAS.

VFR NOT RECOMMENDED– An advisory provided by a flight service station to a pilot during a preflight or inflight weather briefing that flight under visual flight rules is not recommended. To be given when the current and/or forecast weather conditions are at or below VFR minimums. It does not abrogate the pilot's authority to make his/her own decision.

VFR-ON-TOP– ATC authorization for an IFR aircraft to operate in VFR conditions at any appropriate VFR altitude (as specified in 14 CFR and as restricted by ATC). A pilot receiving this authorization must comply with the VFR visibility, distance from cloud criteria, and the minimum IFR altitudes specified in 14 CFR Part 91. The use of this term does not relieve controllers of their responsibility to separate aircraft in Class B and Class C airspace or TRSAs as required by FAA Order JO 7110.65.

VFR TERMINAL AREA CHARTS–
(See AERONAUTICAL CHART.)

VFR WAYPOINT–
(See WAYPOINT.)

VHF–
(See VERY HIGH FREQUENCY.)

VHF OMNIDIRECTIONAL RANGE/TACTICAL AIR NAVIGATION–
(See VORTAC.)

VIDEO MAP– An electronically displayed map on the radar display that may depict data such as airports, heliports, runway centerline extensions, hospital emergency landing areas, NAVAIDs and fixes, reporting points, airway/route centerlines, boundaries, handoff points, special use tracks, obstructions, prominent geographic features, map alignment indicators, range accuracy marks, and/or minimum vectoring altitudes.

VISIBILITY– The ability, as determined by atmospheric conditions and expressed in units of distance, to see and identify prominent unlighted objects by day and prominent lighted objects by night. Visibility is reported as statute miles, hundreds of feet or meters.
(Refer to 14 CFR Part 91.)
(Refer to AIM.)

a. Flight Visibility– The average forward horizontal distance, from the cockpit of an aircraft in flight, at which prominent unlighted objects may be seen and identified by day and prominent lighted objects may be seen and identified by night.

b. Ground Visibility– Prevailing horizontal visibility near the earth's surface as reported by the United States National Weather Service or an accredited observer.

c. Prevailing Visibility– The greatest horizontal visibility equaled or exceeded throughout at least half the horizon circle which need not necessarily be continuous.

d. Runway Visual Range (RVR)– An instrumentally derived value, based on standard calibrations, that represents the horizontal distance a pilot will see down the runway from the approach end. It is based on the sighting of either high intensity runway lights or on the visual contrast of other targets whichever yields the greater visual range. RVR, in contrast to prevailing or runway visibility, is based on what a pilot in a moving aircraft should see looking down the runway. RVR is horizontal visual range, not slant visual range. It is based on the measurement of a transmissometer made near the touchdown point of the instrument runway and is reported in hundreds of feet. RVR, where available, is used in lieu of prevailing visibility in determining minimums for a particular runway.

1. Touchdown RVR− The RVR visibility readout values obtained from RVR equipment serving the runway touchdown zone.

2. Mid-RVR− The RVR readout values obtained from RVR equipment located midfield of the runway.

3. Rollout RVR− The RVR readout values obtained from RVR equipment located nearest the rollout end of the runway.

(See ICAO term FLIGHT VISIBILITY.)
(See ICAO term GROUND VISIBILITY.)
(See ICAO term RUNWAY VISUAL RANGE.)
(See ICAO term VISIBILITY.)

VISIBILITY [ICAO]− The ability, as determined by atmospheric conditions and expressed in units of distance, to see and identify prominent unlighted objects by day and prominent lighted objects by night.

a. Flight Visibility− The visibility forward from the cockpit of an aircraft in flight.

b. Ground Visibility− The visibility at an aerodrome as reported by an accredited observer.

c. Runway Visual Range [RVR]− The range over which the pilot of an aircraft on the centerline of a runway can see the runway surface markings or the lights delineating the runway or identifying its centerline.

VISUAL APPROACH− An approach conducted on an instrument flight rules (IFR) flight plan which authorizes the pilot to proceed visually and clear of clouds to the airport. The pilot must, at all times, have either the airport or the preceding aircraft in sight. This approach must be authorized and under the control of the appropriate air traffic control facility. Reported weather at the airport must be: ceiling at or above 1,000 feet, and visibility of 3 miles or greater.

(See ICAO term VISUAL APPROACH.)

VISUAL APPROACH [ICAO]− An approach by an IFR flight when either part or all of an instrument approach procedure is not completed and the approach is executed in visual reference to terrain.

VISUAL APPROACH SLOPE INDICATOR (VASI)−

(See AIRPORT LIGHTING.)

VISUAL CLIMB OVER AIRPORT (VCOA)− A departure option for an IFR aircraft, operating in visual meteorological conditions equal to or greater than the specified visibility and ceiling, to visually conduct climbing turns over the airport to the published "climb−to" altitude from which to proceed with the instrument portion of the departure. VCOA procedures are developed to avoid obstacles greater than 3 statute miles from the departure end of the runway as an alternative to complying with climb gradients greater than 200 feet per nautical mile. Pilots are responsible to advise ATC as early as possible of the intent to fly the VCOA option prior to departure. These textual procedures are published in the 'Take−Off Minimums and (Obstacle) Departure Procedures' section of the Terminal Procedures Publications and/or appear as an option on a Graphic ODP.

(See AIM.)

VISUAL DESCENT POINT− A defined point on the final approach course of a nonprecision straight-in approach procedure from which normal descent from the MDA to the runway touchdown point may be commenced, provided the approach threshold of that runway, or approach lights, or other markings identifiable with the approach end of that runway are clearly visible to the pilot.

VISUAL FLIGHT RULES− Rules that govern the procedures for conducting flight under visual conditions. The term "VFR" is also used in the United States to indicate weather conditions that are equal to or greater than minimum VFR requirements. In addition, it is used by pilots and controllers to indicate type of flight plan.

(See INSTRUMENT FLIGHT RULES.)
(See INSTRUMENT METEOROLOGICAL CONDITIONS.)
(See VISUAL METEOROLOGICAL CONDITIONS.)
(Refer to 14 CFR Part 91.)
(Refer to AIM.)

VISUAL HOLDING– The holding of aircraft at selected, prominent geographical fixes which can be easily recognized from the air.
(See HOLDING FIX.)

VISUAL LINE OF SIGHT (VLOS)– Condition of operations wherein the operator maintains continuous, unaided visual contact with the unmanned aircraft.

VISUAL METEOROLOGICAL CONDITIONS– Meteorological conditions expressed in terms of visibility, distance from cloud, and ceiling equal to or better than specified minima.
(See INSTRUMENT FLIGHT RULES.)
(See INSTRUMENT METEOROLOGICAL CONDITIONS.)
(See VISUAL FLIGHT RULES.)

VISUAL OBSERVER (VO)– A person who is designated by the remote pilot in command to assist the remote pilot in command and the person operating the flight controls of the small UAS (sUAS) to see and avoid other air traffic or objects aloft or on the ground.

VISUAL SEGMENT–
(See PUBLISHED INSTRUMENT APPROACH PROCEDURE VISUAL SEGMENT.)

VISUAL SEPARATION– A means employed by ATC to separate aircraft in terminal areas and en route airspace in the NAS. There are two ways to effect this separation:

a. The tower controller sees the aircraft involved and issues instructions, as necessary, to ensure that the aircraft avoid each other.

b. A pilot sees the other aircraft involved and upon instructions from the controller provides his/her own separation by maneuvering his/her aircraft as necessary to avoid it. This may involve following another aircraft or keeping it in sight until it is no longer a factor.
(See SEE AND AVOID.)
(Refer to 14 CFR Part 91.)

VLF–
(See VERY LOW FREQUENCY.)

VMC–
(See VISUAL METEOROLOGICAL CONDITIONS.)

VOICE SWITCHING AND CONTROL SYSTEM (VSCS)– A computer controlled switching system that provides air traffic controllers with all voice circuits (air to ground and ground to ground) necessary for air traffic control.
(Refer to AIM.)

VOR– A ground-based electronic navigation aid transmitting very high frequency navigation signals, 360 degrees in azimuth, oriented from magnetic north. Used as the basis for navigation in the National Airspace System. The VOR periodically identifies itself by Morse Code and may have an additional voice identification feature. Voice features may be used by ATC or FSS for transmitting instructions/information to pilots.
(See NAVIGATIONAL AID.)
(Refer to AIM.)

VOR TEST SIGNAL–
(See VOT.)

VORTAC– A navigation aid providing VOR azimuth, TACAN azimuth, and TACAN distance measuring equipment (DME) at one site.
(See DISTANCE MEASURING EQUIPMENT.)
(See NAVIGATIONAL AID.)
(See TACAN.)
(See VOR.)
(Refer to AIM.)

VORTICES– Circular patterns of air created by the movement of an airfoil through the air when generating lift. As an airfoil moves through the atmosphere in sustained flight, an area of area of low pressure is created above it. The air flowing from the high pressure area to the low pressure area around and about the tips of the airfoil tends to roll up into two rapidly rotating vortices, cylindrical in shape. These vortices are the most predominant parts of aircraft wake turbulence and their rotational force is dependent upon the wing loading, gross weight, and speed of the generating aircraft. The vortices from medium to super aircraft can be of extremely high velocity and hazardous to smaller aircraft.

(See AIRCRAFT CLASSES.)
(See WAKE TURBULENCE.)
(Refer to AIM.)

VOT– A ground facility which emits a test signal to check VOR receiver accuracy. Some VOTs are available to the user while airborne, and others are limited to ground use only.

(See CHART SUPPLEMENT.)
(Refer to 14 CFR Part 91.)
(Refer to AIM.)

VR–
(See VFR MILITARY TRAINING ROUTES.)

VSCS–
(See VOICE SWITCHING AND CONTROL SYSTEM.)

VTOL AIRCRAFT–
(See VERTICAL TAKEOFF AND LANDING AIRCRAFT.)

WA–
(See AIRMET.)
(See WEATHER ADVISORY.)

WAAS–
(See WIDE-AREA AUGMENTATION SYSTEM.)

WAKE RE–CATEGORIZATION (RECAT)– A set of optimized wake separation standards, featuring an increased number of aircraft wake categories, in use at select airports, which allows reduced wake intervals.
(See WAKE TURBULENCE.)

WAKE TURBULENCE– A phenomenon that occurs when an aircraft develops lift and forms a pair of counter–rotating vortices.
(See AIRCRAFT CLASSES.)
(See VORTICES.)
(Refer to AIM.)

WARNING AREA–
(See SPECIAL USE AIRSPACE.)

WAYPOINT– A predetermined geographical position used for route/instrument approach definition, progress reports, published VFR routes, visual reporting points or points for transitioning and/or circumnavigating controlled and/or special use airspace, that is defined relative to a VORTAC station or in terms of latitude/longitude coordinates.

WEATHER ADVISORY– In aviation weather forecast practice, an expression of hazardous weather conditions not predicted in the Aviation Surface Forecast, Aviation Cloud Forecast, or area forecast, as they affect the operation of air traffic and as prepared by the NWS.
(See AIRMET.)
(See GRAPHICAL AIRMEN'S METEOROLOGICAL INFORMATION.)
(See SIGMET.)

WEATHER RECONNAISSANCE AREA (WRA)– A WRA is airspace with defined dimensions and published by Notice to Air Missions, which is established to support weather reconnaissance/research flights. Air traffic control services are not provided within WRAs. Only participating weather reconnaissance/research aircraft from the 53rd Weather Reconnaissance Squadron and National Oceanic and Atmospheric Administration Aircraft Operations Center are permitted to operate within a WRA. A WRA may only be established in airspace within U.S. Flight Information Regions outside of U.S. territorial airspace.

WHEN ABLE–

a. In conjunction with ATC instructions, gives the pilot the latitude to delay compliance until a condition or event has been reconciled. Unlike "pilot discretion," when instructions are prefaced "when able," the pilot is expected to seek the first opportunity to comply.

b. In conjunction with a weather deviation clearance, requires the pilot to determine when he/she is clear of weather, then execute ATC instructions.

c. Once a maneuver has been initiated, the pilot is expected to continue until the specifications of the instructions have been met. "When able," should not be used when expeditious compliance is required.

WIDE-AREA AUGMENTATION SYSTEM (WAAS)– The WAAS is a satellite navigation system consisting of the equipment and software which augments the GPS Standard Positioning Service (SPS). The WAAS provides enhanced integrity, accuracy, availability, and continuity over and above GPS SPS. The differential correction function provides improved accuracy required for precision approach.

WIDE AREA MULTILATERATION (WAM)– A distributed surveillance technology which may utilize any combination of signals from Air Traffic Control Radar Beacon System (ATCRBS) (Modes A and C) and Mode S transponders, and ADS-B transmissions. Multiple geographically dispersed ground sensors measure the time-of-arrival of the transponder messages. Aircraft position is determined by joint processing of the time-difference-of-arrival (TDOA) measurements computed between a reference and the ground stations' measured time-of-arrival.

WILCO– I have received your message, understand it, and will comply with it.

WIND GRID DISPLAY– A display that presents the latest forecasted wind data overlaid on a map of the ARTCC area. Wind data is automatically entered and updated periodically by transmissions from the National Weather Service. Winds at specific altitudes, along with temperatures and air pressure can be viewed.

WIND SHEAR– A change in wind speed and/or wind direction in a short distance resulting in a tearing or shearing effect. It can exist in a horizontal or vertical direction and occasionally in both.

WIND SHEAR ESCAPE– An unplanned abortive maneuver initiated by the pilot in command (PIC) as a result of onboard cockpit systems. Wind shear escapes are characterized by maximum thrust climbs in the low altitude terminal environment until wind shear conditions are no longer detected.

WING TIP VORTICES–
(See VORTICES.)

WORDS TWICE–

a. As a request: "Communication is difficult. Please say every phrase twice."

b. As information: "Since communications are difficult, every phrase in this message will be spoken twice."

WS–
(See SIGMET.)
(See WEATHER ADVISORY.)

WST–
(See CONVECTIVE SIGMET.)
(See WEATHER ADVISORY.)

INDEX

[References are to page numbers]

A

[References are to page numbers]

B

C

[References are to page numbers]

D

[References are to page numbers]

E

F

[References are to page numbers]

G

H

I

[References are to page numbers]

J

K

L

M

[References are to page numbers]

N

O

[References are to page numbers]

P

Q

R

[References are to page numbers]

S

[References are to page numbers]

T

[References are to page numbers]

U

[References are to page numbers]

V

W

Federal Aviation
Administration

JO 7110.65AA
4/20/23

BRIEFING GUIDE

U.S. DEPARTMENT OF TRANSPORTATION
FEDERAL AVIATION ADMINISTRATION

Initiated By: AJV-0
Vice President, Mission Support Services

Table of Contents

1. PARAGRAPH NUMBER AND TITLE:
1–2–6. ABBREVIATIONS
5–1–2. ATC SURVEILLANCE SOURCE USE
5–5–4. MINIMA
5–5–7. PASSING OR DIVERGING
5–5–9. SEPARATION FROM OBSTRUCTIONS
5–13–8. CONTROLLER INITIATED COAST TRACKS

2. BACKGROUND: The Standard Terminal Automation Replacement System (STARS) Multi–Sensor Mode display is analogous to a mosaic display based on raw sensor data. The STARS Multi–Sensor Mode displays a target's position from raw sensor data, based on the data from the highest ranked sensor in the sort cell hierarchy. If data from the highest ranked sensor are unavailable, data will be used from the next highest ranked sensor that is available. Safety analysis and safety risk management documentation support the approval of Automatic Dependent Surveillance–Broadcast (ADS–B) and Wide Area Multilateration (WAM) when using STARS Multi–Sensor Mode for 5 NM separation. Enhanced Backup Surveillance (EBUS) has been decommissioned throughout the National Airspace System (NAS).

3. CHANGE:

OLD	NEW
1–2–6. ABBREVIATIONS	**1–2–6. ABBREVIATIONS**
As used in this order, the abbreviations listed below have the following meanings indicated. (See TBL 1–2–1.)	No Change
TBL 1–2–1 **FAA Order JO 7110.65 Abbreviations**	No Change
EBUS . . . . Enhanced Backup Surveillance System	Delete

OLD	NEW
5–1–2. ATC SURVEILLANCE SOURCE USE	**5–1–2. ATC SURVEILLANCE SOURCE USE**
Title through **b**	No Change
c. All procedures and requirements relating to ATC services using secondary radar targets apply to ATC services provided to targets derived from ADS–B and WAM.	**c. Targets derived from ADS–B and WAM may be used for the provision of all terminal services when operating in STARS Fusion, STARS FMA, and STARS Multi–Sensor Mode, including those associated with any published instrument procedure annotated "radar required."**

OLD	NEW
5–5–4. MINIMA	**5–5–4. MINIMA**
Separate aircraft by the following minima:	No Change
a. *TERMINAL.* Single Sensor ASR or Digital Terminal Automation System (DTAS):	No Change
NOTE– *Includes single sensor long range radar mode.*	*NOTE–* 1. *Includes single sensor long range radar mode.*
Add	***2. ADS–B and WAM are not selectable sources when in Single Sensor Mode.***
a1 through **a4** ***NOTE***	No Change

Add

Add

b through **b3**

4. ADS–B may be integrated as an additional surveillance source when operating in FUSION mode. The display of ADS–B targets is permitted and does not require radar reinforcement.

NOTE–
ADS–B surveillance must only be used when operating in FUSION.

5. The use of ADS–B only information may be used to support all radar requirements associated with any published instrument procedure that is annotated "Radar Required".

b6

c. EBUS, Terminal Mosaic/Multi–Sensor Mode

NOTE–
Mosaic/Multi–Sensor Mode combines radar input from 2 to 16 sites into a single picture utilizing a mosaic grid composed of radar sort boxes.

1. Below FL 600– 5 miles.

2. At or above FL 600– 10 miles.

3. Facility directives may specify 3 miles for areas meeting all of the following conditions:

(a) Radar site adaptation is set to single sensor.

(b) Significant operational advantages can be obtained.

(c) Within 40 miles of the antenna.

(d) Up to and including FL 230.

(e) Facility directives specifically define the area where the separation can be applied and define the requirements for displaying the area on the controller's display.

REFERENCE–
FAA Order JO 7210.3, Para 8–2–1, Three Mile Airspace Operations.

5. If TRK appears in the data block, handle in accordance with paragraph 5–3–7, Identification Status, subparagraph b, and take appropriate steps to establish nonradar separation.

NOTE–
TRK appears in the data block whenever the aircraft is being tracked by a radar site other than the radar currently selected. Current equipment limitations preclude a target from being displayed in the single sensor mode; however, a position symbol and data block, including altitude information, will still be displayed. Therefore, low altitude alerts must be provided in accordance with paragraph 2–1–6, Safety Alert.

No Change

Delete

Delete

Delete

Renumber **b4**

c. STARS Multi–Sensor Mode **– 5 miles.**

NOTE–
STARS** Multi–Sensor Mode **displays target symbols derived from radar, ADS–B, and WAM.

Delete

Delete

Delete

Delete

Delete

Delete

Delete

Delete

Delete

OLD	NEW
4. When transitioning from terminal to en route control, 3 miles increasing to 5 miles or greater, provided:	Delete
(a) The aircraft are on diverging routes/courses, and/or	Delete
(b) The leading aircraft is and will remain faster than the following aircraft; and	Delete
(c) Separation constantly increasing and the first center controller will establish 5 NM or other appropriate form of separation prior to the aircraft departing the first center sector; and	Delete
(d) The procedure is covered by a letter of agreement between the facilities involved and limited to specified routes and/or sectors/positions.	Delete
d through **e4(e)**	No Change
f. STARS Multi–Sensor Mode:	Delete
NOTE– **1.** *In Multi–Sensor Mode, STARS displays targets as filled and unfilled boxes, depending upon the target's distance from the radar site providing the data. Since there is presently no way to identify which specific site is providing data for any given target, utilize separation standards for targets 40 or more miles from the antenna.*	Delete
2. *When operating in STARS Single Sensor Mode, if TRK appears in the data block, handle in accordance with paragraph 5–3–7, Identification Status, subparagraph b, and take appropriate steps to establish nonradar separation.*	Delete
3. *TRK appears in the data block whenever the aircraft is being tracked by a radar site other than the radar currently selected. Current equipment limitations preclude a target from being displayed in the single sensor mode; however, a position symbol and data block, including altitude information, will still be displayed. Therefore, low altitude alerts must be provided in accordance with paragraph 2–1–6 , Safety Alert.*	Delete
WAKE TURBULENCE APPLICATION	No Change
g through **j**	Re–letter **f** through **i**

OLD	NEW
5–5–7. PASSING OR DIVERGING	**5–5–7. PASSING OR DIVERGING**
Title through **a2(b)**	No Change
3. Although approved separation may be discontinued, the requirements of paragraph 5–5–4, Minima, subparagraph g must be applied when wake turbulence separation is required.	No Change
REFERENCE– *FAA Order JO 7110.65, Para 1–2–2, Course Definitions.*	No Change

NOTE–
Apply en route separation rules when using multi–sensor mode.

b. *EN ROUTE.* Vertical separation between aircraft may be discontinued when they are on opposite courses as defined in paragraph 1–2–2, Course Definitions; and

Delete

b. *EN ROUTE****, TERMINAL (when STARS Multi–Sensor Mode is selected)***. Vertical separation between aircraft may be discontinued when they are on opposite courses as defined in paragraph 1–2–2, Course Definitions; and

OLD

5–5–9. SEPARATION FROM OBSTRUCTIONS

Title through **a5(b)** ***NOTE***

Add

NEW

5–5–9. SEPARATION FROM OBSTRUCTIONS

No Change

6. STARS Multi–Sensor Mode – ***5 miles.***

OLD

5–13–8. CONTROLLER INITIATED COAST TRACKS

a. Initiate coast tracks only in Flight Plan Aided Tracking (FLAT) mode, except "free" coast tracking may be used as a reminder that aircraft without corresponding computer–stored flight plan information are under your control.

NOTE–
1. To ensure tracks are started in FLAT mode, perform a start track function at the aircraft's most current reported position, then immediately "force" the track into coast tracking by performing another start function with "CT" option in field 64. Making amendments to the stored route with trackball entry when the aircraft is rerouted, and repositioning the data block to coincide with the aircraft's position reports are methods of maintaining a coast track in FLAT mode.

2. EBUS does not have the capability to initiate coast tracks.

NEW

5–13–8. CONTROLLER INITIATED COAST TRACKS

No Change

NOTE–
To ensure tracks are started in FLAT mode, perform a start track function at the aircraft's most current reported position, then immediately "force" the track into coast tracking by performing another start function with "CT" option in field 64. Making amendments to the stored route with trackball entry when the aircraft is rerouted, and repositioning the data block to coincide with the aircraft's position reports are methods of maintaining a coast track in FLAT mode.

Delete

---

1. PARAGRAPH NUMBER AND TITLE:
1–2–6. ABBREVIATIONS
5–3–4. TERMINAL AUTOMATION SYSTEMS IDENTIFICATION METHODS
5–4–6. RECEIVING CONTROLLER HANDOFF

2. BACKGROUND: During an update to FAA Order JO 7110.65Z, "AM" was inadvertently deleted from paragraphs 5–3–4 and 5–4–6. Furthermore, "AM" was omitted from 1–2–6. "AM," while not used by the En Route Automation Modernization (ERAM) and Standard Terminal Automation Replacement System (STARS) platform, is valid and relevant to the Micro–En Route Automated Radar Tracking System (MEARTS) platform. In addition, it was discovered that the current 2 mile disparity value published for the AMB definition is inaccurate as it is locally adaptable and the value could vary depending on the facility.

3. CHANGE:

OLD

1–2–6. ABBREVIATIONS

As used in this order, the abbreviations listed below have the following meanings indicated. (See TBL 1–2–1.)

TBL 1–2–1

FAA Order JO 7110.65 Abbreviations

NEW

1–2–6. ABBREVIATIONS

No Change

No Change

OLD

Abbreviation	Meaning
ALTRV	Altitude reservation
Add	Add
AMASS	Airport Movement Area Safety System
AMB	Ambiguity–A disparity greater than <u>2 miles</u> exists between the position declared for a target by STARS and another facility's computer declared position during interfacility handoff

NEW

Abbreviation	Meaning
ALTRV	Altitude reservation
<u>**AM . . . .**</u>	<u>**Ambiguity–A disparity greater than a locally adapted distance exists between the position declared for a target by MEARTS and another facility's computer declared position during interfacility handoff**</u>
AMASS	Airport Movement Area Safety System
AMB	Ambiguity–A disparity greater than <u>**a locally adapted distance**</u> exists between the position declared for a target by STARS and another facility's computer declared position during interfacility handoff

OLD

5–3–4. TERMINAL AUTOMATION SYSTEMS IDENTIFICATION METHODS

Title through **a1**

2. The aircraft is being handed off using a NAS automated system and one of the following does not appear in the data block: "CST", "NAT", "NT", "AMB", "OLD", or "TRK".

NEW

5–3–4. TERMINAL AUTOMATION SYSTEMS IDENTIFICATION METHODS

No Change

2. The aircraft is being handed off using a NAS automated system and one of the following does not appear in the data block: "CST", "NAT", "NT", "AMB", "OLD", <u>**"AM",**</u> or "TRK".

OLD

5–4–6. RECEIVING CONTROLLER HANDOFF

Title through **e3**

NEW

5–4–6. RECEIVING CONTROLLER HANDOFF

No Change

f. Take the identified action prior to accepting control of a track when the following indicators are displayed in the data block:	No Change
1. "AMB": advise the other facility that a disparity exists between the position declared by their computer and that declared by your STARS system.	**1.** "AMB" **or "AM"**: advise the other facility that a disparity exists between the position declared by their computer and **the position** declared by your STARS/**MEARTS** system.

---

1. PARAGRAPH NUMBER AND TITLE:
2-1-4. OPERATIONAL PRIORITY
2-4-20. AIRCRAFT IDENTIFICATION
9-2-17. SAMP FLIGHTS

2. BACKGROUND: As the lead governmental organization for aerial sampling/surveying missions (SAMP) flights, the U.S. Air Force Technical Application Center (AFTAC) has determined clarity is needed to ensure mission security for SAMP aircraft. Additional characters added to the SAMP flight ID, such as the aircraft tail number, could compromise mission security. A change to this and other FAA orders will designate mission call signs to be "SAMP" followed by a three-digit flight number, i.e., SAMP123. Additional changes associated with "SAMP" missions were coordinated for paragraph 5-3-2, Aerial Sampling/Surveying for Nuclear Contamination, in FAA Order JO 7210.3, Facility Operation and Administration; and paragraph 12-4-3, Aerial Sampling/Surveying for Nuclear Contamination, in FAA Order JO 7610.4, Special Operations.

3. CHANGE:

OLD	NEW
2-1-4. OPERATIONAL PRIORITY	**2-1-4. OPERATIONAL PRIORITY**
Title through **h** ***NOTE***	No Change
i. Provide priority handling to USAF aircraft engaged in aerial sampling/surveying missions using the call sign "SAMP."	**i.** Provide priority handling to USAF **or other government** aircraft engaged in aerial sampling/surveying missions using the call sign "SAMP."
REFERENCE- *FAA Order JO 7110.65, Para 9-2-17, SAMP Flights.* *FAA Order JO 7210.3, Para 5-3-2, Aerial Sampling/Surveying For Nuclear Contamination.* *FAA Order JO 7610.4, Para 12-4-3, Aerial Sampling/Surveying For Nuclear Contamination.*	***REFERENCE-*** *FAA Order JO 7110.65, Para 9-2-17, SAMP Flights.* *FAA Order JO 7210.3, Para 5-3-2, Aerial Sampling/Surveying For* ***Airborne*** *Contamination.*

OLD	NEW
2-4-20. AIRCRAFT IDENTIFICATION	**2-4-20. AIRCRAFT IDENTIFICATION**
Title through **a10(a)** ***EXAMPLE***	No Change
(b) USAF aircraft engaged in aerial sampling/surveying missions. State the call sign "SAMP" followed by the last three digits of the serial number.	**(b)** USAF **or other government** aircraft engaged in aerial sampling/surveying missions. State the call sign "SAMP" followed by **a three-digit flight** number.
EXAMPLE- *"SAMP Three One Six."*	No Change
REFERENCE- *FAA Order JO 7110.65, Para 9-2-17, SAMP Flights.*	No Change

OLD

9–2–17. SAMP FLIGHTS

Provide special handling to U.S. Government and military aircraft engaged in aerial sampling/surveying missions, sampling for nuclear, chemical, or hazardous material contamination. Honor inflight clearance requests for altitude and route changes to the maximum extent possible. Other IFR aircraft may be recleared so that requests by SAMP aircraft are honored. Separation standards as outlined in this order must be applied in all cases.

REFERENCE–
FAA Order JO 7110.65, Para 2–1–4, Operational Priority.
FAA Order JO 7110.65, Para 2–4–20, Aircraft Identification.
FAA Order JO 7610.4, Para 4–4–4, Avoidance of Hazardous Radiation Areas.

NEW

9–2–17. SAMP FLIGHTS

Provide special handling to **USAF or other government** aircraft **using the "SAMP" call sign and** engaged in aerial sampling/surveying missions for nuclear, chemical, or hazardous material contamination. **Approve** inflight clearance requests for altitude and route changes to the maximum extent possible. Other IFR aircraft may be recleared so that requests by SAMP aircraft are **approved**.

REFERENCE–
FAA Order JO 7110.65, Para 2–1–4, Operational Priority.
FAA Order JO 7110.65, Para 2–4–20, Aircraft Identification.
FAA Order JO 7610.4, Para 4–4–4, Avoidance of Hazardous Radiation Areas.
FAA Order JO 7210.3, Para 5–3–2, Aerial Sampling/Surveying for Airborne Contamination.

---

1. PARAGRAPH NUMBER AND TITLE:
2–1–4. OPERATIONAL PRIORITY
9–2–22. OPEN SKIES TREATY AIRCRAFT

2. BACKGROUND: The United States formally withdrew from the Open Skies Treaty on November 22, 2020. Due to current world events, return to the Treaty is unlikely. Therefore, Open Skies Treaty references and procedures are being removed from all FAA orders.

3. CHANGE:

OLD	NEW
2–1–4. OPERATIONAL PRIORITY	**2–1–4. OPERATIONAL PRIORITY**
Title through **k** ***REFERENCE***	No Change
l. Provide priority handling to expedite the movement of OPEN SKIES Treaty observation and demonstration (F and D) flights.	Delete
NOTE– *An Open Skies Treaty (F and D) aircraft has priority over all "regular" air traffic. "Regular" is defined as all aircraft traffic other than:* **1.** *Emergencies* **2.** *Aircraft directly involved in presidential movement.* **3.** *Forces or activities in actual combat.* **4.** *MEDEVAC, and active SAR missions.* **5.** *AIR EVAC and HOSP aircraft that have requested priority handling.*	Delete
REFERENCE– *FAA Order JO 7110.65, Para 9–2–22, Open Skies Treaty Aircraft.* *FAA Order JO 7210.3, Para 5–3–5, Open Skies Treaty Aircraft Priority Flights (F and D).* *Treaty on Open Skies, Treaty Document, 102–37.*	Delete
m through **q**	Re–letter **l** through **p**

OLD	NEW
9–2–22. OPEN SKIES TREATY AIRCRAFT	Delete
a. Open Skies aircraft will be identified by the call sign "OSY" (Open Skies) followed by the flight number and a one–letter mission suffix.	Delete
EXAMPLE– *OSY123D* *Mission suffixes:* **F = Observation Flights (Priority).* **D = Demonstration Flights (Priority).* **T = Transit Flights (Nonpriority).*	Delete
NOTE– **1.** *Observation/Demonstration flights are conducted under rigid guidelines outlined in the Treaty on Open Skies that govern sensor usage, maximum flight distances, altitudes and priorities.*	Delete
2. *Transit flights are for the sole purpose of moving an Open Skies aircraft from airport to airport in preparation for an actual Open Skies "F" or "D" mission.*	Delete
b. Provide priority and special handling to expedite the movement of an Open Skies observation or demonstration flight.	Delete
REFERENCE– *FAA Order JO 7110.65, Para 2–1–4, Operational Priority, subpara l.* *FAA Order JO 7210.3, Para 5–3–5, Open Skies Treaty Aircraft Priority Flights (F and D).* *Treaty on Open Skies, Treaty Document, 102–37.*	Delete
c. Open Skies (F and D) Treaty aircraft, while maintaining compliance with ATC procedures, must have priority over activities in special use airspace (SUA)/Air Traffic Control Assigned Airspace (ATCAA). Open Skies (F and D) Treaty aircraft are nonparticipating aircraft and must be allowed to transit SUA/ATCAA as filed after appropriate and timely coordination has been accomplished between the using agency and controlling agency.	Delete
NOTE– *A letter of agreement is not required for nonparticipating aircraft to transit deactivated/released airspace.*	Delete
REFERENCE– *FAA Order JO 7110.65, Para 9–3–4, Transiting Active SUA/ATCAA.*	Delete
1. Open Skies (F and D) Treaty flights transiting SUA/ATCAA will be handled in the following manner:	Delete
(a) The ATC facility controlling the Open Skies (F and D) Treaty flight must advise the using agency, or appropriate ATC facility, upon initial notification and when the aircraft is 30 minutes from the SUA/ATCAA boundary; and	Delete

(1) For active SUA/ATCAA with an ATC facility, coordinate and execute the transit of Open Skies (F and D) Treaty aircraft.	Delete
REFERENCE– *FAA Order JO 7110.65, Para 9–3–4, Transiting Active SUA/ATCAA.*	Delete
(2) For active SUA/ATCAA without an ATC facility, the using agency must deactivate/re-lease the SUA/ATCAA to permit the Open Skies (F and D) Treaty aircraft to transit as filed in proximity to the active SUA/ATCAA. When de-activating/re–leasing the SUA/ATCAA for this purpose, the using agency is only required to de-activate/release the portion of the SUA/ATCAA to the controlling agency that is necessary to pro-vide approved separation.	Delete
(b) The using agency must deactivate/release the SUA/ATCAA, or portion thereof, no later than 15 minutes prior to the Open Skies (F and D) Treaty aircraft reaching the SUA/ATCAA boundary.	Delete
(c) If the controlling agency is unable to confirm with the using agency that all conflicting activities in the SUA/ATCAA have ceased, the Open Skies aircraft must not be permitted access to the SUA/ATCAA.	Delete
REFERENCE– *FAA Order JO 7110.65, Para 9–3–2, Separation Minima.*	Delete
2. Return SUA/ATCAA to the using agency, if requested, within (15) minutes after the Open Skies (F and D) Treaty aircraft clears the SUA/ATCAA.	Delete
d. Clear the aircraft according to the filed flight plan.	Delete
1. Do not ask the pilot to deviate from the planned action or route of flight except to preclude an emergency situation or other higher priority aircraft.	Delete
2. Do not impose air traffic control delays except to preclude emergency situations or other higher priority aircraft.	Delete
NOTE– *If for reasons of flight safety the route or altitude must be changed, return the aircraft to the filed flight plan route as soon as practical.*	Delete

---

1. PARAGRAPH NUMBER AND TITLE: 2–1–27. PILOT DEVIATION NOTIFICATION

2. BACKGROUND: The March 2021 Air Traffic Procedures Bulletin contained an article on Pilot Deviations, including the phrase "Brasher Notification," sometimes used to reference the phraseology that an Air Traffic Controller will use to notify a pilot of a possible pilot deviation. The article also contained historical information referencing the origins of the phrase "Brasher Notification." While there is no official definition, the use of the phrases "Brasher Notification" or "Brasher Warning" has become prevalent throughout the National Airspace System when referring to the associated phraseology in FAA Order JO 7110.65, Air Traffic Control, paragraph 2–1–27, Pilot Deviation Notification.

3. CHANGE:

OLD	NEW
2–1–27. PILOT DEVIATION NOTIFICATION	**2–1–27. POSSIBLE PILOT DEVIATION NOTIFICATION**
When it appears that the actions of a pilot constitute a pilot deviation, notify the pilot, workload permitting.	No Change
PHRASEOLOGY– *(Identification) POSSIBLE PILOT DEVIATION ADVISE YOU CONTACT (facility) AT (telephone number).*	No Change
Add	***NOTE–*** ***The phraseology example identified in this paragraph is commonly referred to as the "Brasher Notification" or "Brasher Warning," which gives flight crews the opportunity to make note of the occurrence for future reference. The use of these terms during direct pilot communications is not appropriate.***
REFERENCE– *FAA Order JO 8020.16, Air Traffic Organization Aircraft Accident and Aircraft Incident Notification, Investigation, and Reporting, Chapter 11, Para 3, Air Traffic Facility Responsibilities.*	No Change

---

1. PARAGRAPH NUMBER AND TITLE:
2–6–4. ISSUING WEATHER AND CHAFF AREAS
5–4–10. EN ROUTE FOURTH LINE DATA BLOCK USAGE

2. BACKGROUND: The language in FAA Order JO 7110.65, subparagraph 2–6–4k, was in conflict with FAA Order JO 7110.65, supparagraph 5–4–10f Note 2 and Note 3, when coordinating weather deviations using the 4th line of the Full Data Block (FDB) in the En Route Automation Modernization (ERAM) system. Additionally, FAA Order JO 7110.65, subparagraph 5–4–10f, was unclear on the designated characters used when deviating between two headings.

3. CHANGE:

OLD	NEW
2–6–4. ISSUING WEATHER AND CHAFF AREAS	**2–6–4. ISSUING WEATHER AND CHAFF AREAS**
Title through **j** ***REFERENCE***	No Change
k. En Route Fourth Line Data Transfer	No Change

1. The inclusion of a NAVAID, waypoint, or /F in the fourth line data indicates that the pilot has been authorized to deviate for weather and must rejoin the route at the next NAVAID or waypoint in the route of flight.

REFERENCE–
FAA Order JO 7110.65, Para 5–4–10, En Route Fourth Line Data Block Usage.

EXAMPLE–
"Deviation twenty degrees right approved, when able proceed direct O'Neill VORTAC and advise." In this case, the corresponding fourth line entry is "D20R/ONL" or "D20R/F."

1. The inclusion of /(NAVAID) **or /(waypoint), when preceded by the designated characters for weather deviations, indicates that a pilot has been authorized to deviate for weather and rejoin the route at the specified NAVAID or waypoint. The use of /F, following the designated weather deviation characters, indicates that a pilot has been authorized to deviate and rejoin the route of flight at the next NAVAID or waypoint in the flight plan.**

No Change

EXAMPLE–
"Deviation twenty degrees right approved, when able proceed direct O'Neill VORTAC and advise." In this case, the corresponding fourth line entry is "D20R/ONL," or "D20R/F" ***if O'Neill is the next NAVAID in the flight plan.***

OLD

5-4-10. EN ROUTE FOURTH LINE DATA BLOCK USAGE

Title through **d** ***EXAMPLE***

e. Aircraft assigned a heading until receiving a fix or joining a published route must be designated with assigned heading format followed by the fix or route.

EXAMPLE–
H080/ALB, 080/J121, PH/ALB

NOTE–
1. *The notation "PH" may be used to denote present heading.*
2. *The character "H" may be omitted as a prefix to the heading assignment only if necessary due to character field limitations, and it does not impede understanding.*

Add

f. Coordination format for weather deviations must use the designated characters:
D–deviation
L–left
R–right
N–north
E–east
S–south
W–west
/F – direct next NAVAID/waypoint
D+2 headings – deviate between.

NEW

5-4-10. EN ROUTE FOURTH LINE DATA BLOCK USAGE

No Change

No Change

Delete

No Change

No Change

EXAMPLE–
H080/ALB, 080/J121, PH/ALB

f. Coordination format for weather deviations must use the designated characters:
D–deviation
L–left
R–right
N–north
E–east
S–south
W–west
/F–direct next NAVAID/waypoint **in the flight plan**
D**(heading)–(heading)–deviate between two specified headings.**

NOTE–	No Change
1. *Two digits specify turns in degrees and must include direction character(s). Three digits specify heading(s).*	
2. *The inclusion of a /NAVAID, /waypoint, or /F indicates that the pilot has been authorized to deviate for weather and must rejoin the route at the next NAVAID, waypoint, or fix in the route of flight in accordance with the phraseology in paragraph 2–6–4.*	**2.** *The inclusion of* ***/(NAVAID) or /(waypoint), when preceded by the designated characters for weather deviations, indicates that a pilot has been authorized to deviate for weather and rejoin the route at the specified NAVAID or waypoint. The use of /F, following the designated weather deviation characters, indicates that a pilot has been authorized to deviate and rejoin the route of flight at the next fix in the route in accordance with paragraph 2–6–4.***
EXAMPLE– *D90/ATL, DL/KD75U, D090/F*	***EXAMPLE–*** *D90**L**/ATL, DL/KD75U, D090/F*
3. *The absence of a NAVAID, waypoint, or /F indicates that the pilot has been authorized to deviate for weather only, and the receiving controller must provide a clearance to rejoin the route in accordance with subparagraph 2–1–15c.*	**3.** *The absence of /NAVAID,* ***/waypoint, or /F after the weather deviation designated characters indicates that the pilot has been authorized to deviate for weather, and the receiving controller must provide a clearance to rejoin the route of flight in accordance with subparagraph 2–1–15c.***
EXAMPLE– *DN, D20L, D30R, D080+120*	***EXAMPLE–*** *DN, D20L, D30R,* ***D180–210***

---

1. PARAGRAPH NUMBER AND TITLE: 2–6–6. HAZARDOUS INFLIGHT WEATHER ADVISORY

2. BACKGROUND: Airmen's Meteorological Information (AIRMET) is a concise description using abbreviated text of the occurrence or forecast occurrence of specified weather phenomena which may affect the safety of aircraft operations, but at intensities lower than those which require the issuance of a Significant Meteorological Information (SIGMET). Since the 1950s AIRMET information has been issued in text format known also as Traditional Alphanumeric Code (TAC). En route controllers are required to broadcast notification that an AIRMET has been issued or updated when the area affected by the AIRMET is within 150 NM of their sector or area of jurisdiction (50 NM for terminal facilities). Controllers do not broadcast the text of the AIRMET, they only broadcast that the AIRMET exists. In 2010, the FAA approved the G–AIRMET as an alternate way to provide AIRMET information over the contiguous United States (CONUS). For the purposes of this DCP, and in recognition that there are several uses/definitions for the acronym, CONUS, references herein to CONUS are specific to the contiguous United States (i.e., "lower 48"). The Graphical–AIRMET (G–AIRMET) is AIRMET information described at discrete times no more than 3 hours apart for a period of up to 12 hours into the future. The legacy TAC AIRMET over the CONUS is to be retired leaving the G–AIRMET as the only format to advise of AIRMET criteria since the G–AIRMET provides higher resolution weather information to operators. With the retirement of the TAC AIRMET over the CONUS, controllers will no longer receive this advisory; therefore, the requirement in FAA Order JO 7110.65 to broadcast the AIRMET over the CONUS can be removed. Pilots already receive this advisory information through other sources such as Flight Service.

3. CHANGE:

OLD	NEW
2–6–6. HAZARDOUS INFLIGHT WEATHER ADVISORY	**2–6–6. HAZARDOUS INFLIGHT WEATHER ADVISORY**
Controllers must advise pilots of hazardous weather that may impact operations within 150 NM of their sector or area of jurisdiction. Hazardous weather information contained in the advisories includes Airmen's Meteorological Information (AIRMET), Significant Meteorological Information (SIGMET), Convective SIGMET (WST), Urgent Pilot Weather Reports (UUA), and Center Weather Advisories (CWA). Facilities must review alert messages to determine the geographical area and operational impact of hazardous weather information. Advisories are not required if aircraft on your frequency(s) will not be affected.	Controllers must advise pilots of hazardous weather that may impact operations within 150 NM of their sector or area of jurisdiction. Hazardous weather information contained in the advisories includes Airmen's Meteorological Information (AIRMET) **(except over the CONUS)**, Significant Meteorological Information (SIGMET), Convective SIGMET (WST), Urgent Pilot Weather Reports (UUA), and Center Weather Advisories (CWA). Facilities must review alert messages to determine the geographical area and operational impact of hazardous weather information. Advisories are not required if aircraft on your frequency(s) will not be affected.
Add	***NOTE–*** ***In recognition that there are several uses/definitions for the acronym CONUS, references herein to CONUS are specific to the contiguous United States (i.e., "lower 48").***

---

1. PARAGRAPH NUMBER AND TITLE: 5–2–7. VFR CODE ASSIGNMENTS

2. BACKGROUND: Civilian Visual Flight Rules (VFR) standard formation flights often pass through air traffic control sectors unrecognized since the lead aircraft squawks beacon code 1200 with the trailing aircraft squawking standby. This can result in incomplete VFR advisories issued to aircraft that are receiving ATC services. To address this issue, a dedicated beacon code of 1203 is being reserved for VFR standard formation flights that are not in communication with ATC. When controllers observe this beacon code, they can provide more accurate traffic information when providing traffic advisories and safety alerts. Pilots will be instructed via appropriate publications to begin squawking this code when participating in VFR standard formation flights.

3. CHANGE:

OLD	NEW
5–2–7. VFR CODE ASSIGNMENTS	**5–2–7. VFR CODE ASSIGNMENTS**
Title through **a1(b)** *NOTE*	No Change
b. Instruct an IFR aircraft that cancels its IFR flight plan and is not requesting radar advisory service, or a VFR aircraft for which radar advisory service is being terminated, to squawk VFR.	No Change
PHRASEOLOGY– *SQUAWK VFR.* *or* *SQUAWK 1200.*	No Change

NOTE–

1. *Aircraft not in contact with ATC may squawk* ***1255*** *in lieu of* ***1200*** *while en route to/from or within designated firefighting areas.*

No Change

2. *VFR aircraft that fly authorized SAR missions for the USAF or USCG may be advised to squawk* ***1277*** *in lieu of* ***1200*** *while en route to/from or within the designated search area.*

No Change

3. *VFR gliders should squawk* ***1202*** *in lieu of* ***1200****. Gliders operate under some flight and maneuvering limitations. They may go from essentially stationary targets while climbing and thermaling to moving targets very quickly. They can be expected to make radical changes in flight direction to find lift and cannot hold altitude in a response to an ATC request. Gliders may congregate together for short periods of time to climb together in thermals and may cruise together in loose formations while traveling between thermals.*

No Change

Add

4. ***The lead aircraft in a standard VFR formation flight not in contact with ATC should squawk 1203 in lieu of 1200. All other aircraft in the formation should squawk standby.***

REFERENCE–
FAA Order JO 7110.66, National Beacon Code Allocation Plan.

No Change

---

1. PARAGRAPH NUMBER AND TITLE:
5–4–10. EN ROUTE FOURTH LINE DATA BLOCK USAGE

2. BACKGROUND: Language in FAA Order JO 7110.65, 5–4–10g and h, requires that the designation characters "M" or "S" be displayed when assigned speeds are entered in the 4th line of the Full Data Block (FDB). However, En Route Automation Modernization (ERAM) uses several methods to input and process assigned speed data that do not include the display of "M" or "S" due to a four character limit for speed entries in the 4th line of the FDB.

3. CHANGE:

OLD

5–4–10. EN ROUTE FOURTH LINE DATA BLOCK USAGE

Title through **f** ***NOTE 3 EXAMPLE***

g. Coordination format for assigned airspeeds must use the designation character "S" preceding a three–digit number.

NEW

5–4–10. EN ROUTE FOURTH LINE DATA BLOCK USAGE

No Change

g. Coordination format for **specific** assigned airspeeds must use the designation character "S" preceding a three–digit number. **A three–digit number followed by a "+" must be used to denote an assigned speed at or greater than the displayed value, or followed by a "–" to denote an assigned speed at or less than the displayed value.**

NOTE– *A "+" notation may be added to denote an assigned speed at or greater than the displayed value. A "–" notation may be added to denote an assigned speed at or less than the displayed value.*	Delete
EXAMPLE– *S210, S250, S250+, S280–*	*EXAMPLE–* *S210, **250+, 280–***
h. Aircraft assigned a Mach number must use the designation "M" preceding the two–digit assigned value.	**h**. Aircraft assigned a Mach number must use the designation "M"**, "M.", or "."** preceding the two–digit assigned value. **The displayed Mach number shall also be followed by a "+" to denote an assigned speed at or greater than the displayed value, or a "–" to denote an assigned speed at or less than the displayed value.**
EXAMPLE– *M80, M80+, M80–*	*EXAMPLE–* *M80, M80+, M80–**, M.80, .80, .80–***
REFERENCE– *FAA Order JO 7110.65, Para 5–4–10, En Route Fourth Line Data Block Usage, subpara g NOTE.*	Delete

---

1. PARAGRAPH NUMBER AND TITLE:
6–4–3. MINIMA ON OPPOSITE COURSES
6–5–4. MINIMA ALONG OTHER THAN ESTABLISHED AIRWAYS OR ROUTES
6–5–5. RNAV MINIMA– DIVERGING/CROSSING COURSES

2. BACKGROUND: Recently, the Stage 2–4 En Route Training Update team conducted a First Course Conduct (FCC) event for Radar Associate Controller training. During that training, it was discovered that the usage of the term "expanded route" in FAA JO 7110.65Z, subparagraph 6–4–3(c) and (d) and subparagraph 6–5–5(b) was unclear as there is no standard definition for "expanded route" and thus, no way to determine when to apply the 18 mile separation standard. Additionally, while researching the background for these changes it was discovered that FIG 6–5–4 contained incorrect information regarding the degree of the angle used to calculate the expanded route.

3. CHANGE:

OLD

6–4–3. MINIMA ON OPPOSITE COURSES

Title through **b**

c. Two RNAV aircraft have reported passing the same position and are at least *8 miles* apart if operating along a route that is 8 miles or less in width; or *18 miles* apart if operating along an expanded route; except that *30 miles* must be applied if operating along that portion of any route segment defined by a navigation station requiring extended usable distance limitations beyond 130 miles.

d. An aircraft utilizing RNAV and an aircraft utilizing VOR have reported passing the same position and the RNAV aircraft is at least 4 miles beyond the reported position when operating along a route that is 8 miles or less in width; 9 miles beyond the point when operating along an expanded route; except that 15 miles must be applied if operating along that portion of any route segment defined by a navigation station requiring extended usable distance limitation beyond 130 miles; or 3 minutes apart whichever is greater.

NEW

6–4–3. MINIMA ON OPPOSITE COURSES

No Change

c. Two RNAV aircraft have reported passing the same position and are at least *8 miles* apart if operating along a route that is 8 miles or less in width; or *18 miles* apart if operating along **any route segment that is greater than 8 miles in width**; except that *30 miles* must be applied if operating along that portion of any route segment defined by a navigation station requiring extended usable distance limitations beyond 130 miles.

d. An aircraft utilizing RNAV and an aircraft utilizing VOR have reported passing the same position and the RNAV aircraft is at least 4 miles beyond the reported position when operating along a route that is 8 miles or less in width; 9 miles beyond the point when operating along **any route segment that is greater than 8 miles in width**; except that 15 miles must be applied if operating along that portion of any route segment defined by a navigation station requiring extended usable distance limitation beyond 130 miles; or 3 minutes apart whichever is greater.

OLD

6–5–4. MINIMA ALONG OTHER THAN ESTABLISHED AIRWAYS OR ROUTES

Protect airspace along other than established airways or routes as follows: (See FIG 6–5–4.)

NEW

6–5–4. MINIMA ALONG OTHER THAN ESTABLISHED AIRWAYS OR ROUTES

No Change

OLD

FIG 6–5–4

Minima Along Other Than Established Airways or Routes

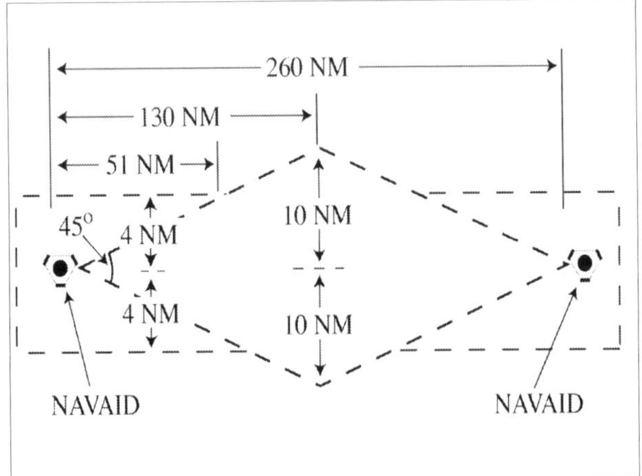

NEW

FIG 6-5-4

Minima Along Other Than Established Airways or Routes

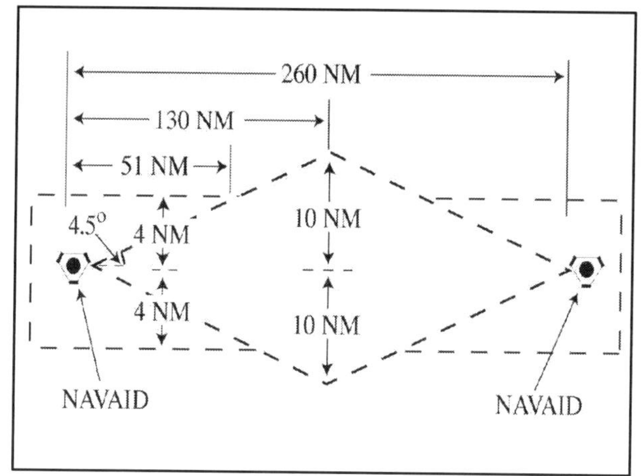

REFERENCE-
P/CG Term- Airway.
P/CG Term- Route.

No Change

OLD

6-5-5. RNAV MINIMA- DIVERGING/ CROSSING COURSES

Title through **a**

b. When operating along an expanded route- *9 miles,* except that *15 miles* must be applied along that portion of any route segment requiring extended usable distance limitation beyond 130 miles of the reference facility.

NOTE-
Except for GNSS-equipped aircraft /G, /L, /S, and /V, not on a random impromptu route, paragraph 5-5-1, Application, requires radar separation be provided to RNAV aircraft operating at and below FL450 on Q routes or random RNAV routes, excluding oceanic airspace.

NEW

6-5-5. RNAV MINIMA- DIVERGING/ CROSSING COURSES

No Change

b. When operating along **any route segment that is greater than 8 miles in width** - *9 miles,* except that *15 miles* must be applied along that portion of any route segment requiring extended usable distance limitation beyond 130 miles of the reference facility.

No Change

1. PARAGRAPH NUMBER AND TITLE:
8–7–4. LATERAL SEPARATION
8–8–4. LATERAL SEPARATION
8–9–4. LATERAL SEPARATION
8–10–4. LATERAL SEPARATION

2. BACKGROUND: To align with ICAO Annex 6, Annex 11, and Procedures for Air Navigation Services, Air Traffic Management (ICAO Doc 4444), the lateral separation minima for air traffic will be reduced from 30 NM to 23 NM for eligible aircraft pairs in oceanic airspaces under the control jurisdiction of Oakland ARTCC, Anchorage ARTCC, and New York ARTCC. For air traffic operating in these airspaces and using this minima, RCP 240 (Required Communication Performance), RSP 180 (Required Surveillance Performance), and at least RNP 4 (Required Navigation Performance) are required. Other requirements include direct controller/pilot communications via voice or Controller Pilot Data Link Communications and that the required ADS–C contracts are maintained and monitored by an automated flight–data processor (e.g., ATOP). FAA Order JO 7110.65, Chapter 8, Offshore/Oceanic Procedures, will be updated to reflect this new minima. This allows FAA to harmonize with its adjacent Air Navigation Service Providers.

3. CHANGE:

OLD	NEW
8–7–4. LATERAL SEPARATION	**8–7–4. LATERAL SEPARATION**
In accordance with Chapter 8, Offshore/Oceanic Procedures, Section 4, Lateral Separation, apply the following:	No Change
a. *30 NM* to (at a minimum, RNP–4, RCP 240, and RSP 180) approved aircraft operating within airspace designated for RNP–4 when direct controller/pilot communications, via voice or Controller Pilot Data Link Communications (CPDLC), and the required ADS–C contracts are maintained and monitored by an automated flight data processor (e.g., ATOP).	**a.** *23 NM* to **approved aircraft** (at a minimum, RNP 4, RCP 240, and RSP 180) operating within airspace designated for ***23 NM* lateral separation** when direct controller/pilot communications via voice or Controller Pilot Data Link Communications (CPDLC), and the required ADS–C contracts are maintained and monitored by an automated flight data processor (e.g., ATOP).
b. *50 NM* between Required Navigation Performance (RNP 4 or RNP 10) approved aircraft which:	**b.** *50 NM* between Required Navigation Performance (RNP 4 or RNP 10) approved aircraft **that operate in the New York Oceanic CTA/FIR or the San Juan Oceanic CTA/FIR or the Atlantic portion of the Miami Oceanic CTA/FIR.**
1. Operate on routes or in areas within WATRS, the San Juan CTA/FIR or the Atlantic portion of the Miami Oceanic CTA/FIR; or	Delete
2. Operate in the New York Oceanic CTA/FIR outside of WATRS.	Delete
NOTE– *This reduced lateral separation must not be used if track–keeping capability of the aircraft has been reduced for any reason.*	No Change

OLD

8–8–4. LATERAL SEPARATION

In accordance with Chapter 8, Offshore/Oceanic Procedures, Section 4, Lateral Separation, apply the following:

a. *30 NM* to (at a minimum, RNP–4, RCP 240, and RSP 180) approved aircraft operating within airspace designated for RNP–4 when direct controller/pilot communications, via voice or Controller Pilot Data Link Communications (CPDLC), and the required ADS–C contracts are maintained and monitored by an automated flight data processor (e.g., ATOP).

b. *50 NM* between Required Navigation Performance (RNP 4 or RNP 10) approved aircraft which:

1. Operate on routes or in area within WATRS, the San Juan CTA/FIR or the Atlantic portion of the Miami Oceanic CTA/FIR; or

2. Operate in the New York Oceanic CTA/FIR outside of WATRS; or

3. Operate in the Houston Oceanic CTA/FIR or the Gulf of Mexico portion of the Miami CTA/FIR.

Add

NOTE–
This reduced lateral separation must not be used if track–keeping capability of the aircraft has been reduced for any reason.

NEW

8–8–4. LATERAL SEPARATION

No Change

a. *23 NM* to **approved aircraft** (at a minimum, RNP_4, RCP 240, and RSP 180) operating within airspace designated for ***23 NM* lateral separation** when direct controller/pilot communications via voice or Controller Pilot Data Link Communications (CPDLC), and the required ADS–C contracts are maintained and monitored by an automated flight data processor (e.g., ATOP).

b. *50 NM* between Required Navigation Performance (RNP 4 or RNP 10) approved aircraft **that**:

1. Operate **in the New York Oceanic CTA/FIR; or**

2. Operate in the **San Juan Oceanic CTA/FIR; or**

3. Operate in the Houston Oceanic CTA/FIR; or

4. Operate in the Atlantic or Gulf of Mexico portion of the Miami CTA/FIR.

No Change

OLD

8–9–4. LATERAL SEPARATION

In accordance with Chapter 8, Offshore/Oceanic Procedures, Section 4, Lateral Separation, apply the following:

a. Within areas where Required Navigation Performance 10 (RNP–10) separation and procedures are authorized, apply *50 NM* to RNP–10 approved aircraft.

b. Apply *30 NM* to (at a minimum, RNP–4, RCP 240, and RSP 180) approved aircraft operating within airspace designated for RNP–4 when direct controller/pilot communications, via voice or Controller Pilot Data Link Communications (CPDLC), and the required ADS–C contracts are maintained and monitored by an automated flight data processor (e.g., ATOP).

NEW

8–9–4. LATERAL SEPARATION

No Change

a. Within areas where Required Navigation Performance separation and procedures are authorized, apply *50 NM* to **RNP 4 or** RNP_10 approved aircraft.

b. Apply *23 NM* to **approved aircraft** (at a minimum, RNP_4, RCP 240, and RSP 180) operating within airspace designated for ***23 NM* lateral separation** when direct controller/pilot communications via voice or Controller Pilot Data Link Communications (CPDLC), and the required ADS–C contracts are maintained and monitored by an automated flight data processor (e.g., ATOP).

OLD

8–10–4. LATERAL SEPARATION

In accordance with Chapter 8, Offshore/Oceanic Procedures, Section 4, Lateral Separation, apply the following:

a. *50 NM* to RNP–10 approved aircraft within areas where RNP–10 separation and procedures are authorized,

b. *30 NM* to (at a minimum, RNP–4, RCP 240, and RSP 180) approved aircraft operating within the Anchorage Oceanic CTA and Anchorage Continental CTA when direct controller/pilot communications, via voice or Controller Pilot Data Link Communications (CPDLC), and the required ADS–C contracts are maintained and monitored by an automated flight data processor (for example, ATOP).

NOTE–
The minimum described in subparagraph b is not applicable within airspace in the Anchorage Arctic CTA.

NEW

8–10–4. LATERAL SEPARATION

No Change

a. Within areas where Required Navigation Performance separation and procedures are authorized, apply *50 NM* to RNP 4 or RNP 10 approved aircraft.

b. Apply ***23*** *NM* to **approved aircraft** (at a minimum, RNP_4, RCP 240, and RSP 180) operating within the Anchorage Oceanic CTA and Anchorage Continental CTA when direct controller/pilot communications via voice or Controller Pilot Data Link Communications (CPDLC) and the required ADS–C contracts are maintained and monitored by an automated flight data processor (**e.g.**, ATOP).

No Change

---

1. PARAGRAPH NUMBER AND TITLE: 9–2–12. LAW ENFORCEMENT OPERATIONS

2. BACKGROUND: In support of national defense, homeland security, intelligence or law enforcement operations, System Operations Security assigns beacon codes and U. S. Special call signs for sensitive government operations. In order to ensure effective air traffic services to these missions, it is necessary the requested and/or displayed beacon codes not be changed and call signs remain unaltered by ATCS during those operations. Paragraph 9–2–12 was also rewritten to eliminate outdated terminology, as well as to harmonize the language contained therein with other orders such as FAA Order JO 7210.3 and FAA Order JO 7110.67.

3. CHANGE:

OLD

9–2–12. LAW ENFORCEMENT OPERATIONS

a. In the event information is received pertaining to stolen aircraft, the controller must forward all information to the OS/CIC for reporting on the Domestic Events Network (DEN).

REFERENCE–
FAA Order JO 7210.3, Para 2–7–7, Cooperation With Law Enforcement Agencies.

Add

NEW

9–2–12. LAW ENFORCEMENT AND SENSITIVE GOVERNMENT MISSIONS

a. Provide the maximum assistance possible to law enforcement aircraft when requested.

Delete

1. If requested by the pilot/flight crew, communicate with law enforcement aircraft on a separate and unique communications frequency whenever possible.

Add

Add

Add

Add

b. Special law enforcement operations.

1. Special law enforcement operations include inflight identification, surveillance, interdiction and pursuit activities performed in accordance with official civil and/or military mission responsibilities.

2. To facilitate accomplishment of these special missions, exemptions from specified parts of Title 14 of the Code of Federal Regulations have been granted to designated departments and agencies. However, it is each organization's responsibility to apprise ATC of their intent to operate under an authorized exemption before initiating actual operations.

REFERENCE–
FAA Order JO 7210.3, Para 19–3–1, Authorizations and Exemptions from Title 14, Code of Federal Regulations (14 CFR).

3. Additionally, some departments and agencies that perform special missions have been assigned coded identifiers to permit them to apprise ATC of ongoing mission activities and solicit special air traffic assistance.

REFERENCE–
FAA Order 7110.67, Air Traffic Management Security Services for Special Operations.

NOTE–
As specified in paragraph 2–1–4, Operational Priority, priority of handling for aircraft operating with coded identifiers will be the same as that afforded to SAR aircraft performing a SAR mission.

Add

2. Ensure assistance to law enforcement aircraft does not compromise approved separation minima or place the aircraft in unsafe proximity to terrain, obstructions or other aircraft.

3. When requested, assist law enforcement in locating suspect aircraft.

4. Forward any information received pertaining to stolen aircraft to the OS/CIC for reporting on the Domestic Events Network (DEN).

REFERENCE–
FAA Order JO 7210.3, Para 2–7–7, Cooperation With Law Enforcement Agencies.

b. Sensitive government missions.

1. Sensitive government missions include inflight identification, surveillance, interdiction and pursuit activities conducted by government aircraft for national defense, homeland security, and intelligence or law enforcement purposes.

2. Provide support to national security and homeland defense activities as specified in paragraph 2–1–2, Duty Priority.

Delete

3. To facilitate accomplishment of sensitive government missions, exemptions from specified parts of Title 14 of the Code of Federal Regulations have been granted to designated departments and agencies. Each organization's exemption identifies its responsibilities for notifying ATC of its intent to operate under an exemption before commencing operations.

Delete

Delete

REFERENCE–
FAA Order JO 7210.3, Para 19–3–1, Authorizations and Exemptions from Title 14, Code of Federal Regulations (14 CFR).

Add	**4. Departments and agencies that conduct sensitive government missions are assigned U.S. special call signs. Additionally, some have pre–assigned beacon codes to permit them to apprise ATC of ongoing mission activities and solicit air traffic assistance. To support these sensitive government missions, ATC must:**
Add	**(a) Not change the sensitive beacon codes requested or displayed by these operators.**
Add	**(b) To the maximum extent possible, ensure the full call sign designator of aircraft conducting sensitive government operations is entered into FAA automation systems.**
Add	**(c) Not alter or abbreviate the U.S. special call signs used by aircraft for sensitive government operations.**
Add	***REFERENCE–*** ***FAA Order JO 7110.67, Air Traffic Management Security Procedures and Requirements for Special Operations.***
c. Assistance to law enforcement aircraft operations.	Delete
1. Provide the maximum assistance possible to law enforcement aircraft, when requested, in helping them locate suspect aircraft.	Delete
2. Communicate with law enforcement aircraft, when possible and if requested, on a frequency not paired with your normal communications frequencies.	Delete
3. Do not allow assistance to law enforcement aircraft to violate any required separation minima.	Delete
4. Do not assist VFR law enforcement aircraft in any way that will create a situation which, in your judgment, places the aircraft in unsafe proximity to terrain or other aircraft.	Delete

---

1. PARAGRAPH NUMBER AND TITLE: 13–1–1. DESCRIPTION

2. BACKGROUND: Recently, the definition of CURRENT PLAN was removed from the Pilot/Controller Glossary (P/CG). The deletion was made as it was discovered that the definition did not meet the intentions of the original authors, nor did it provide an accurate reflection of how it functioned within the En Route Decision Support Tool (EDST) system. However, as "current plan" data is a term used when determining how the EDST functions, the term will be placed into paragraph 13–1–1 and a definition will be added in a NOTE at the end of the paragraph.

3. CHANGE:

OLD

13-1-1. DESCRIPTION

En Route Decision Support Tool (EDST) is an integrated function of ERAM that is used by the sector team in performing its strategic planning responsibilities. EDST uses flight plan data, forecast winds, aircraft performance characteristics, and track data to derive expected aircraft trajectories, and to predict conflicts between aircraft and between aircraft and special use or designated airspace. It also provides trial planning and enhanced flight data management capabilities.

Add

NEW

13-1-1. DESCRIPTION

En Route Decision Support Tool (EDST) is an integrated function of ERAM that is used by the sector team in performing its strategic planning responsibilities. EDST uses **current plan** data, forecast winds, aircraft performance characteristics, and track data to derive expected aircraft trajectories, and to predict conflicts between aircraft and between aircraft and special use or designated airspace. It also provides trial planning and enhanced flight data management capabilities.

NOTE–
For use by the EDST, the current plan is what the En Route Automation System (EAS) predicts an aircraft will fly. This may include clearances that have not yet been issued to the aircraft. Current plans are used to model a flight trajectory and, when applicable, for detecting conflicts.

Federal Aviation
Administration

JO 7110.65AA CHG 1
10/5/23

BRIEFING GUIDE

U.S. DEPARTMENT OF TRANSPORTATION
FEDERAL AVIATION ADMINISTRATION

Initiated By: AJV−0
Vice President, Mission Support Services

Table of Contents

1. PARAGRAPH NUMBER AND TITLE: 2–1–4. OPERATIONAL PRIORITY

2. BACKGROUND: The Department of Defense (DoD) has requested modifications to National Airborne Operations Center (NAOC) and Special Air Missions (SCOOT) mission procedures and information in FAA Orders JO 7610.4, Sensitive Procedures and Requirements for Special Operations; and JO 7110.65, Air Traffic Control.

3. CHANGE:

OLD	NEW
2–1–4. OPERATIONAL PRIORITY	**2–1–4. OPERATIONAL PRIORITY**
Title through **e**	No Change
f. Provide priority handling to NIGHT WATCH aircraft when NAOC (pronounced NA–YOCK) is indicated in the remarks section of the flight plan or in air/ground communications.	**f.** Provide priority handling to NIGHT WATCH **"NAOC" (pronounced NAY–OCK) aircraft when notified via landline or when "NAOC" is used** in air/ground communications. **When the term "NAOC" is used, approve any request(s) as soon as practicable**.
NOTE– *The term "NAOC" will not be a part of the call sign but may be used when the aircraft is airborne to indicate a request for special handling.*	***NOTE–*** *The term "NAOC" will not be a part of the* ***Flight ID in the flight plan or used in conjunction with the call sign but may otherwise be used when the aircraft is airborne.***
REFERENCE– *FAA Order JO 7610.4, Para 12–1–1, Applications.*	No Change
g through **i** ***REFERENCE***	No Change
j. Provide priority handling to Special Air Mission aircraft when SCOOT is indicated in the remarks section of the flight plan or used in air/ground communications.	**j.** Provide priority handling to Special Air Mission **"SCOOT"** aircraft when **notified via landline or when "SCOOT" is** used in air/ground communications. **When the term "SCOOT" is used, approve any request(s) as soon as practicable**.
NOTE– *The term "SCOOT" will not be part of the call sign but may be used when the aircraft is airborne to indicate a request for special handling.*	***NOTE–*** *The term "SCOOT" will not be* ***a*** *part of the* ***Flight ID in the flight plan*** *but may be used* ***during radio communications in conjunction with the call sign****.*
REFERENCE– *FAA Order JO 7610.4, Para 12–6–1, Applications.*	No Change

---

1. PARAGRAPH NUMBER AND TITLE: 5–2–15. VALIDATION OF MODE C READOUT

2. BACKGROUND: FAA Order JO 7110.65, paragraph 5–2–15, Validation of Mode C Readout, makes reference to a "Coast/Suspend Tabular List" that is no longer used in ERAM. The reference will be modified/updated accordingly to reflect the current environment.

3. CHANGE:

OLD	NEW
5–2–15. VALIDATION OF MODE C READOUT	**5–2–15. VALIDATION OF MODE C ALTITUDE READOUT**
Ensure that Mode C altitude readouts are valid after accepting an interfacility handoff, initial track start, track start from coast/suspend tabular list, or during and after an unreliable Mode C readout, except as follows:	**a.** Ensure that Mode C altitude readouts are valid after**:**

OLD	NEW
NOTE– *Consider a Mode C readout unreliable when any condition, not just those that display an indicator in the Data Block, exists that indicates that the Mode C may be in error.*	Delete
Add	**1. Initial track start.**
Add	**2. Track start from coast/frozen status.**
Add	**3. During and after an unreliable Mode C readout.**
Add	**4. Accepting an interfacility handoff, except:**
a. CTRD–equipped tower cabs are not required to validate Mode C altitude readouts after accepting interfacility handoffs from TRACONs according to the procedures in paragraph 5–4–3, Methods, subparagraph a4.	(a) CTRD–equipped tower cabs are not required to validate Mode C altitude readouts after accepting interfacility handoffs from TRACONs according to the procedures in paragraph 5–4–3, Methods, subparagraph a4.
b. ERAM facilities are not required to validate Mode C altitude readouts after accepting interfacility handoffs from other ERAM facilities, except:	(b) ERAM facilities are not required to validate Mode C altitude readouts after accepting interfacility handoffs from other ERAM facilities, except:
1. After initial track start or track start from coast is required, or	(1) After initial track start or track start from coast is required, or
2. During and after the display of a missing, unreasonable, exceptional, or otherwise unreliable Mode C readout indicator.	(2) During and after the display of a missing, unreasonable, exceptional, or otherwise unreliable Mode C readout indicator.
Add	***NOTE–*** ***Consider a Mode C readout unreliable when any condition exists that indicates the Mode C may be in error, not just those that display an indicator in the Data Block.***
c through g	Re–letter as b through f

---

1. PARAGRAPH NUMBER AND TITLE:
5–5–4. MINIMA
5–5–9. SEPARATION FROM OBSTRUCTIONS

2. BACKGROUND: The Surveillance Acquisition and Sustainment Group of the Program Management Office (PMO) is undertaking the Mode S Beacon Replacement System (MSBRS) beginning in 2023. This secondary radar refresh seeks the replacement of all legacy Mode S and Condor MK2 beacon systems associated with ASR–8/9 and ASR–11 terminal airport surveillance radar (ASR) systems. The impending replacement requires the relevant provisions in JO 7110.65 to reflect the new system infrastructure. There will be no changes in separation standards as a result of this system replacement.

3. CHANGE:

OLD	NEW
5–5–4. MINIMA	**5–5–4. MINIMA**
Separate aircraft by the following minima:	No Change
a. *TERMINAL*. Single Sensor ASR or Digital Terminal Automation System (DTAS):	No Change

NOTE– **1.** *Includes single sensor long range radar mode.*	No Change
2. *ADS–B and WAM are not selectable sources when in Single Sensor Mode.*	No Change
1. When less than 40 miles from the antenna– *3 miles.*	No Change
2. When 40 miles or more from the antenna– *5 miles.*	No Change
3. For single sensor ASR–9 with Mode S, when less than 60 miles from the antenna– *3 miles.*	**3.** For single sensor **monopulse secondary surveillance radar (MSSR)**, when less than 60 miles from the antenna– *3 miles.*
4. For single sensor ASR–11 MSSR Beacon, when less than 60 miles from the antenna– *3 miles.*	Delete
NOTE– *Wake turbulence procedures specify increased separation minima required for certain classes of aircraft because of the possible effects of wake turbulence.*	No Change
5. If TRK appears in the data block, handle in accordance with paragraph 5–3–7, Identification Status, subparagraph b, and take appropriate steps to establish nonradar separation.	**4.** If TRK appears in the data block, handle in accordance with paragraph 5–3–7, Identification Status, subparagraph b, and take appropriate steps to establish nonradar separation.
NOTE– *TRK appears in the data block whenever the aircraft is being tracked by a radar site other than the radar currently selected. Current equipment limitations preclude a target from being displayed in the single sensor mode; however, a position symbol and data block, including altitude information, will still be displayed. Therefore, low altitude alerts must be provided in accordance with paragraph 2–1–6, Safety Alert.*	No Change
b through **d3(a)(1)**	No Change
(2) Within 60 NM of the preferred radar when using ASR–9 with Mode S or ASR–11 MSSR Beacon; or	**(2)** Within 60 NM of the preferred radar when using **an** MSSR; or
d3(a)(1) through **e3(b)**	No Change
(c) Within 40 NM of the sensor or within 60 NM of the sensor when using ASR–9 with Mode S or ASR–11 MSSR Beacon and within the 3 NM separation area.	**(c)** Within 40 NM of the sensor or within 60 NM of the sensor when using **an** MSSR and within the 3 NM separation area.
e3(d) through **e4**	No Change
(a) Up to and including FL230 within 40 miles from the antenna or within 60 NM when using ASR–9 with Mode S or ASR–11 MSSR Beacon and targets are from the adapted sensor.	**(a)** Up to and including FL230 within 40 miles from the antenna or within 60 NM when using **an** MSSR and targets are from the adapted sensor.

OLD

5–5–9. SEPARATION FROM OBSTRUCTIONS

a. TERMINAL. Separate aircraft from prominent obstructions depicted on the radar display by the following minima:

1. When less than 40 miles from the antenna– *3 miles.*

2. When 40 miles or more from the antenna– *5 miles.*

3. For single sensor ASR–9 with Mode S, when less than 60 miles from the antenna – *3 miles.*

4. For single sensor ASR–11 MSSR Beacon, when less than 60 miles from the antenna – *3 miles.*

5. FUSION:

(a) Fusion target symbol – *3 miles.*

(b) When ISR is displayed – *5 miles.*

NOTE–
When operating in FUSION, distances from the antenna listed in paragraph 5–5–9, a1 through a4, do not apply.

a6

NEW

5–5–9. SEPARATION FROM OBSTRUCTIONS

No Change

No Change

No Change

3. For single sensor **MSSR**, when less than 60 miles from the antenna – *3 miles.*

Delete

4. FUSION:

No Change

No Change

NOTE–
When operating in FUSION, distances from the antenna listed in paragraph 5–5–9, a1 through a3, do not apply.

Renumber as **a5**

---

1. PARAGRAPH NUMBER AND TITLE: 5–9–7. SIMULTANEOUS INDEPENDENT APPROACHES

2. BACKGROUND: In May 2021, Flight Standards Flight Research and Analysis Branch, AFS–430, completed a supplemental analysis of DOT/FAA/AFS–400/2018/R/22 which provided the foundational analysis for implementation of the revised High Update Rate (HUR) surveillance procedures now published in JO 7110.65 and JO 7210.3. This supplemental analysis was requested after a 2020 safety risk management panel on the subject. It was found that through additional review of ADS–B surveillance accuracy that was not known at the time of the first report, that runway centerline spacing (RCLS) could be further reduced.

3. CHANGE:

OLD

5–9–7. SIMULTANEOUS INDEPENDENT APPROACHES– DUAL & TRIPLE

Title through **HIGH UPDATE RATE SURVEILLANCE**

b. At locations with high update rate surveillance, simultaneous independent approaches may be conducted where the surveillance update rate is 1 second or faster, the system processing time is 3 seconds or faster, and under the following conditions:

1. Dual parallel runway centerlines are at least 3,200 feet apart, or dual parallel runway centerlines are at least 2,500 feet apart with a 2.5° to 3.0° offset approach to either runway.

NEW

5–9–7. SIMULTANEOUS INDEPENDENT APPROACHES– DUAL & TRIPLE

No Change

b. At locations with high update rate surveillance **capable of update rates of 1.2 seconds or faster, and where fusion display mode is utilized**, simultaneous independent approaches may be conducted under the following conditions:

1. Dual parallel runway centerlines are at least 3,100 feet apart, or dual parallel runway centerlines are at least 2,500 feet apart with a 2.5° to 3.0° offset approach to either runway.

OLD	NEW
2. Triple parallel runway centerlines are at least 3,400 feet apart, or triple parallel runway centerlines are at least 2,500 feet apart with a 2.5° to 3.0° offset approach to both outside runways, or triple parallel runway centerlines are at least 2,500 feet apart, a single 2.5° to 3.0° offset approach to either outside runway while parallel approaches to the remaining two runways are separated by at least 3,400 feet.	**2.** Triple parallel runway centerlines are at least 3,**1**00 feet apart, or triple parallel runway centerlines are at least 2,500 feet apart with a 2.5° to 3.0° offset approach to both outside runways, or triple parallel runway centerlines are at least 2,500 feet apart, **and** a single 2.5° to 3.0° offset approach to either outside runway while parallel approaches to the remaining two runways are separated by at least 3,**1**00 feet.
NOTE– *Aircraft without functioning ADS–B Out are restricted from utilizing these high update rate (HUR) procedures unless an alternative HUR surveillance source providing one–second or faster target report updating is utilized.*	No Change
3. A surveillance update rate of at least 1 second is required for monitoring the no transgression zone (NTZ) when conducting simultaneous independent approaches to the runway centerline spacing (RCLS) provided in this paragraph.	**3.** A surveillance update rate of at least 1**.2** seconds is required for monitoring the no transgression zone (NTZ) when conducting simultaneous independent approaches to the runway centerline spacing (RCLS) provided in this paragraph.
NOTE– **1.** *HUR procedures cannot be conducted if notified that a one second update rate is not being provided.*	***NOTE–*** **1.** *HUR procedures cannot be conducted if notified that a* ***1.2-****second update rate is not being provided.*
2. *Where RCLS is ≤3400 feet, the normal operating zone (NOZ) is constant at 700 feet; and for RCLS ≥3400 feet, the no transgression zone (NTZ) remains constant at 2000 feet.*	No Change
b4 through **c**	No Change
1. Dual parallel runway centerlines are at least 3,000 and less than 4,300 feet apart.	**1.** Dual parallel runway centerlines are at least **2,500** and less than 4,300 feet apart.
2. Triple parallel runway centerlines are at least 3,000 but less than 5,000 feet apart.	**2.** Triple parallel runway centerlines are at least **2,500** but less than 5,000 feet apart.

---

1. PARAGRAPH NUMBER AND TITLE: 7–4–6. RNAV VISUAL FLIGHT PROCEDURES (RVFP)

2. BACKGROUND: RNAV Visual Flight Procedures (RVFP) have been approved for use in the National Airspace System (NAS) as special procedures by the Flight Standards Service since 2010. These special procedures leverage the navigation data base and automation on board many modern aircraft. Facility personnel are made aware of RVFPs during the design and implementation process. Due to the nature of these procedures, RVFPs can only be issued to authorized operators.

3. CHANGE:

OLD	NEW
Add	**7–4–6. RNAV VISUAL FLIGHT PROCEDURES (RVFP)**
Add	**RNAV Visual Flight Procedures (RVFPs) are special procedures flown in VMC and clear of clouds and used by authorized operators only. Clear an aircraft for an RVFP when:**

Add	**a. Requested by the pilot, or if necessary, as addressed in a Letter of Agreement (LOA).**
Add	**b. The pilot reports the airport in sight or, at locations with an operating control tower, the preceding aircraft in sight.**
Add	**c. An altitude is assigned at or above the MVA/MIA, before issuing an approach clearance when conducting an RVFP. The pilot should join the RVFP at the beginning of the charted procedure, or if necessary, may join at another waypoint along the path of the charted procedure, except for waypoints beginning or within an RF leg.**
Add	**d. The official weather at the airport of intended landing indicates VFR and should meet or exceed the ceiling and visibility specified on the RVFP.**
Add	**e. The published name of the RVFP and the landing runway are specified in the approach clearance.**
Add	*PHRASEOLOGY–* *(Ident) CLEARED RNAV VISUAL RUNWAY (number) APPROACH*
Add	*NOTE–* *Refer to the facility RVFP LOAs, if applicable, to determine the authorized operators.*
Add	*REFERENCE–* *FAA Order 8260.60, Special Procedures.*
7–4–6	Renumber as **7–4–7**

Federal Aviation
Administration

JO 7110.65AA CHG 2
3/21/24

BRIEFING GUIDE

U.S. DEPARTMENT OF TRANSPORTATION
FEDERAL AVIATION ADMINISTRATION

Initiated By: AJV-0
Vice President, Mission Support Services

Table of Contents

1. PARAGRAPH NUMBER AND TITLE:
3–9–4. LINE UP AND WAIT (LUAW)
3–10–5. LANDING CLEARANCE
3–10–10. ALTITUDE RESTRICTED LOW APPROACH

2. BACKGROUND: United States Air Force (USAF) submitted a Document Change Proposal (DCP) in early 2023 to amend FAA Order JO 7110.65, Air Traffic Control, paragraph 3–9–4, Line Up and Wait (LUAW), for improved clarity.

3. CHANGE:

OLD	NEW
3–9–4. LINE UP AND WAIT (LUAW)	**3–9–4. LINE UP AND WAIT (LUAW)**
Title through **b** ***NOTE***	No Change
c. Procedures.	No Change
1. At facilities without a safety logic system or facilities with the safety logic system in the limited configuration:	**1.** At facilities without a safety logic system or facilities with the safety logic system in limited configuration:
(a) Do not issue a landing clearance to an aircraft requesting a full-stop, touch-and-go, stop-and-go, option, or unrestricted low approach on the same runway with an aircraft that is holding in position or taxiing to line up and wait until the aircraft in position starts takeoff roll.	**(a)** Do not **clear** an aircraft **for** a full-stop, touch-and-go, stop-and-go, **low approach, or** option on the same runway with an aircraft holding in position or taxiing to **LUAW** until the aircraft in position **has exited the runway or** starts takeoff roll.
PHRASEOLOGY– *RUNWAY (number), CONTINUE, TRAFFIC HOLDING IN POSITION,* *or* *RUNWAY (number) (pattern instructions as appropriate) TRAFFIC HOLDING IN POSITION.*	No Change
EXAMPLE– *"American 528, Runway Two–Three continue, traffic holding in position."* *"Twin Cessna Four Four Golf, Runway One–Niner Right, base approved, traffic holding in position."* *"Baron Two Five Foxtrot, Runway One–Niner, extend downwind, tower will call your base, traffic holding in position."*	No Change
Add	***REFERENCE–*** *FAA Order JO 7110.65, Para 3–10–10, Altitude Restricted Low Approach.*
(b) Do not authorize an aircraft to LUAW if an aircraft has been cleared to land, touch-and-go, stop-and-go, option, or unrestricted low approach on the same runway.	**(b)** Do not authorize an aircraft to LUAW if an aircraft has been cleared **for a full-stop**, touch-and-go, stop-and-go, low approach**, or option** on the same runway.
2. Except when reported weather conditions are less than ceiling 800 feet or visibility less than 2 miles, facilities using the safety logic system in the full core alert mode:	No Change

(a) May issue a landing clearance for a full-stop, touch-and-go, stop-and-go, option, or unrestricted low approach to an arriving aircraft with an aircraft holding in position or taxiing to LUAW on the same runway, or

(b) May authorize an aircraft to LUAW when an aircraft has been cleared for a full stop, touch-and-go, stop-and-go, option, or unrestricted low approach on the same runway.

REFERENCE–
FAA Order JO 7110.65, Para 3–10–5, Landing Clearance.

d. When an aircraft is authorized to line up and wait, inform it of the closest traffic within 6 flying miles requesting a full-stop, touch-and-go, stop-and-go, option, or unrestricted low approach to the same runway.

EXAMPLE–
"United Five, Runway One Eight, line up and wait. Traffic a Boeing Seven Thirty Seven, six mile final."

e through **k2**

l. *USAF/USN.* When issuing additional instructions or information to an aircraft holding in takeoff position, include instructions to continue holding or taxi off the runway, unless it is cleared for takeoff.

PHRASEOLOGY–
CONTINUE HOLDING,

or

TAXI OFF THE RUNWAY.

REFERENCE–
FAA Order JO 7110.65, Para 3–10–10, Altitude Restricted Low Approach.

(a) May issue clearance for a full-stop, touch-and-go, stop-and-go, low approach**, or option on the same runway** with an aircraft holding in position or taxiing to LUAW, or

(b) May authorize an aircraft to LUAW when an aircraft has been cleared for a full-stop, touch-and-go, stop-and-go, low approach**, or option** on the same runway.

No Change

d. When an aircraft is authorized to **LUAW**, inform it of the closest traffic within 6 flying miles requesting a full-stop, touch-and-go, stop-and-go, low approach**, or option** to the same runway.

No Change

No Change

l. *USAF/USN.* When issuing additional instructions or information to an aircraft holding in position, include instructions to continue holding or taxi off the runway, unless it is cleared for takeoff.

No Change

No Change

OLD

3–10–5. LANDING CLEARANCE

Title through **b2** ***REFERENCE***

c. Procedures.

1. Facilities without a safety logic system or facilities with the safety logic system inoperative or in the limited configuration must not clear an aircraft for a full stop, touch-and-go, stop-and-go, option, or unrestricted low approach when a departing aircraft has been instructed to line up and wait or is holding in position on the same runway. The landing clearance may be issued once the aircraft in position has started takeoff roll.

NEW

3–10–5. LANDING CLEARANCE

No Change

No Change

1. Facilities without a safety logic system or facilities with the safety logic system inoperative or in the limited configuration must not clear an aircraft for a full-stop, touch-and-go, stop-and-go, low approach**, or option on the same runway with an aircraft** holding in position **or taxiing to LUAW until the aircraft in position has exited the runway or starts** takeoff roll.

2. Facilities using safety logic in the full core alert runway configuration may issue a landing clearance, full-stop, touch-and-go, stop-and-go, option, or unrestricted low approach to an arriving aircraft with an aircraft holding in position or taxiing to LUAW on the same runway except when reported weather conditions are less than ceiling 800 feet or visibility less than 2 miles.

2. Facilities using safety logic in the full core alert runway configuration may **clear an aircraft for a** full-stop, touch-and-go, stop-and-go, low approach**, or option on the same runway** with an aircraft holding in position or taxiing to LUAW except when reported weather conditions are less than ceiling 800 feet or visibility less than 2 miles.

d. Inform the closest aircraft that is requesting a full-stop, touch-and-go, stop-and-go, option, or unrestricted low approaches when there is traffic authorized to line up and wait on the same runway.

d. Inform the closest aircraft that is requesting a full-stop, touch-and-go, stop-and-go, low approach**, or option** when there is traffic authorized to LUAW on the same runway.

EXAMPLE–
"Delta One, Runway One–Eight, continue, traffic holding in position."
"Delta One, Runway One–Eight, cleared to land. Traffic holding in position."
"Twin Cessna Four Four Golf, Runway One–Niner base approved, traffic holding in position."
"Baron Two Five Foxtrot, Runway One–Niner Right extend downwind, tower will call your base, traffic holding in position."

No Change

OLD

3–10–10. ALTITUDE RESTRICTED LOW APPROACH

A low approach with an altitude restriction of not less than 500 feet above the airport may be authorized except over an aircraft in takeoff position or a departure aircraft. Do not clear aircraft for restricted altitude low approaches over personnel unless airport authorities have advised these personnel that the approaches will be conducted. Advise the approaching aircraft of the location of applicable ground traffic, personnel, or equipment.

NOTE–
1. *The 500 feet restriction is a minimum. Higher altitudes should be used when warranted. For example, 1,000 feet is more appropriate for super or heavy aircraft operating over unprotected personnel or small aircraft on or near the runway.*

2. *This authorization includes altitude restricted low approaches over preceding landing or taxiing aircraft. Restricted low approaches are not authorized over aircraft in takeoff position or departing aircraft.*

NEW

3–10–10. ALTITUDE RESTRICTED LOW APPROACH

A low approach with an altitude restriction of no less than 500 feet above the airport may be authorized except over an aircraft **holding** in position or a **departing** aircraft. Do not clear aircraft for restricted altitude low approaches over personnel unless airport authorities have advised these personnel that the approaches will be conducted. Advise the approaching aircraft of the location of applicable ground traffic, personnel, or equipment.

No Change

2. *This authorization includes altitude restricted low approaches over preceding landing or taxiing aircraft. Restricted low approaches are not authorized over aircraft **holding** in position or departing aircraft.*

PHRASEOLOGY–
CLEARED LOW APPROACH AT OR ABOVE (altitude).
TRAFFIC (description and location).

No Change

REFERENCE–
FAA Order JO 7110.65, Para 3–1–5, Vehicles/Equipment/Personnel on Runways.
FAA Order JO 7110.65, Para 3–1–6, Traffic Information.
FAA Order JO 7110.65, Para 3–2–1, Light Signals.
FAA Order JO 7110.65, Para 3–3–3, Timely Information.
FAA Order JO 7110.65, Para 3–9–4, Line Up and Wait (LUAW).
FAA Order JO 7110.65, Para 3–10–3, Same Runway Separation.

No Change

---

1. PARAGRAPH NUMBER AND TITLE:
3–9–8. INTERSECTING RUNWAY/INTERSECTING FLIGHT PATH OPERATIONS
3–10–4. INTERSECTING RUNWAY/INTERSECTING FLIGHT PATH SEPARATION

2. BACKGROUND: Recent inquiries from the Western Service Center Operations Support Group (OSG) concerning Land and Hold Short Operations (LAHSO) indicated misalignment between the current LAHSO order and the content in FAA Order JO 7110.65 regarding intersecting runway operations.

3. CHANGE:

OLD

3–9–8. INTERSECTING RUNWAY/INTERSECTING FLIGHT PATH OPERATIONS

Title through **b2(b)**

Add

(c) Has completed the landing roll and is observed turning at an exit point prior to the intersection, or

(d) Has passed the intersection.

REFERENCE–
P/CG Term – Clear of the Runway.
P/CG Term – Landing Roll.

NEW

3–9–8. INTERSECTING RUNWAY/INTERSECTING FLIGHT PATH OPERATIONS

No Change

(c) Has landed and will hold short of an intersecting runway, intersecting taxiway, intersecting approach/departure flight path, or other predetermined point in accordance with the Land and Hold Short Operations (LAHSO) directive, or

(d) Has completed the landing roll and is observed turning at an exit point prior to the intersection, or

(e) Has passed the intersection.

REFERENCE–
FAA Order 7110.118, Land and Hold Short Operations (LAHSO).
P/CG Term – Clear of the Runway.
P/CG Term – Landing Roll.

OLD

3–10–4. INTERSECTING RUNWAY/INTERSECTING FLIGHT PATH SEPARATION

Title through **a(2)** ***REFERENCE***

NEW

3–10–4. INTERSECTING RUNWAY/INTERSECTING FLIGHT PATH OPERATIONS

No Change

b. "USA/USAF/USN NOT APPLICABLE." An aircraft may be authorized to takeoff from one runway while another aircraft lands simultaneously on an intersecting runway or an aircraft lands on one runway while another aircraft lands simultaneously on an intersecting runway, or an aircraft lands to hold short of an intersecting taxiway or some other predetermined point such as an approach/departure flight path using procedures specified in the current LAHSO directive. The procedure must be approved by the air traffic manager and be in accordance with a facility directive. The following conditions apply:

NOTE–
Application of these procedures does not relieve controllers from the responsibility of providing other appropriate separation contained in this order.

REFERENCE–
FAA Order JO 7210.3, Para 10–3–7, Land and Hold Short Operations (LAHSO).

b. "USA/USAF/USN NOT APPLICABLE." An **arriving** aircraft may be authorized to **land and hold short of an intersecting runway, an intersecting taxiway, an intersecting approach/departure flight path, or other predetermined point in accordance with** procedures specified in the LAHSO directive. The following conditions apply:

No Change

REFERENCE–
FAA Order 7110.118, Land and Hold Short Operations (LAHSO).
FAA Order JO 7210.3, Para 10–3–7, Land and Hold Short Operations (LAHSO).

---

1. PARAGRAPH NUMBER AND TITLE: 5–1–2. ATC SURVEILLANCE SOURCE USE

2. BACKGROUND: Recently, a clarification was issued by Mission Support Services, Policy, AJV–P, to answer questions concerning the ongoing divestiture of select radar site assets. The clarification identified a potential ambiguity related to existing guidance regarding the use of approved ATC surveillance sources. This change is necessary to update the order and account for newer technologies adopted into the NAS within the past decade.

3. CHANGE:

OLD

5–1–2. ATC SURVEILLANCE SOURCE USE

Use approved ATC Surveillance Sources.

REFERENCE–
FAA Order JO 7110.65, Para 5–2–13, Inoperative or Malfunctioning Interrogator.

NEW

5–1–2. ATC SURVEILLANCE SOURCE USE

Use approved ATC surveillance sources. **TERMINAL. When operating in FUSION mode, the provisions of 5–1–2a are not applicable, unless required by facility directive.**

No Change

---

1. PARAGRAPH NUMBER AND TITLE: 5–2–11. CODE MONITOR

2. BACKGROUND: In April 2023, a note was added to FAA Order JO 7110.65 dedicating beacon code 1203 for use by the lead aircraft of visual flight rules (VFR) standard formation flights not in contact with Air Traffic Control (ATC). This code should also have been added to paragraph 5–2–11 containing the list of codes that are specifically monitored by ATC.

3. CHANGE:

OLD

5–2–11. CODE MONITOR

a. Continuously monitor the codes assigned to aircraft operating within your area of responsibility. Additionally, monitor **Code 1200, Code 1202, Code 1255,** and **Code 1277** unless your area of responsibility includes only Class A airspace. During periods when ring–around or excessive VFR target presentations derogate the separation of IFR traffic, the monitoring of VFR **Code 1200, Code 1202, Code 1255,** and **Code 1277** may be temporarily discontinued.

NEW

5–2–11. CODE MONITOR

a. Continuously monitor the codes assigned to aircraft operating within your area of responsibility. Additionally, monitor Code 1200, Code 1202, **Code 1203,** Code 1255, and Code 1277 unless your area of responsibility includes only Class A airspace. During periods when excessive VFR target presentations derogate the separation of IFR traffic, monitoring of **the aforementioned codes** may be temporarily discontinued.

---

1. PARAGRAPH NUMBER AND TITLE:
5–2–15. VALIDATION OF MODE C ALTITUDE READOUT

2. BACKGROUND: The guidance in FAA Order JO 7110.65, 5–2–15e and 5–2–15f, directs the action to be taken when an aircraft displays an invalid Mode C readout, depending on the altitude stratum the aircraft is within. The subparagraphs provide direction to controllers for handling aircraft with invalid Mode C readouts when operating either below or at or above FL 180 and not solely on the Mode C readout.

3. CHANGE:

OLD

5–2–15. VALIDATION OF MODE C ALTITUDE READOUT

Title through **c**

d. Whenever you observe an invalid Mode C readout below FL 180:

d1 through **d2(b)** ***PHRASEOLOGY***

e. Whenever you observe an invalid Mode C readout at or above FL 180, unless the aircraft is descending below Class A airspace:

NEW

5–2–15. VALIDATION OF MODE C ALTITUDE READOUT

No Change

d. Whenever you observe an **aircraft below FL 180 with an invalid Mode C readout**:

No Change

e. Whenever you observe an **aircraft at or above FL 180 with an invalid Mode C readout**, unless the aircraft is descending below Class A airspace:

---

1. PARAGRAPH NUMBER AND TITLE: 5–7–2. METHODS

2. BACKGROUND: In 1990, FAA Order JO 7110.65F, CHG 4, paragraph 5–101, Methods, inserted a speed adjustment example "reduce speed twenty knots" without any reference to expressing numbers in group form in the paragraph. As a result, there was no clear guidance on when speed adjustments must be expressed in single digit or group form.

3. CHANGE:

OLD

5–7–2. METHODS

Title through **a3**

NEW

5–7–2. METHODS

No Change

4. Increase or reduce to a specified speed or by a specified number of knots.

PHRASEOLOGY–
SAY AIRSPEED.

SAY MACH NUMBER.

MAINTAIN PRESENT SPEED.

MAINTAIN (specific speed) KNOTS.

MAINTAIN (specific speed) KNOTS OR GREATER.

DO NOT EXCEED (speed) KNOTS.

MAINTAIN MAXIMUM FORWARD SPEED.

MAINTAIN SLOWEST PRACTICAL SPEED.

INCREASE/REDUCE SPEED:

TO (specified speed in knots),

or

TO MACH (Mach number),

or

(number of knots) KNOTS.

EXAMPLE–
"Increase speed to Mach point seven two."
"Reduce speed to two five zero."
"Reduce speed twenty knots."
"Maintain two eight zero knots."
"Maintain maximum forward speed."

NOTE–
1. *A pilot operating at or above 10,000 feet MSL on an assigned speed adjustment greater than 250 knots is expected to comply with 14 CFR Section 91.117(a) when cleared below 10,000 feet MSL, within domestic airspace, without notifying ATC. Pilots are expected to comply with the other provisions of 14 CFR Section 91.117 without notification.*

4. Increase or reduce to a specified speed **in single-digit form** or by a specified number of knots **in group form**.

No Change

No Change

No Change

2. *Speed restrictions of 250 knots do not apply to aircraft operating beyond 12 NM from the coastline within the U.S. Flight Information Region, in offshore Class E airspace below 10,000 feet MSL. However, in airspace underlying a Class B airspace area designated for an airport, or in a VFR corridor designated through such a Class B airspace area, pilots are expected to comply with the 200 knot speed limit specified in 14 CFR Section 91.117(c). (See 14 CFR Sections 91.117(c) and 91.703.)*	No Change
3. *The phrases "maintain maximum forward speed" and "maintain slowest practical speed" are primarily intended for use when sequencing a group of aircraft. As the sequencing plan develops, it may be necessary to determine the specific speed and/or make specific speed assignments.*	No Change

---

1. PARAGRAPH NUMBER AND TITLE:
8–1–10. PROCEDURES FOR WEATHER DEVIATIONS AND OTHER CONTINGENCIES IN OCEANIC CONTROLLED AIRSPACE
8–7–5. PROCEDURES FOR WEATHER DEVIATIONS IN NORTH ATLANTIC (NAT) AIRSPACE
8–9–5. PROCEDURES FOR WEATHER DEVIATIONS AND OTHER CONTINGENCIES IN OCEANIC CONTROLLED AIRSPACE

2. BACKGROUND: During a recent review of FAA Order JO 7110.65, Chapter 8, Offshore/Oceanic Procedures, it was discovered that procedures for weather deviations were omitted from two of the four ICAO Regions. Weather deviation requests take priority over routine requests regardless of region, and no matter the region, aircraft will not fly into known areas of weather.

3. CHANGE:

OLD	NEW
Add	**8–1–10. PROCEDURES FOR WEATHER DEVIATIONS AND OTHER CONTINGENCIES IN OCEANIC CONTROLLED AIRSPACE**
Add	**Aircraft must request an ATC clearance to deviate. Since aircraft will not fly into adverse meteorological conditions, weather deviation requests should take priority over routine requests. If there is no traffic in the horizontal dimension, ATC must issue clearance to deviate from track; or if there is conflicting traffic in the horizontal dimension, ATC must separate aircraft by establishing vertical separation, then issue clearance to deviate from track. If there is conflicting traffic and ATC is unable to establish required separation, ATC must:**
Add	**a. Advise the pilot unable to issue clearance for requested deviation;**
Add	**b. Advise the pilot of conflicting traffic; and**

Add	**c. Request pilot's intentions.**
Add	***PHRASEOLOGY–*** ***UNABLE (requested deviation), TRAFFIC IS (call sign, position, altitude, direction), SAY INTENTIONS.***
Add	***NOTE–*** ***1. The pilot will advise ATC of intentions by the most expeditious means available.***
Add	***2. In the event that pilot/controller communications cannot be established or a revised ATC clearance is not available, pilots will follow the procedures outlined in the Aeronautical Information Publication (AIP), Section ENR 7.3, Special Procedures for In-flight Contingencies in Oceanic Airspace; and AC 91-70, Oceanic and Remote Continental Airspace Operations.***

OLD	NEW
8-7-5. PROCEDURES FOR WEATHER DEVIATIONS IN NORTH ATLANTIC (NAT) AIRSPACE	Delete
Aircraft must request an ATC clearance to deviate. Since aircraft will not fly into known areas of weather, weather deviation requests should take priority over routine requests. If there is no traffic in the horizontal dimension, ATC must issue clearance to deviate from track; or if there is conflicting traffic in the horizontal dimension, ATC separates aircraft by establishing vertical separation. If there is conflicting traffic and ATC is unable to establish the required separation, ATC must:	Delete
a. Advise the pilot unable to issue clearance for requested deviation;	Delete
b. Advise the pilot of conflicting traffic; and	Delete
c. Request pilot's intentions.	Delete
PHRASEOLOGY– *UNABLE (requested deviation), TRAFFIC IS (call sign, position, altitude, direction), ADVISE INTENTIONS.*	Delete
NOTE– **1.** *The pilot will advise ATC of intentions by the most expeditious means available.*	Delete
2. *In the event that pilot/controller communications cannot be established or a revised ATC clearance is not available, pilots will follow the procedures outlined in the Regional Supplementary Procedures, ICAO Doc. 7030.*	Delete

OLD	NEW
8–9–5 PROCEDURES FOR WEATHER DEVIATIONS AND OTHER CONTINGENCIES IN OCEANIC CONTROLLED AIRSPACE	Delete
Aircraft must request an ATC clearance to deviate. Since aircraft will not fly into known areas of weather, weather deviation requests should take priority over routine requests. If there is no traffic in the horizontal dimension, ATC must issue clearance to deviate from track; or if there is conflicting traffic in the horizontal dimension, ATC separates aircraft by establishing vertical separation. If there is conflicting traffic and ATC is unable to establish approved separation, ATC must:	Delete
a. Advise the pilot unable to issue clearance for requested deviation;	Delete
b. Advise the pilot of conflicting traffic; and	Delete
c. Request pilot's intentions.	Delete
PHRASEOLOGY– *UNABLE (requested deviation), TRAFFIC IS (call sign, position, altitude, direction), SAY INTENTIONS.*	Delete
NOTE– **1.** *The pilot will advise ATC of intentions by the most expeditious means available.*	Delete
2. *In the event that pilot/controller communications cannot be established or a revised AT clearance is not available, pilots will follow the procedures outlined in the Regional Supplementary Procedures, ICAO Doc 7030 and Chart Supplements.*	Delete

---

1. PARAGRAPH NUMBER AND TITLE: 9–2–5. FLYNET

2. BACKGROUND: The agency now responsible for nuclear/radiological emergencies, the Department of Energy (DOE), has provided updated information on the use of the code word FLYNET and how the code word is used.

3. CHANGE:

OLD	NEW
9–2–5. FLYNET	**9–2–5. FLYNET**
Provide expeditious handling for U.S. Government, civil or military aircraft using the code name "FLYNET." Relay the code name as an element in the remarks position of the flight plan.	**ATC personnel at the first facility establishing contact with an** aircraft using the code **word** FLYNET **must:**
Add	**a. Provide expeditious handling.**

Add	**b. Report it to the operations supervisor (OS)/controller-in-charge (CIC), for reporting to the National Tactical Security Operations (NTSO) Air Traffic Security Coordinator (ATSC) through the Domestic Events Network (DEN).**
Add	**c. Add to the remarks section of the flight plan that DEN notification has been accomplished.**
NOTE– *The code name "FLYNET" indicates that an aircraft is transporting a nuclear emergency team or a disaster control team to the location of a potential or actual nuclear accident or an accident involving chemical agents or hazardous materials. It is in the public interest that they reach their destination as rapidly as possible.*	*NOTE–* *The code **word** FLYNET indicates that an aircraft is transporting a nuclear emergency **support** team or **other** disaster **response** teams to a potential or actual nuclear/**radiological incident, or to a potential or actual incident** involving **dangerous** chemical agents or **other** hazardous materials. It is in the public interest that they reach their destination as rapidly as possible.*
Add	***EXAMPLE–*** ***"Miami Center, Energy One Two FLYNET, request clearance direct Dulles."***
REFERENCE– *FAA Order JO 7110.65, Para 2–1–4, Operational Priority.* *FAA Order JO 7610.4, Para 9–4–1, "FLYNET" Flights, Nuclear Emergency Teams.*	*REFERENCE–* *FAA Order JO 7110.65, Para 2–1–4, Operational Priority.* *FAA Order JO 7610.4, Para 9–4–1, FLYNET Flights, Nuclear Emergency **Support** Teams.*

Made in the USA
Middletown, DE
17 June 2024